the **english literature** companion

Palgrave Student Companions are a one-stop reference resource that provide essential information for students about the subject – and the course – they've chosen to study.

Friendly and authoritative, **Palgrave Student Companions** support the student throughout their degree. They encourage the reader to think about study skills alongside the subject matter of their course, offer guidance on module and career choices, and act as an invaluable source book and reference that they can return to time and again.

Palgrave Student Companions – your course starts here ...

Published

The English Language and Linguistics Companion
The MBA Companion
The Politics Companion
The Psychology Companion
The Social Work Companion
The English Literature Companion

Forthcoming

The Anthropology Companion
The Health Studies Companion
The Media Studies Companion
The Nursing Companion
The Sociology Companion
The Theatre, Drama and Performance Companion
Further titles are planned

www.palgravestudentcompanions.com

the **english literature** companion

julian wolfreys

palgrave
macmillan

First published 2011 by
PALGRAVE MACMILLAN

Palgrave Macmillan in the UK is an imprint of Macmillan Publishers Limited, registered in England, company number 785998, of Houndmills, Basingstoke, Hampshire RG21 6XS.

Palgrave Macmillan in the US is a division of St Martin's Press LLC, 175 Fifth Avenue, New York, NY 10010.

Palgrave Macmillan is the global academic imprint of the above companies and has companies and representatives throughout the world.

Palgrave® and Macmillan® are registered trademarks in the United States, the United Kingdom, Europe and other countries.

ISBN 978–0–230–00813–7

This book is printed on paper suitable for recycling and made from fully managed and sustained forest sources. Logging, pulping and manufacturing processes are expected to conform to the environmental regulations of the country of origin.

A catalogue record for this book is available from the British Library.

A catalog record for this book is available from the Library of Congress.

10   9   8   7   6   5   4   3   2   1
20   19   18   17   16   15   14   13   12   11

Printed in China

contents

Preface: how to use this book   ix
Acknowledgements   xvii

1   about literature   1

1.1   literature: fundamental questions   3
Introduction   3
What is literature?   *Bill Overton*   4
Why study literature?   *Kenneth Womack*   10

1.2   your literature course   18
What to expect from your literature course   18
Typical structure and content   18
Literature and language   20
Literature and creative writing   *Jennifer Cooke*   21
Comparative literature   *Doris Bremm*   25
Getting the most from your course   31

1.3   study skills for literature   33
Introduction   33
Study skills   *Christopher Ringrose*   34
    Making the most of seminars and lectures   34
    Using the library   35
    Using IT and the internet   37
    Revising and exams   38
    Coursework and your dissertation   39
Writing and presentation   40
    Writing essays   40
    Presentation skills   44
    Plagiarism   45
    Bibliographies and citation conventions   47

2   literature modules   55

2.1   literature   57
Introduction   57

Critical Studies: an example of a core module   59
Conclusion   63

2.2   periods   65
Old English literature   *Philippa Semper*   65
Medieval literature   *David Griffith*   72
The sixteenth century   *Joan Fitzpatrick*   80
The seventeenth century   *Hugh Adlington*   86
The eighteenth century   *Bill Overton*   93
Romanticism and gothic   *Ian McCormick*   101
The nineteenth century and the Victorians   *Carolyn Kelley*   110
Modernism   *Alex Murray*   120
Contemporary literature   125

2.3   forms, genres and other popular modules   134
Introduction   134
Tragedy   135
Comedy   142
The novel   *Helen Wright*   150
Poetry   *Bill Overton*   157
Drama   *Neal Swettenham and Robert John Brocklehurst*   164
Epic   *Nigel Wood*   171
Lyric   *Nigel Wood*   177
Satire   *Nigel Wood*   181
Realism   *Lawrence Phillips*   186
Fiction   *Lawrence Phillips*   193
Postmodern fiction   *Alex Murray*   198
Gender   *Doris Bremm*   202
Class   *Nick Freeman*   209
Colonial and postcolonial literature   *Jenni Ramone*   215
Subjectivity   *Megan Becker-Leckrone*   221
Children's literature   *Jenny Bavidge*   230
Film studies   *Andrew Dix*   237
Popular fiction   *Jan Baetens*   244
American literature   *Brian Jarvis and Andrew Dix*   250

3   critical approaches and schools of thought   263

3.1   critical approaches   265
Introduction   265
Formalism   *Megan Becker-Leckrone*   267
Archetypal criticism   *Doris Bremm*   270
New criticism   *Megan Becker-Leckrone*   272
Bakhtin and dialogic criticism   *Karine Zbinden*   275
Feminism   *Ruth Robbins*   278
Marxism   *Alex Murray*   286

Structuralism   *Alex Murray*   290
Psychoanalysis   *Brian Jarvis*   293
Deconstruction   *Maria-Daniella Dick*   296
Postcolonialism   *Jenni Ramone*   303
New historicism   *Christopher Ringrose*   304
Cultural materialism   *Alex Murray*   306
African American criticism   *Andrew Dix*   309
Chicano/a studies   *Jenni Ramone*   311
Gay studies and queer theory   *Helen Davies*   314
Cultural studies   *Brian Jarvis*   321
Ecocriticism   *Jenny Bavidge*   324
Postmodernism   *Andrew Dix*   327

4 **key terms and concepts in English literature**   **331**

Julian Wolfreys, Ruth Robbins and Kenneth Womack

5 **career pathways**   **351**

5.1 **career pathways**   **353**
Introduction   353
Careers for English graduates   *Ruth Robbins*   354
The experience of a degree in English   *Claire Bowditch* 359
Interview   *Claire Bowditch*   360
Conclusion   361

6 **learning resource**   **363**

6.1 **chronology**   **365**

Bibliography   395
Notes on contributors   403
Index   408

preface: how to use this book

The English Literature Companion presents a comprehensive introduction to, and exploration of, the discipline of English and Literary Studies. If you're reading this preface, the chances are that you are either just about to begin, have just begun, or are in the middle of a degree in English literature or literatures in English. The purpose of the book is therefore both immediately apparent, and yet perhaps not so obvious. After all, if you know you want to study literature (because you like reading, you enjoy writing, or it was the subject at which you were best in school), then little else need be said, apparently. However, what is – or seems – obvious sometimes, needs restating, casting in a different light, looking at from a different perspective. This book aims to shed that light, looking at the discipline of English literature from a number of different perspectives, all of which have to do with the practical study of the subject, and examining what most, if not all, students, encounter when first taking up a degree in English, or what they find once they are at university.

The nature of studying literature is a diverse experience, made all the more so through modularity, and especially as departments of English allow a great deal of flexibility in module choice, with only minimal compulsory modules. Such diversity is exciting, and to be welcomed – it is often one of the reasons people decide to take up the study of literature. However, the immense wealth of literary texts and the variety of modules reflecting this cultural heritage in all its rich complexity can be to a new student, if not daunting, then at least a challenge. The nature of *The English Literature Companion* is to offer an overview to the nature of its subject. You will therefore find here essays on all aspects of literary study. The first chapter of the first part of the book asks fundamental questions such as 'What is literature?' and 'Why study literature?' The purpose here is to provide both an historical and, let's call it, a philosophical reflection and contextualization on what it is you intend to study or are already studying. The intention is to offer you a sense of what is behind your choice, to give a ground or rationale to that decision. After all, you are going to be spending three or four years reading all manner of prose, poetry and drama.

The second chapter of the *Companion*, 'Your literature course', offers a more pragmatic overview of the relation between literature and language, literature and creative writing and comparative literature courses. Additionally, it offers advice on getting the most from your degree course. This leads into the practical third chapter of Part 1, which addresses the full range of study skills, such as utilizing your time effectively in researching and writing, use of libraries and related resources, and the practical mechanics of writing essays, compiling bibliographies, presenting notes in a formal and consistent manner and so forth. In many ways, this part of the volume, along with Part 4, 'Key Terms and Concepts' (a small dictionary of critical terminology that is often employed in literary criticism), may well be the section you most frequently come back to, refer to, and generally employ in relation to all your modules, regardless of their topics.

Part 2 of *The English Literature Companion* introduces you to the types of modules from which you might have to choose. The introductory part of this section addresses a core module – that is to say, something you are required to study – as a basis for your knowledge of the subject in general, and also as a means of introducing you to certain of the skills that you will employ throughout literary study. These are analytical, interpretative and related skills to do with forms of knowledge themselves, how we think, how we read, and how reading and writing engage with cultural and historical perceptions and beliefs that we sometimes hold without being aware, and which we share with others. The range of modules described here is only a sample; you may not find exactly these, and you may find that your department doesn't offer some of the modules described. This is because the nature of literary study is the least amenable to regimented conformity from institution to institution. In many ways, literary study is an anomaly in universities, and it is the purpose of this volume to highlight that difference. Many English, and English and Drama departments will offer period modules, focusing on a century or part thereof, and the first section of this chapter introduces you to various aspects of period study, including discussion of the kinds of books you might be expected to read. Each module is supplemented with reading lists, one of literary, the other of critical texts. Additionally, each module has a sample syllabus or, at least, a skeletal sketch of one, to give you a sense of how the module might progress. These supplements, which in the case of the bibliographies can be used as reference sources, are also to be found in the second section of the chapter, which addresses some of the other kinds of module you'll have the opportunity to choose, including modules dealing with topics that focus in a very specific way: on a particular literary form, for example, or on the development of a **genre**, such as the novel. There are also modules described here that consider film studies, the nature of fiction, children's literature, gothic literature, and so on. Each of the modules has an indication of which academic year of your degree you might expect to study a particular subject (although, again, this is not hard and fast). Also, most essays contain cross-references to essays on other modules and critical approaches so that you can see possible pathways or relations between what appear at first as ostensibly discrete subjects. These are indicated in the text by the use of small capitals thus: 'see DRAMA'.

Literary study is not simply about taking the same approach to reading and applying it to all forms of literature, film or theatre. If it were, study of literature would be much more formulaic and mechanical. That being the case, you would simply continue to repeat what you have learned in secondary education, and there would, arguably, be little use for a book such as *The English Literature Companion*. What you will encounter fairly early on in your study of literature is that there are many different approaches to the study of literature and related cultural phenomena. The diversity of approaches can be baffling, especially those which have input from other disciplines, or which have a markedly 'theoretical' component. This is because part of the development of literary study has, in the last century or so, been involved in a reflective consideration of the nature of literary criticism itself – how we read, why we read, what we do when we read and interpret texts.

Criticism, in turning to consider its condition and practices, has moved from merely practical or pragmatic concerns, to reflect on historical, ideological, cultural and philosophical forms of knowledge, which either can be employed to inform the act of reading, or which are implicitly part of the work of literature already. (A brief digression: what we call 'literature' is perhaps unique amongst disciplines in that the material that we study is not 'pure'. Literature is made up of political and historical material, the attitudes of one part of society or culture regarding others; it is informed by broad, accepted beliefs, ideas that hold currency at a given historical moment, and which disappear subsequently, or take on another form; literature also imaginatively transfers the language of other aspects of thought so as to construct narratives, imagery, symbols that have cultural relevance or force for the reader.) Thus, you will find modules on criticism itself, its history and development, or particular 'theorized' forms of critical practice. Thus, Part 3 is made up of a series of essays that provide you with brief, illustrative surveys of some of the different critical approaches and schools of thought that you might encounter. As with the essays on modules, you will find supplementary bibliographies of further and suggested reading.

Following this, you will find a section on 'Key Terms and Concepts' and a section on careers that covers what an English degree enables you to do, what possibilities are open to you as a result of literary study. Finally, as a research and reference resource, there is a chronology of key literary works, contextualized through cultural and historical events.

There is no simple way through this book. It is intended to be useful in various and different ways, and you would not expect to read this through from cover to cover. As I have already indicated, certain chapters, and sections, will be 'globally' useful; you will find yourself referring to them regardless of a particular topic or subject that you are studying. Other sections will have local and immediate pragmatic use; you may well wish to find out more about particular types of modules or approaches, and so you will read certain essays from the middle sections of the *Companion*. The logic of the book is that it be useful in various, different ways: it is strategically practical, and will help answer questions, provide information, and serve to clarify aspects of your study, and your experience of your degree.

Let us assume you are just about to begin your degree. Most practically, reading the chapter on study skills and learning those skills will give you a head start, while the chapter on your literature course will contextualize those skills and give you an overview. At the same time, you should take the opportunity to consider why you have chosen a degree; to this end, the first chapter will be of great use, but it is also a chapter to which you will return, for, as you study, questions of what constitutes literature will inevitably arise, and you will be expected to consider such matters. Throughout your introductory year, you will encounter the language specific to criticism, or what is called its **discourse**. Some terms might seem familiar, but others will be strange, and to counter this you will find the glossary of keywords an invaluable resource. When you study particular literary works and reference is made to historical **context**, the chronology can help ground your understanding of those references, and give you a broader view. The module and critical approaches chapters may well help inform your choice of options and highlight how you find yourself favouring certain approaches, and so will begin to take on significance towards the end of your first year. And of course, regardless of where you are in your degree, there are particular sections which you will return to repeatedly, as I have already indicated.

You will notice that the volume is multi-authored;[1] from this, you might also notice that there are different tones, different 'voices', to the various essays here. In taking on *The English Literature Companion*, I made the decision early on that rather than presenting one voice, my own, as a seemingly authoritative one, appearing to offer a single, apparently objective overview, it would be more truly reflective of the diverse nature of an English degree to construct the *Companion* as an edited collection, with many authors. All the authors you will find here regularly teach the modules they write about and introduce you to; more than that, many publish critical works on these subjects, or on the critical approaches on which they have written. In short, the volume attempts to replicate the diversity of approach and experience that is to be found in departments of English today. Reading this volume will give you a sense of what you will encounter first hand: a community of diverse voices, working in concert with one another, and exploring the various affiliations and tensions that give any community its identity. In this, the volume, through its multi-authored nature, reflects on the nature of literature itself.

The English Literature Companion is, then, intended to provide two books in one. Let me recap in more general terms what I have already said. On the one hand, the intention is to offer the student of literature and related subjects a useful, usable overview of what it means to study literature, and how a path can most successfully be navigated through the three or four years of your degree programme. At the same time, the aim is to provide different perspectives on all aspects of studying literature, from developing and honing skills you will require, to the range of courses or modules you will be expected or required to take, or which you can choose for yourself. Additionally, the volume offers both a glossary of useful key terms and concepts, whilst supplementing this with short critical overviews of some of the many different critical and theoretically informed approaches[2] to and methods of literary criticism. Because the *Companion* is written so as to inform and aid all aspects of literary studies, you will also find technical information concerning the conventions of citing research resources, suggestions for different pathways through literature programmes, and information concerning career pathways, following completion of your BA degree. Finally, there is a chronology of significant dates, publications and figures whose work has informed and in no small measure determined the direction and contexts of literary study.

Where, then, might you begin reading this volume, and putting it to work for you in the most effective manner? Because the *Companion* is designed to aid you at various stages of your degree, this is no easy question to answer. If you are a freshman, you might well be best advised to begin with the first chapter of the volume, which covers the question 'Why study literature?', as this will give you a general sense of what matters about literature, why we read it at universities and colleges, and what, if anything, literature can be said to do for you beyond any immediate or pragmatic concerns with earning a degree so as to become more employable. While it is clear that a degree in engineering, in physics, or journalism has practical implications for your future, the uses of literature are not so easily defined. Putting that matter aside for the moment, though, what you do need to know is how you can make sense of your own relation to literature, and this involves a critical reflection on both the more abstract or, let us say, philosophical reasons for what attracts us to literature and also, more practically, what skills a degree in literature both requires and will develop – skills not only to do with lucid and cogent articulation, good writing practices, and so on, but also, the development of abstract logical reasoning, the structuring of a critical argument, etc.

If you read this as a second- or third-year student, as (to use terms more familiar to North American students) a sophomore, junior or senior, you might think you know these things already. Supposing you're right, you may use this section of the book as a means of refreshing your knowledge, allowing yourself to go back over questions to which you thought you already had answers. At the same time, you might have more immediate concerns to do with course or module selection. Allowing for the fact that every institution will have a different approach and pathway through the English degree (however small the differences might initially appear), once you have met the requirements dictated to you by your home department – where I teach it is required that second-year students take a course on Victorian Literature, while in their third year, the same students must sit the compulsory Modernism module – the choices of courses you make are yours. Literature offers a vast range of subjects, forms, historical or cultural areas of interest, and some of you will choose modules based on personal interests, on what student *doxa* suggests is an easy or soft option, on what is culturally relevant. If you're 20 or 21, what is more immediately appealing to you, a course on Science Fiction or one on Early Modern Poetry? Why is that? Some literatures are more relevant because they seem to be 'closer' in some way to your everyday experience; alternatively, what you choose allows you to make a transition from what you read for pleasure to the more 'professionalized' practice of reading. Yet, for all that, such reasons might be the motivational forces behind some students' choices; that which is closest to you (in whatever way this might be defined) is not necessarily most transparently so. It is therefore in part the aim of particular sections (descriptions of courses of modules according to period, form, **genre** or popularity, alongside descriptions of key critical approaches) to offer you a critical insight to what might be studied outside your immediate areas of interest.

All of which comes down to this: there is no one way through the present volume because its uses will change as you become the different reader your Literary Studies degree is designed to make you. How – and why – you study English Literature and Drama is a very different concern, when you are completing final essays and exams in your last term or semester, from the interests that motivated you to choose a degree in English, Drama or Comparative Literature in the first place. Hence, *The English Literature Companion* does not have a single, linear or progressive pathway to be navigated. It is an orientation and reorientation 'device', if you will. It is written in such a way that you can dip in anywhere at any time, treating it like a reference work. But it is also structured in an open fashion to allow you both to gain greater insight into what you do and, at more immediate levels, to become a proficient, attentive, and consistently rigorous reader and analyst, whose goals are to pursue research effectively, to manage the various component skills of reading, writing and research in relation to one another, and to put those competences to work, not only in particular courses, but from one module to another, across the scope of a degree, and beyond, whatever career you choose. The institutional demands of literary study are many and varied, often complex and yet always in some manner related to one another. *The English Literature Companion* aims to enable you to be a good reader of those interconnections. Move around the various sections and chapters of this book as you would your department and the various seminars and lectures offered by that institution. Engage with new material and go back over what you had thought was familiar but with renewed interest or different insights and perspectives.

A note on terminology

As a student reader, particularly a first-year student or one just arriving (or about to arrive) at university, you will find a great difference in the levels of language used throughout the volume. Some of the language will be as familiar as that which you use every day; in other instances, forms of expression or terminology will be difficult, of varying difficulty, and occasionally unfamiliar. This is less a reflection on the diverse authorship of the present volume than it is a reflection on the wide array of 'languages' (or discourses) and the lexicons from which they are drawn. There is a good deal of specialized language and language use in the study of English. This may seem strange, and possibly, initially, estranging; after all, were you studying mathematics, physics or a foreign language you would expect to have to learn new ways of speaking. But English? You are used to speaking and reading English every day, at different levels. The occasional unfamiliarity of expression and the oddity of technical language which you will encounter simply reflects the complexity of some areas of development in the study of English, and, as such, you will be expected both to familiarize yourself with such terminology or expression (hence the presence of a glossary in the book), and to become adept at it, depending on which particular subjects your study of literature in English and approaches to criticism finds you focusing on. This, you will find, is not that different from studying texts from different periods or authors, where you will have to become familiar with different modes of expression and articulation. If you have studied Shakespeare, you will begin to have a sense of what I am indicating. However, rest assured that not only is every author here an expert in their field, each of them teaches such material, and no one is making the language unnecessarily difficult. In order to facilitate comprehension, words, concepts and terms used throughout the book that are defined in Chapter 4, 'Key Terms and Concepts in English Literature', are presented in bold type. Additionally, these keywords are indicated in the index, for comparison and to aid familiarization of use in different contexts.

Notes

1 All material in this book is by Julian Wolfreys, unless otherwise indicated.

2 'Theory' refers to the often systematic borrowing, within the discipline of English studies, from – and adaptation of – discourses and approaches to analysis from other disciplines, such as psychoanalysis, historiography, philosophy, feminism and elsewhere, so as to enable different reading practices and reflections on the means of literary-critical analysis. Such approaches can also be defined as interdisciplinary, in that the approaches adapted from outside literary studies combine traditional reading and interpretative skills necessary to literary criticism with the forms of knowledge from other disciplines. 'Theory' is an imprecise term at best, and, strictly speaking, inaccurate, for a number of reasons. First, the differences between the various approaches, and the diversity that these produce, are too pronounced for a single term, implying their gathering, to work in any efficacious manner, however convenient. Second, many approaches or disciplinary divisions, according to particular intellectual models drawn from other disciplines such as those acknowledged above, are not 'theories', properly understood. A 'theory' is a coherent and self-contained system of ideas, based on general principles, which, once articulated and found to be internally consistent amongst themselves, can be

applied to given objects of study. Various economic models or the different branches of mathematics can claim to have theories. Literature, however, does not abide by rules; nor do the so-called 'theoretical' approaches, which, at best, have certain aims and principles, but about which there is no absolute agreement. Third, there has arisen a somewhat false distinction between what used to be referred to as 'poetics' (from Aristotle onwards, up through the centuries to the twentieth century), which have had concerns with form and aesthetics and what is proper to the work of literature, and what has been considered as 'theory' since the end of the 1960s, whereby 'theory' in the latter case is used as a collective term for the work of various, principally European intellectuals, from a variety of disciplines, few of whom agree unproblematically with one another, and whose work has been employed to transform the practice of literary criticism in a number of places, and in a number of different ways. Certain branches of Marxism or feminism might be considered as more or less 'theoretical', whilst others would distinguish themselves, despite their epistemological and ontological leanings, from what they consider to be 'theory', by which term is usually understood (or rather, I should say, in many examples, misunderstood) a retreat from politics and a focus on language in a formal and ahistorical way. As this note might give you to understand, the question of 'theory', so called, is a fraught, if fascinating one, and one over which there have been many, often heated, debates between academics. However, there are many academics, scholars and teachers who find it convenient to refer to 'theory' as though this umbrella term did, in fact, signal accord, agreement and a generally homogeneous state of affairs and practices. There remain, even today, some academics who either believe that everyone has been 'theorized enough', and so there is no need to talk about or research into questions that do not 'get on' with the process of reading literature, or, perhaps worse still, those who claim that they are not theoretical. This last position is a nonsense, for everyone, however loosely, holds opinions, functions in the world according to received wisdom, codes of morality, attitudes towards humans, has political beliefs, and so forth. If you are thinking at all, and being a human being this is a likelihood, then in some way, to some degree, you work with theoretical principles, however watered down they may have become through your culture and education, by the time you either put them into practice consciously, or otherwise live them in a relatively unthought or at least underthought manner.

acknowledgements

I would like to thank all those who agreed to contribute here (see below) and to my colleagues at Loughborough, whether or not they could be coerced. Thanks to Andrew Dix for pointing out a glaring omission and also for thoughts on other matters relating to the project. Thanks are also due to Bill Overton, Brian Jarvis and Nick Freeman for invaluable thoughts on a particular section of the volume; I would particularly like to thank Nick for suggesting I define 'deconstruction' one more time in my career, even though I declined, and Brian for suggesting I define 'literature' in approximately 100 words; there are no words of thanks enough. Deirdre O'Byrne, Catie Gill and Elaine Hobby also offered advice from which the volume has benefited, and thank you for that. Kate Haines at Palgrave Macmillan deserves a special freely given acknowledgement of gratitude, as she patiently, and with good grace and humour, put up with the often unavoidable but no less unconscionable delays. I would also like to express my gratitude to Frances Arnold, who, at later stages in the project, offered some important insights into the shape of this volume.

Essays in this volume are by the following contributors: 'The seventeenth century' by Hugh Adlington; 'Popular fiction' by Jan Baetens; 'Children's literature' and 'Ecocriticism' by Jenny Bavidge; 'Subjectivity', 'Formalism' and 'New criticism' by Megan Becker-Leckrone; 'Comparative literature', 'Gender' and 'Archetypal criticism' by Doris Bremm; 'Literature and creative writing' by Jennifer Cooke; 'Gay studies and queer theory' by Helen Davies; 'Deconstruction' by Maria-Daniella Dick; 'Film studies', 'African American criticism' and 'Postmodernism' by Andrew Dix, and, with Brian Jarvis, 'American literature'; 'The sixteenth century' by Joan Fitzpatrick; 'Class' by Nick Freeman; 'Medieval literature' by David Griffith; 'Psychoanalysis' and 'Cultural studies' by Brian Jarvis, and, with Andrew Dix, 'American literature'; 'The nineteenth century and the Victorians' by Carolyn Kelley; 'Romanticism and gothic' by Ian McCormick; 'Modernism', 'Postmodern fiction', 'Marxism' 'Structuralism' and 'Cultural materialism' by Alex Murray; 'What is literature?', 'The eighteenth century' and 'Poetry' by Bill Overton; 'Realism' and 'Fiction' by Lawrence Phillips; 'Colonial and postcolonial literature', 'Postcolonialism' and 'Chicano/a studies' by Jenni Ramone; 'Study skills' and 'New historicism' by Christopher Ringrose; 'Feminism' by Ruth Robbins; 'Old English literature' by Philippa Semper; 'Drama' by Neal Swettenham and Robert John

Brocklehurst; 'Why study literature?' by Kenneth Womack; 'Epic', 'Lyric', and 'Satire' by Nigel Wood; 'The novel' by Helen Wright; and 'Bakhtin and dialogic criticism' by Karine Zbinden. The interview conducted by Claire Bowditch with Charlotte was carried out in 2009, and we thank her for her help.

The present chronology is compiled and edited from the chronological tables supplied in the various historical volumes of my 'Transitions' series; I gratefully acknowledge Suntlee Kim Gertz, Marion Wynne-Davies, Kay Gilliland Stevenson, Moyra Haslett, Jane Goldman and John Brannigan for permission to cite the material from those tables.

1 about literature

1.1 literature: fundamental questions   3

1.2 your literature course   18

1.3 study skills for literature   33

1.1 literature: fundamental questions

chapter contents

> Introduction   3
> What is literature?   4
> Why study literature?   10

Introduction

Reading. It is something most of us do, some of the time. You are doing it right now. If you plan to study literature and have bought this book to find out what is expected of you, or if you are studying literature and this book is new to you, then you are – probably – reading most of the time. Reading involves comprehension, analysis, interpretation, evaluation, deciphering, and endless acts of measuring the local, immediate example of what is being read with more general, broader ideas, concepts and notions that inform the world and your relation to that world.

Yet, although we read and we think we know what we are doing, more or less, when we read, how we give value or determine value in our reading has to do with more complex matters, some of which it is the aim of this volume to unfold, and those matters we conveniently gather together in the name 'literature'. This does not mean to say, necessarily, that we know what literature is, even though most people believe they could have a rough stab at definition. The 'what' of literature is intimately bound to the question of why we study literature, why we bother to continue to read – and in some cases, reread – poems, novels or plays, essays or short stories, written, printed and published (mostly) anywhere from last year back to … well, long before anyone bothered to use the term 'literature' – in fact, however far back cultures and civilizations have produced, in one form or another, written or oral forms, in prose or poetry, for the purposes of any or all of the following (though not necessarily in this order): education, information, entertainment, enjoyment, communication, imaginative and emotional escape, or forging links between individuals in particular groups, large or small.

Recognizing this, we begin with a chapter that states, and attempts to answer, the fundamental questions: 'What is literature?' and 'Why study literature?' As you read the following considerations, you might think the reflections and statements a little abstract, difficult to pin down. You might find such answers explaining or justifying 'too much', a little bit like someone describing how a joke works. Certainly, you might be right in part were you to assume that such responses as Bill Overton and Kenneth Womack offer seem to have little to do with the practical study of literature, with the pragmatics of your three- or four-year course, your very real reasons for studying literature, and what, on the ground level, you will be expected to do and how you will be expected to do it. Such empirical issues are not irrelevant, but behind them – haunting them, if you like – are those matters that are at one and the same time fundamental (after all, without such questions there would be no degree programme designed through which one could study literature in the first place) and yet, on reflection, abstract or even abstruse questions. Without this necessary reflection, you may well enjoy or be enriched by your study of literature, but you will not have sufficiently come to terms with the reasons for, and the persistence of, literature (whatever we think we mean by that seemingly obvious and yet, nevertheless, enigmatic term).

What is literature?

Bill Overton

If you are studying Literature, or, as it is sometimes put, English, you may reasonably suppose that the people teaching it will be able to tell you what exactly the subject is. Up to about 30 years ago, they could have done just that, for there was general agreement that certain published writings, and certain kinds of writing, were literature, and others were not. In a degree course in English, for example, you would have expected to read plays by Shakespeare, poems by Alexander Pope or novels by Charles Dickens, but certainly not a seventeenth-century midwifery manual or an autobiography by a freed slave. But now most courses in English are different. The examples I have just given – Jane Sharp's *The Midwives Book* (1671) and Olaudah Equiano's *The Interesting Narrative* (1789) – are books taught in my own institution and elsewhere. And I could easily cite more outlandish specimens, such as Mills and Boon romances, graphic novels and various kinds of film. A look at how texts such as these have found their way into English courses opens up what is at issue in saying what literature is.

The rise of English and the canon

One reason why courses in English changed is that the people teaching them recognized not only that the subject was quite a new one, but also that it could be reinvented. In the 1980s, a number of studies showed that the history of English Literature as an academic subject is pretty short, going back little more than a century (e.g., Baldick 1983; Eagleton 1996). The same studies also claimed that there were powerful ideological motives behind its making. In the classic Marxist sense, 'ideological' means that these motives stem from fundamental social and material interests connected with political and economic power. One motive behind the rise of English was the need, expressed by the Victorian writer Matthew Arnold, among other influential people, to provide a secular substitute for religion. Arnold and others thought that, as organized religion declined, literature might furnish an alternative source of values and morality that would maintain social order and keep people in their place. A related motive was to instil the values of Establishment culture in such subordinate groups as working people, colonial subjects and women. Third, English Literature also helped promote patriotic feeling, important at times of war, unusual class tension or economic depression. As you might imagine, the story is more complex than this. All the same, once it was recognized that English did not exist a hundred years ago as a subject that could be studied at school or university, and once its roots were examined, it became easier to change it.

One of the main ways in which English was understood up to about 30 years ago was as a select body of texts by particular writers. I have mentioned some of these writers already, and anyone studying English at the time would have been able to name many others. The term for such a collection of texts is a **canon**. This sense of the word developed from a much older one meaning, 'The collection or list of books of the Bible accepted by the Christian Church as genuine and inspired', and then, by way of extension, 'any set of sacred books; also, those writings of a secular author accepted as authentic' (*Oxford English Dictionary* [*OED*]). It is a sign of how recent the idea of a general literary canon is that this particular sense only appears among draft additions to the *OED* dating from 2002. It is defined like this: 'A body of literary works traditionally regarded as the most important, significant, and worthy of study; those works of esp[ecially] Western literature considered to be established as being of the highest quality and most enduring value; the classics.' This definition raises questions that go to the heart of what literature is, or is thought to be. You might ask, for instance, why literary works produced in the West should be given priority. You might also ask how it is that certain works come to be recognized as having high quality and enduring value. And there is the problem, too, that works that are not written down do not seem to figure.

All these questions have been subject to hot debate in the last 30 years. In the United States, for example, what came to be known as the Culture Wars raged for a while in universities and the media (see Morrissey 2005). This was a dispute over whether, or to what extent, the kinds of work should be taught that the *OED* defines as 'the classics' and that for generations had made up the traditional curriculum with relatively little change. One of the problems with these, it was argued, is that they are nearly all by dead white European males. A curriculum that more or less excluded work by writers who happened to be still alive, non-white, non-European or female was not only difficult to defend but not worth defending, especially as the fact got around that the **canon** has always been subject to change. To give two examples of such changes, few people now read Robert Southey, yet in his day Southey was one of the leading Romantic poets. On the other hand, Dickens was for long considered a great popular entertainer but hardly an artist. In his book *The Great Tradition*, first published in 1948, the leading British critic F. R. Leavis excluded Dickens from the canon of English novelists, but in a further book, 22 years later, he made amends and put him in.

There are three main reasons why the **canon** changes. The first is that it is culturally produced, and so, as particular cultures change, so too do the works that their members consider important. The other two reasons are more complex. One is that it used to be thought that only the best work survived, like cream collecting at the top. In his *Preface to Shakespeare*, first published in 1765, Samuel Johnson invoked this principle when he declared that any work that people still found interesting after at least a century must have some value. The problem with this, however, is that works do not necessarily survive on merit. Some do not even find a publisher in the writer's lifetime, while others are actively excluded by anthologists or writers of literary histories – as Roger Lonsdale has shown for the work of many eighteenth-century poets, especially women (1984: xxxvi–xxxvii; 1989: xliii–xlvi). The second reason why the canon changes, then, is that valuable work is all the time being rediscovered and brought into the curriculum. Quite different questions are raised by the third reason, because it comes out of a redefinition of what can be read as literature. I mentioned two examples at the start. Jane Sharp's *The Midwives Book* and Olaudah Equiano's *The Interesting Narrative* can be studied in courses of literature not only because they use familiar literary devices such as meta-phors and rhetorical questions, but because they have much to show about the cultures within which they were written. In this sense, distinguishing between works by, say, Sharp and John Milton, or Equiano and Shakespeare, is artificial. All produced different kinds of writing, but the differences between Shake-speare's plays and Milton's poems are scarcely less than the ones between those texts and a midwifery manual or the autobiography of a freed slave.

Literature and literariness

It was in part for such reasons as those just discussed that, in *Literary Theory*, first published in 1983, Terry Eagleton claimed that 'Literature, in the sense of a set of works of assured and unalterable value, distinguished by certain inher-ent properties, does not exist' (1996: 9). That those were not, however, the only reasons for questioning what had been considered as literature is clear from the latter part of the same remark. There, Eagleton disputes whether any text can possess qualities that in themselves define it as literary. A few examples from the world of art may help to show this, for the same question also applies to them. If a rectangular formation of firebricks, a pickled shark or an unmade bed can be offered as works of art – as they have been at the Tate Gallery in London by Carl Andre, Damien Hirst and Tracy Emin respectively – why should not an extract from a telephone directory or a rearranged newspaper article be offered as works of literature? The directory extract would be highly patterned, and it might well contain rhymes and latent metaphors, all qualities that are often held to be literary. The newspaper article might have an even stronger claim to literary status if it could also be seen as raising important human questions, as literature is often thought to do. Consider, for instance, the following poem.

> *Baby abandoned*
> A two-day-old girl was found
> abandoned
> in a plastic bag on the steps
> of a priest's house in the Tox-
> teth district of Liverpool yesterday.
> Police are appealing
> for the mother to
> come forward as she may
> need urgent medical attention.

This looks like a poem on the page, it has a few rhymes ('found' / 'abandoned', 'yesterday' / 'may'), and it raises important questions. Does it matter that it is a short article from the *Guardian* newspaper (25 March 1987) presented with no other changes than splitting it up into lines of unequal length and converting the headline into a title?

One way of resolving this kind of problem was developed by a group of critics known as the Russian Formalists who were active mainly in the Soviet Union in the earlier years of the twentieth century. A leading member of the group, Viktor Shklovsky, argued that the key characteristic of literary texts is what he called 'making strange' or **defamiliarization** (see Rice and Waugh 2001: 50). By this he meant the ability of a text to break through habitual perceptions and make readers or listeners see and think differently. One of his main examples is a story by the Russian writer Leo Tolstoy in which the narrator is a horse who exposes the assumptions behind how he is owned and treated simply by presenting them from his own perspective. Another member of the group, Roman Jakobson, produced a rather abstract but all the same useful formula for defining literariness. Setting out a range of the various functions of language, Jakobson distinguished between them on the basis of their aim or orientation. Examples are the expressive function, in which the orientation is towards the addresser, and which, he said, 'aims a direct expression of the speaker's attitude toward what he is speaking about'; and the conative function, in which the orientation is towards the addressee, and which is aimed at making him or her do something (see Lodge and Wood 2008: 144, 145). 'Conative' means 'expressive of endeavour' (*OED*), and Jakobson's example is the simple command 'Drink!' Jakobson defined the poetic function of language in the same way, though one of the terms he used made this a bit confusing. He said that 'the set […] toward the MESSAGE as such, focus on the message for its own sake, is the POETIC function of language' (146). The confusing bit is that by 'MESSAGE' Jakobson meant not so much the content of the expression as its verbal form. In other words, he argued that literary uses of language are characterized by their orientation towards the way they are expressed rather than to the speaker's state of mind, the content or the audience. One of his examples is the phrase 'I like Ike', a slogan used in the American presidential election campaign of Dwight Eisenhower, whose nickname was 'Ike', in 1956. This illustrates his idea clearly. Although the slogan expresses an attitude on the part of the addresser (the expressive function), although it conveys something about the candidate it names (Jakobson called this the referential function), and although, as a slogan, it aims to have an effect on the addressee (the conative function), its primary orientation, for Jakobson, is poetic. This is because what is most striking about it is its very effective, and memorable, patterning of one vowel sound (long 'i') and two consonants ('l' and 'k').

On the face of it, Jakobson's formula may seem to disprove Eagleton's statement that literary texts have no 'certain inherent properties'. As you will probably have realized, though, it does no such thing, because Jakobson's example is not a recognized literary work but a simple election slogan that happens to use words and their constituent sounds cleverly. For – and this is an important point – the Formalists did not confine literariness to literature. Instead, they claimed it could be found in communications of all kinds, oral as well as written. A better term for the quality of literariness is therefore 'verbal art', because this begs no questions about whether a work has or has not achieved recognition as literature.

Good and bad literature

It may seem, then, that Eagleton is right – that, to repeat his claim, 'Literature, in the sense of a set of works of assured and unalterable value, distinguished by certain inherent properties, does not exist.' If the claim is true, then literature is, as he also says, just 'a highly valued kind of writing' (1996: 9); and the basis on which it is valued is culturally and historically relative, so there may come a time when, for example, 'Shakespeare would be no more valuable than much present-day graffiti' (10). While it is impossible to refute such a statement, it is just a debating point, for a society in which Shakespeare was not valued would be totally different from this one. Instead, it is possible to define literature by considering one of its qualities that Eagleton plays down. This is the fact that it usually takes predetermined forms that are accepted as literary. The plays and poems that Shakespeare wrote are obvious examples. They are clearly not wills, acts of parliament or shopping lists. Provided the reader has some basic cultural knowledge – at the same level as that required to identify a will, an act of parliament or a shopping list – they cannot be mistaken for anything other than literary texts. This is to suggest that literature results not only result from practices of reading and valuing, but also from practices of writing. For instance, writing a sonnet is a self-evidently literary act because a sonnet is a recognized form of poem; and writing a novel is a self-evidently literary act because such a work is a recognized form of narrative fiction.

The French critical theorist Gérard Genette has proposed a pair of very useful terms for these two different ways of identifying literature (1993: 1–29). The kind of theory that defines literature as a specific practice of writing he calls an *essentialist* or a *constitutive* theory. This means that to write a work in an accepted literary form, such as a sonnet, a pastoral elegy, a novel or a short story, is by that token to produce a work of literature, whatever its quality. In other words, the form itself *constitutes* the work as literature. Even if it were also a shopping list, a sonnet would be first and foremost an **aesthetic**, literary, object. To repeat, this is the case even if the work in question is of dismally poor quality. There are many poems, novels and short stories that could not constitute anything other than literature, though you might not find anyone willing to give them house room. These works, usually for very good reasons, are not valued, but they still could not be anything other than literary.

The term proposed by Genette for the other main way of defining literature is *conditionalist*. What this means is that any work of verbal art can, in principle, be recognized as literature *on condition* that it is found to be valuable. On this definition, you could argue that any piece of verbal art has literary value, and you would do that by saying what its particular merits are. This could be even if the piece were in a form not previously established as literary, such as an extract from a telephone directory. To sum up, then, there are works that are *constitutively* literary because they are presented in recognized literary forms; and there are works that are *conditionally* literary because, although not written in conventionally literary forms, they are valued for their aesthetic qualities. In this second category there are many works that were not intended as literature by their writers. These include examples mentioned by Eagleton such as Edward Gibbon's *Decline and Fall of the Roman Empire*, which is history, and George Orwell's essays, which are political and social commentary.

Genette's category of conditional literariness raises the question of value, and this has further implications. You could look at it like this. On the one hand, there are works that, in his terms, are conditionally literary – works that did not necessarily set out to achieve literariness, but, as Eagleton says, quoting Malvolio in *Twelfth Night*, had it 'thrust upon them' (1996: 7). These works will be considered literary as long as they are perceived as possessing aesthetic value. On the other hand, there are works that are constitutively literary – poems, plays, novels and so on. Most of this work varies in quality from undistinguished to dreadful; but a small proportion is read, performed, studied – valued. It is this tip of the iceberg of literature that is called the **canon**.

As a student of literature, many of the works you will be required to study will be parts of the canon. Some, though, may not be; and you may want to study others that are not. If either of the latter alternatives is the case, then it is important to remember that society and culture are constantly changing and are constantly being reinterpreted. You need to be fully aware that they are human constructs that can be altered. 'English' is one such construct, and studying critically is a way of changing it. Because culture is constantly changing, and assumptions about literature change with it, defining literature in any absolute sense is a vain ambition. But knowing why certain works are or might be valued is essential to the study of verbal art. That is one of the main reasons for studying literature.

References

Anon. 1987. 'Baby abandoned', *Guardian*, 25 March 1987, 2.

Baldick, Chris. *The Social Mission of English Criticism, 1848–1932*. Oxford: Clarendon Press, 1983.

Eagleton, Terry. *Literary Theory: An Introduction*, 2nd edn. Oxford: Blackwell Publishers, 1996.

Genette, Gérard. *Fiction and Diction*. Trans. Catherine Porter. Ithaca, NY and London: Cornell University Press, 1993.

Johnson, Samuel. *Preface to Shakespeare*. London: Dodo Press, 2007. Also see 'The Preface to *Shakespeare*'. ebooks @ Adelaide. http://ebooks.adelaide.edu.au/j/johnson/samuel/preface/index.html (accessed 10 May 2010).

Leavis, F. R. *The Great Tradition: George Eliot, Henry James, Joseph Conrad*. London: Chatto and Windus, 1948.

Leavis, F. R. and Q. D. Leavis. *Dickens: The Novelist*. London: Chatto and Windus, 1970.

Lodge, David, and Nigel Wood, eds. *Modern Criticism and Theory: A Reader*, 3rd edn. Harlow: Pearson Education, 2008.

Lonsdale, Roger, ed. *The New Oxford Book of Eighteenth-Century Verse*. Oxford: Oxford University Press, 1984.

Lonsdale, Roger, ed. *Eighteenth-Century Women Poets: An Oxford Anthology*. Oxford: Oxford University Press, 1989.

Morrissey, Lee, ed. *Debating the Canon: A Reader from Addison to Nafisi*. Basingstoke: Palgrave Macmillan, 2005.

Rice, Philip, and Patricia Waugh, eds. *Modern Literary Theory: A Reader*, 4th edn. London: Arnold, 2001.

Why study literature?

Kenneth Womack

'There are more things than poodles in Pomerania.'
(Wallace Stevens)

The study of literature is intrinsically about the act of knowing. It is about knowing the world – a vast, uncharted universe of people and places, ideas and emotions. But in helping us to know the world, literature is mostly about coming to know yourself. It is about exploring the recesses of your mind, the vicissitudes of your memories, the weight and pleasure of your deepest, most personal experiences. It is about getting closer and ever closer to understanding your own essential truths – and yet never quite arriving there. It is, in short, the most intimate and transformative journey that you can possibly take through the lens of your mind's eye. *It is about you.*

In this sense, the reading process may seem mysterious, impenetrable even. Yet for all of its complexity and expansiveness, the act of reading involves a relatively simple transaction between yourself and the literary work. In *The Reader, the Text, the Poem: The Transactional Theory of the Literary Work* (1978), Louise M. Rosenblatt supplies us with an interpretational matrix for explaining the motives of readers and the relationships, for lack of a better word, that you develop with literary texts. Rosenblatt identifies two different types of reading strategies: **aesthetic** reading, in which the reader devotes particular attention to what occurs *during* the actual reading event, and non-aesthetic reading, a reading strategy in which the reader focuses attention upon the traces of knowledge and data that will remain *after* the event.

Rosenblatt designates the latter strategy as a kind of 'efferent' reading in which readers primarily interest themselves in what will be derived materially from the experience (1978: 23–5). Efferent readers reflect upon the verbal symbols in literature, 'what the symbols designate, what they may be contributing to the end result that [the reader] seeks – the information, the concepts, the guides to action, that will be left with [the reader] when the reading is over' (27). Rosenblatt describes the act of reading itself – whether aesthetic or non-aesthetic – as a transaction that derives from the peculiar array of experiences that define the reader's persona: 'Each reader brings to the transaction not only a specific past life and literary history, not only a repertory of internalized "codes," but also a very active present, with all its preoccupations, anxieties, questions, and aspirations,' she writes (144).

Although not always consciously, we employ these different strategies – whether as **aesthetic** or non-aesthetic readers – depending upon our particular needs and purposes. As consumers of literature, we aspire, rather practically, to garner something – *anything* – from our reading events. It is significant that Rosenblatt derives *efferent* from the Latin *effere*, which means 'to carry away'. In our textual experiences, we quite literally take away the efferent freight of reading, which includes not only the plot, characters and setting of the story, but also our highly particularized encounters with the literary work itself. In a sense, you arrive with one set of interior and exterior worlds, only to depart the textual event with an entire range of new and expansive readings of your self in relation to these pre-existing worlds.

In his Cold War poetic opus 'A Duck for Dinner', Wallace Stevens writes that 'There are more things / Than poodles in Pomerania.' At the very least, his words make for an aloof, ambiguous, if not pretentious non sequitur. As with the Beatles' 'I Am the Walrus' – with its hyper-packed nonsensical phrases stacked each atop the other, Lewis Carroll-style – Stevens's spurt of language seems explicitly made up, like cocktail party drivel designed to impress the glitterati through its unexpected randomness.

Let's say it again: *There are more things than poodles in Pomerania.*

But for all its seeming elusiveness, the phrase's implications are fairly simple to parse if we consider our lived experiences, recognizing that life's bounty is often more than it appears, that – if you will forgive the cliché – sometimes there is more than meets the eye. For the speaker in Stevens's poem, the world of language and meaning encompasses

> All the birds he ever heard and that,
> The admiral of his race and everyman,
> Infected by unreality, rapt round
> By dense unreason, irreproachable force,
> Is cast in pandemonium, flittered, howled
> By harmonies beyond known harmony. (1957: 92)

Consider Stevens's notion that through our literary experiences every type of possibility comes into play – that you can catch a glimpse of all the flora and fauna that you can remotely imagine. In Stevens's quixotic universe of literary language, the rhythms of life are 'cast in pandemonium', a place where language flitters and howls all around us – and sometimes, on occasion, in forms vastly more **aesthetically** pleasing than others, creating 'harmonies beyond known harmony'. Whether scrawling upon the walls of caves, pressing ink to parchment, forcing moveable type into paper, emailing, texting, twittering, doodling, howling at the proverbial moon – *you name it* – we grasp for words, reaching out for the language that will make us heard and, just as importantly, that will allow us to *hear*.

Because we need stories

We are, as *Homo sapiens* have always been, desperate for **narrative**. We yearn for stories in which to live, suffer, die and rise yet again with the heroes and villains that come alive in our minds. Indeed, by engaging with narrative, we engage and enliven ourselves. In her important volume of moral philosophy, *The Sovereignty of Good* (1970), Iris Murdoch explores the mysterious fabric of our selfhood. 'The self, the place where we live, is a place of illusion,' she observes, and 'goodness is connected with the attempt to see the unself, to see and to respond to the real world in the light of a virtuous consciousness' (Murdoch 1985: 93). It is through the auspices of narrative that we expand these worlds, that we enlarge our states of being, and – if you will excuse another cliché – that we expand our horizons. But perhaps even more presciently, Murdoch recognizes that 'the world is aimless, chancy, and huge, and we are blinded by self' (100). And it is in this blindness, in this inability to see beyond the margins of our own humanity, that we are most overwhelmed by life, that we are most vulnerable to our natural insularity and inherent anxieties about living.

We need stories to make sense of our inexplicable worlds, to provide contexts and frameworks for our lives. 'We tell ourselves stories in order to live,' essayist Joan Didion remarks in *The White Album* (1979):

about literature

We look for the sermon in the suicide, for the social or moral lesson in the murder of five. We interpret what we see, select the most workable of the multiple choices. We live entirely, especially if we are writers, by the imposition of a narrative line upon disparate images, by the 'ideas' with which we have learned to freeze the phantasmagoria which is our actual universe. (11)

As Didion observes, narrative imbues our lives with structure, artificial as it may be, while transforming chaos into order, nonsensicality into plot. It is how we interpret, how we find solutions, how we derive joy and meaning – even (and especially) when confronted with the bedlam and uncertainty that some-times cloud our worlds.

Because we are jazzed by the majesty of words

In its finest states, the beauty of language, in Stevens's words, ascribes 'harmo-nies beyond known harmony'. It connotes the unusual, the unique and the powerful. The **aesthetics** of the text challenges our intellects – to be sure – but that is only the beginning, the firmament of something larger and more lasting. Language holds the capacity for communicating words of inspiration, of wonder, of love. It is the language of our most reverent, optimistic and fecun-dating selves. As e. e. cummings writes in 'stand with your lover on the ending earth – ', ' – how fortunate are you and i, whose home / is timelessness:we who have wandered down / from fragrant mountains of eternal now' (1994: 743). In cummings's hands, language becomes the stuff of beauty and immortality, a deft and supple means for extolling the richness of human experience. Yet as you carry away the efferent freight of his poem – of his syllables, typography, spacing, even his inverted syntax – his language becomes your own.

In his tragicomic novel *The Good Soldier* (1915), Ford Madox Ford's thick-headed narrator John Dowell trolls, over and over again, through the detritus of his life, searching vainly for the origins of his predicament – namely, that he has been duped by his wife and her lover, his supposedly best friend and the 'good soldier' of the novel's title. Worse yet, they are dead, leaving him alone in his misery to sift through the tatters of his existence. As Dowell seeks out the roots of his doom – the originary moment of his interpersonal demise – the act of reading Ford's novel becomes a brutal and wondrous experience as you find yourself settling into Dowell's highly unsettled skin. When Dowell finally succumbs to the utter hopelessness of his situation, he turns away from his audience in a brash attempt to bargain with a misbegotten universe, and his dreams of an impossible reconciliation with the world become our own: 'Is there any terrestrial paradise where, amidst the whispering of the olive-leaves, people can be with whom they like and have what they like and take their ease in shadows and in coolness?' (2003: 217). In his greatest moment of anguish and uncertainty, Dowell grasps for the poetry of language to sate his weary soul. And as Dowell collapses into a life of rote sameness, we emerge from the text richer for the experience, awash and aglow in the beauty of Ford's language. While the manna of hope is no longer available for Dowell, his life having become irrevocably devoid of meaning, our own lives are made possible – whole even – yet again.

Because we have deep and abiding memories

We find ourselves drawn to literature in order to rediscover ourselves through the windows of the past and our memories. This indelibly human impulse finds its origins in our innate need to situate ourselves in relation to the world, as well as to revivify the past, reconcile ourselves with the present, and plot a course for a seemingly unknowable future of possibility and change. In his valuable work on autobiography and life-writing, James Olney contends that understanding this drive for reflecting ourselves through narrative affords us with a means for comprehending the nature of **other** selves, as well as our own. As Olney observes in *Metaphors of Self: The Meaning of Autobiography* (1972), 'Each of us is still, with experience incorporated into character, what he [or she] was *in potentia* at birth, which is what each of us will still be, only then fully realized, in the moment of death' (280–1). Our encounters with literary works afford us with a means for contextualizing our pasts and refracting through the auspices of the text, for breathing life into the untapped characters of our selves.

For Jerome S. Bruner, the act of achieving selfhood through our textual experiences connotes self-knowledge and our capacity for accomplishing a bounded sense of personal self-construction in relation to the larger worlds in which we live. In addition to arguing that people establish selfhood by 'narrativizing' their experiences, Bruner maintains that individuals often negotiate their sense of self through the act of reading. 'The larger story' of a person's life – consisting of a host of considered and reconsidered 'narrative episodes', Bruner writes in *Acts of Meaning* (1990) – 'reveals a strong rhetorical stand, as if justifying why it was necessary (*not* causally, but morally, socially, psychologically) that the life had gone a particular way.' In Bruner's postulation of 'life as narrative', 'the self as narrator not only recounts but justifies. And the self as protagonist is always,' he adds, 'pointing to the future' – that place where the self-that-will-be resides (1990: 121). For Bruner, it is the journey of the self that matters, that makes our lives ultimately worth living.

The pull of story and the emotional response that it elicits provide us with powerful contexts through which to explore our pasts, our memories, and the mysteries of our futures. Literature reminds us that we do not exist in static, unchanging worlds, but rather, in spaces of swift and often indecipherable change. In her acclaimed novel *The Handmaid's Tale* (1985), Margaret Atwood depicts her narrator, Offred, as she parses through the memories of an increasingly idealized past in relation to a dystopian present in which her own sense of identity has become dispersed and uncertain. Yet as she digs ever deeper, Offred slowly but surely reclaims the threads of her lost self, rebuilding and reinvigorating her selfhood in the process. 'As all historians know, the past is a great darkness, and filled with echoes,' Atwood writes. 'Voices may reach us from it; but what they say to us is imbued with the obscurity of the matrix out of which they come; and, try as we may, we cannot always decipher them precisely in the clearer light of our own day' (2006: 350). For Atwood's narrator, the journey of the self is a transfixing and, at times, soul-destroying mission. Yet for Offred, these very same voices from the past allow her to rediscover herself and usurp the great darkness of her present. As the novel comes to an uncertain close, she is left to ponder the possibilities of an unknown future. But Offred is ready – her sense of self reinvigorated and impatient, even – for the new life that awaits her.

When it comes to the textual excavation of memories, Marcel Proust is literature's gold standard. The French novelist devoted the balance of his life to the art of refracting his memories through the lens of his writerly self. Proust understood implicitly that our memories are triggered by sensory experiences – sights, sounds, smells and touch, to be sure – but most especially through the pleasures of the text. In *Du côté de chez Swann* (1913), the first volume of his epic *À la recherche du temps perdu*, Proust interrogates the ways in which memory is catalysed by the senses, while comprehending, at the same time, the manner in which the reality of our memories becomes shaped by the ruinous work of nostalgia, of a sentimentality that exists beyond our ken: 'How paradoxical it is to seek in reality for the pictures that are stored in one's memory,' Proust writes, 'which must inevitably lose the charm that comes to them from memory itself and from their not being apprehended by the senses' (1992: 606). For Proust, our sense of pastness and the fleeting nature of our memories is both our enemy and our most cherished comrade. On the one hand, our memories taunt us with the reality of an unrealized past; yet on the other, our memories exist as our deepest consolation, as our last best chance for achieving wholeness. And it is our textual experiences, more often than not, that take us there.

Because we will die

But first we must live.

It is uniquely through our encounters with literary works – through novels, poems, plays, films, *whatever they may be* – that we die and yet live again to see another day.

We are eternally vexed by our own mortality. It is the essential condition of being human, and the mysteries of the text afford us with the opportunity to explore, to understand and to appreciate the transitory qualities of our existence. In *Lolita* (1955), Vladimir Nabokov's eccentric narrator Humbert Humbert laments the fleeting qualities of life by reciting a couplet from an 'old poet', who characterizes our mortality as a kind of corporeal tax – or duty – that must be paid for striving for an ethical life and enjoying the simple beauty of human existence: 'The moral sense in mortals is the duty / We have to pay on mortal sense of beauty' (Nabokov 1991: 275). While cummings celebrates the pleasures of living in the moment – of frolicking among 'fragrant mountains of eternal now' – Humbert Humbert recognizes the effortless splendour inherent in the merest of poetic phrases. It is a notion that Paul Bowles realizes intuitively in his deeply philosophical novel *The Sheltering Sky* (1949). For Bowles, it is our memories, not simply our flesh, that render life so precious, so fleeting. 'How many more times will you remember a certain afternoon of your childhood,' Bowles writes, 'some afternoon that's so deeply a part of your being that you can't even conceive of your life without it? Perhaps four or five times more. Perhaps not even that. How many more times will you watch the full moon rise? Perhaps twenty. And yet it all seems limitless' (1990: 238).

As with our lives, literature itself seems so limitless, vast and unquenchable. And yet, as with the 'mortal sense of beauty' that troubles Humbert Humbert, we only have a few vital years in this mortal coil in which to ponder life's mysteries. It is the veritable home of our personal museums of recollections: the past and memories that we have lost, yet regained through the refractive art of literary study. It is the 'terrestrial paradise' of our existence, in Ford's phraseology, and our last best hope for staying a world, in Murdoch's conception, that 'is aimless, chancy, and huge' – a world in which 'we are blinded by self'. It is the illusion, Didion recognizes, that we so desperately crave in order to celebrate life's beauty and to arrest, if only briefly, 'the phantasmagoria which is our actual universe'. It is the story of ourselves.

And that is why we study literature, why we revel in the power of language, why we find ourselves, time and time again, in the arms of narrative.

It is because there are more things than poodles in Pomerania.

References

Atwood, Margaret. *The Handmaid's Tale*. New York: Everyman's Library, 2006.

Bowles, Paul. *The Sheltering Sky*. New York: Vintage, 1990.

Bruner, Jerome S. *Acts of Meaning*. Cambridge, MA: Harvard University Press, 1990.

cummings, e. e. 'stand with your lover on the ending earth – '. *Complete Poems, 1904–1962*. Ed. George J. Firmage. New York: Liveright, 1994. 743.

Didion, Joan. *The White Album*. New York: Simon and Schuster, 1979.

Ford, Ford Madox. *The Good Soldier: A Tale of Passion*. Ed. Kenneth Womack and William Baker. Peterborough: Broadview, 2003.

Murdoch, Iris. *The Sovereignty of Good*. London: Ark, 1985.

Nabokov, Vladimir. *The Annotated Lolita*. Ed. Alfred Appel, Jr. New York: Vintage, 1991.

Olney, James. *Metaphors of Self: The Meaning of Autobiography*. Princeton, NJ: Princeton University Press, 1972.

Proust, Marcel. *Du côté de chez Swann* [*Swann's Way*]. Trans. C. K. Scott Moncrieff and Terence Kilmartin. New York: Modern Library, 1992.

Rosenblatt, Louise M. *The Reader, the Text, the Poem: The Transactional Theory of the Literary Work*. Carbondale: Southern Illinois University Press, 1978.

Stevens, Wallace. 'A Duck for Dinner'. *Opus Posthumous: Poems, Plays, Prose*. Ed. Milton J. Bates. New York: Knopf, 1957. 91–6.

1.2 your literature course

chapter contents

> What to expect from your literature course   18
> Typical structure and content   18
> Literature and language   20
> Literature and creative writing   21
> Comparative literature   25
> Getting the most from your course   31

What to expect from your literature course

While in other chapters we will go on to consider specific modules or courses that your English department should offer in some guise, the present chapter offers an overview of particular broadly defined structures that can inform, with variations, the identity of an English Studies or Literary Studies Department. 'Literature course' is, then, a term describing your degree programme. It is of course impossible to cover all the possible variations that are available to you and, perhaps more than any other discipline, English degrees will differ from one another in their specific structure and content. The purpose of this chapter therefore is to offer a cursory sketch of what content and structure might look like (and you can always compare this with the general overview of modules on offer within your own department, considering requirements, options, pathways and so on). At the same time, this chapter will also offer critical essays that introduce the reader at greater length to the study of creative writing, or comparative literature, as different models of literature or literature-related courses, which – and again this is dependent on the institution at which you are studying – might be offered as part of a double major, as minors to a major in English literature, as majors in their own right, or as pathways within the more general structure of your degree.

Typical structure and content

The first thing to say is that there is no such thing as a 'typical' structure and content for a literature course. This is particularly true now in universities in the United Kingdom, where many literature courses have a modular structure. Modularity is intended to create greater creative flexibility and module choice for students, and is itself a reflection on the understanding that, unlike many other academic disciplines, English literature as a subject does not have a rigid linear–historical, cause-and-effect narrative form, as the clichés have it, from Beowulf to Virginia Woolf or from Plato to NATO. A student may, therefore, whilst completing and following a progressive structure of required modules, also have much freedom – with sufficient organization and forward planning – to shape a course out of which a focus and coherence can be constituted, which will serve to produce both a rigorous and a diverse plan of study.

While it is impossible to speak of what is 'typical', there are, however, shared features, such as the insistence on particular compulsory modules to provide grounding and orientation in the discipline. Module titles (if not content) will be found to be in common across many universities, and it is often the case, where degree programmes (or what we are calling here literature courses) are modelled on a narrative of historical progression or sequence, that you will begin, if not with Anglo-Saxon, then with Medieval Literature in the first year of study, reaching Modernist Literature and beyond in the final year of your course. Another common format is to find in the first year, either as a semester-long or year-long compulsory module, an Introduction to Literary – or Critical – Studies. Frequently, it is the case that such courses offer the student not only a broad and necessarily brief survey sample of **genres** and forms from across the history of English literature, but also an introduction to different critical approaches, preparing the student for a more intensive study of literary criticism or theory as subjects in their own right, rather than simply as means by which to read differently.

Degree programmes and literature courses will all vary according to the number of compulsory modules and optional courses they offer, as well as the ratio between the two. It may be the case that your first year will include a compulsory module on approaches to literature, which stresses theoretically informed modes of analysis (see 'Literature and language', below), and a complementary module on literature and history, or historical approaches. From this introductory point, and in subsequent years of their study, students will usually be able to choose from period modules, such as Victorian or Romantic Literature, Renaissance Literature or Modernism, from modules stressing genre and form (the Renaissance or Early Modern Lyric, the Gothic short story), or other 'special modules', which offer a combination of approaches, such as themes – **gender** and class – in a given period (the 1950s or the 1930s). In some programmes, modules offered in the second, third and fourth year (where relevant) will include film modules and modules on creative writing, drama, and literature in translation.

Teaching is pursued largely through lectures and seminars. Where there are lectures, these are often part of compulsory modules, and students will be divided up into smaller groups for weekly seminars. While all students will be expected to produce written work for the modules they take, the types of assessment will vary in length and form. Some universities still pursue timed exams at the end of semesters, but increasingly it is recognized that English as a discipline is best served by essay writing, in which expository and analytical skills are practised. Essays will of course vary in length, and submission is spread across the academic year. In addition, final-year students may well have to produce an honours dissertation, which is an extended piece of writing.

1 Literature and language

Some degree structures will require first-year students to take an introduction to the study of literature and language at university level. This may well take the form of the Introduction to Critical Studies mentioned above, in which different approaches, with foci on topics such as **gender** and sexuality, nation, race and ethnicity, are given historically contextualized emphasis. Some departments will take a more formal approach to the introduction of literature and language, examining intrinsic aspects of given literary works, such as the nature of literary form, the structure of genre, and the relationship between form and content. What is shared between different programmes, though, is the focus on helping students develop their skills in the analysis of literature and language, with an emphasis being placed on significant approaches to the study of literature and language, and related disciplines.

Another aspect of formal analysis can be attention to particular dimensions of linguistics as these pertain to literature specifically. You will be expected to develop a knowledge of and skill in methods of language analysis relevant to form, period and genre, and this can often be extended through considerations of the historical contexts of the role of language. In such modules, you will be required to hone your **close reading** and analytical skills in a number of different ways, but with the goal of providing you with the intellectual means for producing skilled analysis across the range of your module choices. In other cases, literature and language will develop analytical and language-based approaches in relation to social and cultural **context**, in order to stress how language is a material and historical medium, shaping and being shaped by the complex interactions of history, **power**, class, **gender** and **subjectivity**. In turn, such considerations will be focused through literary examples, whether these are the early modern play *The Witch of Edmonton*, Wordsworth and Coleridge's *Lyrical Ballads*, or a novel such as Bram Stoker's *Dracula*.

All of this is only to give a sense of the broad range of an English degree. Particular pathways or joint honours degrees differ in both small and great ways from institution to institution. The majority of this book addresses certain aspects that are to be found in common across literature degrees. However, this does not address two particular pathways that are offered, whether as pathways belonging to a joint degree programme, or, in some instances, as degree pathways in their own right: creative writing and comparative literature. The remainder of this chapter addresses these, therefore, and what, as a student opting for such degrees, you might expect to find that is different from the conventional degree in English literature.

Literature and creative writing

Jennifer Cooke

More and more students are interested in creative writing: many English Studies courses have responded to this by offering creative writing module options, but there are also an increasing number of joint degrees that combine traditional English Literature courses with the study and practice of creative writing. Such joint degrees can be a great way of exploring two areas of interest simultaneously.

Creative Writing as an academic subject at university level is a relatively recent phenomenon: it began in the United States in the mid-twentieth-century. In the UK, the University of East Anglia was the first to offer a Masters in Creative Writing in 1970 and continues to be one of the most popular places to study the subject, although very many universities have now joined them in providing similar undergraduate and postgraduate courses. Changes in literary theory (see Part 3, 'Critical Approaches and Schools of Thought') over the twentieth century have also contributed to English departments becoming more interested in embracing Creative Writing as part of what they offer. Broadly speaking, in the last 30 years there has been a move away from a preoc-cupation with the author's intentions in his or her work towards a type of reading which is more engaged with the surprising, destabilizing, disruptive and creative possibilities of language and meaning. Traditional discussions, which concerned themselves with topics such as genre, plot and characteriza-tion, have been extended into an acknowledgement that language itself points us beyond the borders of the text. New reading practices seek to engage with a work in ways which emphasize that its meaning is not 'fixed' and therefore 'hidden' somewhere, to be exhumed by academics, but that each reading of a text is a new reading, a new experience, and in some senses a 're-creation' of the work. This affirmation of how the reading experience itself can 'create' new possibilities has led to a greater academic interest in the potential value of crea-tive writing.

What to expect from your course

The teaching

Because you are doing a joint degree, this usually means you get less choice when it comes to optional modules than those who are taking a single honours degree. Both parts of your degree are likely to include core modules, especially the Literature side. For the core Literature courses, you will be with the single honours English students, joining them in seminars and lectures. You may still have choices over some of your Literature modules, though this will vary with the university and it is worth checking first how much choice you get, especially if this is important to you, before you decide on the universities to apply to. For the Creative Writing side of your degree, most universities offer a core course in the first year, which tends to examine different genres and forms, their implications and histories. In the second year, it is usual to have Creative Writing module options that allow you to focus on particular **genres**. Typically, there will be modules on poetry, prose, drama or screen writing and you will do all or a combination of these. In the third year, you will undertake a Creative Writing dissertation. This is an extended piece of work or a portfolio (in the case of poetry, for example) of creative writing, sometimes to be accompanied by a reflective commentary. You will be assigned a tutor who will supervise you as you develop this work through one-to-one feedback sessions, usually over several months. Often there are third-year optional modules too, on more specific genre-related topics, such as writing for children, writing for television or science-fiction writing.

In terms of the kind of teaching you will experience, there will probably be a combination of lectures, seminars and tutorials (small group or one-to-one sessions with a tutor). Additionally, Creative Writing students can expect to participate in workshops. These are group sessions, which may involve writing exercises, discussions of technique, the teaching and practice of methods to help develop your writing ideas, and feedback on your creative work. They are primarily practical, often led by a professional writer, and are aimed at improving your writing.

Feedback on your creative work

What makes Creative Writing courses unique, exciting and often quite scary is the opportunity to use the knowledge you acquire to write and produce individual creative work, to share it with others, to offer it up for comment and, ultimately, to have it assessed by those who are already practitioners. In other words, a good Creative Writing course requires more from its students than a single honours Literature course, both in terms of the scope of what they are asked to do and in braving the vulnerability which is inevitably part of showing one's creative output to other people. Learning how to accept and use feedback is an essential part of your course and even the most confident and prolific of students is likely to feel nervous the first time they present a poem for critique. We tend, rightly or wrongly, to view our creative work as more personal, with more of 'us' in it, than an academic essay. However, a Literature and Creative Writing degree should equip you to see your creative work as being just as much a technical achievement as a personal one. Some institutions will integrate feedback into your courses through assignments and assessment whereas others may run separate seminars or workshops which are designed as forums for the development of ideas and writing, and the sharing and critiquing of it with your peers and tutors. Essential to the success of feedback sessions is for the whole group to display generosity coupled with supportive criticism. It is no good if everyone praises your work since you will learn little about how to improve it, but at the same time it is extremely demoralizing to have creative work ripped apart by someone insensitive to the bravery needed to share it in the first place. The more you share your work and expose it to criticism, the easier it becomes to hear and the more helpful and less painful the process. It is also valuable training: most writers, whatever readership they are aiming at, will have their work rejected or criticized at some point. Feedback also emphasizes the necessity of redrafting: most good work goes through extensive rewriting and editing, reshaping and reorganization, before it can be called finished. The formal route for feedback is, of course, assessment and each Creative Writing module you take will involve an element of your creative work being assessed.

Professional help and guidance

The Creative Writing part of your degree should have elements taught by successful writers. For example, a second-year module on writing drama should be taught by someone who is a playwright and whose work has been publicly performed or broadcast on radio or television. Some English departments have academics who are also published creative writers; others employ writers specifically for the Creative Writing part of the degree; sometimes there is a mixture of these two types of tutor. Many universities with Creative Writing programmes also have a 'writer in residence', usually a recognized author who will be affiliated to the university on a temporary basis for one or two years or more. It very much depends on the institution and the author as to how involved the writer in residence is with the day-to-day departmental teaching. A usual arrangement would be for them to give a talk a term and occasionally run workshops on technique. On the other hand, there are some appointments which require a greater commitment from the author, involving them in teaching or being available at set times for consultation. Many universities, whether or not they have a writer in residence, will have a Royal Literary Fund Fellow. This is an author who has a more active role in the department, often teaching, offering advice on writing and holding consultations. The Fellow, funded by the Royal Literary Fund, not the university, is available to all students in the department who wish to improve their writing, whether creative or academic. As well as this 'in-house' provision, it is equally important that your course offers advice and talks from outside writers and professionals, especially those connected with the publishing industry. This might include visits from editors, publishers and other industry experts who provide valuable counsel about the practicalities of entering the industry and what is required from first-time authors and their manuscripts. In an increasingly competitive market, this kind of advice is invaluable. There should also be regular events where invited authors will read from their work, answer questions about it, and possibly lead workshops giving advice on craft and technique. Often a university will have affiliated authors who regularly contribute to such a series of readings and talks.

Choosing the right Literature and Creative Writing degree

Not everyone is seeking the same thing out of a Creative Writing joint degree and new students display a range of levels. Some may never have shown their work to anyone else before and be unsure about the types of writing they wish to engage in; others may have a very clear idea of what type of writer they are and be seeking commercial recognition and success; still others may be there simply to improve their writing or to attempt to try new types of writing and be more experimental. It is worth asking yourself what you expect from the Creative Writing element of your degree before you begin looking at the courses offered by different universities. Whilst it is not unusual for a student to arrive aspiring to be a novelist but to graduate a poet, if you know that you are primarily interested in a particular **genre**, then it is advisable to look carefully at the tutors and courses which are offered in that area. All university web pages these days give information about the staff who teach on their modules. Ensure you investigate the tutors and writers in residence of the courses that appeal to you. Find out what they have written; if you can, try to read some of their work, and make sure they are published and practising writers. Ask yourself whether the range of tutors and the kind of writing they engage in reflects the kind of writing that interests you, since a tutor's course is likely to reflect their areas of speciality. Find out whether the course has an accompanying programme of invited publishers, writers and industry experts. Most universities that offer Literature and Creative Writing degrees also offer a Creative Writing MA, and you will find that the industry and author talks that are run to accompany the postgraduate courses are open to undergraduates as well. Some institutions even have specific centres, such as The Writing School at Manchester Metropolitan University, or links with specific publishers and agents. Another indication that the university is committed to creative writing is that they host literary festivals or conferences addressing creative writing. It is a good idea to explore whether there is a departmental journal or magazine which publishes student work and whether there are any opportunities where you can read your work: many departments will have performance events and student readings offered alongside those by visiting writers.

One of the most important academic outcomes of a Creative Writing course is that students who have submitted their own creative output to rigorous critique tend, as a result, to have developed acutely attentive reading skills. A good writer is a good reader. In terms of your creative work, you will develop confidence, a good sense of which genres you prefer and where your strengths lie, and you will have met and interacted with other writers, both your peers and your tutors. You will exit your degree with a portfolio of work, built up and improved upon during your three years of study. You may also have been involved with the local events in your area, whether it is reading in public or publishing your work in local or university journals and small presses. You may even have a clear idea of where you want to place your work, the type of writing you wish to produce and the sort of publishing outlets that this can be aimed at. Although all degrees are in some sense a personal journey, creative writing courses are intensely rewarding personally, as you see your work, and that of others, improve and grow. Not all students who complete a Literature and Creative Writing course then go on to become full-time professional writers, but they are all guaranteed to graduate as better creative writers and more adept readers of literature.

Further reading

The bible to the creative writing industry is the annual *The Writer's Handbook*, edited by Barry Turner (Macmillan). It provides invaluable advice on the industry, contact information for agents and publishers, information about courses, grants, festivals and prizes.

A few texts listed below are good introductions to the writing process:

Anderson, Linda, ed. *Creative Writing: A Workbook with Readings*. London: Routledge, 2005.

Bell, Julia, ed. *The Creative Writing Course Book: Forty Writers Share Advice and Exercises for Fiction and Poetry*. Foreword by Andrew Motion. London: Pan Books, 2001.

Bernays, Anne, and Pamela Painter. *What If? Writing Exercises for Fiction Writers*. London: Harper Collins, 1991.

Brande, Dorothea. *Becoming a Writer*. London: Pan Books, 1996.

Lerner, Betsy. *The Forest for the Trees: An Editor's Advice to Writers*. London: Pan Books, 2002. See also http://betsylerner.com/ (accessed 17 May 2010).

Samson, Peter. *Writing Poems*. Tarset: Bloodaxe Books, 1993.

Comparative literature

Doris Bremm

Comparative Literature distinguishes itself from other literary studies in that it does not limit its analysis of literature by nation, language, period or medium. Students of comparative literature do just what the term implies: they compare different national literatures, look at similarities and differences, and make connections across boundaries. The field of comparative literature encompasses the study of literatures in various languages, from all over the world, and from different time periods, which makes it especially difficult to summarize in a few paragraphs what a student of comparative literature can expect.

Furthermore, the discipline itself is in constant flux, redefining itself continuously. What remains the same is the constant crossing of borders, whether they are national, geographical, temporal or linguistic, and as Gayatri Chakravorty Spivak points out, this crossing of borders is always a 'problematic affair' (2003: 16).

One of the principal figures in the field, René Wellek, addressed what he called 'the crisis of Comparative Literature' in the 1960s (1963: 282–96). For many scholars, however, this state of crisis is not a sign of weakness, but points towards the discipline's continued energy and relevance. Critic Jonathan Culler brings it to the point when he says that comparative literature is 'by its very nature a site of crisis' (2006: 241). As such, comparative literature tends to analyse not only literature and the meaning and contexts of cultural production; it also constantly reassesses itself as a discipline. Let's consider a series of questions that you will encounter as a student of comparative literature.

What is comparative literature?

First, what exactly is 'comparative literature'? This is something that has been debated since the term was first coined (the term is usually attributed to a series of French anthologies published in 1816 entitled *Cours de littérature comparée*). The discipline has changed over the past century and has morphed into an interdisciplinary and multidisciplinary area that explores the 'great open space of literature', as Susan Bassnett terms it in *Comparative Literature* (1993: 5). No longer limited to literature, the move towards cultural and area studies has opened comparative literature to other forms of 'cultural productions'. As a student of comparative literature, you will read not only what is traditionally considered to be literature (novels, plays, poems, short stories and **epics**), but also other texts such as films, comics and visual arts. Furthermore, you will analyse them from a multidisciplinary point of view. These other disciplines might include the arts, philosophy, the social sciences and religion, just to name a few. Whereas comparative literature in its beginnings often focused on the study of influences and sources, students today will be asked to make associations and connections between different literatures rather than trying to pinpoint specific lines of influence.

Introductory courses usually cover methods as well as theories of influence, tradition and **intertextuality**. Most departments also require students to take courses on critical theory, familiarizing students with such areas as postcolonial criticism, narratology, structuralism, poststructuralism, new historicism and feminist theory. As for specialized literature courses, many programmes offer a mixture of traditional and non-traditional courses. Whereas traditional courses focus on specific genres, cultural movements or thematic elements across geographical boundaries and historical periods, non-traditional courses will often consider the question of the academic discipline itself.

Here are some examples: traditional genre-based courses might look at the rise of the novel in Europe or the development of the sonnet form from its origins in the sixteenth century to contemporary examples. Another course might focus on the epic poem, comparing such texts as *Gilgamesh*, *The Iliad*, *The Ramayana of Valmiki*, *The Aeneid* and *Paradise Lost*. A period-based course might concentrate on modernisms in different parts of the world, comparing the works of such authors as William Faulkner, James Joyce, Marcel Proust and Virginia Woolf. In general, thematic approaches such as 'the Bourgeois', 'Terrorism', 'Ethnicity and Literature', 'Technology' or 'Representations of

Violence' enjoy great popularity. A thematic course on representations of Empire could include a variety of texts ranging from Virgil's *Aeneid* and *The Song of Roland* to E. M. Forster's *A Passage to India*.

The question of national literature

More traditional courses often start with the question of national literature. Speaking of comparing national literatures naturally implies that different nations produce a distinct body of literature. However, that notion is certainly arguable. Interestingly enough, the term 'comparative literature' was coined during a time of national struggles, when old boundaries disappeared and new ones were erected. For example, when speaking of 'German literature', what effect does it have to consider that the country has changed from an assortment of little states, to a monarchy, to a period of being split into two parts? And what about literature in the German language written by authors from other countries? The question of a cultural and national identity is complicated even more by considering the many examples of 'national literature' that have been 'forged' over the years. One such example is the *Fingal* epic written by the Scottish poet James McPherson in the eighteenth century. He claimed to have found a medieval manuscript by the ancient Irish bard Ossian and translated it from the Gaelic. The fact that he lied about the sources of his work, however, does not alter the fact that McPherson created a piece of literature that became a part of Britain's national literature and had profound effects on the Romantic movement in Europe. Soon after its first publication, it was translated into many European languages, and Goethe even incorporated excerpts of his translation of a part of the work into his novel *The Sorrows of Young Werther*. The example of McPherson shows that national literatures do not simply exist; they are cultural constructions. With these questions in mind, students of comparative literature will not only focus on the analysis of the individual narratives, but also interrogate how cultures are constructed and how they change over time. Instead of looking at literature as a national phenomenon, as many national literature departments do, studying comparative literature gives you the opportunity to look at literature as a transnational phenomenon.

The question of the canon

Another question that you will encounter is that of **canonicity**. Whereas the discipline of comparative literature started out focusing mainly on Western literature, it has now changed to include literatures from all parts of the world. Similarly, many programmes focus on European literature and culture, but more and more schools have developed special modules and courses that look at the literature and cultures of the Americas, Africa, Asia and Australia. Many courses that started out as 'Great Books Courses' now include lesser-known works from a greater variety of cultures. Not only did Norton change the name of its anthology from *The Norton Anthology of World Masterpieces* to *The Norton*

Anthology of World Literature; the new version reflects a similar shift to a focus on giving a greater variety of non-Western texts.

The issue of translation

Depending on the programme, you will need to read literature in at least two different languages, if not more, as well as literature in translation. The field of translation studies itself remains an important area within comparative literature. Each translation changes the original, no matter how much the translator tries to stay as close to the original work as possible. The translator's choices affect and sometimes even change the original meaning and **context** of the work. If you compare various translations of the same text you will see how minor changes can create entirely different meanings.

Whereas all translation is difficult on many levels, the translation of poetry proves to be particularly challenging because, in addition to meaning, the translator has to consider metre, rhyme scheme, and stylistic devices such as puns and metaphors. For example, the various different translations of Sappho's poem on jealousy, praised by Longinus for its evocation of the senses in *On the Sublime*, differ greatly. Let's look at two translations: the first by Sir Philip Sidney (1554–86); the second by Lord Byron (*c.*1920):

> My muse, what ails this ardour?
> Mine eyes be dim, my limbs shake,
> My voice is hoarse, my throat scorched,
> My tongue to this my roof cleaves,
> My fancy amazed, my thoughts dulled,
> My head doth ache, my life faints,
> My soul begins to take leave.
> So great a passion all feel,
> To think a soare so deadly
> I should so rashly rip up.
>
> (Sidney 2002: 94)

> Equal to Jove that youth must be –
> Greater than Jove he seems to me –
> Who, free from Jealousy's alarms,
> Securely views thy matchless charms.
> Ah! Lesbia! though 'tis death to me,
> I cannot choose but look on thee;
> But, at the sight, my senses fly,
> I needs must gaze, but, gazing, die;
> Whilst trembling with a thousand fears,
> Parch'd to the throat my tongue adheres,
> My pulse beats quick, my breath heaves short,
> My limbs deny their slight support;
> Cold dews my pallid face o'erspread,
> With deadly languor droops my head,

My ears with tingling echoes ring,
And life itself is on the wing,
My eyes refuse the cheering light,
Their orbs are veil'd in starless night:
Such pangs my nature sinks beneath,
And feels a temporary death.   (Byron 1864: 19)

Comparing these poems, you might not realize at first that they are translations of the same poem. Kenneth Rexroth has gone so far as to argue that '[t]ranslations of Sappho, until recent years, have been fantastically inappropriate' (1986: 30). Recent translation studies, however, have challenged the traditional idea that a translation is automatically inferior to the original and would not consider Sidney's and Byron's versions lesser works of art because they differ from Sappho's poem. Translations are not considered mere 'copies' of an 'original', but originals in their own right.

Furthermore, it is important to consider the historical **context** of any given translation. Susan Bassnett argues that '[t]ranslations are always embedded in cultural and political systems, and in history ... the strategies employed by translators reflect the context in which texts are produced' (1999: 6). Consider the example of *The Thousand and One Nights*: Edward William Lane's English translation (1838–40) included anthropological notes on Arab customs indicating that the Arabs were far more gullible than European readers (ibid. 6), while excluding content he considered 'immoral'. Sir Richard Francis Burton's version (1885–8), on the other hand, accentuates sexuality within the tales. Both translations create a skewed version of the original that reflects the culture that produced the translation, rather than the culture in which it originated. In cases like these, so Bassnett argues, '[t]ranslation was a means both of containing the artistic achievements of writers in other languages and of asserting the supremacy of the dominant, European culture' (ibid. 6). Critics argue that translations of colonial texts into English are a form of consumption and not a form of reciprocal literary exchange. Ideally, translation should be an ongoing process of intercultural transfer. This aspect of translation studies is especially interesting in the context of postcolonial theory and comparative literature.

Where to start?

As a new student of comparative literature, the sheer scope of the field and the freedom that comes with it might seem paralysing at first. It would be impossible to look at all literatures and cultures of the world, so individual projects need to focus on particular areas, motivated by general theoretical questions that arise when you analyse different kinds of texts. The languages you speak or want to learn will narrow your scope, as will your areas of interest in other fields. The aforementioned *Norton Anthology of World Literature* would be a good start for general reading, since it includes not only a wide variety of texts, but also maps, timelines and images, as well as explanatory material that covers cultural and historical background of the literature and biographical information about the authors. Depending on your area of interest, you will find that critical editions often have excellent introductions as well as bibliographies and suggestions for further reading. As for comparative literature as a discipline, Susan Bassnett's *Comparative Literature: A Critical Introduction* covers the historical development of the discipline as well as recent developments.

As for online resources, I recommend the websites of the British and American Comparative Literature Association. These websites not only gather information about comparative literature departments around the world, but also inform about conferences, journals and publications in the field. Furthermore, you will find further online resources relevant for students of comparative literature.

References

American Comparative Literature Association (ACLA). See www.acla.org (accessed 17 May 2010).

Bassnett, Susan. *Comparative Literature: A Critical Introduction*. Oxford: Blackwell, 1993.

Bassnett, Susan, and Harish Trivedi. *Postcolonial Translation.* London: Routledge, 1999.

British Comparative Literature Association (BCLA). See www.bcla.org/ (accessed 24 May 2010).

Byron, Lord. 'Translation from Catullus. "Ad Lesbiam"'. *The Poetical Works of Lord Byron*, Vol. 1. Boston, MA: Little Brown and Company, 1864. 19.

Culler, Jonathan. 'Comparative Literature, at Last.' *Comparative Literature in an Age of Globalization*. Ed. Haun Saussy. Baltimore, MD: Johns Hopkins University Press, 2006, 237–48.

Rexroth, Kenneth. *Classics Revisited*. New York: New Directions, 1986.

Sidney, Sir Philip. 'Oh muse what ails this ardour'. *Sir Philip Sidney: The Major Works*. Oxford: Oxford University Press, 2002. 94.

Spivak, Gayatri Chakravorty. *Death of a Discipline*. New York, Columbia University Press, 2003.

Wellek, René. 'The Crisis of Comparative Literature'. *Concepts of Criticism*. New Haven, CT: Yale University Press, 1963. 282–96.

Further reading

Ashcroft, Bill. *The Empire Writes Back: Theory and Practice in Post-Colonial Literatures*. London: Routledge, 1989.

Baker, Mona, ed. *Routledge Encyclopaedia of Translation Studies*. London: Routledge, 1989.

Baldwin, E. et al. *Introducing Cultural Studies*. Harlow: Pearson, 2004.

Bassnett, Susan, and André Lefevere, eds. *Constructing Cultures*. Clevedon and Philadelphia: Multilingual Matters, 1988.

Cronin, M. *Translation and Globalization*. London: Routledge, 2004.

Damrosch, David. *What Is World Literature?* Princeton, NJ: Princeton University Press, 2003.

Jefferson, Ann, and David Robey, eds. *Modern Literary Theory: A Comparative Introduction*, 2nd edn. London: Batsford, 1986.

Saussy, Haun, ed. *Comparative Literature in an Age of Globalization*. Baltimore, MD: Johns Hopkins University Press, 2006.

Tötösy de Zepetnek, Steven, ed. *Comparative Literature and Comparative Cultural Studies*. West Lafayette: Purdue University Press, 2004.

Venuti, Lawrence, ed. *The Translation Studies Reader*, 2nd edn. London: Routledge, 2004.

Williams, Jenny, and Andrew Chesterman. *The Map: A Beginners' Guide to Doing Research in Translation Studies*. Manchester: St Jerome, 2002.

Wolfreys, Julian. *Introducing Literary Theories*. Edinburgh: Edinburgh University Press, 2002.

Getting the most from your course

Moving beyond the particulars of comparative literature and creative writing, let us return to the study of literature in general, with a brief conclusion to this chapter addressing how to get the most from your degree. In many ways, this should be the simplest and shortest part of the book you are holding. It should be … but if there is a downside to a degree in English or literary studies it is that with the number of options available to you, it becomes difficult fairly quickly to know how to choose. Something which may have had an appeal from the module description can turn out to be nothing like you'd expected it. On the other hand, something you'd never considered studying could affect many future choices. And it is frequently the case that students, on completing a module, wish they could start over again with the knowledge they have acquired along the way. With the increase in options afforded by modularity, you have then to make choices in a more informed and somewhat structured manner, hence one of the reasons why you are reading this book. However, only your own interests and experiences can be the final arbiter.

To this end, find out as much as you can about options beyond the hand-book definition. Consider which modules would best sit alongside one another to maximize your acquiring a coherent, rather than a disparate body of knowledge. But also be sure to allow yourself breadth of coverage. Too narrow a focus will leave you with large gaps in your knowledge of literature. Once you have chosen your modules, plan your necessary work well in advance. Find out the required reading and, if at all possible, read – at least once, and in however cursory a fashion – all the primary texts on a given module *before* the module begins. If you're uncertain about a particular module, take a look at the reading for that, skimming briefly. Make appointments to ask tutors and lecturers about the modules they teach. Academics will always be happy to talk about their subject and provide you with additional information so that you can make an informed selection from the options.

More generally, make sure you thoroughly familiarize yourself not only with the department and your library, but also with what online resources are available to you. Many libraries, often through lack of physical space, have online subscriptions to publishers and their journal collections (ProjectMuse or JStor are two important examples). With your student ID you'll be able to gain access to tens of thousands of scholarly articles of the highest quality, which can be read online or downloaded.

Additionally, plan your study time. Know how long it takes you to read a novel and ensure that you set aside enough time to study thoroughly for each of your seminars; balance out your work so you don't have to rush. When it comes to research and writing, always allow yourself ample time to plan, to sketch ideas, to revise and correct, proofreading as you go. While many people maintain the myth (if only to themselves) that their best work is done the night before a deadline, this simply isn't true, and where most essays are now written directly onto personal computers, proofing is often slapdash, despite tools for spelling and grammar checking. If possible, always print off a draft of an essay, and read it through for coherence and development of argument, and for consistency in formal aspects (spelling, grammar, getting facts and details write), and make sure that formatting of bibliographical details is correct.

The next chapter will address these matters and related topics at greater length.

1.3 study skills for literature

1

chapter contents

> Introduction 33
> Study skills 34
  ▶ Making the most of seminars and lectures 34
  ▶ Using the library 35
  ▶ Using IT and the internet 37
  ▶ Revising and exams 38
  ▶ Coursework and your dissertation 39
> Writing and presentation 40
  ▶ Writing essays 40
  ▶ Presentation skills 44
  ▶ Plagiarism 45
  ▶ Bibliographies and citation conventions 47

Introduction

In this chapter we address and focus on the major aspects of literary study. We do so in three different ways, looking at various necessary and transferable skills, regardless of particular interest or subject within the study of literature, before moving to a series of practical concerns to do with writing, presentation, avoiding plagiarism and questions of bibliographical and citation convention.

Reading closely in the text at university level is not merely a constant personal engagement. As a student, you are expected to demonstrate, within the **context** of institutional requirements and the demands imposed on you by the parameters of the discipline you have chosen, your singular responses according to particular conventions and frames. With this in mind, Christopher Ringrose explores the study skills you will require through an examination and explication of the different ways and situations in which learning takes place and abilities are developed, and explains how you should function most effectively in these various contexts. The essay reflects on how to get the most from lectures, seminars, using libraries and the internet, and considering how best to approach exams where these are still used. It does so through the construction of the frames of pedagogy within which you will develop appropriately and in a professional manner your own interests in and fascination with literature, literary form and language, and the places out of which literature comes to be produced, and which it, in turn mediates and translates.

Finally, the last part of the chapter presents briefly, and in systematic fashion, a breakdown of the key 'mechanical' aspects of writing essays. With its sections on 'writing essays', 'presentation skills', 'plagiarism' and 'bibliographical and citation conventions', the purpose of this part is to offer you both an introduction and a reminder of what you always need to focus on in producing acceptable university-level work, regardless of the module being taken and the texts being studied.

Study skills

Christopher Ringrose

Making the most of seminars and lectures

Lectures and seminars are (along with tutorials) the traditional ways in which Literary Studies have been taught. There are those who regard lectures as outdated events, driven by a transmission model of knowledge acquisition that ignores the attention span of the average human being, and undermined by the extensive written handouts and web-posted lecture notes which lecturers themselves now use to enhance their delivery, since most of these can be perused at leisure outside the lecture room. Nevertheless lectures do show experts in a particular field arguing a case in a personal way, with all the emphases, pauses, repetitions, inflections and gestures that make communication more memorable, and they encourage students to remember details of an argument by making their own notes in their own style.

As with most study skills, a 'before, during and after' model helps one make the most of lectures. Preparatory reading will situate the lecture in a context and make the lecturer's own approach more evident. It is possible to make a fetish of note-taking during the lecture, but it is surprising how quickly impressions can fade. Most students find that it helps to subdivide their notes into a sequence of steps of the argument, perhaps with the help of subheadings and numbered points. The important thing is to maintain a structure and shape to the notes, without writing too much at first and then tailing off into a series of 'buzz words' and jottings. Notes can be varied and made more memorable through small diagrams and visual representations of key concepts, and by adding one's own queries in the margin or elsewhere. Lecture handouts can be liberally annotated, in a way that will act as an aide-memoire, then checked later the same day, before being filed away for reference. Each of these stages can be recorded on a laptop or other electronic storage device, and the principles remain the same.

Some lecturers post an mp3 or other audio version of their lecture on the web, or add a few further thoughts in an audio file postscript. Such variation in delivery has proved popular with students, who can either listen to this 'extra' on their PC, or download it and listen to it wherever they like.

The seminar is a staple of teaching and learning in literary studies. Though in practice seminars can take many forms, the principle is that they give priority to the student voice, and provide an arena for reflecting on texts and ideas, close reading and discussion through speaking oneself and listening to others. This ideal is harder to achieve than appears at first sight, and its processes depend upon the skill of the tutors and the goodwill and preparedness of the students involved.

Seminar work develops a number of skills which employers value in English graduates, such as the ability to speak articulately and to the point, to listen attentively to others and use their emotional intelligence to judge their own responses and contributions, to sum up an argument or propose new solutions or close readings. Such skills are developed over a number of years, but there are strategies that can help:

> Students who speak early on in a one-hour or 90-minute seminar are more likely to continue to take an active part. If a contribution is delayed too long, it may never be delivered at all. It may help to set yourself a series of targets for speaking out in class.

> Not all the best seminar contributions are spontaneous. It is a good idea to do some specific preparation in the form of notes of statements to be made or issues to be raised.

> Contributions to a seminar need not take the form of brilliant insights, or observations that will impress everyone else. One student can agree or disagree with another's comments, or ask a question – of the seminar group or of the tutor. It is perfectly acceptable to be tentative ('When I first read this I thought … but now I am not so sure') or to ask for others' responses ('Did anyone else find this text disturbing and ambiguous?').

As with lectures, it can be a useful exercise to sit down for 15 minutes *after* a seminar, to write down some reflections on the topics discussed.

Using the library

Suppose that the class has been given an essay to write on narrative form in Emily Brontë's *Wuthering Heights*; how can the library help? The tutor may have provided the titles of one or two important texts or articles; if so, this is probably a good place to start. But it is only the beginning. To formulate ideas on a topic it is necessary to read several critics or theorists. The simplest way to initiate this process is to browse through the relevant section of the literature shelves. Books need to be chosen with care: judicious use of the contents page and index can save time and suggest which books will be most useful. The more recently published books will provide better coverage of current critical debates, but there will be 'classics' of Brontë studies that need to be taken into account; their titles will soon become familiar as they are referred to and debated with in later studies.

More often than not, students are disappointed by what they find on the shelves, in which case they refer to the library catalogue by looking under 'Brontë', or experiment with related search terms such as 'nineteenth-century novel', 'Victorian fiction' or 'narrative'. Any entry there that seems relevant, but is listed as 'on loan', can be recalled. Likewise, books or articles from periodicals that seem interesting (and many critical texts have useful bibliographies at the end) can be requested on inter-library loan or obtained in electronic form.

A more immediate source of information is the library's periodicals section. Again, an initial familiarity with the journals available can be gained by browsing through the display of current issues. The catalogue will of course provide more systematic help in locating relevant literary periodicals. However, electronic publishing and databases have revolutionized access to journal articles and bibliographies. *The MLA Bibliography* and *The Annotated Bibliography of English Studies* are superb ways of searching for recent criticism online. There are many other similar databases that facilitate searching for books and articles on any literary topic. Such resources cover critical essays from books, as well as journal articles. Sometimes a collection of critical essays might contain a gem on a particular topic. Students often miss these because they base their selection on the book title, which may not always give away what is inside.

Online journals such as those available through JSTOR allow students to search for relevant articles and bring them up instantaneously on the screen, and they are often accessible from home. *Project Gutenberg* has ensured that thousands of literary texts are available for download in electronic form, and *Early English Books on Line* allows students to be original in their choice of primary materials to contextualize the set texts. Students who find these and other special collections, or newspapers such as the *Times Digital Archive*, have access to materials which scholars once found hard to obtain. Nevertheless, libraries do specialize in certain areas of literary studies, and it is worth finding out what special collections (of, for example, early books, little magazines, manuscripts, rare editions, or small press editions) might form the basis of a research project.

Despite the digital revolution, paper-based bibliographical resources still have much to offer. Works like *The Year's Work in English Studies* give annotated checklists of contemporary criticism of all periods. On the reference shelves, the major encyclopaedias as well as the various *Guides to ...* and *Companions to ...* are sometimes worth dipping into for a different perspective on the subject (one would find much information on 'narrative form', for instance, and probably some interesting background on Brontë). More advanced students might want to venture outside the English classmark zone to find theoretical texts: Jacques Derrida in Philosophy, Jacques Lacan in Psychology, Ferdinand de Saussure in Linguistics, and Roland Barthes in Media and Culture, for example.

Librarians working in higher education are highly trained specialists who represent an excellent resource for students of literature. As well as providing group workshops on locating resources, they are available for individual consultations, and their guidance can contribute substantially to the success of a project or dissertation.

Though it may be difficult to exhaust the possibilities of the college or university library, it is as well to remember that there may be a good library in town, or a local branch nearby. Why not join it? Small though it might be, you never know what is to be found on the shelves and the librarian will often order books for student readers.

Using IT and the internet

The boundary between 'using a library' and 'using information technology' (IT) is becoming harder and harder to draw, and university libraries have extended their limits through thousands of databases, e-books and e-journals. Similarly, the boundaries between the lecture or seminar room, the library and social internet spaces have become fluid. Most colleges and universities support some form of Virtual Learning Environment (VLE) as a place to post module handbooks and schedules and as a gateway to items in the library catalogue including electronic resources. In addition, VLEs offer a number of communication tools that can be used as part of assessment of students or collaboration between them:

> Blogs are used as learning diaries (assessed or non-assessed) in which students maintain a cumulative reflective account of their encounters with texts and ideas. These can be shared with other students on the course, or just with the tutor, who can add comments.
> Wikis are communal writing spaces which can be used to build a collaborative document – for example a handout for a group presentation or project.
> Discussion boards allow students on a module or course to post observations on a given topic, and to respond to the postings of others in an ongoing dialogue or group discussion, extending the seminar beyond the formal weekly meeting. They have also been used for creative assignments such as 'recreative writing' and role play, which suit some students' learning styles.

Not everyone is enthusiastic about the use of discussion boards to replace some classroom contact hours. In a recent publication Lisa Botshon expresses scepticism about the notion of 'students participating in online conversations about scholarly materials ... so enthralling that these discussions continued well after the courses had ended' (Botshon 2006: 96).

There is a wider issue here, however. The renowned innovator in web-based learning Alan Liu has advanced the idea that humanities scholars are 'knowledge workers' (12), not only because they specialize in information and ways of wielding it (13) but because information technology is an unparalleled instrument for 'speculative vision' that can be adapted for creative ends: 'we would do well to remember that humanities scholars specialize professionally in the history, **tropes**, forms, and, just as importantly, contradictions of poiesis, whether literary or – in the expanded, Percy Shelleyan sense – social' (Liu 2006: 17).

Professor Liu's essay reminds us that information technology is not just a tool for writing literary criticism or locating published critical essays. It is something that is transforming the very textual materials that make up literary studies, both through the 'proliferation of textuality' that has often been noted as a consequence of the World Wide Web (Lee 2006: 59) and through its effect on the nature of writing and publishing, the medium of hypertext, the use of IT to analyse texts, and the creation of specific sites to promote the study of particular literary topics. Examples include George Landow's work on *The Victorian Web*, *The Modern Word*, which is devoted to experimental and avant-garde twentieth-century writers, and The University of Calgary's *Children's Literature Web Guide*. A number of guides to internet resources for English point students to the best of these online communities.

Students in literary studies use PowerPoint in presentations, link written texts to video and visual images, make extensive use of email or text delivered to mobile phones to communicate with tutors and each other, and post their own creative work online. They are invariably consumers of internet resources, for the World Wide Web provides instant access to a bewildering amount of information on almost any writer, text, theoretical approach or critical topic. Finding worthwhile material on the web is a skill worth developing. The first steps can be briefly summarized:

> Combine search terms (Kipling *in relation to* politics) to gain results relevant to your needs.
> Be prepared to use alternative terms (Kipling and *government*) to widen or focus a search.
> Use subject gateways and specialist author sites for assistance in locating material.
> Give more credence to sites with academic affiliations, such as those signified by the URL suffix 'ac.uk' (United Kingdom) or 'edu' (United States). Be aware, however, that such sites can also be used to post student work, which is less authoritative.

Revising and exams

Students often regard examinations as the least enticing form of assessment. Courses which continue to use exams for assessment do so because they see them as testing the ability to remember knowledge about literary studies and access it rapidly, to write fluently and persuasively within a restricted time span, and to set out a case quickly in response to a question.

Examinations have been around for centuries, and there is considerable advice available to students who want to maximize their chances of success. Universities have learning skills units that give sound advice of this kind (the

Universities of Southampton and Melbourne are particularly well organized in this respect, and their web materials are on open access). Anyone convinced that they possess a distinct learning style (whether visual, auditory, active, reflective or intuitive) may wish to adapt their revision methods to match that particular preference. Visually oriented learners might revise with mind maps, sketches and diagrams; those with an orientation towards the auditory might read material aloud, or record it on an mp3 player, and so on. On the other hand, most people benefit from a range of approaches, and writing the major points of a topic on a series of file cards, with brief quotations to support them, is a simple process that often works well. Other traditional suggestions are worthwhile, or even essential: making a revision plan well ahead of time and keeping to it; consulting past exam papers in the library or online database to get a feel for the question style and format; making sure that time is allocated equally between questions in the exam itself. However, exams in literary studies make their own particular demands, and it is worth remembering five key points:

> While most literary exams are in essay question format, there may also be 'passages for comment' or a series of shorter questions that require a different approach.
> Markers will expect a sustained and detailed argument rather than a descriptive approach. The same is true of essays, of course – but in an exam the time limits make extraneous material particularly noticeable.
> To initiate the argument, there should be a thesis sentence in the opening paragraph which sets out a definite response to the question asked. From this follow the various elaborations of the argument, qualifications and evidence.
> While no one should be encouraged to prepare for an examination by learning by heart a large number of quotations, it is equally true that a literary argument loses force if it cannot be linked to brief quotations from primary texts and anchored in some kind of close reading.
> Markers will often look closely at *how* a quotation is used, so the discussion immediately following a citation should be fresh and distinctly related to the quotation itself.

Coursework and your dissertation

The essay, of anything from 1500 to 5000 words, remains the keystone of assessment in Literary Studies. However, the learning outcomes specified for modules and courses often refer to subject-specific and key skills that need to be tested by different forms of assessment: the ability to work in a group, to make an individual or group presentation, to maintain a learning log or blog, to write a creative assignment which may involve pastiche or creative rewriting, the use of IT or the ability to engage with problem-based learning and discussion forums. In practice, this means that a student of literary studies has to write and speak in a variety of modes, from the formal register of the essay to the more reflective personal voice of the learning diary, and adapt to a range of audiences. The learning outcomes for a module, which will often be presented in the handbook or course guide, are well worth consulting, even if they seem to be couched in an unappealing academic **discourse**. They set out the standards which a student is expected to reach by the end of the module, and can put into focus the particular demands of the associated coursework.

The final year of most courses includes a major project or dissertation of some 8000–10,000 words. For most of the previous two years, students have studied the texts their tutors have chosen and written essays on topics set by them. What has been learned in this process should equip them to work on their own, on texts and topics of their own choice, and using methods of research and presentation they have developed throughout the course. Most students find the dissertation a fitting culmination to their studies, and that it allows them to exercise their imagination and display their originality.

If one were limited to four pieces of advice for those embarking on a dissertation, they might be:

> Choose a topic that interests you and that will sustain you over a year's study. It may be defined around an author, a **genre**, a historical period, or a critical and theoretical issue. Try to formulate a genuine question that you think is worth answering and which will give shape to your enquiry.

> Produce a working bibliography and a review of the existing secondary material. This will draw upon all your skills of information gathering, and will begin the process of mapping out the field. Which books and articles and debates are essential points of reference for anyone working in this area?

> Try not to be too stereotyped in your use of theoretical paradigms. Social realism and documentary fiction of the American 1930s may appear self-evidently to lend themselves to a Marxist or **historicist** approach, but an angle of approach via (for example) **queer** theory or postcolonial concerns may be equally productive.

> Be meticulous in recording sources of material. Marking very clearly which passages in your notes are verbatim quotations, copied from the text in question, will help you to avoid plagiarism (see the section on plagiarism at pp. 45–6).

Writing and presentation

Writing essays

When writing essays, you should aim for clarity of expression and make sure you are always responding to the essay title or question on which you have chosen to write. When beginning to plan your essay, ask yourself if you understand the terms of the question or title, how they relate to each other, and what, in their particular form and relation, they demand of you. Formulate an argument or thesis, which can be expressed succinctly, and which will serve as the basis from which to develop your analysis in response to the text or texts about which you are writing. Consider, in presenting an argument or positioning a thesis as a response to the question or title, what you are required to demonstrate, and how, most logically, and in a systematic and orderly fashion, you can do this. Do so through a combination of original argument, careful choice of closely analysed examples from your primary sources, and judicious support from secondary research materials. Do not simply cite a source as though the truth of a published authority were enough as an assertion. Quoted material should enhance, not replace, your own insights, which, from a knowledge of text and its various contexts, are extrapolated from key textual passages.

Formally, whilst also paying close attention to the shape and trajectory of your argument, ensure that you write in a grammatically consistent manner in which standard rules of grammar are employed. Syntax, grammar, punctuation and spelling all have to meet required formal standards and conventions as determined by your department. If you are at all unclear as to these, see your tutor, or a member of staff whose position it is to give professional advice on the standards of written English within an English department. Always work with a dictionary, and always proofread your essay. It is common for students to rely on automated spelling and grammar software that comes with computer word-processing packages, but these will not help assess the logicality of an argument, whether the proofs are sufficient, and whether your thesis, the argument you wish to make, has a coherent trajectory that structures the essay as a whole. You should therefore get into the habit of printing a draft copy, reading it to yourself for sense, clarity and order, and correcting it by hand, then going back to the computer to make necessary changes. Ask yourself always if what you have said is what you intended to say, and whether you have given sufficient attention to your examples. Never assume that your point is obvious. A quotation on its own without analysis from you or some other framing device will look like what it is: a textual fragment that you perceive as being important to your essay, but the significance of which has yet to be explained to your reader.

Here are some steps you should always follow in producing essays.

> Always keep in mind that the essay must be logically and clearly organized. Sound structure will help convey ideas clearly and cogently. I will address this again, below, but I am stating it at the outset since the major crimes against essay writing come from poor organization, weakly developed thought, and casual, lazy or – let's just say – overly idiomatic modes of expression.

> Focus on your ideas about literary texts. Your ideas should be developed as a careful response, on the one hand, to what is in the given text or texts

about which you are writing and, on the other hand, to what is specifically demanded of you by the question or title you have chosen.

> Begin by identifying the necessary primary and secondary sources you will need.

> Remember that it is always better to produce work on the original text than to string together a series of quotations from or references to a critic. It will stand you in better stead if you can refer in relation to your primary text to other literary texts than simply to stack up numerous critical sources, as if others were doing your work for you.

> Bear in mind that reading critics is an important and useful exercise only inasmuch as they serve a preliminary function of allowing you to get your argument more clearly focused. They think through ideas that allow you to formulate your own; they inform your argument, adding to your knowledge of a text, its history, the ways in which its language works, or the philosophical and political ideas that inform the writer's language at a given historical period. However, a critical source should never obscure your argument, and if you use secondary sources think about how you disagree with their position, rather than what you can take from them. One of the cardinal sins in essay writing is citing a critic and saying nothing about the citation. If you insist on using critical material, always attempt to find a position against the source being used. Your own argument will become sharper as a result.

> Always allow yourself enough time to write your essay. Take notes and plan before you begin drafting or writing. Do not simply amass sources in the library and then at the last moment look for the appropriate comment to plug a gap in your essay.

> Do not simply transfer quotations from notebook to essay. Too many students compile quotations and then structure their essays around them. This is passive reading and should be avoided at all costs.

> Take the time to regroup your notes thematically. New ideas will emerge from the process.

> Compile and maintain your bibliography as you work, but also make the effort to maintain a bibliography of sources beyond the immediate context of a particular essay, as this will serve as an invaluable resource over the three or four years of your degree.

> Plan your essay in outline form only when you have gathered your material, thought about it, made notes and rewritten. Of course, in many cases, you will have done the initial research in response to an essay title or question. This does not mean, however, that you are narrowly limited to the constraints of the essay title. A good writer will add torque to the title or question, making it work for him- or herself. This can only happen though, if you're sufficiently well read and have planned clearly.

> Do not allow your plan to be simply a series of points you want to assert. The points you want to show and to prove should be governed by an initial

argument, the assertion of a thesis, which the points, fleshed out through analytical reasoning and logical progression, serve to prove and elucidate.

> Use your opening paragraph to take the key terms of the essay title or question and place them in the **context** of the argument you wish to present. For example, if your question is 'How "Victorian" are the inhabitants of *Cranford*?', your opening paragraph should do something like this:

> In this essay, I will seek to explore the question of the extent to which the inhabitants of Elizabeth Gaskell's short novel, *Cranford*, can be interpreted as 'Victorian'. In order to do this, it will be necessary, first, to define what is meant by Victorian, and whether this is appropriate to thinking about Gaskell's characters. Secondly, in order to answer this question, it has to be asked what evidence there is in the novel that people of the nineteenth century saw themselves as 'Victorian' in the sense we use that word. Third, it will be necessary to ask to what extent we can assume that all the inhabitants think of themselves in the same way. If not, we have to ask what differentiates the different groups of the inhabitants in their habits of thought about their identity and the way Gaskell's narrator, Mary Smith, defines these groups. Last, as this previous comment implies, it is important to assess whether Mary Smith sees herself as 'Victorian'.

> Keep your paragraphs to an appropriate length (approximately a third to half a page – see my example of an introductory paragraph above), developing the points of your plan in logical and coherent fashion. Paragraphs which run on for a page or more are unacceptable, as are paragraphs of one or two sentences. A paragraph should encapsulate a theme, which is worked through carefully. Paragraphs should follow one another logically. The easiest way to make this happen is to bear in mind that the opening sentence of one paragraph should develop from, and refer back to, the close of the previous paragraph.

> Avoid being glib, flippant, overly familiar. At the same time, however, do not be ponderous or verbose. Just because you like a particular writer or critic does not mean you should imitate him or her. Henry James is just fine – for Henry James – as is Jacques Derrida; but you are neither of these writers, so do not try to be. Nothing betrays a paucity of thought so much as a florid or overly busy style. (And never confuse style with the form of thought.)

> Employ quotations by all means, but avoid using them as crutches. You need to illustrate your argument, not substitute someone else's writing for it. If you cite a source, make sure that your argument illuminates what is important. If I had a cash donation for every time a student has, in an essay, presented me with a passage from the primary text, which appears to invite me to intuit what was on the student's mind when I read it, I could give up teaching, and retire somewhere to write a novel.

> Do not simply repeat what you have already said when you get to your final

paragraph. A good opening paragraph should suggest to the reader that, the argument and your ideas having developed in the manner and direction that they have, there is more that remains to be thought about and said. A concluding paragraph should be suggestive of other avenues of research and approach. It should open out promisingly rather than try too rigidly to tie up all the threads.

There are many excellent style guides, and guides on grammar and the conventions of English usage in college and university contexts. A number of these are accessible online. You can find links to these at: vos.ucsb.edu/browse. asp?id=2448. This comes from a website called 'Voice of the Shuttle', one of the most significant and invaluable web resources for humanities research run by scholar Alan Liu. It is as reliable as Wikipedia is not.

Presentation skills

Presentation skills should be learned and developed as early as possible, and then adhered to throughout your academic career. You will invariably find your mark affected for an essay if you don't follow the simple guidelines. While the minutiae may vary from department to school, here are some basic elements of presentation:

> Use standard size unlined paper.
> Keep margins a standard width: on average, an inch on either side and at the top and bottom of each page.
> Always double space your work.
> Avoid using fonts that are too small or too large, but in any case, 12 point is optimal (and use a fairly standard font, like Times).
> Number pages consecutively.
> Always ensure you stay within the word limit (or in some cases page limit) of your particular exercise.
> Do not overuse either first person or contractions, such as 'I've' for 'I have' or 'don't' for 'do not'.
> Ensure you understand departmental rules for avoiding plagiarism (see the section following this one).
> Always provide a bibliography of works used in preparing your essay.
> Present citations in the appropriate form, and do so consistently throughout. With verse, if you are citing more than two lines, these should be presented separated from the body of your text by a line space and indented from the left margin. When offset like this, they should not be placed in quotation marks. If citing two or fewer lines, these should be presented in quotation marks (single; only use double when there is a quotation within a quotation; NB: this rule is reversed for North American students). Furthermore, if you are quoting from two lines (beginning in one and continuing on the next) or if you are citing two lines within quotation marks, indicate the line break with a forward slash between the lines.

> If quoting more than four lines of prose, follow the same rules for offsetting and indenting as with verse. Again, do not place an offset quotation in quotation marks. If you are citing fewer than four lines, these can follow on from your own commentary, but again must be placed in quotation marks.

> Always make sure the passage from which you are quoting works grammatically with your own prose. If you need to add a word to the quotation to maintain good grammar do so by inserting it in the appropriate place, within square brackets. If you need to delete a word or two, again for the purposes of making the grammar function properly, do so, replacing the removed word or phrase with a triple dot ellipsis, thus: ...

> Close a quotation, if the citation amounts to less than a sentence, by placing your punctuation after closing quotation marks. If the citation has one or more completed sentences, place punctuation before closing quotation marks.

> Place your reference after closing punctuation for an offset or indented quotation. If the quotation is given continuously, within the body of your essay, place your reference before closing punctuation.

> Use footnotes, endnotes or author–date reference system (check with your department for the recommended system), but always be consistent. Notes should be numbered consecutively throughout your essay. If citing plays, give act, scene and line numbers, not pages.

> Ensure that titles of books are always in italics or underlined. Book titles should not go in quotation marks. Quotation marks are only to be used for short poems, short stories and essays, and these are not to be presented in italics.

Plagiarism

Let me begin by quoting my own departmental handbook: 'All written work must be your own unless clearly stated to be otherwise. You must identify all quotations as such, and indicate their sources ... you must also point out the source of any idea or item of information you have obtained from elsewhere' (Loughborough Department of English and Drama Department Handbook, 2005). This seems straightforward and, you would imagine, easy to follow. Unfortunately, matters are not so simple.

Plagiarism comes from the Latin, meaning to abduct someone. Originally used in this context, it referred to the kidnapping of another's child or slave. Clearly, this idea is abhorrent today, a crime. In classical Latin, and dependent on the context in which *plagiarius* was used, the intimation was of obtaining a person thought of as property, and with occasional sexual connotations. Today, and indeed since the sixteenth century, when notions of intellectual property and copyright began to be formulated systematically in relation to publication and writing under the law, plagiarism has come to mean literary or intellectual theft, the act of taking someone else's ideas, and especially those ideas as presented in writing, however that writing has been reproduced and disseminated (in books, in newspapers and journals, or through the internet). Even were you to take someone's notes (supposing, for example, you had picked up that person's research in the library and then copied it, adapted it and presented it as your own), this would still, in effect and legally, amount to that specific form of theft known as plagiarism. In the eyes of the law at large and the laws of institutions such as universities specifically, plagiarism is not only the act of turning in someone else's work whilst presenting it as your own; it is also the practice of copying from a published or unpublished work without giving acknowledgement in the form of a citation. This is further compounded by the omission of quotation marks. You may, very occasionally, forget to put in a footnote, endnote or parenthetical reference, but to cite from a source, whether or not you change a few words, omitting in the process to place that citation in quotation marks, is unacceptable and wrong, as is taking ideas and changing all the wording without proper citation. Even if you are alluding in general terms to someone else's argument, to do so without formal and conventional acknowledgement amounts to plagiarism. Finally, in those cases where so much of your work – the majority of it – is presented in your essays and is taken from another source, whether you acknowledge the source or not is irrelevant, because you have gone beyond the rules of what is termed 'fair use' or 'fair dealing', and so have plagiarized. To risk sounding like a bad advertisement, you wouldn't steal a child, so don't steal a sentence.

In recent years, plagiarism has become more of a problem as an indirect result of the internet. Not only do students cut and paste from internet sources, they also buy papers for their topic online. This is not only wrong; it is lazy and stupid. And the really stupid student is so lazy that he or she does not even bother to alter the bought paper in any fashion, thereby presenting something which doesn't answer the question, and submitting a piece of work which, were it his or her own, would fail in any case for not answering the question. Of course, the internet is a gift to the person wishing to commit intellectual property theft. But it has also made it easier for an academic to search for the source, and there are now plagiarism search engines that can track phrases, sentences or passages that catch the eye of the person marking your work. There are of course many nuanced difficulties surrounding this matter, and if you are concerned at all that you may be inadvertently plagiarizing (as in the example above of citing a source and 'forgetting' to put in the accompanying note or reference), you should ask your professor, your tutor or, if your university has one, your writing centre, to clarify for you where a line is crossed. As an immediate place to check, though, take a look at the website www.plagiarism.org, which goes into great detail about all aspects of plagiarism, why it is wrong, and what the consequences can be (everything from getting a fail mark through failing a course or module to expulsion). It is therefore every student's responsibility to learn the bibliographic and citation conventions relevant to their discipline, having found out what is required of them from their department as standard, and to be scrupulous in their use.

Bibliographies and citation conventions

There are several different sets of conventions that explain citation of sources and the proper format for giving bibliographical details. All share certain similarities, and often the differences are minor. In this, the final part of the chapter, two different but important systems of annotation, citation and bibliographical formatting are presented, these being MHRA and MLA, the former used predominantly in the UK, the latter in the United States. Your department will indicate which is the preferred citation method and bibliographical convention.

MHRA (Modern Humanities Research Association)

What follows are general guidelines for consistent citation and bibliographic presentation based on the MHRA style guide (the full guide is downloadable from the MHRA website). When you choose a system of reference (endnote or author–date parenthetical citation) always stick with the one format within your essay or exercise.

If you choose the endnote system, when you first refer to a source, whether the primary work being cited or a secondary source, such as a critical volume or essay, enter an endnote number at the end of the sentence, or if the sentence continues for some time after the citation, following the citation itself. The number must always be superscript, placed after any punctuation, and should be sequential throughout the essay. Endnotes should then appear in sequence at the end of your essay. (Word processing software allows you to choose between endnotes and footnotes.) Endnotes should be numbered in superscript also, corresponding to their counterparts in the body of the essay.

Endnotes

> Endnotes for books: give the full name of the author, with initials or full name first, as this appears on the book. Then give the title and subtitle of the work to which you are referring. Following this, in parentheses, give place of publication, colon, publisher name, comma, and year of publication. Close parentheses, insert volume number, if applicable, then insert another comma, followed by the page numbers for the passage or sentence you are citing or to which you are alluding. Precede page numbers with 'p.' for a single page or 'pp.' for a citation taken from across a page range.

> Endnotes for journal articles: beginning in the same way as with references to books, insert title of journal instead of book, the volume number, the year of publication (in parentheses), a comma, and the page numbers for the reference, but without the abbreviation indicating page or pages.

> Endnotes for an essay, article, or other work in a collection or edited volume: give author as above, but then give the title of the piece in question, in quotation marks, followed by a comma, followed by 'in' and the title of the book; then give the name of the editor or editors, preceded by

'ed. by'; then give publication details for the book as outlined above in the endnotes for books; if there is a volume number, give that, followed by the page numbers as explained in the details on endnotes for books.

> The rules for italicization and use of quotation marks for titles of books, poems, short stories, essays etc., follow those to be applied to such usages in the main text of your essay.

> If you cite or allude to the same work more than once, it is not necessary to give multiple endnotes. To avoid this, when first giving bibliographic details in a note, add a sentence to the effect that 'all subsequent references from this text are given in parentheses following the quotation'. If you use more than one source repeatedly, remember always to reproduce this sentence to indicate subsequent parenthetical reference. If you are discussing several primary texts, it is acceptable, following first citation, to refer to them through abbreviations for the titles, such as *OG* for *Of Grammatology*. You should, however, in the endnote referring to first use, indicate your abbreviation if you plan to cite frequently, thus: 'all further citations will be given parenthetically following citations as *OG*, followed by the page number'.

> Always include a bibliography, even if you are only citing a single text. If you are working from primary and secondary sources, always provide separate bibliographies. A primary source is the literary work or an historical document contemporary with the literary work. A secondary source is any work of criticism, theory or biography, or a critical text addressing the history of the period in which the primary literary text was produced.

Examples of endnotes

Primary source
[1] Charles Dickens, *Nicholas Nickleby*, ed. by Michael Slater (Harmondsworth: Penguin, 1978), p. 271. All subsequent references are taken from this edition, and are given parenthetically following the reference, with the abbreviation *NN*, followed by the page number.

Secondary source (book)
[2] Kelly Hurley, *The Gothic Body: Sexuality, Materialism, and Degeneration at the* Fin de siècle, Cambridge Studies in Nineteenth-Century Literature and Culture (Cambridge: Cambridge University Press, 1996), pp. 123–4.

Secondary source (article from journal)
[3] Jacques Derrida, 'The Animal that Therefore I Am (More to Follow)', trans. by David Wills, *Critical Inquiry*, 28:2 (2002), 399.

Secondary source (essay in collection)
[4] T. J. Clark, 'Phenomenality and Materiality in Cézanne', in *Material Events: Paul de Man and the Afterlife of Theory*, ed. by Tom Cohen, Barbara Cohen, J. Hillis Miller and Andrzej Warminski (Minneapolis: University of Minnesota Press, 2001), p. 110.

Author–date style of citation inserts the relevant publication information into the body of the essay following the quotation. It is keyed through its details to a Works Cited list or Bibliography at the end of your essay. Give surname of author, date of publication followed by colon, and page, without 'p.' or 'pp.' abbreviation, thus: (Derrida 2002: 393). You will still need to provide a full bibliography, of course, with the information that you would put in an endnote, but one of the advantages that author–date style offers is that it allows you to use endnotes for additional information or supplementary discussion not immediately germane to your argument. It is largely a matter of preference whether you use author–date or endnote convention for references, but if choosing the former, do not use endnotes for references. If you refer to other works in any discussion in an endnote, give these details in author–date format, as you would in the main body of the essay.

All works to which you refer or allude must be included in your Bibliography or Works Cited list. If you choose to call your references a bibliography this has the advantage of allowing you to make references to works you have read in any preparatory research, but which have not been cited. There are two principal conventions for the layout of bibliographical references. One is to present each item in the bibliography with a line space between the items. The other is to omit the line space but to indent second and subsequent lines using tabs:

Example 1, with line space

Dickens, Charles, *Nicholas Nickleby*, ed. by Michael Slater, Harmondsworth, Penguin, 1978.

Dickens, Charles, 'Pet Prisoners', in Slater, Michael, ed., *Dickens' Journalism Volume 2: The Amusements of the People and Other Papers: Reports, Essays and Reviews 1834–51*, The Dent Uniform Edition of Dickens' Journalism, London, J. M. Dent, 1996, pp. 227–34.

Example 2, no line space, with indentation

Dickens, Charles, *Nicholas Nickleby*, ed. by Michael Slater, Harmondsworth, Penguin, 1978.
Dickens, Charles, 'Pet Prisoners', in Slater, Michael, ed., *Dickens' Journalism Volume 2: The Amusements of the People and Other Papers: Reports, Essays and Reviews 1834–51*, The Dent Uniform Edition of Dickens' Journalism, London, J. M. Dent, 1996, pp. 227–34.

The style of presentation is similar in some respects to referencing in endnotes, but there are small, crucial differences. Presenting a bibliography, you must place all items in alphabetical order, and separate, as I mention elsewhere, primary from secondary sources. Each bibliographical article should have, in the following order: (i) author surname, comma, initials or first name, as these appear on the title page of the work, all of which is followed by a comma; (ii) title and subtitle of work, followed by a comma; (iii) place of publication, comma, publisher name, comma, date, full stop. Note that if you use the author–date system of citation in the text, the date should be placed immediately following the author's name in the bibliography.

Articles in journals follow the same procedure up to the title, but then follow this with volume number, comma, date of publication in parentheses, comma and page range of article in full, without page abbreviations. Chapters or essays in an edited collection give (i) author surname, comma, initials or name, comma; (ii) this is followed by 'in', followed by the editor's name, given in the same order as the author's name, followed by 'ed.,'; (iii) title of volume, comma, publication details as with a book by a single author; (iv) full page range, with 'pp.' abbreviation.

Primary source (book)

Dickens, Charles, *Nicholas Nickleby*, ed. by Michael Slater, Harmondsworth, Penguin, 1978.

Primary source (essay, short story, poem or other collected source)

Dickens, Charles, 'Pet Prisoners', in Slater, Michael, ed., *Dickens' Journalism Volume 2: The Amusements of the People and Other Papers: Reports, Essays and Reviews 1834–51*, The Dent Uniform Edition of Dickens' Journalism, London, J. M. Dent, 1996, pp. 227–34.

Secondary source (essay or chapter in edited collection)

Clark, T. J., 'Phenomenality and Materiality in Cézanne', in Cohen, T. et al., eds, *Material Events: Paul de Man and the Afterlife of Theory*, Minneapolis, University of Minnesota Press, 2001, pp. 93–114.

Secondary source (article in journal)

Caruth, Cathy, 'The Claims of the Dead: History, Haunted Property, and the Law', *Critical Inquiry*, 28:2 (2002), 419–442.

Internet sources
Give details of the specific article or page you have accessed, followed by the full web address. After the web address, give, in parentheses, the date you accessed the document, thus:
Roberts, Sam, and Groes, Sebastien, 'Ghost Signs: London's Fading Spectacle of History', in *Literary London: Interdisciplinary Studies in the Representation of London* (2007), accessed via http://www.literarylondon.org/London-journal/index.html (23.02.2008).

MLA (Modern Language Association)

Here is a brief summary of the major points of MLA formatting.

Endnotes: For MLA formatting, you should use endnotes for research papers unless you are given instructions that indicate otherwise. For published manuscripts, check with the editorial guidelines. Endnotes should be used primarily to refer readers to a crucial source and/or to provide imperative information that may detract from the essay in some way. You should consecutively number endnotes; furthermore, according to *A Writer's Reference*, 'The text of the paper contains a raised Arabic numeral that corresponds to the number of the note' (Hacker 2008: 446).[1] The number should be placed 'at the end of the sentence, clause, or phrase containing the material quoted or referred to' (Gibaldi 1999: 269).

Parenthetical citations: For a sentence that includes quotations of less than four lines in length (or under three lines in length if poetry), include the page number in parentheses before the period. If the critic or author's name is provided in the sentence, you do not need to include the cited person's last name in the parenthetical citation. If it is not mentioned, you should add the last name before the page number in parentheses. You should neither include a comma to separate the author's name and the page number nor include a p. or pp. Simply use one space to separate the last name and page number.

> Edith Nesbit begins her novel, *The Railway Children*, with the following sentence: 'They were not always railway children to begin with' (1).
> One of the most charming openings of any contemporary British novel is this one: 'Have you ever tasted a Whitstable oyster?' (Waters 3).

Parenthetical citations for two or more authors: For a text written by two or three authors, include their last names in parentheses if they are not included in the sentence with the quotation. For a text written by four or more authors, include all of their names or the last name of the first author. In the latter case, writers should follow the last name with 'et al.'

Parenthetical citations for more than one text: To include quotations from two or more separate texts, you should follow the same guidelines for a parenthetical citation and separate the authors' names and page numbers with a semicolon.

(Waters 87; Nesbit 23)

Parenthetical citations for quotations of more than four lines of prose (or *three lines of poetry*): If a quotation meets these criteria, it remains double-spaced and is offset from the paragraph. The right margin remains ragged; the left margin is indented one inch. For this parenthetical citation, the period comes before the parentheses. You should not use quotation marks.

William Hope Hodgson describes the setting for the frame story of his novel, *The House on the Borderland*, in these words:

> Right away in the west of Ireland lies a tiny hamlet called Kraighten. It is situated, alone, at the base of a low hill. Far around there spreads a waste of

bleak and totally inhospitable country; where, here and there at great intervals, one may come upon the ruins of some long desolate cottage – unthatched and stark. The whole land is bare and unpeopled, the very earth scarcely covering the rock that lies beneath it, and with which the country abounds, in places rising out of the soil in wave-shaped ridges. (1)

Works cited: All bibliographic references should occur at the end of the paper, after the endnotes. This section should be titled, 'Works Cited'. All references should be alphabetized according to the authors' last names. The entire list should be double-spaced; the titles of journals and books are always underlined or italicized. In addition, the first line is left alone while all the lines following it are 'hanging' (indented). A one-author book reference includes the information in the example below:

Waters, Sarah. *Tipping the Velvet*. New York: Riverhead, 1998.

Books with two or more authors or unknown authors: If there are two or three authors, include all their names 'in the order in which they are listed in the source. Reverse the name of only the first author' (Hacker 2008: 422). If a text has four or more authors, you can either list all their names, again reversing only the first name, or just list the first one followed by 'et al.' In the event that the book's author is unknown, 'begin with the work's title' (423).

Book with an editor or translator: You should follow the same format for a book citation, and simply add for editor 'Ed.' and then the name; writers should include this information after the title of the text and before the place of publication. For translator only use 'Trans.' You do not need to reverse the names of the translator or editor. For example,

Barthes, Roland. *Camera Lucida: Reflections on Photography*. Trans. Richard Howard. New York: Hill and Wang, 1981.

Journal article: An academic journal entry looks like the example below. You should note the lack of punctuation between the title of the journal (italicized) and the volume number as well as the second colon that follows the date in parentheses.

Parkins, Wendy. 'Moving Dangerously: Mobility and the Modern Woman.' *Tulsa Studies in Women's Literature* 20:1 (2001): 77–92.

Citing electronic sources: Electronic sources follow a basic format with a few variations. For citing a website with an author, you should include the following information: the author's name; the title of the site; the date of publication or recent update; the name of any organizations affiliated with it; the date the writer accessed the site; and the URL. For example,

Jokinen, Anniina. *Luminarium: Anthology of English Literature*. 4 Feb. 2007. 12 Jan. 2008. http://www.luminarium.org/.

Works cited and parenthetical citations vs. endnotes: If you use endnotes for your bibliographic material, they may not need a 'Works Cited' list or parenthetical citations. This choice is left to the discretion of the style guide approved by your institution. If you use endnotes for all bibliographic information, the formatting is a little different from that of a 'Works Cited' list. The first endnote contains all the bibliographic information and 'ends with the page number or numbers only of the portion you refer to' (Gibaldi 1999: 268). Any endnotes that follow referring to the same work include only the author's last name and page numbers. If you have two or more works by the same author, then you include the author's last name, the name of the work and then the page numbers(s). For example,

> ² Sarah Waters, *Tipping the Velvet* (New York: Riverhead, 1998) 3. [Note that the author's first and last name are not reversed.]
> ³ Waters 18–25. [Note the lack of a comma between the author's last name and the page number.]
> ⁴ Waters, *Affinity* 67. [Note the comma separating the author's last name from the title of the work.]

Note

1   For example, like this.

References

Botshon, Lisa. 'All Aboard Blackboard'. *Teaching, Technology, Textuality: Approaches to New Media*. Ed. M. Hanrahan and D. Madsen. London: Macmillan, 2006. 93–104.

Gibaldi, Joseph. *MLA Handbook for Writers of Research Papers*. New York: The Modern Language Association of America, 1999.

Hacker, Diana. *A Writer's Reference*. Boston and New York: Bedford/St. Martin's, 2008.

http://www.intute.ac.uk/english/

Lee, Stuart. 'Putting IT into the English Syllabus: a Case of Square Pegs and Round Holes?' In *Teaching, Technology, Textuality: Approaches to New Media*. Ed. M. Hanrahan and D. Madsen, 57–68. London: Macmillan, 2006.

Liu, Alan. 'The Humanities: a Technical Profession'. In *Teaching, Technology, Textuality: Approaches to New Media*. Ed. M. Hanrahan and D. Madsen, 11–26. London: Macmillan, 2006.

2 literature modules

2.1   literature   57

2.2   periods   65

2.3   forms, genres and other popular modules   134

2.1 **literature**

chapter contents

> Introduction   57
> Critical studies: an example of a core module 59
> Conclusion   63

Introduction

The purpose of Part 2 of *The English Literature Companion* is to offer you a sense of the range of literature you might study, and which works typically serve to constitute notions of particular periods, **genres**, forms and other academic areas of focus. Through this, you will be offered an introduction to the range of materials, along with their cultural and historical contexts and questions of orientation, which modules can make available. Because every module will have different foci, no two will ever be exactly alike, and modules will frequently be taught with an implicit narrative or other coherent structure running through them. With this in mind, each of the essays here avoids being overly prescriptive or didactic concerning 'what the student can expect from his or her module'. Instead, the aim of these various articles is to give you an informed overview of what might be expected so that, through these critical introductions, you might find an interest in a module that you had not previously considered. As a result – and depending on the extent to which you are free to choose from the variety on offer in departments – you should be able to construct for yourself a pathway through your degree which rewards you and challenges you in a number of unexpected positive ways.

Of course, you would not expect to study everything here in your first year; such a thing would not be possible. Thus, the range of modules, addressing periods of literature, genres and forms, and providing overviews of some of the more frequently offered types of modules, is indicative of many of the aspects of literary study and the options open to you from first to third (or fourth) year. The descriptions of modules are accompanied by basic syllabi, based on a 12-week semester, and given in roughly the order you might study the subjects. Again, this is only, in every example, a rough generalization, as the permutations and variations are almost as infinite as literature itself. Furthermore, because degree programmes can vary so much, from university to university

(English is, in many ways, an anomaly, when compared with other degrees – it does not and cannot be made to assume one or two models of study, as one would find in, for example, the social sciences), the sections on the various modules are not ordered according to a presumed chronological order of study. What has been done, instead, is to assign a provisional year of study in which it is likely that you would take the module in question.

Having made the various cautionary remarks, it can be said that certain features do prevail from department to department, university to university, and it is the case that first-year students will find themselves taking broad overview modules, a number of which will be compulsory. These are intended to introduce you to critical approaches, to give you a sense of history and **context**, to introduce you also to the notion of the relationships between literature and culture, politics, and the ways in which human identity is manifested in literature. Thus, as a first-year student, you might find you are expected to take a module that addresses critical studies, to assist you in learning how to study literature at university level; at the same time, you will be asked to work on different critical approaches, in order to understand how one form of analysis has advantages and blind spots lacking in another, all of which is intended to help you develop your own critical voice. You will be asked to read widely in a range of critical and secondary sources, such as literary criticism, philosophy and the history of ideas, whilst also honing your interpretative and analytical skills. Another module might teach you to read for historical evidence in a literary work, or how to work with form through the close study of poetic form in all its various guises. Yet another first-year module might introduce you to – expecting you to explore – what is referred to as 'fiction', or 'the novel'.

One other remark remains to be made. In reading any module outline provided here, remind yourself of the opening chapter of this book, which discussed what literature is, and why we read it. It is important always to bear in mind why you began a literature degree. In a recent seminar with first-year students, when I asked why they were studying literature, why they had decided on a degree in literary studies, a large number replied that they thought they were good at it, that they had been proven to be good readers, adept in a number of ways, during their high school careers. One of the abiding shocks (if that is not too strong a word) for some students, though, is a sense of bewilderment in the face of encountering critical approaches to literature, which are far more pronounced and nuanced than anything introduced to you whilst in secondary education, where the emphasis is much more on your personal encounter with the form of literature. Literary studies will ask all sorts of questions you could not possibly have anticipated, beginning with such foundational questions such as 'What is literature?' and 'Why study literature?' Keeping in mind the marked difference and, as a result, the gap between secondary and tertiary literary education, which is as wide as any such space in other disciplines, and possibly wider than most, will help to ground what you do.

It is also worthwhile looking for yourself at the various critical approaches discussed in Part 3, as aspects of certain module descriptions will become clearer in the light of an understanding of approaches that you will encounter, some of which you will be expected to be familiar with, or which you might take an interest in for yourself, in the effort to become adept at particular disciplinary approaches to the question of literary interpretation. At more advanced levels of your degree, often in the second but certainly in the third (or fourth) year, it will not only be the case that you are studying a topic, **genre** or period, but that you will be expected to develop more advanced versions of the approaches you have already learned, or the module will be developed in such a way that critical reading is no longer what is conventionally referred to as a secondary source, but constitutes the necessary reading in its own right. The modules on feminism or **subjectivity**, for example, both have highly developed critical perceptions, which are most likely foregrounded in the teaching of the subject, rather than being a background or preparatory aspect of the study. So you might find yourself reading works on linguistics, particular critical discourses from psychoanalysis or Marxism, or those particular, highly diverse critical works generically defined as 'poststructuralism'.

Critical studies: an example of a core module (Year 1)

If you have an introductory module focusing on critical approaches in your first year, and with that the study of literary form, it might take shape in the following manner, to borrow from the description of a compulsory Year 1 module I run at Loughborough. This Critical Studies module introduces the first-year undergraduate to particular critical and analytical skills required to study literature at university. The teaching consists of weekly lectures and seminars. In close conjunction the lectures and seminars explore both literary and critical texts (often referred to as primary and secondary texts), introducing the student to different approaches, methods and perspectives concerned with literary analysis, whilst simultaneously presenting matters of history and form in literary studies. As part of such an introduction, the student is expected to develop an awareness and appreciation of the ways in which the study of literature has developed historically within the university, and how different disciplines, forms of intellectual inquiry, and cultural, theoretical and political concerns from outside the university have called into question and transformed the study of literatures in English. Part of such an introductory training is to help students develop critical faculties concerned with how one constructs an argument and presents evidence. At the same time, the student learns to develop his or her critical voice, through direct engagement with both 'creative' or 'literary' texts, from different periods and different genres or forms, and 'critical' texts, which have been influential, and remain a force within, the critical reading of literature and film, and other related areas of cultural study.

The semester is divided into three sections. Each has its own clearly defined areas and roles, but all are interrelated and are intended to inform one another as part of a whole. In the first part, as a general orientation to the act of close reading in the context of university study of literature, the student is given a critical introduction to the historical and cultural rise of English and literary studies in the university, the philosophical and ideological assumptions underpinning such institutional development, and the question of authorship. Such concerns are intended to introduce the student to the idea that literature is never value free. It asks questions such as: why are some books studied rather than others? Who decides? What are the values that serve traditionally as justification for the study of literature in a university, and where do those values come from? What is the significance of the author in such debates, and what is the role of the reader? Having introduced these questions and the debates that ensue, the module will then, alongside seminar discussion of such concerns, introduce the student to practical skills: how to cite texts appropriately, how to use the library, how to research effectively, and so on.

Part II offers the student an introduction and overview to four critical discourses which they will be expected to engage with, criticize and produce readings from in the second semester of their study, as part of the process of developing their analytical skills and critical voice. In the first instance, these lectures are not aimed at 'teaching' a particular theory (the critical approaches on offer being Feminism, Marxism, Structuralist linguistics and Psychoanalysis), but merely offering an orientation to the disciplinary discourses as these are germane to literary criticism, thereby introducing the student to the question of different perspectives in the practice of criticism. At the same time, and in order that the student keep in mind the literary texts, lectures and seminars guide the student through specific selections from the readers and passages from the literary texts. Having developed critical insight into conventional thematic and formal issues, the student is expected to develop an understanding of how criticism challenges those critical 'truths' that have been introduced in the first five weeks, thereby demonstrating their partiality, their perspectival limits and orientation. As a means both of helping and testing the student's comprehension of critical discourse, which can often seem alienating, unnecessarily jargon-laden or, as some students see it mistakenly, taking the pleasure out of reading, a précis is set as an exercise. If you are not familiar with such an exercise, the purpose is to have you write, in your own words, what the critic is saying, in your own voice, as if the essay were the expression of your ideas. Such critical explication is invaluable in comprehension.

Part III focuses on a small number of literary texts, and, through those, addresses questions of form, theme and history, in relation to one another. The three texts in question, in this particular model, are Christopher Marlowe's tragic drama, *The Tragical History of Dr Faustus*, Alexander Pope's mock-epic poem, *The Rape of the Lock*, and Emily Brontë's novel, *Wuthering Heights*. The three works studied thus represent different periods and different literary forms, with all the questions of convention, historical **context**, and so on, that these bring with them. This part thus introduces the student to the 'creative' or 'literary' texts under consideration, and as preparation for what is to come in the second semester, and the second part of this module, which is the close exploration of how to read from different critical perspectives. Without pre-empting theoretical, critical or ideological discussions, the lectures and seminars in this part of the module discuss the three topics identified as 'form, theme and history'. In doing so, they demonstrate how literature does not develop in isolation: it borrows already existing models, imagery, structures, narratives, cultural values and assumptions. At this stage the student becomes aware that text and context, though distinguishable, are not separable. At the same time, in the discussion of form, theme and history in the three literary texts, the lectures and seminars aid the student in understanding how the different concerns of the module fit together, by referring back to the lectures of the first part of the semester concerning assumptions about authorship, questions of value, and the role of humanist thought in the development of literature as historical category and cultural phenomenon. The purpose in making these connections is to allow the student to carry over the questions of **canonicity**, authorship, institutionalization, and the role of **criticism** – and to begin to question such values. Also, a lecture or seminar at this juncture might well refer to an influential, traditional humanist critical essay that discusses the text, and then demonstrate the limits of that reading. It might equally open debate about the role of the author, and the concomitant question concerning what we receive from a text, over which the author has no control, or which he or she cannot programme. In this way, through providing the student with a clear understanding of the intrinsic aspects of text, the lectures and seminars prepare the student for an introduction to alternative modes of inquiry, as preparation also for their own critical practice throughout the rest of the year.

As you move through a module such as this, you may well be struck repeatedly by the fact that what you took for granted – or perhaps had never thought about, such as what makes a work of literature literature, and why it is considered great, why it is defined as a 'mystery', a 'tragedy', and so on – will be called into question. At times you may well find yourself wishing to resist what, after all, on reflection was so commonsensical as not to be open to interrogation. Such impressions might well come to be magnified when you come to read critical theory, works by Marx, say, or Sigmund Freud, Simone de Beauvoir, or other critics, and theorists, from various backgrounds, these being the kinds of texts you will find in a reader, such as Phillip Rice and Patricia Waugh's *Modern Literary Theory*, to which I refer below. After all, what does Marxism have to do with literature? Why ask political questions about what should be pleasurable? At the very least, some of the language will seem (needlessly, you might think) abstract, or, most simply, difficult.

A good dictionary – and most university libraries will have the *Oxford English Dictionary* (*OED*) or access, through library websites to an online version – is a great help, but much of critical language is what might be called '**discourse** specific' (or what some would complain about in a negative and uncomprehending manner as 'jargon laden'); that is to say, language about a particular subject incorporates particular terms in order more effectively to be able to address as specifically as possible its subject, the subject of its **discourse**. Indeed, it has been the case that words have their meanings adapted to suit a particular purpose in a given **context**, or, on occasions, new words – neologisms – are coined. Because of the breadth of sources of critical language – or discourse – a specialized dictionary or glossary of key words is highly useful. Combined with this, you will find you are being asked to think about what you take for granted: how to read. And you will be expected to question those assumptions, or at least give to those assumptions a more coherent, clearly delineated shape, and to see, additionally, how your reading is neither simply true nor false, but, instead, one perspective, which leaves you blind to others. Those other perspectives can discomfort, initially; however, if given careful consideration in an open-minded manner, they can also indicate to you why we have something at once so magnificently useless as literature, and yet why also we come back to it – whatever it is – over and over.

The current syllabus for such a module, with the required reading list, looks like this. Appended to the lectures is a suggested reading list of the materials that might be covered in seminars:

Critical studies: sample syllabus

Part I: What is 'literature'?

1 Introducing the obvious: an overview and contextualization of the module

2 Defining 'literature': the rise of English Studies
   Reading: Terry Eagleton, Ch. 1 'The Rise of English' in *Literary Theory: An Introduction*

3 'I know what I like ε': humanism, literary criticism and assumed values
   Reading: Terry Eagleton, 'Introduction' in *Literary Theory: An Introduction*; Philip Rice and Patricia Waugh, eds, *Modern Literary Theory*, Part III, Section One: 'Canonicity and Value', pp. 397–409

4 The author's dead, long live the author: assumptions about authorship
   Reading: W. K. Wimsatt and Monroe Beardsley, 'The Intentional Fallacy'; Roland Barthes, 'The Death of the Author' in Rice and Waugh, eds., *Modern Literary Theory*; Michel Foucault, 'What Is an Author?'

5 The importance of the text: why we read, and how literature is different from everything else

Part II: Critical approaches to literary interpretation

6 'Marxism today?': Marxism and literary criticism
   Reading: Terry Eagleton, *Literary Theory*, 'Conclusion: Political Criticism'; Karl Marx, 'From *The German Ideology*', pp. 18–24, and 'Section 3: Marxism' in Rice and Waugh, *Modern Literary Theory*, pp. 103–42

7 'Why, Freud?' Psychoanalysis and literary criticism
    Reading: Terry Eagleton, *Literary Theory*, Ch. 5 'Psychoanalysis'; Sigmund Freud, 'From *Introductory Lectures on Psychoanalysis*', pp. 24–34, in Rice and Waugh, *Modern Literary Theory*; Sigmund Freud, 'The Uncanny'; Geoffrey Hartman, 'The Interpreter's Freud'

8 Here comes the science bit Ɛ concentrate: structuralism, formalism and literary criticism: Reading: Terry Eagleton, Ch. 3 'Structuralism and Semiotics'; Ferdinand de Saussure, 'From *Course in General Linguistics*', pp. 34–40; Viktor Shklovsky, 'From 'Art as Technique', pp. 49–52, and Gérard Genette, 'From *Narrative Discourse*', pp. 65–76, all in Rice and Waugh, *Modern Literary Theory*

9 Feminism
    Reading: Simone de Beauvoir, 'From *The Second Sex*,' pp. 41–3, and 'Section Four: Feminism', pp. 143–74, in Rice and Waugh, *Modern Literary Theory*

Part III: Canonical texts, traditional approaches

10 *Dr Faustus*: Humanism and the (Early Modern) subject

11 *The Rape of the Lock*: an 'Heroi-Comical Poem'

12 *Wuthering Heights*: critical orientations, narrative form, and history

Recommended reading

Brontë, Emily. *Wuthering Heights*. Ed. Helen Small and Ian Jack. Oxford: Oxford World's Classics, 2009.

Eagleton, Terry. *Literary Theory: An Introduction*. Anniversary edn. Oxford: Wiley-Blackwell, 2008.

Marlowe, Christopher. *Dr Faustus*. Ed. Roma Gill. London: Methuen New Mermaids, 2003.

Pope, Alexander. *The Rape of the Lock*. Ed. Elizabeth Gurr and Victor Lee. Oxford: Oxford Student Texts, 2007.

Rice, Philip and Patricia Waugh, eds. *Modern Literary Theory: A Reader*. London: Hodder Arnold, 2001.

Wolfreys, Julian, Ruth Robbins, Kenneth Womack. *Key Concepts in Literary Theory*, 2nd edn. Edinburgh: Edinburgh University Press, 2006.

Conclusion

Of course, it has to be stressed again, this is only one possible example, one form of practice, and your own particular experience might be markedly different. The purpose here, however, is to indicate in this introduction just one of the ways in which literary study at university expects you to engage with, asking particular questions about, what is called 'literature' in a manner that is marked not only by a difference in orientation but also in the attention to detail that is required of you as a student of literature.

You might also think, from the sample syllabus presented above, that the ways in which the literary works and critical works are presented seems somewhat rigidly separated. There are two reasons for this. It is important to present the 'fundamentals', whether one is talking about form, history, context or a school of criticism; thus, the work indicated above is merely that covered in a single semester, the module example given being a two-semester module, lasting a year.

The purpose of the second semester is to develop knowledge of the primary aspects of literary study introduced in the first semester, through the sustained close analysis of literary texts through theoretical models, and simultaneously to examine those theoretical or critical texts for the ways in which their arguments are shaped, how their assumptions are arrived at, what the limitations of their paradigms are, and how they might (a) be combined or argue with other theories and (b) how they might lead critical inquiry into concepts such as class, **gender**, race, **subjectivity**, **power**, identity, and so on. The second semester proceeds in four-week sections, each section devoted to careful rereading of each of the literary works – *Faustus, The Rape of the Lock, Wuthering Heights* – through each of the critical 'lenses' (Marxism, psychoanalysis, structuralism, feminism). In this way, as a student you will be enabled to ask questions of the text according to the critical paradigms with which you are expected to work, the intention also being that as you move repeatedly through the texts and critical approaches, you begin to understand how the critical methodologies do not exist in isolation but engage in a debate amongst themselves, which then enrich and inform the act of critical reading, beyond naive assumptions about 'literature', 'the author', 'history', and other concepts we use to talk about fictional writing, poetry, drama, culture and so forth – and all of which is only to begin to lay the groundwork for what you will be doing during your degree.

With this in mind, we will now turn to the next chapters of Part 2, discussing typical modules you might take, or, in some cases, would be required to take, depending on whether those modules are optional or compulsory.

chapter contents

> Old English literature 65
> Medieval literature 72
> The sixteenth century 80
> The seventeenth century 86
> The eighteenth century 93
> Romanticism and gothic 101
> The nineteenth century and the Victorians 110
> Modernism 120
> Contemporary literature 125

Old English literature

(Years 1–3)

Philippa Semper

What is Old English?

Old English literature is the term used for texts produced during the Anglo-Saxon period: that is, the time (roughly speaking) between the settling of Germanic tribes in England in the fifth century and the invasion of the Normans in 1066. However, most of the texts that survive from this period date from between the eighth and eleventh centuries, and there is some overlap into the twelfth century too, so the boundaries are not exact. Most courses, textbooks and scholarly publications refer to the period and the people who lived in it as 'Anglo-Saxon', while they call the language that was spoken at this time 'Old English'. It will help to keep this distinction in mind right from the start.

Old English literature is a rich and varied body of writing which has an ongoing impact on language and culture: Tennyson and Ezra Pound translated and were inspired by it; Gerard Manley Hopkins used its rhythms and alliteration as the basis for his own development of 'sprung verse'; J. R. R. Tolkien made it the language of the Rohirrim in *The Lord of the Rings*; Nobel prize-winning poet Seamus Heaney wrote a modern poetic version of its most famous work, the **epic** poem *Beowulf*; it has even been used as the basis for the magic spells performed in the recent BBC television drama *Merlin*. Studying Old English provides a fascinating glimpse into the culture of a past society, but also an insight into how much it has affected and continues to affect us today. It is also a good basis for understanding the roots of much of the language, literary forms and cultural constructs which appear in later English writing.

Few people have had the opportunity to find out much about English history before 1066 as part of their school curriculum, so modules in Old English often begin with a brief introduction to the history of the period, showing how the Anglo-Saxons came to be in England and the nature of their society and religion. This will give you a basic framework to help you to organize your learning; you may find it useful to start building your own timeline of the period at this point, adding texts and events to it as you become aware of them. You could read *The Anglo-Saxon Age: A Very Short Introduction* by John Blair, or Peter Hunter Blair's *Introduction to Anglo-Saxon England* to help you with this. Your knowledge and understanding will continue to grow and develop throughout the course as you study Old English texts for yourself and discover more about their original contexts.

Beginning Old English

Some university courses may deal with Old English literature mostly or entirely in translation, but the majority expect students to deal directly with the literature in its original form, at least for selected key texts. Even a quick glance at a piece of written Old English will show that the language has changed considerably over the centuries; it may seem at first to be very different from the English spoken today. Yet many words are identical in Old English and Modern English – in fact, 'word' itself comes from the Old English 'word' – and with a little experience in looking at these kinds of texts you will recognize many more that are very similar indeed to their Modern English forms. To help with this process, most modules include an introduction to the grammar and vocabulary of Old English. The grammar will probably take a little study because Old English is an inflected language. This means that it uses endings on words to mark the subject, object, indirect object, and so on in its sentences; Modern English uses word order to identify these instead. If you have studied a language like German or Latin before, this won't be new; if not, it may take a couple of weeks to get used to it. This might appear something of a challenge to begin with, but practice makes a difference very quickly: a little effort early on in the course will pay dividends later. In fact, it can be very helpful to have your knowledge of grammar refreshed and extended in this way, since it makes it possible to analyse Modern English texts more accurately and with greater confidence.

The alphabet used to write Old English looks slightly different since it contains three extra letters called ash, thorn and eth. These are written æ, þ and ð (or upper case Æ, Þ and Ð). The ash is pronounced like the letter 'a' in 'ash', and thorn and eth are both pronounced as 'th'. These will quickly become familiar, and once you know them you will see more connections between Old English words and their modern equivalents (for example, Old English 'þæt' and Modern English 'that'). Reading Old English texts out loud is always a good idea, because a word that might look strange on the page may sound almost identical to one that you know. Working in a study group with other students can be extremely useful in these early stages; you can help each other to grasp the grammar, look up words and work out how to pronounce them.

There are various guides and textbooks available for those who are learning Old English, and usually one of these will be assigned as the essential book for your course. Very common examples are *An Introduction to Old English* by Peter Baker and *A Guide to Old English* by Bruce Mitchell and Fred C. Robinson. Some of these have online grammar exercises associated with them and increasingly there are entire grammar courses online, which tutors will encourage you to use. Most language textbooks have a large selection of texts in Old English in a section towards the end of the book; these are generally the basis for your study of the literature, saving you from the need to buy other texts. Many texts can also be found online, although without the notes and vocabulary found in the textbooks, they are best kept for quick reference rather than detailed study.

Studying Old English texts

As you read the texts, you will discover that Anglo-Saxons had highly developed ideas about social behaviour, the roles that different people played and the nature of the power governing their interactions. As in other periods, they explored, tested, promoted or challenged such ideas in the stories they told. Family identity (kinship) represented one of the building blocks of their society, and the obligations and issues kinship involves reoccur as themes in many different situations. Often these overlap with themes of lordship (or kingship) and loyalty, since a lord gathers a group of men around him to fight for and with him; in return they gain gifts, status and a place in his hall – a social identity. Sometimes these things may come into conflict, of course: a warrior might be ready to fight to the death for the life of his lord, but what if it is his own family he must take on in the process? What will be remembered about his actions later, whichever side he chooses? The Anglo-Saxons had a strong sense of the importance of personal reputation, of history and of storytelling, which underlies many of the texts in Old English that have survived.

In particular, this may be seen in some of the prose texts often used as good starting points for learning Old English. One of these is the *Anglo-Saxon Chronicle*, an almost year-by-year account of important events. The *Chronicle* was first put together in the ninth century and continuations of it were then made for several centuries. Some years have longer entries, while others are very brief. Students often look at a short selection of entries; a popular choice is the entry for 755/7, which tells the story of power struggles involving two actual kings and one would-be king of the kingdom of Wessex. Entries like this provide a fairly short piece of text to analyse and explore; you can see how narrative is sometimes provided in patterns or repeated structures, and consider how this affects your understanding of the piece as 'history'. Looking closely at the language will reveal how sentences are arranged in clauses, with a strong sense of rhythm, rather than according to word order.

Although pagan when they arrived in Britain, the Anglo-Saxons converted to Christianity for the most part during the seventh century, and the conversion has shaped and filtered our knowledge of everything that happened in the period. Christianity brought with it a new set of ideas, possibilities and constraints; through it, written records and texts became an integral part of Anglo-Saxon culture, yet all that was recorded represented a very particular interpretation – a reshaping even – of that culture. How the Church affected Anglo-Saxons' understanding of their own actions and preoccupations in the world is a key question, and can be examined in some detail through a study of extracts from another text often used: the Old English version of Bede's *Ecclesiastical History of the English People*. Bede was a very learned monk and priest. From his text you might examine several of the different kinds of stories that he weaves together: miraculous healings and events, political manoeuvrings and royal conflicts, religious negotiations, and even an account of how the traditional form of Old English poetry was supposedly first used to express Christian themes. This last story, in which Cædmon the cowherd is divinely inspired through a dream to sing the praise of God the Creator, is very often part of university curricula; this is because Bede included a version of Cædmon's very first poem, thereby providing an ideal place to start learning about the form and content of Old English poetry.

The poetry of the Anglo-Saxons comes mainly from four manuscript anthologies known as the Exeter Book, the Junius Manuscript, the Nowell Codex and the Vercelli Book. This suggests just how much poetry must have been lost simply because other manuscripts have not survived the millennium following their production. Originally this poetry was oral – that is, it was composed out loud, on the spot (although following some very strict rules), in the presence of others, and accompanied by the harp – and some study of the complex nature of oral poetry in general, which exists and has existed in many cultures over many different periods of time, is often provided in university modules. The oral inheritance of Old English poetry is paramount, accounting for the use of alliteration and formulas and for its rhythmic but non-rhyming structure. This poetry is designed to be heard rather than read; we can, therefore, examine the ways in which poems use sound and stress to create poetic effect aimed at the listener rather than the reader. Oral poetry is primarily communal, aimed at a group of people rather than one person alone; it is valuable to investigate the various kinds of community who might have listened to these poems, even after they had been written down, and what kinds of uses or responses might have resulted.

Christianity provided written versions of the oral tradition of memory and history, both in Latin and Old English. Before the conversion, the oral poetry of the Anglo-Saxons was concerned with promoting a heroic tradition, producing stories concerned with battles, heroes, kings, treasure and, sometimes, monsters; many university modules will emphasize the nature of heroic society. There are not many 'heroic' poems left but we do, fortunately, still have *Beowulf*, the longest and most important poem surviving in Old English. The deeds of the hero form the basis of this tale of brutal fights and gruesome deaths, but there is a surprising amount of polite discussion, wise advice and philosophical pondering too. Because *Beowulf* is an epic poem in every sense (see EPIC), it is not possible to study more than a few extracts in an introductory course, and in some universities you might not study it at all until later on in your degree programme. However, its themes and ideas inform any understanding of other poems from the period. In addition, *Beowulf* and stories like it in Old English have influenced later writing to a huge extent, from medieval romance right through to modern fantasy and science fiction.

After the conversion to Christianity, the traditional poetic form and themes were adapted to present Christian content, and so there are several poetic versions of Bible stories in Old English, such as the poems known as *Genesis*, *Daniel* and *Judith*. These show how these stories of creation, exile, testing and battle were rewritten in terms that would make sense to an Anglo-Saxon audience, and how this interaction of cultures resulted in a new and creative form of poetry. Introductory modules often include *The Dream of the Rood*, an extraordinary dream-vision poem which describes the crucifixion from the viewpoint of the cross itself and portrays Christ as a triumphant hero rather than a suffering saviour. Study in this area might entail close comparisons between the biblical texts and the Old English versions, but could also include research into the many other representations of these ideas in Anglo-Saxon art.

Old English literature includes a group of texts often described as 'wisdom poetry', and you might encounter famous poems like *The Wanderer* and *The Seafarer*, as well as those like the *Maxims* that explain everyday life in terms both of nature and of human behaviour. These introduce questions about the interaction of traditional ideas with Christian ones, including whether the Christian consolation of an eternal, enjoyable afterlife seems to balance out the transitory nature of human experience. This wider perspective on life and death can then inform your reading of other texts, enabling further possible interpretations of secular poems like *Beowulf* as well as of those more obviously concerned with religious matters.

Critical approaches

When you first begin reading Old English texts, you will probably concentrate on working out what they mean, perhaps translating them into Modern English. However, you should expect to work with them in the same ways as any other literary texts too; like modern novels or poetry, you will analyse their language and imagery, style, tone, form and **genre**. It's important to avoid over-simplifying either the Anglo-Saxons themselves or the texts they produced. Collections of essays such as *A Companion to Anglo-Saxon Literature* will give you a detailed and wide-ranging insight into the literature of this period and the culture that produced it. For a volume that will fit in your bag, try *The Cambridge Companion to Old English Literature*.

Various critical approaches can be used effectively on these texts – it doesn't matter that they postdate the texts by over a millennium. If an approach is valid it should provide valuable insights into Old English writing as well as more recent textual productions. Books like *Reading Old English Texts* provide examples of how you can try different kinds of approach to specific issues and areas. For example, Claire Lees's chapter on feminist criticism and Old English would give you a sound introduction to the area and also to Lees's own groundbreaking work on **gender**. This is an important area for research into Old English; feminist readings have sought to recover or re-examine the roles and voices of women in both poetry and prose, while other scholars have re-examined male sexuality in the period and also produced **queer** readings of Old English texts. Similarly, Nicholas Howe's introduction to historicist approaches is a clear exposition of the ways in which Old English texts can be opened up by attention to the interactions of **power**, material culture and **ideology**, while acknowledging the difficulties inherent in accessing and discussing a period so far removed from our own. His book *Migration and Myth-Making in Anglo-Saxon England* might in turn cause you to apply to Old English literature some of the questions asked by critics dealing with colonialism and postcolonial literature. Alternatively, you might use *Of Giants: Sex, Monsters and the Middle Ages* by Jeffrey Jerome Cohen as a starting place for various readings, including psychoanalytical ones, of the interactions of men and monsters in Old English texts. Even a very brief summary such as this indicates the potential for applying a range of critical approaches to poetry and prose of this period, and the fascinating outcomes that follow.

By the end of the module, you should be comfortable with reading and analysing the language, and may wish to engage more deeply with the meanings and etymology of words. If you decide to take further modules in Old English, there are a range of subjects you might focus upon. Some universities might save one or more elements discussed above for second- or third-year modules, often alongside other types of Old English text such as homilies (sermons) or saints' lives. In a more advanced module you would also have more opportunity to investigate the Anglo-Saxons' love of wordplay and verbal games of all sorts, especially in relation to their composition of riddles and their use of runes to create more complex written puzzles. A final step might be to read Old English texts against their own modern versions and retellings (of which there are many) and to study the different ways in which these texts have been received at various times.

Summary

Although you may need a little effort to come to terms with the language at the beginning, Old English literature offers a varied and fascinating body of texts for study. From the heroic tradition and Anglo-Saxon culture to textual games or the nature of storytelling, there is plenty of material to work with. Learning about Old English also provides a valuable basis for the understanding of later literary production, and thus forms a key part of any English degree programme.

Old English: sample syllabus

Semester 1: Old English prose

Week 1   Introduction to the Anglo-Saxons
Week 2   Introduction to Old English: letters and sounds
Week 3   Introduction to Old English: grammar
Week 4   Reading Old English: starting translation
Week 5   Tales of the beginning: history, origins and identity in *The Anglo-Saxon Chronicle* and Bede's *Ecclesiastical History*, Book 1
Week 6   Kings and kin in the *Anglo-Saxon Chronicle:* 'Cynewulf and Cyneheard'
Week 7   The coming of Christianity: Bede's *Ecclesiastical History*
Week 8   Why Christianity? Bede's account of the conversion of King Edwin
Week 9   Fighting and learning: King Alfred's preface to 'Pastoral Care'
Week 10   The Anglo-Saxons at school: Ælfric's 'Colloquy'
Week 11   Translating from Latin to Old English: Ælfric's 'Preface to Genesis'
Week 12   The conversion of Old English poetry: Bede's account of Cædmon

Semester 2: Old English poetry

Week 1   Introduction to oral poetry
Week 2   Old English poetry: metre, alliteration, formulas, kennings
Week 3   Celebrating heroes: *The Battle of Brunanburgh*
Week 4   Celebrating heroes? Extracts from *Beowulf*
Week 5   The hero in context: *The Battle of Maldon*
Week 6   The hero in defeat: spinning *The Battle of Maldon*
Week 7   Christ as hero: *The Dream of the Rood*
Week 8   Appropriating Anglo-Saxon culture: Christianity in *The Dream of the Rood*
Week 9   Dream visions: *The Dream of the Rood*
Week 10   Seeking wisdom: *The Wanderer*
Week 11   Speaking wisdom: *The Seafarer*
Week 12   Orality, poetry and manuscript copies: the nature of Old English poetry

Bibliography

(a) Literary works

Gordon, Ida L. *The Seafarer*, rev. edn. Exeter: University of Exeter Press, 1997.

Jack, George. *Beowulf: A Student Edition*, rev. edn. Oxford: Clarendon, 1997.

Krapp, G. P. and E. V. K. Dobbie. *The Anglo-Saxon Poetic Records*. 6 vols. New York: Columbia University Press, 1931–53.

Leslie, R. F. *The Wanderer*, 2nd edn. Exeter: University of Exeter Press, 1985.

Marsden, Richard. *The Cambridge Old English Reader*. Cambridge: Cambridge University Press, 2004.

Miller, Thomas, trans. *The Old English Version of Bede's Ecclesiastical History of the English People*. Cambridge, Ontario: In Parentheses Publications, 1999; www.yorku.ca/inpar/Bede_Miller.pdf

Muir, Bernard. *The Exeter Anthology of Old English Poetry*. 2 vols. Exeter: University of Exeter Press, 1994.

Scragg, D. G., ed. *The Battle of Maldon*. Manchester: Manchester University Press, 1981.

Shippey, T. A. *Poems of Wisdom and Learning in Old English*. Cambridge: D. S. Brewer, 1976.

Swanton, Michael, trans. and ed. *The Anglo-Saxon Chronicle*. London: Dent, 1996.

Swanton, Michael, ed. *An Anglo-Saxon Chronicle*. Exeter: University of Exeter Press, 1990.

Swanton, Michael. *The Dream of the Rood*. Manchester: Manchester University Press, 1970.

Treharne, Elaine. *Old and Middle English: An Anthology*, 3rd edn. Oxford: Blackwell, 2009.

(b) Further reading

Campbell, James, ed. *The Anglo-Saxons*. London: Penguin, 1991.

Donoghue, Daniel. *Old English Literature: A Short Introduction*. Oxford: Blackwell, 2004.

Fulk, Robert D., and Christopher M. Cain. *A History of Old English Literature*. Oxford: Blackwell, 2004.

Godden, Malcolm, and Michael Lapidge, eds. *The Cambridge Companion to Old English Literature*. Cambridge: Cambridge University Press, 1991.

Liuzza, R. M., ed. *Old English Literature: Critical Essays*. New Haven, CT: Yale University Press, 2002.

North, Richard, and Joe Allard, eds. *Beowulf and Other Stories: An Introduction to Old English, Old Icelandic and Anglo-Norman Literature*. London: Longman, 2007.

O'Brien O'Keeffe, Katherine, ed. *Reading Old English Texts*. Cambridge: Cambridge University Press, 1997.

Pulsiano, Philip, and Elaine Traherne, eds. *A Companion to Anglo-Saxon Literature*. Oxford: Blackwell, 2008.

Medieval literature

(Year 2)

David Griffith

For many students medieval literature possesses magnetic qualities: an ability to attract and repel in equal measure. You may find first acquaintances quite baffling. It can seem rather daunting if your only premodern landmark is something called 'Chaucer' and the natives in this uncharted territory appear to speak a foreign language. But to recognize the distinctive qualities of medieval literature is to begin to understand the relevance – and pleasure – of reading books from a 'half-alien' culture (Medcalf 1981: 1). Your tutors will point towards the beauty of its language, to its ability to grapple with both abstract ideas and pressing human concerns, its array of technical innovations (in **genre**, form, style and mode of expression), and its habit of anticipating contemporary critical concerns such as issues of **gender** and identity. If

Chaucer is still the main component of medieval literature courses it is because he is a poet of incomparable wit and insight into the human condition, but it is important to recognize that the term 'medieval' collapses into a single category a huge body of verse and prose that spans the arrival of the Normans in 1066 and the Reformation of the sixteenth century. Today many ·courses look beyond notions of Chaucer as the only significant poet of the age, beyond the notion of static feudal society waiting for the Renaissance to happen, to reveal the dynamic historical and linguistic processes by which literature of the medieval period was formed.

Early Middle English

Students approaching medieval literature for the first time often address the underlying causes of language change across this period and their impact upon literary activity. Indeed, you are likely to encounter passages from texts of the immediate post-Conquest period on language modules that explore how and why Old English (the language used for the English of the Anglo-Saxon period) becomes Middle English (the term scholars use to describe the language of post-Conquest England). The story of English at this time is complicated and under constant revision but there are a number of key developments. Most obviously, there is a new linguistic order and for some centuries English ceased to be the language of the ruling classes. The Norman aristocracy spoke a version of French and, quite naturally, this became an official language of their new domains. Latin remained the language of the Church and of government and record keeping, but Anglo-Norman (the form of French spoken in England) very largely displaced English as the language of education, the Court, the legal system, and of literature. The speed and extent of the decline of English literary activity is debatable – the relatively small number of surviving manuscripts obscures the larger picture – but certainly English lost prestige; to gain significant preferment English speakers were forced to speak and write in French.

Without any centralized authority to govern its written forms early Middle English reflected the regional dialect of individual scribes (Burnley 1992: 63–4). Writing after arrival of the Normans in 1066 is thus marked by a variety of Englishes rather any one standard form, and by vastly reduced opportunities to copy and circulate English texts. You will find careful analysis of this transitional period in the 'After the Norman Conquest' section of *The Cambridge History of Medieval English Literature* edited by David Wallace. Particular emphasis here is placed upon the 'afterlife' of Old English, by which is meant the ways in which the literary traditions of the Anglo-Saxon period continued to shape and inhabit Middle English texts. One important continuation is the descendant of the *Anglo-Saxon Chronicle* written at Peterborough Abbey (*c.*1140), but religious texts such as the *Ancrene Riwle* (*The Rule for Anchoresses*) (*c.*1220) and the 'Katherine' group (*c.*1225), all from the north and west midlands, also emerge from the pre-Conquest prose tradition. That this region also preserved something of the Anglo-Saxon poetic inheritance, perhaps nurtured by local monastic centres, is shown by Layamon's *Brut* (*c.*1200–25). This history of Britain in alliterative verse echoes Old English **epic** but its immediate source is the Anglo-Norman *Roman de Brut* (1155) by the Channel Islander Wace, itself an adaptation of Geoffrey of Monmouth's Latin *Historia Regum Britanniae* (*The History of the Kings of Britain, c.*1136). This triangulation of texts exemplifies the close relations between the post-Conquest languages. A more intimate exchange is seen in the debate poem *The Owl and the Nightingale* (1190s), which, though distinctively English in setting and vocabulary, adopts a genre favoured by Latin authors and uses the short **couplet** form developed by French poets. Elaine Treharne's anthology *Old and Middle English c.890–c.1400* presents a variety of witnesses to the major English genres during this period and is an excellent classroom text.

While these and other texts demonstrate the diversity of early Middle English, it must be remembered that they represent a modest return on two centuries of literary activity and that French and Latin remained the preferred languages of the political and cultural elite. However, a marked shift in attitudes had taken hold by the later thirteenth century, and by the early 1300s English had emerged in some quarters as the national language. One attractive reading suggests that this development is part of a growing sense of English identity and a belief that 'national sentiment is most properly expressed in English' (Turville-Petre 1977: 22). This cultivation of 'Englishness' is often coupled with a desire to write in the mother tongue for the good of the individual and the greater cohesion of the country. The Northumbrian *Cursor Mundi* (*c.*1300) proclaims that it is translated 'For the love of Inglis lede [people], / Inglis lede of Ingland, / For the commun at understand' (234–36), while the Lincolnshire monk Robert Mannyng presents his *Chronicle* (finished 1338) as 'not for þe lerid but for þe lewid' [not for the educated but for the unlearned]. The kinds of linguistic choices made by medieval readers have proved to be compelling areas of research and higher-level classes often address the significance of multilingual manuscripts and poems. For example, the manuscript now known as British Library, Harley 2253 – a collection of English, Latin and Anglo-Norman materials from *c.*1330 – demonstrates how knowledge of book production and the means by which texts circulated and were copied by scribes is vital for any true understanding of the reception and readership of literary works.

The romance genre

One particularly sensitive index of the changing demand for English texts is the romance genre, the most popular form of secular literature of the period and one that features on many courses. Originating in the aristocratic courts of northern France at the end of the twelfth century (the term derives from the romance languages), the romance narrative typically charts the adventures of a hero whose chivalric and courtly behaviour validates the power, status and value systems of its readers. These exploits have often been seen as timeless and non-specific but recent criticism has shown how romance reveals the particular concerns of its own historical moment. Thus, while a text like the Anglo-Norman *Gui de Warewic* (*c.*1240) espouses the political and social outlook of a baronial class of reader, later English versions of Guy's legend point towards an audience with 'a wider perception of national identity and the importance of national interests' (Crane 1986: 59). The sub-generic strands – Arthurian legend, Breton lays, the so-called 'Matters' of England, France and Rome – all inflect the central issues of history and chivalric values to lesser or greater degrees. Set against hagiography's muscular Christianity, the prominence of religious ideals and overt piety in many English romances also indicates sustained crossover between the genres.

Poetry in the age of King Richard II

These fertile conditions gave rise to the experimental, often radical English writing of the later fourteenth century. Collectively William Langland, the *Gawain*- or *Pearl*-poet, John Gower and Geoffrey Chaucer are termed 'Ricardian poets' (from the age of King Richard II, 1377–99) and many undergraduate courses focus exclusively upon their formal and thematic interests; in all cases good student editions are on hand (respectively Schmidt 1995; Anderson 1996; Peck and Galloway 2003–6; Benson et al. 2008). Driven by the simple question 'How may I save my soul?' *Piers Plowman* describes Langland's alter ego Will journeying through the contemporary secular world and biblical history. By turns naturalistic, **allegorical** and visionary, Langland's poem typifies the social and political engagement of the so-called 'revival' of alliterative verse of the west midlands first seen in *Winner and Waster* (*c.*1352). These poems share the lexical and technical brilliance of their Old English antecedents but both *Piers Plowman* and the four poems attributed to the *Gawain*-poet, including the finest medieval English romance *Sir Gawain and the Green Knight*, are also suffused with a deep knowledge of Latin and French literary culture. Putter's *An Introduction to the Gawain-Poet* (1996) and Simpson's *Piers Plowman: An Introduction* (2007) offer detailed analyses of the poets and their contexts and are good starting places from which to begin your personal exploration. Londoners both, Chaucer and Gower write in the rhymed verse popular in the south and east of the country. They too share a profound interest in form and employ multi-layered narrative structures to contain an array of generic and stylistic experiments. *Confessio Amantis*, Gower's major English poem in a trilingual output, uses the simple device of a lover's confession to frame a set of individual narratives. Chaucer's writing is marked by complex narratorial voices, generic hybridity and a pervasive ironic tone. These can be seen in dream visions like *The Book of the Duchess* and in the tragic classical love story of *Troilus and Criseyde*, but they find greatest expression in his last work, the polyvocal and open-ended *Canterbury Tales*. For pursuing the myriad critical responses to Chaucer – his anticipation of postmodern preoccupations of meta-fiction, the

2

construction of sexual identities, and so on – the collection of essays in Ellis's *Chaucer: An Oxford Guide* (2005) makes an excellent companion.

Chaucer's legacy

A crucial factor in the reinvention of the English tradition at this time is the act of translation by which readers were given access to works in Latin and other European languages. Chaucer's writing, in particular, is thoroughly **intertextual** and rooted in adaptation of other works. The allusion to 'Virgile, Ovide, Omer, Lucan and Stace [Statius]' at the end of *Troilus and Criseyde* (Benson et al. 2008: 584, l. 1792) reveals how he is at once acutely aware of his role in the aggrandizement of the English vernacular and of the processes by which his own writing is authorized, that is, how it achieves the authorial or authoritative status traditionally associated with Latin texts. To describe this Anglicization of European literature as a cultural transference of power neatly captures these literary dynamics and it is nowhere more apparent than in the generations of Ricardian writers (Wogan-Browne et al. 1999: 314–30).

Such was Chaucer's status among his immediate successors that his death in 1400 seemed to them to mark the end of imaginative writing in England. This kind of negativity has clouded much critical thinking about fifteenth-century literature, which has traditionally been seen as imitative and uninspired. Latterly, many critical studies have reassessed these rather sterile responses by reading, for example, the self-abasement of poets like Thomas Hoccleve and John Lydgate as an inventive modesty **trope** (see, for example, Lerer 1993). So, rather than taking Hoccleve's admissions of dullness and inferiority in *The Regement of Princes* at face value – 'my worthy mayster Chaucer' and 'The first findere of our fayre langage' (Pearsall 1998: ll. 4978, 4983) – we can detect strategies of self-assertion that authorize his own work through alignment with the father of English poetry. That these early fifteenth-century poets were encouraged to elevate Chaucer to the status of a national poet by a Lancastrian monarchy keen to use English to promote national identity against a backdrop of internal rebellion and foreign war is an intriguing aspect of this complex process of **canon** building. It should also remind us that poets are integral to literary activity at this time, not merely in writing for patrons for financial gain but in nurturing the moral and intellectual vitality of the nation.

Later Middle English

The re-evaluation of late medieval literature has led to renewed appreciation of its diversity and innovation. Though many of its examples are presented in abbreviated or extracted form, Pearsall's *Chaucer to Spenser: An Anthology of Writings 1375–1575* features many significant and landmark texts and authors and is a key student edition. Here you will find further evidence of the repackaging of classical wisdom in Lydgate's *Troy Book* (1412–20) and *The Fall of Princes* (1431–8); the first stirrings of autobiographical writing in Hoccleve's

The Series (1421–2) and the *Book of Margery Kempe* (*c*.1436), in which the eponymous author throws over family life to devote herself to God; the continued appetite for lyric poetry, secular and religious, including the sustained love **allegories** of the French nobleman Charles d'Orléans who was held captive for 25 years after the battle of Agincourt in 1415; and Thomas Malory's postcolonial *Le Morte d'Arthur* (1460s), the definitive version of the Arthurian legend in English and a meditation upon the loss of the English empire in France and the civil strife of the Wars of the Roses. More specialized anthologies are Boffey's *Fifteenth Century English Dream Visions*, which shows the adaptability and enduring popularity of the genre, and Wogan-Browne's *The Idea of the Vernacular: An Anthology of Middle English Literary Theory 1280–1520*, in which the 'prologue' is used to describe contemporary approaches to the vernacular tongue; the latter volume is accompanied by an excellent set of critical essays. Barratt's edition of *Women's Writing in Middle English* presents a range of female-authored texts, including translations of the French works of Christine de Pizan (*c*.1365–*c*.1434), perhaps the most influential late medieval woman writer, and the letters of the Norfolk-based Paston family, which perhaps more than any contemporary writing give us the impression of eavesdropping across time. For plays, Walker's *Medieval Drama: An Anthology* illustrates the vibrant dramatic traditions of late medieval England – from the biblical retellings of the mystery plays that are rooted in the urban culture of East Anglia and the north to the allegories of morality plays like the comic but disturbing *Mankind* (1460–5). Many of these texts, and earlier ones too, are freely available in online editions by The Consortium for the Teaching of the Middle Ages (TEAMS).

The final phase of medieval writing can be measured by the same continuations, ruptures and paradoxes of earlier centuries. On the one hand, a breed of self-confident authors doff their poetic caps to tradition; on the other, there is a new set of literary agendas largely determined by the rise of European humanist thought and the religious and political reformations instigated by Henry VIII. Once again it is rewarding to trace these changes through responses to Chaucer, though now we find more explicitly competitive or revisionary readings. Perhaps the most intriguing is Robert Henryson's *Testament of Cresseid* (before 1492), a Middle Scots reworking of *Troilus and Criseyde* that questions Chaucer's moral authority in the aphoristic 'Quha wait if all that Chauceir wrait was trew?' [Who knows if all that Chaucer wrote was true?] (Pearsall 1998: 471, l. 64). An English contemporary of Henryson, and one equally attuned to the moral dimensions of storytelling and notions of self-worth, is the poet-priest John Skelton whose poetic persona is crowned laureate in *The Garland of Laurel* (*c*.1495, printed 1523), leaving Chaucer, Gower and Lydgate trailing in his wake. Skelton is often described as a transitional writer, profoundly attached to the religious and intellectual structures of the Catholic world yet possessed of an abiding interest in the classical learning that stood at the heart of humanist endeavours.

Literature and the Reformation

It is perhaps only with Thomas Wyatt that we stand for the first time in the presence of a literary figure with distinctly Protestant tendencies. Like Chaucer before him, Wyatt was a court poet whose works figure political and cultural struggles through personal relationships such as his aborted affair with Anne Boleyn (Pearsall 1998: 609). So, too, formal experimentation leads him to Italian literature, reworking Petrarchan sonnets just as Chaucer had adapted Dante and Boccaccio. But it is in the paraphrases of the Penitential Psalms – 'From depth of sin and from a diepe dispaire ... / The have I cald, O Lord, to be my borow' [guarantor] (Pearsall 1998: 629, ll. 1, 4) – that the Reformed theology of personal penitence and dependence upon God's grace is given its first distinctive voice (Heale 1998: 154–5). The break from Rome largely dismantled the intellectual and material culture of medieval England but the energy and resourcefulness of its literary tradition continues to inform and inspire.

Medieval literature: sample syllabus

Semester 1: After the Conquest

Week 1   After the Conquest: fragmentation and variety
Week 2   Making history: *The Peterborough Chronicle*; Layamon, *The Brut*
Week 3   *The Owl and the Nightingale* and debate poetry
Week 4   Women and God: *Ancrene Riwle* and the Katherine Group
Week 5   Poetry and experimentation: the lyric tradition
Week 6   Genre, mode and audience: early Middle English romance
Week 7   Drama and community (1): the York and Wakefield mystery plays
Week 8   Langland, *Piers Plowman* (1): visions of England
Week 9   Langland, *Piers Plowman* (2): visions of Heaven and Hell
Week 10   *Sir Gawain and the Green Knight*: an alliterative romance
Week 11   Poetry and morals: John Gower, *Confessio Amantis*
Week 12   Chaucer and France: *The Book of the Duchess*

Semester 2: Chaucer and after

Week 1   Chaucer and Italy: *Troilus and Criseyde*
Week 2   Chaucer and England: the *Canterbury Tales* (1)
Week 3   Chaucer and England: the *Canterbury Tales* (2)
Week 4   Writing after Chaucer: John Lydgate and Thomas Hoccleve
Week 5   Mystics and pilgrims: Dame Julian of Norwich and Margery Kempe
Week 6   Drama and community (2): *Mankind* and the morality play
Week 7   The Arthurian legend: Sir Thomas Malory, *Morte d'Arthur*
Week 8   Scots writings: William Dunbar and Robert Henryson
Week 9   Satire and politics: John Skelton
Week 10   English humanism: Sir Thomas More
Week 11   The Courtly poet: Sir Thomas Wyatt and Henry Howard, Earl of Surrey
Week 12   The end of Catholic England: *The Examinations of Anne Askew*

Bibliography

(a) Literary works

Anderson, J. J., ed. *Sir Gawain and the Green Knight, Pearl, Cleanness, Patience*, new edn. London: Dent, 1996.

Barratt, Alexandra, ed. *Women's Writing in Middle English*, 2nd edn. Harlow: Longman, 2010.

Benson, L. D. et al. eds. *The Riverside Chaucer*, 3rd edn. Foreword by Christopher Cannon. Oxford: Oxford University Press, 2008.

Boffey, Julia, ed. *Fifteenth-Century English Dream Visions: An Anthology*. Oxford: Oxford University Press, 2003.

Burrow, J. A. and Thorlac Turville-Petre, eds. *A Book of Middle English*, 3rd edn. Oxford: Wiley-Blackwell, 2004.

Pearsall, Derek, ed. *Chaucer to Spenser: An Anthology of Writings 1375–1575*. Oxford: Blackwell, 1998.

Peck, R. A. and Andrew Galloway, ed. and trans. *John Gower: Confessio Amantis*. 3 vols. Kalamazoo, MI: Medieval Institute Publications, 2003–6.

Schmidt, A. V. C., ed. *William Langland: The Vision of Piers* Plowman, B-Text, new edn. London: Dent, 1995.

Treharne, Elaine, ed. *Old and Middle English c.890–c.1450: An Anthology*, 3rd edn. Oxford: Blackwell, 2009.

Turville-Petre, Thorlac, ed. *Alliterative Poetry of the Later Middle Ages: An Anthology*. London: Routledge, 1989.

Walker, Greg, ed. *Medieval Drama. An Anthology*. Oxford: Blackwell, 2000.

Wogan-Browne, Jocelyn et al., eds. *The Idea of the Vernacular. An Anthology of Middle English Literary Theory 1280–1520*. Exeter: Exeter University Press, 1999.

(b) Further reading

Aers, David. *Community, Gender and Individual Identity: English Writing 1360–1430*. London: Routledge, 1988.

Barron, W. R. J. *English Medieval Romance*. Harlow: Longman, 1987.

Cooper, Helen. *Oxford Guides to Chaucer: The Canterbury Tales*, 2nd edn. Oxford: Oxford University Press, 1996.

Salter, Elizabeth. *Fourteenth Century English Poetry. Contexts and Readings*. Oxford: Oxford University Press, 1984.

Scanlon, Larry, ed. *The Cambridge Companion to Medieval English Literature 1150–-1500*. Cambridge: Cambridge University Press, 2009.

Simpson, James. *The Oxford English Literary History*, Volume 2: *Reform and Cultural Revolution, 1350–1547*. Oxford: Oxford University Press, 2002.

Spearing, A. C. *Medieval to Renaissance in English Poetry*. Cambridge: Cambridge University Press, 1985.

Strohm, Paul, ed. *Oxford Twenty-First Century Approaches to Literature: Middle English*. Oxford: Oxford University Press, 2007.

Treharne, Elaine, and Greg Walker, eds. *The Oxford Handbook of Medieval Literature in English*. Oxford: Oxford University Press, 2010.

Wallace, David, ed. *The Cambridge History of Medieval English Literature*. Cambridge: Cambridge University Press, 1999.

Online resource

TEAMS Middle English Texts:
   www.lib.rochester.edu/camelot/teams/tmsmenu.htm

The sixteenth century

Joan Fitzpatrick

Terminology

The sixteenth century is notable for its engagement with a phenomenon that emerged in Italy two centuries earlier: the 'Renaissance', meaning 'rebirth'. This refers to a revival of art and literature under the influence of classical models which began in Italy in the fourteenth century and which occurred between roughly 1500 and 1650 in England. Renaissance humanists were keen to emphasize cultural links with ancient Greece and Rome; 'humanist' from the Latin *humanitas* indicated learning or literature concerned with human culture, including grammar, rhetoric and poetry, and especially the study of ancient Latin and Greek classics (*OED* humanity II. 4.). In the course of your study you might come across the term 'early modern', which is sometimes used by critics in an attempt to get away from the patronizing notion that the Renaissance came just after the cultural lull of the Middle Ages, yet neither term is free of ideological implications since 'early modern' has the flaw of suggesting that everything that came earlier was before the 'modern' and thus somehow inferior.

The printing press

There was a distinct shift in the sixteenth century towards a literature that was less exclusive than much of what had gone before. This was essentially due to the invention of the printing press in the fifteenth century by Johannes Gutenberg. Manuscript culture produced books that were beautifully crafted objects but they were inordinately expensive and thus exclusive. The impact of the printing press was remarkable: for the first time, books were a commodity rather than a specially commissioned, precious and exclusive work of art. Although books were still relatively expensive, printing meant that they could be produced more quickly and at a lower cost than was previously the case. The invention of the printing press had an enormous impact upon English cultural life but literature also became less exclusive because of a fresh effort to re-establish literature for English people in the vernacular, that is, the language commonly spoken by the people. There emerged an increasing number of texts translated from Latin into English, not least the Bible, and an interest in adapting foreign forms to suit an English audience. This was in no small part due to the English Reformation, which demoted Latin, the recognized language of the Roman Catholic Church, and brought about a renewed interest in English.

More's *Utopia*

Sir Thomas More's *Utopia*, first published in Latin in 1516, was translated into English and published in 1551. *Utopia* is a prose work in which a fictional traveller, Raphael Hythloday, whose second name means 'dispenser of nonsense' in Greek, describes the social organization of the island of Utopia, which in Greek means 'no place' but might also be a pun on *eutopos*, meaning 'good place' (More 1992: 3). Some critics claim that Utopia constitutes a blueprint for perfect social organization but others that More meant *Utopia* as a grand joke at your (the reader's) expense, which mocks the ideal of communal ownership of wealth (see SATIRE). Certainly the text is full of contradictions and conflicts, such as the name of the island itself, which suggest that More wanted the reader to consider carefully if Utopia really is an ideal place. In 1535 More was executed for his refusal to swear to the Act of Succession and the Oath of Supremacy, which made Henry VIII and his heirs, not the Pope, head of the Church of England. It is perhaps ironic that the split from Rome that led to More's downfall was part of the process that led to the wider dissemination of his writings and all texts formerly only available in Latin.

The Court and patrons

Before the emergence of the professional theatre industry in the late sixteenth century, literary dissemination was via the Court; therefore authors who were not aristocratic and thus wealthy and well-connected depended on patrons to promote and fund their creativity. Amongst notable sixteenth-century aristocratic courtiers and authors were Sir Philip Sidney, whose *Apology for Poetry* (sometimes called *The Defence of Poesy*) presents a philosophically informed treatise praising the virtues of poetry and poets. Arguing against Plato, who claimed that poets should be omitted from his model state, Sidney contends that the poet creates anew that which in nature is flawed: 'Her world is brazen, the poets only [that is, only poets] deliver a golden' (Sidney 2002: 85). Sidney also wrote the influential sonnet sequence *Astrophil and Stella* and the hugely popular romance *The Arcadia*, sometimes termed *The Countess of Pembroke's Arcadia* after his sister Mary Herbert for whom he wrote the text, or *The Old Arcadia*, to distinguish it from the revision begun by Sidney but left unfinished (Sidney 1970; 1985).

Winning favour at Court depended upon behaving according to specific rules and an important prose text from the period is Baldesar Castiglione's *The Book of The Courtier*, translated into English from Italian by Sir Thomas Hoby and published in 1561. The text outlines the basic requirements of a successful courtier: '... beside noblenesse of birth, I will have him ... by nature to have not onely a wit, and a comely shape of person and countenance, but also a certaine grace ... that shall make him at the first sight acceptable and loving unto who so beholdeth him' (Castiglione 1974: 33). These are the kinds of attributes one might expect from a lover, and a romantic frisson between courtier and prince was fully exploited in the court of Queen Elizabeth. The female monarch, the Virgin Queen, presented herself as chaste mistress to a host of male suitors, a behaviour undoubtedly influenced by sixteenth-century love poetry, specifically the kind of poetry influenced by Francesco Petrarch.

Petrarch

Petrarch (or 'Petrarca'), the fourteenth-century Italian poet, had an enormous influence on sixteenth-century English poetry (see POETRY). He made commonplace the convention of love poetry being addressed to a chaste lady who was the epitome of beauty and unresponsive to pleas for love. His sonnet sequence the *Rime Sparse* (or the 'scattered rhymes') became a primary **canonical** text in the Renaissance (Petrarch 1980). Henry Howard, Earl of Surrey and Sir Thomas Wyatt were the first to introduce the sonnet into English in the early sixteenth century. In the Petrarchan or Italian sonnet the first eight lines describe a specific situation or problem and the last six provide a commentary on it or a solution. Most of Wyatt's finest poems are translations or imitations of Petrarch's sonnets but with three quatrains and a concluding couplet. In Wyatt's Sonnet 11, 'Whoso list to hunt', the speaker complains, 'Yet may I by no means my wearied mind / Draw from the deer, but as she fleeth afore / Fainting I follow.' Punning on the word 'deer', Wyatt tells the reader about his problem, which is unrequited love for a particular woman, and then comments on it, noting that there is no point pursuing her because

> ... graven with diamonds in letters plain
> There is written her fair neck round about:
> '*Noli me tangere* for Caesar's I am,
> And wild for to hold though I seem tame.' (Wyatt 1978: 77)

Wyatt served in the court of Henry VIII and it is thought by some that the woman being written about in this sonnet is Anne Boleyn, Henry's mistress and later his wife.

The anti-Petrarchan tradition

Petrarch's influence was pervasive but towards the end of the sixteenth century his poetry had come to be perceived as rather old-fashioned and there was a firmly established anti-Petrarchan tradition. Shakespeare's sonnets in praise of dark beauty are part of that tradition and, unlike Petrarch's clichéd verse, contain protestations of a very sincere love. You will notice that Shakespeare undermines what the reader expects to hear about his love object by refusing to describe her in traditional ways. For example, in Sonnet 130 Shakespeare refuses to describe his lady in terms of the religious hyperbole adopted by Petrarch by denying that she is any kind of ethereal creature: 'I grant I never saw a goddess go; / My mistress when she walks treads on the ground.' But despite his refusal to flatter her – indeed perhaps because of it – Shakespeare's poem is more heartfelt. To him she is exceptional: 'I think my love as rare' – and here he takes a swipe at the Petrarchan conventions of false flattery – 'As any she belied with false compare.' Petrarch's overworked clichés are replaced with something heartfelt and sincere.

Spenser's *Faerie Queene*

The adoption and adaptation of older forms is evident also in Edmund Spenser's *Faerie Queene*, the first three books of which were published in 1590 (Spenser 2001). The poem is an epic (see EPIC) but Spenser adapts this classical form so that he can present himself as a kind of English Homer, telling stories of heroic confrontations with monsters and witches but, crucially, in a Christian **context** and in the English language. Although it is likely that he was influenced by his Italian sources, Ludovico Ariosto's *Orlando Furioso* and Torquato Tasso's *La Gerusalemme Liberata*, Spenser used an entirely original verse form: the Spenserian stanza. *The Faerie Queene* is an allegorical poem, which means that it has hidden meanings behind the obvious story being told. As a Christian poet, Spenser begins his epic poem with a focus on Holiness, which is the overall theme of Book 1. Given England's break with the Roman Catholic Church, many critics have interpreted this book as an **allegory** of Protestant England's fight against Roman Catholicism. There is a certain irony in Spenser using Italian (and thus Catholic) sources to construct a Protestant epic for an English readership but, as we have seen, it was usual in this period for writers to reshape older forms and thus make them speak in fresh ways to their readers.

Renaissance theatre: Shakespeare and his contemporaries

The sixteenth century saw the first purpose-built theatres in England since the time of the Romans and they echoed the open-air circular style of the Roman amphitheatres. These amphitheatres were all in London and included the Rose (1587), the Swan (1595) and the Globe (1599). Both kinds of theatre were open to the public, although the considerably higher cost of entrance to the indoor theatres kept out all but the middle and upper classes. Before the emergence of the open-air theatres drama was performed either on makeshift stages built in public places such as the town square or in large private houses or public buildings which usually served another purpose. Plays available to the public – morality plays, mystery plays and miracle plays – were religious and didactic in nature whilst Latin plays, interludes and masques were performed in great houses or the universities.

We have seen the importance of patronage and gaining influence at court but this pertained to published literary works only. The emergence of professional playing companies and professional dramatists meant that a writer need worry only that his play would appeal to the theatre-going public who paid to see it. William Shakespeare was not a courtier, nor was he an aristocrat, but he wrote plays that the public wanted to see and thus he proved a successful play-wright; the professional theatre was a market and the principles of the marketplace – most importantly, supply and demand – dictated literary success or failure (see MARXISM). Like his contemporaries, Shakespeare made use of classical and Italian source material: for example, *Titus Andronicus* is indebted to Ovid's *Metamorphoses*, *The Comedy of Errors* to the comedy *Menaechmi* by the Roman dramatist Plautus, and *The Merchant of Venice* to an Italian collection of stories called *Il Pecorone*, meaning 'the big sheep', or 'dunce' (Shakespeare 1988: 125, 257, 425). In the sixteenth century Shakespeare wrote a prolific number of comedies, tragedies and histories and he continued writing plays, including some in collaboration with other dramatists, until his death in 1616.

William Shakespeare's plays remain popular but his contemporary play-wrights are unfairly neglected, amongst them Thomas Kyd, Christopher Marlowe, Francis Beaumont, John Fletcher and Thomas Middleton. It is not possible here to trace the achievement of all Shakespeare's sixteenth-century dramatic contemporaries so Marlowe will serve as an example. In the 1590s Marlowe offered real competition to Shakespeare and was, in fact, already an established name when Shakespeare was just beginning to make his mark. Marlowe differed quite markedly from Shakespeare: he was university educated and had a reputation for religious and sexual radicalism. It is difficult not to be influenced by Marlowe's biography when seeing or reading his drama because, like the man himself, his plays are exciting, challenging and, even (perhaps especially) today, have the ability to cause controversy: the anti-hero Tamburlaine claims he is known as 'the scourge and wrath of God' (Marlowe 1981: part 1, 3.3.44) and burns a copy of the Koran on stage (Marlowe 1981: part 2, 5.1.171–84), whilst in *Dr Faustus* the devil takes Faustus's soul in exchange for worldly power (Marlowe 1993). It is difficult to know whether, had he lived longer and written more plays, Marlowe would today present a serious challenge to Shakespeare as the best known and most admired play-wright of the sixteenth century. It is arguable, however, that, like Ben Jonson, whose best plays were written and staged in the seventeenth century, his tendency to display classical learning, in particular his repeated use of Latin, would appeal less to a modern audience than Shakespeare's ability to present the erudite in a more accessible manner and without apparent effort.

Summary

The sixteenth century saw a rebirth of classical models and an appropriation of Italian forms but with a focus on reshaping them for an English-speaking, Protestant audience. Classical influence was also apparent with the building of England's first theatres since Roman times but, crucially, the plays written and performed in these spaces were English. The invention of the printing press saw a significant rise in the availability of printed books and, later in the century, literary dissemination shifted from the insular and privileged Court to the public stage, where success was dictated not by birth, wealth or connections but by the market. These phenomena indicate a democratization of literary and dramatic art, just as there had been a democratization of the Bible via its translation from Latin into English. Although literary works, even those written in English, were still only available to the educated minority who could read, the plays of Marlowe, Shakespeare and others were available to all.

The sixteenth century: sample syllabus

Week 1   An introduction to the major events of the Renaissance
Week 2   More's *Utopia*: manifesto or satire?
Week 3   Sidney's *Apology for Poetry*: theories of literature
Week 4   Castiglione's *The Courtier*: theories of manners
Week 5   Sonnets by Petrarch: traditions of romantic love poetry
Week 6   Sonnets by Shakespeare: challenging traditions
Week 7   *The Faerie Queene* Book 1: allegory and holiness
Week 8   *The Faerie Queene* Book 3: allegory and chastity
Week 9   *The Merchant of Venice*: Shakespeare's sources (1)
Week 10 *The Comedy of Errors*: Shakespeare's sources (2)
Week 11 Marlowe's *Dr Faustus*: Shakespeare's contemporaries and tragedy
Week 12 Jonson's *The Alchemist*: Shakespeare's contemporaries and comedy

Bibliography

(a) Literary works

Castiglione, Baldassare. *The Book of the Courtier*. Trans. Sir Thomas Hoby. London: Dent, 1974.

Jonson, Ben. *The Alchemist and Other Plays*. Ed. Gordon Campbell. Oxford: Oxford University Press, 2008.

Marlowe, Christopher. *Doctor Faustus A- and B- Texts (1604, 1616)*. Ed. David Bevington and Eric Rasmussen. Manchester: Manchester University Press, 1993.

More, Thomas. *Utopia: A Revised Translation, Backgrounds, Criticism*. Trans. and ed. Robert M. Adams. New York: W. W. Norton, 1992.

Petrarch. *Petrarch and Petrarchism: The English and French Traditions*. Ed. Stephen Minta. Literature in Context. Manchester: Manchester University Press, 1980.

Shakespeare, William. *The Complete Works: Compact Edition*. Ed. Stanley Wells, Gary Taylor, John Jowett and William Montgomery. Oxford: Clarendon Press, 1988.

Sidney, Philip. *An Apology for Poetry (or The Defence of Poesy)*. Ed. R. W. Maslen. Manchester: Manchester University Press, 2002.

Sidney, Philip. *Astrophel and Stella*. Menston: Scolar Press, 1970.

Sidney, Philip. *The Countess of Pembroke's Arcadia (The Old Arcadia)*. Ed. Katherine Duncan-Jones. Oxford: Oxford University Press, 1985.

Spenser, Edmund. *The Faerie Queene*. Ed. A. C. Hamilton, Shohachi Fukuda, Hiroshi Yamashita and Toshiyuki Suzuki. London. Longman, 2001.

Wyatt, Thomas. *Sir Thomas Wyatt: The Complete Poems*. Ed. R. A. Rebholz. Harmondsworth: Penguin, 1978.

(b) Further reading

Belsey, Catherine. *The Subject of Tragedy: Identity and Difference in Renaissance Drama*. London: Methuen, 1985.

Davis, Alex. *Chivalry and Romance in the English Renaissance*. Studies in Renaissance Literature. Cambridge: D. S. Brewer, 2003.

Greenblatt, Stephen. *Renaissance Self-Fashioning: From More to Shakespeare*. Chicago and London: University of Chicago Press, 1980.

Gurr, Andrew. *Playgoing in Shakespeare's London*, 2nd edn. Cambridge: Cambridge University Press, 1996.

Hadfield, Andrew, ed. 1996. *Edmund Spenser*. London: Longman, 1996.

Healy, Thomas. *Christopher Marlowe*. Writers and Their Work. Plymouth: Northcote House, 1994.

Knapp, Jeffrey. *An Empire Nowhere: England, America, and Literature from* Utopia *to* The Tempest. Berkeley: University of California Press, 1992.

Matz, Robert. *Defending Literature in Early Modern England: Renaissance Literary Theory in Social Context*. Cambridge Studies in Renaissance Literature and Culture. Cambridge: Cambridge University Press, 2000.

Rivers, Isabel. *Classical and Christian Ideas in English Renaissance Poetry*, 2nd edn. London: Routledge, 1994.

Ryan, Kiernan, ed. *Shakespeare: Texts and Contexts*. Basingstoke: Palgrave Macmillan, 2000.

Waller, Gary. *English Poetry of the Sixteenth Century*. London: Longman, 1986.

The seventeenth century

(Year 2)

Hugh Adlington

The seventeenth century is a golden age in the history of English literature. From the glories of Shakespeare's great tragedies to the stunning achievement of Milton's *Paradise Lost* (1667), the era oozes a literary confidence and ambition that few other periods can match. But the centrality of the seventeenth century in any degree course in English literature is not only due to the brilliance of particular plays or poems. It is also due to the fact that the world changed beyond recognition between 1600 and 1700, in politics, religion, society, art and knowledge itself. Fierce battles for political power and religious freedom broke out in the civil wars in Britain (1642–8), and in the Thirty Years' War in continental Europe (1618–48). Bold new ideas in astronomy, medicine, philosophy and economics – pioneered by famous names such as Galileo, Newton, Harvey, Descartes and Bacon – overturned centuries-old customs and traditions. Technology spurred a host of advances: the printing press widened access to knowledge; the compass aided exploration and colonization; improved farming methods and better sanitation (after the Great Plague of 1665) led to a surge in population. Each of these seismic changes left its imprint on the English literature of the period; each contributed to the verbal energy, stylistic variety and lightning wit characteristic of seventeenth-century writing.

How much of this can you expect to cover in a 12-week course? Not very much, is the short answer. But for a more tangible sense of what to expect, see the sample syllabus at the end of this chapter. In what follows, you will be introduced to some of the most important authors, works and topics dealt with on that syllabus. A list of further reading is intended to guide your independent study.

Jacobean and Caroline drama

From the outset of your course, you will consider how broad cultural trends are reflected in particular literary **genres** (or 'kinds'). One of the most important of these genres is Jacobean drama (see DRAMA). Through close study of the language and structure of plays such as Shakespeare's *The Tempest* (1611) and John Webster's *The Duchess of Malfi* (1614), you will discover a defining characteristic of the drama of this period: namely, a persistent fascination with what it means to be human, and an equally persistent inquiry into the value and limits of verbal art. 'You taught me language,' Caliban retorts to Prospero in *The Tempest*, 'and my profit on't / Is I know how to curse' (Shakespeare 1999: I.ii.364–5). Other kinds of values and limits are also being tested in these plays. Inspired in part by accounts of sea voyages to the newly established colonies in America ('The New World'), *The Tempest* is as much an exploration of old and new habits of thought as it is of a particular place on a map.

Similarly, in *The Duchess of Malfi* Webster's brilliant poetry plumbs the depths of human immorality in an exposé of avarice, lust and cruelty. Webster's bold heroine refuses to submit to male authority, and is brutally murdered as a consequence. Thus Webster's play satisfies his audience's taste for both lurid violence *and* moral courage. And, most characteristic of Jacobean drama, the threat of divine retribution hangs over all: 'Other sins only speak; murder shrieks out: / ... blood flies upwards, and bedews the heavens' (Webster 1972: IV.ii. 260–2). If you have read or seen Christopher Marlowe's tragedy *Dr Faustus* (1604), you may recognize here an echo of the doomed Faustus's despairing cry, 'O I'll leap up to my God! Who pulls me down? / See, see where Christ's blood streams in the firmament!' (Marlowe 1989: 13.71–2). To recognize such echoes is to begin to appreciate the ways in which authors imitated one another in the period, when the concept of authorial virtuosity lay as much in the skill of adaptation and translation, as in what we might understand today as 'originality'.

Lyric poetry: Donne and Herbert

Following Jacobean drama, many courses look at another of the period's great literary achievements: lyric poetry (see LYRIC). In the 1590s, poets such as Sir Philip Sidney, Edmund Spenser and Shakespeare had written sequences of 14-line sonnets, drawing on classical and Italian poetic models (such as Petrarch), and dealing chiefly with the topics of love, death and literary fame. In the early seventeenth century a new kind of poetic voice emerged. Colloquial, ardent and fiercely intelligent, poems by John Donne such as 'The Sun Rising', 'The Canonization' and 'To His Mistress Going to Bed' captivated readers with their frank expressions of **desire**: 'For God's sake hold your tongue, and let me love' (Donne 1994: 10); and equally candid outbursts of hate: 'and since my love is spent, / I'had rather thou shouldst painfully repent, / Then by my threatnings rest still innocent' (1994: 44).

Donne is especially renowned for his use of elaborate images, or **conceits**, to cast fresh light on familiar situations. One of the most well-known examples comes in 'A Valediction: Forbidding Mourning', in which separated lovers are compared to the two legs of a pair of compasses. Later poets such as John Dryden and Samuel Johnson gave the name of '**metaphysical** poetry' to this tendency for far-fetched comparison, and a number of other seventeenth-century poets, such as Richard Crashaw, Thomas Carew and Henry Vaughan are often described in such terms. Donne and these poets are also known as 'metaphysicals' due to their preoccupation with religion, and, in particular, with their use of erotic imagery to imagine human relations with God. In one of Donne's most notorious holy sonnets, 'Batter my heart', the poem's speaker goes so far as to plead for God to 'break, blow, burn' his reason, and to enact a kind of spiritual possession: 'Except you enthral me, never shall be free, / Nor ever chaste, except you ravish me' (1994: 348).

In studying the religious poetry of the period, you will be certain to encounter George Herbert's unique collection of poems, *The Temple* (1633). If Donne's depictions of relations between male and female, and between man and God, shock us by their violent intensity, Herbert is the poet who speaks most profoundly and resonantly about spiritual doubt and consolation: 'I struck the board, and cry'd, '"No more. / I will abroad"' (Herbert 2007: 526). The poems in *The Temple* are astonishing for their formal innovation (every poem's stanza form or versification is in some way unique), and notable for their passionate avowal of a purity of poetic style, stripped of rhetorical ornamentation.

New genres: the country-house poem and court masque

Following study of lyric and religious poetry, it is likely that you will be introduced to writing specifically by women. Spiritual diaries, prayers and devotional literature were some of the few acceptable areas of writing by women in the male-dominated culture of the period. In particular, you will probably encounter Aemilia Lanyer, whose poem 'The Description of Cooke-ham' (1611) inaugurated the minor genre of English 'country-house' poems. 'Cooke-ham' is an elegiac celebration of the crown estate of Cookham in Berkshire, a place where Lanyer had enjoyed the hospitality of the Countess of Cumberland. Lanyer's poem is particularly notable for its focus on the virtues of Cookham's female community, and as such the poem touches on a number of the most urgent ideological conflicts in the period: country vs. city, male vs. female, feudal vs. monetary land ownership. Other important female writers you are likely to encounter in the period 1603–40 include Elizabeth Cary, Mary Wroth and Rachel Speght.

The most important country-house poem written by a male author in this period is Ben Jonson's 'To Penshurst' (1616). A prolific writer of plays, poems and prose, Jonson made one of his most distinctive literary contributions in the **genre** of the court masque. Performed at the courts of James I and Charles I, works such as Jonson's 'Masque of Blackness' (1605) and 'Pleasure Reconciled to Virtue' (1618) were lavish theatrical performances involving song, dance, ingenious stage machinery and the participation of courtiers themselves (as dancers). Highly symbolic in nature, referring extensively to Roman and Greek myths and legends, and virtually always performed in celebration of royalty, masques were firmly a part of elite culture (as opposed to popular plays performed at London theatres such as The Globe or The Rose). Nevertheless, masques still reveal much about the mentality of the age, particularly in their explorations of the function of art and dramatization of abstract concepts such as truth, beauty and virtue.

Literature and politics: cavalier poets

With the victory of the parliamentary forces in the civil wars of the 1640s, the predominant themes of royalist writing of the period are of defeat, exile and loss. And yet in the poems of the so-called 'cavalier poets' such as Robert Herrick, Edmund Waller or Abraham Cowley, you can expect to find such themes concealed beneath a witty celebration of sociable pleasures. At first sight, poems such as Herrick's 'Corinna's Going A-Maying' and Waller's 'Song ('Go, lovely rose!')' seem to have little to do with politics. Yet the delight they take in sensual pleasure and in time-honoured rural customs and festivities (many of them pre-Christian in origin), are an implicit rebuke to Puritan disapproval of anything that distracted from the worship of God (parliament closed the theatres between 1642 and 1660 because plays were thought to encourage immorality and vice). Cavalier poetry, therefore, is only superficially licentious: at a deeper level it reinforces traditional concepts of absolute monarchy and aristocracy, the virtues of obedience and duty, and an established state church. With the restoration of Charles II in 1660, royalist poetry and its stylistic hallmark the heroic couplet once again became the predominant fashion in court literature of the period, with poems by John Wilmot, Earl of Rochester proving some of the most lasting and most outrageous.

Epic poetry: John Milton's *Paradise Lost*

At some point in any course on seventeenth-century literature you will study what is perhaps the greatest single work of the period, John Milton's epic poem *Paradise Lost* (see EPIC). Milton's poem is over 10,000 lines long and deliberately aims to emulate and surpass the great epic poems of antiquity, such as Homer's *The Iliad* and Virgil's *The Aeneid*. Milton's poem retells the biblical story of the creation of the world and the temptation of Adam and Eve by the serpent in the Garden of Eden. Milton's ambition is dizzying: his stated aim is to 'justify the ways of God to men' (Milton 2007: I.26). As well as being a religious drama, however, the poem is also a political one. Milton was a committed supporter of the republican cause, and in the heroic status given in the poem to Satan, leader of the rebellion against God, it is tempting to see a contemporary parallel with Cromwell's defiance of Charles I: 'Will ye submit your necks, and choose to bend / The supple knee? Ye will not, if I trust / To know ye right' (2007: V.787–9). Yet the poem is also a domestic drama, in which the love and marriage of Adam and Eve takes centre stage. And unlike other epics, such as *The Aeneid* and Spenser's *Faerie Queene* – which serve to explain and glorify a nation's history and purpose – *Paradise Lost* dares to provide an account of the origin of the human race itself. The epic's powerful blank verse poetry, monumental drama and profound learning proved an inspiration and challenge to generations of succeeding poets and critics, including Dryden, Samuel Johnson, William Blake and Percy Shelley.

Civil war and restoration: parody and politics

Following *Paradise Lost*, you can expect to be introduced to Restoration literature more broadly. The new emphasis in this period on classical poetic models is advertised in the title of Andrew Marvell's 'An Horatian Ode: Upon Cromwell's Return from Ireland', written in about 1650, but not published until 1681. Marvell's ode is notable for its even-handed portrayal of both Cromwell's victory over the Irish after the execution of Charles I, *and* its admiration for Charles's courage on the gallows: 'He nothing common did, or mean, / Upon that memorable scene' (Marvell 2007: 276). You can expect to study this poem both for its important and subtle reflection of political currents in the period, and for the formal emphasis it places on the classical values of balance and proportion, the watchwords of the new literary era.

In this period you are also likely to encounter one of the most important poems of a new genre: John Dryden's *Mac Flecknoe* (1682), the instigator of a type of satire known as mock-epic (see SATIRE). The target of Dryden's satire here is Thomas Shadwell (1640–92), a minor playwright who considered himself a worthy successor to Ben Jonson as a writer of comedies. Through parodic imitation of the solemn tone of epics such as *The Aeneid* and *Paradise Lost, Mac Flecknoe* is a wickedly funny denigration of Shadwell's hubris, poetic ability, and literary and political opinions. In its skilful use of heroic couplets (two consecutive rhyming lines in iambic pentameter), Dryden's poem exemplifies the Restoration combination of correctness of method with quickness of mind, or wit: 'Shadwell alone, of all my sons, is he / Who stands confirmed in full stupidity' (Dryden 2007: 131).

Seventeenth-century prose

At some point, your course is also likely to consider the seventeenth-century revolution in the status and style of English prose. Traditionally considered inferior to poetry, prose benefited in the period from a number of factors. Sir Francis Bacon's grand plans for a thorough reconsideration of all human knowledge, proposed in works such as *The Advancement of Learning* (1605), called for a new plainness and utility in prose style, influenced by the aphoristic prose styles of Roman writers such as Seneca and Tacitus. Bacon's *Essays*, first published in 1597, also initiated a new prose form in English, drawing on a wide range of classical and medieval authors to offer counsel for the successful conduct of life. At the same time, English prose was enriched by the massive influence of the Authorized Version of the Bible (AV). The AV popularized a scriptural prose style, characterized by phrasal parallelism and incantatory prose rhythms: 'I cried unto the Lord with my voice; with my voice unto the Lord did I make my supplication' (Psalm 142.1). Unlike Baconian prose style, which conforms to our modern notions of sentence structure and punctuation, the scriptural style adhered to what was known as the 'periodic' or 'rounded' style, in which lengthy, meditative passages of prose are subdivided by commas and colons. Perhaps the most famous exponent of periodic prose style in the seventeenth century was Sir Thomas Browne. Works such as Browne's *Religio Medici* (1643) revel in intricate, interwoven coils of language and thought, which lend themselves to philosophical speculation: 'I love to lose myself in a mystery, to pursue my reason to an *O altitudo*!' (Browne 1968: 14).

Other important prose **genres** that you may encounter include history, biography and religious prose (e.g. sermons, devotions and meditations, and religious tracts). Prose fiction remained in embryo in the period, although Aphra Behn's *Oroonoko* (1688) transformed earlier romances into a remarkable fictional protest against the slave trade, and John Bunyan's *The Pilgrim's Progress* (1678), an **allegory** that takes the form of a dream by the author, proved to be fabulously successful with a popular audience (see THE NOVEL).

Summary

This essay has offered just a brief glimpse of the 'infinite riches in a little room' that is seventeenth-century English literature. A number of ideas recur throughout the literature of this period. Some of the most important of these include:

> **the purposes of writing**: for patronage; to induce virtue; to persuade;
> **the kinds of writing**: how literary genres evolve (including the emergence of new forms such as the court masque, country-house poem, mock-epic and prose essay);
> **concepts of literature**: that it should imitate, translate and adapt previous literary forms, rather than strive for pure 'originality';
> **gender**: the emergence of women writers in the period;
> **literary contexts**: politics (civil war and Restoration); religion (Reformation debates over the nature of man's relation with God); travel, exploration,

colonization; increasing literacy; textual transmission by manuscript and print;

> **shift in worldview**: from gods, monsters, witches and angels (Spenser, Shakespeare, Milton) to scientific empiricism and mechanical materialism (Hobbes, Newton, Locke).

The seventeenth century: sample syllabus

Week 1   Introduction: major texts and contexts of the seventeenth century
Week 2   Shakespeare's *The Tempest*: drama for a new world
Week 3   Webster's *The Duchess of Malfi*: Jacobean revenge tragedy
Week 4   Lyric poems by John Donne: sacred and profane
Week 5   Religious poems by George Herbert: formal innovation
Week 6   Lanyer's 'The Description of Cooke-ham': the country-house poem
Week 7   Jonson's *Pleasure Reconciled to Virtue*: court masque
Week 8   Herrick, Waller, Cowley: cavalier poets
Week 9   Milton's *Paradise Lost*, Books I & II: biblical epic
Week 10 Marvell's 'An Horatian Ode': political poetry
Week 11 Dryden's *Mac Flecknoe*: mock-epic
Week 12 Bacon, Browne, Bunyan: seventeenth-century prose

Bibliography

(a) Literary works

Browne, Sir Thomas. *Selected Writings*. Ed. Sir Geoffrey Keynes. London: Faber & Faber, 1968.

Donne, John. *Complete English Poems*. Ed. C. A. Patrides. London: J. M. Dent, 1994.

Dryden, John. *Selected Poems*. Ed. Paul Hammond and David Hopkins. Harlow: Longman, 2007.

Herbert, George. *The English Poems*. Ed. Helen Wilcox. Cambridge: Cambridge University Press, 2007.

Marlowe, Christopher. *Dr Faustus: Based on the A Text*. Ed. Roma Gill. London: A & C Black, 1989.

Marvell, Andrew. *The Poems*, rev. edn. Ed. Nigel Smith. Harlow: Longman, 2007.

Milton, John. *Paradise Lost* (1667), rev. 2nd edn. Ed. Alastair Fowler. Harlow: Longman, 2007.

Shakespeare, William. *The Tempest* (1611). Ed. Virginia Mason Vaughan and Alden T. Vaughan. London: Arden, 1999.

Webster, John. *The Duchess of Malfi* (1614). In D. C. Gunby (ed.), *John Webster: Three Plays*. Harmondsworth: Penguin, 1972.

(b) Further reading

Corns, Thomas N., ed. *The Cambridge Companion to English Poetry: Donne to Marvell*. Cambridge: Cambridge University Press, 1993.

Evans, Robert C. and Eric J. Sterling, eds. *The Seventeenth-Century Literature Handbook*. London: Continuum, 2009.

Fowler, Alastair, ed. *The New Oxford Book of Seventeenth-Century Verse*. Oxford: Oxford University Press, 2008.

Hattaway, Michael. *Renaissance and Reformations: An Introduction to Early Modern English Literature*. Oxford: Blackwell, 2005.

Keeble, N. H., ed. *The Cambridge Companion to Writing of the English Revolution.* Cambridge: Cambridge University Press, 2001.

Norbrook, David. *Writing the English Republic: Poetry, Rhetoric and Politics, 1627–1660.* Cambridge: Cambridge University Press, 1999.

Pooley, Roger. *English Prose of the Seventeenth Century, 1590–1700.* Harlow: Longman, 1992.

Smith, Nigel. *Literature and Revolution in England, 1640–1660.* New Haven, CT: Yale University Press, 1994.

Stevenson, Jane and Peter Davidson, eds. *Early Modern Women Poets: An Anthology.* Oxford: Oxford University Press, 2001.

Wilcox, Helen, ed. *Women and Literature in Britain, 1500–1700.* Cambridge: Cambridge University Press, 1996.

The eighteenth century

(Year 3)

Bill Overton

Introduction

The eighteenth century long languished as the Cinderella of English literary studies, all the more neglected because her siblings are not ugly. Her closest elder sisters, Renaissance and seventeenth-century literature, have more than kept their attractions, while her younger sisters – Romantic, Victorian and twentieth-century literature – have always proved seductive. But, though no Prince Charming has arrived to transform her from put-upon to princess, a host of other helpers have finally brought her to the ball. Part of Cinderella's problem has always been her dress. The various garments she has worn have never fitted very well. If measured in dates, 1700–1800 seems accurate but is too tight at one end and too loose at the other. For this reason, she is often called 'the long eighteenth century' and given a larger size, from 1660 to 1780 or even 1800. Though the effect is rather tent-like, it gives plenty of room. But the style has often been wrong, too. 'The Age of Reason' is far too sensible, 'The Augustans' too classical. Worse still, both clash with other costumes she has had to wear, 'The Age of Sensibility' and 'The Enlightenment' among them. Instead, the scholars and critics who have helped bring out her natural qualities have worked hard to identify what these really are. The way in which they have done this most successfully has been through close study of the different forms of writing in the period.

Novels and other narratives

One reason why the eighteenth century is an exciting period to study is that it was from about 1680 to 1750 that what we now know as 'the novel' became established. A further reason is that recent critics have shown that women writers played an important part in this. The standard account, stemming especially from Ian Watt's *The Rise of the Novel,* is that the English novel began with Daniel Defoe, Samuel Richardson and Henry Fielding. Thanks to such books as Jane Spencer's *The Rise of the Woman Novelist*, the role of women writers, among them Aphra Behn and Eliza Haywood, is now much better recognized. At the same time, studies including Michael McKeon's *The Origins of the English Novel 1600–1740* and Brean Hammond and Shaun Regan's *Making the Novel* have made the definition of what a 'novel' is, or was, much more subtle and inclusive. Yet the new form – the word itself means 'new thing' – took root at a time when many older kinds of **narrative** were still current, so the subject is more complex and inviting still if the term is stretched to include prose narrative in general. Such a move makes sense, because many examples of these other types of narrative are so interesting. They include travel narratives and criminal (auto)biographies, which fed into Defoe's *Robinson Crusoe* (1719) and *Moll Flanders* (1722) respectively; prose satires such as Jonathan Swift's *Gulliver's Travels* (1726) aimed in part at the kinds of new thing represented by *Crusoe*; oriental tales such as *The Arabian Nights* (1704–17), translated from a version in French; and works such as Olaudah Equiano's *Interesting Narrative* (1789), which is now understood as a slave narrative and which blends autobiography, travel writing and abolitionist campaigning with a type of spiritual autobiography known as the conversion narrative. Works of these kinds, and others, rubbed shoulders with the novel, both influencing it and, in turn, influenced by it. Paula Backscheider and Catherine Ingrassia's *Companion to the Eighteenth-Century English Novel and Culture* demonstrates the variety of narrative culture at the period.

Those studying the eighteenth-century novel need, then, to be aware of its range and complexity. This includes romances such as those by Eliza Haywood early in the period – for example, her lively and entertaining *Love in Excess* (1719–20) – and, later on, gothic fiction, originated in 1764 by Horace Walpole's *The Castle of Otranto*. A good reason for reading works now understood as novels alongside examples of other and older narrative forms is that this helps understanding of how the novel developed. Another is that it enables the new form to be defined more clearly. A key criterion for Ian Watt, in *The Rise of the Novel* (1957), was 'formal realism', and, although 'realism' is a slippery term that begs various questions, it has its uses. Eighteenth-century novels on the whole aimed at a closer representation of contemporary life than other narrative forms, they did so in more everyday language, and, in order to suggest that they were authentic, they often employed such devices as a first-person narrator or a collection of apparently genuine letters. For this reason, it is especially important in studying them to analyse the kinds of language they use and their narrative methods. It is, for instance, instructive to compare Swift's first-person narrator in *Gulliver's Travels* with Defoe's in *Robinson Crusoe*, and Behn's in *Oroonoko* (1688) with both; to examine how third-person narrative works in Sarah Fielding's *Adventures of David Simple* (1744, 1753) and her brother Henry's *Tom Jones* (1749); and to trace Richardson's development of the novel in letters from *Pamela* (1740–41), dominated by a single correspondent, to *Clarissa* (1748–49), which has many. Epistolary fiction is particularly significant because, following the development of the Post Office, founded in 1660, and the general expansion of trade and communications, the eighteenth century was the great age of the letter. In Britain it was the most popular narrative form for much of the 1770s and 1780s. Tobias Smollett wrote *The Adventures of Humphry Clinker* (1771), which is a sort of satirical travel narrative, in the form of letters, and Frances Burney told a famous half-truth in pretending to be writing letters when composing her first novel, *Evelina* (1778), which is also epistolary.

The varieties of narrative form are so rich, not only in the eighteenth but also in other centuries, that advanced study requires more accurate terms than those such as 'first-' and 'third-person' in the paragraph above. It is important, for example, to be able to distinguish between different kinds of personal and impersonal narrators (the terms I prefer), as when comparing Behn's narrator in *Oroonoko* with Robinson Crusoe, or those of the two Fieldings in *The Adventures of David Simple* and *Tom Jones* as already mentioned – or even those in *Tom Jones* and a later novel by Henry Fielding, *Amelia* (1751). Similarly, the amount of dialogue – the representation of direct speech – and its distribution is significant in any narrative text. So too is what Gérard Genette describes as 'focalization', a much more precise and productive term for studying what older theories of narrative call 'point-of-view' (1980: 185–94). In an impersonal narrative, for instance, it makes a difference if some characters are allowed to focalize and not others; and in personal narratives it makes a difference if the story is focalized from a time soon after or long after the events took place. For this second distinction, which can determine the whole effect of a narrative, F. K. Stanzel introduced the terms 'experiencing self' and 'narrating self' (1984: 80–83). It is worth applying these to novels by Defoe among others, including epistolary novels, in which parts of the action are often narrated very soon after it took place – or even while it is still happening. Though advanced students may wish to study the works by Genette and Stanzel that originated these concepts, Shlomith Rimmon-Kenan provides a clear, concise and surprisingly comprehensive introduction to narratology in her *Narrative Fiction: Contemporary Poetics*.

In studying the eighteenth-century novel, it must also be borne in mind that the form thrives on parody (see SATIRE). It has often been pointed out that, if Cervantes's *The Adventures of Don Quixote* (1605, 1615) is the first novel, it is at the same time the first anti-novel. While Swift reacted satirically to Defoe, so that *Gulliver's Travels* may be considered as an anti-novel in certain respects, so, in *Shamela* (1741) and *Joseph Andrews* (1742), did Henry Fielding to Richardson's *Pamela*, turning himself into a novelist in the process; and *Tom Jones* delights in parody too. It was not only Fielding who looked back to Cervantes; Charlotte Lennox produced a female eighteenth-century counterpart in *The Female Quixote* (1752). Yet the most systematically parodic of all novels of the period is Laurence Sterne's *The Life and Opinions of Tristram Shandy* (1759–67), deeply imbued in ancient satirical traditions but, as the first English anti-novel, astonishingly up to date. It can stand on its own as an example of why study of this period is so exciting.

Poetry

Although the novel is now the dominant literary form, in the eighteenth century it was considered, if considered at all, as a mongrel and an upstart. The most prestigious literary form, though it rarely paid well, was poetry. It would be a mistake, however, to assume that eighteenth-century verse is characteristically pretentious or remote. During the past 20 or so years, the work of Roger Lonsdale and others has brought to light just how lively and various much of it is. Lonsdale set himself the task of reading all the verse published in the century as far as he possibly could, and from this huge mass of material he compiled two anthologies that are often, and rightly, termed groundbreaking: *The New Oxford Book of Eighteenth-Century Verse* and *Eighteenth-Century Women Poets: An Oxford Anthology*. These collections make clear that people at all levels of society wrote verse, and that they did not always do so for publication but for their own amusement and that of their friends and acquaintances. They strikingly juxtapose poems and verse extracts from such **canonical** writers of the period as Alexander Pope, Thomas Gray and Samuel Johnson with work by women writers, labouring-class writers of both sexes, and now all but anonymous figures who had something interesting to say and expressed it vividly or inventively in verse. Other scholars have extended Lonsdale's research, so that it is now much easier to read neglected verse of the period.

Just as the study of narrative requires adequate analytical concepts and terminology, so does that of verse. This is all the more important with eighteenth-century poetry because it often either follows or, more interestingly, adapts, varies or turns upside down one or more formal or generic conventions. Formal conventions have to do with the way a poem is written – for example, the choice of verse form and the way that form is used. Different verse forms tended to have different functions and implications, so that epics (including translations) and poems on serious subjects in general are typically in closed pentameter couplets, while tetrameter couplets are more frequent in light or occasional verse, and hymns and songs are often in various kinds of quatrain. Blank verse, established by Milton's *Paradise Lost* (1667, 1674) as a proper medium for verse narrative as well as drama, was also used for poems on serious subjects, as by James Thomson in *The Seasons* (1726–48), though it could be turned to parody or pastiche, too, as in John Philips's *The Splendid Shilling* (1705). Other serious forms include the Pindaric ode, occasionally parodied as well. It is not just the choice of a particular verse form that is important, but how it is handled. In mock-epics, for example, such as Pope's *The Rape of the Lock* (1712, 1714) or *The Dunciad* (1728, 1743), the closed pentameter couplet is adjusted in order to undermine or to produce bathos (a lapse into the ridiculous, in this context deliberate); while tetrameter couplets in anapaestic or trochaic metre are capable of quite different effects from those in iambics. Open couplets, too, are more informal, and so are often used for occasional poems including familiar letters.

Generic conventions have to do with different kinds of poem, such as epic, satire and different types of lyric. An obvious example is the mock-epic, which applies epic ways of writing to such unworthy subjects as the theft of a lock of hair or, in *The Dunciad*, the triumph of stupidity. But there were also accepted styles and protocols for writing all sorts of other poem, from epigram to pastoral and panegyric (a poem of praise, common in a period when it could earn the writer money or favour). In the introduction to his anthology *English Augustan Poetry*, Paul Fussell gives thumbnail sketches of no fewer than 20 examples of what he calls 'the eighteenth-century genre system' (1972: 7–13). These include not only the genres already mentioned, but also the moral narrative or fable, the essay and the inscription; and as many as seven are mock forms, including travesties not only of epic but ode and elegy. This is significant because it shows poets of the period adapting old forms to new subject matter, such as pastoral to the city (as in Swift's 'Description of a City Shower' [1710] or John Gay's *Trivia* [1716]), and also because it highlights their inventiveness and often too their playfulness. For instance, in the 1720s Lady Mary Wortley Montagu produced two heroic epistles about contemporary scandals, 'Epistle from Arthur Glra]y to Mrs M[urra]y' and 'Epistle from Mrs. Y[onge] to her Husband'. Conventionally, this type of poem is written by a male author but presents a woman from legend or history writing to the lover who has abandoned her. Wortley Montagu's break the rules not only in dealing with events in the present but also in that they are satirical, and 'Arthur G[ra]y' goes further in that its supposed writer is a man. The *Blackwell Companion to Eighteenth-Century Poetry*, edited by Christine Gerrard and produced in part to complement *Eighteenth-Century Poetry: An Annotated Anthology*, is a guide to virtually all of the various forms and **genres** in the period, as well as to some key writers and poems. Another excellent detailed introduction to the subject is *English Poetry of the Eighteenth Century 1700–1789*, by Gerrard's co-editor for the *Anthology*, David Fairer; and Paula Backscheider's *Eighteenth-Century Women Poets and their Poetry* is a very wide-ranging study of poetry by women of the period.

Drama and theatre

While the most stimulating developments in eighteenth-century literary criticism have taken place in studies of the novel and other prose narrative forms, and, more recently, of poetry, drama of the period also has a lot to offer. It is divided, however, by the fissure produced by the Stage Licensing Act of 1737, which required all plays to be submitted for pre-production censorship and which, astonishingly, was not repealed until 1968. Until 1737, it was possible to produce satirical drama and serious political plays. Afterwards, dramatists had to steer clear of risky or sensitive subjects, so that the kind of drama that is considered most characteristic of the later eighteenth century is comedy of manners, as in Oliver Goldsmith's *She Stoops to Conquer* (1773), and Richard Brinsley Sheridan's *The Rivals* (1775) or *The School for Scandal* (1777). As a result, later eighteenth-century drama is comparatively neglected. While students of Restoration drama, especially Restoration comedy, are well served by anthologies and secondary sources – among them Deborah Payne Fisk's *Cambridge Companion to English Restoration Theatre* (2000), and Susan J. Owen's *Companion to Restoration Drama* – there are no comparable works for the later part of the period. This emphasis is unfortunate, for it disguises the fact that much more was happening in later eighteenth-century theatre than light comedy. Tragedies, often centring on a suffering, victimized woman, continued to be popular, but other forms, such as tragicomedy, farces and afterpieces, flourished and music often played a key part, especially in ballad operas, inaugurated by Gay's *The Beggar's Opera* (1728), and, later, in comic operas such as Sheridan's *The Duenna* (1775).

The importance of theatre to later eighteenth-century culture is suggested by Gillian Russell, who points out that, by the early nineteenth century, 'there were over three hundred licensed theatres in Great Britain and Ireland' (2004: 100), as compared with a handful a hundred years earlier. Russell goes on to remark that 'the networks of exchange in personnel, repertoire, and finances between the theatres of North America, the West Indies, the Cape Colony, India, and Australia, paralleled the networks of colonial trade, producing a recognizable and transportable category of British cultural identity' (2004: 100–1). Plays from the Renaissance and Restoration continued as part of the theatrical culture, though the politer tastes of the period led to much bowdlerization of Restoration comedy in particular; and it was in the 1760s that Shakespeare became definitively established as the national bard. This, too, was the period in which a structure known as the proscenium arch stage, separating performers from audience, became the norm for theatres, a norm that has become old-fashioned only within the last 40 years. A further anticipation of later developments is the star system, which effectively began with the career of David Garrick (1717–79), and continued through others including the Kemble family, especially Sarah Siddons (1755–1831) and her brother, John Philip Kemble (1757–1823). Richard Bevis's *English Drama: Restoration and Eighteenth Century, 1660–1789* is a very full introduction to the whole subject.

Kinds of course

Courses on eighteenth-century literature most often divide into three main types. Some are survey courses, either of the period itself or as one among several neighbouring periods; others focus on specific forms such as the novel, poetry or drama, as this chapter has done; while others still are generic or thematic, based on topics such as satire, or the representation of travel or **gender**. Courses that include more than one kind of writing are especially valuable, because they bring into play important texts that are otherwise easily neglected, such as Addison and Steele's *Spectator* papers (1711–12, 1714), or

Lady Mary Wortley Montagu's Turkish Embassy Letters, stemming from her stay in Turkey in 1717–18. Thematic courses create the same opportunity, which is crucial to study of a period in which new and hybrid ways of writing arose and in which many writers – Wortley Montagu, Samuel Johnson and Oliver Goldsmith among them – by no means confined themselves to a single form. It was also a great period for translations, ranging from Alexander Pope's translations of Homer to *The Arabian Nights*, already mentioned. The mingling of different forms and genres, and the experimentation and innovation that went on within them, horrified Pope, who, in his *Dunciad*, deplored 'How Tragedy and Comedy embrace; / How Farce and Epic get a jumbled race' (I, 69–70). In *Pope to Burney, 1714–1779: Scriblerians to Bluestockings*, probably the best single introduction to the literature of the period, Moyra Haslett presents a more generous view, emphasizing the sociability of this period's writing. More specialized studies are Roy Porter's *English Society in the Eighteenth Century* and W. A. Speck's *Literature and Society in Eighteenth-Century England*, both very readable and informative; while John Brewer's *The Pleasures of the Imagination* is a rich and wide-ranging study, as stimulating as it is scholarly.

Summary

The chief reason why studying the eighteenth century is fascinating is that it was during this period that much of what we now know as the modern world took shape. It did so through, among other factors, the industrial and agrarian revolutions, the massive expansion of trade and communications, the increasing concentration of people in urban areas, the growth of a reading public, the development of a consumer culture, and what has been described as a process of cultural 'feminization' (Eagleton 1982: 13–17; Clery 2004). Literary forms of all kinds responded to these changes and were informed by them, leading to works that rival those of any period in their richness and vitality. If eighteenth-century literature still is a Cinderella, she is now on much more equal terms with her siblings. As a result of new approaches and discoveries over the past 25 or so years, there is no more exciting time to study the writing of the period.

The eighteenth century: sample syllabus

Semester 1: Narratives

Week 1   Introduction to 'the eighteenth century'
Week 2   Romance, slave narrative or novel? Aphra Behn, *Oroonoko*
Week 3   Economic versus spiritual man: Daniel Defoe, *Robinson Crusoe*
Week 4   Satire and narrative: Jonathan Swift, *Gulliver's Travels*
Week 5   Women and the novel: Eliza Haywood, *Love in Excess*
Week 6   The novel in letters: Samuel Richardson, *Pamela*
Week 7   The narrator in the novel: Henry Fielding, *The History of Tom Jones*
Week 8   The philosophical tale: Samuel Johnson, *Rasselas*
Week 9   Laurence Sterne, *The Life and Opinions of Tristram Shandy* as an anti-novel

Week 10 Sterne, *The Life and Opinions of Tristram Shandy* as a Menippean satire
Week 11 Revisiting gender, rank and the novel in letters: Frances Burney, *Evelina*
Week 12 Abolitionist narrative: Olaudah Equiano, *The Interesting Narrative*

Semester 2: Poetry and drama

Week 1 Anne Finch, Countess of Winchilsea, and varieties of eighteenth-century verse
Week 2 Alexander Pope and mock-epic
Week 3 Jonathan Swift and satirical verse
Week 4 Subversions: Lady Mary Wortley Montagu and Mary Leapor
Week 5 Poetry at mid-century: Thomas Gray and William Collins
Week 6 Forms of satire, forms of pastoral: Samuel Johnson and Oliver Goldsmith
Week 7 Harking back, harking forward: Anna Letitia Barbauld and William Cowper
Week 8 Restoration comedy reformed? William Congreve, *The Way of the World*
Week 9 Restoration comedy reframed: Susannah Centlivre, *The Basset-Table*
Week 10 Words and music: John Gay, *The Beggar's Opera*
Week 11 Comedy of manners (1): Oliver Goldsmith, *She Stoops to Conquer*
Week 12 Comedy of manners (2): Richard Brinsley Sheridan, *The School for Scandal*

Bibliography

(a) Literary works

Behn, Aphra. *Oroonoko*. In *Oroonoko and Other Writings*. Ed. Paul Salzman. Oxford: Oxford University Press, 1994.

Burney, Frances. *Evelina*. Ed. Edward A. Bloom and Vivien Jones. Oxford: Oxford University Press, 2002.

Centlivre, Susannah. *The Basset Table*. Ed. Jane Milling. Peterborough, ON: Broadview Press, 2009.

Congreve, William. *The Way of the World*, 3rd edn. Ed. Brian Gibbons. London: Methuen, 2002.

Defoe, Daniel. *Robinson Crusoe*. Ed. Thomas Keymer and James Kelly. Oxford: Oxford University Press, 2007.

Equiano, Olaudah. *The Interesting Narrative and Other Writings*, rev. edn. Ed. Vincent Carretta. London: Penguin, 2003.

Fairer, David and Christine Gerrard, eds. *Eighteenth-Century Poetry: An Annotated Anthology*, 2nd edn. Malden, MA and Oxford: Blackwell, 2004.

Goldsmith, Oliver. *She Stoops to Conquer*. Ed. James Ogden. London: Methuen, 2003.

Haywood, Eliza. *Love in Excess; Or, The Fatal Enquiry*, 2nd edn. Ed. David Oakleaf. Peterborough, ON: Broadview Press, 2000.

Johnson, Samuel. *The History of Rasselas, Prince of Abissinia*. Ed. Tom Keymer. Oxford: Oxford University Press, 2009.

Sheridan, Richard Brinsley. *The School for Scandal*, 2nd edn. Ed. Ann Blake. London: Methuen, 2004.

Swift, Jonathan. *Gulliver's Travels*. Ed. Claude Rawson and Ian Higgins. Oxford: Oxford University Press, 2005.

(b) Further reading

Backscheider, Paula R. *Eighteenth-Century Women Poets and Their Poetry: Inventing Agency, Inventing Genre*. Baltimore, MD: Johns Hopkins University Press, 2005.

Backscheider, Paula R. and Catherine Ingrassia, eds. *A Companion to the Eighteenth-Century English Novel and Culture*. Malden, MA, and Oxford: Blackwell, 2005.

Bevis, Richard. *English Drama: Restoration and Eighteenth Century, 1660–1789*. Harlow and New York: Longman, 1988.

Fairer, David. *English Poetry of the Eighteenth Century 1700–1789*. London and New York: Longman, 2003.

Gerrard, Christine, ed. *A Companion to Eighteenth-Century Poetry*. Malden, MA, and Oxford: Blackwell, 2006.

Hammond, Brean and Shaun Regan. *Making the Novel: Fiction and Society in Britain, 1660–1789*. Basingstoke and New York: Palgrave Macmillan, 2006.

Haslett, Moyra. *Pope to Burney, 1714–1779: Scriblerians to Bluestockings*. Basingstoke and New York: Palgrave Macmillan, 2003.

McKeon, Michael. *The Origins of the English Novel 1600–1740*. Baltimore, MD: The Johns Hopkins University Press, 1987.

Price, Cecil. *Theatre in the Age of Garrick*. Oxford: Oxford University Press, 1973.

Rimmon-Kenan, Shlomith. *Narrative Fiction: Contemporary Poetics*, 2nd edn. London: Routledge, 2002.

Spencer, Jane. *The Rise of the Woman Novelist: From Aphra Behn to Jane Austen*. Oxford and New York: Basil Blackwell, 1986.

Romanticism and gothic

(Years 1 & 2)

Ian McCormick

From romantic encounters to definitions

Your first encounter with romanticism is likely to be a close analysis of a short poem by William Blake, John Keats or William Wordsworth. As your familiarity with romantic writing expands you are likely to pick up a sense of recurring themes and topics: mind, spirit, memory, rebellion, nature, sensibility, innocence, wanderers, terror, **sublime** (see below), beauty, fancy, imagination. Faced with such a variety of themes you will start to wonder how it all fits together. As you continue taking notes you will build up a picture of romanticism but there will also be an uneasy sense that the concept is exceeding itself. Your picture of romanticism bursts its own frame and the task of defining romanticism coherently and concisely appears doomed to failure. But have courage: the movement from simplicity to complexity is part of the learning process. Rather than being a one-stop idea, romanticism is lots of different things; that's part of its appeal and part of its endurability over the last 200 years.

Based on your wider readings of romantic writers, you might want to argue that the pursuit of structure, order, fixed categories, tidy definitions and stable classifications works against the romantic project. In historical terms the romantic writings that emerged in the 1780s are sometimes cast as a rebellion against the values established in the previous century: a **culture** of rules and restraint; the primacy of reason and the sense of an ordered world informed by scientific progress sometimes collectively known as the 'Enlightenment'; the pursuit of harmony, proportion and symmetry, taken as a revival of the classical values of Ancient Greece; the polite and mannered society of the prosperous middle classes. Romanticism's 'sensibility' – its characteristic spontaneity, originality, individuality, its rebel creativity and dynamic energy refuses to submit to the prison-house of definition. Romanticism romanticizes itself; romanticism is different from itself. It is different also, but sometimes similar, to what came before it. There is a long critical history of disagreement on the meaning of 'romantic' or 'romanticism'. When you come to write about a romantic text, try to demonstrate your awareness of the variety of romantic writers and their writings. Avoid the one poem/one straitjacket approach. Ideally, compare and contrast two or more writers and provide a sense of the critical debate between romantic writers, and between critical approaches. The following section briefly outlines the most salient contours in the romantic landscape but notes that these are pictures bursting out of their frames; romanticism exceeds tight containment. The second part of this essay outlines the emergence and development of gothic writing and draws parallels with romantic contexts.

It does not help that many of the earliest writers who are generally accepted as having romantic credentials seldom defined themselves as romantic, nor did they agree on the dating of their first emergence from history. The romantic 'period' has also been difficult to limit. If the English romantic period falls somewhere in and between the reigns of George III (1760–1821) and George IV (1821–30), then anything after that can be safely categorized as 'Victorian' rather than romantic. Given the anti-royalist or at least anti-hierarchical predisposition of many romantics, dynastic markers are surely a perverse strategy for defining romanticism(s). A different strategy might take the radical ruptures of revolution as a starting point for romanticism. Accordingly, there are two pivotal dates of considerable significance: the American Revolution (1776) and the French Revolution (1789). A focus on these events leads us through the radical writing of William Godwin, Tom Paine and Mary Wollstonecraft (with Edmund Burke thrown in as the token political reactionary). The historical contexts along these lines are helpful for our understanding as they illuminate the reading of many texts, including those that on first appearance are deemed to be purely **aesthetic** or non-referential. At the same time we need to build into a period-based approach to English romantic texts the notion of early or first-generation romantic writers and a second generation; the difference between William Blake, Samuel Taylor Coleridge and William Wordsworth, on one side; John Keats, Lord Byron and Percy Shelley, on the other. In this line of categorization, Coleridge and Wordsworth are presented as exponents of revolutionary ideals and enthusiasms that turn to disenchantment as the French Revolution moves through the period of the Terror and on to the hegemony of Napoleonic dictatorship. The long period of Wordsworth's writing suggests also a transition through the 'second generation' romanticism into a romantic Victorianism. Blake's radical and religious fervour is so idio-syncratic as to resist the precise linkage of historical events; these are in any case transmuted into mythical energy forces. The narrative in romantic writers is not purely one of youthful enthusiasm leading to an adult sense of disen-chantment. Rather, there is the sense that radical energies are being reconstructed; poetry gives them a new 'pulse' that is felt 'along the heart'.

The underlying ideological forces at work in romanticism can be seen as a staging of the self or the individual against a repressive culture of sameness; privileging the margins against the centre; innovation against tradition; origi-nality against imitation. The negotiation of these oppositions varies significantly between romantic writers. In some cases the emphasis appears to be more on the political and the revolutionary; in others the preoccupation is more one of **aesthetics**. Admittedly, and importantly, politics becomes aestheticized or the aesthetic is politicized. Those who do not 'belong'; those who lack power and influence, or have been deprived of it – such as women, children, beggars, wanderers, hermits, the imprisoned, the insane – begin to be a new focus and space of representation, sometimes awkwardly, second-hand, their voices and thoughts ventriloquized, their appearance voyeuristically 'presented'. Their vivid political presence is one aspect of romanticism's grotesque inclusivity – it breaks decorum by mixing tragic and comic compo-nents. But these recurring figures or types are also mental and aesthetic categories – a way of reaching beyond conventional truths and traditional representations. Perhaps the prisoner's or the child's eyes see something that those who take freedom or adulthood for granted have missed. Perhaps our minds are being closed by artificial traditions and by conventional thought, by William Blake's 'mind forg'd manacles'. On one level, then, there is a new subject matter, and on another there is an attempt to rethink literary forms and styles. The programme for reform is noteworthy in the renewed interest in oral folk literature such as songs and ballads, which become a major area of interest for antiquarian collectors during the eighteenth century. William Wordsworth, in particular, experimented with such forms in his *Lyrical Ballads* (1798). For the modern reader unschooled in the traditions of English poetry, Wordsworth's lyrical ballads are still striking for their literariness rather than their closeness to the ordinary language of the common people (the reader turns to Burns for examples of invented poetic decorum *and* ordinary dialect). Yet there is a move away from the tired conceits of 'polite' classical poetry in which breeze becomes Zephyr and girls turn nymphs.

Romanticism is often presented as a return to nature. This notion is indeed very complicated. For the French writer Jean-Jacques Rousseau there was a return to the sources of our being that is less a primitive aggression than a return to the state of the 'noble savage'. It is at once striking how far Nature has become a mythically constructed category that becomes a rallying cry against Art, artifice and artificiality. Romantic poets have often been specifically attached to nature, and even to a location, such as the Lake District. But it would be a mistake to identify the romantics as the familiar 'worshippers of nature' who have existed throughout history. The first difference is that nature is more than the 'town versus country' debate; the urban is increasingly the Satanic or prison-like world enslaved to the factory and the first wave of the Industrial Revolution. Nature, then, is a resistance to these dehumanizing forces of the contemporary world. On another level, nature is a species of artlessness, of spontaneity and freedom rather than caprice and restriction. These notions are recognizable as elements in a romantic sensibility – *being* your self, rather than submitting to hierarchies and dead conventions. Yet there are few manifestations of romantic culture that fully embody spontaneous composition or the 'automatic writing' of the surrealists. Romanticism is partly defined by its failure to be itself; great poems remain unfinished or are just a beginning (William Wordsworth's *Prelude*). They fail to live up fully to the gigantic inspiration at their source. The problem of being hurried out of oneself by the force of strong natural feelings is one that Wordsworth resolves through his notion of a poetry that is 'emotion recollected in tranquillity'. A naive adherence to nature is seldom enough to constitute a definition of romanticism. What we are more likely to find is a debate between the phenomenon of nature and the mind, the presence or selfhood of the observer. The vastness of nature frequently occurs in romanticism as the infinite dimension – the sublime. The **sublime** is not a new notion: writers of the classical period, such as Longinus, were attracted to and wrote on the notion of the sublime. But the renewed interest in the gigantic, in exceeding limits, in a notion of the infinite so disturbing that it might inspire awe and terror and vertigo (Edmund Burke – see below) was in many respects well suited to the heroic obsession with self, power and authority that supports the masculine gender of romanticism. In its political dimension the sublime is sometimes the mythological force of the revolutionary hero, violently tearing down oppression and sweeping away centuries of injustice (the Napoleon Bonaparte idea). The beautiful, in contrast, is nature on a human scale and often more feminine (life affirming), the stream rather than the river torrent; a sea tranquil not stormy; the breeze rather than the hurricane; meadows not mountains. The masculine–feminine oppositions of landscapes and ideologies feature in Mary Shelley's *Franken-stein* as alternative sides in a debate about the nature of romanticism and man or woman's place in that world. Driven by pride and ambition, the hero usurps the female role in conception and subsequently must face the monstrous consequences of his actions.

The narrowness of romanticism perceived purely in terms of English writings has to be addressed with reference to an acknowledgement of European writers, the New World, and indeed the rest of the world. (Maurice Cranston's *The Romantic Movement* has chapters on German, English, French, Italian and Spanish romanticism; the graphic beginner's guide *Introducing Romanticism* by Duncan Heath and Judy Boreham also takes a Eurocentric approach, but does devote two pages to Latin American Nationalism.) Emerging from

Eurocentric roots, romanticism informs the emerging constitutionalism and conflict in the nineteenth century. If there is, in one sense, a fascination with common humanity and a resistance to oppression, then romanticism shares with gothic an element of critique directed at an aristocratic society. Also worthy of consideration here is the role of romantic writers in defining and celebrating regional identities, local customs and practices and, on a larger scale, serving as the inspiration for the rise of nation states in the later nineteenth century – Germany and Italy being noteworthy examples. The transition from a state of healthy patriotism to one of strident national interests is also instructive in exploring the sinister contribution of romanticism to modern political identities such as neo-fascism.

From romanticism to gothic

If romanticism sometimes appears to be a journey through dreams and **idealism**, gothic is the nightmare trip from calm to terror; its demons and monsters and the forces of the unconscious set loose upon us. But many **aesthetic** terms and cultural markers that have been attributed to romantic writings could also be attached to the notion of the gothic. Before proceeding to gothic ideologies and psychologies, you will often come across 'the gothic' as the opposite of classical/rational/Enlightenment mentioned at the beginning of this essay. In its early phases, 'Gothick' moves beyond ordinary commonsense experiences to embrace romance; the marvellous; the fantastic; dream and nightmare. Accordingly, Samuel Johnson's definition of 'Romantick' in his *Dictionary* of 1755 could serve as a precursor of the gothic writings that were to emerge a decade or so later: 'Resembling the tales or romances; wild, improbable; false; fanciful; full of wild scenery.' Even earlier, romantic imagination has a precursor in gothic, 'an imagination naturally fruitful and superstitious'; for Joseph Addison the characteristics are gloom, melancholy and the propensity for 'wild Notions and Visions' (*The Spectator*, 1 July 1712). Many of these features are present in the early writings of gothic: Horace Walpole's *The Castle of Otranto* (1764), Matthew Lewis's *The Monk* (1796), Ann Radcliffe's *The Mysteries of Udolpho* (1794) and Charles Maturin's *Melmoth the Wanderer* (1820). Insofar as gothic is defined by a notion of the past, the comparison with 'pre-romanticism' and 'Enlightenment' is also worth consideration: 'whereas the Enlightenment represents a critique of the old, Pre-Romanticism is inspired by a real revulsion from all that the Neo-classicism was thought to stand for: dull rules, superficial elegance, formality, orderliness, finite views, artificiality, convention, didacticism, courtly civilization, the preservation of the status quo' (Furst 1969: 24–5).

The first major gothic text is generally agreed to be Horace Walpole's *The Castle of Otranto* (1764). This short novel has many of the figures and themes identified in what follows that constitute a recipe for gothic writing. Briefly, the gothic text usually has one or more of the following ingredients. Its setting tends to be in South or Eastern Europe; the period is often medieval or pre-Enlightenment; the dominant religion is Catholic, or is based on rituals and on oral superstition; the social class structure is based around tyranny or aristocracy; landscapes are often wild and sublime, often functioning as psychological analogues; buildings are equally awesome and often threaten to imprison their inhabitants. Characteristically confined spaces include castles, dungeons, monasteries, towers, cellars and prisons.

Working against these themes in gothic writing are the notions of contemporary empirical common sense; Protestant and liberal values; notions of individual choice and freedom to innovate. Insofar as these elements are present, gothic writings remind us of a recent past; tyranny and violence come back to the surface, are clothed and given life, only to be exorcized and sent back with the triumph of modern liberal protagonists and progressive values. Accordingly, gothic is a process or ideology haunting that ultimately renews a belief in the inevitable victory of the bourgeoisie and its sociocultural values. That is to say, gothic is politicized history; it unrepresses a society's past.

Alongside the historicist and ideological approaches to gothic are to be found the recurring repressed elements that relate to the psychological and the psychoanalytic. In gothic the calm and peace of daytime is replaced by inquietude and nightmare; the life forces are encroached on by death and decay; sanity is threatened by trauma and the return of the repressed; civilization is challenged by violence unleashed, by sexual perversions, decadence and extremism. Gothic texts frequently present an **aesthetic** of terror based on **patriarchy** and may therefore interrogate notions of female as victim, or at least as vulnerable. In some cases (Ann Radcliffe is an example) gothic explores the unfamiliar, but then returns us safely to the base camp of reflective reasoning. Psychoanalytic and feminist interpretations are often intertwined with other ideological factors, and this in turn may explain the popularity of gothic fiction. Walpole's novel fits these definitions well in several respects: its core narrative of the aristocratic Manfred's obsession with primogeniture and the theme of daughter-in-law incest. Racial and identity qualities are embodied in the obsessions that pervade the cultural markers of family, race and identity: blood and semen. These factors become a potent mixture in tales such as Dracula and the ever-multiplying vampires and the literature that portrays them.

As soon as we attempt to apply such models their coherence becomes less stable. A recipe of gothic ingredients is easier to assemble than an inclusive theoretical construct. But there are also aspects of the gothic style of writing that require consideration. First, there is a question about the quality of gothic writing. Is it literature? Michael Alexander noted in his *History of English Literature* that, 'For all its curiosity value, the literary merit of 18th-century Gothic fiction is negligible compared with the use made of Gothic in the 19th-century novel' (2000: 202). Many early commentators noted the appeal of the novel, and subsequent gothic writings, for a female readership. The popularity and mass appeal of gothic leads to criticism that it panders to pleasure rather than profit, it delights but fails to instruct. Gothic is bad taste; it satiates and satisfies, but it based on idle fantasy and irresponsible invention. The gothic writer deals in absurdities and abandons truth to nature. Yet we can point to a major gothic tradition without which our literary heritage would be diminished: Charles Dickens, James Hogg, Bram Stoker's *Dracula*, Sheridan Le Fanu, Ambrose Bierce, horror in M. R. James, Henry James's *The Turn of the Screw*, R. L. Stevenson's *The Strange Case of Dr Jekyll and Mr Hyde* and so on. For those who want to keep a sense of the entertainment value of gothic in the foreground, we need to recall how often the gothic has tended to poke fun at itself; gothic excess and insecurity lends itself to parody. Early examples include Jane Austen's *Northanger Abbey*, a romance-realist response to Ann Radcliffe's *The Mysteries of Udolpho*. Another feature of gothic fiction is its tendency to present absurd caricatures; two-dimensional characters; recurring types; **allegorical** representations, and artificial melodrama. Nonetheless, these components will be present in different degrees; they correspond to the romance rather than the realism of gothic fiction. The gothic or the supernatural is in one sense the **binary opposition** to nature, the copying of nature, and the aesthetics of realism. It would take some time to explore each of these charges against the gothic presented in such criticism. Ultimately we are faced with a case of different tastes. But briefly in defence, let it be noted that gothic has a fine place in our greatest poetry; in the contribution of poems with gothic themes, notably in examples such as Coleridge's *Rime of the Ancient Mariner*, Keats's *Lamia* and *Eve of St Agnes*, Byron's *Manfred*. Many of our greatest novelists have used gothic themes in their best works (Charles Dickens's *Great Expectations*); gothic is a worldwide phenomenon in colonial and postcolonial writings; it has proliferated into highly significant sub-genres such as the gothic of the American South; it has been a major force moving into multimedia, and was present and influential with the birth of film (see FILM STUDIES). The monsters of gothic keep coming back to life.

The enduring legacies of terror, abjection and horror

From an **aesthetic** perspective it is worth noting the enduring relevance of Edmund Burke's classic *A Philosophical Inquiry into the Origin of our Ideas of the Sublime and the Beautiful* (1757). It is worth dipping into the book if you are interested in how our feelings work, how the mind works, and how we react to what we read. It was a popular book in its time and there is plenty of evidence that notions of terror and the grotesque were taken up subsequently by gothic and romantic writers and that they became a prevailing popular fashion. Important in this regard was the notion of the sublime composed of the twin forces of awe and terror. More recently, feminist critics have explored the idea further as 'the unspeakable' and 'the abject' (see Julia Kristeva's work for more on that topic). Briefly, to summarize these developments in theory we would define terror as the sublime component but see **abjection** holding a radical potential for cultural reconstruction; it becomes a zone of creative crossing over and a way of moving between categories. Horror is more associated with claustrophobic fiction: Edgar Allan Poe's fiction frightens and disgusts, and horror is sometimes twinned with impotence. Terror often comes from a fear of in-carnation or organization, or a re-membering of bodies and experience – most memorably as presented in Mary Shelley's *Frankenstein*. Film has often made the shift from the literariness of terror into the manifestation of horror; perhaps in this regard texts can suggestively withhold meaning in a way that film does not. In the work of deconstruction the theory that language (writing) represents but also stands in for its absent **other** is being explored in relation to the philosophy of gothic; texts become tales of terror/absence – a form of haunting (see DECONSTRUCTION). Jacques Derrida and his followers have begun to uncover the notion of 'haunting', starting with the spectre of revolution that Marx raised at the beginning of his *Communist Manifesto* (1848). No matter how far back the gothic turns in our history, nor how deep it ventures into our repressed selves, the contemporary gothic is a versatile, popular, accessible and dynamic phenomenon. Modern exponents such as Anne Rice and Angela Carter carry on any number of postmodern games, and play **gender** politics in revamped fairy tales. For the creator, the reader and the critic, gothic writing is a rich field for invention and innovation. Gothic, like romanticism, is far from dead.

Romanticism and gothic: sample syllabus

Introduction

Week 1   Romanticism and revolutionary contexts: Milton and the English Revolution; the American Revolution (1776) and the French Revolution (1789): selections from the writings of Tom Paine; Edmund Burke; Mary Wollstonecraft; William Godwin; John Thelwall

Week 2   Political fiction: the novel, gothic and terror: William Godwin: *Caleb Williams*

Weeks 3–6: The first movement

Week 3   The poetry of rebellion: poems by William Blake: *Songs of Innocence* (1789) and *Songs of Experience* (1793); *The Marriage of Heaven and Hell* (1790)

Week 4   Selected poems of William Wordsworth from *Lyrical Ballads*; *The Prelude*

Week 5   Edmund Burke on the sublime (selections): poems by William Wordsworth and Samuel Taylor Coleridge

Week 6   Women and romanticism: selected poems and writings by Anna Laetitia Barbauld; Hannah More; Charlotte Smith; Ann Yearsley; Mary Robinson; Helen Maria Williams; Joanna Baillie; Ann Batten Cristall; Dorothy Wordsworth; Charlotte Dacre

Weeks 7–12: The second movement

Week 7   Beyond sense and reason: opium and the East: selections from Thomas De Quincey; Samuel Taylor Coleridge

Week 8   Romanticism and satire: selections from Lord Byron's *Childe Harold's Pilgrimage* and *Don Juan*

Week 9   Selected poems of Percy Bysshe Shelley: 'To Wordsworth'; 'Hymn to Intellectual Beauty'; 'Ozymandias'; 'Ode to the West Wind'

Week 10 Selected poems of John Keats: 'On First looking into Chapman's Homer'; the Odes; 'To Autumn'

Week 11 Mary Shelley's *Frankenstein*

Week 12 Review and reflection. An opportunity to create your own mind map or collage of romantic people, places, images, themes and concepts.

Bibliography: romanticism

(a) Literary works

Austen, Jane. *Mansfield Park*. Ed. James Kinsley and Jane Stabler. Oxford: World's Classics, 2008.

Brontë, Charlotte. *Jane Eyre*. Ed. Margaret Smith and Sally Shuttleworth. Oxford: World's Classics, 2008.

Brontë, Emily. *Wuthering Heights*. Ed. Ian Jack and Helen Small. Oxford: World's Classics, 2009.

Bygrave, Stephen. *Romantic Writings*. London: Routledge, 1996.

Godwin, William. *Caleb Williams*. Ed. Pamela Clemit. Oxford: Oxford University Press, 2009.

Shelley, Mary. *Frankenstein*. Ed. Marilyn Butler. Oxford: Oxford University Press, 2008.

Wu, Duncan, ed. *Romanticism: An Anthology with CD-ROM*. Oxford: Blackwell, 1998.

(b) Further reading

Curran, Stuart, ed. *The Cambridge Companion to British Romanticism*. Cambridge: Cambridge University Press, 1993.

Day, Aidan. *Romanticism*. London: Routledge, 1995.

Heath, Duncan and Judy Boreham. *Introducing Romanticism*. Cambridge: Icon Books, 1999.

Kelly, Gary. *English Fiction of the Romantic Period, 1789–1830*. Harlow: Longman, 1989.

O'Flinn, Paul. *How to Study Romantic Poetry*. Basingstoke: Palgrave Macmillan, 2000.

Roe, Nicholas. *Romanticism: An Oxford Guide*. Oxford: Oxford University Press, 2005.

Stabler, Jane. *Burke to Byron, Barbauld to Baillie 1790–1830*. Basingstoke: Palgrave Macmillan, 2001.

Bibliography: gothic

(a) Literary works

Austen, Jane. *Northanger Abbey*. Ed. John Davie and Terry Castle. Oxford: World's Classics, 1998.

Godwin, William. *Caleb Williams*. Ed. Pamela Clemit. Oxford: Oxford University Press, 2009.

Poe, Edgar Allan. *Selected Tales*. Ed. David Van Leer. Oxford: World's Classics, 2008.

Radcliffe, Ann. *The Italian*. Ed. Frederick Garber and E. J. Clery. Oxford: World's Classics, 1998.

Shelley, Mary. *Frankenstein*. Ed. Marilyn Butler. Oxford: Oxford University Press, 2008.

Stevenson, Robert Louis. *Dr Jekyll and Mr Hyde*. Ed. Roger Luckhurst. Oxford: World's Classics, 2008.

Stoker, Bram. *Dracula*. Ed. Maud Ellman. Oxford: World's Classics, 2008.

Walpole, Horace. *The Castle of Otranto*. Ed. W. S. Lewis and E. J. Clery. Oxford: World's Classics, 2008.

2

(b) Further reading

Baldick, Chris. *In Frankenstein's Shadow: Myth, Monstrosity and Nineteenth Century Writing*. Oxford: Clarendon, 1987.

Botting, Fred. *Gothic*. London: Routledge, 1996.

Cavallaro, Dani. *The Gothic Vision: Three Centuries of Horror, Terror and Fear*. London: Continuum, 2002.

Cornwell, Neil. *The Literary Fantastic: From Gothic to Postmodernism*. Brighton: Harvester, 1990.

Ellis, Markham. *The History of Gothic Fiction*. Edinburgh: Edinburgh University Press, 2000.

Hogle, Jerrold E., ed. *The Cambridge Companion to Gothic Fiction*. Cambridge: Cambridge University Press, 2002.

Mulvey-Roberts, Marie, ed. *The Handbook of Gothic Literature*. Basingstoke: Palgrave Macmillan, 1998.

Punter, David. *The Literature of Terror: A History of Gothic Fictions from 1765 to the Present Day*. 2 vols. London: Longman, 1996.

Punter, David, ed. *A Companion to the Gothic*. Oxford: Blackwell, 2000.

Sage, Victor, ed. *The Gothick Novel: A Casebook*. Basingstoke: Palgrave Macmillan, 1990.

Wolfreys, Julian. *Victorian Hauntings: Spectrality, Gothic, the Uncanny and Literature*. Basingstoke: Palgrave Macmillan, 2002.

The nineteenth century and the Victorians

(Year 2)

Carolyn Kelley

Introduction

In *Middlemarch,* George Eliot directly addresses her readers: 'Your pier-glass or extensive surface of polished steel made to be rubbed by a housemaid, will be minutely and multitudinously scratched in all directions' (Eliot 1977: 182). The Victorian era is, metaphorically, like Eliot's 'minutely and multitudinously scratched' pier-glass. Trying to compartmentalize and condense Victorian events and literary achievements, these past 'scratches' left by this era, remains a daunting task. The Victorian era cannot be captured with any kind of strict ordering. In turn, this review does not proceed with any kind of strict linear or temporal integrity. I will attempt, however, to provide some form of cohesiveness in order to orient you if you are new to, or continuing, your journey into Victorian studies.

Victorian studies: what to expect as a student and current trends in scholarship

The woman who gives her name to this era, Queen Victoria, reigned 64 years, from 1837 until her death in 1901. Many scholars align the era to the years of Victoria's reign, although these dates are arbitrary, as are any proposed 'dates' of an era. Some scholars believe Victorian studies should encompass 'the long century'; namely, beginning with romantic poets who lived through the

Industrial Revolution, like William Wordsworth, and ending with 1914, the year the First World War began. Therefore, be prepared to work with texts that go beyond the years of Victoria's reign. Victorian studies remains popular due to the diverse and exciting texts created during this time period. The sample syllabus below contains examples of Victorian primary texts (novels, plays, poems and prose essays) you might encounter in a first-level or beginning course. Keep in mind that an advanced class would most likely incorporate these primary texts and secondary texts too. Secondary texts are theoretical or critical texts that interpret and suggest insights into primary texts, often in relation to a type of theoretical framework, such as feminism, postcolonialism or gender studies. I have provided a list of secondary texts in the 'further reading' section.

As a student of Victorian studies, you should be aware of current trends in the Victorian scholarship. Presently, most scholars concentrate on a small area of Victorian primary texts and read them through a critical theoretical lens. Current popular critical approaches include gay and lesbian theory, masculinity studies, anti-feminism (looking at woman authors who were anti-feminist) and postcolonial issues (the effects of the Victorian British Empire's subjugating and colonizing people from around the world) (see GAY STUDIES AND QUEER THEORY, GENDER, POSTCOLONIALISM). Although postcolonialism is mostly a twentieth-century phenomenon, it is rooted in the colonialism practised in the nineteenth century. For example, scholars look at Rudyard Kipling's colonial text 'The Man Who Would Be King' (1888), in which an Indian character, Billy Fish, has his identity co-opted by white, British characters and loses his life in the service of 'The Empire'. Another popular scholarly trend involves recovering forgotten authors. Scholars uncover and study authors who have not received proper attention. It is often the case that these authors were very popular in the Victorian era, but Victorian scholars have ignored them until presently.

You must also be prepared to undertake a large amount of reading, particularly in relation to Victorian novels, such as Charles Dickens's *The Pickwick Papers* (1836–7) and George Eliot's *Middlemarch* (1871–2). If you take an advanced Victorian literature class, be prepared to have some understanding of the formal elements of the novel and the poetic devices employed by Victorian poets (see THE NOVEL, POETRY). You should also expect to work heavily with secondary texts. Since events and artistic productions cannot be neatly packaged and never exist in a vacuum, you should have an awareness of how the social, cultural and political aspects of the era shaped its production of artistic texts. Most anthologies of Victorian literature, such as *The Norton Anthology to British Literature: The Victorian Age*, do a good job of familiarizing students with the Victorian background. When you take any module in Victorian studies, you must consider these contextual aspects to understand what motivated and inspired Victorian writers who lived, to borrow a phrase from Dickens's *A Tale of Two Cities*, in 'the best of times' and 'the worst of times' simultaneously.

The Industrial Revolution: the consequences of urban growth

Victorians lived in a time of staggering cultural, scientific and political transformations, and the art produced by Victorian artists reflects and critiques how these changes affected and shaped this era. Perhaps the most profound event shaping the era was the Industrial Revolution, which began to gather momentum around 1830. Prescient 'romantic era' (ROMANTIC AND GOTHIC) writers like William Wordsworth threaded poems with both a celebration and a sense of dread about 'Nature' and its future. In his sonnet 'The World is too much with us' (1803), Wordsworth claims he would rather give up his Christianity than live without Nature's beauty: 'Great God! I'd rather be / A Pagan suckled in a creed outworn; / So might I standing on this pleasant lea, / Have glimpses that would make me less forlorn' (9–12). The alarm in this (blasphemous) oath indicates that Wordsworth correctly intuits that the rural England he cherishes will soon disappear. Starting in the early nineteenth century, political and technological changes led to a wholesale upheaval, in which many rural dwellers moved to urban, industrial centres. Unlike the wealthy landed gentry and the poor who farmed on the land of the gentry, this new group was rootless and unfettered to the land. This landless class causes anxiety in the Victorian consciousness.

One way this anxiety manifests itself is through the literary figure of the orphan, such as Charlotte Brontë's Jane Eyre (*Jane Eyre*, 1847), Emily Brontë's Heathcliff (*Wuthering Heights*, 1847), and Dickens's Oliver (*Oliver Twist*, 1838) and Pip (*Great Expectations*, 1860–1). The orphan symbolizes the rootless group of people migrating to the city and facing an uncertain future. These new urban dwellers no longer had direct access to food through their family farm. They depended on wages, which were low, making poverty and starvation common occurrences. Orphan literature often emphasizes hunger. Literary orphans manage to rise socially and/or economically despite their uncertain future. Jane Eyre marries her former employer, Rochester. Pip fulfils his 'Great Expectations' and becomes upwardly mobile. Likewise, some farmers achieved upward mobility, rising to management positions in factories, or becoming wealthy through entrepreneurial trade ventures. In postindustrial England, class and station achieve a fluidity not experienced by previous generations.

Victorian novel I : advocating social and moral change – Dickens, Eliot and Gaskell

The novel as a literary form achieves its own upward mobility in the Victorian era. Poetry dominated the literary scene in the eighteenth and early nineteenth centuries, but several changes in the Victorian age make the novel the new prevailing literary form. First, more people attend school and achieve literacy, so the reading audience itself becomes larger. Second, with limited media available, novels serve as a primary source of entertainment for this new 'reading' class. Thirdly, the rise of the literary magazine, which publishes novels in serialized form, makes reading affordable. Dickens's first novel, *The Pickwick Papers*, was published in serial form between 1836 and 1837. Dickens then establishes his own periodical, *Household Words*, in which he publishes his own novels and the texts of other writers like Elizabeth Gaskell. Dickens and Gaskell, along with Eliot, cared about social and moral issues and created realistic characters and situations in order to instil a sense of concern, and sometimes outrage, in their readers. Dickens's novels often have sympathetic characters that emotionally affect readers. In *Great Expectations*, Joe treats Pip with love and understanding, even after Pip treats him disrespectfully. Joe's first wife beats him, and the audience, by developing sympathy for Joe, celebrates Joe's second marriage to the equally kind Biddy. Dickens is particularly adept at creating child characters who evoke sympathy, such as Pip, Little Nell (*The Old Curiosity Shop*, 1841) and Tiny Tim (*A Christmas Carol*, 1843). Victorian novelists also use sentiment to convey messages about pain, suffering and injustice.

Gaskell's novel *North and South* (1855) is set in Milton, a fictive counterpart for Manchester, and concerns life in a large industrial city from a middle-class perspective. The novel focuses on a textile factory owner, Thornton, and the woman he eventually marries, Margaret Hale. Margaret raises Thornton's consciousness about the working conditions in his factory and eventually saves him from being killed by a mob of strikers. Dickens's *Hard Times* (1854) also deals with life in a factory town. Dickens depicts the harsh ugliness of fictional Coketown and also satirizes the Victorian utilitarianism which highlights the loss of creativity and individuality. Urban workers become cogs in machinery, engaged in monotonous factory labour. The Gradgrind children in *Hard Times*, choked with facts by their father and the appropriately named schoolmaster, M'Choakumchild, lead unimaginative, unhappy lives. By opening his work of *fiction* with the praise of *facts*, Dickens ironically plays with the idea that people cannot survive on a mental diet of facts alone. In *Middlemarch*, Eliot shows that marrying for reasons other than love causes unhappiness. Dorothea marries Casaubon because she admires his intellect, but soon learns he does not respect her intelligence. After Casaubon dies, Dorothea finally finds love with Will and surrenders her rights to Casaubon's estate so she can be with him. For Dorothea (and Eliot), love and compatibility bring happiness in marriage; wealth and admiration do not provide strong enough bonds to make marriage work.

Victorian novel II: the sensation novel – Braddon and Collins

One major sub-genre of the Victorian novel to emerge midway through the century is the sensation novel, typified by the works of Mary Elizabeth Braddon and Wilkie Collins. The sensation novel takes 'the gothic mansion' of the eighteenth-century novel 'into the new industrialized city' (Adams 1999: 293). Sensation novels involve sexual intrigue and lurid crimes. Mary

Elizabeth Braddon's *Lady Audley's Secret* (1862) is a prime example of the sensation novel: the beautiful Lucy weds wealthy Sir Michael Audley. She appears to be the perfect upper-class wife. As the novel unfolds, however, the reader learns that Lucy is a bigamist who attempts to murder anyone who interferes with her comfortable life. Braddon's novel was considered scandalous, but its reputation did not stop it from becoming a bestseller.

Wilkie Collins is another famous purveyor of the sensation novel, penning the popular *The Moonstone* in 1868. Collins's novel tells the story of a stolen sacred Indian jewel, the titular moonstone gem, which the novel's young heroine, Rachel Verinder, inherits upon her eighteenth birthday. An unknown thief steals the jewel on the day she receives it. The question of who stole the gem becomes the central focus as the novel unfolds through first-person **narratives** of various characters, under the editorial gaze of the novel's hero, Franklin Blake. Collins finally reveals that Franklin is the thief who stole the gem while under the influence of opium, so he has no memory of committing the crime. The moonstone gem eventually makes its way back to its rightful place in India. *The Moonstone* blended aspects of the sensation novel, such as shocking crimes and romantic intrigue, with concepts that became essential to the detective novel of the twentieth century, such as having a 'whodunnit' crime serve as the centrepiece of a novel, and detectives as major characters. Collins's novel served as a harbinger for the popular texts of Arthur Conan Doyle and Agatha Christie.

Victorian poetry I: Tennyson and Browning

Victorian poets had to overcome the legacy of the great early nineteenth-century century romantic poets, so they experimented with new forms, such as the dramatic monologue, in order to make their own claim on the **genre**. The dramatic monologue features a solitary speaker addressing an audience and/or another person in the poem. The speaker tells a story, giving his unique perspective of an event. Alfred Lord Tennyson and Robert Browning, two of the most eminent Victorian poets, used this poetic format expertly and effectively. In Tennyson's *Ulysses* (1842), Homer's Ulysses addresses the reader, lamenting the ennui he experiences since returning home to Ithaca: 'How dull it is to pause, to make an end, / To rust unburnish'd, not to shine in use!' (21–2). Ulysses will be succeeded by a tepid inheritor, his son Telemachus, who will take 'a rugged people, and through soft degrees / Subdue them to the useful and the good / Most blameless is he, centered in the sphere / Of common duties' (37–40). Telemachus represents the new generation of Victorians who view 'common duties' such as maintaining the 'spheres' of proper society, as major life goals. The penchant for normalcy and calmness, instead of adventure and excitement, make Ulysses (and perhaps Tennyson) long for a past he cannot repeat.

In Browning's 'Fra Lippo Lippi' (1855), the speaker, a painter who lived in fifteenth-century Italy, is caught sneaking out at night by his patron's guards.

He tries to talk and charm his way out of being arrested. Lippi argues that exceptional artists provide an invaluable service because they allow people to see the world in a defamiliarized way. **Defamiliarization** involves taking something familiar, often in relation to nature, and reproducing it in a work of art, so that the familiar becomes defamiliar and can be re-experienced as new. Lippi says: 'nature is complete: / Suppose you reproduce her – (which you can't) / There's no advantage! You must beat her, then.' He continues, explaining that 'We're made so that we love / First when we see them painted, things we have passed / Perhaps a hundred times nor cared to see; / And so they are better painted' (297–303). Lippi emphasizes that art should not merely imitate the beauty of nature, but 'beat her'. Art, then, does not imitate life, but makes people experience life in a more profound way. Through Browning's poem, poetry turns 180 degrees from Wordsworth's 'The World is too much with us', in which he implies that nature cannot be equalled, let alone 'beat'.

In the poem *In Memoriam A.H.H* (1850), Tennyson struggles with his faith after the death of his friend: 'Are God and Nature then at strife, / That Nature lends such evil dreams?' (55:5–6). In other words, nature exerts herself as being predominant over God, so how could God have created nature? Tennyson's referral to 'Nature' as 'red in tooth and claw' (56:15) presages Charles Darwin's 'survival of the fittest' theory. Darwin changes how human beings view the 'facts' of their own existence. Darwin's first major text, *The Origin of Species* (1859), introduces the concept of natural selection, the process of adaptability in which a species must evolve in order to survive in its environment. Although Darwin avoids explicitly discussing humans in this first book, his subsequent book, *Descent of Man* (1871), connects his theories to humans. Darwin's findings made it difficult for people to believe in the Genesis stories of creation – suddenly the idea of the world as God's creation is called into question. Darwin's work shows how new ways of thinking were blossoming throughout the mid-Victorian era.

Victorian poetry II: Elizabeth Barrett Browning and Christina Rossetti

The mid-Victorian era also experienced a flowering of women's poetic voices. Elizabeth Barrett Browning, wife of Robert Browning, and the 20-years-younger Christina Rossetti create narrative poems with strong women characters who fight against sexual oppression. Two poems especially, Browning's *Aurora Leigh* (1857) and Rossetti's *Goblin Market* (1862) demonstrate that traditional notions about the two distinctive spheres of men and women were slowly changing. Victorians believed that women and men maintained separate 'spheres' in society. Men operate in the outside sphere, interacting with other men and facing contamination from earthly temptations, such as alcohol and prostitutes. Women create a domestic sphere in which a 'woman's virtuosity lay in her containment, like the plant in the pot, limited and domesticated, sexually controlled, not spilling out into spheres in which she did not belong nor being overpowered by "weeds" of social disorder' (Davidoff and

Hall 1987: 192). The 'potted' Victorian woman's domestic sphere creates a comfortable haven in which men retreat to weed out the taint of the outside sphere. Barrett Browning's 11,000-line novelistic poem *Aurora Leigh* depicts a woman character who has ambitions to enter the masculine outside sphere. Her eponymous heroine wishes to be a poet, despite the odds against her succeeding in this masculine profession. She tells her cousin Romney: 'I choose to walk at all risks. – Here, if heads / That hold a rhythmic thought, must ache perforce, / For my part I choose headaches' (2: 106–8). Aurora suffers the 'headaches' that come with being a tortured poet because she, like any male poet worth his words, will suffer for her art.

Christina's Rossetti's proto-feminist poem *Goblin Market* extols the bonds of female friendship while also serving as a cautionary tale warning young women to resist illicit sensual pleasures. In this narrative poem, the fruits of the Goblin Men represent sexual experience. After hearing the repeated calls of 'Goblin Men', Laura ignores her sister Lizzie's warning to ignore the calls and gives into temptation: 'She sucked and sucked and sucked the more / Fruits which that unknown orchard bore; / She sucked until her lips were sore' (134–6). Lizzie never hears the calls of the Goblin Men, as women who have not eaten the fruits cannot hear them. Laura's intense longing to taste these fruits again leave her near death. To save Laura, Lizzie endures the tortures of the Goblin Men, who 'Twitched her hair out by the roots, / Stamped upon her tender feet, / Held her hands and squeezed their fruits / Against her mouth to make her eat' (404–7). By withstanding the torture and by refusing to give into temptation, Lizzie redeems Laura and makes her well. Lizzie's ability to save her sister demonstrates the intense friendship bonds that form between women and suggests that mid-Victorian women did possess a degree of **agency**, despite that agency being limited only to the ability to say 'no'.

Christina Rossetti finds inspiration in the art of her brother Dante Gabriel Rossetti. She writes her sonnet 'In an Artist's Studio' (1856) after visiting her brother's art studio. Christina writes: 'One face [Elizabeth Siddal's] looks out from all his canvases' (1). Dante paints Siddal's face over and over, on canvas after canvas, and in the poem, Christina captures her brother's obsession: 'He feeds upon her face by day and night' (9). Dante Gabriel Rossetti finds in 'life' the 'stunner', the woman who embodies his artistic vision: a woman so stunningly beautiful that she seems capable of existing only in art, not in life. Rossetti and other artists of the Pre-Raphaelite Brotherhood find the embodiment of the 'stunner' in Elizabeth Siddal, Rossetti's first wife, and model for a number of Millais's paintings, particularly *Ophelia* (1852). In turn, Rossetti finds inspiration in his sister's poetry. He creates a frontispiece for *Goblin Market*, in which two beautiful Pre-Raphaelite 'stunners' embrace passionately, reflecting the close friendship between the Lizzie and Laura as well as hinting at the poem's homoerotic undertones. When Lizzie returns to the ailing Laura after undergoing the Goblin torture, she calls to Laura: 'Did you miss me? / Come and kiss me. / Never mind my bruises, / Hug me, kiss me, suck my juices' (465–8). The sexual boldness of Christina Rossetti's poem and the sumptuous sexuality seen in her brother's paintings and those of the Pre-Raphaelite Brotherhood anticipate the sea change in ideas of morality that will intensify in the final decade of the nineteenth century, referred to as the *fin de siècle*.

Fin-de-siècle

The *fin de siècle* of the nineteenth century ushered in the Decadent and **Aesthetic movements**, which venerated 'art for art's sake', praising art for its aesthetic value alone – luxuriating in its excessive (decadent) beauty while dismissing its possible instructive value. The towering *fin-de-siècle* artistic figure is Oscar Wilde. Wilde and other writers of this period were greatly influenced by the work of critic Walter Pater. Pater represents the antithesis of mid-century critic John Ruskin, who believes art should be tied to instruction. Pater, 30 years later, suggests that 'the poetic passion, the **desire** of beauty, the love of art for it's own sake' (Pater 1967: 224) epitomizes the artist's goal. Wilde's play, *The Importance of Being Earnest* (1895), pokes fun at the 'earnestness' so much, already in the 1880s and 1890s, a stereotypical feature of the mid-Victorian era. Wilde (in)famously writes in the preface to his novel *The Picture of Dorian Gray* (1891): 'There is no such thing as a moral or an immoral book. Books are well written, or badly written ... All art is quite useless' (2003: 3–4). In his prose essay 'The Decay of Lying', Wilde notes: 'The only beautiful things ... are the things that do not concern us. As long as a thing is useful or necessary to us ... it is outside the proper sphere of art' (Wilde 1891: 40). Art must exist solely for its own sake, not as a tool for teaching or as an attempt to reproduce 'life', because this endeavour, according to Wilde, is not possible: 'Life imitates art far more than Art imitates Life' (2003: 56).

At the same time as the rise of the Decadent movement, the image of 'the New Woman' becomes popular and pervasive. The New Woman is an independent-minded woman who wears trousers, rides bicycles, smokes and desires to participate in the masculine sphere. These 'new' women wanted the same freedom longed for by the fictional characters of Barrett Browning's *Aurora Leigh* and Rossetti's *Goblin Market*. They wanted to unfetter themselves from the role of 'angel in the house'. These 'angels' were content with their roles in the domestic sphere, and were eulogized in Coventry Patmore's poem, *The Angel in the House* (1854–62). As the century progressed, traditional-minded Victorians express anxiety about the breakdown of the spheres. Eliza Lynn Linton frets about 'The Girl of the Period', who possesses 'the love of pleasure and indifference to duty' (Linton 1868: 358). Linton laments: 'It used to be an old-time notion that the sexes were made for each other, and that it was only natural for them to please each other. ... But the girl of the period does not please men. She pleases them as little as she elevates them' (Linton 1868: 360). Popular (and scandalous) plays, like Arthur Wing Pinero's *The Second Mrs. Tanqueray* (1893), and George Bernard Shaw's *Mrs. Warren's Profession* (1893), feature New Woman heroines. Nevertheless, both plays' heroines are prostitutes, albeit sympathetic and likable prostitutes. This aligning of the 'new' woman with the **trope** of the 'fallen' woman indicates that old attitudes about women and sexuality still prevailed at the end of the century, despite some advancement.

Summary

Circling back to where I began, with George Eliot, I return to the lines of *Middlemarch* and Eliot's example of the 'minutely and multitudinously scratched' pier-glass. Eliot, after observing that the pier-glass is 'scratched in all directions', continues on to write, 'but place now against it a lighted candle as a centre of illumination, and lo! The scratches will seem to arrange themselves in a fine series of concentric circles … and it is only your candle which produces the flattering illusion of a concentric arrangement … These things are a parable. The scratches are events, and the candle is the egoism of any person now absent' (1977: 182). Eliot's words propose that any person who puts his/her 'candle' under the scratched surface of the Victorian era will encounter a different 'series' of clues. We continue to attempt to decipher these clues in order to understand the paradoxical and complex Victorian era, which is still changing in relation to the ways we try to present and preserve it.

The nineteenth century and the Victorians: sample syllabus

Semester 1: The novel and drama

Week 1   Introduction to Victorian literature; begin *The Pickwick Papers*
Week 2   Charles Dickens, *The Pickwick Papers* (1836)
Week 3   Charlotte Brontë, *Jane Eyre* (1847)
Week 4   Anthony Trollope, *The Warden* (1855)
Week 5   George Bernard Shaw, *Mrs. Warren's Profession*; Arthur Wing Pinero, *The Second Mrs. Tanqueray* (both 1893)
Week 6   Elizabeth Gaskell, *North and South* (1855)
Week 7   Charles Dickens, *Great Expectations* (1860)
Week 8   Wilkie Collins, *The Moonstone* (1868)
Week 9   George Eliot, *Middlemarch* (1871)
Week 10   Oscar Wilde: *Salome* (1894), and illustrations by Aubrey Beardsley; *The Importance of Being Earnest* (1895)
Week 11   Thomas Hardy, *The Mayor of Casterbridge* (1886)
Week 12   Robert Louis Stevenson, *The Strange Case of Dr. Jekyll and Mr. Hyde* (1886)

Semester 2: Poetry and prose

Week 1   Thomas Carlyle: excerpts from *Sartor Resartus* (1833); *On Heroes, Hero-Worship and the Heroic in History* (1841)
Week 2   Alfred Lord Tennyson: 'The Lady of Shalott', 'Ulysses', 'St. Simeon of Stylites'; excerpts from *In Memoriam A.H.H.* and 'The Charge of the Light Brigade'
Week 3   Robert Browning: 'Porphyria's Lover', 'My Last Duchess', 'Fra Lippo Lippi', 'A Grammarian's Funeral' and 'Caliban upon Setebos'

Week 4   John Stuart Mill: 'What is poetry?' (1833); excerpts from *On Liberty* (1859) and *The Subjection of Women* (1869)

Week 5   Elizabeth Barrett Browning: 'The Runaway Slave at Pilgrim's Point', excerpts from *Aurora Lee* and 'Mother and Poet'

Week 6   John Ruskin: excerpts from *The Stones of Venice* (1853) and *Modern Painters* (1856); George Eliot: excerpts from 'Silly Novels by Lady Novelists' (1856)

Week 7   Gerard Manley Hopkins: 'Wreck of the Deutschland', 'God's Grandeur', 'Pied Beauty' and 'Spring and Fall'; Matthew Arnold: excerpts from *Culture and Anarchy* (1869) and poems 'The Buried Life' and 'Dover Beach'

Week 8   Charles Darwin: excerpts from *Origin of the Species* (1859) and *Descent of Man* (1871)

Week 9   Poetry and art: Christina Rossetti: 'In An Artist's Studio', *Goblin Market* and 'No Thank You, John'; Dante Gabriel Rossetti: 'The Blessed Damozel' and paintings by D. G. Rossetti and other Pre-Raphaelite Brotherhood artists

Week 10   Walter Pater: excerpts from *Studies in the History of the Renaissance* (1873); Oscar Wilde: 'The Decay of Lying' (1891)

Week 11   'The New Woman': essays by Eliza Lynn Linton, Mona Alison Caird, Sarah Grand and Ouida (1889–94)

Week 12   Rudyard Kipling: 'The White Man's Burden' and 'The Man Who Would Be King' (1888); Ernest Dowson: 'They Are Not Long'

Bibliography

(a) Literary works

Brontë, Charlotte. *Jane Eyre*. Ed. Stevie Davies. London: Penguin, 2006.

Browning, Elizabeth Barrett. *Aurora Lee*. Ed. Kerry McSweeney. Oxford: Oxford University Press, 2008.

Browning, Robert. 'My Last Duchess', 'Fra Lippo Lippi', 'A Grammarian's Funeral' and 'Caliban upon Setebos'. In *Robert Browning: Selected Poems*. Ed. Daniel Karlin. London: Penguin, 2004.

Collins, Wilkie. *The Moonstone*. Ed. John Sutherland. Oxford: Oxford University Press, 2008.

Dickens, Charles. *Great Expectations*. Ed. Robert Douglas-Fairhurst and Margaret Cardwell. Oxford: Oxford University Press, 2008.

Dickens, Charles. *The Pickwick Papers*. Ed. Mark Wormald. London: Penguin, 2004.

Eliot, George. *Middlemarch*. Ed. B. G. Hornback. New York: Norton, 1977.

Eliot, George. *Silas Marner*. Ed. David Carroll. London: Penguin, 2003.

Gaskell, Elizabeth. *North and South*. Ed. Sally Shuttleworth and Angus Easson. Oxford: Oxford University Press, 2008.

Hardy, Thomas. *The Mayor of Casterbridge*. Ed. Pamela Dalziel and Dale Kramer. Oxford: Oxford University Press, 2008.

Stevenson, Robert Louis. *The Strange Case of Dr. Jekyll and Mr. Hyde and Other Tales*. Ed. Roger Luckhurst. Oxford: Oxford University Press, 2008.

Tennyson, Alfred Lord. *Ulysses, In Memoriam and Other Poems*. Ed. John Jump. London. Everyman, 1991.

Wilde, Oscar. *The Importance of Being Earnest and Other Plays*. Ed. Peter Raby. Oxford: Oxford University Press, 2008.

(b) Further reading

Altick, Richard D. *Victorian People and Ideas: A Companion for the Modern Reader of Victorian Literature.* New York: Norton, 1973.

Anger, Suzy, ed. *Knowing the Past: Victorian Literature and Culture.* Ithaca, NY: Cornell University Press, 2001.

Christ, Carol T. and Catherine Robson, eds. *Norton Anthology of English Literature – The Victorian Age.* New York: Norton. 2006.

Gilbert, Sandra M. and Susan Gubar. *The Madwoman in the Attic. The Woman Writer and the Nineteenth-Century Literary Imagination.* London: Yale University Press, 1979.

Houghton, Walter E. *The Victorian Frame of Mind 1830–1870.* New Haven, CT: Yale University Press, 1957.

Miller, J. Hillis. *The Form of Victorian Fiction.* Notre Dame, NC: University of Notre Dame Press, 1968.

Otis, Laura, ed. *Literature and Science in the Nineteenth Century.* Oxford: Oxford University Press, 2002.

Poovey, Mary. *Making a Social Body: British Cultural Formation 1830–1864.* Chicago: University of Chicago Press, 1995.

Thomson, David. *England in the Nineteenth Century 1815–1914.* Harmondsworth: Penguin, 1978.

Warwick, Alexandra and Martin Willis. *The Victorian Literature Handbook.* London: Continuum, 2008.

Modernism

(Year 3)

Alex Murray

Modernism refers to a loosely associated group of writers who experimented with literary form, largely in England, during the period 1900–45. As a student new to modernism you can easily identify it as the collection of authors you're likely to study: James Joyce, Virginia Woolf, T. S. Eliot, Ezra Pound, Joseph Conrad, Wyndham Lewis, D. H. Lawrence and Katherine Mansfield. But when one examines this modernist **canon**, the sense of it being a unified movement, or even a descriptive term for a literary style, starts to collapse. But then we can definitively state that it locates texts produced between 1900 and 1945. Or can we? These dates are in many ways arbitrary, using events, namely the beginning of the twentieth century and the end of the Second World War, to delimit a literary 'period' that arguably began in the late Victorian period and didn't 'end' until the late 1960s, if at all. So, locating modernism as either a literary 'period' or 'movement' seems redundant, an attempt to compartmentalize and homogenize a disparate range of writers and literary forms. So when faced with the task of defining modernism, how is one to proceed? In what follows I will suggest that you can locate modernism under the two rubrics of *aesthetic innovation* and *cultural politics*. These are far from exhaustive and in themselves fail to cohere as stable categories, yet I hope they can help us to see how modernism itself works to undo the forms of neat and stable labelling that underpin many of our ideas of literature.

Aesthetic innovation

In poetics, modernism signalled the decisive collapse of the traditional poetic form and the emergence of a verse form that, despite using internal rhythms, denied the reader the traditional crutches of rhyme and standardized metre to guide the reading of a poem (see POETRY). They were now replaced by excessive and obscure allusions to literary texts, classical myths, historical events and other extratextual sources, which produced a true questioning of the nature of the poetic and of reading.

This impetus towards innovation, newness and destruction characterizes modernism in poetry. It is important to remember that the injunction to 'make it new' meant that modernist poetics moved very quickly, with different styles and forms being experimented with in a short period. Therefore it remains difficult to provide a description of modernist poetics, or to hold up a single poem as exemplary. This, however, does not stop most twentieth-century literature courses from wheeling out T. S. Eliot's *The Waste Land* as the representative modernist poem. With its impossible depth of allusions, shifts in style and voice, as well as its perpetual **ambiguity**, it will always occupy the central place within the modernist **canon**. Yet there were a whole host of differing styles that characterize modernist poetics. Perhaps imagism can provide us with a sense of an alternative modernist style, and by looking at some of the manifesto-like work written by Ezra Pound, we can get a glimpse of how modernism saw the challenge of creating a new poetics.

Imagism is largely associated with Ezra Pound and Hilda Doolittle (H.D.). The moniker was primarily Pound's and it described the means by which the writers associated with the movement described objects with a clarity and precision. As Pound stated in the non-manifesto 'A Few Don'ts by an Imagiste', 'Use no superfluous word, no adjective which does not reveal something' (Rainey 2005: 95). This command underlines the idea of stripping language down to a bare minimum needed to describe, with clarity, an object. Importantly, this injunction comes at the expense of traditional poetic form. A traditional ballad form, for instance, stipulates a rhyming structure to the quatrain and often a rhythm. The imagists suggested that these imposed formulae denied what they saw as the task of poetry, namely the description of the thing itself. Their poetry was therefore short, focused, and characterized by a musical cadence. The contrast between the imagists and Eliot should underline that modernist innovation takes many differing forms, and that it is perhaps best to think of modernism as an intention towards formal experimentation, rather than as having a definitive style by which it can be identified.

If modernist innovation is complex and varied in poetics, it is no less true in the field of fiction (see THE NOVEL). Perhaps here it will be most useful to examine the beginning of two classic novels, one Victorian, one modernist, to understand how modernism is regarded as a dramatically innovative literary moment. Our first example comes from Charles Dickens's novel *Our Mutual Friend* (1864–5):

> In these times of ours, though concerning the exact year there is no need to be precise, a boat of dirty and disreputable appearance, with two figures in it, floated on the Thames, between Southwark Bridge which is of iron, and London Bridge which is of stone, as an autumn evening was closing in. (Dickens 1998: 1)

Dickens places us in time and space, giving us a tone, themes and symbolism that will be repeated throughout the novel. It works to orient the reader, but also to place them at the start of a narrative. Even if the narrative is to reach back into the past, or to look forward to a future, we still feel that the beginning is giving us a place, within the text, to grasp the action. Compare this opening to one of the most celebrated texts of the modernist **canon**, Virginia Woolf's *To the Lighthouse* (1927):

> 'Yes, of course, if it's fine to-morrow,' said Mrs Ramsay. 'But you'll have to be up with the lark,' she added.
> To her son these words conveyed an extraordinary joy, as if it were settled the expedition were bound to take place, and the wonder to which he had looked forward, for years and years it seemed, after a night's darkness, and a day's sail, within touch. (Woolf 1992: 7)

Woolf's novel begins by plunging the reader into the narrative of the story, giving them neither time nor place – no **context** at all. Whereas the Victorian novel led the reader in, lulling her into a sense of comfort, Woolf seeks to force the reader dramatically into a far more active mode of textual engagement. No longer will the action unfold in a setting, but through action we can piece together something like the components of a setting. Yet these differences don't truly hold across either author's *oeuvre*. The start of *Great Expectations* (1860–1), with Pip ruminating on why he's known as Pip, is hardly setting a deliberate scene. Likewise, the start of Woolf's final novel *Between the Acts* is, even if a parody, more reminiscent of a Victorian novel that the modernist.

More broadly, the modernist novel refuses to provide the familiar expectation of narrative closure, linearity, fully formed characters, definitive moral perspective or judgement and a consistent style. At its extremes, as in the case of James Joyce's *Finnegans Wake*, it sought to destroy the very idea of the novel and to force an interrogation of literary language more broadly. Holding up a work of extreme experimentalism in fiction such *as Finnegans Wake* as an example of modernist innovation is misleading. Instead it would be far more effective to look at the modernist novel as a continuum of experimentation. Here we may want to place a seemingly traditional novella like Joseph Conrad's *Heart of Darkness* (1899) as an example of subtle modernist experimentation. While Conrad's subject matter – the nature of colonialism and its relation to broader issues of human nature and social values – was groundbreaking, his use of literary technique remained, for the most part, within traditional fictional conventions. While the use of a multi-textured narrative – the narrator giving his account of Marlowe's story, who at times relays the stories of others – plays with ideas of narrative authority and perspective, the text as a whole locates itself within a traditional prose style, a clearly identifiable narrative perspective, a sense of time and place, a clear use of traditional symbolism and a denouement that leaves the action of the story enclosed. Between Conrad and Joyce there lie hundreds of different experimentations of style, all of which can be identified as modernist, but which collectively hardly give us a solid definition of modernism as a programme of **aesthetic** innovation.

Cultural and social politics

The seeming **ambiguity** that characterizes modernist aesthetics is no less apparent when we turn to its cultural and social politics. If modernism conjures up dazzlingly complex texts on the one hand, it often elicits impressions of elitism and conservatism on the other. Modernist politics, in particular the politics of English modernism (unlike German, for instance), are tainted by the infamous dalliances with fascism by Wyndham Lewis and Ezra Pound. While both cases are complex and prone to exaggeration, particularly Lewis, both writers were drawn by fascism's **desire** to reinvigorate the lives of the working class through an authoritarian implementation of social and economic development, which arguably struck a chord with a writer such as Pound. Many modernists were deeply critical of the rise of a mass culture that they saw as vulgar. In many ways, their elitist forms of cultural production (limited numbers of difficult texts printed for a discerning audience) emerged out of a deep-seated distrust of the unknown mass. Fascism's desire to give direction to the masses through the imposition of the state and the **ideology** of the nation thus dovetailed with many modernists' ideals.

Yet to allow the relation between fascism and modernism to dominate our understanding of the movement is both inaccurate and irresponsible. Modernism coincided with an unprecedented period of social change. The moralism and seeming stability of the Victorian period gave way to a tumultuous period of social change that saw, amongst other things, two world wars, universal suffrage, the Russian Revolution, the Great Depression, and dramatic scientific and technological advancement. Modernism was one of many responses to these events, and their responses must be seen as varied and complex. For instance, many modernist writers saw the rapid development of technology as filled with a dramatic potential. It was the futurist, Marinetti, who declared that 'A racing car with a hood that glistens with large pipes resembling a serpent with explosive breath … a roaring automobile that rides on grape-shot, this is more beautiful than the *Victory of Samothrace*' [a classical Greek statue] (Rainey 2005: 4). In the clean lines of the automobile Marinetti saw a new future in which speed completely changed our understanding of reality. On the other hand, a writer such as D. H. Lawrence saw in the industrialization of modernity a deadening and weakening of the vital spirit in man. As the character Dionys in the novella *The Ladybird* states, 'I have found my God. The God of anger, who throws down the steeples and the factory chimneys' (Lawrence 1994: 186). This desire to destroy modernity, as opposed to an uncritical faith, marks one instance of the dramatic polarization that existed within modernist responses to the social.

If modernism was ambivalent about changes in technology, it was even more so in its **gender** politics. The modernist **canon** only includes one, or at the most two, female authors – Virginia Woolf and Katherine Mansfield – and critics now argue that the gendered bias of modernism worked to actively exclude females. In addition, the canon has also come to seem deeply Eurocentric and elitist. A great deal of work in recent modernist studies has sought to call into question these biases, blowing apart the idea of modernism as a small set of elite cultural cliques. In doing so, our understanding of what the very term signifies has expanded and shifted, widening its scope and time frame as we come to contemplate the politics and ethics of radical **aesthetics**.

Modernism: sample syllabus

Week 1   From impressionism to modernism: Joseph Conrad, *Heart of Darkness*
Week 2   Modernist poetry (1): Pound; Eliot; H.D.; Yeats
Week 3   Virginia Woolf, *To the Lighthouse*
Week 4   D. H. Lawrence, *Three Novellas*
Week 5   James Joyce, *Ulysses* (1): nationalism, history, modernity
Week 6   James Joyce, *Ulysses* (2): language and literary form
Week 7   Modernist poetry (2): American modernism – Wallace Stevens; William Carlos Williams; Gertrude Stein
Week 8   Modernist magazines: excerpts from a range of modernist 'little' magazines
Week 9   Djuna Barnes, *Nightwood*
Week 10 European modernism: Franz Kafka, *Metamorphosis and Other Stories*
Week 11 Colonial modernism: Patrick White, *Voss*
Week 12 After modernism?: Samuel Beckett, *Waiting for Godot*

Bibliography

(a) Literary works

Dickens, Charles. *Our Mutual Friend*. Oxford: Oxford University Press, 1998.

Lawrence, D. H. *The Fox / The Captain's Doll / The Ladybird*. London: Penguin, 1994.

Rainey, Lawrence, ed. *Modernism: An Anthology*. Oxford: Blackwell, 2005.

Woolf, Virginia. *To the Lighthouse*. London: Penguin, 1992.

(b) Further reading

Baker, Jr, Houston A. *Modernism and the Harlem Renaissance*. Chicago and London: Chicago University Press, 1987.

Bradbury, Malcom, and James McFarlane, eds. *Modernism: A Guide to European Literature, 1890–1930*. Harmondsworth: Penguin, 1976.

Carey, John. *The Intellectuals and the Masses: Pride and Prejudice Among the Literary Intelligentsia, 1880–1939*. London: Faber & Faber, 1992.

DeKoven, Marianne. *Rich and Strange: Gender, History, Modernism*. Princeton, NJ: Princeton University Press, 1991.

Leveson, Michael, ed. *The Cambridge Companion to Modernism*. Cambridge: Cambridge University Press, 1999.

Nicholls, Peter. *Modernisms: A Literary Guide*. London: Macmillan, 1995.

North, Michael. *Reading 1922: A Return to the Scene of the Modern*. Oxford: Oxford University Press, 1999.

Rainey, Lawrence. *Institutions of Modernism: Literary Elites and Popular Culture*. New Haven, CT: Yale University Press, 1998.

Scott, Bonnie Kime, ed. *The Gender of Modernism: A Critical Anthology.* Bloomington: Indiana University Press, 1990.

Stevens, Hugh, and Caroline Howlett, eds. *Modernist Sexualities.* Manchester: Manchester University Press, 2000.

Contemporary literature

(Year 3)

What is contemporary literature?

Contemporary literature can be defined most basically as literature published after the Second World War. This has been, and in some cases remains, the implicit basis on which modules on contemporary literature are founded. Equally implicit in this assumption, and something which a teacher of such a module might stress to you, is the idea that, unlike other formal or period-dictated groupings of English literature, or literature in English, there are no discernibly dominant trends or forms to offer more precise definitions (such as 'modernism' or 'Victorian fiction'). What might also be suggested to you is the idea that, unlike the period of the first 30 years of the twentieth century, or the nineteenth century, we are not, as readers, sufficiently far enough away historically from the late 1940s, 1950s or subsequent decades to be able to give a label that can encompass both the diversity and the similarity of a cultural moment smaller than the 50–60 years that constitute the second half, roughly speaking, of the twentieth century. Moreover, this does not take into account the first decade of the twenty-first century, some of the literature of which is already finding itself on modules of contemporary literature, as the 1950s and 1960s appear to begin to recede.

The first problem that any module on 'contemporary' literature should confront, therefore, is the difficulty we have in defining the 'contemporary', which in some cases has not been well defined but taken as a rather loose synonym for 'recent'. 'Contemporary' also does not simply mean 'postmodern', itself a notoriously vague and problematic term (see POSTMODERNISM). If it is possible to say anything about the 'contemporary' in contemporary literature, therefore, it might be that a module would begin by acknowledging the difficulty, but also suggest that if we take as the period of our inquiry 1945 or 1950, for argument's sake, to 2009 (Liverpool University defines its MA in contemporary literature as being from *c.*1960 to the present day), we have to acknowledge that 'contemporary' literature is always subject to a historical shifting and revision.

If you were to look at the journal *Contemporary Literature*, which celebrates its fiftieth anniversary in winter 2010 (see contemporaryliterature.org), you would find a banner definition at the head of its website. This states that it publishes articles on multiple genres including novels, drama, poetry, creative non-fiction, digital literature and other 'new' media, and graphic novels. As precedent and history – this is both justification and definition of contemporary literature – the website observes that it was the first to publish essays on North American poet Susan Howe and novelist Thomas Pynchon; it has also published on Don DeLillo and Margaret Drabble, Kazuo Ishiguro and South African novelist J. M. Coetzee. Additionally, the journal publishes articles and reviews not only on 'creative' writing but also concerning critical discussions. In the current issue (as I write) there are articles on Lyn Hejinian, J. M. Coetzee, Vikram Seth, Toni Cade Bambara and 'contemporary British writing'. You may not recognize all the names here, but a sense of the eclecticism of 'contemporary literature' can be gleaned if you reflect that the small group of authors named here are American, South African, Indian, African American, and English, of Japanese birth.

While *Contemporary Literature* offers one picture of what you might expect contemporary literature to be, modules being taught at universities provide other possible broad definitions. Liverpool University offers an MA in the subject, and starts from a premise of studying 'Anglophone' writers, whose backgrounds are Irish, American and British. Additionally, it includes study of the relation between literature and film, and debates the nature of postmodernism. It promises to provide the historical, political, generic and philosophical contexts of contemporary fiction, and amongst the writers it offers for study are to be found Ian McEwan, A. S. Byatt, Margaret Atwood, Don DeLillo, Paul Auster and Carol Ann Duffy. The modules into which Liverpool divides its MA are 'contemporary Irish poetry', 'contemporary English fiction', 'postmodern fiction' and 'contemporary women's poetry'. The MA in contemporary literature at Leeds University has similar parameters but offers modules in 'Caribbean and Black British writing', 'contemporary poetry', 'critical theory', 'culture and anarchy 1945–1968' (which covers drama and film from Noel Coward and David Lean to Joe Orton), 'Graham Greene', and 'psychoanalysis in cultural theory'. Hull University also has an MA in what it defines as 'modern and contemporary literature', and offers modules on the 'literary north', 'poetry and the spirit of place', 'women, writing, travel', 'domestic violence /colonial violence', the 'neo-Victorian novel', 'gender in popular culture'.

Thinking about diversity: strategic approaches to the contemporary

You might wonder why I've been referring to MA courses when this is a companion to undergraduate study. A brief 'google' of the phrase 'contemporary literature module' immediately threw up ten MAs, with no initial reference to undergraduate modules. This, in itself, reflects the breadth, diversity and, quite seriously, the undefinability of the topic. 'Contemporary literature' defines that which cannot be defined, except through an all-encompassing gathering up, from which, in order to be practical, a teacher might winnow one of several possible trajectories, according to a specific theme or other defining recurrent topic. At its broadest, such an approach might be to examine how literature in English around the world addresses major social and political issues in the past two decades. Another approach might be to focus on **gender**, sexuality, sexual orientation and gender difference, including novels by, amongst others, Alan Hollinghurst, Sarah Waters and Jeanette Winterson. While I've been illustrating the diversity of contemporary literature, and the attendant problem of defining it through specialized postgraduate courses and their modules, none of these modules in modified form might be out of place on undergraduate syllabi. What an undergraduate module on contemporary literature might be expected to cover, not unreasonably, then, would be a little, if not of everything, then at least a selection of some of what such modules focus on. Of course, depending on which university you attend, you might find that your English department has suitably wide parameters for the definition of its own contemporary literature module, which can allow for highly focused themes as a strategic means of instituting a pathway through the topic. Given that 'contemporary literature', arguably more than any other module, can be about almost anything published, printed, digitized or even filmed in the last 60 or so years, the rest of this essay will set out possible ways of approaching the subject of contemporary literature modules, and defining one such module.

Outlining a module

Given the date range that remains as the 'borders' of contemporary literature's chameleon identity, you might perhaps expect to find a module structured through the choice of 'exemplary' texts from each decade. While MA modules emphasize particular themes and offer a concentrated focus, any undergraduate module should offer a critical introduction, survey and overview. To this end, a module that progresses across the decades can offer a strong sampling, which while not defensibly typical, nonetheless can introduce you to certain key texts, which, whether having a large or small readership, whether having become **canonical** or having retained a cult or coterie status, remain fascinating singular textual forms, indicative of the breadth of literary interests. Were we to begin with the 1950s or 1960s, this would mean that you would be expected to read two, perhaps three key texts – novels, poetry, drama – from each decade, and study these with a view to determining the significant cultural events, trends, beliefs. A question that immediately arises here is whether to limit the study of contemporary literature to one nation or to take works from different countries and different cultures as key works of a particular generation. Given that what has become known as globalization may be understood as a post-Second World War phenomenon, it is feasible that the module should address not simply English literature, but literature in English and also literature in translation.

Beginning in the late 1940s, historically and politically, such a module might start from the end of British rule in Palestine in 1948 and, in the same year, the founding of the National Health Service and the nationalization of the railways in Great Britain. Such historical events might be used to contextualize a change in cultural perspectives as a strategic narrative for introducing the idea of contemporary literature. An introductory lecture or seminar would address such historical events, providing commentary on roughly a decade of postwar change, indicating events such as the advent of the Cold War, the beginnings of large-scale immigration in the United Kingdom, communist paranoia in the United States, the proliferation of nuclear testing, and the erection of the Berlin Wall in 1961.

The 1950s could be studied equally through a play such as *The Entertainer* by John Osborne, which contrasts the contemporary events of the Suez crisis (as these provide the 'backstory' to the play) and the decline of English colonial power as figured, unusually, through the decline of music hall; the poetry of Philip Larkin or W. H. Auden would serve to highlight the change of focus in poetry away from modernist experimentation and oblique language or classical/mythological reference to a more accessible poetry; while a novel such as Günter Grass's *The Tin Drum* (1959) exemplifies particular aspects of contemporary writing (and indeed is a major influence on many subsequent novelists, such as Salman Rushdie) by introducing mythical and anti-realistic elements into a narrative concerned with Germany's Nazi and wartime past. Vladimir Nabokov's *Lolita* (1955) would also be a possible text, as would Friedrich Dürrenmatt's play, *The Visit* (1956), both being, if not satires proper, then certainly satirical in their exploration of social weaknesses and transgressions. William Golding's *Lord of the Flies* (1954) can be read as both a commentary on atomic culture and the threat of nuclear weapons, and a critique of what Golding takes to be the inherent savagery underlying British middle-class society, as represented through its schoolboys.

From such choices you might be expected not only to examine such works for what they tell you about the given period, but also to read them in the **context** of the traditions on which they borrow, to which they allude, and from which they depart or react against, in their efforts to make literature new. There are thus to be considered elements that are simultaneously conservative and traditional, and also radical, experimental and innovative. Here, you might find you are approaching a cautious, provisional definition of contemporary literature: that it seeks at the same time to be both accessible and to draw upon its precursors and antecedents, and also to invent something different. Without being as formally experimental as modernism, contemporary literature might well attempt to experiment with form, address new subjects and approach old subjects in a new way, whilst also appearing to take on older forms of representation. In some contemporary literature, therefore, there is to be read a reaction against the avant-garde of modernism.

If the 1950s can be read as emphasizing hybridity (as I've been implying), work in the 1960s might be taken as moving back towards a more radically or obvious avant-garde position. Plays by Samuel Beckett or Harold Pinter would be studied to explore and emphasize experimentation and departures from obviously signposted traditions. A novel such as Gabriel Garcia Marquez's *One Hundred Years of Solitude* (1967) might be studied for both its formal experimentation, heralding what has become known as 'magic realism', and its critical observation, albeit in somewhat mythical and symbolic fashion, on the history of Latin America, whilst also acknowledging Spanish and, generally, European traditions in the novel. Jean Rhys's *Wide Sargasso Sea* (1966) offers a postcolonial retelling of, and commentary on, the colonial assumptions of *Jane Eyre*, being told from the perspective of Mr Rochester's first wife, Bertha Mason, while Sylvia Plath's poetry or her novel *The Bell Jar* (1963) looks to examine questions of **gender** and identity within cultures that are still strikingly patriarchal, or which, despite the rise of feminism in the 1960s, remain paternalist in their determination of normative selfhood (see POSTCOLONIALISM, GENDER, SUBJECTIVITY). Both Rhys and Plath address questions of women's identity and place in contemporary culture, as does American confessional poet Anne Sexton.

By the 1970s, there are to be found more radical experiments in poetry. Most prominent is the work of the Language Poets in the United States, who emphasized method and, in this at least, demonstrated an affiliation with modernist poetics. Susan Howe's work is particularly remarkable in its experimentation with language and form, especially the more striking aspects of type manipulation on the page, where lines are imposed over one another at odd angles, for example. *Frame Structures* (1996) by Howe presents an anthology of Howe's work from the 1970s. Regarding fiction, it is arguable that while poetry became more avant-garde, novels returned to more traditional storytelling values. This is given a somewhat ambiguous, if not ambivalent, exploration by John Fowles. A novel such as the neo-Victorian *The French Lieutenant's Woman* (1969) takes on the problems of historical retrospect and the narration of the past in the light of, then, recent French theories of authorship, specifically those being asserted by literary critic Roland Barthes. Against this, you might also read a collection of short stories such as *The Book of Sand* by Jorge Luis Borges, an experimental, some would say surreal, Argentinian writer, whose writing acknowledges both experiments in Latin American tradition and also displays an indebtedness to 'high' literary culture and tradition in Europe. And speaking of European writers, as a contrast to the North American avant-garde poetry of Howe and the Language Poets, there is Paul Celan, the Jewish Romanian poet who experienced the concentration camps, a major contemporary poet. Writing his poetry exclusively in German, and confronting the limits of language in the wake of the experience of the Holocaust, Celan killed himself in 1970, and while he may more properly be considered in a contemporary literature module as belonging to the 1950s or 1960s, when the majority of his works were published, mere historical reference is only that, and cannot tell the whole story. Reading Celan offers the student a reflection on personal and **existential** struggles covering the entire postwar period for writers who struggled with the question of the necessity of poetry after Auschwitz. For Celan, language remained the only thing that was secure against loss, as he put it.

Umberto Eco's *The Name of the Rose* and Salman Rushdie's *The Satanic Verses*, both published in the 1980s, are amongst the most visible novels of the decade. Alongside Milan Kundera's *The Unbearable Lightness of Being* (1984), they represent a high-water mark in the popularity (or at least sales, no evidence being available concerning whether all those who bought these titles actually read, or finished, these bestsellers) of the 'novel of ideas'. Were you to be assigned these, you would find two extremely playful, intellectually informed novels, each in its own way playing games with the form of narrative and the identity of the novel. In the case of Eco, *Rose* addresses various theories and philosophical arguments, ancient and modern, while Rushdie's novel concerns itself with questions of faith, the impossibility of asserting truths, and the power of **narrative** itself. Both are **metaphysical** novels; they address abstract ideas concerning identity and being, exploring these through narratives that question the limits of knowledge. Both, equally, are novels addressing intolerance and belief.

Portuguese novelist José Saramago's *Blindness* (1995) is a disquieting fantasy about a mass epidemic of blindness, which is also a parable about the nature of society. Saramago's writing is itself a challenge for the reader, with long, lyrical sentences. At the end of the twentieth century, it would present you with questions that are both political and historical, and formal. In an ostensibly wittier manner, John Banville's *Ghosts* (1993) asks similar questions. Another writer who, like Saramago, is known as a lyrical stylist whose writing draws on classical **myth** and literary tradition, Banville invites us to ask questions about the nature of representation, the purpose of art, and the nature of being. Does the world I imagine have a reality that, though different from material reality, can have, nevertheless, a profound effect on my sense of self? Lyricism and **irony**, qualities he shares with Saramago, inform Banville's narrative representations of worlds which, though fantastic, are familiar to us as readers. Both men present worlds where the real and imagined, the everyday and the literary, are closely entwined with one another, as does the work of another writer, Turkish author Orhan Pamuk (who came to prominence in the English-speaking world in the 1990s), not least his late 1990s novel, *The New Life*, in which a character becomes so enamoured of a 'new life' in a novel he has read, that he sets off in search of it. While Saramago's novel is not an example of 'metafiction' – fiction which addresses the status and condition of fiction, of what it is and what it can do, how it achieves its effects, and so forth – it does, like Banville and Pamuk's more obviously metafictional works, use fiction and narrative to ask ethical and moral questions that situate fictional protagonists in an oblique and tense relationship to the societies in which they exist, but which they also reveal to you as a reader, with a critical distance that is significant in all three novels.

Such ethical or moral questions reappear at the beginning of the twenty-first century, albeit in a more immediate fictional manner. The first decade of the twenty-first century has seen a return to novels seemingly driven by more conventional forms of narrative, once again. Both Ian McEwan's *Atonement* (2001) and Sarah Waters's *Night Watch* (2006) are historical novels, set in the years before the Second World War and during it, respectively. This return to the past might be considered a return to a point from where 'contemporary literature' sprang, and you might consider questions already raised in a module such as the one I am imagining here, having to do with how one bears witness to the past through narrative, what in narrative can be relied on, and, more generally, what purposes the novel might serve.

Summary

If you contemplated taking a contemporary literature module, there would be questions you might ask yourself, and which I have tried to position in present-ing one possible module outline, above. To start with, you might wish to consider what, if anything, can be said to connect the works I've indicated (or some, at least), despite their very obvious differences. Putting this another way, are there themes in common, even though these themes are handled in diverse, different ways? What your module might explore, placing this at the beginning as an open-ended question that it is the purpose of the module to contemplate, are questions concerning the relation between literature, history and philo-sophical reflections on being, identity, society and the past, following the Second World War, the Holocaust, and the first use of nuclear weapons. 'What can literature do?' is a broad, but necessary question in the second half of the twentieth century, and if literature has the right, in principle, to say anything, what responsibilities, what ethical duties does literature have? Other concerns in a contemporary literature module might have to do with form, experimenta-tion and balances or tensions between accessibility and experiment, popularity and intellectual inquiry. How, in a commercial world, and with changes in media, can literature remain viable as a mode of intellectual investigation *and* as a form of popular entertainment, without sacrificing readership to avant-garde experiment on the one hand, and without falling into the most formulaic and obvious of poetic or fictional devices on the other? If, as we began by saying, contemporary literature is diverse, in another way, it shares certain interests – in the effects of the past, for example, in the possibilities and limits of narrating that past, for another. Your contemporary literature module might formulate its questions differently, but at bottom it should have in mind the

2

question of how individuals form identities within, or in tension with, communities and societies that bear a certain historical weight or burden.

Contemporary literature: sample syllabus

Week 1   Introduction: literature after Auschwitz
Week 2   1950s: horror, the grotesque, and history: Günter Grass, *The Tin Drum*
Week 3   1960s (1): rewriting the colonial past (1): Gabriel Garcia Marquez, *One Hundred Years of Solitude*
Week 4   1960s (2): rewriting the colonial past (2): Jean Rhys, *Wide Sargasso Sea*
Week 5   1970s (1): bearing witness through a poetics of the limit: Susan Howe, *Frame Structures*; Paul Celan, *Selected Poetry*
Week 6   1970s (2): history, narration and undecidability: John Fowles, *The French Lieutenant's Woman*
Week 7   1980s: Salman Rushdie, *The Satanic Verses*
Week 8   1990s (1): occasional morality: José Saramago, *Blindness*
Week 9   1990s (2): the ethics of fiction: Orhan Pamuk, *The New Life*
Week 10 2000s (1) history and myth: Ian McEwan, *Atonement*
Week 11 2000s (2): history and myth: Sarah Waters, *The Night Watch*
Week 12 Conclusion: experiment and tradition

Bibliography

(a) Literary works

Celan, Paul. *Selected Poetry*. Trans. Michael Hamburger. London: Penguin, 1996.

Fowles, John. *The French Lieutenant's Woman*. London: Vintage, 2004.

Garcia Marquez, Gabriel. *One Hundred Years of Solitude*. Ed. Gregory Rabassa. London: Penguin, 2007.

Grass, Günter. *The Tin Drum*. London: Vintage, 2004.

Howe, Susan. *Frame Structures*. New York: W. W. Norton & Co., 1998.

McEwan, Ian. *Atonement*. London: Vintage, 2002.

Pamuk, Orhan. *The New Life*. London: Faber and Faber, 2002.

Rhys, Jean. *The Wide Sargasso Sea*. London: Penguin, 2000.

Rushdie, Salman. *The Satanic Verses*. New York: Random House, 2008.

Saramago, José. *Blindness*. London: Harvill, 1997.

Waters, Sarah. *The Night Watch*. London: Virago, 2006.

(b) Further reading

Brannigan, John. *Orwell to the Present: Literature in England, 1945–2000*. Basingstoke: Palgrave Macmillan, 2003.

English, James F. *A Concise Companion to Contemporary British Fiction*. Oxford: Blackwell, 2006.

Gasiorek, Andrej. *Post-war British Fiction: Realism and After*. London: Arnold, 1995.

Head, Dominic. *The Cambridge Introduction to Modern Fiction, 1950–2000*. Cambridge: Cambridge University Press, 2002.

Lane, Richard, Rod Mengham and Philip Tew, eds. *Contemporary British Fiction*. London: Polity, 2003.

Lee, Alison. *Realism and Power: Postmodern British Fiction*. London: Routledge, 1990.

Mengham, Rod. *An Introduction to Contemporary Fiction: International Writing in English Since 1970*. Cambridge: Polity Press, 1999.

Nicol, Brian, ed. *Postmodernism and the Contemporary Novel: A Reader*. Edinburgh: Edinburgh University Press, 2002.

Taylor, D. J. *A Vain Conceit: British Fictions in the 1980s*. London: Bloomsbury, 1989.

Tew, Philip. *The Contemporary British Novel*, 2nd edn. London: Continuum, 2007.

2

2.3 forms, genres and other popular modules

chapter contents

> Introduction   134
> Tragedy   135
> Comedy   142
> The novel   150
> Poetry   157
> Drama   164
> Epic   171
> Lyric   177
> Satire   181
> Realism   187
> Fiction   193
> Postmodern fiction   198
> Gender   202
> Class   209
> Colonial and postcolonial literature   215
> Subjectivity   221
> Children's literature   230
> Film studies   237
> Popular fiction   244
> American literature   250

Introduction

The previous chapter moved chronologically through the history of English literature. Such an historical survey is useful, but does not serve to explain fully, if at all, the interconnectedness, in literary relations, between form and content. Unlike dodos or royal families, literature does not develop in an evolutionary or genetic manner.

You will doubtless have noticed that module descriptions thus far (and this will continue) contain cross-references to other modules. One reason for this is to indicate the extent to which literature, whether you consider period, form or **genre**, does not exist in isolation. While successive generations may well read authors belonging to previous periods – in her essay 'Modern Fiction', Virginia Woolf announces her indebtedness to Henry Fielding and Jane

Austen, but directs us to Joseph Conrad, Thomas Hardy and Russian novelists of the nineteenth century as her spiritual predecessors in their exploration of the human spirit and psyche – each period consolidates or experiments with form. Tragedy and comedy of one type or another will be found in almost every century, in most cultures with oral or written traditions; equally, novels, plays, poems, short stories, or works of prose not otherwise easily placeable into categories, gain precedence, come into being in particular manifestations that remain more or less recognizable up to the present day. What follows looks at some of the more abiding forms, and their major features. While the modules you take may vary in content from department to department, what you will find in this chapter is a reliable overview of the broad parameters of such modules.

Tragedy (Year 2)

What's so tragic about tragedy, anyway?

Tragedy is one of those terms we take for granted. The death of a soldier in Helmand Province is 'tragic'. It is a 'tragedy' when a plane or bus crashes. But the term 'tragedy', referring to a largely dramatic form, originates in ancient Greece and combines two words, *tragos*, meaning *goat*, and *oide*, signifying *song* or *ode* – so *goat song*, from which it is assumed that the earliest tragedies were part of a festival, resulting in the prize of a goat for the best play, or otherwise that the word referred to a choric tradition of song competitions and festivals. This hardly sounds like what you might associate with the notion of tragedy, or that of the tragic, even though those ancient Greek plays that have survived have narrative elements that we would conventionally associate with 'tragic' events (death, calamity, catastrophe, and so on). Importantly, therefore, a small part of what a module concerning itself with tragedy should do is help define this term, even though its usage and meaning rapidly became multiple. That both Middle English and Medieval French retained *tragedie*, more or less unchanged from the transliteration of the Greek, however, should suggest to you that something of significance is maintained across translations. To put this differently, something, let us call it a trace, persists and remains, from the past, to haunt successive presents, each present leaving its own trace as a spectral manifestation in the future of its own present moment. Taking a module on tragedy, then, will involve you in coming to terms with its practical manifestations, in dramas, and perhaps some poetry or even novels; such a module should, in addition, address both meaning and concept.

In the process of definition, you will have to consider those early plays, dramas by Aeschylus (*c.*525 BCE–*c.*455 BCE), Sophocles (*c.*496 BCE–406 BCE) and Euripides (*c.*480 BCE–406 BCE) (see DRAMA). Not only will the process of reading such plays help define the iterable aspects of dramatic form belonging to tragedy in general in the period in question; it will also serve to form for you a sense of those elements that have changed and those that have remained constant in tragedy. Aeschylus's tetralogy of plays, known collectively as the *Oresteia*, consists of *Agamemnon, Choephoroi* (or *The Libation Bearers)* and *The Eumenides*. The fourth play of the tetralogy is no longer extant, and so the trilogy, telling the story of Agamemnon, King of Argos, and the misfortunes of his family, is all that remains. Sophocles wrote many plays, fragments of a number of which survive. His most famous play, however, remains the tragedy of the nobleman who, unwittingly, killed his father and married his mother, thereby bringing about ruin to his house and line, *Oedipus Rex*. Euripides, the third of the famous Athenian tragedians, is responsible for a number of trage-dies, not least among which are his *Medea, Electra* and *The Trojan Women*. If you know the proper names here, amongst these play titles, one thing that might strike you is that Euripides, unlike his two near contemporaries, focuses on female characters, thereby suggesting gendered characterization and, with that, plays which introduce female perspectives into tragic form.

Theories of tragedy

One of the first things to observe about Greek tragedy is that it focuses on the sufferings of individuals in circumstances over which they have no control. Such plays also frequently demonstrate supernatural intervention as part of the protagonist's destiny. As a way of theorizing such an empirical understand-ing that reading these plays affords, it would be helpful to consider the *Poetics* of Aristotle (384 BCE–322 BCE), which, if not the first example of literary criti-cism, 'theory' or poetics, remains an essential critical appreciation of form and content. Aristotle suggests that tragedy is defined by the seriousness of its treatment of its subject. In addition to this 'appropriate tone', Aristotle also remarks that the subject of tragedy should be someone of high or noble birth who undergoes a reversal of fortune, which is referred to by Aristotle as *peri-peteia*. The change from good to bad should be handled with dignity, but its purpose for Aristotle is to invoke feelings fear or pity in the audience. The reversal or change is usually the result of some unfortunate, but inevitable and unforeseen event, allied to what is conventionally understood as a character flaw in the heroic and noble protagonist. This sequence of events, Aristotle believes, produces – or should aim to produce – the effect known as **catharsis**, the process of releasing and purging strong feelings that are normally kept in check. So, we see in *Oedipus Rex* the story of a king (*rex*) who, unwittingly, kills his father (he does not know his victim is his father) and marries the man's wife, not knowing also that this is his, Oedipus's, mother.

Such a model might not always be the case, and your reading in the history of tragic dramas will show you the inventiveness with which playwrights adapt the conventions, distort them for dramatic purpose, or even subvert them in various ways. At the same time, the paradigm Aristotle proposes has easily been reduced to some fairly simple, not to say clichéd narrative tricks, so that tragedy has, in some cases of literature or film, become rendered merely as a sad story with an unhappy ending, at the witnessing of which we end up in tears. This fairly debased variation has become known as the 'three Kleenex movie', signifying the number of tissues you'll need as you blub at the misfortunes of the hard-done-by hero.

Tragedy is not, however, just about making us feel bad, or getting us to weep. Aristotle, it should be remembered, stresses the appropriateness of action, the seriousness of subject and the dignity of rank of the protagonist, and, within the contexts of genre transformation in different cultures and centuries, such devices tend, until the twentieth century at least, to remain more or less constant. The other principal philosopher of tragedy is the nineteenth-century German thinker, Friedrich Nietzsche. His *The Birth of Tragedy* (1872) is a major reconsideration of tragic art form and its philosophical underpinnings. No study of tragedy can claim to be comprehensive without a consideration of Nietzsche, for whom tragedy, through its suffering and elements of irrational narrative exposition, provided a powerful affirmation of the life force, often in the face of terrors, the inexplicable, and the painfulness of existence.

Early modern tragedy

Some modules focusing on tragedy might well move away from drama to consider particular long narrative poems or novels, in order to emphasize how tragedy is not simply a dramatic **genre** but a conceptual frame for presenting types of story involving misfortune. Critics, in their turn, have pointed to particular novelists, such as Thomas Hardy, for example, who have drawn on the structures and plots of classical or Shakespearean tragedy to shape their fictions. These are not unreasonable, perfectly fair ways of approaching the topic, but the module I am proposing here has the advantage of remaining true to the dramatic heritage. My reason for this is to indicate how, culturally and historically, some basic premises adhere, while the stories themselves are quite radically transformed over time, and show that tragedy, as a dramatic mode, survives because it is at once both historically specific and also mutable enough to maintain itself in quite different social and cultural **contexts**.

In the second part of the module I am imagining here, you would move to the study of early modern tragedy, the first notable highpoint in secular drama in the Christian epoch. Shakespeare would obviously be central to such a consideration but throughout Europe and in England, tragedy as a dramatic form proliferated and produced many great dramatists, poets and plays themselves. Often, plays from Elizabethan or Jacobean England reiterate the reversal of fortune of noble figures typical of classical tragedy, but you will often find variations on these themes, where discontented figures, known as malcontents, climb the social ladder within the courtly cultures that the plays depict, often through corrupt actions – plotting, scheming, murder, seduction and so forth. Becoming a critique of Elizabethan realpolitik, early modern tragedy explores through its variations the nature of political power, and transforms our understanding of tragedy by demonstrating worlds in which

Protestant doctrine and **humanist** philosophy play a part. Behind many tragedies produced in Elizabeth's England there is to be found a strong, not to say virulent anti-Catholicism, so that early modern tragedy takes on an **ideological** role at the end of the sixteenth, and beginning of the seventeenth, centuries.

Kyd's *The Spanish Tragedy*, which influenced Shakespeare in the writing of *Hamlet*, introduces devices such as the play within the play; it is also a specific type of tragedy, known as a revenge tragedy, in the plot of which several murders occur. If for Aristotle tragedy had been intended to purge the emotions of the audience, for the Elizabethans it became a vehicle for exciting the emotions, producing vicarious thrills, and exploring not the nobler, but the darker aspects of human behaviour. Shakespeare's *Macbeth* adheres to the traditions of supernatural intervention, but it does so in order to demonstrate how ambition, getting above one's station or destiny, can bring about tragic consequences, and also how political power corrupts and encourages ambition. John Webster's 1612 tragedy, *The White Devil*, is a more powerful, ambivalent play yet, featuring characters guilty of debauchery and murder, violent passions, infidelity, and a host of other crimes. If Kyd and Shakespeare had appeared to adapt and modify the conventions of tragedy, Webster might be said to have abandoned them altogether, to depict a wholly corrupt Catholic courtly world, where tragic events are the result of corruption of those who should be noble, have dignity and behave according to their station. The final play in this part of the module is Middleton's *Women Beware Women* (date of authorship is uncertain and has been placed anywhere between 1612 and 1627; the play text was not published until 1657). It is again set in the Italian court, and based on real events, involving not a male protagonist but a female one.

Bourgeois tragedy

The plays of the early modern period may be seen to have transformed classical tragedy in what were, if not unrecognizable ways, at least sufficiently radical. The changes were due to culturally and historically different interests and expectations. In this, you would come to understand how literature, while maintaining particular forms over centuries and cultures, nevertheless survives and evolves because it adapts to its times, the pleasures or interests of its audiences, and the material conditions of the culture that serves to produce it.

Nineteenth-century tragedies are no different, and are principally, and initially, notable in the most general terms for the ways in which they adapt tragic form to bourgeois, or middle-class interests and modes of behaviour, cultural mores, and so forth. It is in the Scandinavian countries that tragedy is given new impetus in dramatic form, chiefly through the work of Henrik Ibsen, but also August Strindberg, and the lesser-known, but no less significant Victoria Benedictsson, whose play *The Enchantment* (1888), like Ibsen's *Hedda Gabler* (1890), utilizes tragic narrative to explore the limits of women's freedom within hypocritical, **patriarchal** societies, where sexual and sexist double standards prevail (see GENDER).

Outside of Sweden, Russian playwright and short-story writer Anton Chekhov wrote a number of significant plays at the turn of the nineteenth century, such as *The Seagull, Three Sisters* and *The Cherry Orchard*, which are often featured on tragedy modules. Though Chekhov himself did not consider his plays tragic, they nevertheless explore the end of a culture and era in Russia, with their stories of landowners forced to leave and sell their properties, unable to comprehend fully the ramifications of historical and social change going on around them in Russian society.

Tragedy in modern times

The implications of Chekhovian drama are, in hindsight, political – that is to say, broadly political in historical terms – whilst the plays of Ibsen, Benedictsson and Strindberg place in tragic contours matters of sexual and class politics, which ideological issues in turn produce tragedy as a result of the material conditions of middle-class life towards the end of the nineteenth century (see CLASS). However, what Chekhov shares with his Swedish counterparts is a sense of the ways in which the world sweeps up individuals and brings tragic consequences because of their unpreparedness in the face of the forces of history. In this, you might reflect, what in Greek or even early modern plays, such as *Macbeth* or Christopher Marlowe's *The Tragical History of Dr Faustus*, is attributed to supernatural or **metaphysical** forces, becomes, by the nineteenth century, a question of the social, economic and cultural forces by which societies and individuals have change forced on them.

Dying in 1904, Chekhov failed to see the Russian Revolution of 1917, but the tragicomic disorder of his fictional families and their friends, their inability to understand what is happening to them and why they can no longer live in the way in which their families have for generations, hints repeatedly at the broad discontent and unrest in Russian society in the early twentieth century. In this, if you pause to reflect on the beginnings of tragedy, it might be said that though much has changed, there is also that in tragedy that has remained the same: the staging of family crises as expositions of political turmoil and transformation. Whether a monarch or a landowner, an Italian count or a Scottish king, all tragedies mediate conditions in which history produces painful transformations that are felt in the family. Tragedy, it might be said, does not present the personal as political but rather it connects the two, the family home becoming a site analogous with government or court. The one departure from this is in the plays of Ibsen and his two Swedish compatriots. Ibsen's protagonists are doctors, lawyers or pastors. However, each is a prominent social figure in Ibsen's 'democratic' reinvention of the tragic.

In the twentieth century, a number of playwrights are worthy of consideration in the **context** of tragedy. Harold Pinter has, not infrequently, been taught on tragedy modules. The two chosen here are Brecht and Beckett. Bertolt

Brecht, German dramatist and playwright, sought to push against notions of **catharsis** and what he would have seen as the essentialist and humanist aspects of conventional tragedies. For Brecht, all human conditions, all human suffering, was a result of material and economic conditions, and his plays sought to unfold this in deliberately estranging ways that proscribed emotional identification on the part of the audience. Developing a technique known as *verfremdungseffekt*, or distancing effect, Brecht sought to produce a critical audience capable of comprehending the material causes of human tragedy. In *Mother Courage and Her Children* (1939), Brecht's play (adapted loosely from an early novel dated approximately 1670), which chronicles the efforts of the titular character to make a profit from the Thirty Years' War, and protect her children unsuccessfully, offers a critique of the business of war and the ways in which humans are co-opted, used by political and economic situations, often with tragic consequences despite, or because of, their complicity in the dominant ideologies of the day.

Samuel Beckett's work, in contrast with that of Brecht's, could not be more dissimilar. Beckett's plays are, or *seem to be*, relentlessly closed off, for the most part, from immediate identification with, or attention to, the everyday world of history, politics and society. His dramas do, however, address in very intimate and often private ways what it means to exist in a world, which, after the Second World War, appeared to have lost purpose or meaning. Sometimes associated with **existentialist** philosophy, Beckett's plays reduce humans to bare living beings, whose condition is taken as tragic because they continue to exist in the face of no larger apparent purpose or meaning in their lives, and only the most dimly expressed sense of memory of a past when things might have been better. A play such as *Waiting for Godot* (1952) does not appear to conform in any manner to the conventions of tragedy, save for the fact that it presents characters whose very existence is tragic – that is to say, who exist after some catastrophic downfall. The notion of tragedy as dramatic form is thus implied, rather than presented.

Summary: why we are entertained by tragedy

It is not easy to understand why we might be entertained by tragedy. Perhaps, like comedy, tragedy entertains because, in witnessing the downfall of others, we have a sense of relief that what we see is not happening to us. Perhaps Aristotle's notion of catharsis still holds true: in identifying with a character's misfortunes, and understanding that the world around him or her has brought about this downfall, our sense of good fortune is mixed with empathy for the suffering of an individual not unlike us. Whether that collapse or reversal of fortunes is seen to be **metaphysical** or material, supernatural or as a collateral effect of economics and politics, the sense remains one of personal recognition. Theatre, as Eva Figes observes in *Tragedy and Social Evolution*, plays 'a central function in giving expression to and perpetuating the beliefs and ideologies of that society' (1976: 13). In this, it stages that which we are familiar with, but gives us insight into what, by habit, we tend to ignore, on a daily basis. Heightening the real, through theatre and tragic drama, provides poetic insight into the politics of our selfhood, understood in relation to larger social groups, and illuminates for us how every action, however personal, always has social consequences beyond our immediate concerns.

Tragedy: sample syllabus

Week 1   Introduction: theories of tragedy: Aristotle, *Poetics*, and Nietzsche, *The Birth of Tragedy*

Week 2   Greek tragedy (1): Aeschylus, *Agamemnon*

Week 3   Greek tragedy (2): Sophocles, *Oedipus Rex*

Week 4   Greek tragedy (3): Euripides, *Medea*

Week 5   Elizabethan tragedy and Jacobean revenge tragedy (1): Thomas Kyd, *The Spanish Tragedy*

Week 6   Elizabethan tragedy and Jacobean revenge tragedy (2): William Shakespeare, *Macbeth*

Week 7   Elizabethan tragedy and Jacobean revenge tragedy (3): John Webster, *The Duchess of Malfi*

Week 8   Elizabethan tragedy and Jacobean revenge tragedy (4): Thomas Middleton, *Women Beware Women*

Week 9   Tragedy in the nineteenth century (1): Victoria Benedictsson, *The Enchantment*

Week 10 Tragedy in the nineteenth century (2): Henrik Ibsen, *Hedda Gabler*

Week 11 Modern tragedy (1): Bertolt Brecht, *Mother Courage and Her Children*

Week 12 Modern tragedy (2): Samuel Beckett, *Waiting for Godot*

Bibliography

(a) Literary works

Aeschylus. *The Oresteia*. Trans. Robert Fagles. London: Penguin, 1977.

Beckett, Samuel. *Waiting for Godot*. London: Faber and Faber, 2006.

Benedictsson, Victoria. *The Enchantment*. London: Nick Hern Books, 2007.

Brecht, Bertolt. *Mother Courage and Her Children*. Trans. and int., Ralph Manheim and John Willett. London: Eyre Methuen, 2000.

Euripides. *Medea and Other Plays*. Trans. Philip Vellacott. London: Penguin, 2002.

Ibsen, Henrik. *Four Major Plays*. Trans. James McFarlane and Jens Arup. Oxford: Oxford University Press, 2008.

Kyd, Thomas. *The Spanish Tragedy*. Int. J. Mulrayne. London: Methuen, 2003.

Shakespeare, William. *Macbeth*. Int. Nicholas Brooke. Oxford: Oxford University Press, 2008.

Sophocles. *Selected Plays*. Trans. Edith Hall and H. D. F. Kitto. Oxford: Oxford University Press, 2008.

Webster, John. *The White Devil*. John Russell Brown. Manchester: Manchester University Press, 1996.

(b) Further reading

Aristotle. *Poetics*. Ed. and int. Gerald F. Else. Ann Arbor: University of Michigan Press, 1967.

Bushnell, Rebecca, ed. *A Companion to Tragedy*. Oxford: Blackwell, 2005.

Eagleton, Terry. *Sweet Violence: The Idea of the Tragic.* Oxford: Wiley-Blackwell, 2002.

Nuttall, A. D. *Why Does Tragedy Give Pleasure?* Oxford: Clarendon Press, 1996.

Poole, Adrian. *Tragedy: A Very Short Introduction.* Oxford: Oxford University Press, 2005.

Steiner, George. *The Death of Tragedy.* London: Faber and Faber, 1961.

Wallace, Jennifer. *The Cambridge Introduction to Tragedy.* Cambridge: Cambridge University Press, 2007.

Williams, Raymond. *Modern Tragedy.* London: Chatto and Windus, 1966.

Comedy

(Year 2)

Introduction

It's a funny thing, comedy. Or not. Because when you try to explain it, whatever is humorous, witty or amusing about it seems, if not to disappear, then, at the very least, to have lost its ability to tickle you, cause you to smile, or roar out loud. If you take a module on comedy, in all likelihood it may not make you laugh; neither will it explain the workings of a joke so that you get to see it as being humorous. But you should come to understand why comedy survives over centuries, and returns in different guises. You might even understand why we appear to 'need' the comic, why jokes get reinvented repeatedly. What you will discover is that comedy is a **genre** that, having evolved, has come to exploit, and be shaped by, certain conventions. These, changing over time, remain readable, in part or in whole, from one guise to the next.

Before going further, it should be said that comedy is not merely what is funny. It is a genre, and as such has distinct structures and forms, which reiterate themselves and which are reinvented from culture to culture, age to age. One of the most basic generic conventions of comedy is a tendency to focus on community rather than an individual – though there are exceptions to that; or perhaps it is fairer to suggest that where the individual is highlighted, as in Ben Jonson's *Volpone* or Molière's *The Misanthrope,* then that attention serves as a prism through which to see a particular community in given historical circumstances. That said, however, comedy considered as a genre is almost impossibly broad for us to make too precise a definition here. While in Ancient Greece comedies were, loosely speaking, dramas staged as part of seasonal festive celebrations, and were often vulgar, if not obscene, in the Middle Ages 'comedy' named a genre of narrative poetry, the convention of which was to conclude with a happy ending. The idea of a dramatic form that concentrates on groups of people tends to stem from the early modern period, or Renaissance. Comedy might also be defined through its attention to those of low station or class, and comic plots rely on confusion, misunderstanding and potential (though not serious) disasters, before a resolution solves the difficulties and closure is reached. In the examples of those narratives where an individual is seen at odds with the society or community, resolution typically involves the recovery of that individual into the society against which he or she has opposed himself.

One other remark remains to be made concerning genres. Some critics would distinguish satire from comedy, because it is, arguably, a different genre, with its own laws and conventions (see SATIRE). However, when you read a playwright such as Ben Jonson, then you're reading a satirical comedy: it relies on many of the same structures as other comedies, but the key is sharper, harder, the emphasis more on human vice and weakness. What this points to is my last initial definition of comedy as a **genre**: it is impossibly mixed; there is no pureness to the genre, especially today (although this is true of much of comedy's history). Therefore, there will be some reference to satire in this chapter, and I will focus on some of the fundamental elements of what makes us laugh and (hopefully) why that is so.

Cultural and historical specificity

What appears to amuse one group of people can strike others as distinctly unfunny. Take Radio 4. If you're reading this chapter, the chances are slim that you actively listen to comedy, or 'light entertainment' shows as they used to be called. You may have encountered *The News Quiz* in your family home, perhaps *Just a Minute, I'm Sorry, I Haven't a Clue, The Unbelievable Truth*, but do you go out of your way to listen to them? Do you download podcasts, play them back on the BBC iPlayer? Demographically, social scientists and marketing people tell us, you, as an 18–21-year-old, are less likely to be doing this than I am. But then again, this remains far too broad a division, because while – I confess it – I find the shows I've mentioned witty, to varying degrees, there are others that make me question why I pay the licence fee.

My point is this: comedy has a degree of cultural specificity, and part of its appeal is that specificity – as if comedy, whatever its form (the game or quiz show, the sitcom, a play, a novel, jokes), and whichever historical periods its examples come from, arrives encoded in ways that don't necessarily bear the burden of explanation. If you laugh at something, that's because it's funny, you're in on the secret, there is a 'fit' between the codes and tricks of the comic medium, and the cultural and historical knowledge you possess and the extent to which you belong to, or reject, given facets of society, particular communities or groups. In short, comedy has to do with the shared identity you believe yourself to have.

This, in turn, means that the specificity of whatever comic example or form we might want to discuss is specific to a given culture and a given historical moment; it concerns also matters of social station and class, of ethnicity and **gender**, and to seem to belong to self-identifying imaginary 'communities' within a given culture, historical instance or national formation. If you are told that a joke or comic scene in a play by Shakespeare is uproariously amusing but you don't find it so, this is less a sign that you lack the requisite intelligence to 'get the point', than that, on the one hand, the person telling you this has spent a good deal more time than you researching the contexts of the play and its sources, knows what the allusions are by heart, and so has an 'access' to the codes which you have yet to acquire; or, on the other hand, it is an indication that a joke or comic scene is 'for an age' and not for all time.

Understanding the codes, having a familiarity with the contexts, the history, the culture, may not make whatever it is you're reading or watching amusing. It will, however, give you insight into why comedy reinvents itself repeatedly and endlessly; why it remains as potent a cultural **discourse** and form as any other, such as tragedy. Indeed, in comparison with the novel, which in the history of cultural entertainment is something of a parvenu, comedy has a much older pedigree. Long before any literary historian or critic sought to define comedy, there was comedy, or manifestations of the comic.

This was the case, even if it did not know it was comedy, or if the earliest forms defined the 'comic' in a manner wholly, or almost completely, alien to our comprehension. In the same way that before the first geometer ever existed – the first person or persons to define geometry as a particular, scientific discourse with its own language and logic – there was already geometry and there had always been geometry in practical terms, so there has always been comedy. And while comedy, in all its various different practices and forms in the twenty-first century may have little, immediately, to do with the comedy of, say, Aristophanes' *The Birds* or Chaucer's Wife of Bath, yet the codes of comedy accrete; they leave in the sediment of human culture various deposits, little notes about knowledge, society, human relations, which, however transformed, remain as traces, to be unearthed in present-day forms.

What such traces tell us is this: the comic defines the human animal in particular situations; it exposes the human's behaviour, his or her motivations; it points out psychological reasons for actions even if the word 'psychology' is unknown to a given historical community or society; and it provides the glue that binds groups together, if only in demonstrating what takes place when one member of a community comes unstuck. In brief, comedy illuminates what it means to be human through an eccentricity or deviation from the normal and everyday, thereby highlighting normality as merely a series of learnt conventions. Comedy is there to expose the workings of the everyday. Comedy tells us who we are, and it does so not by making us into heroes, but by showing us as little human beings, just like everyone else. Comedy shines a light onto us, often in our misfortunes.

Schadenfreude, comic karma or the pleasures of bad luck

Frequently, comedy invites us to feel superior by staging the misfortunes of others, so that we experience what some refer to as *Schadenfreude*. This German word, appropriated into English, means the pleasure one derives from another's misfortune, often when a mishap or bad luck is of the physical kind. Witnessing someone else's bad luck is comic to us because, the argument runs, we identify with the misfortune, but feel lucky to have escaped the accident. Some might argue that the pleasure is derived from some atavistic superstition; buried somewhere deep in our psyches is the sense that the gods have let us off the hook.

An example might be when we see a man walking about in his home, trying to recall the past, slipping over on a banana skin – what is known in comic discourse as a pratfall – that he has absent-mindedly left on the floor. A stock comic device used in music hall of the nineteenth century, and subsequently in silent films, the banana skin joke is used by Samuel Beckett in his play *Krapp's Last Tape* (1958). In the midst of seriousness we are in slapstick, you might say. ('Slapstick' is a term used for very physical comedy or humorously embarrassing events, and comes from the practice in pantomime, music hall or vaudeville of simulating the sound of a slap or punch by means of two pieces of wood joined at one end that are brought sharply together.) Other examples of the use of *Schadenfreude* can be found throughout history.

To go back to Chaucer's Wife of Bath: she recalls the tale of how Xanthippe, wife of the Greek philosopher Socrates, allegedly 'cast pisse upon his [Socrates'] heed' (*Prologue*, l. 729). Obviously, this is amusing because the drenching Socrates endures is not happening to us, hence the experience of *Schadenfreude*. This tale, told to the Wife for moral instruction on the behaviour of 'unruly' women, is used by her against the grain of the moral purpose to illustrate the fools men make of themselves when they try to assert authority (the first word of the Wife's prologue) over women. The scene itself is funny for a number of reasons: woman makes a fool of man, his 'mastery' and 'authority' being undercut (women in the Ricardian court might well have enjoyed such a subversive idea); additionally, here in Socrates is a great figure in the history of thought, familiar to at least some of the learned members of Chaucer's audience, being brought low by an action as far removed from philosophy as it is possible to get. If there were an hierarchical cultural scale, where philosophy is 'high' and bodily waste 'low', then a single action, recounted in a narrative, is witty precisely because the scale is traversed in a single gesture, where woman has the upper hand, silencing the great talker and rendering his **discourse** purposeless (philosophy has had little to say about piss or shit). Lastly, the structure of low overcoming high, thereby inverting socially determined order, is played out visually in the imagination because Xanthippe would be imagined as emptying the pot from an upper window, perhaps, onto her husband below.

Whatever Chaucer's intentions, Xanthippe was not to survive in comedy as a proto-feminist protagonist. Shakespeare attempts to put her back in her place in *The Taming of the Shrew*, when Petrucchio compares Katherina to her. In the eighteenth century, the novelist Henry Fielding exploits a similar sexist logic in describing Mrs Partridge as one of the followers of 'Xantippe', her husband never being 'master' in her presence (*The History of Tom Jones*, Book II, Ch. iii). It is easy to see that cultural assumptions about **gender** roles play a part in forms of comedy. There are assumptions historically about the roles of men and women in society and in relation to one another. Part of Fielding's point to his male readers is to intimate that 'we' are lucky in not having Mrs Partridge for a wife; 'we' have escaped Mr Partridge's misfortune. Or, if it turns out that 'we' haven't, then we may have a sympathetic laugh in reading of Mrs Partridge, as women are satirized or parodied through Fielding's caricature.

Comedy on the couch

This is not to suggest that all comedy is sexist or misogynist, any more than it is (or has been) racist, xenophobic, homophobic or otherwise fuelled in some manner by fear or hatred of anyone not ourselves, belonging to our social groups. It is true that a great deal of comedy relies on such fears or anxieties, and part of the cultural and historical specificity of comedy has to do with its power to offer imaginary projections of a community identity by playing on that community's phobias of particular '**others**'. Your module should explore this dimension of comedy, its historically darker side, if you like. This is useful for illustrating the historical **context**, the ideological drive and singularity of particular comic texts. If jokes come from anxieties and fears, those fears have to do with whatever might be termed the *phobia du jour*. They operate by releasing or promising to release the pressure valve that is kept closed in our psyche, so that we don't act negatively based on our repressed fears.

If you think this all sounds a little bit psychoanalytical, you'd be right. As if to prove the assertion I began with – that explaining comedy is not in the least bit amusing – you may well be expected to read on your module excerpts from *Jokes and Their Relation to the Unconscious* (1905) by Sigmund Freud, the 'father' of psychoanalysis (see PSYCHOANALYSIS). In this Freud examines how humour and jokes work through association between different things, things we have difficulty speaking of in public or in so-called 'polite' society; or the displacement of a forbidden thing or word with an acceptable one, so that if I speak about being a pheasant plucker, I might just be telling you about my job (writing academic texts is just a sideline), or I could be deliberately toying with a spoonerism, in order to get a laugh because you have made a transgressive association in your mind, whilst I was speaking completely innocently. A spoonerism, named after the Reverend W. A. Spooner (1844–1930) who apparently made such errors frequently, is a verbal slip which accidentally transposes the initial sounds of two words. Freud would say that my uncon-scious makes me do this; that I really want to say something rude, disgusting, filthy, but I'm too repressed to do so. Eric Idle, in the Tourism sketch from *Monty Python's Flying Circus*, exploits this mercilessly, through a character who is unable to say the letter 'C' and so substitutes the letter 'B'. In the words of the sketch, 'What a silly bunt'.

Freud goes on to distinguish between such verbal jokes, puns and double entendres (phrases with a double meaning, one 'clean', the other not). An unintended double entendre – a Freudian would say nothing is truly unin-tended – might be found in a line from Jane Austen's *Northanger Abbey*, a comic pastiche of the gothic novel you might study for its elements of parody.

Catherine Morland, the heroine's, growth is described thus: 'at fifteen, appearances were mending; she began to curl her hair and long for balls' (Ch. 1). (Almost) for sure, Jane Austen meant nothing by this innocuous remark; but examine the following dialogue from *Oliver Twist*, and consider one of the two characters' names:

> 'And what have you got, my dear?' said Fagin to Charley Bates.
> 'Wipes,' replied *Master Bates*; at the same time producing four pocket-handkerchiefs. (Ch. 9; emphasis added)

You might think this very amusing; I could not possibly comment. The fact that Dickens refers to Charley about 50 times in this manner might help you decide on what is meant. Whatever the case, conceptual jokes fall into this category, the purpose of which is far harder to explain for the psychoanalyst. What he does argue, though, is that such forms of humour operate in order to get round difficulties or obstacles in society, or at particular historical moments. Thus, humour circumvents taboos, and serves to create a favourable impression. However, comedy also allows the possibility of identifying a scapegoat, by which process the humour gives a sense of power to those who believe themselves to be under threat, and this often takes place through an economy of dehumanization. If comedy takes away some dimension of the human, then those we laugh at are easier to dismiss, and it is 'our' superiority that is asserted. This is why Shakespeare's play uses the – what we now define as sexist – convention of calling a woman a 'shrew'. Anyone who is identified with a 'small mouse-like insectivorous mammal' because of the perception of bad temper and allegedly aggressive assertiveness is not likely to be treated as fully human. And the use of 'shrew' in this way may have deeper etymological roots, for its Germanic origin indicates it to have the senses of dwarf, devil or fox.

Forms and types of comedy

I have spent quite some time examining two aspects of comedy, the physical and the verbal. While comedy changes throughout history, the roots of humour rely on verbal play and physical action, both of which are seen to deviate from the everyday, and, in doing so, tell us a great deal about how we think – about ourselves, about **others**. Unlike tragedy, comedy is not about heroic deeds, notions concerning the actions of supposedly great men or woman, the gods, or some universal truth – or if it is, it's about how such ideas are inevitably illusory, based on generalizations rather than the perspicacious observation of human minutiae.

Comedy, though, is also based on the way in which, if you try to do an heroic deed, you will end up with egg on your face (metaphorically speaking), be misunderstood, or otherwise get yourself into an embarrassing situation which you find it hard to explain. Take Mr Pickwick, in Dickens's first, and for me, wittiest novel. Going at night to a girls' boarding school to prevent an elopement (so he thinks), he is mistaken by the occupants of the school for a burglar (with possibly even more nefarious designs, which Dickens never spells out), the whole heroic endeavour going badly – and very funnily – wrong. The comic is what we are, every day, despite our best intentions.

This being the case, history has thrown up – no pun intended – all manner of comedic modes and genres: parody, satire, burlesque and the carnivalesque, to identify just a few. I have already exemplifed the **carnivalesque** – a term coined by Russian critic Mikhail Bakhtin (BAKHTIN AND DIALOGIC CRITI-CISM) – through the inversion of social order typified in Chaucer's Wife of Bath in *The Canterbury Tales*. It therefore remains to say only a little more here. Bakhtin traces the origins of this mode to the medieval concept of carnival. It is defined through inversion of social order, subversion of hierarchy and the destabilization of assumed meaning through humour and chaos. The carnivalesque is what Bakhtin terms a representation of the world turned upside down, where societal norm and convention are questioned through displacement and replacement, such as a king becoming a fool, or a fool or pig being crowned monarch.

Your module should identify and explain these different kinds, but, repeatedly, you will come back to the fundamentals of linguistic infelicity, errors of perception based on the interpretation of actions without full knowledge, and the inability to do something as you had intended. Parody involves exaggeration of style, imitation of language or behaviour, which amplifies or mimics in a distorted manner to make fun, to produce a laugh. Such false or absurd representation is known as travesty, and can involve caricature, in which aspects of a person's mannerisms, behaviour, way of speaking, are exaggerated. Similarly, burlesque also imitates absurdly or in an inflated, hyperbolic way.

Such practices, along with elements of surrealism, have, in the twentieth century, developed into strategies for ideological critique, in forms of narrative or drama which are identified as belonging to their own **genre**, the **Absurd**. In this category, plays such as Eugene Ionesco's *Rhinoceros*, some of the earlier plays of Beckett, or Luigi Pirandello's *Six Characters in Search of an Author*, might be studied. The Absurd, or Absurdism, is taken to have developed from **existentialist** and **nihilist** branches of philosophy, which hold, very broadly, that any effort to find meaning in the universe by humans ultimately fails. While this doesn't sound particularly comic, it enables the possibility of the presentation of absurd actions, or to suggest that humans simply are absurd in their social constructs, and that this offers the possibility of humour.

Of course, comedy did not have to wait until the late nineteenth and twentieth centuries for such possibilities. As I have suggested, parody and its component devices already did this, as did satire. Satire, from its earliest examples onwards, has relied on the power of humour, ridicule, hyperbole and **irony** to expose human stupidity, greed and vice, and to do so, moreover, not as merely a critique of the individual, but through the dramatization of narration of a given individual, to present a sustained critique of contemporary political and related topical matters. The television show *Spitting Image* drew on a rich satirical tradition in its grotesquely caricatured puppet-representations of politicians, not least in the image of Tory minister Norman Tebbit as a skinhead thug in a leather jacket. If you don't see why this might be funny, you're either not old enough to remember the days when Margaret Thatcher was Prime Minister, or you're a Tory. But in satirical comedy at least, there is nothing new under the sun.

A possible module

Language, action, mode, and historical development and change: a module on comedy must seek to address all such aspects. Thus, you might find a comedy module that moves chronologically, beginning with Juvenal and Horace, coming up through the centuries, to early modern England, and then on through the eighteenth and nineteenth centuries, to the present. In order to develop your understanding, your module might well assign, alongside literary texts, some of the 'theoretical' texts I have mentioned, or extracts at least, from Freud, Bakhtin, the theoretical essays of playwrights, or essays by novelists explaining how they go about their work. Another possible organization might be one where the theoretical reflections on what constitutes comedy are considered first, before moving onto the particular literary texts to be read.

Comedy: sample syllabus

Each week's primary text(s) will be supplemented with critical reading.
Week 1   Introduction: what's so funny about comedy, anyway? Some theories of comedy
Week 2   Festive drama: Aristophanes, *Birds and Other Plays*
Week 3   Satire: Horace, *The Satires of Horace and Persius*; Juvenal, *The Satires*
Week 4   Laughing at the world (1): Ben Jonson, *The Alchemist and Other Plays*, LadyMary Wortley Montague, *Simplicity, A Comedy*
Week 5   Laughing at the world (2): John Dryden, selected poems; Aphra Behn, *The Emperor of the Moon*
Week 6   Scenes from everyday life (1): 18th-century comedy: extracts from Laurence Sterne, *The Life and Opinions of Tristram Shandy*
Week 7   Scenes from everyday life (2): 18th-century laughter: Tobias Smollett, *The Expeditions of Humphrey Clinker*
Week 8   Sentimental humour: Dickens, *The Pickwick Papers*
Week 9   Comedy of manners: Oscar Wilde, *The Importance of Being Ernest*
Week 10   The screwball tradition in Hollywood: film screenings of *Bringing up Baby*; *Mr Blandings Builds His Dream House*
Week 11   Nothing's funny: farce and the Absurd: Ionesco, *Rhinoceros*, Beckett, *Waiting for Godot*
Week 12   The politics of comedy: Trevor Griffiths, *Comedians*

Bibliography

(a) Literary works

Aristophanes. *The Birds and Other Plays*. Ed. David Barrett and Alan H. Sommerstein. London: Penguin, 2003.

Beckett, Samuel. *Waiting for Godot*. London: Faber and Faber, 2006.

Behn, Aphra. *The Emperor of the Moon*. In *The Rover and Other Plays*. Ed. Jane Spencer. Oxford: Oxford University Press, 2008.

Dickens, Charles. *The Pickwick Papers*. Ed. Mark Wormald. London: Penguin, 2004.

Dryden, John. *Selected Poems*. Ed. Steven N. Zwicker and David Bywaters. London: Penguin, 2001.

Griffiths, Trevor. *Comedians*. London: Faber and Faber, 1979.

Jonson, Ben. *The Alchemist and Other Plays*. Ed. Gordon Campbell. Oxford: Oxford University Press, 2008.

Juvenal. *The Satires*. Ed. Peter Green. London: Penguin, 2004.

Smollett, Tobias. *Humphrey Clinker*. Ed. Jeremy Lewis. London: Penguin, 2008.

Sterne, Laurence. *The Life and Opinions of Tristram Shandy*. Ed. Melvyn New. London: Penguin, 2003.

Wilde, Oscar. *The Importance of Being Ernest and Other Plays*. Ed. Peter Raby. Oxford: Oxford University Press, 2008.

Wortley Montague, Lady Mary. *Essays and Poems and 'Simplicity', A Comedy*. Ed. Isobel Grundy. Oxford: Oxford University Press, 1993.

(b) Further reading

Charney, Maurice. *Comedy High and Low: An Introduction to the Experience of Comedy*. New York: Oxford University Press, 1978.

Cordner, Michael, Peter Holland and John Kerrigan, eds. *English Comedy*. Cambridge: Cambridge University Press, 1994.

Finney, Gail, ed. *Look Who's Laughing: Gender and Comedy*. Langhome, PA: Gordon and Breach, 1994.

Harper, Graeme, ed. *Comedy, Fantasy, and Colonialism*. London: Continuum, 2002.

Heilman, Robert Bechtold. *The Ways of the World: Comedy and Society*. Seattle: University of Washington Press, 1978.

Leggatt, Alexander. *English Stage Comedy 1490–1990: Five Centuries of a Genre*. London: Routledge, 1998.

Medhurst, Andy. *A National Joke: Popular Comedy and English Cultural Identities*. London: Routledge, 2007.

Olson, Elder. *The Theory of Comedy*. Bloomington: Indiana University Press, 1968.

Purdie, Susan. *Comedy: The Mastery of Discourse*. Hemel Hempstead: Harvester Wheatsheaf, 1993.

Stott, Andrew. *Comedy*. London: Routledge, 2005.

The novel

(Year 1)

Helen Wright

What is a novel?

If you find yourself taking a module on 'the novel', you might be surprised to find that your tutor avoids telling you exactly what a novel is. This would certainly not be because s/he doesn't know. On the contrary: admitting that the novel doesn't have an exact definition is – however strange it may seem

– probably considered to be one of its best and most accurate definitions (Eagleton 2005: 1). Yet it hasn't always been this way. During the period traditionally thought to be the most important in the history of the novel's emergence as a fully formed literary **genre**, the eighteenth century, female novelist Clara Reeve observed that '[t]he novel is a picture of real life and manners, and of the times in which it is written' (Reeve cited in Cross 1899: xiv). The novel is therefore marked out as the form of fiction that reflects a realistic engagement with what we could term 'the everyday': people's real lives as they live them. Here, then, you can see why the novel resists definition. If you think about what constitutes our everyday lives, you'll see that what was everyday in 1785 was certainly not the same as what was everyday in 1885; nor will what was everyday in 1885 be the same as what will be everyday in 2185. The novel's focus on the everyday aspects of our lives and 'of the times in which it is written', means that it is a constantly shifting **genre**. Its connection to people's everyday lives makes it impossible to define once and for all. What you are therefore likely to encounter when studying the novel is a set of texts that will offer you an insight into both when and how the novel emerged, and how, whilst remaining indefinable, it has come to be one of the most popular and enduring forms of literature.

Romance

Many courses on the novel will begin with a study of the literary genre of romance. At first, this might seem odd, as romance was popular amongst the ruling elite in the Middle Ages, long before the novel even existed. Yet as romance is traditionally viewed as the genre against which the novel defines itself in opposition, no course on the novel can afford to underestimate its significance (Hammond and Regan 2005: 7). Indeed, if we look at one of the most famous texts of English romance, you will see the tension between romance and the novel by looking at romance's fundamental nature (see MEDIEVAL LITERATURE). Thomas Malory's *Le Morte d'Arthur* (1485) is a text which draws together the various tales of Arthurian legend. However, one the most noticeable things about *Le Morte d'Arthur* is that it is based upon figures of ancient historical legend: King Arthur belongs, of course, to sixth-century Britain, and this makes the material for Malory's romance outdated by nearly a thousand years by the time he actually came to write it. Beyond doubt, then, Malory's text could not possibly detail the everyday lives of the elite fifteenth-century audience who would read it. In light of this, Malory's text might therefore be used to show the formal contrast between romance and the everyday realism that is characteristic of the novel. Whatever form the study of this contrast between romance and the novel takes, it will become clear that, unlike the novel, romance is characterized by a lack of engagement with the real lives of people in the time in which it was written (McCarthy 1988: 14). Such a study will therefore leave you well placed to see how the novel began to emerge in opposition to romance during the following centuries.

Once the fundamental nature of romance has been established, you will find it easier to make sense of the anti-romantic nature of the picaresque tradition, which first emerged in sixteenth-century Spain. Although a late example of the **genre**, most courses on the novel will probably make substantial reference to Miguel de Cervantes' *Don Quixote*. First published in Spain in 1605 (part I) and 1615 (part II), *Don Quixote* represents a conscious attempt to discredit the romance genre by throwing the unreality of romance together with the often harsh realities of real life (Cross 1899: 9). In *Don Quixote* you will thus see one of the first texts to adopt a critical – and a highly literary – perspective on the failings of traditional romance. By writing a character who is obsessed with chivalric tales from history, Cervantes creates the ultimate, or 'proto-typed', figure of romance in Don Quixote, and then unleashes him on the real world. From this position, you will therefore find that *Don Quixote* allows you to analyse the conflict between romance and reality that Cervantes and the picaresque tradition attempt to foreground. For instance, when Don Quixote charges at the windmills, thinking they are giants simply because that is the sort of adventure romance has led him to expect, what sort of comment is Cervantes making about the tension between reality and the romance? By contrasting Don Quixote's behaviour with that of his servant, Sancho Panza, you might see elements of everyday reality creeping into the text. Through this, you will thus get an insight into the role that *Don Quixote* plays in preparing the way for the shift from the unreality of romance to the everyday realism of the novel that begins to emerge in the next couple of centuries.

Seventeenth-century prose

If you are studying the novel as part of an English degree, it's likely that you will move back to studying English prose when you reach the seventeenth century. Whilst looking at prose from this period, you will encounter a range of texts that illustrate the increasing shift onto the realities of everyday existence. For instance, although not published until the nineteenth century, you might study Samuel Pepys's *Diaries* (1825), as it gives a good indication of the extent to which writers of the seventeenth century were beginning to engage with the realities of everyday life (Allen 1954: 29). By increasing the degree of focus that prose writing could now have on real life, texts such as Pepys's *Diaries* opened the way to putting prose and reality together, and this was particularly significant in the development of the novel as a form (Allen 1954: 28). Indeed, one text that will give you a good insight into how the real-life focus of prose contributed to the emergence of the novel is Aphra Behn's *Oroonoko* (1688). A tragic story of enforced slavery, *Oroonoko* takes the autobiographical emphasis of seventeenth-century prose and fuses it with an indeterminate degree of fiction. This introduction of – arguably – fictional elements into a text that claims to be 'a true history' pushes prose writing even closer to the fictional realism that would become typical of the novel (Todd 1999: 4). By looking at this blurred distinction between what is real and what is fictional in Behn's text, you will begin to see that the blending of fact and fiction in *Oroonoko* makes it identifiable as one of the most important precursors of the eighteenth-century novel, and heralded the arrival of the novel as we would recognize it today (Woodcock, cited in Todd 1999, 6).

The modern novel

Most scholars identify the eighteenth century as the time in which the novel made its first appearance as an established literary form. Indeed, the 'rise of the novel' at this time is often correlated with the rise of the middle class (Watt 2001: 35–59). Up until the eighteenth century there had never been such a literate audience, or one with as large a disposable income to spend on literature. Frequently cited as early examples of the novel in English, you will hear mention of texts such as Henry Fielding's *Tom Jones* (1749) and Samuel Richardson's *Pamela* (1740). However, there is a good chance that you will look at Daniel Defoe's *Robinson Crusoe* (1719) in some depth. Not only does *Robinson Crusoe* offer crucial insights into the relationship between author and reader in what was now considered the 'literary marketplace', but it also offers an insight into the challenges posed by the novel's extreme realism, or *verisimilitude*. Defoe's fictional representation of one man's life in a specific time and place results in a text that is so lifelike that it created a deal of confusion when it was first published as to whether it was actually fictional (Baines 2007: 8–14; Marsh 1998: 181–2). You will therefore see that the novel was not wholly unproblematic as a form of fiction when it first emerged, and in order to see how the reading public finally overcame this initial confusion, you will perhaps look at novels from later in the eighteenth century, or even the early nineteenth century. A likely text here might be Jane Austen's *Northanger Abbey* (completed in 1798). A darkly comic analysis of the connections between reality and the plots of novelistic fiction, *Northanger Abbey*'s focus on the inherent reality of what are even the most seemingly fictional of fictions could well be used to illustrate the eventual acceptance of the novel's fundamental nature of realistic representation (see ROMANTICISM AND GOTHIC). Regardless of what texts you study from this period, though, you will observe the establishment of the novel as the most popular literary form, and that which – as Clara Reeve would remind us – offers 'a picture of real life and manners, and of the times in which it is written'.

The Victorian novel

Once officially established as the form of everyday life, it is often argued that the novel really came of age in the nineteenth century: 'the period was, and is, for many, the *age* of the novel' (O'Gorman 2002: 1). For this reason, it is difficult to predict what texts you might be likely to study from the Victorian period (see THE NINETEENTH CENTURY AND THE VICTORIANS). Increasingly popular amongst the expanding middle – and now also lower – classes, the novel at this time is so diverse that it is impossible to cover all the sub-genres that had developed. For example, you may study Elizabeth Gaskell's *Mary Barton* (1848), which engages with the struggle between factory workers and their employers in the industrial city of Manchester. Yet, equally, you may study Emily Brontë's highly original *Wuthering Heights* (1847), quite a different style from that of Gaskell. Then, of course, there is also the social comment of Charles Dickens's novels, the religious doubt of Mrs Humphrey Ward's *Robert Elsmere* (1888), and the height of intellectual realism that is George Eliot's *Middlemarch* (1871–2). Even a quick glance at this diversity reveals the breadth of focus you can expect to see within the novel of the Victorian period; but what unites these texts is that they all engage with the realities of people's existence and the types of challenge they would encounter every day as people of the Victorian period. For instance, Gaskell's *Mary Barton* details the horrors of extreme poverty brought about by industrialization and offers a harrowing account of the human cost of such conditions. Similarly, Ward's *Robert Elsmere* engages with the religious doubt that was common in the latter half of the nineteenth century, and illustrates the type of disruption that many people felt at this time in relation to their own beliefs. Here then, by studying one or even a variety of texts from the Victorian period, you will see how its characteristic realism results in the novel of this time giving the Victorians an insight into their own lives and times and, thus, becoming a significant vehicle for social comment and criticism (O'Gorman 2002: 1).

Modernism

By the end of the nineteenth century, however, the realism of the Victorian novel had hit a crisis. During the late nineteenth and early twentieth centuries, a number of scientific and philosophical developments led to new ways of thinking about – and, indeed, experiencing – everyday life. Because of this, the realism of the Victorian novel was no longer suited to capturing or reflecting the everyday lives of modern people (see REALISM). Indeed, it is for this very reason that Ezra Pound coined the phrase 'make it new' in relation to modernist art (Pound cited in Goldman 2004: 1) (see MODERNISM). Many courses on the novel will show the effect that this injunction had on the modernist novel by introducing a text like James Joyce's *Ulysses* (1922). With its odd flow of events and textual interruptions by signs, song lyrics, and even music at one point, you may find that *Ulysses* makes no real sense in comparison with the solid realism of the Victorian novel. Yet this apparent lack of realism is not really a lack of it at all, it is just realism of a different – or 'modern' – kind. For instance, alongside other significant advances in philosophy and science in the early twentieth century, Freudian ideas about human consciousness were beginning to be translated into English and thus inspire both intellectuals and writers alike (Goldman 2004: 60). Joyce's *Ulysses* will certainly illustrate this significant influence, as too will a text like Virginia Woolf's *Mrs Dalloway* (1925). Often referred to as a **stream of consciousness**, you will see that the prose of *Mrs Dalloway* is structured in such a way as to suggest the reality of the characters' inner experience of their everyday existence, from Mrs Dalloway's recollections of her youth as she plans her party, to Septimus's painfully distorted perceptions through the mental confusion of shell shock (Bradbury and McFarlane 1991: 26). Through a study of texts such as Joyce's *Ulysses* and Woolf's *Mrs Dalloway*, it will emerge that the modernist novel experimented with form in order to try and capture not just real life as an 'external' reality or material situation, but – much more specifically – real life as the inner experiences of the human consciousness in the **context** of the ever-demanding modern world.

Summary

If you recall, we began this discussion by stating that 'if you find yourself taking a module on the novel, you might be surprised to find that your tutor avoids telling you exactly what a novel is'. By this point, you will have seen exactly why the novel is inherently indefinable: it is the form of everyday reality, and is, therefore, ultimately defined by its contemporaneity (Hammond and Regan 2005: 25). Ever changing, the time to which the novel connects and from which it takes its themes is so much 'now' that any definition will always be playing catch-up with the pace of the novel's formal and thematic reinventions (Hammond and Regan 2005: 124). If you just look at the speed at which writers reinvented the novel between *Robinson Crusoe* in 1719 and – say – *Ulysses* in 1922, you will see that it is constantly changing in order to accommodate and show us ourselves as we really are, right now. Indeed, it is for this very reason that this discussion concludes with texts from the modernist period. After modernism comes, of course, *post*modernism (see POSTMODERNISM); but this particular phase of time is yet to end. We are, ourselves, still postmodern, and this means that whatever suggestions are made as to postmodern novels you may study, you may actually end up studying some that have yet to be written at the time I am writing this. What is certain, though, is this that regardless of the theme or form of the postmodern texts you study, you will inevitably see yourself in them, in some way at least. Indeed, it is perhaps this peculiar ability of the novel to show us our own everyday experiences through characters that don't necessarily resemble us that continues to make – or, rather, keep – the novel the most popular form of literature today (Hammond and Regan 2005: x).

The novel: sample syllabus

Week 1   Introduction: what is a novel? – theories of the novel and its history
Week 2   Romance: legends and histories: *Le Morte d'Arthur*
Week 3   Romance vs. reality, or fighting windmills: *Don Quixote* and the Spanish picaresque

Week 4 Seventeenth-century prose (1): 'The condition of the state was thus': Pepys's *Diaries*
Week 5 Seventeenth-century prose (2): from prose to prose fiction: *Oroonoko*
Week 6 Modern origins: 'The rise of the novel': *Robinson Crusoe*
Week 7 Novels and the real (1): 'Flights of fancy?': *Northanger Abbey*
Week 8 Novels and the real (2): 'Giving some utterance to the agony': *Mary Barton*
Week 9 Novels and the real (3): 'Hidden lives' and everyday heroics: *Middlemarch*
Week 10 Modernism: One day in June (1): *Mrs Dalloway*
Week 11 Modernism: One day in June (2): *Ulysses*
Week 12 Conclusion: from modernism to postmodernism Ɛ and beyond?

Bibliography

(a) Literary works

Austen, Jane. *Northanger Abbey*. Ed. Marilyn Butler. London: Penguin, 2003.

Behn, Aphra. *Oroonoko*. Ed. Janet Todd. London: Penguin, 2003.

de Cervantes, Miguel. *Don Quixote*. Trans. Charles Jarvis and ed. E. C. Riley. Oxford: Oxford University Press, 1992.

Defoe, Daniel. *Robinson Crusoe*. Ed. Thomas Keymer. Oxford: Oxford University Press, 2007.

Eliot, George. *Middlemarch*. Ed. Rosemary Ashton. London: Penguin, 1994.

Gaskell, Mary. *Mary Barton*. Ed. Macdonald Daly. London: Penguin, 1996.

Joyce, James. *Ulysses*. Ed. Jeri Johnson. Oxford: Oxford University Press, 1998.

Malory, Thomas. *Le Morte d'Arthur*. Ed. Helen Cooper. Oxford: Oxford University Press, 2008.

Pepys, Samuel. *The Diaries of Samuel Pepys: A Selection*. London: Penguin, 1983.

Pepys, Samuel. *The Diary of Samuel Pepys: A New and Complete Transcription*. 11 vols. Ed. Robert Latham and William Matthews. London: Bell and Hyman, 1970–83.

Woolf, Virginia. *Mrs Dalloway*. Ed. David Bradshaw. Oxford: Oxford University Press, 2000.

(b) Further reading

Allen, Walter. *The English Novel: A Short Critical History*. London: Phoenix House, 1954.

Booth, Wayne C. *The Rhetoric of Fiction*. London: University of Chicago Press, 1983.

Eagleton, Terry. *The English Novel: An Introduction*. Malden, MA: Blackwell, 2005.

Hammond, Brean and Sean Regan. *Making the Novel: Fiction and Society in Britain, 1660–1789*. Basingstoke: Palgrave Macmillan, 2005.

Keymer, Thomas and Jon Mee, eds. *The Cambridge Companion to English Literature, 1740–1830*. Cambridge: Cambridge University Press, 2004.

McKeon, Michael. *Origins of the English Novel 1600–1740*. Baltimore, MA: Johns Hopkins Press, 2002.

Moretti, Franco. *Atlas of the European Novel, 1800–1900*. London: Verso, 1998.

O'Gorman, Francis, ed. *The Victorian Novel*. Oxford and Malden, MA: Blackwell, 2002.

Shiach, Morag, ed. *The Cambridge Companion to the Modernist Novel*. Cambridge: Cambridge University Press, 2007.

Watt, Ian. *The Rise of the Novel: Studies in Defoe, Richardson and Fielding*. Berkeley: University of California Press, 2001.

Poetry

Bill Overton

If you are unsure what poetry is, consider the following text by Thomas Hardy:

> Any little old song
> Will do for me,
> Tell it of joys gone long,
> Or joys to be,
> Or friendly faces best   5
> Loved to see.
> Newest themes I want not
> On subtle strings,
> And for thrillings pant not
> That new song brings: 10
> I only need the homeliest
> Of heartstirrings.   (Hardy 1976: 702)

The text is short, and its language simple. There are no similes and no metaphors, nor does any striking thought seem expressed. Instead, the text asks for something quite ordinary – a familiar tune to evoke the 'homeliest' emotions. Although a reader will recognize it as a poem from its layout, and although a listener might do so from noticing that it rhymes, it seems otherwise to have few literary qualities.

What makes the text a poem is, in part, its metre. Anyone familiar with how English is spoken will notice patterns of emphasis that seem connected with the number of syllables in each line. In each stanza, for example, the first and third lines have six syllables, and, in each of these lines, three syllables are emphasized, including the first. The pattern in the second and fourth lines is simpler: each has four syllables, and the only ones emphasized are the second and fourth. In these four-line units that open each stanza, two tensions result: between alternating lines with different lengths and different patterns of emphasis. While the odd-numbered lines begin with a falling rhythm, because the stronger emphasis comes first, the even-numbered lines have a rising rhythm, because they move from a lighter to a heavier stress. These kinds of metre are called, respectively, trochaic (heavier stress followed by lighter) and iambic (lighter stress followed by heavier). In the four lines that begin each stanza, then, a quick and lilting line is twice brought up short. The effect, like the poem's subject, is musical.

The facts that the text has regular patterns of emphasis – in other words that it is in metre – and that it rhymes, make it verse. Poetry is normally considered to be verse with special qualities of expressive subtlety and complexity, and the text has these too. For instance, there are delicate metrical variations within each stanza and between the two stanzas. An example of a variation between stanzas is that, unlike lines 1 and 3, lines 7 and 9 are regularly trochaic and end with double rhymes. The last two syllables of line 1 put the lighter stress before the heavier, as do the last four syllables of line 3, so that the stress pattern changes to iambic before each of the short iambic lines that follow. As a result, the first stanza has a more hesitant movement than the second, because the trochaic pattern is interrupted earlier. An example of a variation within a stanza is that the shift to iambic metre takes place earlier in line 3 than in line 1. This helps usher in the fifth line, which, in both stanzas, keeps to the iambic metre of the even-numbered lines, instead of conforming to the mainly trochaic metre of the previous odd-numbered ones. Yet there are variations here too. While the line closing each stanza follows the same pattern as the other even-numbered lines, in the first it has only three syllables instead of four, bringing the stanza to a halting end that suggests a kind of emotional catch of the breath. In contrast, line 11 has two extra syllables, so adding animation at the climax. These differences, and the changes of pace and emphasis they create – especially when the poem is read out loud – affect its tone and meaning. Another example of intricate variation is that, although the second word in the phrases 'old song' (1) and 'gone long' (3) carries a heavier stress than the first, the first word in each phrase carries a heavier stress than the second syllables of 'Any' and 'little' in the first line and the words 'it' or 'of' in the second. The effect is to lay special emphasis on both these phrases, suggesting a wistful harking back. More subtly still, the poem uses the words 'gone long' instead of the usual phrase, 'long gone'. The reversal of the order that would normally be expected calls attention to the phrase and invites the reader to dwell on it.

Other sound patterns produce extra resonances. The phrase 'gone long' is an example, for it shows another of the poem's musical qualities in its aural patterning. It begins and ends similarly, for the ear and, even more, for the eye (the repeated 'g' constituting a kind of eye-rhyme), and so encloses the repeated sound 'on', with its prolonged and plangent vowel. This further kind of rhyme is known as internal rhyme, and here it is emphasized by the fact that the second word is also an end-rhyme. There is another example in the second stanza in 'strings' and 'thrillings', as 'strings' begins another end-rhyme, picked up in lines 10 and 12. But this is not just a matter of sound, because, through the rhymes, a semantic connection is suggested: 'strings', 'thrillings', 'brings', 'heartstirrings'. There is a similar and even more subtle link between the lines in each stanza that seem unrhymed. Not only do the two lines rhyme with each other, across the break between the stanzas, but again this carries semantic value: 'best', 'homeliest'. Further sound patterns include alliteration, in 'friendly faces', and assonance, which is a play on vowel sounds, as with the long 'o' in 'only the homeliest'. The phrase 'gone long', with its repeated consonant and vowel sounds, is a combination of consonance and assonance.

Kinds of poetry

In his essay 'Why study literature?' in the first part of this book, Kenneth Womack suggests that it is the enigmatic and undecidable qualities of texts that make them interesting and engaging. 'Any Little Old Song' has those qualities, and it is through recognizing its metrical and aural pleasures and intricacies that it may best be appreciated. What is enigmatic about the poem is its ability to imply complex emotions with seemingly simple materials. There is no way of knowing what lies behind the wish to hear a familiar song. From that wish the poem produces verbal music.

The kind of poetry that does this is called lyric (see LYRIC). Originally the word referred to words sung to the accompaniment of a kind of musical instrument called a lyre, and this sense continues in the word 'lyrics' today. A lyric poem is essentially an expression of thought or feeling, or a mixture of the two, and for this reason it is usually quite short – modern poetry magazines reckon on a maximum of 40 lines, though some lyric poems from the past are considerably longer. But it is important to recognize that, although lyric poetry is the commonest kind of verse today, it is not the only kind. The word 'verse' refers to metrical form, and almost any kind of writing may be in metre. Obvious examples are the plays of Shakespeare and most of his contemporaries, and narrative works in verse such as Chaucer's *Canterbury Tales*, Milton's *Paradise Lost*, or, to give an example closer to the present, Vikram Seth's *The Golden Gate* – which is a novel about life in Berkeley, California – in the very hard-to-do but enjoyable form known as the Pushkin stanza. As recently as the eighteenth century, verse has even been used for philosophical and scientific texts. The reason it is important to be aware that different kinds of work may be written in verse is that such works, if they are any good, will require attention to their metrical qualities, because it is in part through those qualities that they communicate. In other words, a play or a narrative written in verse, let alone a poem of any type, cannot properly be studied solely on the basis of its action, themes, characterization or imagery. The way it uses verse will be fundamental to its mode of expression and its meaning.

Learning about poetry

It follows that a course in poetry ought to teach two main kinds of knowledge and skill. First, it must be able to explain how poems are organized metrically, and to develop the ability not only to recognize and analyse this but also to understand how it is significant to their meanings and effects. There is no inherent difficulty in this, because anyone familiar with spoken English knows how different words are pronounced, and this includes not only their sounds but their patterns of stress – the fact, for example, that the names 'Chaucer', 'Shakespeare' and 'Milton' are all pronounced with the first syllable more heavily emphasized than the second. In this process, learning the technical vocabulary – words such as 'iambic' and 'trochaic' – is not enough. Although such a vocabulary is necessary to describing a poem's metre, it is only a kind of notation. The really important aim is to understand how particular metres, or particular metrical variations, produce different effects. For this reason, it is essential to have a clear sense of how a poem sounds. This may mean reading it out loud, though those with good auditory imaginations may be able to hear it, as it were, inside their heads. Without a sense of how the poem sounds, it is difficult, and may even be impossible, to identify where the main stresses are or where patterns of sound are repeated. The great benefit of carrying out this kind of analysis is that it enables deeper insight into how a poem works and what it means. It also equips anyone who becomes reasonably competent in metrical analysis to make original discoveries, even about poems that are quite well known.

The second key requirement of a course in poetry is that it teach what distinguishes different kinds of poem, and also poems written in different historical periods. Lyric poems, for example, work differently from narrative poems or from poems in such genres as satire or pastoral; and poems written in the romantic period tend to use different language and either to develop new verse forms or to renew, often radically, those used in earlier periods. It is important to know about poetic genres, because poems written within these will invite particular kinds of expectation and then confirm, challenge or even overturn them. For instance, a pastoral will invite the expectation that it will present a more or less idealized view of life in the countryside, but the poem may either do this in an unusual way or put it in question, as Sir Walter Raleigh did in his poem answering Christopher Marlowe's 'The Passionate Shepherd to His Love'. It is important to know about the special kinds of language and verse form that poems tended to use in different historical periods because they too had their own associations, and because this knowledge enables the reader to recognize innovation. Those who have read some eighteenth-century poetry and have noticed that its language is often quite elaborate will be able to feel some of the shock of the new that Wordsworth and Coleridge's *Lyrical Ballads* would have had on readers when it was first published in 1798. Those who have read some Victorian poetry will be able to measure the parallel shock of T. S. Eliot's *The Waste Land*.

Form and meaning

To give a more specific example, Milton indicated in a note to a reissue of *Paradise Lost* in 1668 that he had chosen blank verse for his poem rather than rhyming couplets because of its greater freedom. This was not only a literary but an ideological challenge, because the heroic couplet, the dominant form for serious verse at the period, tended to imply a conservative politics through its cultivation of balance and order. Wordsworth and Coleridge, like Blake in his *Songs of Innocence and of Experience*, did something similar in choosing ballad form, because its associations were with ordinary people and not with the elite. Even short quotations from poems in these forms give some idea of how sharply they differ and how forcefully they can convey meaning. For example, a characteristic heroic couplet is this one from Dryden's *Absalom and Achitophel*, a long narrative poem in the form of a biblical **allegory** that sought to influence the trial of the Earl of Shaftesbury for treason against Charles II: "Gainst Form and Order they their Power employ; / Nothing to Build, and all things to Destroy' (1972: II, 21; ll. 531–32). Here, not only the choice of key words such as 'Form' and 'Order' is important, but also the ordered form in which they are arranged: the two words complement each other, and they name the qualities that the King's opponents allegedly threaten. Similarly, the second line not only develops this idea, and distils it into the seventeenth-century verse equivalent of a soundbite, but, through its balanced structure ('Nothing' / 'all things', 'to Build', 'to Destroy'), presents an example of the values it claims are under attack. Milton's blank verse, on the other hand, celebrates not only freedom from what he regarded as the constraint of rhyme but also the self-discipline that he commended in its place. This is shown especially by its use of run-on lines, as in these from the description of Satan's flight into Chaos:

> At last his Sail-broad Vannes
> He spread for flight, and in the surging smoak
> Uplifted spurns the ground, thence many a League
> As in a cloudy Chair ascending rides
> Audacious, but that seat soon failing, meets
> A vast vacuity: all unawares
> Fluttring his pennons vain plumb down he drops
> Ten thousand fadom deep, and to this hour
> Down had been falling. (1674: Book II, 927–35)

It is difficult to imagine such movements described so compellingly in any kind of couplet. Milton's use of run-on lines and mid-line pauses is crucial to the effect. This short extract is part of a sequence of no fewer than 11 consecutive run-on lines that provide a stunning impression first of mounting into the air and then of plummeting helplessly. It is the choice of where to break the line that does much of the expressive work, as in 'surging smoak / Uplifted', or 'ascending rides / Audacious', where words to do with triumphant ascent begin both new lines, in the second case preceded by a powerful verb; and, even more, in 'down he drops / Ten thousand fadom deep', and 'to this hour / Down had been falling', where the ending of one line at the word 'drops' invites the reader to look into a chasm, and the beginning of another with the word 'Down', after another run-on line, reverses the normal metrical emphasis. But the mid-line pause, or caesura, contributes strongly too, especially when, after five run-on lines, the reader, like Satan, is stopped short by 'A vast vacuity'. If space permitted, it would be easy to provide further examples, or to illustrate the different expressive potentials of other verse forms. There are as many as there are good poems, and all those interested in poetry will be able to find them for themselves.

Kinds of poetry course

Poetry may be taught in a wide range of courses. At one end of the spectrum, there are courses devoted to the study of poetry as a form of literary expression. Such courses may emphasize prosody, which is the study of metre, while others may focus primarily on **genre** or on historical survey. All will also be likely to pay attention to figurative language – simile and metaphor – and to other uses of language that tend to occur more often or more systematically in poetry, such as changes of word order or sound patterns. At the other end of the spectrum are courses in which poetry is taught among other kinds of writing. Perhaps the most common of these are courses concerned with the literature of a particular historical period. These may have a very wide focus, in which case they will offer a general survey; but others, especially the more advanced ones, will be more specialized – dealing with the Renaissance, for instance, or the romantic period. While courses of this type will often cover a range of different kinds of writing – plays or even novels, as well as poems, and sometimes, too, texts that are not normally considered as 'literature' – it is important to bear in mind that each of them works differently and requires different kinds of skill and knowledge. In the case of poems, this means reading closely for the various kinds of metrical and aural effects already mentioned. Other types of course include the thematic, such as representations of the city, or the generic, such as satire (see SATIRE). The study of poetry will also be taught in courses on creative writing, though with a more practical emphasis.

It may seem obvious, but the best way to become a competent reader of poetry is to read as many poems as you can. Good anthologies, such as the *Norton Anthology of Poetry*, are easily available, and the better ones, including the *Norton Anthology*, have explanatory notes and other material. It helps to get into the habit either of reading aloud or of imagining the sound of the poem in your head. Further guidance may be obtained not only from courses but from books on the subject. Books that are least likely to be useful are those arranged on an historical, period-by-period basis, because it is not by reading older poems first that knowledge about poetry is best developed. The most effective such books work by moving from simpler to more complex topics, so enabling readers to build their knowledge and awareness by stages. I strongly recommend two in particular. First, although Stephen Fry's *The Ode Less Travelled: Unlocking the Poet Within* is aimed at people who wish to write poetry, as its subtitle indicates, I know of no more instructive, accessible or entertaining an introduction to prosody. It may be read without carrying out the exercises offered to budding poets, though even people without an interest in creative writing will learn from completing them because, as John Lennard remarks, 'You will learn more about prosody by trying to write metrically than in any other way' (2005: 29). Lennard's *The Poetry Handbook: A Guide for Reading Poetry for Pleasure and Practical Criticism* is my second recommendation. Not only is it a comprehensive introduction to the subject, packed with knowledge and examples, but its range is much wider than the title suggests. Six of the twelve chapters, for example, cover Punctuation, Diction, Syntax, History, Biography and Gender, all of which are important to the study of writing in any form. Because it is so full of information, it makes sense to heed Lennard's advice to work through it slowly, going on to another chapter only when the previous one has been absorbed (2005: xxiii). For those wanting a more technical introduction to prosody, the best one is Timothy Steele's *All the Fun's in How You Say a Thing*. This, too, requires careful reading, although it is certainly not a dry academic book but one that sets out the subject clearly and without unnecessary jargon.

Observant readers will have noticed that the quotations above from Dryden and Milton are from original editions. I agree with John Lennard in preferring these to attempts at modernizing that often mislead, though I also strongly recommend using good scholarly editions where these are available. But another reason is that now, thanks to such databases as *Early English Books Online* and *Eighteenth-Century Collections Online*, it is possible to read facsimiles of original editions without visiting a major research library. These databases, along with *Literature Online*, are transforming the study of poetry as well as other literary and historical subjects. They offer exciting opportunities not only to researchers but to students at all levels.

2

Poetry: sample syllabus

Semester 1: Versification

Week 1   Introduction to verse and versification
Week 2   Iambic verse
Week 3   Trochaic verse
Week 4   Anapaests and dactyls
Week 5   Stanza form: couplets and quatrains
Week 6   Rhyme and more complex stanza forms
Week 7   Ballad metre
Week 8   Pentameter couplets
Week 9   Blank verse
Week 10 The Elizabethan sonnet
Week 11 The sonnet from the 17th to the 20th century
Week 12 Case study: W. B. Yeats, the ballad and ottava rima

Semester 2: Kinds of poetry

Week 1   Introduction to genre
Week 2   The languages of poetry
Week 3   Lyric
Week 4   Dramatic monologue
Week 5   Satire
Week 6   Elegy
Week 7   Ode
Week 8   Love poetry
Week 9   Pastoral verse
Week 10 Narrative verse

Bibliography

(a) Literary works

Dryden, John. *Absalom and Achitophel*, in *The Works of John Dryden*. 20 vols. Vol. II: *Poems 1681–1684* (1972), 2–36. Ed. H. T. Swedenberg, Jr and Vinton A. Dearing. Berkeley: University of California Press, 1956–2002. Also in *Norton Anthology of Poetry*.

Early English Books Online (EEBO). See: http://eebo.chadwyck.com/home (accessed 24 May 2010).

Eighteenth-Century Collections Online (ECCO). See: http://www.cengage.com/ EighteenthCentury (accessed 24 May 2010).

Ferguson, Margaret, Mary Jo Salter and Jon Stallworthy, eds. *The Norton Anthology of Poetry*, 5th edn. New York and London: W. W. Norton, 2005.

Hardy, Thomas. *The Complete Poems*. Ed. James Gibson. London: Macmillan, 1976.

Literature Online (LION). See: http://lion.chadwyck.com (accessed 24 May 2010).

Milton, John. *Milton: Paradise Lost*, 2nd edn. Ed. Alastair Fowler. London: Longman, 2006.

(b) Further reading

Carper, Thomas and Derek Attridge. *Meter and Meaning: An Introduction to Rhythm in Poetry*. Abingdon and New York: Routledge, 2003.

Fenton, James. *An Introduction to English Poetry*. London: Penguin Books; New York: Penguin Putnam, 2002.

Hobsbaum, Philip. *Metre, Rhythm and Verse Form*. London and New York: Routledge, 1996.

Hollander, J. *Rhyme's Reason: A Guide to English Verse*. New Haven, CT: Yale University Press, 1989.

Lennard, John. *The Poetry Handbook: A Guide for Reading Poetry for Pleasure and Practical Criticism*, 2nd edn. Oxford: Oxford University Press, 2005.

Nowottny, Winifred. *The Language Poets Use*. Corr. edn. London: Athlone Press, 1965.

Peck, John and Martin Coyle. *Practical Criticism: How to Write a Critical Appreciation*. Basingstoke: Palgrave Macmillan, 1995.

Steele, Timothy. *All the Fun's in How You Say a Thing: An Explanation of Meter and Versification*. Athens, OH: Ohio University Press, 1999.

Strand, Mark and Eavan Boland, eds. *The Making of a Poem: A Norton Anthology of Poetic Forms*. New York: W. W. Norton, 2000.

Williams, Rhian. *The Poetry Toolkit: The Essential Guide to Studying Poetry*. London: Continuum, 2009.

Drama

(Year 1)

Neal Swettenham and Robert John Brocklehurst

Theatre and drama

Drama and Theatre Studies, though obviously related to Literary Studies, offer distinctive approaches to text. Whilst Drama may also on occasion focus on literary aspects, Theatre Studies directly addresses the fact that plays are written for performance. A small number of authors have, of course, written plays for what might be called the 'theatre of the mind', where public performance was never the intended aim, and others have sought to 'defy' the very possibility of performance (Artaud's *Spurt of Blood* [1925] is one such example). However, the vast majority of playwrights write in the understanding that their works are incomplete without theatrical realization.

For a long time, students of English literature were encouraged to read plays as primarily literary objects: dramatic characters were psychoanalysed to reveal their essential behavioural traits; stories were interrogated for their central themes and meanings. With the emergence of **semiotics** (the study of 'signs') and phenomenology (the study of 'presence'), during the early part of the twentieth century, the emphasis gradually shifted from the literary to the performative, and the question of meaning(s) became less straightforward.

From the perspective of drama, it is a given that a play text must be considered as an unfinished work: a blueprint for performance. (As Martin Esslin suggests in *The Field of Drama*, 'Definitions of concepts like "drama" should never be treated as normative, but as merely outlining the somewhat fluid boundaries of a given field' [1987: 23]). Directors, designers, technicians and performers are all co-creators, with the author, in bringing that text to life, and yet by adding all the elements of body-voice performance – gesture, facial intonation, vocal emphasis, light, sound, prop and set – they inevitably take the work significantly beyond the author's original idea and intention (sometimes beyond recognition altogether).

The turn of the century saw an increased acceptance of what might be termed 'non-standard texts' into the mainstream due in part to a breakdown in boundaries between art, video and theatre (art in performance, performance as art). Such alternative approaches in drama (body, object, image foci) contribute to a healthy debate as to what a text can be as part of the continuing histories of theatre and drama where technical media and other performative elements help extend the realms of form and presentation, of what can be presented where, how and to whom. Rather than such ideas becoming a panacea for the performing arts, increasingly directors and artists alike are looking to the possibilities of an interplay between the traditions of analytic reading and writing and the adaptive potential of the 'combined arts', of past and present to inform innovative textual development and staging for the future.

It therefore follows that students of literature who wish to engage confidently and appropriately with dramatic texts need to be familiar with the many different languages of the stage, even if they have no intention of becoming theatrical practitioners themselves. To read plays, it is not necessary to *make* theatre; but it *is* necessary to understand it.

Staging Shakespeare

To make the ideas of dramatic interpretation more concrete, let's consider one very simple aspect: the casting process and the effect this might have upon the reading of a play. In Shakespeare's *A Midsummer Night's Dream*, Titania, the

Queen of the Fairies, is attended by a group of minor fairies, whose names are Peaseblossom, Cobweb, Moth and Mustardseed. How would you cast those roles? The names are rather playful and suggest the possibility of using very young actors, possibly even children. Bottom addresses them all as 'Monsieur', suggesting that they are to be played by male performers (as indeed would have been the case in Shakespeare's time). But perhaps it would be more fitting if the Queen of the Fairies had female attendants? Bottom's reading of the situation is not necessarily to be trusted, after all. Or the fairies might be portrayed quite ambiguously in respect of **gender**.

Behind all of these possibilities lies the more basic question of how we are picturing the fairies in the first place. In Peter Brook's landmark production at the Royal Shakespeare Company (1970), they were played by three male performers and one female, all dressed in loose-fitting, drab costumes. They were of no particular time or place and used physicality, their acrobatics defining their status, their difference, as fairies. Jonathan Miller's version of the play for the Royal Shakespeare Company, produced in 1996, used much older actors. These performers, in their sixties and seventies, conveyed the notion that the fairies were more than mortal through the obvious fact that they had lived many lifetimes: they had seen it all before, nothing could surprise them. In the RSC's 2008 production the fairies were portrayed as leather-jacketed punks, invisible to humans, manipulating child puppets, adding another layer of 'conduit' between the reality and fantasy of the forest scenes. So: playful children? Anonymous acrobats? Jaded pensioners? Mischievous punks? Which of these, or many other possibilities, might it be? The permutations are endless; but each new reimagining of the characters portrays the fairy realm in a different light and transforms the experience of the play for its respective audience.

Staging your own texts

Let's consider how a student of dramatic literature might set about the task of interpreting a text written for the stage. It is helpful to think in terms of three overarching considerations: *content, form* and *production*.

1 Content

Content takes us back to the first principles of literature: what is the story being told and what are its key themes? Who are the main/secondary characters? What issues do they raise? What happens in what order and what triggers act and action? What is the central crisis of the play and how is it resolved? And how are all these issues made concrete through the actions and events of the narrative? These are primarily questions of story and character: the 'what' and the 'who'. It is also important for any student of drama to spot the moments within the script that gain their power precisely because of their physical qualities.

From the earliest Greek plays, with their rhythmic, musically underscored Chorus speeches, right up to present-day performance art, the physical presence of the actors' bodies has been a critical element of any theatrical experience and good writers know when to reduce language to a minimum and allow the actual bodily presence of the performers to achieve their effects. The first appearance of the blinded Oedipus in Sophocles' *Oedipus Rex* would be an early instance of this at work. (It is important to remember that this would have been achieved through the use of masks rather than make-up.) Shakespeare offers many such examples in his plays, one of the most striking of which, perhaps, is an equivalent moment from *King Lear* when Gloucester's eyes are 'gouged out' in front of the audience. Finally, an even more extreme and shocking version of this would be the point in Sarah Kane's play *Blasted* (1995) at which the Soldier, having first raped Ian, then 'sucks out' his eyeballs and 'eats' them. Such visceral shocks may be obvious at first reading (it is hard to miss the effect of that last example), but they may also be much more elusive and require closer reading before they yield up their full power.

Finally, there are the 'when' and 'where' questions of time and place. What effect does geography, period and cultural location(s) have upon the text? What impact does this have on the characters' behaviour and their value systems, and is it believable? Is there a particular political **context** that needs to be taken into account (think of Caryl Churchill's work on Thatcherism)? Or is the play set in a much less specific location (Samuel Beckett's *Waiting for Godot* [1952])? Gathering all these aspects together, we must ask big 'why' questions: why is this particular story being told? Why should we engage with these issues again now, and what might the audience response be? What might the play actually 'mean'? (We should resist the idea, of course, that a play has just one meaning that can be excavated and put on display. A good text will suggest many potential meanings, some quite contradictory, and it should also be clear that the particular questions we ask of a text will determine the meanings we find.)

2 Form

Form shifts our attention from 'what, who and where' to the question of 'how' – from the story elements themselves to how that story is being told. These are issues of **genre**, dramatic structure, tone and pace, and the ability to ask these questions intelligently and attentively is developed over time. It is vital for a student of drama and theatre studies to understand how many times the rules of 'good' playwriting have changed over the centuries. What may seem, to a modern reader, to be crude and clumsy construction may, in fact, be a highly sophisticated mastery of unfamiliar genre conventions. Someone encountering the medieval Mystery Cycles for the first time is more likely to be unsettled by the absence of psychologically plausible characters than impressed by the plays' subtle use of poetic language and profound theological grasp. So we first need to understand what kind of play we are looking at (theatre studies) and how the dramatic rules work in this particular story-universe.

Initial genre questions are concerned with overall dramatic form, the simplest categories being *tragedy* (which ends with the death or punishment of the main characters), *comedy* (which ends with the main characters getting married), and *drama* (a more modern category which is unlikely to resolve as 'neatly' as the two classic forms), though there are, of course, many more sub-divisions below these three primary categories (see TRAGEDY, COMEDY). Then there are questions of structure. Does the play follow an Aristotelian story arc from exposition (setting the scene), through catalyst (the event that sparks the action into life), development, crisis and resolution (the restoration of social balance)? Or is it structured using the 'epic' form (primarily associated with the writer Bertolt Brecht, though, in fact, he borrowed many key ideas about the form from earlier Elizabethan and Jacobean playwrights), which can typically encompass a longer timeframe and which divides the story into discrete narrative units, or story 'parcels', each of which can be considered separately? Finally, pace and tone are often missed or misused by the inexperienced reader, where intelligent dialogue intended to have an ironic edge may be wrong when delivered with deadly earnestness or flippant speed. This has implications for all aspects of the text, but is most critical when related to vocal and physical delivery.

3 Production

Never a mere 'add-on', production considerations are about facilitating an interpretation of text from its content and form into realization. Consider how choices such as who you cast, how they deliver the text, and the look of your overall stage design might fashion and affect the final presentation. You may have chosen to relocate the play in both period and place; you will need to research the 'feel' and the 'look' of these other worlds. Shakespeare's dialogue spoken on the stage of the modern Globe Theatre on London's South Bank has given contemporary audiences a sense of his time, of how his text 'feels' in that environment, but equally, what of the many new intimacies possible when staging such work in the black-box studio setting? (The 1976 production of *Macbeth*, starring Judi Dench and Ian McKellen, gained much of its impact from its claustrophobic, black-box setting at The Other Place in Stratford.) There are potential pitfalls when attempting large-scale production designs within the context of a student production. Not uncommon is the design 'epic' that fails, ending up as an approximation of the imagined effect. On the other hand, with the right kind of creativity and an imaginative use of resources, student productions, just as much as any others, are able to unlock whole new meanings within the text.

Media as text in performance

With increased quality and access to portable recording technologies and the influence of theatre on media art (drama in video artworks; Peter Greenaway is a good example of an artist becoming a 'mainstream' director, bringing drama into close proximity with his artworks using film and video), art on theatre media (screen-based media art in theatrical settings; see, for example, the theatre project work of The Builders Association: www.thebuildersassociation.org) has become accepted and valid as a 'text' unto itself. Media can be as much the premise or start point for performances or plays in development as any published work.

The idea of creating your own ideas, roles, and writing your own scripts raises awareness not just of how 'scripts' come into being but whether or not the content 'belongs to you' in the first place. It is easy to understand how media as text has filtered into the theatre space something that can be traced back to 1960s experiments in theatre performance where collectives and collaborators such as The Wooster Group or John Cage and Merce Cunningham created 'texts' formed of things other than the written word (audio-visuals, body movement, memories, events). Today such approaches are no longer seen as radical, alternative 'dramas' existing in settings other than just the formal theatre space, such as in the art gallery (Tim Crouch's *My Arm* and *An Oak Tree* performed at the Tate Modern, London, 2006) or in site-specific settings (Punchdrunk's *Tunnel 228*, a collaboration with the Old Vic Theatre set inside a railway arch, London, 2009). Despite such works being experientially different, they are no less tangible or readable than any other form of text. It may only be that audiences have 'work to do' in making narrative sense of the performance, perhaps confronting the spontaneity of improvisation as believable reality, or dealing with their own physical proximity to the act/action, where audiences drawn in, whether willingly or unwillingly, become part of a text in the making.

Despite the seeming difference, such performances often still adhere to prepared and considered orders, philosophical concepts, lists and schedule plans, effectively still very content–form–production driven. The difference from traditional writings is that processes may occur less formally, be more fluid, developmental and devised. The adaptive possibilities and available choices in mediation are still very much considered even if the process has shifted in terms of its chronology. A particular subject or approach may have *production* needs that can create *forms* resulting in 'new' *content*. Equally *form* can demand a certain *production* approach creating final *content*.

Let's return to a production of Sarah Kane's play *Blasted*: when dealing with the text formally as a single play, the central themes and ideas of mental illness in and as society can be discussed, extracted and emphasized in the development of the piece, from the earliest discussion through to final realization in production (*content–form = production*). However, it is possible to encompass the same ideas in a different way. In a recent student production, the focus was on the author's life, extracting visual/dialogue moments from sources including television interviews and news excerpts reporting her death. The students explored ideas of 'mirroring', taking narrative ideas from *all* her play works (*production–form = content*) and illustrating Kane's life using character 'conversations' between screen and stage. In this way, similar end ideas (as content) were produced but with the relationship between media and movement (production–form) being the main driver. The complexities of approach to text are clear to see for the dramaturge though true to all forms of writing and adaptation, choices of start point, emphases, movement and prop/media elements have a huge bearing on the success of a piece of work in terms of its effectiveness.

Summary

A student of Drama and Theatre Studies may have many and different tools at their disposal but what remains constant is the need to do all the close textual study and research needed for the interpretation of any other literary work and then also bring to bear additional questions to do with production and performance. These core issues must be borne in mind: (1) In what ways is this play (theatre) or text (drama) *similar* to other plays/texts (**genre**, structure, content and so on)? (2) In what plays is this play/text *different* from other plays or texts (the unique qualities of this writer, the telling of the story, the subtexts of object, place and time, maybe the subtle twists in the conventions of a particular genre)? (3) And how might the theatrical realization of this play or text influence its many possible meanings? These are core considerations in the use and application of textual ideas in the practical arena but may also be useful to writers before they head out on their own creative, textual journeys.

Drama: sample syllabus

Week 1   Introduction: The origins of drama: Sophocles, *Oedipus Rex*
Week 2   Approaches to drama – content: Timberlake Wertenbaker, *The Love of the Nightingale*
Week 3   Approaches to drama – form: *The Love of the Nightingale*
Week 4   Approaches to drama – production: *The Love of the Nightingale*
Week 5   Script into performance: theories of interpretation: Richard Hornby, *Script into Performance*
Week 6   The dramatic text: William Shakespeare, *Hamlet*
Week 7   Body as text: Stephen Berkoff, *Metamorphosis*
Week 8   Space as text: Tom Stoppard, *Arcadia*
Week 9   Media as text: Martin Crimp, *Attempts on Her Life*
Week 10 Drama, theatre and performance – W. B. Worthen, 'Disciplines of the Text: Sites of Performance'
Week 11 The role of the audience: Peter Handke, *Offending the Audience*
Week 12 Beyond the text – the relationship with the real: Tim Etchells and Forced Entertainment

Bibliography

(a) Literary works

Berkoff, Steven. *The Trial; Metamorphosis; In the Penal Colony. Three theatre adaptations from Franz Kafka*. Oxford: Amber Lane, 1988.

Crimp, Martin. *Attempts On Her Life*. London: Faber and Faber, 2007.

Handke, Peter. *Plays*. London: Methuen Drama, 1997.

Shakespeare, William. *Hamlet*. Ed. Ann Thompson and Neil Taylor, 3rd edn. London: Arden Shakespeare, 2005.

Sophocles. *The Theban Plays*. Trans. Robert Fagles. Harmondsworth: Penguin, 1984.

Stoppard, Tom. *Arcadia*. London: Faber and Faber, 1993.

Wertenbaker, Timberlake. *Plays 1*. London: Faber and Faber, 1996.

(b) Further reading

Etchells, Tim. *Certain Fragments*. London and New York: Routledge, 1999.

Goldberg, RoseLee. *Performance Art: From Futurism to the Present*, 3rd edn. London: Thames and Hudson, 2001.

Hornby, Richard. *Script into Performance*. New York: Applause, 1995.

Leach, Robert. *Theatre Studies*. London and New York: Routledge, 2008.

Lennard, John and Mary Luckhurst. *The Drama Handbook: A Guide to Reading Plays*. Oxford: Oxford University Press, 2002.

Wallis, Mick and Simon Shepherd. *Studying Plays*, 2nd edn. London: Arnold, 2002.

Worthen, W. B. 'Disciplines of the Text: Sites of Performance'. In *The Performance Studies Reader*. Ed. Henry Bial. London: Routledge, 2007.

Epic

(Year 2)

Nigel Wood

Classical definitions and characteristics

An epic poem usually consists of a sustained narrative description of heroic actions or themes. The events might be unified by their relationship to a central heroic character, who is caught up in interesting and even fantastic contexts, or to a significant, mythical, train of events. For example, in the classical epic form, Homer's *Odyssey* traces the 10-year travels of Odysseus to reach his home in Ithaca after the Trojan War; his *Iliad* covers the main event in the last year of that conflict, including Achilles' desertion from the Greek front line in Book I, and his slaying of Hector in Book XXII; and Virgil's *Aeneid* tracks Aeneas's wanderings from Troy to Italy, and then the Trojans' victories over the Latins. The events are grand and typically interest the gods, who intervene or debate the complexities of war and chance. Thus, Athena directly helps break the fragile Greco-Trojan truce in Book IV of the *Iliad* and, despite Zeus's explicit instruction to the gods to desist in aiding one or other side in the conflict, Hera, Athena and Poseidon defy him (Books VIII, XIII) until the gods enter the battle in Book XX. Similarly, Athena is a protector of Odysseus in the *Odyssey*, and also helps his son Telemachus in his project to protect his mother, Penelope's, interests in resisting the suitors gathered in Ithaca. For Virgil, divine intervention is less consistent in his plot, yet Aeneas's difficulties in navigation are due to the antagonism of the goddess Juno, who enlists Aeolus, King of the Winds, against his fleet in releasing strong and unpredictable winds that blow his ships off course. When tempted to tarry in Carthage with its Queen, Dido, in Book IV of the *Aeneid*, Aeneas is reminded of his destiny to found Rome by Mercury, the messenger of the Gods, and he leaves reluctantly.

There are obvious attractions in the epic form: stirring events and heroic actions demand the highest forms of poetic description and figurative power. As a means of drawing a reader's attention to the potential for grand human aspirations, the form is unrivalled, and, in its earliest forms, these were wedded to strong military virtues. These are, however, linked to a certain resourcefulness and the charity of the gods – Aeneas, Odysseus and Achilles, as well as Beowulf in the medieval epic poem of that name, cannot get by on moral rectitude alone. For example, Aeneas does not only triumph over the Latins because of the Trojans' valour but because he had secured the support of the Tuscans; Odysseus and his crew escape the clutches of the one-eyed giant Polyphemus (the Cyclops) by deception and, having eventually secured mastery of the winds captured (all but the West Wind) in a bag by Aeolus, his crew open it, believing it to contain gold, and the advantage is lost, with Ithaca in sight; Achilles is so enraged at the death of his friend, Patroclus, that he takes immense risks in pursuing Hector, and kills him in a savage fit of temper that owes little to strategy. In short, these are not primarily Christian virtues and firmly belong to a previous religious climate.

As Barry B. Powell, in his study of *Homer* (2004), and Robin Lane Fox, in *Travelling Heroes: Greeks and Their Myths in the Epic Age of Homer* (2008), have made plain, the Greek classical epic poem values a distinct model of heroism, one that lays great store by adaptability and pragmatism and one well attuned to sudden political upheavals. Primarily handed down by oral memory, these first epics are often called *primary* examples, more a collection of tales with a looser narrative thread than in subsequent instances (including the *Aeneid*) that have come to be regarded as *secondary* or literary. Although the travels of Virgil's Aeneas seem similar to those of Homer's Odysseus, there is a subtle difference, however, in that the former has to remain true to his national destiny, to be the founder of Rome; Odysseus wants more simply and personally just to get home to Ithaca and his family. Virgilian heroism lays claim to more abstract aims and Aeneas has, more than once, to sacrifice immediate comfort and friendship in order to pursue a higher calling. This is most succinctly expressed in Francis Cairns's *Virgil's Augustan Epic* (2008) and Eve Adler's *Vergil's Empire* (2003), both of whom trace an appreciation of the Emperor Augustus's attempts to bring peace to a vast empire – and to impose stability on sometimes rebellious peoples.

The early modern English epic

Creating an English equivalent to classical precedent, though, was another matter. How might one adapt primary epic heroes to Christian manners? What native myths were available for English epics? These were not easily answered since a national mythology was not clearly available. The best description of the pagan interest in the epic and its myths is probably given by Sallustius, a fourth-century thinker on the attractiveness of pre-Christian thought. In his *On the Gods and the World* (*c*.365), he felt that 'the myths represent the gods themselves and the goodness of the gods ... since, just as the gods have made the goods of sense common to all, but those of intellect only to the wise, so the myths state the existence of gods to all, but who and what they are only to those who can understand'. In this sense, the whole world is a **myth**, deserving, not scientific analysis, but rather the awakening of wonder and a higher perception, and this supreme achievement could only be attained by the highest reaches of poetry. For Sir Philip Sidney, in his *Apology for Poetry* (1595), the poet creates another 'nature', reflecting not the world of the senses in which we are captive most of the time, but, with the 'zodiac of his own wit', creating a world that reflects a mythical reality: 'Nature never set forth the earth in so rich tapestry as divers poets have done; neither with pleasant rivers, fruitful trees, sweet-smelling flowers, nor whatsoever else may make the too much loved earth more lovely. Her world is brazen, the poets only deliver a golden' (Sidney 2002: 85). For the early modern period, the epic was quite simply the most 'golden' artistic form, and, whereas we often now distrust rhetoric, Sidney saw something elevated in its power and symbolic suggestiveness. Reading epic verse is thus an exercise in a higher poetic appreciation (see POETRY).

Edmund Spenser's *The Faerie Queene* (1590, 1596) and John Milton's *Paradise Lost* (1667, 1668) are generally recognized as the most successful English epic poems. Both embrace generally accepted – and understood – myths: Spenser looks to Arthurian legend for his organizational principle, whereas Milton immerses himself in the Genesis account of Adam and Eve and their disobedience of God's strict prohibition against tasting the apple from the tree of the Knowledge of Good and Evil. Recent scholarship has, however, uncovered several references to each author's immediate political situation and his understanding of English nationhood.

The Faerie Queene

Spenser intended his poem to have a civilizing influence both on the Elizabethan court and the Queen's gentry. In his letter to Sir Walter Raleigh of 1589, prefixed to the first edition, he hopes that its 'continued' **allegory** – or 'dark conceit' – will not be misinterpreted, for its 'general end' was to 'fashion a gentleman or noble person in virtuous or gentle discipline'. His scheme for the unfinished work was to celebrate 12 'private' virtues derived from the adventures of 12 knights, and then 12 'public' virtues derived from the character of

King Arthur. Believing that the work would recommend him to the Court after dutiful work in Ireland subduing the second Desmond rebellion there in 1580–4, he intended to present it to Court through the good offices of Raleigh, but the Queen's principal secretary, Lord Burghley, was not impressed, and the most its author received was a smaller pension than expected in 1591. It is, however, a poem that interests itself in courtly virtues, each extant Book devoting itself to one main trait: Holiness (I), Temperance (II), Chastity (III), Friendship (IV), Justice (V) and Courtesy (VI), and it is also clear that it aims to glorify the Tudor dynasty, drawing parallels with Augustus's Rome. Elizabeth is most consistently figured as Gloriana throughout the poem, yet she also appears in Books III and IV as the virgin Belphoebe, a twin of Amoret, representing married love. Several have also traced a less-than-flattering image of her in Book I as Lucifera, a 'maiden queen' who presides over a garish Court of Pride, ignoring dungeons full of prisoners.

Thus, it would not do to regard the work as merely Elizabeth-worship; as Willy Maley has most recently reminded us, the poem takes as its subject the whole set of issues surrounding national, Protestant, identity – for a fragile, 'new', state founded on separatist principles and feeling its way without Roman Catholic support, both in earthly and spiritual matters. In Maley's work (1997, 2003), the codes that Spenser embedded into his moral **allegory** are examined afresh, as are his complex religious and political principles. Andrew Hadfield places the work within a national tradition of moral rearmament (2009), and the most succinct biographical account of how Spenser regarded his ethical bearings is contained in Gary Waller's *Edmund Spenser: A Literary Life* (1994) and John N. King's 'Spenser's Religion' in Andrew Hadfield's collection, *The Cambridge Companion to Spenser* (2001), pp. 200–16.

Paradise Lost

John Milton's interest in the epic is similarly affected by national concerns. It is likely that he witnessed the execution of Charles I in 1649, and, during his king's trial, he drafted a fiercely republican piece, *The Tenure of Kings and Magistrates*. Whilst not directly advocating regicide, he allowed such a step some legitimacy. It was published just two weeks after Charles's momentous death, and captures much of Milton's distrust of tyranny: 'all men naturally were born free, being the image and resemblance of God himself, and were by privilege above all, the creatures born to command, and not to obey' (Milton 1953, 3:198). Note the sense that 'all' men, according to nature, were 'born free'. The Cromwellian government appointed him Secretary for Foreign Tongues later that year, and one of his first tasks was to formulate an answer to Charles I's apology for sacred kingship, *Eikon Basilike* (1649). Milton set to work immediately and his *Eikonoklastes* (translated as 'image-breaker') was published that October. In Book VIII of *Paradise Lost*, Adam requests of God a companion of equal kind, for no 'societie … harmonie or true delight' can exist between 'unequals' (VIII: 383–4) – but by 1667 the political landscape had altered drastically.

With the restoration of Charles II in 1660, Milton's position was precarious; he had been imprisoned for a short time during the autumn of 1659, and several of his more outspoken pamphlets publicly burned. One can see how the Edenic parable of how Man fell by wanting to know too much and daring to reach for knowledge appealed to him. Even the blank verse he used was an image of liberty, as his remarks prefixed to the 12-book version of 1668 made clear: the refusal of rhyme was an embrace of 'ancient liberty' and a strike against the 'troublesome and modern bondage of rhyming'. William Blake's verdict on *Paradise Lost* is a resonant one: '[The reason Milton] wrote in fetters when he wrote of Angels & God, and at liberty when of Devils & Hell is because he was a true Poet and of the Devils party without knowing it' (*The Marriage of Heaven and Hell* [1790, Plate 1]). This indicates a split in Milton's own imaginative grasp of the Genesis myth, for it is a common reading experience to find the positive Satan of the first four books stirring and engaging (in an almost Homeric sense) and the more abstract divine process of the rest of the 12 books, where he is belittled and the divine plan for fallen Man outlined, less dramatic. To get a sense of how Blake's reading might be understood, one might contrast Satan's vivid speeches when rallying his fallen legions at I: 622–62 or at II: 11–42 with the description of creation at VII: 243–632. It is as if Milton was bowing the head to the new order, yet recognizing the Satanic, rebellious traces in himself as well.

The decline in epic

The lack of an epic with the same mythic power as that in Spenser and Milton was often discussed in the eighteenth century (see THE EIGHTEENTH CENTURY). Indeed, some tried to emulate the past but discovered that they wrote rather empty if bombastic rhetoric. Dustin Griffin (2009) has argued that the very excellence that was recognized in Milton (especially) inhibited all would-be epic writers, and that the way forward was to mock the form, and build a new foundation for that same expansiveness of expression in an ironic vein. In Alexander Pope's *The Rape of the Lock* (1712, 1714) and his *Dunciad* (1744), there is the same understanding of epic gestures, but the mood is more analytic, poring scorn on social pretension and bad art.

The reason why there has been no more recent epic could be that the attention of all serious art has been placed on the individual self and not on national or religious myth; the interior consciousness is the big adventure. Consequently, there is heroism in the newer art forms – such as the novel or film – but poetry has perhaps found different voices, more lyric and inward-looking. Take the example of William Wordsworth's *The Prelude*, which only made it into print after his death, in 1850. Designed as a 'prelude' to a much larger philosophical poem, to be called either *The Ruined Cottage* or *The Recluse*, the poet could not finish the project, despite several separate attempts in 1799 and 1805 to write it up for publication. Stuart Curran (1986) has also pointed to the intense revival of interest in the romance form that displaced other interests. In William Blake's *Jerusalem* and *Milton* (both 1804), there is vision and scope, yet the myths are more private than in the regular, classical epic. To this day, we expect the epic to exist outside poetry.

Epic: sample syllabus

Week 1   Some definitions; the distinction between primary and secondary epic
Week 2   Primary epic: Homer, *Odyssey*, Books IX and X
Week 3   Secondary epic: Virgil, *Aeneid*, Books IV, V and VI
Week 4   *Beowulf* (in translation)
Week 5   Either Edmund Spenser, *The Faerie Queene* (*FQ*) or John Milton, *Paradise Lost* (*PL*)
Week 6   Either *FQ*, Books III–IV, or *PL*, Books V–VIII
Week 7   Either *FQ*, Books V–VI, or *PL*, Books IX–X
Week 8   Either *FQ*, Book VII ('The Mutabilitie Cantos') or *PL*, Books XI–XII
Week 9   Either *PL*, Books I–IV, or *FQ*, Books I–II
Week 10   William Wordsworth, *The Prelude*, especially Books I–II and IX–X
Week 11   William Blake, *Milton: A Poem*
Week 12   Concluding comments; screening of Robert Zemeckis's 2007 film of *Beowulf*

Bibliography

(a) Literary works

Anon. *Beowulf.* Trans. Seamus Heaney. London: Faber and Faber, 2000.

Blake, William. *Milton: A Poem. The Illuminated Books of William Blake*, Vol. 5. Ed. Robert N. Essick and Joseph Viscomi. Princeton, NJ: Princeton University Press, 1998.

Homer, *Odyssey.* Trans. Robert Fagles. London: Penguin, 2006.

Milton, John. *Complete Prose.* Ed. D. M. Wolfe et al., 8 vols. New Haven, CT: Yale University Press, 1953–80.

Milton, John. *Paradise Lost.* Ed. Stephen Orgel and Jonathan Goldberg. Oxford: Oxford University Press, 2008.

Sidney, Philip. *An Apology for Poetry (or The Defence of Poesy).* Ed. R. W. Maslen. Manchester: Manchester University Press, 2002.

Spenser, Edmund. *The Faerie Queene.* 2nd edn. Ed. A. C. Hamilton. Text eds, Hiroshi Yamashita and Toshiyuki Suzuki. Harlow: Longman, 2001.

Virgil, *Aeneid.* Trans. Robert Fagles. London: Penguin, 2007.

Wordsworth, William. *The Prelude: The Four Texts (1798, 1799, 1805, 1850).* Ed. Jonathan Wordsworth. London: Penguin, 2004.

(b) Further reading

Abrams, M. H. 'The Prelude and The Recluse: Wordsworth's Long Journey Home'. In *The Prelude: A New Casebook*, 209–24. Ed. Stephen Gill. Basingstoke: Palgrave Macmillan, 2006.

Blessington, Francis C. *Paradise Lost and the Classical Epic.* London: Routledge & Kegan Paul, 1979.

Feeney, D. C. 'Epic Heroes and Epic Fable'. *Comparative Literature*, 38 (1986): 137–58.

Hadfield, Andrew. *Shakespeare, Spenser and the Matter of Britain*. London: Palgrave Macmillan, 2003.

Hadfield, Andrew. *Literature, Politics and National Identity: Reformation to Renaissance*. Cambridge: Cambridge University Press, 2009.

Worden, Blair. *Literature and Politics in Cromwellian England: John Milton, Andrew Marvell, Marchamont Needham*. Cambridge: Cambridge University Press, 2009.

Lyric [Year 2]

Nigel Wood

Definitions and forms

Lyric poetry is notoriously difficult to define because it has nowadays come to designate any short form of verse. For the classical Greeks, however, it signified verse accompanied by the lyre; in other words, it could only be fully appreciated when you heard the accompaniment. This also meant that one looked for varieties of melody in lyric work – as opposed to writers of plays (that were spoken not sung), of elegies (accompanied by the flute not the lyre), and writers of epics. We now retain a sense of a lyric as where the words are designed to complement music, as Sir Philip Sidney noted in his *Apology for Poetry* (1595): the poet 'cometh to you with words set in delightful proportion, either accompanied with, or prepared for, the well enchanting skill of music' (Sidney 1965: 113). We come across lyrics every day in popular music, printed to accompany CDs. Lyrics enchant; the metre can create mood as well as the usual verbal resources of repetition and assonance (see POETRY).

This is one probable excellence of lyric poetry: it fascinates by its intricacy of metre, the way it is stressed or how it sounds. There are others, though. The brevity of a lyric can mean that it distils the special power of a moment or realization; there is a minimum of scene setting and narrative context – just the strong impression of a personal feeling. You might be impressed by the emotion but you might also have to admit that you would not be quite so impressed if there had not been care in the arrangement of metre and choice of words. This is what Shakespeare meant when he has his Touchstone declare that 'the truest poetry is the most feigning' (*As You Like It*, III.iii.17–18).

There are at least three main kinds of lyric that have their own subset of guidelines: the *ode*, the *elegy* and the *sonnet*. Lyrics may also simply be called *songs* or *ballads*, but here the definition is looser. The *dramatic monologue* involves us in detective critical work, whereby we eventually come to judge the character speaking as well as her/his situation.

The ode

Odes are usually addressed to an object or quality, such as to Autumn (John Keats) or Evening (William Collins). They explore its qualities or what it means to the poet; typically, they start with the description of conventional associations and then progress to more individual connotations. Take one example: William Collins's 'Ode to Evening' (1746, rev. 1748; see Ferguson 2005.).

Collins starts by evoking the stillness of evening: 'Now air is hushed, save where the weak-eyed bat, / With short shrill shriek flits by on leathern wing' (ll. 9–10). The passage of the bat is rendered by the sound as well as signified by the words. It is an exercise in pausing and in trying to capture that moment of change before night fully falls: sunset with its 'bright-haired sun' (l. 5 – the streaks of its faltering rays resembling strands of hair), and the appearance is noted of the 'folding-star' (l. 21 – the evening star that warns shepherds to drive their flocks to their pens for the night). There is a 'turn' in the poem, though, at line 33, for it is there that the poet imagines other, more forbidding, evenings, when he may have to take shelter from 'blustering winds, or driving rain' (l. 33). From this hut, his vantage point throughout the seasons, he takes stock of the change in seasons, and perhaps his own change in fortune, and finds a necessary coherence, embracing 'Fancy, Friendship, Science, rose-lipped Health' (l. 50). Further lucid demonstrations can be found in Jump (1974).

This is a relatively private and calm example, yet the ode could embrace political themes in the form of the *Horatian ode*, and one of the most successful of these was 'An Horatian Ode Upon Cromwell's Return From Ireland' (1650) by Andrew Marvell. Horace, the classical Roman poet, was renowned for his cool and dispassionate style, and his odes are balanced and even in temper.

Its polar opposite was the thrillingly irregular and digressive *Pindaric ode*. Modelled on the intricacies of the odes of the Roman poet Pindar (518–438 BCE), such odes often appear to be without a plan and entirely random. To some extent, they are virtuoso exercises, although you should try to trace the deeper consistencies in John Dryden's 'Threnodia Augustalis' (1685) or Thomas Gray's 'The Bard' or his 'The Progress of Poesy' (both 1757).

The elegy

The need to encapsulate what one feels when someone dies and the desire to sum up just what that person has meant to us is a common impulse, and an elegy meets that need – even when the person is not personally known to us. In the broadest terms, these lyrics are formal exercises in containing pain and loss. As Alastair Fowler has it, an elegy is 'passionate meditation' leading to a 'recognition … of feeling' (Fowler 1982: 207). Indeed, the less one has direct knowledge of the deceased, the more one can see the death in a wider frame or include less personal or anecdotal reflections. This is best instanced in two examples: John Milton's 'Lycidas' (1638) and Thomas Gray's 'Elegy Written in a Country Churchyard' (1751).

'Lycidas' is a variant of the form called a *pastoral elegy*, wherein the life of the departed and the present circumstances of the poet are assumed to be equivalent to the simplest and purest form of existence, found in the unsophisticated rural affairs of shepherds and nymphs. It is a device to suggest an uncalculated purity of emotion, yet it is very unlikely that Milton actually knew Edward King (the subject of the poem) well; he was a fellow student at Cambridge who had drowned a few months before. Milton notes a change with the death that affects us all and reminds the poet of the fragility of all human hopes and concerns, especially in the world of poetry: 'Alas! What boots it [of what profit is it] with incessant care, / To tend the homely slighted shepherd's trade' (ll. 64–5). The Christian consolation of the last section is all the more effective for rising out from this unpretentious ground: Lycidas 'is not dead, / Sunk though he be beneath the wat'ry floor;' (ll. 166–7); he is surely resurrected through Christ's sacrifice for mankind. Indeed, the poet enters the poem directly at the end, setting his compass for 'fresh woods, and pastures new' (l. 193), as all mourners should eventually. Occasionally, a poet can almost play a double bluff by ending her/his elegy before the anticipated consolation; the last line of John Dryden's 'To the Memory of Mr. Oldham' (1684) ends with the consideration that 'fate and gloomy night encompass [him] around' (l. 25).

2

The point of Gray's 'Elegy' is that he does not know the dead buried in the 'Country Churchyard'. They are not famous, but that does not mean that they do not have their own story, contained in the 'short and simple annals of the poor' (l. 32). Their nobility is not less because it is a daily and unsung fact;

> Far from the madding crowd's ignoble strife,
> Their sober wishes never learned to stray;
> Along the cool sequestered vale of life
> They kept the noiseless tenor of their way. (ll. 73–76)

At the poem's close, the poet himself becomes the subject of an imagined future elegist – as humble and unregarded as the lives commemorated on the headstones. In a poem with more pointed **irony** – Jonathan Swift's 'Verse on the Death of Dr. Swift' (1739) – the poet imagines his own death and the temporary impact it will have, even on his own friends. His 'character impartial' is eventually drawn by one 'quite indifferent in the cause' (ll. 305–6), one who is imagined as genuinely compassionate, but not gushingly so. These last two examples introduce some traits we usually associate with the *dramatic monologue*, where we overhear a speaker (whose character we gradually deduce) addressing someone – or us. The full meaning of these poems emerges when we have detected what the full **context** of the utterance might be (sometimes deriving from information given us in the last few lines)

The sonnet

The sonnet is 14 lines in length. There is some precision in this, as the number of lines is enough to allow change in idea or mood, but not long enough to allow a certain diffuseness that would possibly reduce the intensity of the emotion represented or explored. The best sonnets are exact in what they have to say whilst at the same time long enough to introduce variety or scope. There are two main arrangements of these 14 lines: the *Petrarchan* or the *Shakespearean sonnet*. Petrarch was an Italian poet of the fourteenth century whose reputation was based on the *Canzoniere* (*c.*1351–3), a sonnet sequence in praise of a woman called Laura. His most frequent sonnet form was an opening octave (unit of eight lines) followed by a sestet of six lines. The rhyme scheme was similarly segregated: *abbaabba* for the octet, and either *cdcdcd* or *cdecde* for the sestet. The Shakespearean variety has three quatrains (units of four lines) followed by a closing couplet, rhymed *abab cdcd efef gg*.

The poems chosen for Week 3 below show how much might be accomplished by deft changes in emphasis, and, in the examples of Elizabeth Barrett Browning, how your expectations of a strict division between octet and sestet might be defeated and the breathlessness of her sonnets enhanced.

Lyric: sample syllabus

The best method of understanding and sampling the variety of lyric forms is to read closely several examples and attempt to compare and contrast them. A scheme that is organized in exact historical terms might end up in some duplication and overlap.

Week 1   Introduction – types of lyric. Examples of: dramatic monologue, Browning; elegy, Heaney; sonnet, Shakespeare; ode, Anne Finch, Countess of Winchelsea

Week 2   Medieval lyrics: selected poetry by Chaucer

Week 3   The sonnet: selected poetry by Sidney; Shakespeare; Wyatt; Smith; Barrett Browning; extracts on the role of poetry in Sidney, *The Defence of Poesy*

Week 4   Selected poetry by John Donne and Ben Jonson; T. S. Eliot, 'The Metaphysical Poets'

Week 5   Religious lyrics: selected poetry by Donne; Herbert; Vaughan; Hopkins. Lewalski, *Protestant Poetics and the Seventeenth-Century Religious Lyric*, on the role and rules of religious meditation

Week 6   The song: selected poetry by Wroth; Marvell; Blake; Byron. Blake, *Marriage of Heaven and Hell* (1790), plates 5 and 11

Week 7   The ode: selected poetry by Marvell; Collins; Wordsworth; Coleridge; Keats; Shelley. Coleridge, *Biographia Literaria*, Ch. 13

Week 8   The elegy: selected poetry by Dryden; Gray; Tennyson; Hardy; Yeats; Auden; Dunn, 'Second Opinion', *Elegies*

Week 9   The dramatic monologue: selected poetry by Browning; Tennyson; Plath; Duffy; Armitage. Glennis Byron, *Dramatic Monologue*, Ch. 2

Week 10 Selected poetry from *The Lyrical Ballads*. Wordsworth, 'Preface to the *Lyrical Ballads*'; Coleridge, *Biographia Literaria*, Ch. 14

Week 11 Hope and loss: selected poetry by Hardy; Owen; Yeats; Smith; McNeice; Larkin; Heaney; Armitage

Week 12 Conclusion: student discussion either of lyrics not discussed in the module or explanation of three favourite lyrics.

Bibliography

(a) Literary works

Of the poems detailed in the foregoing syllabus, many are readily available online or can be found in anthologies such as the *Norton Anthology of Poetry* listed below.

William Collins's 'Ode to Evening'. In *The Norton Anthology of Poetry*.

Ferguson, Margaret, ed. *The Norton Anthology of Poetry*. 5th rev. edn. New York: Norton, 2005.

Sidney, Philip. *An Apology for Poetry*. Ed. Geoffrey Shepherd (Manchester, 1965); 3rd edn by R. W. Maslen. Manchester: Manchester University Press, 2002.

Wordsworth, William and Samuel Taylor Coleridge. *Lyrical Ballads*. Ed. Michael Schmidt. London: Penguin, 2006.

(b) Further reading

Bold, Alan. *The Ballad*. London: Methuen, 1979.

Brewster, Scott. *Lyric*. London: Routledge, 2009.

Hallberg, R. V. *Lyric Powers*. Chicago: University of Chicago Press, 2008.

Johnson, W. R. *The Idea of Lyric: Lyric Modes in Ancient and Modern Poetry*. Berkeley: University of California Press, 1982.

Lindley, David. *Lyric*. London: Methuen, 1985.

Ramazani, Jahan. *Poetry of Mourning: The Modern Elegy from Hardy to Heaney*. Chicago and London: University of Chicago Press, 1994.

Spiller, Michael. *The Development of the Sonnet*. London: Routledge, 1992.

Vendler, Helen. *The Art of Shakespeare's Sonnets*. Cambridge, MA: Harvard University Press, 1999.

Vendler, Helen. *Our Secret Discipline: Yeats and Lyric Form*. Oxford: Oxford University Press, 2007.

Welsh, Andrew. *Roots of Lyric: Primitive Poetry and Modern Poetics*. Princeton, NJ: Princeton University Press, 1978.

Satire

Nigel Wood

Definitions and styles

Efforts to define satiric writing are rarely satisfactory; the term describes an approach and sometimes a subject, but there is no such thing as satiric form or even a consistent set of satiric methods. Compared to the penning of a tragedy or an epic, there are few rules available for the budding satirist; you write satire in order to disconcert and/or ridicule and this is best accomplished when you know the expectations and assumptions of your readers or audience well. You may encounter several satiric works in any historical survey of the Restoration and eighteenth century, for example, and it could be that the amount of initial explanation about the author and her/his situation may seem like unnecessary throat-clearing when what you want to do is hear the voice clear and full. Depending on your literary taste, this is either going to be a hurdle or a fascinating test of your powers of deduction. Satiric works frequently rely on a reader's recognition of **irony** – and you may not trace this simply by even the closest attention to textual detail. So, here are three questions to ask yourself about any satiric work:

> What are its targets? Try to be precise about this, as the usual suspects recur

across the ages: perhaps corruption in high places, or bad writing or modishness in all its forms. A second set of enquiries may help here, for we should be interested in what riled the satirist *then*, and we often have to look at the author's own life for help with this: was she or he politically active? Who were her/his friends or circle? How did the work get published?

> Is it an *imitation* of another work or author? This does not sound like work of the first order – as if it lacks completely original inspiration – yet the satirist may be quite deliberately bringing another well-known author or work into the equation by allusion or even translation. For example, in the 1730s, Alexander Pope turned to the example of Horace (65–8 BCE) in his *Imitations of Horace* (1733–7), a series of poems where the basic reference back to the Roman poet's example helped establish a set of honoured norms of reason and moderation against which to measure eighteenth-century foolishness. Nearly 200 years later, Wilfred Owen referred to a Horatian phrase from his second ode in his third book (l. 13) to help amplify the ironic savagery of his poem 'Dulce et decorum est' (1920). Horace's full phrase, 'dulce et decorum est pro patria mori' ('it is sweet and fitting to die for one's country') was a straightforward exhortation to bravery in war; for Owen, it is the 'old Lie' (l. 27). In short, the allusion to Horace can be an extension of the original, or a deliberate subversion of its original sense.

> Is there a projection of the author's 'character' in the work? I put speech marks round the word because it may be a purely fictional persona or one that builds upon some traits in the writer's biography but embellishes them to suggest an ideal that stands in stark contrast to folly or vice. In the work of Maynard Mack (1951), it was shown how satirists often spoke through a persona, a fictional projection of a self that was calculated to win the reader's assent or sympathy, but not to be associated with the 'real', biographical self at all.

Whether it be the salutary exercise of finding a scapegoat to offer a sense of social cleansing (see Girard 1986) or the ritual of exorcism (Elliott 1960), or a form of sanctioned sadism (Bentley 1967), satire operates as if from a higher moral ground; the problem is one of intention, for there may be something exemplary about the satirist, but then again there may not be. In the 1950s and 1960s, the study of satire exhibited a fascination with the author's rhetoric; well-planned strategies were used to entrap the reader and much seemed artful and predetermined. This was clearest in the satire of Jonathan Swift and Alexander Pope, and yet there were problems with this because it implied that all was orderly about satiric expression. Take Swift's most widely read works, *A Tale of a Tub* (1704), *A Modest Proposal* (1729) or *Gulliver's Travels* (1726); each proceeds by way of a fictional self. The Teller of the *Tale* is (deliberately) so disorganized a narrator, the Modest Proposer so outrageous in his suggestion that Irish famine might be cured by the Irish eating their young, and

Gulliver so lacking in human focus and certainty that we could simply laugh at them safely. And yet, the range of the *Tale* is enviable and sketches out wider issues that exceed a simple attack on bad writing: of a lack of order throughout life in general and the difficulties in believing in traditions that are set apart from the contemporary or 'relevant'. Similarly, Gulliver is tragically torn between his human self and his love for the enlightened race of horses, the Houyhnhnms, that he encounters on his fourth voyage – he ends up sniffing dung in his own stable, a deliberate affront to humankind. The Modest Proposer ends his pamphlet in tones indistinguishable from Swift's other Irish Tracts: 'But, as to myself, having been wearied out for many years with offering vain, idle, visionary thoughts, and at length utterly despairing of success, I fortunately fell upon this proposal …'. In each case, the persona is both the author and is not, in that Swift cannot be Gulliver, say, but the sudden stylistic savagery and visceral detail discloses a literary personality that is compulsive, uttering a form of truth in jest, in each case unmistakably Swiftian. To know more would take us into the less conscious areas of writing and reading.

2

Satiric models

English literary satire has drawn upon several classical and Renaissance models. There were two principal Roman sources, much studied in grammar schools and universities for their stylistic distinctiveness: Horace and Juvenal.

Quintus Horatius Flaccus, or Horace, wrote two books of *Satires*, in which he exploited aspects of his own life. His good fortune in attracting the notice of an enlightened patron, Maecenas, and one friendly with the emperor, Augustus, led to the award of a farm to him in Tibur in the Sabine hills. This independence (best exemplified by his second satire in Book 2), and the perspective of one not directly within the whirl (and compromises) of active political life, modulates in his work into a number of recurrent themes and styles: an urbanity that shows amusement at the lengths others will go to in order to gain high office; an easy, conversational style (he dubbed his satires *sermones* or chats) that apparently rambles through loosely connected topics, and a gradually unfolding preference for temperance and good humour. Pope's identification with Horace in the 1730s is apt; he, too, a Roman Catholic and deformed from birth, suffered a similar exile, purchasing a property in Twickenham, just outside (then) the western suburbs of London, equivalent to Horace's Sabine farm. In his *Horatian Epistles and Satires* (1731–8), Pope found a means of amplifying his comments through other accents than his own, dignified by the passage of time as well as Horace's own skill in apparently off-the-cuff and disengaged wit.

In sharp contrast, there is Decimus Iunius Iuvenalis (*fl.* late first to early second century), or Juvenal, whose firebrand vituperation in his 16 *Satires* is unrelenting and targeted at the commercial and pagan spirit that suffused Rome at the moment of its decline. Here there is a breathless invention that is relentless in its detail, constructed out of free associations, personal lampoons and attacks on the high and apparently mighty. But would 'comfortable' satire be successful? Although translated by many, there are few who capture that power of unrelenting conviction. In Samuel Johnson's *London* (1738, an imitation of the Third Satire) and *The Vanity of Human Wishes* (1749, an imitation of the Tenth), on the other hand, we trace less of the rant than the glance towards the universal; in place of much of the idiomatic detail, Johnson supplies an abstract and thus elevated, even epic, scope – a reminder that imitations can be unpredictable.

For the Elizabethans, satire tended to mean something rather more Juvenalian; for both Thomas Lodge, in his *Defence of Poetry* (1579), and George Puttenham, in his *Arte of English Poesie* (1589), satire derived from the vogue for dramatic invective, supposed to be the defining feature of Satyrs, who lived a reclusive and embittered life in woodland, away from the city (see THE SIXTEENTH CENTURY). As Dustin Griffin has made clear in his informative and yet still adventurous *Satire: A Critical Reintroduction* (1994), this identification promoted a rather narrow set of possibilities; at the same time, there was available another possible etymology, that from the *lanx satura*, a dish of mixed fruits or a medley (1994: 6–34). This allowed formal variety; the reader marvelled at the variety of style and the rush of associations, often redolent of the best conversation. In John Dryden's *Discourse on the Original and Progress of Satire* (1693), this change of emphasis marks a watershed in satiric writing. It was now possible simply to write of ideas and issues, free of the need to indulge in personalized abuse. The fullest account of this strategy might perhaps be found in Howard Weinbrot (1969, 1982), both of whose critical works provide invaluable context for the allusions of most of the period's satirists.

Dramatic satire

Drama is potentially a radical art form and one that governments or certain religious orders have occasionally striven to suppress, yet its satirical power is intense only in certain eras (see DRAMA). In works such as Thomas Dekker's *The Shoemaker's Holiday* (1599; pub. 1600), Ben Jonson's *The Devil Is an Ass* (1616; pub. 1631), *Every Man in His Humour* (1598) and *Bartholomew Fair* (1614), Thomas Middleton's *Michaelmas Term* (1604; pub. 1607) and *A Chaste Maid in Cheapside* (*c.*1613; pub. 1630), the norms for the most realistic and thus most reliable judgements are those adopted by the middle classes in their struggle to survive successfully in the bustle and drastic environments of the city. In Brian Gibbons's *Jacobean City Comedy* (1980), he shows how constructed this sense of the 'City' actually was, and in Raymond Williams's *The Country and the City* (1973) and Jean E. Howard's *Theater of a City: The Places of London Comedy, 1598–1642* (2006) this contrast with pastoral idylls and courtly pageants or masques is analysed closely for its more radical comments on a tradition of social distinction that was increasingly diluted and questioned by new social formations. This survives in Restoration comedy, so called for its sudden prevalence after the restoration of the monarch (Charles

II) in 1660. Those rich enough to do so departed country estates for the city to lose old selves as well as find new ones. Peter Thomson summarized a Restoration comic plot line as the inclusion within one narrow space, 'sexually predatory well-born men, adulterously inclined well-born women, well-born husbands who generally deserve to be cuckolded and well-born ingénues who are not as ingenuous as all that' (2006: 31). In the plays of William Wycherley, George Etherege, Sir John Vanbrugh, Thomas Shadwell and Aphra Behn, the main fulcrum for such criticism are libertine figures who have no time for the restraints of religion or social order; their free thinking is a challenge to any cosy sense of social continuity.

The Licensing Act of 1737 brought in the licensing of stage performances and forced a certain obedience on new plays. The careers of John Gay and Henry Fielding were irrevocably changed by it. Gay, in *The Beggar's Opera* (1728), sailed too close to the wind in supplying the Beggar's view of events, exposing 'greatness' for the sham that it was in government as well as in society at large; his sequel, *Polly*, was not produced until 50 years had passed. Fielding might have written considerably more works for the stage; at least, we have his novels. And yet, the political invective found in *The Modern Husband* (1732) and *Rape upon Rape* (1730) indicates a rough effectiveness that might have led to a new satiric idiom had it been allowed to mature.

With the repeal of this Act in 1968, we are, perhaps, rediscovering satiric power in its newer forms: television, DVD and internet. According to Humphrey Carpenter (2002), the 1960s saw a resurgence of faith in iconoclasm and in a 'juvenile' and 'immature' refusal to 'grow up'. In *Monty Python* and *Saturday Night Live*, the delight is less in the justness of the targets than the inventive silliness that is part of the protest. This does not mean that committed drama does not exist nowadays. David Hare, in his *Stuff Happens* (2004), is unsparing in his exposure of the illegality of the Iraq conflict, and, with Howard Brenton, was precise and prophetic in his analysis of the effects of the 'Murdochization' of our newspapers in *Pravda* (1985). This is satire that is both aligned and inventive. As Swift put it, in his Preface to *The Battel of the Books* (1704), 'Satire is a sort of glass [mirror] wherein beholders do generally discover everybody's face but their own', and the satirist's mission is to dismantle the defences of the knowing and complacent reader.

Satire: sample syllabus

Week 1   Introduction – the consequences of satire: extracts from Bentley, 'Satire and the Rhetoric of Sadism' (1967); Elliott, *The Power of Satire* (1960)

Week 2   Johnson reads Juvenal: Juvenal, Third and Tenth satires; Johnson, *London*, *The Vanity of Human Wishes*

Week 3   Pope reads Horace: Horace, Book I, Satire 6, Book II, Satires 1 and 6; Pope, *Moral Essays*

Week 4   The mock-heroic (1): Pope, *The Rape of the Lock* (1712, 1714), *Dunciad*, Book IV (1744); Virgil, *The Aeneid*, Books IV and VI

Week 5   The mock-heroic (2): Dryden, *MacFlecknoe* (1682); John Gay, *Trivia* (1716); Dryden, *Discourse on the Original and Progress of Satire* (1693)

Week 6   Dramatic satire (1): Jonson, *The Alchemist* (1612); Middleton, *A Chaste Maid in Cheapside* (1630)

Week 7   Dramatic satire (2): Aphra Behn, *The Feign'd Courtesans* (1679); William Wycherley, *The Country Wife* (1675); John Wilmot, Earl of Rochester, 'A Satyr: on Mankind' (1680)

Week 8   Dramatic satire (3): John Gay, *The Beggar's Opera* (1728); Henry Fielding's *The Modern Husband* (1732)

Week 9   Jonathan Swift, *Gulliver's Travels* (1726), 'Digression on Madness' from *A Tale of a Tub* (1704)

Week 10   Modern stage satire: Howard Brenton and David Hare, *Pravda* (1985); David Edgar, *Destiny* (1976)

Week 11   David Hare, *Stuff Happens* (2004)

Week 12   Conclusion

Bibliography

(a) Literary works

Behn, Aphra. *The Feigned Courtesans*. In *The Rover and Other Plays*. Ed. Jane Spencer. Oxford: Oxford University Press, 2008.

Brenton, Howard and David Hare. *Pravda*. London: Methuen, 1985.

Gay, John. *The Beggar's Opera*. Ed. Bryan Loughrey and T. O. Treadwell. London: Penguin, 2003.

Hare, David. *Stuff Happens*. London: Faber and Faber, 2006.

Jonson, Ben. *The Alchemist*. Ed. Elizabeth Cook. London: Methuen, 2004.

Middleton, Thomas. *A Chaste Maid in Cheapside*. Ed. Alan Brissenden. London: Methuen, 2002.

Pope, Alexander. *The Rape of the Lock*. Ed. Elizabeth Gurr and Victor Lee. Oxford: Oxford University Press, 2007.

Swift, Jonathan. *Gulliver's Travels*. Ed. Claude Rawson and Ian Higgins. Oxford: Oxford University Press, 2008.

Wycherley, William. *The Country Wife*. Ed. James Ogden. London: Methuen, 2003.

(b) Further reading

Elliott, Robert C. *The Power of Satire: Magic, Ritual, Art*. Princeton, NJ: Princeton University Press, 1960.

Girard, René. *The Scapegoat*. Baltimore, MD: Johns Hopkins University Press, 1986.

Griffin, Dustin. *Satire: A Critical Reintroduction*. Lexington: University of Kentucky Press, 1994.

Howard, Jean E. *Theatre of a City: The Places of London Comedy, 1598–1642*. Philadelphia: University of Pennsylvania Press, 2006.

Mack, Maynard. 'The Muse of Satire'. *The Yale Review*, 41 (1951): 80–92.

Weinbrot, Howard. *The Formal Strain: Studies in Augustan Imitation and Satire*. Chicago: University of Chicago Press, 1969.

Weinbrot, Howard. *Pope and the Traditions of Formal Verse Satire*. Princeton, NJ: Princeton University Press, 1982.

Williams, Raymond. *The Country and the City*. London: Paladin, 1973.

Realism

Lawrence Phillips

What is realism?

Realism as a **genre** and critical term promises great simplicity – we all know what we mean by realism – but in truth it is a rather diffuse term that covers a range of writing practices that tend to multiply the more they are scrutinized. Perhaps the place to start is to deal with the 'naive' interpretation of the word which most people have shared at some time, and that is: 'realism is in some way a representation – or worse, reflection – of the "real world" or reality'. On a formal level, of course, this is nonsense. Literary realism is a series of techniques, a writing style, which readers have come to accept as an evocation of a realistic as opposed to a fantastic fictional world. Realism in formal terms is every bit as artificial as a sonnet; they are both, of course, artifice. There is no essential link between the techniques of realistic fiction and its subject. As Wallace Stevens (1879–1955) famously noted, 'Realism is a corruption of reality.'

By reflecting on the preceding paragraph it will become apparent that 'realism' as a genre is determined by both form (more on that in a moment), and also content: it is a series of literary techniques *and* the evocation of a realistic fictional world. When we use it in relation to literature it is most immediately likely to be in reference to prose fiction, novels or short stories (although one might also come across it in relation to drama). As a writing practice it reached its technical apogee in the nineteenth-century novel and short story, but it has been around since the birth of the novel in the eighteenth century (see THE NOVEL). That the novel and realism as a literary technique rapidly develop in the eighteenth century is no accident. It is in that intellectually turbulent century that fundamental questions began to be asked concerning philosophical assumptions about reality and perception (see THE EIGHTEENTH CENTURY). Yet, Damian Grant argues, realism traditionally served **idealism** as a way to argue that universals such as justice, goodness, etc. have a real existence 'independent of the particular objects in which they are found' (Grant 1970: 3). For someone new to thinking about realism, this appears to be diametrically opposed to the usual promise of realism which supposes that it will somehow be an engagement with the grittiness of a warts-and-all 'real life', and nothing to do with anything so idealistic – and unrealistic – as universal truths. Yet one can see the legacy of that doctrine in eighteenth- and nineteenth-century prose fiction – for example, all those happy, neat endings where truth, justice and/or love prevail (see THE NINETEENTH CENTURY AND THE VICTORIANS, FICTION).

Origins

However, the roots of a specifically literary notion of **realism** can be traced to the development of ideas during the eighteenth century derived from

Descartes and Locke. It was the work of the Scottish philosopher Thomas Reid, particularly his notion of 'common sense realism', that was to provide the strongest attraction to writers. Reid's position was quite literal: the world and the objects in it are real and our senses merely report that reality to our minds. In philosophical terms this is referred to as **materialism**, which is opposed to **idealism**. Here one can discern the origins of the naive realism I mentioned above. Following Reid, one reaches the presumption that by merely recording it, writing (or any other form of representation) can somehow produce an objective view of reality. Yet even the briefest intellectual reflection on the notion of common sense reveals all sorts of problems; common sense is really little more than the ideologically determined presumptions of a given group. So, rather than 'reality', one is really getting a construction of it. And this is the key point that forcibly reminds us that writing is artifice: art is a means of representation not reflection. To ignore the 'frame' or the means of representation, the medium – in this case writing – is to wilfully forget that literature is art and not a valueless conduit through which the 'real world' flows into the mind. It is all too easy to forget this, as Ian Watt observes: 'since almost everyone in all ages, has in one way or another been forced to some such conclusion about the external world by his own experience, literature has always been to some extent exposed to the same epistemological naïveté' (Watt 1957: 12). At the risk of labouring the point, writing does not provide a *reflection* of the world as if it were a mirror: writing shapes its material which is then further filtered by whatever preoccupations the writer consciously or unconsciously subjects it to, expressed through the characters and narrator of the text. Moreover, one can still see the **idealism** behind naive realism since it is based on the presumption that the 'real' or objective world is in some way universally meaningful. The assumed opposition between idealism and **materialism** is far from clear cut when one considers realism as a literary practice and form.

As students of literature we have to be acutely sensitive to these issues, but it is certainly true that writers and readers do produce and consume literary realism under this genuine or assumed naive outlook. That is of course a huge generalization, but to borrow a phrase more often associated with dramatic realism, one suspends disbelief to read realism on its own terms if reading for entertainment or even under the desire to be informed about an experience beyond your own. Literary critics, on the other hand, want to understand what's going on – how literary art works and what it means. So, in that spirit, among the constellation of new ideas and attitudes that would fuel the rise of the novel in the eighteenth century is another factor we need to consider in relation to realism: originality.

The question of 'originality'

As a general rule, literature prior to the eighteenth century was based on the creative repetition of traditional stories from **myth**, religion, folk tales, history or earlier literature, particularly that of the classical world of Greece and Rome.

A selection of Shakespeare's plays demonstrates the point: *King Lear* is based on legend, *Henry V* on history, and *Romeo and Juliet* on an existing story. A great artist like Shakespeare can produce strikingly original results even from unoriginal source material. Yet this is also another manifestation of the universalism associated with philosophical idealism that held sway until the eighteenth century: because certain experiences and ideas are true and universal for all time, the stories that transmit them, it was argued, are equally as timeless. But the rise of the novel shifts the balance of interest away from proving oneself against traditional sources and towards originality of experience. Moreover, as we saw above, it was an originality of experience through the senses shaped by **ideology** that point the way to one of the enduring features of realism: experience is historically and personally specific.

This emphasis on originality in these terms is an enduring feature of the novel, while the influence of the history of the genre both in terms of content and form in poetry and drama, for example, remain important. By contrast, an unoriginal novel is seen as flawed as a work of art. As Ian Watt concludes: 'What is often felt as the formlessness of the novel, as compared, say, with tragedy or the ode, probably follows from this: the poverty of the novel's formal conventions would seem to be the price it must pay for its realism' (1957: 13). The earliest exponent of modern literary realism is therefore Daniel Defoe in *Robinson Crusoe* (1719), a novel which pays little attention to traditional literary form, but shapes itself around what his character might plausibly do next after being marooned on a deserted island. The *representation* of experience (which is, of course, not the same as actual experience) shapes both the form and content of realism and of the novel. It is also significant that the main producers and consumers of literary realism in the novel during the eighteenth century were the very pragmatic commercial middle classes, who only rarely benefited from the type of classical education that sustained the insider knowledge needed to follow the older literary paradigm that valued traditional form and adaptations of well-known stories. In fact, an early novelist with aristocratic pretensions, Henry Fielding, tried to convince himself and his readers that they were reading anything but a novel. In the Preface to *Joseph Andrews* (1742) Fielding argues that what he has written is not a novel at all but a 'comic-epic' formed from the very best classical influences. Writers and readers would have to wait until the nineteenth century for realism – and the novel – to gain recognition and respectability as a legitimate form of artistic expression.

Nineteenth-century realism

For many readers it is nineteenth-century prose fiction that has shaped their perception of literary realism. One of Fielding's anxieties about the novel form of which he was such a successful early practitioner was the perception that it was vulgar and dealt with the baser human instincts, lower-class characters, and appealed as a result to a vulgar readership – the under-educated commercial middle classes. Indeed, despite Fielding's protestation, this was how his own productions were seen. As one correspondent of Fielding's rival Samuel Richardson claimed, *Joseph Andrews* 'will entertain none but Porters or Watermen'. Yet this reminds us that even at an early stage in the development of the form, the novel and realism held the promise of a great democratic literary art accessible to the widest possible readership, as Pam Morris observes: 'realism participates in the democratic impulse of modernity' (2003: 3). All that was required to access this art was the ability to read and the wherewithal to afford to buy or to subscribe to the books themselves. The nineteenth century, with innovations like serial publication and the increasingly inexpensive mass production of books, provided such access to an ever wider audience, and a nascent state education would see ever more people able and eager to read. For the first time, an art form had a genuinely mass market.

Yet the directions that realism took in the nineteenth century continued to be influenced by the dichotomy of its origins forged between **idealism** and **materialism**, which the Victorian poet Algernon Charles Swinburne distinguished as 'prosaic realism' (materialism) and 'poetic reality' (idealism) (Morris 2003: 4). The distinction is, of course, far from being so clear cut in practice, but one can see in the nineteenth-century realist novel a distinction between those like George Eliot's 'state of the nation' novel *Middlemarch* (1871) and the gritty urban realism of George Gissing's *The Nether World* (1889). The former has something of realism's roots in idealism and universalism at its heart, in which the specific experience of a limited range of characters in a small town is generalized into a commentary on the nation as a whole. Such social commentary is still apparent in Gissing's novel, but here it is formed into a scathing social commentary on the debasement of human nature as a consequence of poverty. Eliot's realism is a means to remind the reader of 'universal' moral benchmarks as a shared aspiration, whereas Gissing's novel suggests that human morality is rotten to the core, at least as soon as it becomes compromised by the material dictates of economic existence. Yet what brings both novels back together is that the consequences and experience of human society is traced through the perceptions and thoughts of individual characters. While realism might be accompanied by a narrator providing a commentary on both character and events, which might range in perceptibility from overtly critical and opinionated to subtle and self-effacing, literary realism invariably comes back to the individual.

Naturalism

However, the element of fatalism that can be detected in Gissing's novel leads us to another branch of realism that emerged in the nineteenth century. Gissing is influenced by the French writer Émile Zola, who is associated with a school of realism known as naturalism. In fact, never shy of self-promotion, Zola coined the term himself and the sub-variety of the **genre** was overtly influenced by an adaptation of scientific methodology founded on observation and experimentation. 'The novelist,' Zola argued, is both an observer and an experimenter. The observer in him presents the data as he has observed them. ... Then the experimenter appears and institutes the experiment, that is, sets the characters of a particular story in motion in order to show that the series of events therein will be those demanded by the determinism and of the phenomenon under study. (Becker 1963: 166)

Zola's claims to method bring to the fore a notion of realism that has been implicit in the form since its emergence in the eighteenth century. It is no accident that the eighteenth century saw not only the birth of the novel and realism, but also the popularization of modern scientific method following Newton and others, collectively understood as the Enlightenment. Realism as much as modern science emerges from this profound reformulation of human understanding of the material world.

Defoe's *Robinson Crusoe* conforms quite well to the structure Zola elaborates here: Crusoe is marooned on an island and learns to survive by a methodical exploration of and accommodation with his environment. The enticement to the reader is: 'How would I behave in such a situation?' Yet where Zola substantially differs from Defoe is in the scientific theory he is consciously referencing in his work. The clue lies in his reference to 'determinism'. In Zola's work and those writers influenced by him, like Gissing and Thomas Hardy, can be discerned the underlying influence of Charles Darwin's ideas on heredity and environment applied directly to human society. His characters behave as they do, not necessarily as individuals, but involuntarily in response to the fictional situation he creates for them. Of course, this is far from good science; a fictional plot can hardly be accepted as independent verification of the laws of hereditary and environment (Morris 2003: 71), but it makes for a powerful if rather depressing fiction.

Modernism and beyond

Yet naturalistic realism presents something of a problem for the representation of character. Since environment and situation determines behaviour, there is little left to do but feel sorry for the suffering characters; there is little enduring interest in the choices they make since their fate is inevitably circumscribed by their circumstances and environment. Moreover, the early twentieth century would see a sustained attack by a new generation of modernist authors, such as Virginia Woolf, on what was perceived as the rather hackneyed preoccupation with the surface of things by an earlier generation of realist writers such as Arnold Bennett and John Galsworthy. Woolf's essay 'Mr Bennett and Mrs Brown' (1924) famously attacks Bennett, claiming instead that the interest for the literary artist 'lies very likely in the dark places of psychology. ... Examine for a moment an ordinary mind on an ordinary day. The mind receives myriad impressions – trivial, fantastic, evanescent, or engraved with the sharpness of steel. From all sides they come, an incessant shower of innumerable atoms.' On the face of it, the lively and sometimes disturbing experimentation of modernist writers would indeed appear to be a resounding rejection of realist practices – as seen in modernist prose techniques such as **stream of consciousness**. Yet Woolf's claim to champion a satisfying break with literary continuity is not quite so clear cut as she thinks. Certainly, she argues powerfully for a change of point of view in the novel from contemplating character at a discrete narrative distance to inhabiting the interior of the character's mind and filtering perception and experience through their fictional consciousness. While this leads to a rejection of tired narrative techniques that were associated with realism in the nineteenth century, this obscures the fact that she is arguing for a new degree of realism based on a greater understanding of human psychology following the popularization of Sigmund Freud's ideas (see PSYCHOANALYSIS). Not unlike Zola's adaptation of scientific method and Darwinism, Woolf is arguing for a psychological realism and an expansion of realist literary technique to accommodate this in response to the new conceptual ground opened up by Freud.

Summary

As will have become clear by this point, realism has a remarkable capacity to adapt and adopt conceptual, political and scientific shifts in human perception and understanding, which in turn makes it a slippery concept to define exactly. This is not surprising: born alongside the novel in a historical moment which saw human comprehension of existence and experience change profoundly, realism remains the bedrock of modern prose fiction. Its popularity with both readers and writers is undiminished. Indeed, it is the departure point by which all prose innovation is measured, and it is such that it seems unlikely that the novel will ever do without it some form or fashion. When Watt refers to the 'formlessness of the novel', he is also referring to the peculiar formlessness – or better, adaptability – of realism. To return to Wallace Stevens's criticism of realism as a corruption of reality, it becomes part of the conceptual and psychological nexus by which we mediate our apprehension of reality and, as such, it is a literary **genre** that continues to attract and move us. As Henry James observed in the preface to *The Ambassadors*, 'the novel remains still, under the right persuasion, the most independent, most elastic, most prodigious of literary forms', as does the form of writing most closely associated with the novel: realism. The tension it sustains between idealism and materialism is the very stuff of Western society and its art.

Realism: sample syllabus

Week 1   Introduction: criticism and realism/critical realism – assessing the form
Week 2   The pre-history: adventures in early English prose
Week 3   Early masters (1): Daniel Defoe
Week 4   Early masters (2): Henry Fielding
Week 5   Questioning the form: *Tristram Shandy*

Week 6   Women novelists and the new literary form (1): Fanny Burney
Week 7   Women novelists and the new literary form (2): Jane Austen
Week 8   Charles Dickens and sensational realism
Week 9   Realism and naturalism
Week 10 Modernism and the new psychological realism
Week 11 Realism and the postmodern – magical realism
Week 12 Realism and the short story

Bibliography

(a) Literary works

Austen, Jane. *Mansfield Park*. Ed. Kathryn Sutherland. London: Penguin, 2003.

Defoe, Daniel. *Robinson Crusoe*. Ed. John Richetti. London: Penguin, 2004.

Dickens, Charles. *Bleak House*. Ed. Nicola Bradbury. London: Penguin, 2003.

Eliot, George. *Middlemarch*. Ed. Rosemary Ashton. London: Penguin, 2003.

Fielding, Henry. *Joseph Andrews and Shamela*. Ed. Judith Hawley. London: Penguin, 2003.

Forster, E. M. *Howards End*. Ed. David Lodge. London: Penguin, 2000.

Gissing, George. *The Nether World*. Ed. Stephen Gill. Oxford: Oxford University Press, 2008.

James, Henry. *What Maisie Knew*. Ed. Adrian Poole. Oxford: Oxford World's Classics, 2008.

Sterne, Laurence. *The Life and Opinions of Tristram Shandy*. Ed. Melvyn New. London: Penguin, 2003.

Woolf, Virginia. *Mrs Dalloway*. Ed. Elaine Showalter. London: Penguin, 2000.

(b) Further reading

Barrish, Phillip. *American Literary Realism, Critical Theory, and Intellectual Prestige*. Cambridge: Cambridge University Press, 2001.

Becker, George J. *Documents of Modern Literary Realism*. Princeton, NJ: Princeton University Press, 1963.

Grant, Damian. *Realism*. London: Methuen, 1970.

Kearns, Katharine. *Nineteenth-Century Literary Realism: Through the Looking Glass*. Cambridge: Cambridge University Press, 1996.

Morris, Pam. *Realism*. London: Routledge, 2003.

Villanueva, Dario. *Theories of Literary Realism*. New York: State University of New York Press, 1997.

Watt, Ian. *The Rise of the Novel: Studies in Defoe, Richardson, and Fielding*, Berkeley: University of California Press, 1957.

Fiction

(Year 2)

Lawrence Phillips

Truth in fiction

In 1889, while travelling in the South Pacific, the great adventure writer Robert Louis Stevenson visited the Gilbert Islands. Seeking permission of the ruler of one of the islands to visit his island kingdom (to which outside access was strictly controlled), the latter's judgement was 'I look your eye. You good man.

You no lie', of which Stevenson wryly comments, 'a doubtful compliment to a writer of romance'. So, is 'fiction' literally lying, a falsehood? Certainly, 'fiction' has been a sobriquet literary artists have been keen to avoid in the past. It is no accident that early novelists invariably claimed their writing to be 'true histories', no less. But why the anxiety, which is scarcely shared by the contemporary author or reader, although to the budding as well as the accomplished literary critic it is a question of some significance? Lying behind Stevenson's rather glib observation is a very old opposition between 'truth' and 'fiction'. The stories presented as fiction are not, of course, expected to be literally true. But in the realm of literature, a form of art, the enduring value of the work is that it does indeed impart some sort of 'truth'. It is worth pausing for a moment to think about what we mean by truth. There is a central tenet of philosophy hiding here which gives some hint of what is at stake for the writer, the reader and the literary critic. Perhaps one way of approaching the debate is to start with the notion that it is entirely different from 'fact'. A fact is, on the one hand, a piece of verifiable information or, on the other, the record of a material event – night follows day (or does it precede day?) or England won the World Cup in 1966. Fiction can encompass facts, of course, and transform them, but the truth to be found in fiction or in art more generally is about *meaning*. The significance of that meaning in a given work itself – although there is a hot debate to be had here – leads to notions of value. In one sense, it is part of the literary critic's role to debate the role of 'truth' in literature and, as such, it is a central focus of literary studies at university (see WHAT IS LITERATURE? and WHY STUDY LITERATURE?).

It is a debate as old as the entire notion of artistic interpretation. In his study of tragic drama, Aristotle reformulates artistic 'truth' as knowledge and perhaps the value of a thoughtful engagement with literature is a matter of the old adage, 'know thyself' or, looking outwards, 'know thy culture' and gain an insight into other experiences and cultures. This might mean being challenged, often uncomfortably, by a given text as its reading pushes the limits of your own knowledge and beliefs. There is a distinction to be drawn here, perhaps – although that gives an illusion of solidity to some pretty porous borders – between literary fiction as a form of art that challenges the reader, and popular fiction that plays safe within predictably mapped **genre** boundaries. However, before we feel too comfortable with that formulation, it is as well to recall Daniel Herwitz's deft articulation of the downside to such neat distinctions:

> Art is a mode of knowing, but this also means a signal of everything ideological in an age, a cipher for its prejudices, forms of arrogance, grandiosity, delusion. If art is an expression of human aspiration the aspiration has often been one of domination, control, repression, and art has played its role in those human disfigurements. (Herwitz: 2008 153)

Ideology, we might remind ourselves, is the principle – the 'truths' – which guide our understanding of society in the interests of its dominant groups. So, if art, and more specifically literary fiction, is potentially a collective delusion – a lie, to return us to Stevenson – where does that leave 'truth' in fiction? One could argue that in giving shape and contour, a form, to ideology, literary fiction exposes the shallowness of the ideological constructions of that which passes itself off as 'truth'. Such a debate doesn't end there, but if literary fiction cannot easily reveal truth, it can, at its best, rob the ideological straw men that masquerade as the truth of their false clothes. Perhaps the island king that Stevenson encountered was not so wide of the mark in his judgement of the writer of romance.

A matter of form?

Another way of approaching the conundrum of fiction is to ask whether it possesses any formal – as opposed to philosophical – qualities that could define it. Most references to fiction you will encounter as a student are, sadly, less about the understanding of truth in fiction we have discussed so far, but shorthand for a rather different thing – narrative fiction. In fact, so persuasive is this loose meaning of fiction that it subsumes just about any literary form in prose. However, such baggy monsters are invariably inaccurate, which demands a moment of reflection. Narrative is, simply put, the succession of one event by another.

Narrative fiction is, then, the relation of a succession of fictional events: although a text may reorder the telling of those events, it still relies on the original chronology. Such a definition takes us further than just prose, though. Any poem expressing a fictional narrative is also, by definition, narrative fiction, as are satires, dramatic dialogues and film, as well as other mixed media forms such as the comic book or graphic novel. In fact, narrative fiction does not necessarily need words at all – think of silent movies, mime, or a series of narrative paintings such as Hogarth's *The Rake's Progress*. Yet such is the strength of the commonplace use of the word 'fiction' to refer to narrative prose fiction, the word is rarely used in conjunction with work in these other media. Nonetheless, they are self-evidently narrative fictions. This is often tacitly recognized in university literature courses, where it is quite common to encounter film and other visual forms as part of the curriculum. You might even encounter opportunities to compare the same narrative fiction in different media, for example the original dramatic version of Shakespeare's *Hamlet* alongside film and graphic novel adaptations. Narrative poetry is all too often seen by students as part of that larger and exclusive category 'poetry', which forms the basis of many an examination neurosis. It also sets up an artificial and absolute distinction between prose and poetry around the question of fiction. Since narrative fiction can be articulated in poetry or prose, many of the same literary qualities will be present in both and thence receptive to the same critical probing.

Beyond these subtleties of **genre** within narrative fiction that can be obscured by the collapse of fiction as shorthand for narrative prose fiction, there is also the risk that one is cut off from the deeper question of the nature of fiction touched on above – but also another question of form. If in a very basic definition narrative is the relation of a succession of events, how secure is the distinction between fictional and non-fictional forms of narrative at the level of form? The answer is 'not very'. This then begs the question of how secure the distinction between fact and fiction might be. In recent years this has caused something of an upheaval in other disciplines, greatly extending the remit of Literary Studies even if this may not be immediately apparent on English courses that stick to variations of the literary **canon**. For example, the historian Hayden White concluded, in an exhaustive study of nineteenth-century narrative histories (1973), that the form and techniques of literary fiction, particularly the novel, strongly influenced how such histories were told, drawing upon plot techniques and methods of characterization that would have been familiar to Dickens and the Brontës. Some writers have quite deliberately and sometimes brilliantly exploited the intersection between fictional and non-fictional forms such that one can see the influence on both their 'factual' and 'fictional' writing. The great exemplar of this in English literature is George Orwell. Alongside 'factual' narrative such as *The Road to Wigan Pier* (1937) and *Down and Out in Paris and London* (1933) one can compare *Animal Farm* (1945) and *Nineteen Eighty-Four* (1949). It is no accident, perhaps, that the two fictional books have at their centre a preoccupation with textual truth: the pigs use **rhetoric** to distort the ideals of the farmyard revolt in the former, while Winston Smith is actively engaged with rewriting the past (often quite creatively) in the latter. Likewise few would argue that Orwell's non-fictional works are anything less than very finely written and share, technically and stylistically, many similarities with his fiction. What White points to not only challenges his fellow historians but raises an important issue for the literary critic: our techniques for analysing literary texts can be just as effective as a means to interpret texts that are identified as 'factual' but exhibit qualities of fine writing and/or narrative, which may encompass narrative history, political speeches, anthropological accounts, sociological narratives, journalism, advertisements, travel writing, diaries, biographies and autobiographies, etc. Fiction in turn, it should be noted, can borrow successfully from all or any of these forms and others. The *forms* of fiction are widely travelled or, as Thomas Pavel observes: 'Far from being well defined and sealed off, fictional borders appear to be variously accessible, sometimes easy to trespass, obeying different sorts of constraints in different contexts' (Pavel: 1983).

Perhaps we come back again to a question of 'truth', not at the level of content but at the level of form. Content or factual information require interpretation. The forms of narrative fiction can be adapted to add persuasiveness to any given interpretation. Literary fiction appears to do much the same thing, but whereas literary fiction may or may not deal with verifiable facts – it often does and when it does it is often called mimetic (from the Greek word *mimesis*)

– it is certainly trying to get at the truth of something. While factual writing may be trying to convince you that a certain argument or interpretation is the truth, literary fiction by its nature is trying to interrogate the very nature of the truths we adhere to.

Summary

Fiction in literary terms is both the gateway to fundamental questions about the nature of art and literature, but also something of a trap or a misnomer. The very term raises key questions about truth and literature, but can just as easily be passively accepted as a category limited to narrative prose fiction, or the criteria for the arrangement of books in your favourite bookshop or library. It is a category that is intensely familiar and rarely questioned, but one that cannot be passed over by the literary critic. So what does fiction do? At its best – and when it is at its best we can rightly refer to it as literature – it does what all great art aspires to: it makes us think.

Fiction: sample syllabus

Week 1   Introduction – art, fiction and truth
Week 2   Fiction and the self (1): James Joyce, *A Portrait of the Artist as a Young Man*
Week 3   Fiction and the self (2): Henry David Thoreau, *Walden*
Week 4   Formal interrogations: Laurence Sterne, *Tristram Shandy*
Week 5   History and fiction: Daniel Defoe, *A Journal of the Plague Year*
Week 6   Fiction and history: Graham Swift, *Waterland*
Week 7   Fiction and the question of objectivity: George Orwell, *The Road to Wigan Pier* and *Nineteen Eighty-Four*
Week 8   Adventures in genre (1): the Arthur legend part 1 – Sir Thomas Malory, *Le Morte d'Arthur*; Mark Twain, *A Connecticut Yankee in King Arthur's Court*
Week 9   Adventures in genre (2): the Arthur legend part 2 – *The Sword in the Stone* (1963; dir. Wolfgang Reitherman); *Excalibur* (1981; dir. John Boorman)
Week 10 Adventures in genre (3): *The Tempest* part 1 – William Shakespeare, *The Tempest*; Paul Duffield, William Shakespeare and Richard Appignanesi, *Manga Shakespeare: The Tempest*
Week 11 Adventures in genre (4): *The Tempest* part 2 – *Forbidden Planet* (1956; dir. Fred McLeod Wilcox); *Prospero's Books* (1991; dir Peter Greenaway)
Week 12 The epic tradition in poetic fiction: Homer, *The Iliad*; Derek Walcott, *Omeros*

Bibliography

(a) Literary works

Defoe, Daniel. *A Journal of the Plague Year*. Ed. Anthony Burgess. London: Penguin, 2003.

Homer. *The Iliad*. Ed. E. V. Rieu. London Penguin, 2003.

Joyce, James. *The Portrait of the Artist as a Young Man*. Ed. Seamus Deane. London: Penguin, 2003.

Malory, Sir Thomas. *Le Morte d'Arthur*. Ed. Stephen H. A. Shepherd. New York: W. W. Norton, 2003.

Orwell, George. *The Road to Wigan Pier*. Ed. Richard Hoggart. London: Penguin, 2001.

Sterne, Laurence. *The Life and Opinions of Tristram Shandy*. Ed. Melvyn New. London: Penguin, 2003.

Swift, Graham. *Waterland*. London: Picador, 2008.

Thoreau, Henry. *David Walden*. Ed. Stephen Allen Fender. Oxford: Oxford University Press, 2008.

Twain, Mark. *A Connecticut Yankee in King Arthur's Court*. Ed. Dan Beard and Justin Kaplan. London: Penguin, 2007.

Walcott, Derek. *Omeros*. London: Faber and Faber, 2002.

(b) Further reading

Gelder, Ken. *Popular Fiction: The Logics and Practices of a Literary Field*. London and New York: Routledge, 2005.

Lewis, David. 'Truth in Fiction'. *American Philosophical Review*, 15.1 (January 1978): 37–46.

Lodge, David. *The Art of Fiction*. London: Penguin, 1994.

McHale, Brian. *Postmodernist Fiction*. London: Routledge, 1987.

Riffaterre, Michael. *Fictional Truth*. Baltimore, MD: Johns Hopkins University Press, 1990.

Rimmon-Kenan, Shlomith. *Narrative Fiction: Contemporary Poetics*. London and New York: Routledge, 2002.

Sheppard, Anne. *Aesthetics: An Introduction to the Philosophy of Art*. Oxford: Oxford University Press, 1987.

Waugh, Patricia. *Metafiction: The Theory and Practice of Self-Conscious Fiction*. London: Methuen, 1984.

White, Hayden. *Metahistory: The Historical Imagination in Nineteenth-Century Europe*. Baltimore, MD: Johns Hopkins University Press, 1973.

Postmodern fiction

(Year 3)

Alex Murray

Postmodernism

The literature that came to typify the 1980s can be read as an attack on the very idea of authenticity, originality and experience. The term 'postmodernism' has now come to stand as a synecdoche for these fictions, and I will deploy it here as a descriptive category despite having extreme reservations over precisely what it means. The most notable writers of this new generation were Martin Amis, Salman Rushdie, Graham Swift, Julian Barnes, Angela Carter and Peter Ackroyd. Many may argue that postmodernism peaked in the 1960s and 1970s with the publication of the great American postmodern novels, such as Kurt Vonnegut's *Slaughterhouse Five* (1969) or Thomas Pynchon's *Gravity's Rainbow* (1973), but it is arguably not until a literary trend has filtered down through a literary culture that it truly exists, and I would suggest that in England it was a slightly later development, and that it didn't hit its apotheosis until the period between 1983 with the popular postmodernism of Graham Swift's *Waterland* and 1988/9, when the publication of Salman Rushdie's *The Satanic Verses* and the ensuing controversy marked a very public clash between the deconstructive relativism of the postmodern and a broader global culture.

Defining the literary qualities of postmodernism is notoriously difficult, but one could summarize them as an ironic tone; black humour; narrative experimentation (of varying degrees); a tendency towards creating pastiches of other **genres** and texts; the denial of originality; metafiction; radical historiography; paranoia. While it is impossible to go into any or all of these features in depth here, it may be of use to suggest textual examples. **Irony** is perhaps the master **trope** of the postmodern: in a world of pure relativism, how can one take anything seriously? The answer of course was not to. Perhaps one could turn to Martin Amis's novel *London Fields* (1989), where the narrator, Samson Young, seeks to document the self-willed murder of Nicola Six as a cure to writer's block. The relativism of his morality, as well as that of other characters in the novel, is used by Amis to ironically question the contemporary malaise, as well as the source of much dark humour. Many novels of this period utilize dramatic narrative experimentation, and in so doing call into question our reliance on coherent narratives as organizational practices. An example here could be Rushdie's *The Satanic Verses*, where a number of parallel narratives run alongside one another, blending forms of realism with the fantastical, and creating a form known as magical realism, which challenges readers to piece together a coherence to the differing narrative strands.

The postmodern novel also revels in pastiche and appropriation of **canonical** texts, as well as other cultural forms, in order to call into question notions of cultural value, along with denying the possibility of originality. There are many examples, including Peter Ackroyd's novel *Chatterton* (1987), where the eponymous poet's infamous literary forgeries are utilized as a paradigm for the essentially parasitic and derivative nature of textual production. The questioning of literary authority and originality is often coupled with a self-reflexive interrogation of the nature of literary production A famous case in point is Italo Calvino's *If on a Winter's Night a Traveller* (1979), where the novel revolves around a character's experience of reading a book that shares the same name as the novel. The gesture here is a wonderful example of metafiction, where the writer places attention on the very act of reading in order to explore the nature of textual consumption in relation to literary production. This reflection on the nature of fiction is part of a larger interrogation of the ways in which reading relates to broader practices of cultural knowledge. This questioning of our perceptions is also a feature of historiographic fiction, that sub-genre which utilizes the novel as a space for casting light upon the constructed nature of history. Graham Swift's *Waterland* (1983) is a classic example of this literary form, where the suggestion that history is a matter of storytelling unites the historical and the fictional as a means of making sense of the past, calling into question the idea that history can ever be empirical, and that its narratives should carry any more weight than those of literature. Swift's novel also asks us to consider the nature of the future, and the extent to which we still believe in universal progress: 'There's this thing called progress. But it doesn't progress. It doesn't go anywhere' (Swift 2008: 291).

Jean-Francois Lyotard famously diagnosed this postmodern **trope** as 'incredulity towards meta-narratives' (xxiv). The calling into question of our ways of making sense of both the past and the future can often lead to a degree of paranoia invading the postmodern novel. If our realities are seen to be constructed and representational, it can be assumed that these realities are the work of governments and corporations. This fear of covert power can be seen in a range of postmodern novels, particularly the work of Thomas Pynchon.

The contemporary in the wake of postmodernism

The prevalence of postmodern themes and styles continued into the 1990s, but it soon became apparent that the fictional landscape was altering. Whereas the postmodern novel called into question the values of authenticity and sincerity, the fiction of the 1990s began to reinstate them, largely through concerns of identity politics. The 1990s also saw a move away from experimentalism and a return to forms of realism in many 'literary' texts. In a sense it is difficult to fully characterize the nature of the fiction that followed postmodernism. This is due in part to a diffusion of styles and approaches, but also to an increasing blurring between 'popular' and 'literary' fiction (see POPULAR FICTION, FICTION). In addition to these problems is the near proximity of these fictional tendencies, whereby we remain uncertain if we have entered into a new cultural and fictional landscape, or if we remain in that bequeathed to us by the 1990s.

The questioning of hegemonic forms of authority and narrative in the postmodern novel dovetailed with fictions that wished to explore the nature of marginalized forms of identity. These include racial minorities, those of a non-heterosexual orientation, those displaced and culturally altered through colonialism and the concerns of particular subcultures. The 1990s, in particular the late 1990s, saw the rise of these modes of fiction with novels such as Arundhati Roy's *The God of Small Things* (1997), Ahdaf Soueif's *The Map of Love* (1999) and Monica Ali's *Brick Lane* (2003), representing the rise of a second-wave and arguably more populist postcolonial fiction, with non-English-born writers who were often educated in an English system writing about forms of cultural dislocation experienced as the margins of those colonial empires moved back to the centre. Undoubtedly the most important book in this **genre** of postcolonial fiction was Zadie Smith's phenomenally successful *White Teeth* (2000). This novel remains the centre of 'contemporary' British fiction, lauded for having its finger squarely on the cultural zeitgeist (see CONTEMPORARY LITERATURE). Its plot revolves around two families, the Iqbals and the Joneses, and their experiences of postwar life in north London. Spanning two generations and some 45 years, the novel, almost Dickensian in scope, manages to capture the cultural shifts and developments in postwar Britain with both humour and sensitivity. Its focus on the fluidity of identity, parodic tone, ambivalent ending and concentration on what can be defined as 'the new Britain' cemented its place in the modern **canon**.

There has been an argument made recently by Philip Tew (2007: 194–7) that the world of optimism that characterized this image of a new Britain in *White Teeth* has come to seem, if not inaccurate, then certainly questionable in the cultural climate that followed the bombing of the World Trade Center on 11 September 2001 and the following 'war on terror'. There has certainly been a shift in the tone of cultural production, with many novelists displaying a far darker and more pessimistic view of our contemporary world. Simultaneously there has also been a move towards the spiritual as a space in which some form of redemption is possible. Where fluidity of cultural identity once seemed the site for an affirmative politics of multiculturalism, it now appears as a site of contestation and potential disaster. The style that characterizes contemporary fiction has moved further away from experimentalism and the fantastical, becoming more realistic and descriptive in form.

The writer who currently stands at the centre of British fiction is Ian McEwan. While McEwan has been publishing short stories and novels since the 1970s, it was only really with the publication of *Enduring Love* (1997) that he became well known; and with *Amsterdam* winning the Booker Prize in 1998, he cemented his place at the forefront of British letters. Since then, novels such as *Atonement* (2001) and *Saturday* (2005) have increased his popularity, with his form of reserved and descriptive prose, and his focus on dark and troubling events, raising ethical questions in an accessible fashion. Similarly, the work of J. M. Coetzee has come to figure heavily in our under-standing of contemporary fiction, sharing some similarities with McEwan, as does the work of Jim Crace, whose sparse prose and excessively descriptive narratives mark out an investigation of the **materiality** of existence without denying the potential for some form of redemption.

Beyond these writers there have been few new voices to emerge in recent years in the same way that Smith did at the turn of the millennium. This has lead to the impression that contemporary fiction has hit a wall, that it is in a state of exhaustion. Yet these claims seem inevitable in a culture that has its gaze fixed firmly towards the past, constantly feeling the need to measure ourselves against the great innovators of modernism and even postmodernism, rather than to turn our attention towards fiction to come.

Postmodern fiction: sample syllabus

Week 1 Introduction to theories of the postmodern: Lyotard, Jameson, Hutcheon
Week 2 John Fowles, *The French Lieutenant's Woman*
Week 3 Salman Rushdie, *Midnight's Children*
Week 4 J. M. Coetzee, *Waiting for the Barbarians*
Week 5 Graham Swift, *Waterland*
Week 6 Jeannette Winterson, *Sexing the Cherry*
Week 7 Zadie Smith, *White Teeth*
Week 8 Ian McEwan, *Saturday*
Week 9 Yan Martel, *The Life of Pi*
Week 10 Kazuo Ishiguro, *Never Let Me Go*

Week 11 The current Booker Prize winner

Week 12 Conclusion: reflections on the postmodern and the contemporary

Bibliography

(a) Literary works

Coetzee, J. M. *Waiting for the Barbarians*. London: Vintage, 2004.

Fowles, John. *The French Lieutenant's Woman*. London: Vintage, 2004.

Ishiguro, Kazuo. *Never Let Me Go*. London: Faber and Faber, 2006.

Martel, Yan. *The Life of Pi*. Edinburgh: Canongate, 2003.

McEwan, Ian. *Saturday*. London: Vintage, 2006.

Rushdie, Salman. *Midnight's Children*. London: Vintage, 2008.

Smith, Zadie. *White Teeth*. London: Penguin, 2001.

Swift, Graham. *Waterland*. London: Picador, 2008.

Winterson, Jeannette. *Sexing the Cherry*. London: Vintage, 1990.

(b) Further reading

Connor, Steven, ed. *The Cambridge Companion to Postmodernism*. Cambridge: Cambridge University Press, 2004.

Currie, Mark, ed. *Metafiction*. London: Longman, 1995.

Gasiorek, Andrej. *Post-war British Fiction: Realism and After*. London: Arnold, 1995.

Head, Dominic. *The Cambridge Introduction to Modern Fiction, 1950–2000*. Cambridge: Cambridge University Press, 2002.

Hutcheon, Linda. *A Poetics of Postmodernism: History, Theory, Fiction*. New York: Routledge, 1988.

Lane, Richard, Rod Mengham and Philip Tew, eds. *Contemporary British Fiction*. London: Polity, 2003.

Lee, Alison. *Realism and Power: Postmodern British Fiction*. London: Routledge, 1990.

Mengham, Rod. *An Introduction to Contemporary Fiction: International Writing in English since 1970*. Cambridge: Polity Press, 1999.

Nicol, Brian, ed. *Postmodernism and the Contemporary Novel: A Reader*. Edinburgh: Edinburgh University Press, 2002.

Taylor, D. J. *A Vain Conceit: British Fictions in the 1980s*. London: Bloomsbury, 1989.

Wells, Lynn. *Allegories of Telling: Self-Referential Narrative in Contemporary British Fiction*. Amsterdam: Rodopi, 2003.

Gender

(Year 2)

Doris Bremm

If somebody asked you, 'What is your sex?', you might answer 'I am male' or 'I am female', or you might say, 'I am a man' or 'I am a woman'. Would your answer change if the question were, 'What is your gender?'? As a student of gender you will critique the concept of **gender** as it is commonly conceived. You will start by changing your notion of gender to include not only the biological concept of sex, but also the way somebody dresses, how they speak, what they do in their free time, and what they do for a living. Questions you will encounter in this field are concerned with how gender is understood, constructed, represented and imagined in a given culture and time. Besides discussing genders separately, you will also analyse the relationships between genders. This interdisciplinary field intersects with other areas such as sociology, anthropology, philosophy, psychology, history and politics as well as literary and cultural studies.

What is gender?

Consider the opening lines of Jeffrey Eugenides' novel *Middlesex*: 'I was born twice: first, as a baby girl, on a remarkably smogless Detroit day in January of 1960; and then again, as a teenage boy, in an emergency room near Petoskey, Michigan, in August of 1974' (2002: 1). The example of the novel's protagonist, Calliope or Cal, illustrates the issue at the heart of gender studies. Born a hermaphrodite, it seems that s/he is neither male or female, or both at the same time. So what is gender? Is there such a thing as natural or innate gender? And what is the difference between sex and gender? These questions will be addressed in introductory courses that analyse the social creation as well as cultural representations of gender.

Furthermore, in such a course you will question if there are 'natural' or 'normal' associations between concepts such as men/masculine and women/feminine. Gender critics usually define 'sex' as a biological term, and 'gender' as a social and psychological term. Thus, one is male or female in biological terms, but masculine and/or feminine in social and cultural terms. Gender critics reject the notion that gender is inherent; they do not see it as something we are born with but as something we learn. Significantly, they use gender not just as a noun but also as a verb: 'to gender'. Judith Butler even talks about the processes of 'boying' and 'girling'. This idea is not entirely new, since as early as 1949 French philosopher Simone de Beauvoir wrote in *The Second Sex*: 'one is not born, but rather becomes a woman' (1988: 267).

Gender criticism vs. feminist and lesbian & gay criticism

Gender criticism views gender as a social and cultural construct, unlike feminist theorist and gay and lesbian critics who look at gender and sexuality respectively as innate and natural (see FEMINISM). Whereas gender critics can be called *constructionist* because they see gender and sexuality as social and cultural constructs, feminist critics can be regarded as *essentialists* because they believe that women are inherently different from men. The same can be said about many lesbian and gay critics who see homo- and heterosexuality as something that is innate. While gender criticism draws heavily on feminist theory, it rejects some of it, such as the concept of gender as something that is innate, and commonly held beliefs among feminists such as the existence of a specific in the way women write (*écriture feminine*). Whereas feminist criticism looks at men and women as fundamentally different, gender criticism focuses on critiquing the very categories of gender.

Constructionist gender critics disagree fundamentally with French feminists critics who insist on a specific female way of writing. Peggy Kamuf posits in 'Writing like a Woman' (1980) that it is possible for a man to write like a woman and for a woman to write like a man. Whereas feminist critics believe in the existence of a specifically female way of writing, some lesbian and gay critics explore the way a woman *reads*. In *On Lies, Secrets, and Silence* (1979), Adrienne Rich reads Emily Dickinson's poetry as a lesbian, a method that reveals a very different poet than that illustrated in readings of heterosexual critics.

In her seminal study *Gender Trouble* (1990), Judith Butler takes the distinction of constative and performative language from J. L. Austin's speech act theory and applies it to gender. In 'Imitation and Gender Insubordination' she writes, '[g]ender is not a performance that a prior subject elects to do, but gender is performative … It is a compulsory performance in the sense that acting out of line with heterosexual norms brings with it ostracism, punishment, and violence, not to mention the transgressive pleasures produced by those very prohibitions' (1991: 23–4).

Gender and (homo)sexuality

Another influential text is Michel Foucault's *The History of Sexuality* (1990). Although he is generally associated with the critical school known as new historicism, Foucault's study of the distinction between heterosexuality and homosexuality is significant for gender studies in that it discusses sexuality as a continuum rather than a **binary opposition**. For Foucault, sexuality encompasses a range of behaviours including sadomasochism and bestiality. He historicizes sexuality and argues that homosexuality is an invention of the nineteenth century. Before that time people would talk of a sodomite as someone who commits an isolated act. However, the word 'homosexual' doesn't signify an act but a person.

Lesbian and gay studies focus on the textual representations of issues of homo- and heterosexuality. Eve Kosofsky Sedgwick's *Between Men: English Literature and Male Homosocial Desire* (1985) was an important step for feminist theory that is primarily interested in foregrounding women writers, representations of women, and a specific female way of writing (*écriture feminine*). She adapts feminist theory to look at relationships between male characters in novels as well as between men in general based on gender and sexuality. It is a study of men's same-sex bonds in nineteenth-century English literature and the oppressive effects on women and their relationships to men. Lesbian and gay studies engage in readings of the textual representations of issues of homo- and heterosexuality.

In the context of film, Teresa de Lauretis's *Technologies of Gender: Essays on Theory, Film, and Fiction* (1989) offers important insights. As a constructionist gender critic she argues that gender is 'the product of various social technologies, such as cinema,' and not 'a property of bodies or something originally existent in human beings' (1989: 2). For de Lauretis one of the 'social technologies' most influential in (re)constructing gender is film (see FILM STUDIES). Other film critics such as Laura Mulvey also critique the representation of women as spectacle in film. In her influential essay 'Visual Pleasure and Narrative Cinema' (1975), Mulvey introduces the concept of the 'male gaze' in film and discusses the way women are presented as passive objects to be looked at rather than as active **agents**.

Possible courses

So what might a course on gender encompass? Gender might be taught in a wide variety of courses. At one end of the spectrum, there could be courses focusing entirely on theory. Other courses might focus primarily on texts and how they construct, perpetuate, question or challenge gender roles. Most courses will offer a combination of both theory and texts. You will read different genres from different time periods and different geographical areas. Possible texts are not limited to what is generally included under 'literature' such prose, lyric or drama, but can include film, media and other art forms.

The fact that gender studies is a very interdisciplinary field will also be reflected in your courses on gender. Possible topics may include romantic love and marriage, sexuality, parenthood, violence, the scientific study of sexual differences, body image, as well as popular culture, sexual division of labour and economic development, and feminist movements. As a critic of gender you might ask the following questions about any given text: How does this text construct cultural notions of femininity, masculinity, motherhood, romantic love or marriage? How do genders or sexual orientations intersect with social status or ethnicity or national identity?

Often courses in gender modules might look at the work of female authors from a specific time period and geographical area such as 'African-American women writers' or 'Victorian women writers'. Other courses might focus on female characters in fiction such as 'Women in literature: lesbian fictions'. Another possibility would be a concentration on relationships between the genders in families or society in general. However, concentrating on women and the way they are represented is just one side of gender studies. Other courses might specifically focus on male characters within novels or how masculinities are constructed within a given text. Relationships between men are also of interest whether within a homosocial or homosexual **context**. Other potential courses might look at certain life stages such as boyhood or girlhood as well as mother and father roles.

Let us consider the example of Charlotte Brontë's *Jane Eyre* (1847). Brontë's novel is both a Cinderella story and a gothic tale. It would fit any number of classes within a gender module such as a class on British women writers, or a class that focuses specifically on Victorian women writers (see THE

NINETEENTH CENTURY AND THE VICTORIANS). Such a course might have a general gender studies approach or a more specific point of interest. Two general approaches would be to look at Brontë's novel as a work *by* a woman or as a work *about* a woman. Within the latter possibility, the course might focus on female characters and the specific female roles they personify or work against: Bertha Rochester (wife, madwoman), Blanche Ingram (lady, possible wife), Adèle (daughter, ward), Jane (orphan, governess, bride). Another course might take the novel as an example of *écriture féminine* and analyse the specific 'female' attributes of Brontë's prose. Yet another class might look at it as an example of the madwoman in the attic after Sandra M. Gilbert and Susan Gubar's *The Madwoman in the Attic: The Woman Writer and the Nineteenth-Century Literary Imagination* (1979), in which they examine the notion that the restrictive gender categories of the nineteenth century imposed on female writers are reflected in the metaphors of anger and madness in their heroines.

Jane can be read as a feminist character because she refuses to marry St. John Rivers and only marries Rochester when she is convinced they will be equals. Early on in the novel Jane points out her belief in the equality of the sexes:

> Women are supposed to be very calm generally: but women feel just as men feel; they need exercise for their faculties, and a field for their efforts as much as their brothers do; they suffer from too rigid a restraint, too absolute a stagnation, precisely as men would suffer; and it is narrow-minded in their more privileged fellow-creatures to say that they ought to confine themselves to making puddings and knitting stockings, to playing on the piano and embroidering bags. It is thoughtless to condemn them, or laugh at them, if they seek to do more or learn more than custom has pronounced necessary for their sex. (1971: 96)

A gender critic would focus on this passage to analyse gender and the social hierarchy of the novel. Jane criticizes gender roles when she points out that it is wrong to think that women 'ought to confine themselves to making puddings and knitting stockings'. Even though she is educated, as an orphan her opportunities are very limited and her only option to support herself is to work as a governess. Her inferior social status makes her doubt a possible marriage with Rochester. The gender relations within the novel are informed by the patriarchal society it is set within. Throughout the novel Jane tries to assert her identity in a society dominated by men, while the male characters such as Mr Brocklehurst, Edward Rochester and St. John Rivers try to keep Jane in a subordinate position. Their masculinity is defined largely through their power over the female characters. In general, one could argue that the novel reflects nineteenth-century gender roles and that Brontë works against Victorian gender stereotypes of women at the same time. When Jane tells her audience in the final chapter, 'Reader, I married him', the question remains whether she has finally found an equal partner, or whether she fails as she succumbs to society's pressures (395).

Another focus for an analysis of Brontë's novel could be sexualities/sexuality. A critic approaching the novel from a queer theory point of view might propose that Jane's close friendship with Helen Burns has lesbian overtones because of Jane's adoration of her profound Christianity (see GAY STUDIES AND QUEER THEORY). Jane's years at the orphanage would also be interesting for a course focusing on girlhood in Victorian England.

Yet another approach would be to look at the novel from an ecofeminist perspective, examining the relationship of women and nature in the novel (see ECOCRITICISM). The opening lines of the novel introduce the parallel between nature/freedom and culture/confinement: 'There was no possibility of taking a walk that day' (5). In this story of enclosure and escape, Jane moves from one state of confinement to the other. Interestingly enough, Jane meets Rochester for the first time not at his home Thornfield, but while she is outside walking to the next town to deliver a letter to the post office (ch. 12).

From a postcolonial point of view, Bertha Rochester's character would be especially interesting. In this **context**, Brontë's novel might be paired with Jean Rhys's prequel, *Wide Sargasso Sea* (1966), which tells the story of how Bertha meets Rochester. Rhys calls her Antoinette Cosway and has Rochester rename her as a sign of colonial power. Through her rewriting of the master narrative, Rhys gives Bertha and thus the colonial subject the voice she is denied in Brontë's text (see COLONIAL AND POSTCOLONIAL LITERATURE).

As has been briefly demonstrated, there are a range of possible approaches that feminist criticism, in its diversity, makes possible.

Gender: sample syllabus

All readings for a module such as this would be drawn from two volumes, listed below; due to the constraints of space in the present volume, only author names can be supplied, and the reader is referred to those volumes for the pertinent articles.

Susan M. Shaw and Janet Lee, eds. *Women's Voices, Feminist Visions*. Columbus, OH: McGraw-Hill, 2001.

Estelle B. Freedman, ed. *The Essential Feminist Reader*. New York: Modern Library, 2007.

Week 1   Introduction: Baumgardner and Richards; hooks; Quindlen; Frye; Hogeland
Week 2   Gender, race and sexuality in the media & early theories of gender difference: screening of *My Feminism*; Douglas and Orenstein; Kilbourne; Wollstonecraft; Mill; de Beauvoir
Week 3   History of the women's movement – the first wave: Grimké; Cady Stanton; Truth; Cooper; Anthony
Week 4   History of the women's movement – the second wave: Baxandall and Gordon; Friedan; Murray
Week 5   Feminism, race and intersectional analysis: Combahee River Collective Statement; Lorde; Anzaldúa; McIntosh; Rich
Week 6   Gender socialization and gender difference: Fausto-Sterling; Lorber; Chodorow
Week 7   LGBT politics and movements: Pharr; Greenaway; 'World Report 2002: Lesbian, Gay, Bisexual, and Transgender Rights'; Deihl and Ochs
Week 8   Feminist issues and activism around the world: Freedman; Neuwirth; UN, 'Convention on the Elimination of All Forms of Discrimination Against Women'; UN,

'Fourth World Conference on Women'; Revolutionary Association of the Women of Afghanistan

Week 9 Masculinity: Connell; Kimmel; Schacht; St. John

Week 10 Sex and sexuality: Schwartz and Rutter; hooks; Ilkkaracan; Meengleshi

Week 11 Reproductive rights and abortion: Sanger; Silliman et al.; Cooney

Week 12 Work, economics and employment: Hesse-Biber; Ehrenreich; Hawkes; Burk, Hays

Bibliography

Because this module is designed to focus on theories and discussions of gender, literary works and critical texts are combined here. Therefore the bibliography is limited to the critical reading.

(a) Key texts

de Beauvoir, Simone. *The Second Sex*. Trans. and ed. H. M. Parshley. London: Pan, 1988.

Brontë, Charlotte. *Jane Eyre*. New York: Norton, 1971.

Butler, Judith. 'Imitation and Gender Insubordination'. In *Inside/Out*, ed. Diana Fuss, 13–31. New York: Routledge, 1991.

Eugenides, Jeffrey. *Middlesex*. New York: Farrar, Straus and Giroux, 2002.

Foucault, Michel. *The History of Sexuality*. Trans. Robert Hurley. New York: Vintage Books, 1990.

Gilbert, Sandra M. and Susan Gubar. *The Madwoman in the Attic: The Woman Writer and the Nineteenth-Century Literary Imagination*. New Haven, CT: Yale University Press, 1979.

Kamuf, Peggy. 'Writing Like a Woman'. In *Woman and Language in Literature and Society*, ed. S. McConnell-Ginet et al., 284–99. New York: Praeger, 1980.

de Lauretis, Teresa. *Technologies of Gender: Essays on Theory, Film, and Fiction*. Basingstoke: Macmillan, 1989.

Mulvey, Laura. 'Visual Pleasure and Narrative Cinema'. *Screen*, 16(3) (1975): 6–18.

Rhys, Jean. *Wide Sargasso Sea*. New York: Norton, 1999.

Rich, Adrienne. *On Lies, Secrets, and Silence: Selected Prose, 1966–1978*. New York: Norton, 1979.

Sedgwick, Eve Kosofsky. *Between Men: English Literature and Male Homosocial Desire*. New York: Columbia University Press, 1985.

Voices of the Shuttle <http://vos.ucsb.edu/browse.asp?id=2711>

(b) Further reading

Butler, Judith. *Gender Trouble: Feminism and the Subversion of Identity*. New York: Routledge, 1990.

Chodorow, Nancy J. *Feminism and Psychoanalytic Theory*. Cambridge: Polity, 1989.

Cixous, Héléne. *The Héléne Cixous Reader*. Ed. Susan Sellers. London: Routledge, 1994.

Friedan, Betty. *The Feminine Mystique.* Harmondsworth: Penguin, 1991.

Greer, Germaine. *The Female Eunuch.* London: MacGibbon & Kee, 1970.

hooks, bell. *Feminist Theory from Margin to Center*. Boston, MA: South End Press, 1984.

Kristeva, Julia. *The Kristeva Reader*. Ed. Toril Moi. Oxford: Blackwell, 1986.

Mulvey, Laura. *Visual and Other Pleasures*. Basingstoke: Macmillan, 1989.

Sedgwick, Eve Kosofsky. *Epistemology of the Closet*. Berkeley: University of California Press, 1990.

Defining 'class'

Class governs writing and interpretation in complex ways – indeed for centuries it determined whether someone could read or write at all. The study of literature and class is typically associated with Marxist criticism, though it is not confined to it. For good examples, see Adorno, Bourdieu, Day, Eagleton, Marx.

Tracing the meaning of 'class', Raymond Williams notes that it entered English from the Latin, *classis*, 'a division according to the property of the people of Rome' (Williams 1963: 60). Used initially in a learned elite's discussions of Roman history, 'class' spread to encompass ecclesiastical organization and then a 'division or group' of plants or animals. This usage does not convey merit; it merely identifies. Hence 'students belong to the class of 2009'.

During the Industrial Revolution, 'class' acquired social implications. People still spoke of 'rank', 'order', 'estate' or 'degree', but 'class' categorized and *judged* individuals. The shift was caused by an 'increasing consciousness that social position is made rather than merely inherited' (Williams 1963: 61). The complexities surrounding 'working class', 'middle class' and 'upper class' are considerable, as are questions of identity raised by belonging to a class or moving to another. Karl Marx and Friedrich Engels' theories emerged from the world of these labels and assumptions, and their vocabulary articulates the tensions they observed (see MARXISM). Rather than pursuing their ideas, however, we will turn to some literary and critical implications of class structures.

Literature and class

'Class' only began to acquire its modern connotations in the late eighteenth century, so it is anachronistic to apply it to earlier literature. Nevertheless, social hierarchy shapes older texts in striking ways. Chaucer's *The Canterbury Tales* (begun *c.*1387) emerged from a society that distinguished between the 'estates' of clergy and the laity, further dividing the latter on feudal lines with nobles at the top and peasants at the bottom (see Mann 1973; Day 2001). Elevated pilgrims – the Knight, for instance – tell serious tales, while 'commoners' such as the Miller and the Wife of Bath narrate racier stories of sexual farce (see MEDIEVAL LITERATURE).

Elizabethan and Jacobean drama was performed before audiences of diverse literacy levels and social privilege, and playwrights often allowed great and humble, e.g. Hamlet and the gravedigger, to converse. Nevertheless, most characters know their place. They may transcend it in comedies, but attempts to do so in tragedies or histories usually involve skulduggery and end in tears. Fixed positions are reinforced by theatrical convention dictating that common people – soldiers, servants and clowns (i.e., country folk as well as comedians) – speak prose, whereas kings, bishops and nobles speak blank verse. Blank verse dramatizes higher emotions or displays of wit, while prose is the vehicle for comedy, often coarse in style (think of the porter in Shakespeare's *Macbeth* [1606]).

Social status may influence subject matter, but this is rarely straightforward, not least because the steady rise of the middle class from the 1750s disrupted the traditional pairing of class with money. William Wordsworth was a 'gentleman' educated at Cambridge University, but the 1802 preface to his *Lyrical Ballads* insists that poetry should 'choose incidents and situations from common life' and present them, if possible, 'in a selection of language really used by men' (Wordsworth 2006: 263–74). Wordsworth experienced the initial euphoria of the French Revolution, and its radicalism is reflected in an enthusiasm for demotic speech and 'ordinary' characters in his early poetry. Jane Austen's novels, by contrast, although written around the same time, are less interested in such figures. You may wonder why, when Emma Woodhouse in *Emma* (1816) must have servants, they rarely appear, much less speak.

When you read literary works with class issues in mind, details acquire new significance. A good example occurs in Chapter 27 of George Eliot's *Middlemarch* (1870–1). Eliot, an intelligent, politically aware writer whose adoption of a male pseudonym (her given name was Mary Ann, later Marian, Evans) is itself revealing, gives a probably unconscious glimpse of her intended audience in a scene usually studied in terms of characterization. Eliot's narrator suggests that we tend to think the world revolves around us by noting how scratches on a mirror apparently circle a lighted candle. This example illuminates Eliot's narrative method, but it is also significant that 'Your pier-glass [...] is made to be rubbed by a housemaid' (Eliot 2004: 232). Clearly, *Middlemarch*'s readers have time to ponder the niceties of egotism (and to read a long, complex book), but female servants are too busy catering to the needs of their mistresses to be quizzed on such matters. Whether housemaids had the leisure and education to read *Middlemarch* demonstrates the problematic intertwining of class and gender relations.

Critics, class(ics) and the canon

Class often conditions critical reaction to literature. An extreme example concerns the response to John Keats's poetry by the aristocratic *Quarterly Review* and *Blackwood's Magazine* in 1817. Keats and his fellow poet, Leigh Hunt, were judged less on their talent than on their background and political sympathies: Keats's father managed a livery stable (note how mothers tend to be considered irrelevant in the social classification of their sons) and Keats was a Whig rather than a Tory. Not being 'men of some rank', as *Blackwood's* put it, 'cockneys' like Keats and Hunt could never be great poets. So savage was the press's treatment of Keats that reviewers, rather than tuberculosis, were blamed for his early death.

Twenty years later, the young Charles Dickens was regarded as vulgar: he liked jewellery, colourful waistcoats and picking his teeth. Dickens's 'social betters' enjoyed his work, but his background initially made it difficult for him to be admitted into elite society. Middle and upper-class Victorians were hyper-conscious of rank. Parentage and ancestry, pronunciation, accent and dialect, cleanliness, clothing (style/fashion, quality, degree of wear, cost), address, education and mastery of etiquette all helped define an individual's 'place' (see THE NINETEENTH CENTURY AND THE VICTORIANS). Dickens's father was imprisoned for debt, and the young Charles worked in a factory, labelling bottles. This was not widely known in his lifetime, but his employment as a parliamentary reporter and journalist was quite enough to bar him from the ranks of 'gentlemen'.

Alfred Tennyson's life was very different. The Cambridge-educated son of a clergyman, Tennyson's classical learning and commitment to poetry rather than fiction marked him as someone capable of mixing in society despite periods of melancholia and heavy drinking. Tennyson succeeded Wordsworth as Poet Laureate in 1850, and it is a telling reflection on Victorian society and the relative status of poetry and prose that he received a civil list pension of £200 a year from 1845 and was eventually made a baron, while the hard-working journalist, magazine editor and novelist Dickens received only the adulation of the reading public. Any money coming his way was earned by his pen rather than governmental largesse.

The English **canon**, the works readers and critics deem central to literary tradition and cultural heritage, is dominated by the work of socially privileged, 'classic' authors. This is not to deny the worth of Alfred, 1st Baron Tennyson, but to point out that class and **gender** inequality, chiefly in the field of education and access to publication, means many authors survive only as 'Anon' in anthologies. Writers from marginal positions have occasionally won a measure of fame in their lifetimes – the poet and agricultural labourer John Clare did so in the 1820s – but their work was rarely taught in universities until the late twentieth century. Such omissions distort literary history. It is easy to assume that readers of the 1840s 'must' have been reading Tennyson, Dickens, Emily Brontë's *Wuthering Heights* (1847) and W. M. Thackeray's *Vanity Fair* (1847–8), because these works have retained their popularity and critical standing. This view neglects Brontë's mixed critical reception, the popularity of writers such as Harrison Ainsworth and 'penny dreadfuls' such as Thomas Preskett Prest's *Varney the Vampire* (1845–7), as well as the political popular poetry of Chartists such as Ernest Jones.

Literacy levels have increased markedly since the mid-nineteenth century, and the power and wealth of the gentry has declined as a consequence of economic and political change. This has affected the development of English writing and criticism. Literature reflects and shapes the society from which it emerges, and the last century or so has seen significant changes in literary hierarchies. One might note, too, how the backgrounds of academics and students are altering. Nowadays, although academia confers an honorary middle-class status on its practitioners, individuals may not have come from the same world as the largely white, male, middle-class university teachers of the earlier twentieth century. This growing, if still limited, element of diversity has surely had an effect upon the choice of texts set for school examination and studied in English departments, as well as on the critical methods used for their analysis.

Reader positions

When we read the fiction, poetry and plays of past ages, we do not always judge them according to the sociopolitical norms of their own time. We are also inclined to forget that however highly we regard them today, their reputations were often made and defended by a relatively small number of privileged readers able to write and publish their opinions. Our own backgrounds and prejudices may well influence our critical responses, as we can see from a brief reading of E. M. Forster's *Howards End* (1910). 'We are not concerned with the very poor,' says the narrator. 'They are unthinkable, and only to be approached by the statistician or the poet. This story deals with gentlefolk, or with those who are obliged to pretend that they are gentlefolk' (Forster 1983: 58). The cultured Schlegels look down on the wealthy but vulgar Wilcoxes. Caught between the two is Leonard Bast, a self-educated working-class clerk whose appetite for culture is whetted by the Schlegel sisters and who is thrown into poverty by the dealings of Henry Wilcox. The Schlegels see Bast as their comic inferior, failing to appreciate his hardships or the social 'abyss' waiting to swallow him if he became unemployed.

Forster intertwines material and spiritual wealth, prompting debate about their worth and relationship: the cultivated but impractical Schlegels' lifestyle depends on businessmen such as Wilcox, while Wilcox's elevation above Bast is complicated by his having had an affair with Bast's wife, Jackie. Forster's narrator and characters patronize Bast, but is he so laughable? You may find the Schlegels' cultural enthusiasms have little relevance for your own life, or conversely, that you have little direct knowledge of poverty, inequality or discrimination. How might these factors influence your reaction to the novel?

If Forster encourages debate, D. H. Lawrence, the son of a Nottinghamshire miner, adopts a more explicitly combative approach to class relations in *Lady Chatterley's Lover* (1928), pitting a physically and sexually vigorous working class against an etiolated aristocracy in an exploration of the national malaise that followed the 1914–18 war. You might consider the implications of Lawrence's title – how might we react if it were entitled *Tenderness* (his first idea), *The Gamekeeper* or even *Oliver Mellors*? You might also wonder whether *Lady Chatterley* was read by gamekeepers, disabled aristocratic men or their sexually unfulfilled wives, not least because it was banned in Britain until 1960. Even then, when it was tried as an obscene publication on the grounds of explicit sexual content (E. M. Forster spoke in its defence), the prosecuting counsel asked the jury, five of whom apparently struggled to read the oath, whether Lawrence's novel was one 'you would ... wish your wife or your servants to read?' (Sutherland 1982: 23). The connection between literature, reading and class was here rendered explicit, albeit to the amusement of many.

Lawrence presented elements of working-class life sympathetically, but there has long been a belief that 'working-class literature' is a contradiction in terms. From the chapbooks and street ballads of the eighteenth century to 'penny dreadfuls' and on to sexually explicit and violent paperbacks of the 1970s, such as Richard Allen's *Skinhead* (1970), those outside the working class, and indeed, some readers within it, have adhered to the belief that the working class has little time for 'high' culture and that its needs are best met by what George Orwell cynically terms 'prole food' in his *Nineteen Eighty-Four* (1949). Commentators such as Richard Hoggart and, more recently, Michael Collins have argued that a culturally dominant middle class, which controls higher education and substantial sectors of the culture industries (publishing and television, for example) is unlikely to take the cultural achievements of the working class very seriously, although it may lionize a writer such as James Kelman, winner of the Booker Prize with *How Late It Was, How Late* (1994). An education system that articulates a fundamentally bourgeois notion of 'culture' means writers from working-class backgrounds who do not leave school at the first opportunity to enter the workplace or vocational training can be caught between two very different worlds. The poets Tony Harrison and Simon Armitage have written movingly about their difficult relationships with Yorkshire working-class communities and the cultural dislocation caused by going to university.

At the same time, however, many writers actively exhibit their own prejudices or encourage those of their implied readership. Lawrence's depiction of the impotent aristocrat and the virile though uneducated gamekeeper is but one example of a recurrent tendency in English writing to present social stereotypes. It can be hard for writers to cast off the ingrained assumptions of their own backgrounds. Orwell's *The Road to Wigan Pier* (1937) addresses this explicitly, with Orwell lamenting how he was brought up to believe that '*the lower classes smell*' (Orwell 2001: 118) even as he gives queasily detailed accounts of life in a Wigan boarding-house.

Class, race and **gender** are intricately interrelated, and even today elaborate hierarchies exist that differentiate and stratify people who ostensibly seem to have much in common. While some people identify strongly with a particular social class, others resist such affiliation. Neither group is able to read literary texts with complete immunity from their sociopolitical **context**, and it is worth considering the implications of this for your own reading. Are you an adversarial reader who takes sides, consciously or otherwise, or do you attempt to retain a sense of equilibrium? Neither approach is right or wrong in itself, but all readers need to maintain an awareness of their own reading position and the part that class plays in its formulation.

Class: sample syllabus

The following is a brief outline of a 12-week module on class which combines a focus on 'class issues' with a broad historical spread.

Week 1 Introduction to key issues of reading with an awareness of class issues
Week 2 Kings and commoners (1): Shakespeare's *Henry V*
Week 3 Kings and commoners (2): the English Civil War: Andrew Marvell, 'An Horatian Ode Upon Cromwell's Return from Ireland' (1650); Gerrard Winstanley, 'A New Year's Gift Sent to Parliament and the Army' (1650)
Week 4 Eating the underclass: Jonathan Swift, *A Modest Proposal* (1729)
Week 5 New voices (1): Preface to the 1802 edition of Wordsworth and Coleridge, *Lyrical Ballads*; Wordsworth, 'Resolution and Independence' (1807)
Week 6 New voices (2): Marx and Engels, *The Communist Manifesto* (1848); selections from Tennyson; Ernest Jones's 'The Song of the Low' (1852)
Week 7 Industrial voices: Elizabeth Gaskell, *North and South* (1855)
Week 8 Class and 'culture': E. M. Forster, *Howards End* (1910)
Week 9 England from below: George Orwell, *The Road to Wigan Pier* (1937)
Week 10 How the other half loves: Alan Hollinghurst, *The Line of Beauty* (2004)
Week 11 Modern times? Linda Grant, *The Clothes on Their Backs* (2008)
Week 12 Conclusions: a re-examination of the issues of the module.

Bibliography

(a) Literary works

Eliot, George. *Middlemarch*. Ed. Gregory Maertz. Toronto: Broadview, 2004.

Forster, E. M. *Howards End*. Ed. Oliver Stallybrass. Harmondsworth: Penguin, 1983.

Gaskell, Elizabeth. *North and South*. Ed. Patricia Ingham. London: Penguin, 1995.

Grant, Linda. *The Clothes on Their Backs*. London: Virago, 2008.

Greenblatt, Stephen et al., eds. *The Norton Anthology of English Literature, Volumes I and II*. New York: Norton, 2006.

Hollinghurst, Alan. *The Line of Beauty*. London: Picador, 2005.

Marx, Karl and Friedrich Engels. *The Communist Manifesto*. London: Penguin, 2002.

Orwell, George. *The Road to Wigan Pier*. London: Penguin, 2001.

Wordworth, William. *Preface to Lyrical Ballads with Pastoral and Other Poems*. In *The Norton Anthology of English Literature, Volume II*, ed. Stephen Greenblatt et al., 263–74. New York: Norton, 2006.

Wordsworth, William. 'Resolution and Independence'. In *The Norton Anthology of English Literature, Volume II*, ed. Stephen Greenblatt et al., 302–5. New York: Norton, 2006.

(b) Further reading

Adorno, Theodore. *The Culture Industry*. London: Routledge, 1991.

Bourdieu, Pierre. *The Field of Cultural Production*. Cambridge: Polity Press, 1993.

Butler, Marilyn. *Jane Austen and the War of Ideas*. Oxford: Clarendon Press, 1975.

Carey, John. *The Intellectuals and the Masses: Pride and Prejudice amongst the Literary Intelligentsia 1880–1939*. London: Faber, 1992.

Eagleton, Terry. *Ideology: An Introduction*. London and New York: Verso, 1991.

Greenslade, William. 'Socialism and Radicalism'. In *The Cambridge Companion to the Fin de Siècle*, ed. Gail Marshall, 73–90. Cambridge: Cambridge University Press, 2007.

Keating, Peter. *The Working-Classes in Victorian Fiction*. London: Routledge, 1971.

Light, Alison. *Mrs Woolf and the Servants*. London: Fig Tree, 2007.

Rose, Jonathan. *The Intellectual Life of the British Working Classes*. New Haven, CT: Yale University Press, 2001.

Thompson, E. P. *The Making of the English Working Class*. London: Gollancz, 1963.

Colonial and postcolonial literature (Year 2)

Jenni Ramone

Introduction

Before the middle of the twentieth century, countries like Britain, France and Spain celebrated the powerful status afforded them by the territories that they had colonized. It was believed that by colonizing countries in South Asia and in Africa, for example, less 'developed' nations could benefit from the more advanced ideas and cultural practices of their European governors. Many English novels written during this colonial period involve European characters like Allan Quatermain in H. Rider Haggard's *King Solomon's Mines* (1885), an explorer who encounters (and wins over) savage and superstitious tribes people during his quest through Africa. European adventurers in what is known as 'colonial literature' routinely tame wild and hostile native peoples and landscapes, inspired by non-fictional (though not necessarily accurate) accounts in histories, travel writing, and the diaries and letters of wealthy European travellers and explorers. Such stories perpetuated the notion of the white man's superiority.

In recent decades, people started to question these ideas. Who is to say that one nation's idea of education, religion and law is superior or more civilized or more developed than another's? Why should one nation impose its values on another? And aren't such arguments simply excuses for profiteering through unfair trade with the colonized nations? When many colonial governments started to break down (for example, Britain withdrew from India in 1947 and from Nigeria in 1960), literature and other writing from within former colonies started to question the assumptions on which colonialism had been based. Literature of this kind, produced by newly independent citizens of formerly colonized nations, is called 'postcolonial literature'.

Scope

In the context of a Literary Studies degree (or an English degree), the scope of a colonial/postcolonial literature module is usually restricted to the countries which were formerly British colonies, and were colonized by English speakers. The writing produced in these regions is known as Anglophone writing (Anglophone simply means English-speaking). Studying only these texts avoids the need to study texts in translation. It is possible that some modules will include important works by writers from places that were once colonized by other nations, especially France, which you will read in English translation. These are known as Francophone (French-speaking) writers.

There are a number of ways that you might take a module on colonial or postcolonial literature – or both – in the course of a Literary Studies degree. Usually, this material would form an optional module in the second or final year of a three-year degree but it is also likely that you will come across examples of postcolonial novels, short stories or plays in a more general or **genre**-based, first-year module. As well as modules that encompass both colonial and postcolonial texts, you may have the opportunity to study modules on postcolonial literature alone, on postcolonial literature from a specific geographical location (typically Africa or South Asia, where the majority of prominent authors have come from, but also Singapore, Australia, Ireland, Canada and the Caribbean), or postcolonial **diaspora** literature, which focuses on the writing of first or later generation migrants living in, and writing about, their new location.

Colonial to postcolonial

Unlike many modules, this one is not confined to one historical period. Instead, it straddles a vast time frame which begins with texts written in the earliest colonial period. For instance, Shakespeare's *The Tempest*, written and performed during the Elizabethan period when expansion of trade routes and of overseas colonies was growing, has been seen by many scholars as commentary on colonialism. Prospero is the colonial master of the enslaved native, Caliban. In fact, for many Postcolonial Studies scholars, Shakespeare's works became an important part of the colonial project when, in the Victorian period, they were regularly performed in India in an effort to justify colonialism by giving something that British people considered valuable to the Indian upper and middle classes. It was taken for granted that Shakespeare's plays were what people in India wanted to watch, and ultimately what these performances did (though not explicitly) was to impose European values and stories on a non-European audience. This is very similar to missionary work: missionaries who entered the colony believed that their way of life was morally superior to that of the 'native' inhabitants. 'Native', of course, is a very loaded term in relation to Colonial and Postcolonial Studies, because it was often used in colonial literature in **binary opposition** with the colonial settlers, and came to mean wild, uncivilized, undisciplined and inferior, as postcolonial thinkers have since pointed out.

Shakespeare has an ongoing relationship with colonial and postcolonial literature; there have been a number of postcolonial rewritings or adaptations of Shakespeare's plays, such as, among many others, Aimé Cesaire's *A Tempest* (originally written in French and called *Une Tempête*), which was written during the author's struggle to renegotiate the colony status of Martinique; the influential but frequently out-of-print novel by G. V. Desani, *All About H. Hatterr*, which opposes a man's travels through India with numerous quotations (and misquotations) from Shakespeare's plays; and Salman Rushdie's short story 'Yorick', a retelling of *Hamlet* from the perspective of the migrant descendant of the old court jester. The extension of Shakespeare's influence throughout such varied adaptations indicates another reason for the appeal of this field of literary study: the current and ongoing relevance of the field which includes present-day literature dealing with the experience of the migrant, with the postcolonial subject, and with communities living under the influence of global corporations, often called economic **imperialism**, or neocolonialism.

The field covers literature from many regions of the world: even if restricted to the literature of former British colonies, the world map of former British colonies is vast, as many colonial and postcolonial texts will point out. Colonial literature studied on a module might include those which are written by British authors and are set in South Asia, in a number of African countries, North and South America and the Caribbean, the Pacific Islands, Australia and Ireland. Postcolonial literature is written by inhabitants from the same locations, writing after the end of colonial rule, and the closely related postcolonial diaspora literature deals with issues of migrating from colonies or former colonies. Postcolonial literature is often described as an interdisciplinary field of study, because it involves studying other kinds of texts (histories, travel writing and anthropological studies, for example) and this means that you need to think about all those texts and the literary texts (plays, poetry, novels, short stories) together, asking questions about how they work together to create an image of a colonized state, or to identify the colonizers' problematic assumptions about the colony, from a critical, postcolonial perspective.

In a module that considers both colonial and postcolonial literature, texts could range widely in both period and **genre**, and might include any of the following: Elizabethan plays; 'pioneer' texts; nineteenth-century novels either challenging or promoting the Victorian age of trade and empire; modern short stories and novels; contemporary writing from postcolonial territories, including writing which examines the language of English-speaking and -writing members of postcolonial states; diaspora writing and new literatures in English; and later neocolonial and romantic popular fiction and film. On a course which focuses only on postcolonial literature, much of the earlier literatures would not be covered in depth, and the focus would be on examining new, postcolonial and diaspora writing while making reference to earlier, colonial literatures and documents in order to demonstrate some of the colonial assumptions set up in those texts, and undone by newer writing.

Key questions

As well as the vast body of literature available for study on a colonial/postcolonial literature module, there are some key critical questions that make the field unique. Much early colonial writing is invested with problematic assumptions about colonized territories and their inhabitants, portraying the colonizer as a paternal, taming force in a wild and infantile landscape. This portrayal was part of the colonial project, which involved the attempt to transform the colonies into emergent replications of Europe, while using their resources for profit. Postcolonial literature and criticism is writing that interrogates colonialism and colonial writing in the **context** of the end of imperial control of former colonies. It aims to demonstrate the flawed colonial vision of colonized territories and inhabitants by demonstrating how those texts set up and maintained colonial binaries, and by revising the stories and histories in new writing and in theoretical explorations.

There are a number of commonly occurring things done by postcolonial literary texts, which offer a starting point for understanding the body of literature. These include the use of a 'native informant' who is a character in the novel or short story who understands the culture and location towards which the reader's attention is directed, but who has some distance from it, perhaps due to a period of time spent living elsewhere. This distance allows the character to discuss their location more objectively in order to convey information to an unfamiliar reader. Literary genres popular in postcolonial literature include magic realism, used, for example, in *Midnight's Children* (1981) by Salman Rushdie, where magical happenings take on political significance in an otherwise realistic text, as opposed to a more traditional use of magic in the fairy tale, the gothic novel, or science fiction fantasy.

Postcolonial literature aims to challenge literary forms, sometimes by writing texts in English that conform in part to the structure of oral narrative, which is more cyclical and repetitive with multiple narrative perspectives. Perhaps the most common feature of postcolonial literature is that, like postcolonial theory, it is engaged in retelling commonly held versions of history. Many contemporary writers from formerly colonized locations are conscious of the way that their writing functions specifically as postcolonial literature – in other words, instead of just seeing their novel as a unique piece of writing, they understand its context and the way that it might be read by university students and Literary Studies scholars. Sometimes, it is suggested that the postcolonial novel can cross over the boundary between literary text and postcolonial critique to become an interdisciplinary text which creates, as it comments critically about, the postcolonial subject. So the novel can stand in for postcolonial literary theory.

Rereading and rewriting

The learning outcomes of modules in colonial and postcolonial literature might include rereading established 'classic' texts from a new perspective, and reading emerging literature by new and experimental writers. This involves close analysis of the literary text in the context of its historical period and the historical periods in which it has been read, while developing a familiarity with key concepts including exile, diaspora, hybridity, mimicry, **orientalism**, the

Other, neocolonialism, anti-colonialism and the subaltern. Modules endeavour to engage with colonial and postcolonial constructs such as the Oriental, the Global and the Third World. Key to achieving these aims is questioning the assumed authority of the literary **canon**. This perspective also requires an awareness that the nation is an unstable construction and not a fixed and permanent category. All of these concepts and terms guide the engagement with the literary texts expected by written assignments.

Many literary theorists have engaged with the way that the English language is used in postcolonial literature, suggesting that it resists the dominant standard form that represents the colonial English language. Rushdie's use of the English language does not replicate or conform to the standard, but instead recreates the language so that it becomes a new language, owned by the postcolonial speaker. One of the ways in which postcolonial literature has attracted this kind of attention is by experimenting with the language used in the literature. Though some writers have considered writing in the language of the colonizer (usually English or French) to be an act of submission to colonial rule, others have used the imposed language to present a challenging linguistic debate. Another popular approach to the subject is to engage with the prominent theorists who have shaped the field, and with contemporary theorists who are further developing the subject, including Homi Bhabha, Edward Said, Frantz Fanon, Gayatri Spivak and Neil Lazarus. Collections of short essays by postcolonial theorists are commonly available in university libraries, and these offer a good starting point for students on encountering the subject.

Migration is a key area for the study of colonial and postcolonial literature. Population movements and migrations are many, but primarily studies involve examining migrations from Europe to colonial territories, and from postcolonial territories back to the lands of former colonizers, or to new locations. Much postcolonial literature has examined the migrant whose identity has been affected by contact with his or her new location.

Practical advice

You will enjoy this module if you like to place texts in their historical and political **context**, and to demonstrate that a text can be read from a number of different perspectives. Novels and other literary texts are read alongside histories and other kinds of writing, but work in assignments and in seminars will still involve close, critical reading.

It is a good idea to consult collections of short essays by postcolonial theorists and collections of colonial writing to gain knowledge of the field and its debates. Good glossaries of literary and critical terms will be helpful for initial definitions, but the best way to become familiar with the concepts discussed in postcolonial literary theory is to read essays on the subjects, and to identify them at work in literary texts.

Summary

To summarize, a module on colonial and postcolonial literature involves:

> reading texts from a broad historical period and from a number of geographical locations;

> reading literary texts alongside other texts like diaries, travel writing, histories, newspapers, maps, legal transcripts and letters;

> questioning the concept of nation, and considering past and present global expansion and trade critically;

> becoming familiar with a number of colonial and postcolonial concepts and debates, such as hybridity, exile, diaspora, the native informant, mimicry, orientalism, the Other, neocolonialism, anti-colonialism, the subaltern, the oriental and the global.

Colonial and postcolonial literature: sample syllabus

Week 1   Colonialism, an introduction: Edmund Spenser, *A View of the State of Ireland*; Rudyard Kipling, 'White Man's Burden'

Week 2   Thinking about colonial representation (1): Edward Said, *Orientalism*

Week 3   Thinking about colonial representation (2): Ngugi wa Thiong'o, *Decolonising the Mind*; Joseph Conrad, *Heart of Darkness*

Week 4   Language (1): Derek Walcott, 'Omeros'

Week 5   Language (2): Salman Rushdie, *Midnight's Children*

Week 6   Nation: Sara Suleri, *Meatless Days*; Bessie Head, *Collector of Treasures and Other Botswana Village Tales*

Week 7   Postcolonialism: readings from Ashcroft, Griffiths and Tiffin, eds, *The Postcolonial Studies Reader*

Week 8   Postcolonial literature (1): Chinua Achebe, *Anthills of the Savannah*

Week 9   Postcolonial literature (2): Arundhati Roy, *The God of Small Things*

Week 10 Diaspora and beyond (1): Hanif Kureishi, *The Buddha of Suburbia*

Week 11 Diaspora and beyond (2): Zadie Smith, *White Teeth*

Week 12 Conclusion: a reassessment of the positions and ideas studied through the semester

Bibliography

(a) Literary works

Achebe, Chinua. *Anthills of the Savannah*. London: Picador, 1988.

Conrad, Joseph. *Heart of Darkness*. London: Penguin, 1994.

Forster, E. M. *A Passage to India*. London: Penguin, 1979.

Haggard, H. Rider. *King Solomon's Mines*. London: Penguin, 2007.

Head, Bessie. *Collector of Treasures and Other Botswana Village Tales*. London: Heinemann, 1992.

Kureishi, Hanif. *The Buddha of Suburbia*. London: Faber and Faber, 1991.

Levy, Andrea. *Small Island*. London: Headline Review, 2004.

Roy, Arundhati. *The God of Small Things*. New York: Harper Perennial, 1997.

Rushdie, Salman. *Midnight's Children*. London: Vintage, 1995.

Smith, Zadie. *White Teeth*. London: Penguin, 2000.

Soyinka, Wole. *The Man Died*. London: Arrow, 1985.

(b) Further reading

Bhabha, Homi K, ed. *Nation and Narration*. London: Routledge, 2000.

Boehmer, Elleke, ed. *Empire Writing: An Anthology of Colonial Literature 1870–1918*. Oxford: Oxford World's Classics, 1998.

Childs, Peter and Patrick Williams. *An Introduction to Post-Colonial Theory*. London: Prentice Hall, 1997.

Fanon, Frantz. *Black Skin, White Masks*. London: Pluto, 1986.

Gandhi, Leela. *Postcolonial Theory: A Critical Introduction*. New York: Columbia University Press, 1998.

Gilroy, Paul. *The Black Atlantic: Modernity and Double Consciousness*. London: Verso, 1993.

Harrison, Nicholas. *Postcolonial Criticism: History, Theory and the Work of Fiction*. Cambridge: Polity Press, 2003.

Landry, Donna and Gerald MacLean, eds. *The Spivak Reader*. London: Routledge, 1996.

Said, Edward. *Orientalism*, London: Penguin, 1991.

Spivak, Gayatri. *A Critique of Postcolonial Reason: Toward a History of the Vanishing Present*. Cambridge, MA: Harvard University Press, 1999.

Young, Rober. *White Mythologies: Writing History and the West*. London: Routledge, 1990.

Subjectivity

Megan Becker-Leckrone

Introduction: who am I?

The question and thus definition of 'subjectivity' is dauntingly enormous, which is why you would probably find such a module in the final year of your studies, although this doesn't mean we should – or possibly could – avoid it. So let's start, as we would in a module on this subject, with the simplest way in which the word is used these days, especially within the discourses of literary study: to invoke the term 'subjectivity' (or, just as often, the 'subject') is to raise the issue of the self, 'I', point of view, or even merely to refer to a given work's character(s), narrator or lyric voice. Subjectivity, simply put, is yourself, your subjectivity is who you are, not as an isolated being, but as someone who, in referring to themself, refers also to their **culture**, ethnicity, **gender**, beliefs, along with everything else that determines them.

In the basic rules of grammar, the subject of a sentence is that which the sentence is about, the agent the verb obeys and the predicate describes. But from here things get complicated, not least because literature creates imaginary selves out of a multiplicity and infinite variety of such grammatical units. Even within English grammar, subjects are not only 'actors or **agents**', possessors of 'a free subjectivity that does things', but also beings who are acted upon, '*subjected*, determined' (Culler 1997: 111–12). One may be a subject *of* the queen or an experiment; or subject *to* the laws of the state, nature, God, fate or ideology. In literature, subjects are also subjects *of* their author and reader, and subject *to* interpretation. Both author and reader, of course, are in turn subjects themselves, both actors and acted upon. Thus, a module addressing subjectivity should begin by addressing the extent to which you think of yourself as an individual and to what extent that individuality is, itself, a construction.

Philosophical and related perspectives

In philosophy, subjectivity refers most generally to the human mind, thinking or perceiving – in other words, to the fact of individual cognition. The concept comes up particularly in debates about the forms and possibilities of human perception ('subjectivity' vs. 'objectivity', in shorthand), knowledge, mind and being. Sociologically, politically, economically or psychoanalytically, 'subjectivity', you will find, can refer to the **context** and conditions, dictated by myriad structures and events, by which your individuality (the I, subject, or self) gets specifically shaped. In these disciplines, the subject – that is to say, you – comes into being dynamically through various sets of relations, forces of power, and accretions of experience. In all these fields of study, there has been wide and vigorous disagreement about the nature of those dynamics, usually around the question of both how 'dynamic' these determinants really are and which one predominates: is subjectivity, in other words, something predetermined (like one's race or sex) or constituted (like one's racial or **gender** identity)? Out of the general human sciences' attention to subjectivity, there has also emerged an enormously influential array of theoretical discourses: feminism, queer theory, gender and ethnic studies, postcolonialism, and more. All such topics, you might find, have become modules in university literature courses. Indeed, many have entries in the present chapter and volume, so central is the notion of your subjectivity, what constitutes it, and how it is formed.

Critical views of the subject

You can see from this long list how easily any initial definitions might well fly afield from what 'subjectivity' would connote in the specific act of reading a specific literary work. But indeed the history of literature is expansive enough itself to have explored subjectivity in all these forms and more. All the above fields of study investigate something literature itself relentlessly puzzles through in the travails of a main character, the voice of a narrator, and in the 'I' of a sonnet. Just ask yourself, as no doubt a module on subjectivity might expect you to explore, what is happening any time you read a poem, where the apparent speaker says 'I', as in the line 'I sing the body electric', or in a novel where someone says, 'whether I shall turn out to be the hero of my own life or whether that station will be held by anyone else, these pages must show'. Or what happens when, opening a book, you find a voice saying 'Call me Ishmael'? In each case, you read of a subject, someone at the centre of the text, who seems to speak that text. How does this person, this subject, come into being, what makes it possible for them to speak, and how does the language of the text construct them so that you imagine them to exist?

French critic Roland Barthes and French historian Michel Foucault, following in the footsteps of French thinker Maurice Blanchot, argue that any given literary unit, so to speak – a sentence, an utterance, an example, an assertion – requires the reader to ask 'Who is speaking?' It turns out this is no simple question and that the answer matters. Barthes memorably asks this question, and a cascade of others that come with it, in his essay, 'The Death of the Author' (1977). Quoting a single, deceptively simple sentence from a story by Honoré de Balzac, *Sarrasine*, Barthes asks, 'Who is speaking thus?' In so doing, he demonstrates that reading requires imagining many possible subjectivities, none simply locatable in a figure literary criticism has heretofore conveniently called the 'author'.

So then, your module will ask: is subjectivity aggregated or singular, essential or constructed, fixed or mutable, given or made? You might believe yourself to be an individual, your opinions your own. One resounding response favouring the former in each of the above pairs would be the proposition put forward by René Descartes, so famous it is typically referenced as a single noun: the *cogito*. That is to say, 'I think, therefore I am'. René Descartes' formula, put forth in *Meditations on First Philosophy* (1641), has become a cornerstone of Western thought, and to speak of the *cogito* is to reference, among other things, an assumption dominant since at least the Renaissance: that the individual subject exists insofar as and because he or she *thinks*; that this thinking subject is singular, internal, self-determined, self-present and essentially rational. As it has done with so many of the bedrock concepts of Western thought, literature has long been a means of both creatively reinforcing *and* subverting this understanding of subjectivity. Indeed, some would argue it is possible altogether to *define* a given period or literary **genre** solely according to how it conceives of the subject. It is a constitutive feature of the rise of the novel, for example, and arguably of British romantic poetry also. Your module might well expect you, having read Descartes, to test out the philosophical premises through critical readings of literary works (see THE NOVEL, POETRY).

Different approaches

What should be clear to you, and what your module will stress, is that, historically or philosophically, politically or culturally, there is little consensus on what constitutes subjectivity. Many influential thinkers assert their theory by way of distinctively defining subjectivity. Michel Foucault provocatively declares, in the last pages of *The Order of Things* (1966), that before the eighteenth century 'man did not exist' prior to the birth of the human sciences, which is to say before the eighteenth century (Foucault 1994: 344). Nancy Armstrong offers a similar point of origin, though she ties her justification of this date more explicitly to the rise of the novel, a relatively young genre that she argues not only reflects but indeed *produces* the modern individual (1987).

In her 1924 essay, 'Mr. Bennett and Mrs. Brown', Virginia Woolf even more precisely declares that '[o]n or about December 1910 human nature changed' (Woolf 1984: 193). What she means to establish by such hyperbole is a revolutionary distinction of the twentieth-century from the nineteenth-century centred on the question of subjectivity – on 'subjects and objects and the nature of reality', as one character puts it in her 1927 novel, *To the Lighthouse* (Woolf 1989: 23). For her, what has changed, what makes the modernist novel 'modern' is precisely the shift from a novelistic subject treated largely 'externally' (defined by her **context** within a broader social reality and adumbrated through plot), to a subject whose internal, usually unspoken consciousness takes centre stage. The modern subject of both theory and literature – from Sigmund Freud to James Joyce – comes into view out of the corner of our eye, in fleeting impressions and epiphanies, dreams, slips of the tongue, **desires**. In stark contrast to Descartes, this modern literary subject is often irrational, associative, unreliable, a creature of ephemeral and conflicting drives, a consciousness expressed by thoughts and actions that constitute the subject because the subject is subject *to* them.

Woolf's works are exquisitely intricate explorations of a subjectivity so defined; **stream of consciousness** is the clichéd term attached to her narrative style, but in fact most of her works weave in and out of the 'consciousness' of several characters, where impressions, associations, interactions and desires issue from a place we could call 'consciousness' only with a number of careful provisos in place. James Joyce's work proceeds similarly, culminating in a 'novel' (*Finnegans Wake*) where one would be hard pressed even to identify a unified narrator or main character, much less one organized around (a) consciousness or subjectivity. In the third chapter of his penultimate novel, *Ulysses* (1922), Joyce presents the reader with a world seen through the eyes and musings of (an arguably semi-autobiographical) Stephen Dedalus, who, in thinking about the relation of perception to identity – of 'subjects and objects and the nature of reality', as Woolf puts it – demonstrates its radically elusive fragility: 'Ineluctable modality of the visible: at least that if no more, thought through my eyes.' This first line of the chapter Joyce calls 'Proteus' nicely describes – but also articulates the emphatic difficulty, if not impossibility, of – the modernists' project of capturing something at all like the nature of reality through the lens of such a radically protean subjectivity, 'thought through my eyes'. Throughout the chapter, when not distracted by the mud beneath his feet or other ephemera, Stephen worries through this 'ineluctability', the unstoppable, unceasing qualities upon which subjectivity is to be built.

The example of Walter Pater

No consideration of subjectivity would be complete without a study, however brief, of the Victorian essayist Walter Pater. You can learn a lot from Pater about how we think about ourselves, and who we believe ourselves to be. Pater, considerably prior to Woolf's modernist statute of limitations, had similar concerns for the **aesthetic** subject (both author and audience). In his famous 'Conclusion' to *The Renaissance*, composed in 1868, Pater acknowledges the modern (he too considered himself 'modern') tendency to 'consider all things and principles as inconstant', but worries as well about how a subject is to express itself at all, given that he (Pater's subject generally seems to be male) must contend with not just an external ineluctability and flux, but with a similarly mutable perceptive experience. In other words, how can the subject be more than merely the sum of his fleeting and unique impressions? If it is the case that 'I perceive uniquely, therefore I am', then a modern subjectivity defined by perceptive uniqueness or singularity threatens to settle into sheer solipsism:

> Experience, already reduced to a group of impressions, is ringed round for each one of us by that thick wall of personality through which no real voice has ever pierced on its way to us, or from us to that which we can only conjecture to be without. Every one of those impressions is the impression of the individual in his isolation, each mind keeping as a solitary prisoner its own dream of a world. (Pater 1980: 187–8)

Pater's dense prose proves hard to excerpt, and a fuller presentation of it would show more emphatically how indebted Woolf and Joyce truly are to his own exquisitely wrought understanding of the expression of subjectivity in and through art. For now, it is helpful to notice that Pater, like the Stephen of 'Proteus', regards inconstancy not merely as external, something that threatens 'to bury us under a flood of external objects', but as a thoroughly anxious function in the formation of subjectivity itself. Like the sea or time, so too are our impressions of them and all things 'unstable, flickering, inconsistent, which burn and are extinguished with our consciousness of them' (187).

Pater's image of this internal and external flux as a 'flood' that threatens to engulf the subject recalls an important if misleading term ascribed to the modernist narrative of Woolf and Joyce: 'stream of consciousness'. Because they are really neither linear ('stream'), nor conscious, nor singular, I advise against using the label altogether, or at least putting them under a heading more truly descriptive: such experiments in modern narrative subjectivity are perhaps best understood by way of Sigmund Freud's (contemporary) term, the **unconscious**.

Sigmund Freud and the psychoanalytic legacy

No one has been more influential *and* controversial in shaping or provoking our thinking of subjectivity than Sigmund Freud. As a student, it is entirely unlikely that you will get through your time as an undergraduate reading for an English degree without encountering Freud.

Freud spent a lifetime of groundbreaking work exploring and elaborating, debunking irrevocably the manifest and knowable Cartesian *cogito*. For Freud, the **unconscious**, which *is* us, is also never *present* to us. It is always occluded, elsewhere. Literary theorists have liked to stress that one of Freud's greatest articulations of this concept comes from literature: his readings of *Oedipus Rex* and *Hamlet*. In *The Interpretation of Dreams* (1900), where the Oedipus complex is introduced by way of those readings, Freud states unequivocally:

> The unconscious is the true psychical reality; *in its innermost nature it is as much unknown to us as the reality of the external world, and it is as incompletely presented by the data of consciousness as is the external world by the communications of our sense organs.* (Freud 1965: 165–6)

What Freud here announces – which is not to say invents – is a distinctly twentieth-century understanding of subjectivity as *decentred*. That is, if Descartes' subject is centred on the first, undeniable fact that 'I think, therefore I am', the definition of the modern subject rests precisely on an inability to locate him or her according to such a stable, fundamental and self-present rationality. Jacques Lacan, the French theorist who regarded his work as a rigorous 'return to Freud', provides a rewriting of the Cartesian formula that nicely articulates the tremendous force of this shift. 'In what might be called the Freudian universe,' Lacan writes, 'I think where I am not, therefore I am where I do not think […] I am not wherever I am the plaything of my thought; I think of what I am where I do not think to think' (Lacan 1977: 165–6). If these lines happen to remind you, incidentally, of Joyce or Beckett, that is probably not by accident. Lacan professed a fascination with both, and indeed acknowledges Arthur Rimbaud's poetic articulation of subjectivity – 'I is an **other**' (*'Je est un autre'*) – as an inspiration for his own (Lacan 1977: 23).

Without belabouring too much any assertion that the modernists were specifically Freudian, nor that Freud and Lacan were specifically modernists, what I mean to highlight for you is the way in which literature not only echoes broader or supposedly deeper understandings of subjectivity circulating in the intellectual air of the day, but actually helps to articulate that understanding. Yet we should also recognize that, Woolf's blunt historicizing aside ('December 1910'), the issue of subjectivity suffuses literature, arguably from its beginning. Oedipus struggles because he cannot appropriately divine the distinction between the preordained path his life is to take and his personal ability to outwit it. Shakespeare's most memorable tragic heroes suffer similarly. At the hands of his bastard son (who himself wonders whether 'bastard' is an inborn or earned designation), Gloucester ironically laments his fate in thoroughly Sophoclean terms, implying an ultimate subjective impotence in the face of greater forces: 'As flies to wanton boys are we to th' gods / They kill us for their sport' (IV.i.36–7). The pendulum seems to shift away from Gloucester's fatalism with the next two centuries' development of the British novel, whose plots are often driven by their main characters' survival, self-definition, development and discovery.

The politics of subjectivity

In *Capital*, Volume I (1867), Karl Marx identifies, with considerable derision, the powerful myth of the 'self-made man' in Daniel Defoe's *Robinson Crusoe* (1719). Sole survivor of a shipwreck, an absolutely solitary human being (or so he thinks) for many years, he has no ties to his former life. In order to survive, the utterly individual Robinson must redefine himself; he must begin again. What strikingly underscores the novel's central theme of self-generated subjectivity is the way in which the narrative/generic form of *Robinson Crusoe* mirrors the plot of Robinson Crusoe's life. The initial journal entry in Robinson's self-preservative journal (self-preservative in that it will at once preserve his sanity, mark out his existence in time, and immortalize him to his readers) looks substantively like the first paragraph of the novel itself: both offer a date, a naming, a situating by place, an explanation of where he came from and how. The beginning of the novel describes by what genealogical circumstances Robinson is born; the beginning of this journal, analogously, describes and self-authorizes by what circumstances Robinson is – by his own making – born again.

There is so very much to say about the dynamics of subjective construction in the British novel: how Tom Jones's adventures and missteps all guide him eventually to the noble 'self' he did not know was his actual birthright, for example; or how Tristram Shandy so ineptly and subversively undoes any certainty about the relationship between such genealogical 'fortune' and the individual's role in realizing it. There is just as much if not more to say about such ambivalences and explorations in verse: Coleridge's agonizing effort in 'Dejection: An Ode' to puzzle out the distinction between a poetic voice generated from within versus that given to him by a divine nature, for example, or Wordsworth's creation of an epic, *The Prelude*, that *solely* traces the journey of an individual mind (his own). We have world enough but not time – which might be a convenient way of saying that, in some way, all the literary considerations I outline here, no matter how singular or self-possessed a subjectivity they posit, hinge at some point on the issue of the subject's relation not just to the world, but to time.

Another name for the 'ineluctability' Stephen Dedalus ponders or Walter Pater worries over is 'mutability', which the romantics themselves worried over beautifully. Like Pater, Percy Bysshe Shelley observes in his lyric, 'Mutability', that our perceiving, creative minds are 'as the clouds that veil the midnight mood'; both 'restlessly … speed, and gleam, and quiver' (ll. 1–2). In his own powerful 'Mutability', a sonnet, Wordsworth calls this great struggle to assert a self, poetic and **existential**; it must somehow articulate itself within and in spite of 'the unimaginable touch of Time' (l. 14).

In his 1967 introduction to *Tristram Shandy* (1768), Christopher Ricks praises Laurence Sterne's novel in large part because it encompasses all of what I survey above, calling it a masterful depiction of a 'doomed and heroically absurd battle against time' (Sterne 1978: xxiii). Its central power, for Ricks, stems from its illustration of the novel's specific relationship to the construction of narrative identity as well as its seemingly prescient, and certainly subversive, understanding of all such identities as precariously constructed at best. (James Joyce, incidentally, admired it for the same reasons.) Throughout the novel, Tristram's anguished first-person narrative is sabotaged by the question, 'Where to begin?' So too is his identity hobbled by an uncomfortable amalgam of poor timing (his conception and birth), shaggy dog stories, hobby horses, digressions, and so on. What Tristram can never quite settle on is whether 'Where to begin?' is a temporal question or a question about the limits (or limitations) of the subject as such.

The question persists to this day. In 'A Lie That Tells the Truth: Memoir and the Art of Memory' (2007), writer Joel Agee is forced to think about 'literature' as it has been defined – especially in recent decades – by Anglo-American publishers, as he finds himself struggling to write in some anxious middle ground between what his editors want to call a 'memoir' and what he thinks is something closer to a 'novel' – or rather, something 'serious' he wants to call 'literature', which his editors insist a 'memoir' is not. Raised in a Germanic tradition that exalted 'literature' without making the implicit, and implicitly hierarchical, Anglo-American distinction between one narrative's allegiance to fact (memory, lived experience) and another's to fiction (imagination, creation), Agee struggles even within his own memory to separate out his remembrance of events as they happened from the way they come to settle into his consciousness once he writes about them. Again and again, he locates this struggle squarely within the question of subjectivity itself. Forcing himself to write about a particularly nightmarish period of his life without risking self-exposure, he tried to '[m]ake it a novel', modelled on Faust, but 'It wasn't possible: the pronoun "I" would not be replaced by any other. And it wasn't just anyone's "I", it was mine. The subject of this novel – in both senses of the word "subject" – was my self. I dared not write it' (Agee 2007: 54).

Agee's point, and in turn mine, is that the difficulty with which he aimed to be 'true' to and about himself in his writing had as much to do with literary terms, fact and fiction, as it did with the very question of what constitutes his subjectivity, himself as a subject. Just as his writing seems to traffic uneasily in both fiction and fact, so does his consciousness itself. 'Memory' is at once lived experience, subjectively perceived and remembered, and itself the product of a subjective creative act. Through writing literature – even if the 'literary enterprise' (publishers, marketers, bookstores and libraries) had relegated his work to a subordinate generic distinction, 'merely' memoir – Agee discovers that the distinctions, practically speaking, are impossible to separate. He finds, while he's writing, that 'to remember is, at least in part, to imagine, and that the act of transposing memory into written words is a creative act that transforms the memory itself' (2007: 58, 55). This creativity is necessary because '"is" becomes "was" in the blink of an eye, and memories are shadows' (55). A particular writer's subjectivity, in this sense, is not just the subject, the 'I', of a memoir. Its subject is the very question of memory, which is in turn a version of all the powerful ways in which literature has historically regarded subjectivity – of whether the self is acted upon (by experience, recorded by memory) or actor (imaginative creator of memories). It is the question of how the subject constitutes itself by writing, how the thing we call 'I' affirms itself. Agee describes this **writerly** 'I' as something that holds itself perpendicular to the 'horizontal plane of time' – of 'Where to begin?' in the midst of mutability. Literature, by this definition, could simply be the effort to imagine – which means, for Agee, both to recall and create – the subject out of and in spite of 'the unimaginable touch of Time'.

Summary

As I hope this short essay indicates to you, subjectivity is a complex and often contentious issue. Doubtless, a number of students reading this will question, or simply think wrong, the notion that who they are is constructed or produced in some way. You are, after all, an individual, with free will, aren't you? If you were to pause and consider to what extent your Facebook page – you do have one, don't you? – is, well, really quite similar to everyone else's who you have as your friend, but that, at the same time, it differs in small ways; considering this, you might reflect on the fact that something has brought about those similarities. Equally, if you read literature and find yourself empathizing with a character or, conversely, find yourself unable to understand why a character does or thinks what they do, you might begin to understand why the matter of what constitutes your subjectivity is not always as cut and dried as you might, initially, have believed. To put this another way, taking a module, taking a degree, you're not the same person, quite, as you were when you began.

Subjectivity: sample syllabus

Week 1   Introduction: what is subjectivity?
Week 2   Descartes' *cogito*
Week 3   The premodern 'subject': Oedipus vs. Hamlet
Week 4   The lyric subject (1): early poetic forms
Week 5   The lyric subject (2): romanticism
Week 6   Other forms of the poetic 'I'
Week 7   Subjectivity in the early novel: Defoe
Week 8   Subjectivity in the Victorian novel: omniscience, unreliability
Week 9   Subjectivity in modern literature: 'stream of consciousness', modernism and postmodernism
Week 10 Memoir and autobiography: writing the 'self'
Week 11 The psychoanalytic subject
Week 12 Subjectivity and power: media, politics, ideology

Bibliography

(a) Literary works

Joyce, James. *Ulysses*. New York: Modern Library, 1992.

Pater, Walter. *The Renaissance: Studies in Art and Poetry, the 1893 Text*. Ed. Donald L. Hill. Berkeley: University of California Press, 1980.

Sterne, Laurence. *The Life and Opinions of Tristram Shandy, Gentleman*. New York: Penguin, 1978.

Woolf, Virginia. 'Mr. Bennett and Mrs. Brown'. *The Virginia Woolf Reader*. New York: Harvest Books, 1984.

Woolf, Virginia. *To the Lighthouse*. New York: Harvest Books, 1989.

(b) Further reading

Blanchot, Maurice. 'Where Now? Who Now?'. *The Siren's Song: Selected Essays by Maurice Blanchot*. Ed. Gabriel Josipivici, trans. Sacha Rabinovitch. Bloomington: Indiana University Press, 1982.

Foucault, Michel. 'What Is an Author?' *The Foucault Reader*. Trans. Paul Rabinow. New York: Pantheon, 1984.

Freud, Sigmund. *The Interpretation of Dreams*. Trans. and ed. James Strachey. New York: Avon, 1965.

Lacan, Jacques. *Écrits*. Trans. Alan Sheridan. New York: Norton, 1977.

Children's literature

(Year 2)

Jenny Bavidge

What is children's literature?

The recent commercial success of children's books such as the *Harry Potter* and *His Dark Materials* series has brought children's literature a new visibility and sharpened interest in questions that literary critics in the field have been pursuing for some time. Until fairly recently, it might have seemed odd for adults to read and discuss books written and primarily marketed to children. For the moment, children's books are being published with optional 'adult' covers to allow commuters to catch up with the latest in boy wizardry while retaining their grown-up dignity. A national enthusiasm for children's books was uncovered in the BBC's 2003 'Big Read' poll to discover Britain's favourite fiction: six out of the top ten were children's books. Despite this 'amateur' interest, children's literature still occupies a marginal position within academic English courses, although an opening out of the subject to literary criticism, literary theory and interdisciplinary approaches continually recasts the subject. It's probable that you'll come across children's literature in your English degree even if you don't take a course in it: you may discuss *Alice's Adventures in Wonderland* (1865) on a literary theory class in connection with psychoanalytic theory or **deconstruction**, or study the works for children of authors such as Rudyard Kipling or Ted Hughes. Books which were once 'just' for children in their own historical moment acquire gravitas and significance with the passing of time, so you may read *Uncle Tom's Cabin* (1852) or *Little Women* (1868) on an American Literature course. It's also the case that boundaries between adult and children's literature are porous: the children's author Michael Morpurgo recently included Dickens's *Oliver Twist*, a text you're more likely to encounter on a nineteenth-century novel course, on his list of favourite children's books. Some texts such as Mark Twain's *The Adventures of Huckleberry Finn* (1884) or Jonathan Swift's *Gulliver's Travels* (1726) begin their literary lives as adult books but are adapted or abridged in order to be offered to children.

Unless you're studying children's literature in the context of an Education or Childhood Studies course, you're unlikely to spend much time thinking in an empirical way about the intended readership, 'children' in terms of literacy or language acquisition. Instead, you'll study the writing as you would any other – as texts which can be analysed, decoded and discussed. And, as with any broad category of literature, there are many different routes into studying under the broad heading of children's literature. In terms of *what* you study, you might look at the **canonical** texts of 'classic' children's literature or range widely though poetry, film or any manifestations of children's contemporary culture, from the 'Bratz' dolls to skateboarding. You might focus particularly on fantasy fiction, realist narratives, picture books or fairy tales. A course may confine itself to Anglo-American work, or consider a range of national literatures. Now, *how* you study whatever makes it onto your reading list is a weighted question. Of course, the arsenal of literary close reading can be utilized to analyse children's literature. We can talk about rhetorical style, imagery, narrative structure, generic elements and so on as fruitfully in regard to Maurice Sendak's *Where the Wild Things Are* (1964) as with any other literary text. After the *what* and the *how*, however, comes the *why*, and this is where the Little Red Riding Hood of children's literature meets the Big Bad Wolf of theory.

The children's literature canon

The history of children's literature is most commonly broken into periods organized around the so-called Anglo-American 'Golden Age' of children's literature. The 'Golden Age' describes a period roughly between the second half of the nineteenth century and the First World War, when a mode of writing for children emerged which addressed its audience in a new way. Previously, children's books had often had a didactic intent, even if they were also entertaining. Early examples of literature written for children such as James Janeway's *A Token for Children. Being An Exact Account of the Conversion, Holy and Exemplary Lives, and Joyful Deaths of Several Young Children* (1692) set the tone for much of the eighteenth and nineteenth centuries. Authors such as Charlotte Younge and Maria Edgeworth aimed to teach child readers moral or religious lessons, and, with few exceptions, depicted child characters of unlikely piety. From the 1860s onwards, however, books appeared which established a new tone for writing for children, and one which is recognizably 'modern'. Works such as Charles Kingsley's *The Water Babies* (1862), Lewis Carroll's *Alice in Wonderland* (1865), Frances Hodgson Burnett's *The Secret Garden* (1911) and the novels of E. Nesbit both reflected and established a new idea of childhood. To a certain extent, the category of 'children's literature' is itself created by the books published in this period. The interwar period, the years between 1920 and 1939, saw a continuation of the newly modern tone of children's literature. The characters created in this period – Peter Hunt provides a list which includes Mary Poppins, Bilbo Baggins, Richmal Crompton's William, Winnie the Pooh – are still with us, recreated and rebranded for later audiences by cinema and television (Hunt 1991: 106). The books of the Golden Age and the interwar period are most often those cited as the 'classics' of the **genre** and they have formed the basis of the canon of children's literature, against which subsequent works are judged. Later children's literature from the 1960s onwards attempted to break free from the somewhat cosy and protected worlds of these books, moving into a period of 'new realism'. Subjects which had hitherto been out of bounds in children's books – sex, violence, political and social issues – were now addressed by writers such as Robert Cormier, Jan Mark and Judy Blume (see REALISM). Books had in part been defined as being for children because they evaded such subject matter, but now a new term, 'Young Adult' (YA), came into use to describe books written specifically for teenagers. Often dealing with issues of self-definition and social alienation, the 'coming of age' narrative can be traced across manifold genres, and also literary forms, with graphic novels and other non-traditional forms deserving attention. Perhaps as a reaction to this gritty realism, **fantasy** fiction has become dominant in children's fiction once more. Fantasy has always been an important element of children's literature, from its earliest classics, through C. S Lewis's Christian **allegories** in the Narnia series, to the 1960s and 1970s, which saw the complex works of Susan Cooper and Alan Garner drawing on British folklore and **myth**. In the late twentieth century, the world-conquering *Harry Potter* series appeared and since then a new industry in children's fantasy fiction has emerged. There are ongoing and fierce public debates about the subjects and style proper to children's literature, which even if they have moved on from earlier preoccupations with innocence or religious training, still operate through the same discourses of morality and propriety. Contemporary authors such as Jacqueline Wilson and Melvyn Burgess are often criticized – by adults – for their 'inappropriate' or negative subject matter or characterization.

Children's literature criticism

The brief history of children's literature given above conforms to the 'canonical' view of literary studies. That is, it highlights the works which have been agreed (by whom?) to be the classics of a given period. Children's literature scholars have a complicated relationship with the idea of **canon**. On one hand, in order to have the subject taken seriously, scholars might wish to establish key works as texts worthy of adult attention. It would be 'respectable' to study, or at least admit to having read, Golden Age classics like *Alice in Wonderland* or *Peter Pan* (1904), but do children's literature scholars then have to produce different justifications for the study of, for example, a picture book such as Judith Kerr's *The Tiger Who Came to Tea* (1968) or the sparkly vampires of Stephenie Meyer's YA *Twilight* series. As Hunt points out, there are two different kinds of children's literature scholars, and the idea of a canon of children's literature is problematic for both (Hunt 1991: 17). One group, linked to librarians, educationalists and child development experts, is interested in children themselves as readers and in assessing the suitability and effect of books on those readers. This raises a whole set of questions: what are good books for children? What is it that we think literature should do for children? What are the politics behind projects to promote literacy such as the Blair/Brown Labour government's Bookstart scheme? Often the 'anything to get them reading' approach is adopted in public discussions about children's reading habits, but the idea lingers that there are certain books that children *should* have read in order to be culturally as well as functionally literate. The other group of scholars interested in children's books are those working within literature departments who have had to justify why children's literature has a place alongside their colleagues' courses on *Paradise Lost* or the nineteenth-century novel. The application of literary theory has, however, more recently moved the debate on from an anxiety about children's literature's place in the pantheon of great works, offering a multitude of other ways of approaching the texts.

This development raises its own difficulties about approach and methodology. It's likely that people who end up studying English Literature at university were first enthused about narrative and imagery by the books they read as children. You probably remember the passionate intensity of your childhood reading experiences and might have books that you reread again and again through the years. Perhaps because readers' first encounter with children's literature normally occurs outside of academic approaches, there is sometimes a reluctance to bear down on the fragile-seeming children's book with the scalpel of literary analysis. Deborah Cogan Thacker, for example, talks about how some critics may feel reluctant 'to perform literary surgery on the beloved texts of childhood, suggesting a need to preserve a sense of magic surrounding children's books that might draw scholars to them in the first place' (Cogan Thacker and Webb 2002: 7). Inflicting literary theory on children's literature may seem even more inappropriate if the preservation of 'a sense of magic' is at stake.

Theory asks some very difficult questions of these precious texts. To begin with, there's the problem of whether children's literature exists at all. The term 'children's literature' is problematic: like the term 'women's literature' it seems to suggest that 'children' are a quantifiable, knowable body of readers, about whom observations can be made and conclusions drawn. It also suggests that this is literature that *belongs* to children, even that it is produced by them. As critics have often pointed out, of course, children's literature is (with a few exceptions) defined, produced and promoted by adults, and academic studies of children's literature are part of this process of classification. Books such as Kenneth Grahame's *Wind in the Willows* (1908) may always be included on lists of classic children's literature but be relatively unread by contemporary child readers who are being entertained by Jacqueline Wilson or David Almond, or disreputable generic series such as the *Point Horror* books or Cecily von Ziegesar's *Gossip Girl* series. Prominent children's literature critic Jack Zipes says, 'There is no such thing as children's literature [...] there has never been a literature conceived *for* children *by* children, a literature that belongs to children, and there never will be' (Zipes 2002: 40). Of course, children produce their own creative writing in school or privately, but it rarely becomes public. In terms of responding to literature, children are trained to be literary critics at school and they may informally discuss their reading preferences in book groups or online communities. What Zipes means is that there is a distinction between the literary classification 'children's literature' and the books that children might read or the writing they might themselves produce. This is an important point: because we have all at one point been child readers there's a temptation to make judgements about 'what children think' or 'how children read' in a way that we would never do about other groups of readers based on criteria such as **gender** or race, rather than age. Lapses into sentimentality about children's books are also a problem for children's literature critics. Karin Lesnik-Oberstein comes down hard on critics who indulge in the 'widespread use' of hazy and self-justifying terms such as 'dreaming' and 'wonder' (Lesnik-Oberstein 1994: 117) when discussing the nature of children's literature. There has also been a problematic emphasis on the role of the author of children's literature. The effectiveness of an author's text is assigned to a somewhat vague idea that they have retained some degree of 'childishness' or a sometimes prurient interest in the details of their psychologies, which perhaps betrays something of our culture's anxiety about the relationships between adults and children. An over-emphasis on the personality of the author also elides some of the most interesting issues around the construction of narrative voice in a children's book – where an author speaks through a child character, for example.

If we can agree for a moment that there is a grouping of texts united by an implied audience of 'children', we can start looking at what specific critical approaches can do with them. Reader-response theory, which focuses on the role of the reader in constructing the meaning of a text, has illuminated theories of what it is to read as a child (an approach Peter Hunt has called 'childist criticism'). Structuralist approaches have been particularly applicable for the study of fairy tales, and for the fantasy literature which continues to use the **archetypes** and generic forms of older literature. Psychoanalytic approaches can look for the *unconscious* motivations or **desires** of the text, the reader or the author. Feminist and Marxist criticism can reveal the ideological underpinnings of children's fiction. Postcolonial criticism can take apart, for example, the overt orientalism of much Golden Age literature's treatment of the colonies in Victorian and Edwardian boys' adventure stories (see COLONIAL AND POSTCOLONIAL LITERATURE). Comparative approaches note that much of literary criticism's discussion of 'children's literature' is based on a handful of Anglo-American texts, and ignores the literatures of other countries and languages. Aside from these literary concerns there is also a growing body of interesting interdisciplinary approaches. Common ground is emerging between literary criticism, social science and cultural studies, so literature can be considered within a network of children's culture. For example, Henry Jenkins's *The Children's Culture Reader* includes a very broad range of **discourses**, social practices and texts, including popular fiction and video games.

Poststructuralist approaches to children's literature vary widely but are particularly apposite for asking the question raised above: is there such a thing as children's literature? For that matter, is there such a thing as a child? Viewing the 'child' identity as one created and constructed differently within various **cultures**, historical periods and political ideologies suggests that adults continually project an *idea* of childhood onto 'children' and all their activities, and that children's literature is one of the main tools of this process of idealization, colonization and construction. The 'child' is a blank space against which adults can define themselves and around which all sorts of troubling issues about identity, **power** and **subjectivity** cohere. (Such an argument works in a very similar way to the postcolonial theory of **orientalism**, or feminist analyses of **gender**, as outlined by Edward Said and Judith Butler respectively.) It's easy to see how a text called *Little Women* is going to treat its heroines, and to draw out the ideas of childhood that might be informing the text, but even beyond the historical period when children's literature was very obviously didactic or romanticizing, such an approach is applicable to any system of representation which claims knowledge of the 'child' it itself constructs.

Such discussions begin to edge children's literature criticism away from the straight path through the woods and into the more dangerous (but exciting) areas of philosophy and theory where no category – child, text, meaning – is stable and straightforward.

Children's literature: sample syllabus

Week 1   Introduction: critical approaches to children's literature
Week 2   Introduction: children's literature and concepts of childhood
Week 3   Defining children's literature: nursery rhymes and picture books
Week 4   Origins: fairy tales, folk tales and fables
Week 5   18th- and 19th-century didactic moral literature
Week 6   Fantasy and subversion: Lewis Carroll, *Alice in Wonderland*; J. M. Barrie, *Peter Pan*

Week 7   The 'Golden Age' of children's literature: Frances Hodgson Burnett, *The Secret Garden* and E. Nesbit, *The Story of the Treasure Seekers*

Week 8   Narrative voice: comparing C. S. Lewis and Roald Dahl

Week 9   Modern children's literature: Philip Pullman, *His Dark Materials* trilogy

Week 10   Defining the YA novel: realism and dystopia

Week 11   Contemporary audiences: who reads *Harry Potter*?

Week 12   Contemporary children's culture: gaming, online narratives, comic books and graphic novels

Bibliography

(a) Literary works

Barrie, J. M. *Peter Pan: Peter and Wendy and Peter Pan in Kensington Gardens*. Ed. Jack Zipes. London: Penguin, 2005.

Carroll, Lewis. *Alice's Adventures in Wonderland and Through the Looking Glass*. Ed. Hugh Houghton. London: Penguin, 2003.

Dahl, Roald. *Charlie and the Chocolate Factory*. London: Penguin, 2001.

Edgeworth, Maria. *The Parent's Assistant*. London: J. Johnson and Co., 1813.

Lewis, C. S. *The Lion, the Witch and the Wardrobe*. New York: HarperCollins, 1978.

Nesbit, E. *The Story of the Treasure Seekers*. London: Puffin, 1995.

Opie, Iona and Peter, eds. *The Classic Fairy Tales*. New York: Oxford University Press, 1980.

Pullman, Philip. *His Dark Materials Trilogy*. London: Scholastic, 2008.

Rowling, J. K. *Harry Potter and the Philosopher's Stone*. London: Bloomsbury, 1997.

Sendak, Maurice. *Where the Wild Things Are*. London: Red Fox, 2000.

Twain, Mark. *The Adventures of Huckleberry Finn*. Ed. Emory Elliott. Oxford: Oxford University Press, 2008.

Wilson, Jacqueline. *The Illustrated Mum*. New York: Random House, 2007.

(b) Further reading

Cogan Thacker, Deborah and Jean Webb. *Introducing Children's Literature: From Romanticism to Postmodernism*. London and New York: Routledge, 2002.

Foster, Shirley and Judy Simons. *What Katy Read: Feminist Re-Readings of 'Classic' Stories for Girls*. Iowa City: University of Iowa Press, 1995.

Jenks, Chris. *Childhood*. London: Routledge, 1996.

McGillis, Roderick. *The Nimble Reader: Literary Theory and Children's Literature*. New York: Twayne, 1996.

Reynolds, Kimberley, ed. *Modern Children's Literature: An Introduction*. Basingstoke: Palgrave Macmillan, 2005.

Rose, Jacqueline. *The Case of Peter Pan or the Impossibility of Children's Fiction*. Philadelphia: University of Pennsylvania Press, 1992.

Tucker, Nicholas. *The Child and the Book: A Psychological and Literary Exploration*. Cambridge: Cambridge University Press, 1981.

Wall, Barbara. *The Narrator's Voice: Dilemmas in Children's Fiction*. London: Macmillan, 1991.

Zipes, Jack. *Fairy Tales and the Art of Subversion: The Classical Genre for Children and the Process of Civilisation*, 2nd edn. New York and London: Routledge, 2006.

Film studies

(Year 2)

Andrew Dix

Introduction

You may be wondering what a piece on film studies is doing in a companion to the study of literature. If you have such doubts, you are in good company. For Ingmar Bergman, the great Swedish director who worked in both cinema and theatre, 'Film has nothing to do with literature; the two art forms are usually in conflict' (Bergman 1960: 17). Bergman sets out a rigid division of cultural labour: while written texts engage 'the intellect', films, by contrast, activate 'the imagination and the emotions'. Such a distinction, of course, is liable to collapse as soon as it is examined: the viewer of, say, *Eternal Sunshine of the Spotless Mind* (2004) is cerebrally challenged, as well as emotionally rewarded, by the film's experiments with narrative patterning. Nevertheless, Bergman's separation of film and literature exemplifies a way of thinking that, even now, you may find making its mark upon your course. Some lecturers in English still conceive of Film Studies as a foreign body within the curriculum, something that endangers the host's health by promoting an inferior art form and by substituting immersion in images for the arduous reading experience initiated by literary texts. Yet what such divisive, hierarchical thinking boasts in longevity, it lacks in coherence. I hope in this chapter to discuss where you might expect to find film in your English course, and also to indicate several ways in which, far from being an unwelcome guest, the study of film has actually *enriched* the methods and projects of literary scholarship.

Cinematic literature

Film's footprint is visible everywhere in twentieth- and twenty-first-century writing. Contemporary blockbuster fictions, such as J. K. Rowling's Harry Potter series, or the novels of writers as varied as Dan Brown, John Grisham and Stephen King, already seem marked by their future cinematic adaptation: turning the pages, the reader sees in advance vivid screen locations, story-boarded action sequences and opportunities for special effects. To describe written texts of this kind as 'cinematic' appears less than complimentary, implying that they are too heavily saturated by the conventions and pleasures of mainstream film. Yet your course may take you to other moments in literary history when the affinities texts show with film actually mark their radical, innovatory quality, rather than any such commercial-mindedness. Writing in 1926, Virginia Woolf deplored cinema's vulgarizing tendency whenever it adapts literary fiction; nevertheless, she was excited by the temporal and spatial flexibility of film: 'The past could be unrolled, distances could be annihilated' (Woolf 1994: 352). The cinematically informed work you do on Woolf, then, will be interested not only in assessing what happens to her 1928 novel *Orlando* when it is adapted for the screen by Sally Potter in 1992, but in tracking film's structuring processes across all of her fiction. Similarly, you might find yourself studying Woolf's American contemporary John Dos Passos, who borrows from cinematic montage in his novels *Manhattan Transfer* (1925) and *U.S.A.* (1930–6) in order to convey the discontinuous impressions of modern urban life. As well as making space specifically for the study of innovatory films made in Europe and the United States after the First World War, your modules in modernism will explore the ways in which the literary practice of the period lends itself to reading through a filmic framework (see MODERNISM).

Film studies will not only enhance your approach to modern and postmodern literary work, but, more radically still, may allow you to produce new readings of literary texts written *before* moviemaking began in the last decade of the nineteenth century. The radical Soviet director Sergei Eisenstein envisaged such study in 1942 when he referred provocatively to 'Dickens' cinema' (Eisenstein 1996: 205). For Eisenstein, certain of Dickens's strategies – especially his multiply-centred narratives and his organization of scenes into an array of longer and closer 'shots' – do not display the mechanics of conventional Victorian novel writing but, rather, anticipate the syntax of film. From this perspective, cinema's future invention may be glimpsed not only in early optical apparatuses such as the magic lantern, but in the experiments of literary artists also – including, besides Dickens, Hardy and many other Victorian and even pre-Victorian writers. Borrowing the title of Robert Stam's 2005 book, you may find yourself reading literature *through* film.

Literary cinema

Many of the cinematically oriented modules you will take in your English course focus upon *adaptation*. Here your concern will be with what occurs when novels, short stories, plays, biographies, newspaper articles, even poems are translated into the medium of film. Film's entry into literary curricula under cover of the subject of adaptation actually echoes a strategy by which the medium sought to achieve cultural respectability early in the twentieth century. Exhibited at first in venues such as fairgrounds, circuses and music halls, film had **connotations** of popular entertainment and so looked for an alliance with literature to improve its own standing as an art form. Fledgling studios adapted both European and American classics for the screen. Such reliance upon literary sources seemed to cinema's avant-garde to be a betrayal of the new medium's particular creative possibilities. For other early theorists of film, however, cinema's turn to literature was neither timid nor disappointing: the Russian Formalist critic Boris Eikhenbaum declared in 1926 that '[e]ven though the storyline may be borrowed, plot takes unique shape in film, inasmuch as the methods themselves are original, i.e. the very elements of film speech, its very semantics' (Bann and Bowlt 1973: 124) (see FORMALISM).

Eikhenbaum awakens us to the fact that cinematic adaptation of literature is complex rather than simple; as your modules will show, adaptation is always a process of *transformation*, not of automatic or unproblematic transcription from one medium to the other. Even the slightest reflection on the respective narrative processes of literature and film shows why this is necessarily the case. Against the single means of verbalization which literary narration has at its disposal, we need to juxtapose what one writer calls 'the multiplexity of the cinematic narrator' (Chatman 1990: 134). Film narration, especially in the post-1927 sound era, is 'multi-track': its storytelling is achieved by a complex meshing of visual and aural devices, comprising in the first instance words on screen and photographic images in colour or monochrome, and in the second, dialogue, sound and music.

You will discover, however, that the study of adaptation was surprisingly slow to pick up on such fundamental differences in the DNA of literature and of film. Early scholarship in this area which you may still come across is marked by *fidelity criticism*, an interpretive mode in which the literary 'original' is given pride of place and the success or otherwise of an adaptation for the screen is gauged by how 'faithful' it is to this source text. Yet your adaptation modules should show how and why this static, hierarchical model of literary–cinematic relations has come under increasing challenge during the past 15 years. Studies such as Brian McFarlane's *Novel to Film* (1996) and Deborah Cartmell and Imelda Whelehan's *Adaptations* (1999) have pioneered a richer conceptualization of the screen adaptation of literary materials. As well as insisting upon the equality of the literary and cinematic works involved in any such transaction across media, current writers on the subject employ a wide range of models and metaphors to evoke the process of adaptation. Robert Stam's catalogue is especially full and instructive:

> adaptation as reading, rewriting, critique, translation, transmutation, metamorphosis, recreation, transvocalization, resuscitation, transfiguration, actualization, transmodalization, signifying, performance, dialogization, cannibalization, reinvisioning, incarnation, or reaccentuation. (Stam and Raengo 2005: 25)

For an example of the kind of work your adaptation module might do on a film's 'rewriting' and 'critique' of a literary text, take Steven Spielberg's 1991 film, *Hook*. Here fidelity criticism's dubious presumption of the authority of the literary 'original' is even more suspect than usual: J. M. Barrie's *Peter Pan* is a strikingly unstable rather than fixed source text, existing in different versions as both play (1904) and novel (1911). Literature's privilege dissolves further when we appreciate that, like any adaptation for the screen, *Hook* is connected **intertextually** not only to a written model but to *a host of other films*. When Robin Williams, playing the protagonist, shouts 'Good Morning, Neverland!', the words rhyme not with anything Barrie wrote but with the title of an earlier Williams film, *Good Morning, Vietnam!* (1987). Similarly, Julia Roberts's vivid transformation scene as Tinker Bell relates first of all to a cinematic rather than literary precursor, echoing the same star's magical change of image in *Pretty Woman* (1990). There is even cannibalization in *Hook* of moments from other

Spielberg films – above all, perhaps, the low-angle shot of Peter in flight that reprises the best-known image from *E.T.* (1982).

In this welter of cinematic referencing, *Peter Pan* loses its status as the singular point of origin for *Hook*, and is downgraded to just one of the film's many source texts. As with all the study of adaptations you will undertake, it is important in this instance to avoid simple statements of preference for the literary work over the film, or vice versa, and instead to aim more analytically at reconstructing the complex **aesthetic** and ideological conditions in which first Barrie's 'text', then Spielberg's, emerges. Some of Barrie's darker psycho-analytic themes – notably the thesis of a child's monstrous egotism – cannot be replicated in the film, given Spielberg's wholesome, anti-Freudian construc-tion of childhood across his directorial career. More positively, *Hook* rewrites for the modern cosmopolitan West the retrograde racial politics of *Peter Pan*. In Barrie's work, a 'gigantic black' is the most frightening of the pirates; at least symbolically, Hook too is Africanized, possessing 'a black voice' and a facial expression described as 'blackavized'. Spielberg's adaptation rereads the early-twentieth-century literary material from a contemporary perspective of racial sensitivity: for example, the film shows authority over the Lost Boys delegated to a black youth after Peter's departure.

Reading films

In his groundbreaking essay 'The Work of Art in the Age of Mechanical Repro-duction' (1935–9), the German Marxist Walter Benjamin describes film's disruptive effects upon a cultural order long established in the West: the upstart medium threatens in fact 'the liquidation of the traditional value of the cultural heritage' (Benjamin 1968: 221). What film particularly endangers is the protocol of *reading* itself. Cinema's dispersal of its products to audiences of millions seems to do away with the notion of a privileged caste of interpreters, since every spectator now is potentially in the critic's position. Ominously, Benjamin adds that 'at the movies this position requires no attention. The public is an examiner, but an absent-minded one' (237–8).

Despite Benjamin's accurate cultural forecasts in this article, his sense of film as a medium that incorrigibly resists reading, a form that provokes distrac-tion rather than attentiveness, has worn less well. Indeed, you might fairly describe as *reading* the activity with respect to film that will be solicited by your English course. As well as options specifically in adaptation, you are likely to be offered modules in which literary and cinematic works are conjoined as objects of study since both are presumed to be amenable to serious reading. The concept of **genre**, for example, nicely mediates between the two art forms, making some of their obvious differences appear relatively trivial: thus your study of the western might take you from Zane Grey's novel *Riders of the Purple Sage* (1912) to Clint Eastwood's film *Unforgiven* (1992), while your module in American noir fiction is likely to interpret with equal sensitivity both the hard-boiled prose of Raymond Chandler and the iconography and lighting of 1940s crime films. If genre has proved productively 'intermedial', so too has the notion of *representation*. A module on the representation of disability in twentieth-century America, for example, could range from William Faulkner's linguistic experiments in his novel *The Sound and the Fury* (1929) to Tom Hanks's performance style in *Forrest Gump* (1994). Similarly, a strand on Holocaust representation might well juxtapose the written testimonies of Primo Levi and Elie Wiesel with such films as *Schindler's List* (1993) and *Life Is Beautiful* (1997). The syllabus in representations of the American city that is given at the end of this chapter offers an opportunity for precisely such mixed study of literature and film.

There is a risk, in the cross-media identification of shared thematic materials, that a sense of film's formal specificity may be lost. This would be an alarming development, since meaning in cinema emerges only through precise interactions of image and sound. It is crucial, then, that even while doing your film studies work inside departments of literature, you acquire a technical vocabulary which is as carefully calibrated as the language of practical criticism you deploy upon literary texts. At times, of course, analytical terms may be exchanged across the two media: for instance, the optical metaphors favoured by narrative analysis – *focalization, point of view, perspective* – prove effective in both cinematic and literary contexts. Elsewhere, however, film studies has accumulated a rich lexicon of its own to enable detailed interpretation of both the visual and sound tracks of the works it analyses: for literary study's *iambic pentameter, enjambment* and *free indirect **discourse***, substitute film criticism's *zooming, deep focus* and *non-diegetic sound*. Mastering such terms will enable you to read a sequence of *Titanic* (1997) as fully and precisely as you analyse a passage of Jane Austen's prose.

Beyond film reading?

Describing a film as a 'text' – something, that is, which is amenable to 'reading' – has, for obvious reasons, helped to consolidate cinema's place on English courses. This textual **analogy**, however, is currently under suspicion within film studies itself. Films, after all, lend themselves not only to a mode of formal interpretation which mimics literary analysis, but also to sociologically and economically oriented work which may have little or no interest at all in uncovering nuances of meaning. Cinema is not just a collection of texts to read but, in Stam's phrase, 'a multi-dimensional socio-cultural fact' (Stam 2000: 110). Charles Acland wittily suggests, in fact, that 'the problem with film studies has been *film*, that is, the use of a medium in order to designate the boundaries of a discipline' (Acland 2003: 46). From this perspective, film studies has historically petrified around protocols of textual interpretation more suited to literature; as a result, it has, until recently, had relatively little to say about institutions of cinematic production and consumption.

To encounter contemporary film studies, then, is sometimes to uncover methodologies and research questions distinct from the kind of film work carried out within literature departments. Film studies as a specialist discipline is interested, for example, in *political economy*, in tracing the economic and industrial contours of film production (topics here might include the synergies between cinema and the music industry, or the contemporary globalization of Hollywood). Film studies has also developed an *ethnographic* strand, gathering and analysing spectator testimony about the experience of cinema-going. Finally, the discipline has turned to *cultural geography*, as when exploring the different impacts of viewing spaces that extend from the 1930s 'picture palace' through the modern multiplex to the present-day living-room equipped with high-definition image and auditorium-quality sound. Taken within English departments, however, your own cinematically oriented modules are very unlikely to follow these recent conceptual turns taken by film studies itself; instead, the protocols of textual and ideological analysis remain intact here. Rather than being asked to think about the effects of changing cinema archi-tecture, therefore, you could find yourself assessing the representation of the figure of the enemy in American war films from *The Deer Hunter* (1979) to *The Hurt Locker* (2009). Rather than analysing the ratio of box-office revenue to DVD sales in contemporary Hollywood, you are much more liable to be given the enjoyable task of uncovering the political implications of *The Incredibles* (2004).

Sample syllabus

The sample syllabus that follows is for a second-year module entitled 'Representing the American City', which moves fluidly between literary and cinematic materials, and aims to develop a comparative approach to the narrative and representational strategies of prose fiction on the one hand and of film on the other.

Week 1 Introduction to the module
Week 2 Prehistory of the modern American city: Martin Scorsese (dir.), *Gangs of New York* (2002)
Week 3 Naturalistic fiction and the city: Theodore Dreiser, *Sister Carrie* (1900)
Week 4 The American city and female desire: Dreiser, *Sister Carrie*; Terence Davies (dir.), *The House of Mirth* (2000)
Week 5 The classic American gangster film and the city: William Wellman (dir.), *The Public Enemy* (1931); Howard Hawks (dir.), *Scarface* (1932)
Week 6 Mapping the modernist city: John Dos Passos, *Manhattan Transfer* (1925)
Week 7 The politics of the modern American city: Dos Passos, *Manhattan Transfer*
Week 8 A brief history of L.A. in film noir: Howard Hawks (dir.), *The Big Sleep* (1946); Ridley Scott (dir.), *Blade Runner – The Director's Cut* (1992)
Week 9 James Ellroy's L.A. noir: James Ellroy, *The Big Nowhere* (1988)
Week 10 Ellroy's noir in fiction and film: Ellroy, *The Big Nowhere*; Curtis Hanson (dir.), *L.A. Confidential* (1997)
Week 11 American suburbia: Tim Burton (dir.), *Edward Scissorhands* (1991); Sam Mendes (dir.), *American Beauty* (1999)
Week 12 White identity in the postmodern city: Joel Schumacher (dir.), *Falling Down* (1992)

Bibliography

Because of the nature of film studies and the reading involved, it is not possible to make the kinds of distinction between primary and critical materials as is done with other modules, which clearly separate 'creative' forms of writing from the critical. This being the case, all reading is listed here as 'further reading'.

(a) Further reading

Acland, Charles. *Screen Traffic: Movies, Multiplexes, and Global Culture*. Durham, NC and London: Duke University Press, 2003.

Bann, Stephen and John E. Bowlt, eds. *Russian Formalism*. Edinburgh: Scottish Academic Press, 1973.

Benjamin, Walter. 'The Work of Art in the Age of Mechanical Reproduction'. In *Illuminations: Essays and Reflections*, ed. Hannah Arendt, 217–52. New York: Harcourt Brace Jovanovich, 1968.

Bergman, Ingmar. *Four Screenplays*. New York: Simon and Schuster, 1960.

Bignell, Jonathan, ed. *Writing and Cinema*. Harlow: Longman, 1999.

Bordwell, David and Kristin Thompson. *Film Art: An Introduction*, 8th edn. Boston, MA: McGraw-Hill, 2007.

Cartmell, Deborah and Imelda Whelehan, eds. *Adaptations: From Text to Screen, Screen to Text*. London and New York: Routledge, 1999.

Corrigan, Timothy and Patricia White. *The Film Experience*. Boston, MA: Bedford/St. Martin's, 2004.

Eisenstein, S. M. *Selected Works*, Vol. 3, ed. Richard Taylor. London: British Film Institute, 1996.

Hammond, Paul, ed. *The Shadow and Its Shadow: Surrealist Writings on the Cinema*, 2nd edn. Edinburgh: Polygon, 1991.

Hutcheon, Linda. *A Theory of Adaptation*. New York and Abingdon: Routledge, 2006.

Lothe, Jakob. *Narrative in Fiction and Film: An Introduction.* Oxford and New York: Oxford University Press, 2000.

Marcus, Laura. *The Tenth Muse: Writing about Cinema in the Modernist Period*. Oxford and New York: Oxford University Press, 2007.

Stam, Robert. *Film Theory: An Introduction*. Malden, MA and Oxford: Blackwell, 2000.

Stam, Robert. *Literature through Film: Realism, Magic, and the Art of Adaptation*. Malden, MA and Oxford: Blackwell, 2005.

Stam, Robert and Alessandra Raengo, eds. *Literature and Film: A Guide to the Theory and Practice of Film Adaptation*. Malden, MA and Oxford: Blackwell, 2005.

Stam, Robert and Alessandra Raengo, eds. *A Companion to Literature and Film*. Malden, MA and Oxford: Blackwell, 2007.

Trotter, David. *Cinema and Modernism*. Malden, MA and Oxford: Blackwell, 2007.

Wexman, Virginia, ed. *Film and Authorship*. New Brunswick, NJ and London: Rutgers University Press, 2003.

Woolf, Virginia. 'The Cinema'. *The Essays of Virginia Woolf*, Vol. 4, ed. Andrew McNeillie, 348–54. London: The Hogarth Press, 1994.

Popular fiction

(Year 3)

Jan Baetens

What is popular fiction, and where does it come from?

Suppose you are taking a course on popular fiction. The titles that appear on your reading list may be books like *Harry Potter, The Lord of the Rings, The Big Sleep, Bridget Jones's Diary*, one of the many *Star Wars* books, *Watchmen, eXistenZ* (the novel by Christopher Priest), a Barbara Cartland novel, and so on. Yet, not all these books are identified as 'popular fiction': they are classified, for example, as children's literature, **fantasy**, detective fiction, chick lit, science fiction, graphic novel (a very complex category, by the way), novelization and romance. Nevertheless, the fact that such books all belong to very different **genres** does not mean that they do not belong to the same cultural universe, 'popular fiction'.

Spontaneously, we identify 'popular' as the opposite of 'high-brow' or 'elitist', but such a definition is far too simple. It overlooks a very crucial feature of popular fiction, which is its relationship with the publishing industry. Popular fiction, in a way, is a special category to which fiction that makes the bestseller lists has been made possible by the rise of industrial techniques in the publishing business. In other words, even if some texts had proven to be extremely popular before the emergence of the industrialization of publishing –one may think here of Shakespeare, who was not considered in his time the epitome of high-brow literature – it is the merger of literature and the Industrial Revolution that has produced a new category of book, which has become labelled 'popular fiction'. For this reason, the phrase 'popular fiction' does not refer simply to fictional works that enjoy a large readership, such as Jane Austen's *Pride and Prejudice*, James Joyce's *Ulysses* or Salman Rushdie's *Satanic Verses*.

Instead, you will find on your module that 'popular fiction' names a specific type of fiction targeting a broad audience, whose very form and existence are inextricably linked with the specific features of mass culture as it emerged after the Industrial Revolution. 'Popular fiction' is associated with specific sub-genres such as detective fiction, science fiction, fantasy or romance. The reasons for this are perfectly understandable. On the one hand, most popular sub-genres of fiction emphasize entertainment and evasion, or escapism. On the other hand, they obey strong genre formulas, which not only make them predictable or 'formulaic' (you read one, and then read more because they fulfil your expectation and the experience of pleasure) but also make them easy to identify, to market and to read. A metaphor might be helpful here: if fiction can be compared to *music*, then popular fiction can be compared to *muzak*, the kind of thing you hear in the background at supermarkets or in elevators.

But let's have a look at popular fiction from the viewpoint of the author. This viewpoint is not arbitrary, for according to traditional notions of literature, it is the author who occupies the centre of the system. One of the most salient features of popular fiction will be that this situation no longer applies. In popular fiction, the author is just one of many cogs of a much bigger machine. However, the author's prominence was itself an historical phenomenon, brought about by particular manufacturing changes and related technological and cultural factors.

These factors included the introduction of new printing techniques (the rotary printing press); the drastic cutting of paper prices (thanks to the use of wood pulp); the rise of the modern press (mainly in the form of newspapers and magazines); the gradual spread of literacy (due to compulsory public education); the overall movement towards more democracy and liberalism; and, finally, the collapse of the traditional economic and legal system that characterized and ruled literary production till the end of the eighteenth century. Such factors determined, in the 1820s, a totally new situation in which writers could become professionalized, without being dependent on the traditional pursuit of authorship as a result of the privilege of personal wealth or official sponsorship.

If the new situation meant freedom, it was one that came at a huge price. From the beginning of the nineteenth century to today, the author has had to sell his or her writing, and he or she can only do so with the help of the publisher, who ceases to be a printer, as he had been in the seventeenth and eighteenth centuries, catering to the needs of the author under strict legal, state-ruled conditions, and who becomes very rapidly an entrepreneur in the modern sense of the word, taking personal risk in the launching of new products for increasingly broader markets and considering the author an employee rather than a partner. Authors who didn't enjoy a personal income from rent (such as Flaubert or Proust) were obliged either to accept a daytime job (often linked to writing, like journalism, as in the case of Walt Whitman), or to cater for a broad audience (the work of Charles Dickens is a good example here). Thus, a necessary component in any module on popular fiction must be one that emphasizes and explores these historical dimensions of publication, authorship and market.

Popular fiction as a literary issue

It is as a result of this **context** in its full historical scope that we have witnessed the division of the literary field into various categories, the extremes of which have been defined as 'high' culture and 'popular' culture. According to John Storey, 'popular' has been used since the nineteenth century to designate forms of art and entertainment that appealed to 'ordinary' people. But given the fact that the popular was most of the time defined in relationship to high culture, it was then suggested that popular culture 'is the culture which is left over after we have decided what is high culture' (Storey 2001: 6). Many discussions on popular culture in general and popular fiction in general have been focusing on the allegedly essential inferiority of the popular as well as on the threats of its success for the position of high culture. The names of Mathew Arnold, in the nineteenth century, and F. R. Leavis, in the twentieth century, are often associated with these debates on the popular as the culture of the 'philistines'. With the rise of visual culture and the promotion of cinema as the dominating cultural form of the twentieth century, the opposition between high culture and popular culture is no longer reduced to that of elite literature and popular fiction, but takes more and more the form of a conflict between the literary and the visual (most defenders of classic views on high literary have also a strong anti-visual bias, as demonstrated exemplarily by Postman 1985 and Birkerts 1995). The very dichotomy of popular and high culture, which may have been a reality in the nineteenth century, even though there were already many signs of the opposite, has been challenged systematically for more than a century. Modern art, as we know today, has been dramatically influenced by all of that which advocates of high art had been denouncing as typically popular: images (and all the – female – seductiveness it implied), machines (and all the dehumanization it was said to involve) and commercialism (and all the artistic **alienation** it supposedly involved). However, contemporary scholars no longer accept the social, artistic and ontological gap between literary innovation and mass culture (Suarez 2007; Trotter 2007). It would be a mistake, though, to believe resistance to popularization of the literary heritage has all but disappeared, and this resistance has to be identified with right-wing politics. Today, these debates may seem out of fashion, but the systematic return of this debate is witnessed each time an effort is made to communicate between high-cultural models and products in popular form (literary talk shows on television, film adaptations of classic books, reuse of literary material in musicals, etc.). And it would be an illusion to believe that the formulaic aspects of much popular fiction are now warmly welcomed by all critics.

It is undoubtedly cultural studies that has played a key role in this thorough re-evaluation of the relationships between the popular and the high-cultural model. This has come about through proposing new models for a sociologically inspired approach of the literary production and by making a plea for a non-evaluative description of the popular as cultural practices (see CULTURAL STUDIES, CLASS). In the field of literature, these discussions have evolved in two different, but nevertheless related areas.

The first of these areas has to do with the very definition of what literature is, and what it is not (and if there are still forms of expression that do *not* belong to the all-embracing field of literature). Since the gap between high and low literature is less broad than before, it is now possible to include genres and media like the graphic novel, the lyrics of a rock song, the photo-novella, or the novelization, to pick just a few examples, as valuable forms of literature. The same goes for non-fictional genres such as editorial columns, blogs, music reviews or the photo-essay (here too, the set of examples and genres could be extended almost indefinitely). Moreover, the collapse of the distinction between popular fiction and high literature has been reinforced by parallel debates on the relationship between Western and non-Western literature. And even more radically, what contemporary definitions of literature are abandoning is the exclusively verbal character of its object. Films, soap operas on radio and television, and even video games are valuable forms of storytelling, and now considered as forms of literature that cut across media and therefore exceed the boundaries of what was traditionally called literature. In short, the opening of the literary field to popular forms, the culture wars that have criticized the Western **canon** and the increasing intermediality of literature are all part of the same cultural shift that shatters our age-old ideas of the literary. The consequences for classic ways of evaluating literature seem dramatic, for it is now possible to claim the Nobel prize for, say, Leonard Cohen or Bob Dylan. Yet in practice, one has to observe that the traditional vertical distinctions between higher and lower genres have not so much disappeared as have been integrated in the horizontal juxtaposition of all types of writings: avant-garde poetry and detective pulp fiction may occupy the same position on the global cultural scale, yet within either of them the distinction between the highly valued and the less valued forms is still there and is still functioning according to the classic values of high literature (innovation, originality, personality, multi-layeredness, and so on).

The second shift does not concern the content of popular fiction, but offers one of the more legitimate ways to study it. The classic evaluative way of approaching popular fiction has been abandoned. Popular fiction is no longer seen as 'the **other**' of high, good, legitimate writing, but considered from a more descriptive viewpoint which tries to foreground the contextual and historical determinations of how popular fiction is produced as well as consumed. Given the pre-eminence of industrial, technological and commercial aspects in the rise of the popular fiction market, it is understandable that the logic of writing and reading is likely to become completely different from the traditional view of literature as the expression of one's personal self (from the viewpoint of the author) and the desire for personal self-fulfilment (from the viewpoint of the reader). Following, for instance, Dominique Kalifa (2001), the mere description of popular culture as the transformation of a work of art into a commodity is far from sufficient. Such an evaluative and moralizing judgement pre-empts an in-depth analysis of the cultural impact of the **semiotics** of the object, which has now to obey the triple law of novelty, seriality and adaptation. New forms of popular fiction must be circulated continuously for a public in constant search of new stimuli that wants to consume in order to fill up empty leisure time, hence the programmed short-livedness of much popular fiction and the always increasing pace of product innovation. Those objects that are well received by the public are then serially reproduced for a greater return on investment, whose costs are more and more linked to advertisement campaigns (contrary to the 'cheap' but slow system of book reviewing in traditional systems). And successful items are exploited as much as possible in different media. Adaptation, in this view, represents the culminating logic of the combination of novelty and seriality, for an adaptation is a product that is new and serialized at the same time; and which, furthermore, can be considered profitable for this double reason.

Between constraint and rhetoric

The strictly economic underpinnings of this vision can be further detailed with the study of what R. A. Peterson in a seminal article (1982) has called the 'constraints' on the production of culture, and whose relevance for popular fiction is much stronger than for high literary art: (1) law (investors cannot take the risk that the circulation of cultural products might be hindered by legal restrictions, hence the frequent use of internal censorship codes in the various fields of mass culture art); (2) technology (the current state of production and reception technology has an impact on what is produced and how it is brought to the audience: it should come as no surprise if the success of the iPod and other storage devices brings with it a spectacular return of the audio book); (3) market (the initiative of the making of a work of art is taken by the publisher and his or her editors, not by the author of popular fiction, while the former rely for their decisions on at least an intuitive knowledge of the market); (4) organizational structure (the position of the author is for instance determined by the shifting relationships between publisher, editor and agent, who all have their word to say in the production of the work; by corollary, the formulaic aspects of popular fiction are a side-product of the ever-increasing production speed of this type of writing, where any traditional mode of writing and editing is superseded by the higher necessities of cost reduction); and (5) occupational careers (which will encourage or discourage beginning authors, for instance, to embrace this or that medium, to practise this or that **genre**, or to adopt this or that style).

The triple law of novelty, seriality and adaptation, as well as the multiple constraints that burden popular culture, should not, however, make us neglect the fundamental importance of rhetoric in popular fiction. If non-popular fiction is supposed to be author-oriented (the role of the reader is here to live vicariously through what has been felt and expressed by the author), popular fiction is definitely reader-oriented, hence the alleged affinity with sensationalism. This concept is dangerous, however, for its moralizing overtones. Moreover, it would not be very difficult to demonstrate that many forms of classic or traditional literature are no less sensationalist, not to say sentimental, gory or even 'trashy', or emotionally exploitative in some way. Yet it is undeniable that ideas of suspense and emotional involvement are key to the understanding of what popular fiction is – or, should we say, what popular fiction *does*, for this is finally the major revolution brought by our new ways of looking at the popular: rather than broadening the **canon**, it has forced us to rediscover that literature, like art, is in the very first place an experience (Shusterman 1992).

Popular fiction: sample syllabus

Week 1   How do readers identify this field? How do they approach popular fiction?: one *Star Wars* book; a Barbara Cartland novel

Week 2   Which books are marketed as popular fiction and how do publishers structure this field?: Christopher Priest, *eXistenZ*; Alan Moore and Dave Gibbons, *Watchmen*

Week 3   How is the profile of the typical author of popular fiction defined?: R. A. Peterson, 'Five Constraints on the Production of Culture'

Week 4   History of popular fiction (1): the emergence of popular fiction

Week 5   History of popular fiction (2): 20th-century genres: Juan Antonio Suarez, *PopModernism: Noise and the Reinvention of the Everyday*

Week 6   History of popular fiction (3): contemporary forms of popular fiction

Week 7   Critical voices against the success of popular fiction: Sven Birkerts, *The Gutenberg Elegies*

Week 8   Critical voices in defence of popular fiction: John Storey, *Cultural Theory and Popular Culture*

Week 9   What can we learn from popular fiction if we want to redefine literature in general?: Richard Shusterman, *Pragmatist Aesthetics*

Week 10 Relationships between popular fiction and visual culture + reading: Neil Postman, *Amusing Ourselves to Death*

Week 11 Which methods and theories are most appropriate to the study of the field?: Richard Shusterman, *Pragmatist Aesthetics*

Week 12 Popular fiction and the tension between freedom and constraint

Bibliography

(a) Literary works

Fielding, Helen. *Bridget Jones's Diary*. London: Penguin, 2009.

Moore, Alan and Dave Gibbons. *Watchmen*. New York: DC, 1987.

Priest, Christopher. *eXistenZ*. New York: Harper, 1999.

Rowling, J. K. *Harry Potter and the Philosopher's Stone*. London: Bloomsbury, 1997.

Tolkien, J. R. R. *The Lord of the Rings*. 3 vols. London: Allen and Unwin, 1954–5.

(b) Further reading

Birkerts, Sven. *The Gutenberg Elegies: The Fate of Reading in an Electronic Age*. Winchester, MA: Faber and Faber, 1995.

Kalifa, Dominique. *La Culture de masse en France*, *1860–1930*. Paris: La Découverte, 2001.

Peterson, R. A. 'Five Constraints on the Production of Culture: Law, Technology, Market, Organizational Structure and Occupational Careers'. *Journal of Popular Culture*, 16(2) (1982): 143–53.

Postman, Neil. *Amusing Ourselves to Death: Public Discourse in the Age of Show Business*. New York: Viking Press, 1985.

Shusterman, Richard. *Pragmatist Aesthetics: Living Beauty, Rethinking Art*. Oxford: Blackwell, 1992.

Storey, John. *Cultural Theory and Popular Culture. An Introduction*. Harlow: Pearson, 2001.

Suarez, Juan Antonio. *PopModernism: Noise and the Reinvention of the Everyday*. Chicago: Illinois University Press, 2007.

Trotter, David. *Cinema and Modernism*. Oxford: Blackwell, 2007.

2

American literature

Brian Jarvis and Andrew Dix

'Who reads an American book?' asked the nineteenth-century British critic Sydney Smith. The tone of his question reflects not simply personal scorn but a widespread, long-lasting disregard in Britain for American writing compared with the established literatures of England, France, Germany, Russia and other European centres. Even as literary study became institutionalized in the United Kingdom during the twentieth century, writings from the United States remained at best disparaged, at worst neglected entirely. In the past four decades, however, pioneered by scholars including Tony Tanner at Cambridge and Malcolm Bradbury at East Anglia, the study of American literature in British universities has expanded hugely. Now, wherever you pursue your course, you will have many opportunities to read 'an American book'.

According to the US poet Walt Whitman, writing about his homeland, 'Here is not merely a nation, but a teeming of nations.' A similar claim can be made about the study of American literature now: you will find not merely *a* module but a *teeming* of modules. Depending on your institution, these may be organized by *period* ('Nineteenth Century'); by *geography* ('The American West'); by *race and ethnicity* ('African American'); by *gender and sexuality* ('Women's Writing'; 'Gay and Lesbian Literature'); by *theme* ('The American Dream'); by *form and genre* ('American Detective Fiction'); by *literary school* ('Dirty Realists'); by *specific writer* ('Henry James'); or by *interdisciplinary combination* ('Literature, Film and Music of the Vietnam War'). This essay cannot aspire to cover every kind of study of American literature you will undertake; yet it offers, we hope, an introduction to the most important names, themes and contexts in this exciting field.

Ethnic American literatures

Many of the modules you will be offered in American literature cohere around types of racial and ethnic identity. Opportunities are increasingly emerging to study *Native American* work from a time before white settlement on the American continent to the present. Referring to a thing called 'Native American literature' is not, however, without its problems. The verbal art historically produced by Indians is not always easily assigned to the categories which underpin conventional literary study; it may instead take such varied forms as tribal chant, prayer, folk tale and oratory (well-studied examples from the nineteenth century include the defiant speechmaking of Chief Seattle). Nevertheless, much of your work in this area will focus upon modern Indian interventions into familiar Western forms of fiction and poetry. Modules on the Native American novel might range from N. Scott Momaday's *House Made of Dawn* (1968), through Leslie Marmon Silko's *Ceremony* (1977) and Louise Erdrich's narrative cycles, to the contemporary, stylistically freewheeling fiction of Sherman Alexie. Major Native American poets you may read include Paula Gunn Allen and Simon Ortiz.

If Native American writing has still only a patchy presence in British universities, the study of *African American* literature is, by contrast, firmly established. Modules that you take in this tradition will have a significant historical range, frequently reaching back to mid-nineteenth-century slave narratives by Frederick Douglass, Hannah Crafts and Harriet Jacobs (and sometimes, in cross-ethnic fashion, reading these alongside *Uncle Tom's Cabin*, by the white novelist Harriet Beecher Stowe, which we discuss below). From the first half of the twentieth century, you may study the blues-influenced poetry of Langston Hughes, the vernacular fiction of Zora Neale Hurston and other productions – musical and painterly, as well as literary – of 'the Harlem Renaissance'. Richard Wright's *Native Son* (1940), an incendiary novel of a proletarian black man on the run for murder in racist Chicago, will give you a further sense of African American literature's freeing itself from politeness and conformism (as, in different ways, will Ralph Ellison's mapping of black inner life in his novel *Invisible Man* and James Baldwin's intelligent rage across a body of novels and essays). From nearer our own moment, it is likely you will read two novels above all others: Alice Walker's *The Color Purple* (1982), which revives for new political purposes the eighteenth-century form of the **epistolary novel**, and Toni Morrison's *Beloved* (1987), which combines structural innovation and verbal beauty with harrowing examination of slavery as America's original sin. The best modules in the black US tradition are also generically wide-ranging, extending perhaps to oratory by Martin Luther King, Jr. and Malcolm X, or to the prison writings of Black Panther activists. You may get a chance as well to explore rap and hip hop: one of the present authors, indeed, tries implausibly to pretend in the seminar room that he is an expert on Jay-Z and Kanye West.

Other 'minority' literatures of the United States might also figure on your syllabus. A traditional object of study is *Jewish American* literature, ranging chronologically from early fictions of the immigrant experience like Abraham Cahan's *Yekl: A Tale of the New York Ghetto* (1896) to postwar meditations on assimilation and inter-ethnic relations by such novelists as Saul Bellow, Bernard Malamud and the still-productive Philip Roth.

Modern migrations, however, have seen the growth of other ethnic American literatures that will be reflected in your modules. You may, for example, study *Asian American* literature, assessing the pitfalls as well as potentials of a critical label that is affixed to diverse figures like the Chinese American novelist Maxine Hong Kingston and the Indian-born writer of novels and short stories Bharati Mukherjee. Modules are also emerging in the increasingly prominent literatures known as *Hispanic*, *Latino/a* and *Chicano/a*. 'Hispanic' and 'Latino/a' signify US populations having ethnic and cultural affiliations to the Spanish-speaking Americas and Caribbean, with 'Chicano/a' reserved for those of specifically Mexican descent; the feminine 'a' gives important recognition to female members of the communities. Your work on these literatures might take you to the fiction of the contemporary Chicana Sandra Cisneros; to the crossing of cultures, languages and forms performed by Chicana intellectual Gloria Anzaldúa in *Borderlands/La Frontera* (1987); or to *The Brief Wondrous Life of Oscar Wao* (2007), a playful, yet abidingly political novel by the Dominican American Junot Díaz (see CHICANO/A STUDIES).

Early American literature (1620–1830)

Rather than organized by race or ethnicity, your study of American literature may be arranged chronologically. While many modules have later starting points, some will introduce you to the first white-authored texts in America, produced during the phase of Puritan settlement that began early in the seventeenth century (see THE SEVENTEENTH CENTURY). These foundational texts vary in **genre**, sometimes testing conventional understandings of what constitutes 'literature'. They include William Bradford's account of the Pilgrims' arrival in the New World in *Of Plymouth Plantation* (1630); John Winthrop's 'City upon a Hill' sermon (1630); the best-known 'Indian captivity narrative', *Narrative of the Captivity and Restoration of Mrs. Mary Rowlandson* (1682); and the work of America's first published poet, Anne Bradstreet. Study of these writings will develop your knowledge of three key areas: the nature and significance of American Puritanism; the social, economic and environmental hardships of everyday life in the colonies; and the colonists' fervent commitment, even so, to creating a new society.

Materials you may study from the eighteenth and early nineteenth centuries indicate the legacy of Puritan vision and rhetoric (see THE EIGHTEENTH CENTURY). The voice of an emerging national identity can be heard, variously, in Benjamin Franklin's *Autobiography* (1771); in the *Declaration of Independence* (1776), written primarily by Thomas Jefferson; and in Hector St. John de Crèvecoeur's *Letters from an American Farmer* (1782). Following the political secession of the United States from Britain, literature was key to the development of American *cultural* independence, and three pioneering figures in this regard you may encounter are Charles Brockden Brown, Washington Irving and James Fenimore Cooper. Brown's novels, particularly *Wieland* (1798), and Irving's short stories, including 'The Legend of Sleepy Hollow' and 'Rip Van Winkle' (both 1820), achieved popularity by their adapting of European gothic and folk tale to American settings. Cooper's 'Leatherstocking' novels, notably *The Last of the Mohicans* (1826), remodelled Sir Walter Scott's romances about medieval Britain for the purposes of reflecting on nation, race and progress in the United States.

Romanticism and realism (1830–1910)

While some institutions do not cover writings of Puritan and revolutionary America, almost all offer modules in the nation's literature from the mid-nineteenth century onwards. Three writers are likely to be especially prominent in your study of fiction produced during the two decades before the Civil War (1861–5). For Nathaniel Hawthorne, in novels including *The Scarlet Letter* (1850) and many short stories, the Puritan period, mingling utopian aspiration with disquieting cruelty, proved especially compelling for re-examination. Edgar Allan Poe figures in a variety of syllabuses: for example, in modules devoted to American gothic, with his delirious fictions of mental and moral collapse that include 'The Fall of the House of Usher' and 'The Tell-Tale Heart'; or in strands on US detective fiction, given his pioneering trio of stories featuring the amateur sleuth Dupin. Although Herman Melville may crop up as author of texts like 'Bartleby the Scrivener' (1856), the fable of a New York clerk's mysterious intransigence, he will enter your courses above all as writer of *Moby-Dick: or, The Whale* (1851). Encyclopaedic in its contents and concerns – mingling Shakespeare with harpoons, clam chowder with pointed critique of America's growing power – *Moby-Dick* provides an early entrant for title of 'the Great American Novel' (a term coined in 1868 and still current in the framing of some modules).

Obsessive in their personal visions, Melville's Captain Ahab and Poe's Roderick Usher dwell on the morbid wing of American romanticism (see ROMANTICISM AND GOTHIC). Other, less destructive strains of the nineteenth-century romantic tradition in the US will figure in your studies, with the most significant of these being *Transcendentalism*. Based in New England during the 1840s and 1850s, Transcendentalism was a literary and philosophical movement dominated by three figures: Ralph Waldo Emerson, Henry David Thoreau and Walt Whitman. Emerson's essays (especially 'Nature' [1836], 'The American Scholar' [1837] and 'Self-Reliance' [1841]), Thoreau's autobiographical *Walden, or, Life in the Woods* (1854) and Whitman's poetry in *Leaves of Grass* (first edition 1855) comprise the indispensable reading list of Transcendentalism. Modules in this area will focus on subjects such as Transcendentalist understanding of connections between nature, art, spirituality and the body; Transcendentalism as critique of rising capitalism, industrialization and urbanization; and Transcendentalism as precursor of contemporary environmentalism and green politics.

Variants of romanticism are also apparent in writing by nineteenth-century American women which you should have occasion to study. The emergence of the female writer in the United States was not universally welcomed: writing in 1855, Hawthorne complained about the 'damned mob of scribbling women' which was often outselling male contemporaries. Hawthorne's particular target was practitioners of *sentimental fiction*, a **genre** intended largely for a female audience, and characterized by melodramatic plotting and emotional excess. Still-studied examples include Louisa M. Alcott's *Little Women* (1869) and Stowe's *Uncle Tom's Cabin* (1852). The latter is a landmark in nineteenth-century American literary history: the first US novel to sell over a million copies due to its deftly combining the pleasures of sentimental fiction with the moral urgency of anti-slavery polemic. While Stowe did not challenge the institutions of marriage and motherhood, other female writers in America made suggestive links between slavery on the one hand and patriarchal oppression on the other. Late in the nineteenth century, and early in the twentieth, they offered piercing diagnoses of the condition of American women, exploring not only the politics of the family but also such subjects as female sexuality, female labour, and the pleasures and dangers of a new, female-centred consumerism (see GENDER). Work in this vein you will meet includes the innovative poetry of Emily Dickinson; Charlotte Perkins Gilman's gothic story, 'The Yellow Wallpaper' (1890); Kate Chopin's novel of female rebellion, *The Awakening* (1899); and Edith Wharton's subtle explorations of gender, money and manners in *The House of Mirth* (1905) and *The Age of Innocence* (1920).

Concurrent with these strains of women's writing were versions of male-authored *realism* (see REALISM). For Ernest Hemingway, writing in 1935, 'All modern American literature comes from one book by Mark Twain.' Extravagant as the claim is, it nevertheless recognizes the importance of Twain's attempt in *Adventures of Huckleberry Finn* (1884–5) to purge American writing of any lingering nostalgia for English style and ground it instead in local speech. Twain's key novel is studied variously, according to institution: it crops up, for instance, in modules on the American South, or on the literature of slavery, or on comedy in US fiction. If Twain is indelibly associated with the South, his friend William Dean Howells – in still-studied novels like *A Hazard of New Fortunes* (1890) – was a realist of commercialized, urbanized New England. Your course may, however, allow you to explore how Howells's mode of realism fell into crisis at the end of the nineteenth century. For *naturalist* novelists, on the one hand, realism's attention to the contours of everyday life was insufficient to register the environmental forces that, pessimistically, they saw crushing the human subject: fiction in this vein you may study includes Frank Norris's *McTeague* (1899) and Theodore Dreiser's *Sister Carrie* (1900). For American *modernists*, on the other hand, both realism and naturalism were ill equipped to uncover the complexities of consciousness. Here a major transitional figure you will encounter is Henry James. Initially a realist in such novels as *The Portrait of a Lady* (1881), James moved in later texts like *The Ambassadors* (1903) towards symbolism, impressionism and other strategies associated with the modernist novel (see MODERNISM). Such is the richness of James, however, that he may fill several slots in your curriculum: as gothic writer, say, with *The Turn of the Screw* (1898), or, given his mapping of Anglo-American cultural relations, as a figure well suited to American literary study's current interest in the *international* dimensions of US writing.

Modernism and its discontents (1910–45)

It is likely that you will have many opportunities to study American modernist fiction and poetry of the first half of the twentieth century. Although modernist novels of the US should be set alongside work produced in Europe by Virginia Woolf, James Joyce and others, they also have distinctive national qualities. Your studies here will uncover diverse techniques, atmospheres and ideologies. Writers' strategies range from the unobtrusive symbolism of F. Scott Fitzgerald's *The Great Gatsby* (1925) to the collages through which John Dos Passos registers modern urban life in *Manhattan Transfer* (1925), or from the stripped-down prose of Hemingway to the labyrinthine sentences and temporal dislocations by which William Faulkner, notably in *The Sound and the Fury* (1929) and *Absalom! Absalom!* (1936), elaborates the complexities of the post-Civil War South. The mood of American modernist fiction varies, too: if these novelists are sometimes euphoric in the face of modernity, they are also adepts of apocalyptic imagery, from the dead Gatsby floating in his swimming pool to Hollywood burning at the end of Nathanael West's *The Day of the Locust* (1939). You will explore, too, the variable politics of American modernist fiction. While the early Dos Passos is fiercely leftist, Fitzgerald, for example, seems unsure whether to snarl or swoon at the conspicuous wealth of 'the Jazz Age'. There is also a **patriarchal** strain in this work, exemplified by the machismo with which Hemingway pursued not merely big game but laconic, manly sentences. Gertrude Stein will give you a healthy, if challenging, experience of female-authored modernist prose.

Following the Wall Street Crash of 1929 and the onset of the Great Depression, some American novelists came to feel that modernist difficulty and abstraction were unsuited to tough times. While much of the political fiction of the 1930s is now little studied, you may well read John Steinbeck's *The Grapes of Wrath* (1939). Still indebted to modernist innovation, Steinbeck's novel nevertheless reinvigorates realism and political narrative in its account of the epic journey to California of Oklahoma farmers uprooted by poverty.

As with US modernist fiction, so in America's modernist verse you will encounter a stimulating variety of forms and contents. The modernist American poetic is, adapting Whitman, 'large and contains multitudes'. It can be ecstatic or despairing in mood; radical or reactionary in politics; and epic or minimalist in scale (Ezra Pound's 120 *Cantos* [1915–62] compared with his two-line 'In a Station of the Metro' [1913]). Pound exhorted his contemporaries to 'make it new', and tracing the several phases of innovation in his own work will allow you to grasp how American poetry was both a laboratory and a battleground during this period. Early in his career, Pound attempted to import aspects of classical Chinese and Japanese poetry, particularly the *haiku*, into his verse. Emphasizing brevity, precision and the foregoing of both 'ornamental' language and rigid rhyme schemes, the resulting *imagist* poetic was taken up by other writers you may study, including H.D. (Hilda Doolittle) and Amy Lowell. After the First World War, however, in work such as *Hugh Selwyn Mauberley* (1920) and the accumulating *Cantos*, Pound moved away from imagism. Crucially, besides advancing his own poetry, he advised T. S. Eliot in the composition of *The Waste Land* (1922). This notoriously 'difficult' long poem is marked by radical disjunctions in time and space, and interweaves numerous dramatic voices with an encyclopaedia of allusions to literary, mythological, religious and philosophical sources. Sometimes placed on English syllabuses, because of Eliot's later British citizenship, *The Waste Land* is also central to the study of US poetry.

William Carlos Williams was one of those American modernist poets profoundly affected by Eliot, likening the impact of *The Waste Land* to that of 'an atom bomb'. Initially an imagist – as in the much-anthologized poem, 'The Red Wheelbarrow' (1923) – Williams regrouped after his reading of Eliot. However, your course may allow you to explore his later attempts to distance himself from 'European' modernism and develop a distinctively 'American' poetic. Here the key text is *Paterson* (1963), a five-volume verse meditation on the modern US city. Other modernist American poets you will encounter include the verbal and typographical experimentalist e. e. cummings, the philosophically meditative Wallace Stevens, and Marianne Moore, whose poetry combines precise focus on objects and images, often animals, with scrutiny of the power of the imagination. An American poet more antagonistic towards modernism, but still liable to crop up in your study of this period, is Robert Frost, who tends to use traditional verse forms and frequently focuses on lives and landscapes of rural New England.

Postwar American writing (1945 to present)

Many of the modules open to you in American literature will be dedicated to modern and contemporary work. Here we offer brief discussion of three major fields of study.

Postwar poetry

Your work on postwar American poetry will typically survey a number of 'schools' and 'movements'. The earliest and arguably most famous of these is the *Beat generation*. First glimpsed emerging from artistic communities in New York, San Francisco and Los Angeles during the late 1940s, and active in fiction as well as poetry, the 'Beats' were eclectic in personality and achievement, but shared certain commitments, including hostility towards capitalism, conformity and the state; adherence to 'alternative' lifestyles, including drug use and sexual experiment; fascination with jazz and blues; interest in Eastern and Native American religions; and respect for the American environment. The two most distinctive poetic voices in the Beat generation belong to Allen Ginsberg and Gary Snyder. Ginsberg's 'Howl' (1956) attracted much attention for its wild union of social protest, religious ecstasy and homosexual yearning. Snyder's work combines Zen Buddhism, Native American mythology and environmentalism in a lyrical exploration of the connections between people and the land. Alongside the Beat generation are the *Black Mountain poets* (Robert Creeley, Robert Duncan, Denise Levertov and Charles Olson). As well as their poetry, you may read Olson's manifesto essay, 'Projective Verse'

(1950), which rejected fixed metres in favour of a more flexible, 'natural' poetic line based on breath.

Whilst the Beats engaged with public and political issues, the *Confessional poets* were renowned for unveilings of often painful personal experience. Robert Lowell's *Life Studies* (1959) and *For the Union Dead* (1964), Sylvia Plath's *The Colossus* (1960) and *Ariel* (1965), John Berryman's *The Dream Songs* (1969) and Anne Sexton's *The Death Notebooks* (1974) draw on intimate autobiographical detail whilst also fashioning masks and personas to explore **desire**, illness, depression, madness and suicide. Elizabeth Bishop was a close friend of Lowell but avoided 'Confessional' style and focused instead, like her mentor Marianne Moore, on precise, often painterly depictions of the physical world. Although Bishop's lesbianism does not feature directly in her work, you may engage with explicitly lesbian concerns in the politically engaged poetry and essays of Adrienne Rich. Another poetic current you might study is the *New York School*, flourishing especially in the 1950s and 1960s. The work of its leading members, such as Frank O'Hara and the still-prolific John Ashbery, is influenced by visual art and characterized by a **stream of consciousness** style. Its formal complexity and linguistic playfulness are replicated by the *Language poets*, amongst whom Susan Howe is a leading figure.

Fiction of the 1950s, 1960s and 1970s

Exuberant in its forms and voices, and resonant in its concerns, postwar fiction is probably the most popular, widely studied strand of American literature. Your work on fiction of the 1950s is likely to circle around three texts in particular. J. D. Salinger's *The Catcher in the Rye* (1951), intimately voiced by its 16-year-old protagonist Holden Caulfield, has proved iconic for young people confronting the absurdities of social power. Jack Kerouac's *On the Road* (1957) – the key Beat novel – has been an equally indispensable item in the backpacks of American (and global) nonconformists. Although recently subjected to scrutiny by feminist, postcolonial and ecological critics, *On the Road* remains appealing in its vision of open spaces as an escape from the capitalist, bureaucratic and military structures cohering in postwar America. Requiring of the reader both a strong stomach and a resourceful brain, William Burroughs's *Naked Lunch* (1959) is still much studied for its searching examination of American conformity in a narrative that descends into hallucinatory worlds of drug use.

Optimistic currents in the United States during the 1960s will not necessarily be reflected in the novels you study. Instead, you are likely to read texts that explore, directly or indirectly, the decade's darker historical developments, including the Vietnam War, political assassinations, race riots and nuclear anxieties. Novelists of this period are inventive in finding metaphors of state and corporate coercion: Joseph Heller turns to a Second World War airbase in the **absurdist** *Catch-22* (1961), Ken Kesey and Sylvia Plath to the mental institution in *One Flew Over the Cuckoo's Nest* (1962) and *The Bell Jar* (1963) respectively, while Kurt Vonnegut has Vietnam in mind as much as the 1945 firebombing of Dresden that he revisits imaginatively in *Slaughterhouse-Five* (1969). Given sufficient stamina, you might also study a number of novels that attempt on a gargantuan scale to trace the origins and consequences of the postwar 'military-industrial complex': chief examples here – mingling historical seriousness with cartoonish play – are Thomas Pynchon's *Gravity's Rainbow* (1973) and Robert Coover's *The Public Burning* (1977). You will find E. L. Doctorow **historicist** in a different vein, turning to the US past in a series of novels in order to locate both the seeds of national destruction and resources for political renewal. But if these writers are often drawn to the grotesque and apocalyptic, other novelists you may study take less sensational paths. Anne Tyler, for example, deals subtly with the changing lives of Middle American women. In the *Rabbit* tetralogy of novels (1960–90), and numerous other fictions, John Updike tracks shifts in small-town America through conventional narrative modes that he nevertheless endows with lyrical resonance.

Fiction of the 1980s, 1990s and 2000s

The field here is vast and, of course, still growing. The Vietnam veteran Tim O'Brien has been writing since the early 1970s about war and trauma, as well as the relationship between history, narrative and the imagination: *The Things They Carried* (1990) appears regularly on modules in both war and postmodern literature. Different varieties of traumatic violence and their relationship to masculine identity figure centrally in Bret Easton Ellis's fiction. In *Less Than Zero* (1985) and *American Psycho* (1991), Ellis links violence with consumerism, sex and drug taking (a toxic cocktail also served up by Chuck Palahniuk's *Fight Club* [1996]). In Ellis's *Glamorama* (1998), the lives of over-sexed, permanently 'wasted' supermodels are connected provocatively to international terrorism. The fiction of terrorism has become a burgeoning sub-genre after the events of September 11, 2001, and examples include Jonathan Safran Foer's *Extremely Loud and Incredibly Close* (2005), Updike's *Terrorist* (2006), Joseph O'Neill's *Netherland* (2008) and Don DeLillo's *Falling Man* (2007). In a 40-year career, DeLillo has returned regularly to the theme of terrorism, as well as to issues of power in consumerist, media-dominated America. David Foster Wallace's *Infinite Jest* (1996) is a massive, seriocomic critique of a near-future society governed by advertising and various forms of addiction. A comparably ambitious critique of capitalism, globalization, technology and their impact on family life is central to Jonathan Franzen's *The Corrections* (2001). Whilst Foster Wallace and Franzen work on an epic scale, Raymond Carver is a major American miniaturist, his short stories – as in *Cathedral* (1984) – finding revelations in the mundane experiences of everyday life. In Paul Auster's fiction, including *The New York Trilogy* (1987) and *Moon Palace* (1989), you will find further engagement with the everyday, alongside self-reflexive meditations on the writing process and the relationship between words and reality. If many of these writers are predominantly concerned with New York and L.A., some contemporaries map other American spaces. Cormac McCarthy's novels, for example *Blood Meridian* (1985) and *No Country for Old Men* (2005), offer gothic revision of the mythology of the American West. Annie Proulx's 'Brokeback Mountain' (1997) and other Wyoming-set short stories explore previously neglected lives on the Western frontier.

Your course may also introduce you to popular novels in the crime, horror and sci-fi genres. James Ellroy's *L.A. Confidential* (1990) extends and sometimes critiques the tradition of noir detective fiction which began with Raymond Chandler, Dashiell Hammett and Mickey Spillane. Walter Mosley's *Devil in a Blue Dress* (1990) and other 'Easy Rawlins' crime novels cumulatively construct an African American counter-history of postwar L.A. Thomas Harris's 'Hannibal Lecter' series (notably *The Silence of the Lambs* [1988]) fuses the police procedural with horror. From the horror genre itself, Stephen King's novels, such as *Misery* (1987), may appear on modules in American gothic. The best modules in contemporary US writing will also embrace science fiction, where two of the most important figures – their visions and terminologies influential well beyond genre boundaries – are Philip K. Dick and William Gibson. You may study many of these popular novels alongside their film adaptations. Given American Studies' interdisciplinary orientation, however, there should also be opportunities elsewhere in your course for you to read US literature at the same time as US cinema (and US music, painting and photography).

American drama

A handful of landmark plays aside, drama is less conspicuous than fiction and poetry in programmes of American literary study. Nevertheless, even institutions lacking a specialism in theatre studies may offer opportunities to engage with twentieth- and twenty-first-century drama of the United States. As well as linking to each other, plays you might read connect to chronological or thematic strands discussed above. Eugene O'Neill's innovative work, from *The Emperor Jones* (1920) to *Long Day's Journey into Night* (1956), fuses modernist interest in structure, symbol and myth with concerns of race and class. Clifford Odets's agitprop play, *Waiting for Lefty* (1935), has endured in the curriculum longer than much of the Depression-era's protest fiction. *Death of a Salesman* (1949) is one of the most poignant reckonings of 'the American Dream', and, along with *The Crucible* (1953) and *A View from the Bridge* (1955–6), central to Arthur Miller's dramatizing of postwar American malaise. Contrasts are sometimes overdone between the 'naturalistic' Miller and two other major playwrights of mid-century in the United States: Tennessee Williams and Edward Albee. In formally and verbally dextrous plays like *The Glass Menagerie* (1944) and *A Streetcar Named Desire* (1947), Williams enacts the collision of romance and brute power in the modern South. Albee is best known for his dispatches from the gender wars in *Who's Afraid of Virginia Woolf* (1962), but you might also sample his later, post-realist work.

Study of two younger American dramatists will uncover disparate preoccupations. In plays including *Glengarry Glen Ross* (1983), David Mamet reflects on the state of national masculinity. Sam Shepard's elliptical, frequently surreal plays meditate on the American West as its landscapes become urbanized and its icons atrophy into clichés. Your work may also show you alternatives to what – Williams aside – can sometimes seem a long line of playwriting by straight white American males. Tony Kushner's *Angels in America* (1992) remains one of the most important responses in any medium to the decimation wrought by AIDS. Significant African American drama includes Lorraine Hansberry's *A Raisin in the Sun* (1959) and August Wilson's 10-play *Pittsburgh Cycle* (1982–2005). Female American dramatists might be represented by Lillian Hellman and Marsha Norman, each ranging well beyond gender in her thematic preoccupations.

American literature: sample syllabus for 'American gothic writing'

Because the range of American literature is almost as wide as its English counterpart, and modules on American literature many and varied, what follows is a sample syllabus for one topic only, American gothic:

Week 1   Introduction to the module: histories and definitions of the gothic
Week 2   'The love of the horrible': short stories by Edgar Allan Poe (1840–5)
Week 3   American poetry and the gothic (1): selected poems by Emily Dickinson (1858–86)
Week 4   Feminist gothic: Charlotte Perkins Gilman, 'The Yellow Wallpaper' (1890)
Week 5   'The most helplessly evil story we have ever read': Henry James, *The Turn of the Screw* (1898)
Week 6   Southern gothic (1): Eudora Welty, 'Clytie' (1941); Flannery O'Connor, 'A Good Man is Hard to Find' (1955)
Week 7   Southern gothic (2): Cormac McCarthy, *Child of God* (1974)
Week 8   American poetry and the gothic (2): poems by Sylvia Plath (1958–63)
Week 9   Reading the vampire: Anne Rice, *Interview with the Vampire* (1981)
Week 10 African American gothic: Toni Morrison, *Beloved* (1987)
Week 11 Gothic reading and writing: Stephen King, *Misery* (1987)
Week 12 Postmodern gothic: Bret Easton Ellis, *Lunar Park* (2005)

Bibliography

(a) Literary works

Chopin, Kate. *'The Awakening' and Selected Stories*. Oxford: Oxford University Press, 2000.

Cooper, James Fenimore. *The Last of the Mohicans*. Ed. John McWilliams. Oxford: Oxford University Press, 1994.

Dickinson, Emily. *The Complete Poems*. Ed. Thomas H. Johnson. London: Faber and Faber, 1976.

Fitzgerald, F. Scott. *The Great Gatsby*. Ed. Ruth Prigozy. Oxford: Oxford University Press, 2008.

Kerouac, Jack. *On the Road*. Ed. Ann Charters. London: Penguin, 1991.

Melville, Herman. *Moby-Dick: or, The Whale*. Ed. Tony Tanner. Oxford: Oxford University Press, 1988.

Miller, Arthur. *Plays: One – 'Death of a Salesman', 'The Crucible', 'All My Sons', 'A Memory of Two Mondays', 'A View from the Bridge'*. London: Methuen, 1988.

Morrison, Toni. *Beloved*. London: Vintage, 1997.

Silko, Leslie Marmon. *Ceremony*. New York: Penguin, 2006.

Steinbeck, John. *The Grapes of Wrath*. Ed. Robert DeMott. London: Penguin, 1992.

Stowe, Harriet Beecher. *Uncle Tom's Cabin: or, Life Among the Lowly*. Ed. Jean Fagan Yellin. Oxford: Oxford University Press, 1998.

Twain, Mark. *Adventures of Huckleberry Finn*. Ed. Emory Elliott. Oxford: Oxford University Press, 1999.

Whitman, Walt. *Leaves of Grass*. Ed. David S. Reynolds. New York: Oxford University Press, 2005.

Wright, Richard. *Native Son*. London: Vintage, 2000.

(b) Further reading

Altieri, Charles. *The Art of Twentieth-Century American Poetry: Modernism and After*. Oxford: Blackwell, 2006.

Bercovitch, Sacvan and Myra Jehlen, eds. *Ideology and Classic American Literature*. Cambridge: Cambridge University Press, 1987.

Bradbury, Malcolm. *The Modern American Novel*, 2nd edn. Oxford: Oxford University Press, 1982.

Brown, Gillian. *Domestic Individualism: Imagining Self in Nineteenth-Century America*. Berkeley: University of California Press, 1992.

Davidson, Cathy N. *Revolution and the Word: The Rise of the Novel in America*, 2nd edn. Oxford: Oxford University Press, 2004.

Fiedler, Leslie A. *Love and Death in the American Novel*. Champaign, IL: Dalkey Archive Press, 1998.

Gray, Richard. *A History of American Literature*. Oxford: Blackwell, 2004.

Lee, A. Robert. *Multicultural American Literature: Comparative Black, Native, Latino/a and Asian American Fictions*. Edinburgh: Edinburgh University Press, 2003.

Smith, Susan Harris. *American Drama: The Bastard Art*. Cambridge: Cambridge University Press, 2006.

Tanner, Tony. *The American Mystery: American Literature from Emerson to DeLillo*. Cambridge: Cambridge University Press, 2000.

3 critical approaches and schools of thought

3.1 critical approaches 265

3

chapter contents

> Introduction   265
> Formalism   267
> Archetypal criticism   270
> New criticism   272
> Bakhtin and dialogic criticism   275
> Feminism   278
> Marxism   286
> Structuralism   290
> Psychoanalysis   293
> Deconstruction   296
> Postcolonialism   303
> New historicism   304
> Cultural materialism   306
> African American criticism   309
> Chicano/a studies   311
> Gay studies and queer theory   314
> Cultural studies   321
> Ecocriticism   324
> Postmodernism   327

Introduction

Throughout the years of your degree you will study – or, for some readers, will have already studied – a broad number of topics and subjects. In this process, sooner or later, you'll encounter the phrase 'literary theory'. I have already discussed this matter in the preface, in a lengthy note aimed at clarifying the terminology. As I remarked in the introduction to Chapter 2.1 concerning your modules, many of which will be optional for you, 'theoretical' paradigms or approaches will be either implicitly or explicitly employed in framing the discussion and reading of literature, film and other related texts and media.

To come back to the question of 'theory', though. This somewhat nebulous phrase signifies a number of ways of approaching the matter of critical analysis from varied and different perspectives. Criticism in its more theoretical forms has developed from a number of disciplines beyond English and Literary Studies. Therefore, what comes under the heading of literary theory can encompass work related to historical, political or philosophical forms of, and approaches to, study, and from various branches of academic knowledge such as psychoanalysis or linguistics, or more obviously political discourses such as feminism and Marxism.

There are quite a number of different approaches, some interacting with others or overlapping with one another in a number of ways. Such approaches vary in the degree to which they might be said to be properly 'theoretical' – that is to say, to the extent that they have fully worked out logical processes and practices that are repeatable across a wide range of interpretative or analytical acts. What all share, though, are constellations of perspectives informed by concepts, which help place the reader and direct him or her to examine literary work with an eye to adopting the perspective of a particular approach. In some cases, what we call literary criticism or literary theory can have assumed at an historical moment a coherent identity shared by a number of practitioners. In such cases, we might refer to schools of thought, rather than to theory as such.

The point here is that the act of reading is never just a neutral appreciation of a work of literature, a film, or other '**aesthetic**' form. Indeed, one of most surprising things to students when they arrive at university to study literature is that such study is not simply a matter of taste, aesthetics or appreciation. If you are studying literature at university, presumably you already have learned to appreciate it in broad ways. You have various beliefs about what it is, what it does, and even what it should or shouldn't do. These are not natural values, though; you have learned them, and, this being the case, already occupy a 'theorized' role as a reader, even if you only claim to read for pleasure. We all read not only according to our tastes, but also in relation to where we are historically or culturally, and how we identify or reject particular values that are common in society. Education has already developed our tastes, whether formally, through the process of school, or less formally, as a result of what we learn in being a member of a family, culture, particular social groups, and so on.

How you come to understand this in English study is through being introduced to the critical approaches, methods and schools of thought that shape how you are taught, directly or indirectly. No academic ever assumes a neutral or objective position, even if they believe they do. What follows therefore is a series of short essays designed to introduce you to a number of approaches, methods and schools, and to show you the main aspects of the respective approaches, with illustration of what such methods or reading activities look for in literature, as well how such approaches to literary study can illuminate a text in a manner that sheds new light on what you might assume you have some familiarity with.

In reading these essays you will notice some areas of overlap. You might also consider for yourself how some are antagonistic towards one another. This is inevitable because the practice of criticism can often engage in a critique of another critical perspective. In the essays presented here, there are some approaches which remain widely practised, while there are others which, for one reason or another, have become consigned to modules focusing on the history and practice of criticism itself, rather than being taught with a view to having you try such approaches. Sometimes, it is the case that a critical mode has simply developed or evolved, or otherwise been transformed through the interaction between two different critical modes. What follows therefore is just an introductory sample of the ways in which critical **discourse** in English departments has grown and been transformed in the last few decades. These essays, each with a bibliography for suggested further reading, are not intended to be exhaustive. Indeed, the fact that this is merely a brief, selective guide should give you a sense of the vitality of critical discourse, which, in one manner or another, will not only inform how you read and interpret, but also give you insight into yourself as a reader, and cause you to reflect on and analyse both literary works and the world in which you live.

Formalism

Megan Becker-Leckrone

Formalism focuses privileged attention on the way a given literary work functions poetically, narratively and linguistically. It operates from the assumption that discovering *how* a literary text operates is the best way to understand *what* it means. Or, to borrow from Cleanth Brooks's pithy aphorisms, formalism begins with the credo '*That form is meaning*' ('The Formalist Critics', 1951). To this end, Brooks explains, 'the formalist critic is concerned primarily with the work itself', and while examinations of literature based in biography, psychology or history might be 'worth making', they are nevertheless *not* – and 'should not be confused with' – the true job of the literary critic. Literary language, formalists maintain, is markedly distinct from practical language. It does not necessarily aim literally to describe a real thing or convey a true fact. Rather, it operates according to 'independent' principles of reference; more simply put, formalists pay attention to *the way* literary language refers to things or ideas, real or imagined, and believe that it does so uniquely (see REALISM, THE NOVEL). The words 'My love is like a red red rose / That's newly sprung in June', for instance, *mean* in a way quite unlike the words 'if I plant the rose bush in early spring, it will bloom in June'. That is because literature produces different associations than the usual ones between a given word and the thing or idea to which it refers. Describing literary language thus requires identifying the specific elements of a given work's signifying mechanisms – its so-called 'literariness', the particular ways in which it, through figure and form, 'defamiliarizes' so-called 'normal' or 'practical' language.

Though other methods, like the New Criticism, might fit the description above, 'Formalism' usually refers to a critical movement developed by Russian literary scholars and linguists in the early decades of the twentieth century (specifically from the mid-1910s to about 1930). Some worked in a couple of collaborative groups, others worked independently, but all share the basic principles outlined above. In his essay 'The Theory of the "Formal Method"' (1926), Eichenbaum appoints himself spokesman for a critical movement he says is defined neither dogmatically nor 'in advance' by some unified 'method' per se, but rather by a set of provisional objectives, borrowed in part from modern linguistics, and founded chiefly on the premise that there may exist 'a science of literature that would be both independent and factual', a discipline free from the 'antiquated aesthetic, psychological, and historical "axioms"' of prevailing academic research. Against the psychological and biographical **subjectivity** they saw in the late-nineteenth- and early twentieth-century criticism – **aestheticism**, impressionism, symbolism – Russian formalists aim for objectivity. Perhaps related, but not identical, to the kind of objectivity Matthew Arnold famously aimed for in the previous century ('to see the object as in itself it really is'), formalists, too, see the literary text as an *object*, or in their words a 'positive' entity, made up of 'facts' that – while emphatically distinct from a fact like 'roses bloom in June' – demand their own kind of attention.

Rejecting an 'old scholarship' that read novels and short stories solely for their 'content', Russian Formalists shift their focus to elements and 'motivations' of narrative form such as the techniques of plot construction (for example, the ordering, framing and selection of a story's details) and the use of generalizable character 'types'. Vladimir Propp's influential *Morphology of the Folk Tale* (1928) takes the scientific ambitions of formalist narratology to their logical extreme. For him, the elements of a folk tale – 31 of them, he says, no more, no less – can be mapped, arranged and isolated like the elements on the periodic table.

Rejecting verse criticism that regards poetry as 'a language of images', Russian Formalists sought to shift poetic inquiry to matters of rhythm, syntax and sound. Osip Brik explains, in 'Sound Repetitions' (1964), that the poetic work itself demands such a focus, and that we miss much of a poem's meaning if we regard its acoustic qualities as nothing more than 'accessories of meaning', when in fact they are 'also the result of an independent poetic purpose'. Victor Shklovsky similarly advocates attention to seeming 'nonsense words' – such as the fanciful, make-believe words often employed in children's literature. For him, the sound and texture of words are important in themselves – 'even words without meaning are necessary' – to the sense of a poem, and that our habit of ignoring them impoverishes the prevailing critical **discourse**. Indulging that habit of misreading, he argues, erroneously judges all forms of language, from fable to political treatise, with the same yardstick; in so doing, such reading is blind to the **defamiliarizing** effects of poetic language, where the practical laws of meaning no longer apply. To seek out and puzzle through such processes in a literary work is to discover its specific 'literariness' (Jakobson), that which renders it strange and demands of its audience 'a special perception of the object' it represents.

As we might predict from its emphasis on the fundamental strangeness of literary language, Russian Formalism favours art that was, at the time, strange. Many write about specifically avant-garde art and explicitly present themselves as working in concert with the artistic agitators and innovators of the day. Eichenbaum regards the formalist critic and the avant-garde Russian poet as 'bound together by history' in the service of a common cause. Both are fighting a generational 'battle' against antiquated poetic forms and 'Impressionistic criticism'; both are revolutionaries whose weapons are 'categorical thes[es], merciless irony, and bold rejections'. Writing in the wake of the 1917 Russian Revolution, Eichenbaum's manifesto-like rhetoric is no doubt deliberate.

In that Eichenbaum speaks for so many in 'The Theory of the "Formal Method"', it is an excellent synthesis of the major concepts, theses and theorists of the Russian Formalist movement. All quotations here are taken from the essay's appearance in *The Norton Anthology of Theory and Criticism*, translated by Lee T. Lemon and Marion J. Reis and taken from their collection, *Russian Formalist Criticism: Four Essays* (1965). Quotations from Brooks's essay also derive from its appearance in *Norton*. Useful critical histories and analyses include Victor Erlich's *Russian Formalism: History – Doctrine* (1980) and Peter Steiner's *Russian Formalism: A Metapoetics* (1986). Fredric Jameson's *Prison-House of Language: A Critical Account of Structuralism and Russian Formalism* (1972) was extremely influential in bringing Russian Formalism to an English-speaking audience, if not in the most favourable light; Jonathan Culler's *Structuralist Poetics: Structuralism, Linguistics, and the Study of Literature* (1976) was similarly influential, though he is more centrally concerned with the way French structuralism grew out of a response to formalism. The early chapters of Peter Brooks's *Reading for the Plot: Design and Intention in Narrative* (1992) bring formalism into dynamic conversation with more recent psychoanalytic and **deconstructive** theory, producing a suggestive theory of 'narrative desire'.

Further reading

Bann, Stephen and John E. Bowlt. *Russian Formalism: A Collection of Articles and Texts in Translation*. New York: Barnes and Noble, 1973.

Jakobson, Roman. *Language and Literature*. Ed. Krystyna Pomorska and Stephen Rudy. Cambridge, MA: Belknap Press of Harvard University Press, 1987.

Medvedev, P. N. *The Formal Method in Literary Scholarship: A Critical Introduction to Sociological Poetics*. Trans. Albert J. Werhle. Cambridge, MA: Harvard University Press, 1985.

Steiner, Peter, ed. *The Prague School: Selected Writings, 1929–1946*. Austin: University of Texas Press, 1982.

Thompson, Ewa M. *Russian Formalism and the Anglo-American New Criticism*. New York: Walter De Gruyter, 1971.

Wellek, René and Austin Warren. *Theory of Literature*, 3rd edn. New York: Harvest Books, 1984.

Archetypal criticism

Doris Bremm

An introduction to the field of archetypal criticism needs to start with a definition of the term **archetype** (from the Greek *arche*, first, and *typum*, to impress, stamp, type). Generally, an archetype is defined as the original model or prototype from which copies are made. In literary theory, an archetype refers to a pattern that commonly recurs in literary works. Archetypal, or myth, critics argue that archetypes determine the form and function of literary works. Such patterns can include character types, plot lines, settings, themes and images. For example, the archetype of the journey can be found in narratives from Homer's *Odyssey* and John Bunyan's *The Pilgrim's* Progress to Virginia Woolf's *To the Lighthouse*.

Archetypal criticism is primarily informed by Carl Gustav Jung's theory of archetypes in the field of psychology and James G. Frazer's work in social anthropology. Jung's theory of the unconscious differentiates between two levels of unconscious: the personal unconscious of the individual psyche that comprises repressed memories, and the archetypal unconscious that includes what Jung calls humanity's 'collective unconscious'. This repository contains primordial images, or archetypes, as they are manifested in dreams and **myths** and shared by people across cultures. Examples of such archetypal forms are prototypical figures such as a mother, father or sibling. Jungian scholars also use the term 'archetype' to describe patterns of the life cycle that begins with childhood and ends with death. One of the most powerful archetypes is the animus figure (male side of the female psyche) and the anima figure (female side of the male psyche). Jung posits that, when reading a narrative featuring such archetypes, readers are subconsciously affected in a powerful way because these images evoke memories of primordial feelings that do not have a logical explanation. The second important influence is the social anthropologist James G. Frazer's work *The Golden Bough* (1890). This comprehensive study of rituals, myths and folklore juxtaposes parallel practices in cultures around the world. For example, Frazer argues that the circle of life and death found in many fertility cults forms the common basis for a number of mythologies.

Literary critics influenced by Jung's theory first emerged in the 1930s, but archetypal or myth criticism became especially popular in the late 1950s and early 1960s. Whereas Jungian scholars take the presence of certain recurring images as evidence of their status as part of the collective unconscious, other myth critics such as Northrop Frye discuss such persistent elements without referring to Jung's theories. Frye, who is probably the most influential myth critic, defines archetypes as 'a symbol, usually an image, which recurs often enough in literature to be recognizable as an element of one's literary experience as whole' (2001: 365). He explores archetypes in a very complex and systematic way and focuses on the analysis of the nature, function and significance of the archetype and its manifestations in literature across cultures and time.

According to Frye, these images 'derive from the epiphanic moment, the flash of instantaneous comprehension with no direct reference to time' (2001: 23).

In his influential study *Anatomy of Criticism* (1957), Frye devises a complex system that pairs literary genres with the myths and archetypal patterns associated with the four seasons: **comedy** (spring), romance (summer), **tragedy** (autumn), and **irony**/satire (winter). Examples of **archetypes** he singles out are universal motifs such as birth and death, marriage, and the change of seasons. Furthermore, Frye looks at certain **genres** as archetypes, examples being the quest and the journey narrative.

Frye sees literature as a rewriting of the stories of the past and accordingly his archetypal criticism is very much **intertextual**. His work differs from previous Jungian criticism such as Maud Bodkin's *Archetypal Patterns in Poetry* (1934) in that he attempts to give more than just 'fragmentary insights' but instead a comprehensive conceptual framework. Furthermore, Frye challenges the conventional terrain of literary criticism and theory as he devises a complex and comprehensive system that encompasses any work of literature and helps to place individual texts in a relationship with each other.

In recent years, archetypal or myth criticism has found itself under attack for being reductive and for ignoring the historical and cultural **context** of literary works. However, the area of criticism still has a place in the literary tradition and has had an effect on other disciplines and branches of literary study such as gender studies, comparative literature, cultural studies and narrative theory. Any study looking at specific roles of women and men (such as mother/father or daughter/son), it could be argued, is a form of myth or archetypal criticism. Any comparative literature project that looks at a certain genre, character or theme across cultural boundaries and across periods, in a way analyses archetypes. Scholars of narrative theory that look at a specific kind of narrative such as the epic or the quest are also engaging with similar topics that Frye was interested in.

Only a few contemporary critics still engage in strictly Jungian or 'Fryeian' readings, though. Whereas Frye tried to establish a comprehensive system for all literature, many contemporary scholars do not make such universal claims when analysing patterns that Frye would have called archetypes. Often such arguments pertain to a certain time period and culture. For example, a study on marriage in literature might focus on this specific pattern in Victorian literature, such as Rachel Ablow's *The Marriage of Minds: Reading Sympathy in the Victorian Marriage Plot* (2007). Another example that looks at myth in a very specific context is Jeffrey B. Leak's *Racial Myths and Masculinity in African American Literature* (2005), which not only identifies some of the myths and stereotypes that persist in the work of black writers from Frederick Douglass to Toni Morrison, such as intellectual inferiority, criminality, sexual prowess, but, more importantly, analyses how these narratives reflect and construct black masculinity. These recent studies show an interest in archetypes, but instead of making universal claims about them, they analyse them within their cultural and historical context.

Further reading

Ablow, Rachel. *The Marriage of Minds: Reading Sympathy in the Victorian Marriage Plot*. Stanford, CA: Stanford University Press, 2007.

Bodkin, Maud. *Archetypal Patterns in Poetry*. London: Oxford University Press, 1934.

Fiedler, Leslie A. *Love and Death in the American Novel*. New York: Criterion Books, 1960.

Frazer, James G. *The Golden Bough* (1890). New York: Macmillan, 1922.

Frye, Northrop. *Anatomy of Criticism*. Princeton, NJ: Princeton University Press, 1957.

Frye, Northrop. *Fables of Identity: Studies in Poetic Mythology*. New York: Harcourt Brace & World, 1963.

Frye, Northrop. *Fearful Symmetry: A Study of William Blake*. Princeton, NJ: Princeton University Press, 1947.

Frye, Northrop. *The Great Code: The Bible and Literature*. New York: Harcourt Brace Jovanovich, 1982.

Frye, Northrop. *Spiritus Mundi: Essays on Literature, Myth, and Society*. Bloomington, IN: Indiana University Press, 1976.

Jung, Carl Gustav. *The Archetypes and the Collective Unconscious*. Trans. R. F. C. Hull. New York: Pantheon, 1959.

Krieger, Murray. *Northrop Frye in Modern Criticism: Selected Papers from the English Institute*. New York: Columbia University Press, 1966.

Leak, Jeffrey B. *Racial Myths and Masculinity in African American Literature*. Knoxville: University of Tennessee Press, 2005.

New criticism

Megan Becker-Leckrone

Like Russian Formalism, the New Criticism treats literary criticism as an examination of the form and functions of the 'text itself' at the principled exclusion of biographical, psychological, historical and political considerations. 'Close reading', critics maintain, is the proper method for discovering the workings of the text. Such reading, furthermore, attends to form and language, paradox, **irony**, figures of speech, the structures of narrative that generate what Wayne Booth called 'the rhetoric of fiction' (1983). Spanning several decades and two continents, some of the most influential projects placed under the heading of Anglo-American New Criticism tell the story of their aims in their very titles. I. A. Richards's *Principles of Literary Criticism* (1924) and *Practical Criticism* (1929) indicate that the New Critics see their projects as hands-on, teachable and foundational – producing *the* books to read on how to read books. *Seven Types of Ambiguity* (1930) by Richards' student, William Empson, suggests that this project regards language as at once multiform ('**ambiguity**', like 'irony' and 'paradox', being a pervasive concern for these critics) *and* in some sense containable ('seven types') – though only superficially; it's in fact quite a complex and open-ended work. Cleanth Brooks's *The Well-Wrought Urn: Studies in the Structure of Poetry*

(1941) is arguably Richards's principles in action, a collection of influential close readings of Keats's 'Ode on a Grecian Urn' (perhaps most famously) among other works. W. K. Wimsatt's and Monroe C. Beardsley's *The Verbal Icon: Studies in the Meaning of Poetry* (1982) reminds us that 'meaning' comes from the 'icon'-ographic richness of literary language itself.

New Critics believe that literary criticism might operate by means of certain generalizable 'principles', that the 'practical' work of criticism may proceed at least to some extent normatively – in other words, that a kind of critical objectivity is not only possible and desirable, but also *necessary* if literary critics are to justify their work as a professional discipline in and of itself. These claims, by extension, maintain that the literary text also exists as an *object* in and of itself, like a 'well-wrought urn' or an 'icon'. The New Criticism, in fact, often defines itself by this supposedly fundamental fact: that its task is to study objects, and that insofar as these objects exist in concrete form – on the page or out there in the world, as 'verbal icons' – so too is it both possible and necessary to consider a thing such as a poem *objectively*. The New Critics regard literary analysis, so defined, as a positive science, with distinct critical principles. Chief among them was the notion, which they shared with the Russian Formalists, that arriving at the 'meaning' of a specific poetic object involves, above all, examining its 'structure'.

The New Critics' emphasis on 'the text itself' made them vulnerable to charges by later generations of critics that they inexcusably ignore history, politics, authors' biographies, readers' experiences and a host of other 'extrinsic' concerns. Certain formidable critiques – such as Frank Lentricchia's *After the New Criticism* (1980) – have done much to shape a contemporary reputation of the New Criticism as a dead end. Lentricchia in fact ascribes it a precise expiration date: 1957. By then, he declares, 'the New Criticism had done all that it could do' and 'newer movements were waiting in the wings to take its place on the center stage' (1980: 3). While the latter announcement is historically correct, the general assessment is reductive, if not unfair, and misrepresents both the project and the enormous institutional influence the New Criticism has had (for good or ill) on the way literary texts are read and taught to this day.

Not only did people like I. A. Richards change the way generations, including our own, go about reading literature, they wrote the how-to guides themselves. And in the process, the New Critics were instrumental in asserting literary study's disciplinary and institutional right to exist. John Crowe Ransom provides a vigorous justification for 'professors of English', and by extension, of course, departments of English, in his spirited 1938 essay, 'Criticism, Inc.'. Here, he argues that it is crucial that teachers of literature, if they are to be considered 'professionals', must labour towards the 'erection of intelligent standards of criticism. It is their business' (Leitch 2001: 1108–9). In this effort, Ransom insists, '[c]riticism must become more scientific, or precise and systematic', just as the formalists call upon literary study to be. Ransom acknowledges that this effort 'will never be a very exact science, or even a nearly exact one', and warns that any illusions to the contrary would be 'hollow and pretentious' (1109). Aspiring towards something like a 'scientific' method is predicated, as I say above, on the belief that the literary text positively exists as an *object* available for study; but it also helps Ransom distinguish literary study specifically from what it is *not*: science, sociology, economics (1109).

William K. Wimsatt Jr. and Monroe C. Beardsley, in their enormously influential essay 'The Intentional Fallacy' (1946), further assert literary criticism's distinctions from other ways of reading, especially through their memorable thesis that knowing what an author 'intended' is *not* – despite widespread assumptions to the contrary – the proper way to 'judge' a poem's meaning (Leitch 2001: 1375). Their assertion lends force to the New Critical insistence on the text above all else (such as author, reader or context) is the central and proper source of meaning. The essay's seemingly unsentimental banishment of authorial intent from the literary experience scandalized many – particularly those who do not read past its title or take it to mean, literally, that authors have nothing to do with the production of a literary text. Wimsatt and Beardsley exclude the question of 'what the author intended' from the work of literary interpretation because it fails to yield anything like the kind of reliable, objective, consensus-built 'data' Ransom's enterprise requires. Of course there is such a thing as intention, they say, but finding it is the work of a psychologist or biographer, not the literary critic. 'Intention' is unreliable, impossible to delimit and, further, tells us nothing truly 'critical' about the words on the page in the form of, say, a sonnet.

Not even a poet's own commentary on the meaning of his poem constitutes critical data, like asking T. S. Eliot what he meant by his supposed allusions to Donne and Marvell in 'The Love Song of J. Alfred Prufrock'. 'Critical inquiries are not settled by consulting the oracle' (Leitch 2001: 1387). Again, the thrust of this argument is not to knock the author off some pedestal. After all, T. S. Eliot's 'Tradition and the Individual Talent' is the arguable point of reference for their very own point about 'Prufrock', and indeed Eliot's criticism was a crucial touchstone for much of the New Criticism. Rather, it is to acknowledge a certain radical autonomy to the text, separate not just from the author but ultimately from the critic as well. This is an acknowledgement that finds different but genealogically recognizable articulation in the very usurpers Lentricchia favours for being newer than the New. In a striking, *Frankenstein*-like image (we of course can't ask them if they intended it), Wimsatt and Beardsley sum up their position thus: 'The poem is not the critic's own and not the author's (it is detached from the author at birth and goes about the world beyond his power to intend about it or control it). The poem belongs to the public' (1376). In light of this statement, at once liberating yet subtly ominous, it is perhaps ironic, or perhaps perfectly apt, that so many of the genuinely subtle and influential texts produced by the New Critics have been treated so roughly – or, that these often virtuoso close readers are these days rarely closely read.

Further reading

Booth, Wayne C. *The Rhetoric of Fiction.* London: University of Chicago Press, 1983.

Eliot, T. S. *On Poetry.* New York: Noonday Press, 1957.

Eliot, T. S. *Selected Prose* of *T. S. Eliot.* Ed. Frank Kermode. London: Faber, 1975.

Hartman, Geoffrey. *Beyond Formalism: Literary Essays, 1958–1970.* New Haven, CT: Yale University Press, 1970.

Ransom, John Crowe. *The New Criticism*, 2nd edn. Westport, CT: Greenwood Press, 1979.

Richards, I. A. *Principles of Literary Criticism.* Routledge Classics Series, 2nd edn. London: Routledge, 2001.

Thompson, E. M. *Russian Formalism and the Anglo-American New Criticism.* New York: Walter De Gruyter, 1971.

Wellek, René, and Austin Warren. *Theory of Literature*, 3rd edn. New York: Harvest Books, 1984.

Wimsatt, W. K. and Cleanth Brooks. *Literary Criticism: A Short History.* New York: Vintage, 1957.

Wimsatt, W. K. *The Verbal Icon: Studies in the Meaning of Poetry.* Lexington: University of Kentucky Press, 1982.

Bakhtin and dialogic criticism

Karine Zbinden

3

As you progress in your literary studies you may well hear of Mikhail Bakhtin and/or of **dialogism**. Bakhtin was a Russian thinker and cultural theorist and his life spans most of the twentieth century and therefore the Soviet era. This accounts for a lot of the difficulties in identifying his philosophical sources – mostly German idealist philosophers at odds with the dogma of the Soviet period – and also for the fact that most of his work was discovered rather late in the day, since he had great difficulty getting anything published during his lifetime. You may also have heard the terms 'Bakhtin Circle' or 'Bakhtin School', which refers to a group of scholars he was closely associated with. (In case you are interested in finding out more about other members of the Circle, the group also includes the linguist Valentin Voloshinov (1895–1936), the literary scholars Pavel Medvedev (1891–1938) and Lev Pumpianskii (1891–1940), the philosopher Matvei Kagan (1889–1937), the pianist Mariia Iudina (1899–1970) and the musicologist Ivan Sollertinskii (1902–44).) However, Bakhtin is without doubt the most prominent of the scholars forming the Bakhtin Circle, who are noted for their writings dealing with issues as diverse as ethics and **aesthetics**, the theory of the novel, the foundations of the human sciences, and linguistics. You may be interested in following up some of the varied philosophical positions, on which they drew as a group, including neo-Kantianism (especially Ernst Cassirer and the Marburg School), Hegelianism and phenomenology (in particular Max Scheler). Other influences include Russian Formalism (Lev Iakubinskii) and the Marxism of Georg Lukács, and Marrism. I will explain some of the major aspects of Bakhtin's incredibly diverse range of works in the following pages.

Bakhtin was at one time frequently referred to as a formalist, and you may well have encountered this yourself, but, although he began his scholarly career in the late 1910s–early 1920s and was thus a contemporary of the Russian Formalists, he was never associated with them, and indeed wrote an extensive critique of formalism in his 1924 essay 'The Problem of Content, Material and Form'. In this piece he claims that the over-evaluation of the material characteristic of formalism (which privileges form over content, i.e., considers that what matters about literature and poetry is how things are written rather than what a novel or poem is about) leads to the replacement of **aesthetics** by linguistics and to the isolation of the arts from one another. In opposition to this, Bakhtin thought that art can only be truly grasped in the correlation of the aesthetic with the ethical and the cognitive, a correlation that makes it possible to understand how they relate in the whole of human culture (Bakhtin 1990: 259). To put things more simply, what is valuable about art is the relationship between its form and its meaning, *how* art says something about the world, or human experience, but also *what* it says about them, and that it is only when these two aspects are apprehended together that art can be meaningful. (But it was Medvedev who produced the most constructive and scholarly criticism of Russian Formalism with his monograph *The Formal Method in Literary Scholarship: A Critical Introduction to Sociological Poetics* (1928), where he emphasized the primacy of **genre** over specific literary devices for the study of literature and the importance of sociological factors (as well as internal factors) in the shaping of literature.) Voloshinov's main publication, *Marxism and the Philosophy of Language* (1929), studies language as a product of social interaction and takes the utterance as its focus. More specifically, the utterance expresses in discursive form the worldview of the various participants (and social groups) in dialogic interaction. Voloshinov's analysis had seminal importance for Bakhtin's own theory of the polyphonic novel in his *Problems of Dostoevsky's Poetics* (1929). Here he claims that in Dostoevsky's novels the voices of characters, including that of the narrator, are given equal importance and interact dialogically in the structure of the novel, whereas a monologic novel such as Tolstoy's would subject all voices to the authorial consciousness. Here you can see how dialogue in social interaction relates to dialogism as a theory of the novel.

The Bakhtin Circle ceased to meet and function as a coherent group after 1929, when a number of its members were arrested, including Bakhtin, who was sentenced to six years' internal exile in Kazakhstan (his original sentence to 10 years' hard labour was commuted on the grounds of ill health). In the 1930s and 1940s Bakhtin concentrated on literary history and the theory of the novel, writing a series of essays where he showed the novel as rooted in popular discursive genres that exploit the heteroglossia of language (its internal stratification or diversity due to regional, social, professional variety but also to age, education etc.), in contrast to poetry and the **epic**, which promote a monologic use of language. Laughter and parody are driving forces for the language of the novel to gain self-awareness of its own subversiveness. These essays include 'Discourse in the Novel' (1934–5), 'From the Prehistory of Novelistic Discourse' (1940), 'Epic and Novel' (1941) and 'Forms of Time and of the Chronotope in the Novel' (1937–8), published in English under the title *The Dialogic Imagination* (1981).

These concerns culminate in Bakhtin's major study in literary and cultural history, which you may have heard of, *Rabelais and His World* (1965), in which he develops the themes of carnival as expression of unchecked unofficial culture, laughter as profoundly ambivalent and as expression of and release from humankind's fear of death, and the public square as a space where all are at the same time spectator and participant in the **carnivalesque** debasing of official culture and language. Once the carnivalesque has entered literature, its relativizing spirit serves to invigorate official culture and to restructure the relationship between official and popular cultures.

In brief, you can see that although dialogism is steeped in sociality (understood as the social aspect of language, thought and self-consciousness, including the complex relationship of the individual with social groups and institutions, and of the individual thought with **ideology**), commentators of Bakhtin's works have tended to reduce dialogism to the unidimensional realm of the text. In this they followed the interpretation of Julia Kristeva in the late 1960s (when his works were still largely inaccessible to a readership in the West), where, in 'Word, Dialogue and Novel', which introduced Bakhtin to the Western world, she recast dialogism as **intertextuality**. Put simply, this means that Kristeva took dialogism from the richness of social diversity, from all the social tensions and interactions that shape up dialogism, and projected it onto the text. She reduced dialogism to only one of its aspects, that of the relations between words and texts. This made Bakhtin relevant not only to French structuralist thought but also to poststructuralism, but at the expense of a proper understanding of his complex intellectual affiliations.

Further reading

Bakhtin, Mikhail. 'Author and Hero in Aesthetic Activity'. In *Art and Answerability: Early Philosophical Essays by M. M. Bakhtin*. Ed. M. Holquist and V. Liapunov, trans. K. Brostrom, 257–325. Austin: University of Texas Press, 1990.

Bakhtin, Mikhail. *Speech Genres and Other Late Essays*. Ed. C. Emerson and M. Holquist, trans. V. McGee. Austin: University of Texas Press, 1986.

Bakhtin, Mikhail. *Toward a Philosophy of the Act*. Ed. M. Holquist and V. Liapunov, trans. V. Liapunov. Austin: University of Texas Press, 1994.

Brandist, Craig. *The Bakhtin Circle: Philosophy, Culture and Politics*. London and Sterling, VA: Pluto Press, 2002.

Hirschkop, Ken. *Mikhail Bakhtin: An Aesthetic for Democracy*. Oxford: Oxford University Press, 1999.

Hirschkop, Ken and David Shepherd, eds. *Bakhtin and Cultural Theory*, 2nd rev. edn. Manchester and New York: Manchester University Press, 2001.

3

Kristeva, Julia. 'Word, Dialogue and Novel'. In *Desire in Language: A Semiotic Approach to Literature and Art*, ed. L. S. Roudiez, trans. T. Gora et al., 64–91. New York: Columbia University Press, 1980.

Tihanov, Galin. *The Master and the Slave: Lukács, Bakhtin, and the Ideas of Their Time.* Oxford: Clarendon Press, 2000.

Zbinden, Karine. *Bakhtin between East and West: Cross-Cultural Transmission.* Oxford: Legenda, 2006.

Feminism

Ruth Robbins

In his essay on 'Femininity' (1933), Sigmund Freud commented: 'When you meet a human being, the first distinction you make is "male or female?" and you are accustomed to make the distinction with unhesitating certainty' (Freud 1986: 413). This is a comment about both the biological markers that determine sex – the primary and secondary sexual organs – and a commentary about the cultural marks of **gender** (the clothes one wears which signal masculinity or femininity). The former is to a large extent unchangeable (at least without surgical intervention), and 'natural'; the latter is variable depending on the culture in which it takes place. To be fair to Freud, he went on immediately to point out that the biological clues and the social markers of 'male and female' were not nearly so secure as generally presumed; but he also insisted that biological sex and its cultural markers (which we usually term 'gender') were strongly linked, at least in our minds. And he wrote of gender – masculinity and femininity as culturally constructed as opposed to the naturally made biological sex organs – that it had become fixed in its meaning:

> We are accustomed to employ 'masculine' and 'feminine' as mental qualities ... Thus we speak of a person, whether male or female, as behaving in a masculine way in one connection and in a feminine way in another. But you will soon perceive that this is only giving way to anatomy or to convention. You cannot give the concepts of 'masculine' and 'feminine' *any* new connotation. ... when you say 'masculine' you usually mean 'active', and when you say 'feminine' you usually mean 'passive'. (Freud 1986: 414)

Two questions arise out of this commentary. The first is: if Freud is right (and I rather suspect he is), why do we need to know if our interlocutor is male or female? Why does it matter? And second: how did 'masculine' come to mean 'active' and 'feminine' come to mean 'passive'? I hope it is obvious why the second question matters. I also hope that it is obvious that new **connotations** for masculinity and femininity are part of what feminism is about. For if culture is variable then gender too can change. Freud dismisses this possibility in part because of the moment in history in which he was writing. He suggests that gender is fixed in meaning because he is describing what he sees around him as a privileged middle-class figure who came to maturity in the nineteenth century. His attitude is, one might say, 'Victorian'. For feminist thinkers, however, giving new meanings to gender is part of what the project is about.

I begin here because it is with questions of sex (biology) and gender (culture) that feminism as an approach to literature is crucially concerned. It seeks to understand and change the ways in which sex and gender have become connected to such an extent that it is presumed that women are 'naturally' 'passive' and men 'naturally' 'active'. Feminism is a political project at least as much as it is an approach to literature and it has its origins in campaigns for women's rights in the political arena. The politics matter, and one cannot and should not dismiss or underplay the relationships between literary and imaginative representations of the world and the actual world in which we live. Like Marxist approaches, feminism when it reads literature takes for granted that there is some relationship between the literary imagination and the real world; sometimes this is a reflective relationship in that the text mirrors the world it sees around it, and sometimes this is a transformative relationship: to some extent, the feminist argues, the text makes the world we live in because it is part of it. It is these relationships between the real and the **imaginary** that feminism takes as a given, but which it also seeks to interrogate.

In this essay, borrowing from an essay by Elaine Showalter, I want to suggest that there are three main features which feminist thought addresses when it approaches the literary text. In her 1981 essay 'Feminist Criticism in the Wilderness', Showalter writes:

> English feminist criticism, essentially Marxist, stresses oppression; French feminist criticism, essentially psychoanalytic, stresses repression; American feminist criticism, essentially textual, stresses expression. All, however, have become gynocentric. All are struggling to find a terminology that can rescue the feminine from its stereotypical associations with inferiority. (Showalter 1986: 249)

The geographical locations of emphases have probably shifted in the intervening 30 years. It is no longer true, for example, that British feminist theory is most strongly marked by a commitment to socialist or Marxist politics. There has been territorial leakage across the borders of the national traditions Showalter identified, with American and British critics becoming increasingly interested in psychoanalysis and psychical accounts of women's lives, and with all feminisms having some investment in the **materiality** of the word and the world. But the key element of this commentary which remains useful and true to the contemporary feminist critic is the identification of the sites of interest for feminists – in the diagnosis of the multiple oppressions women have suffered (on the grounds of their gender, but also of class, race, ethnicity, economic and social disprivilege, denial of education and rights, and so on); in feminism's interest in the mechanisms by which patriarchal societies persuade women into the repression of their own **desires** and best interests; and – because feminist literary critics are *literary* critics as well as politically motivated ones – in the focus on *how* writers expressively represent the world in their literary words. Any feminism worth its salt must be able to deal with the material world since it is the material world which feminism as a political project seeks to change. But feminism must also be alive to the problematic ways in which women have engaged with a world which has often been hostile and aggressive to their interests. Thus, although psychoanalysis often feels like an approach which is apolitical (though it should not be when well practised), it has been successfully co-opted into the practice of feminist **discourses**. Finally, oppression and repression leave their marks on expression: on what can be said and on how it is said. The three areas are connected, as their common etymological roots might suggest.

Oppression

It is a fact that remains rather less than universally acknowledged that women have had a raw deal out of the history of **patriarchy**. They have been defined as goods and chattels, owned by fathers and husbands. They have been denied education and access to the professions. They have not been permitted to vote. They have been legally beaten and raped within marriage. They have been excluded from the ownership and inheritance of property. They have been sexual slaves and prostitutes, usually unable to benefit even from the sale of themselves. In the West, many of these abuses have been criminalized; sadly, there are large parts of the world where such horrors continue, which is one of the many reasons why feminist thought is still necessary and urgent. The battles have not been won, not for everyone, and in some parts of the globe, partial victories have been reversed: I am glad, for instance, not to be a woman in Taliban-controlled areas of Afghanistan.

Early versions of feminist criticism concentrated on identifying the wrongs of woman through a process of looking at representations of the feminine condition. Images of woman criticism in its first guises treated the literary text as a mirror of the human condition and pronounced outrage at the ways in which women had been treated in fiction, in fact and in criticism. A notable early example of this kind of critique can be found in Charlotte Brontë's *Villette* (1853), when the heroine Lucy Snowe is left to browse the pictures in a Belgian gallery. There are five images she considers: a masculine sexual fantasy in the form of a voluptuous *Cleopatra*, and a series of four paintings entitled *La vie d'une femme* [The Life of a Woman], which are equally masculine fantasies of the feminine in the guise of domesticated angel. Lucy's comments on these male-authored images are excoriating. She rejects the sensuous model of the Cleopatra, dismissing her as grotesque. But she also loathes the four portraits of a maiden, a bride, a mother and a widow, commenting that they are images of hypocrisy, lifeless and gothic – 'All four *Anges* [angels] were grim and gray as burglars, and cold and vapid as ghosts. What women to live with! insincere, ill-humoured, brainless nonentities!' (Brontë 1985: 249).

There are, however, some pretty fundamental problems with a form of critique which limits itself to saying 'women have been badly treated, how disgraceful it all is'. The first problem is that its tendency is to look at the images of women largely in male-authored texts to demonstrate that men have traditionally misunderstood the female condition. Thus whilst it offers an opportunity to diagnose a particular problem in the cultural representations of women, it does not offer any solution to that problem. The second is that it does tend to be a repetitive gesture. The critic repeats her critique because the images themselves are repeated, as the example from *Villette* suggests: the ancient dichotomy of the angel and the whore is writ large in Brontë's novel, suggesting that the old, old story is the only one that can be told. Lucy Snowe's outrage is important in the novel, but she struggles for the whole of the text to find an alternative way of being a woman in a world that offers such limited exemplars – in Showalter's terms, she is seeking a terminology that will not insist on her inferiority simply because she is a woman. But she is also to a very large extent trapped by the images she sees around her. Lucy's intelligent diagnosis of the problem does not make it easy for her to escape the implications of the images around her. Until she is able to make new images of women, the old story will continue to have its force.

One of the shifts that took place quite early in the wake of 'second wave' feminism's entries into the academy, therefore, was that feminist critics began to look more closely at women writers to escape from the simplistic representations that the male-authored **canon** offered them. This led to a sustained effort in the recuperation of a female tradition in literature, including the raiding of dusty library shelves to recover the names and the works of women whose writings had been neglected. Showalter named this emphasis on female authorship 'gynocritics' and contrasted it with the more 'passive' mode of criticism that images of women produced. If the emphasis in image criticism is on the reader's response to images, the emphasis in gynocritics is on the woman as author. The process of recuperation had impressive effects on the materials available to criticism since it led to a major effort in republishing lost works of interest to feminism. The establishment of both The Women's Press and Virago, for example, produced a massive range of reprinted texts, and in their early incarnations, these imprints were specifically aimed at women readers and at republishing women authors. (Sadly, that particular feminist experiment is now over, and The Women's Press is defunct; Virago is now a minor arm of the HarperCollins corporation.) Just as significantly, the gynocritical impetus enabled a generation of critics to seek out a variety of female traditions of engaging with literature, including traditions of working-class writing, of politically engaged fiction (especially suffrage fiction), of lesbian identity fictions and of black writing. There were, after all, some alternative ways of seeing the world than those sanctioned by the masculine tradition.

That said, the movement towards considering the woman as writer could also be a fairly naive activity. In their quest for the continuities between women authors of different generations, some gynocritical studies risked the charge of

essentialism, the assumption that all women are essentially the same, that all women's experiences are similar and that they transcend historical, socio-economic, ethnic and geographical specificities. As Nancy Armstrong writes, in a fair-minded but pointed critique of Sandra M. Gilbert and Susan Gubar's *The Madwoman in the Attic* (1979), Gilbert and Gubar suggest that 'the conditions for women's writing appear to remain relatively constant throughout history because the authors in question were women and because the conditions under which they wrote were largely determined by men' (Armstrong 1987: 7). When we actually look at women's lives, however, there are other determinants than patriarchy, some of which may be even more important than **gender**: race in the slave-owning society of nineteenth-century America, for instance, or class, which has particular effects on access to education and the materials for literary production. Moreover, an author-centred criticism does have some attendant risks, including the presumption that the author writes in a relatively unmediated way about her own experience. It can lead to the text being treated as mere transcription, rescuing a feminist account of human activity at the expense of any serious attention being paid to its literariness or **aesthetic** qualities. Message is valued over medium.

Repression

Why do readers (especially female readers) admire Heathcliff, the motive force in Emily Brontë's *Wuthering Heights* (1848)? What's to like or admire about a man who brutalizes and steals the inheritance of a young boy; who terrorizes his wife (and casually hangs her dog); who terrifies his own son; who may even murder his housemate? This is a female-authored novel which presents us with masculine brutality in all its foulness. In the text, the woman who knows him best and who could choose Heathcliff to marry, Cathy Earnshaw, does not do so, and even warns her sister-in-law Isabella Linton against him in no uncertain terms: Heathcliff is, in her words 'an unreclaimed creature, without refinement – without cultivation; an arid wilderness of furze and whinstone … He's not a rough diamond – a pearl-containing oyster of a rustic; he's a fierce, pitiless, wolfish man' (Brontë 1992: 103). This from his best and perhaps only friend. And yet Heathcliff remains a figure for whom relatively large numbers of young women seem to fall. There are a number of possible explanations. One is that that women readers feel maternal pity for the outcast gypsy boy who arrives at Wuthering Heights at the novel's outset. Like that of Frankenstein's monster, Heathcliff's outrageous behaviour is the result of impoverishment: he too might claim that he is vicious because he is miserable. Or, perhaps more plausibly (since, after all, the maternal Nellie Dean does not want to mother him), his disenfranchised, dispossessed status reminds us of the position of women. Thus women readers identify with him, just as Cathy herself does in her earlier declaration that 'I *am* Heathcliff' (Brontë 1992: 87). But perhaps the most obvious reason – given that it is the well-trained lady, Isabella, who marries Heathcliff in the novel – is the training that well-bred women appear to receive in masochism and self-sacrifice. Cathy, whose own training has been in the school of hard knocks at the Heights, recognizes that marriage to Heathcliff would consume her. Isabella, on the other hand, who has learned the lessons of femininity only too well, believes that he is strong rather than brutal, and sexualizes his violence into an attractive though ultimately deceptive masochistic fantasy. She probably also believes that she can civilize him, tame him – how wrong she is.

What is interesting about Cathy Earnshaw is that she is not repressed into the means and manners of femininity as most women would have been. Although she does receive some training in the appropriate forms of the feminine, following her savaging by the Lintons' dog, the training does not stick, coming as it does rather late in the day. She returns from Thrushcross Grange as a passable imitation of a lady, but it does not take long for the influence of the Heights and Heathcliff to reassert itself. From the outset, she is active not passive, demanding from her father a whip as a present from his travels as her first articulate statement in the novel. She means to be the mistress of her own destiny, to have the whip hand. For her, the world of Thrushcross Grange is a beautiful but alien landscape in which she is a stranger who does not understand the conventions by which the genteel world of the squires operates. She chooses this world freely, disliking the brutality of her home under the aegis of her drunkard brother who has destroyed Heathcliff's always tenuous humanity: 'It would degrade me to marry Heathcliff now,' she says, the result of 'that wicked man' her brother, bringing him low (Brontë 1992: 86). She is also deceived in her choice, of course; life at the Grange stifles her – repression is made manifest in her struggles against the limits of propriety that her position as a lady now imposes on her, and she is literally driven mad by it. But at least her husband does not beat her or terrorize her. Isabella, on the other hand, has received an utterly appropriate training in the realm of the feminine and it makes her choose the role of sacrificial victim. Brontë provides a very thorough critique of the destructiveness of her preference to be victim rather than mistress. Neither of the women survives their choice, however, even in this quasi-fantasy world: Cathy dies in childbirth – victim of biology as well as psychic pain; Isabella dies of consumption, her family's disease, but only at the point at which she has been completely humiliated by her monstrous husband. It is a double bind – choose civilization and you die; choose untamed nature – you die as well.

What psychoanalytical accounts of the construction of femininity give us, at the level of content, is a partial explanation of how and why women behave as they do, and *Wuthering Heights* offers us some interesting examples of the processes of fatal acculturation into the feminine passivity which is the norm for the Victorian period. The Freudian story, along with its various rewritings by different critics and theorists, tells us that women suffer from conflicting versions of selfhood far more than men do, since biologically they are always already 'castrated', lacking; and culturally, that lack is rendered painful by the denial of the rights and privileges that attach to the phallus (both a real biological penis, and a symbol of worldly power in culture). Choices are limited for them, since their identity (in much fiction, but also in a great deal of historical reality) is bound up with their choice of marriage partner. To assert a personality for a woman may well mean, therefore, choosing a mate with a personality to live through vicariously (Isabella's mistaken choice) or choosing a mate one might dominate (Cathy's choice, though she forgets that the worldly power that Linton wields – he is a wealthy man, a magistrate and therefore the representative of the law and these symbolic potencies – more than compensates for his physical impotence and watery personality). But psychoanalysis is much more than an account based on the manifest content of a given text. It is also concerned with the hidden or latent content, the story that is not quite on the surface. As such, it is also centrally interested in 'expression' – in how repressed **desires** come to the surface.

Expression

In a famous passage in Charlotte Brontë's *Jane Eyre*, the heroine describes her dissatisfaction at Thornfield Hall. 'I desired more,' she tells us, as she outlines her habit of climbing to the top of the house to pace out her frustrations on the battlements, like a caged lion. Needing to justify her longings and desires – after all, many readers would have assumed that she should be satisfied with what she had, a job, a home, an income – she writes:

> Women are supposed to feel very calm generally; but women feel just as men feel; they need exercise for their faculties, and field for their efforts, just as much as their brothers do; they suffer from too rigid a restraint, too absolute a stagnation, precisely as men would suffer; and it is narrow-minded in their more privileged fellow-creatures to say that they ought to confine themselves to making puddings and knitting stockings, to playing on the piano and embroidering bags.

> While thus alone I not unfrequently heard Grace Poole's laugh. (Brontë 1996: 125–6)

Writing about this passage 50 years later in *A Room of One's Own*, Virginia Woolf argued that its tone rang false to her. 'She left her story … to attend to some personal grievance,' she wrote. 'She remembered that she had been starved of her proper due of experience – she had been made to stagnate in a parsonage mending stockings when she wanted to wander free over the world. Her imagination swerved from indignation and we feel it swerve' (Woolf 1977: 70). And it is the shift between the demoniac laughter of the madwoman in the attic and the impassioned plea for women's rights that particularly exercised her. There is, however, another way of reading this passage. Rather than seeing it as artistically flawed because it is not seamless and well made, one could equally argue that Brontë has found a way to express the dangers that attend dissatisfaction with one's lot. The juxtaposition of the articulate discussion of women's needs and desires with the inarticulate 'low, slow ha! ha!' which thrills and frightens Jane is the symptom of the fate that awaits any 'mad-cat' who dares to demand more; rather literally, that way madness lies. Jane is at once fascinated and fearful of the lack of restraint. She has seen, despite her relative inexperience, that the training in femininity that her schooling has provided her with is a training in restraint. But all this quiescence and passivity has led to the deaths of nigh on half the school. Miss Temple, the headmistress, admonished by the 'benefactor' Mr Brocklehurst for nourishing the children's starved bodies, is a model of restraint:

> Miss Temple ... gazed straight before her, and her face, naturally pale as marble, appeared to be assuming also the coldness and fixity of that material; especially her mouth closed as if it would have required a sculptor's chisel to open it, and her brow settled gradually into petrified severity. (Brontë 1996: 75)

She maintains her dignity but does not save the girls who die of typhus. Yet if she spoke out against her master, she would lose her job and no one would even try to protect the girls. Pragmatism matters as much as principle in the expression (and the repression) of feminist principles in *Jane Eyre*. Sometimes, however, the price of repression is a breaking out of the unspoken **desires**. In Miss Temple's case, she feeds her charges with bread and cheese against the express orders of her boss and is admonished for it. In Jane's case, she speaks out against the brutality of her cousin (and is punished for it), and for the desire she feels for Rochester (which her second cousin roundly disapproves). She has to find a way to express her desires without putting herself in harm's way, either physically or mentally. For Jane this comes in the first instance with her paintings, fantasy landscapes which speak of freedom and of the dread that can come with it. The awkward break that Virginia Woolf identifies is in fact a symptom of the psychological situation of which the novel speaks: restraint is confinement which offers an illusory form of safety; self-expression is a risk as well, to psychic good health and to physical well-being. The novel oscillates between these poles, seeking equilibrium, and perhaps almost finding it in the wish-fulfilment fantasy of the ending.

Over the last 40 years or so, feminism has found its way into the academy to the extent that it is now so embedded in the consciousness of students and their teachers that it is rather easy to forget the radical political meanings the word once had, and the often bitter history of feminism's incorporation into the standard accounts of what literature might be. This is both a cause for celebration and a cause for concern: celebration because, intellectually, if not practically, feminism has won the argument; concern because the practical should still be at the core of what feminism is for, and its adoption as an orthodoxy perhaps undoes its political potential. If the study of literature has a purpose, it is that it reminds us that the cultural products of a given society

3

reflect that society, operating both as a mirror (sometimes distorting) of the world as it is, and as a space in which that society can be shown how to change, where injustice and oppression intervene in real people's lives. 'Doing' feminism is more than just a discussion of an abstruse set of principles. It is an ongoing series of political gestures – and don't let its position as orthodoxy tell you any different.

Further reading

Brennan, Teresa, ed. *Between Feminism and Psychoanalysis*. London and New York: Routledge, 1990.

Butler, Judith. *Gender Trouble: Feminism and the Subversion of Identity*. London: Routledge, 1990.

Fuss, Diana, ed. *Inside/Out: Lesbian Theories, Gay Theories*. London and New York: Routledge, 1991.

Gilbert, Sandra M. and Susan Gubar. *The Madwoman in the Attic: The Woman Writer and the Nineteenth-Century Literary Imagination*. New Haven, CT and London: Yale University Press, 1979.

Greene, Gayle and Coppelia Kahn, eds. *Making a Difference: Feminist Literary Criticism*. London and New York, 1985.

Hull, Gloria T., Patricia Bell Scott and Barbara Smith, eds. *All the women are white, All the black are men, But some of us are brave: Black Women's Studies*. New York: The Feminist Press, 1982.

Jacobus, Mary. *Reading Woman: Essays in Feminist Criticism*. London: Methuen, 1986.

Moi, Toril. *Sexual/Textual Politics: Feminist Literary Theory*. London: Methuen, 1985.

Morris, Pam. *Literature and Feminism: An Introduction*. Oxford: Blackwell, 1983.

Robbins, Ruth. *Literary Feminisms*. London: Macmillan, 2000.

Marxism

Alex Murray

One of the most common critical approaches you will encounter in literary studies is Marxism, a theoretical tradition that asks questions of the material conditions under which a text was produced and consumed, and the power relations that underpin these processes. Many other critical perspectives, such as postcolonialism, cultural **materialism**, gender studies, etc. are influenced by Marxism. Why? Marxism provides us as readers with a means of reading literature against itself, not simply accepting the assumptions, values and perspectives that a writer gives us. Instead, it wants to ask how the writer came to be in a position in which they could write. Who are they writing for? Whose voices were they ignoring or silencing?

Marx and the essence of man

Marxism is the generic name for a diffuse body of work that is either the work of Karl Marx and Fredrick Engels (see their *Communist Manifesto*), or is deeply indebted to these two nineteenth-century political theorists. Karl Marx was born in Prussia in 1818 to a middle-class family of Jewish origin, although rather lax and liberal in their outlook. He was educated at the University of Bonn before moving to Jena University where he wrote a thesis on Ancient Greek philosophy. He later become editor of a radical journal, *Rheinische Zeitung*. Marx's radical views led to government censorship and he moved to Paris to start up a new newspaper before he was expelled from France in 1845. Marx's early life as a student of philosophy and as a political radical and activist is important here. It was from his study of classical and modern philosophy that he was able to provide a philosophical foundation for his political thought, providing a universalizing approach to society, both ancient and contemporary. It was Marx's conviction that philosophy could change the world. As he stated in his famous thesis XI from the theses on Feuerbach: 'The philosophers have only *interpreted* the world in various ways; the point is to *change* it.'

So, how does philosophy change the world? For Marx, human existence is fundamentally about action, what he terms (from the classical Greek philosopher Aristotle) *praxis*: not about the relation between object and understanding, or self-perception, but about doing. Marx is then able to view man by his relation to his own action. If the essence of man is doing, or creating, then the concern of philosophy is not with some abstract principle of the 'good life' but, more importantly, with helping man to realize that capacity for doing. From this perspective Marx can explore the ways in which comparative models of social organization allow man to work and to create in the most effective ways. Marx then has a basis for both a view of the past and a model for the future – what is known as a teleological view of history – in which humankind is working to a goal (in Marx's case socialist utopia) and can see the past and the future in relation to that goal.

History and class

Marx's view of history is known as materialist. Our usual view of history is measured according to events or by reference to those in power, i.e., Victorian, Elizabethan, postwar, etc. – indeed, this is often how your courses will be organized. For Marx this is a history written by the winners, a narrative imposed from those above, rather than with the lived experience of the past for the majority of people. Marx was concerned instead with the material conditions of the past, with how life was lived under certain social and economic conditions. This understanding is known as historical **materialism** and is at the core of how Marx was to categorize historical development. According to Marx, history had been a continual process of developing and refining these modes of organization and he was able to plot the model of social and cultural organization he lived in – capitalism – within a process of development. This is also known as a 'scientific' view of history in which the future is determined by the past. So for Marx, capitalism, due to its inherent contradictions, would eventually end, being replaced by organized socialism and communism before being realized in a utopian society that would be the end of history.

This notion of an end of history is tied to the other great premise of Marx's view of history: class struggle. Marx followed what is known as a **dialectical** view of history, which was adapted from the German philosopher Hegel. According to Hegel, history moved through a series of struggles. He claimed that two opposing forces would meet and clash, before this antithesis produced a new synthesis, which would find a new adversary with whom it would clash, out of which would emerge a new synthesis, and so on until a point where opposition ended and we reached something like the end of history. Marx saw capitalism as a clash between the bourgeoisie – those who owned the means of production – and the working class who were controlled by them. This unequal arrangement would result in a dialectical clash, out of which the proletariat would emerge, a synthesis of the working class and those sympathetic bourgeois. So Marx was interested in social struggles in which the working class rose up against the bourgeoisie, seeing them as essential in the progression of history.

The production of literature

Marx proposed that our experience of living in capitalism was determined, as in any social and economic system, by the relation between a **base** and a **superstructure**. The base is the economic relations of a particular social system. This is divided into a tripartite system of the means of production, the relations of production and the forces of production. For Marx the **mode of production** that constituted the base in a system was simultaneously preserved and obscured by the superstructure: the set of institutions, conventions and phenomena that constitute a society. These can range from educational institutions and practices to the police force, religion, the judiciary, the system of political organization, cultural production, etc., and of course the production of literature. All of these aspects of a society were designed to condition those who live under it to exist within the economic mode of production, without challenging – or preferably being aware of – its existence. This superstructure forms the **ideology** of a society. An ideology is the collective set of beliefs that condition one's perspective on the world. If perfectly effective, ideology will be like a pair of permanent contact lenses we never knew we had, a means of conditioning our perspective of the world around us that is so complete it seems natural.

For Marxist critics such as Terry Eagleton, literature is intrinsically caught up in the production of ideology (see his *Marxism and Literary Criticism*, 1976). Instead of seeing literature and art as a free and autonomous sphere of creativity (the genius in the garret), Marxist critics want to know why the writer was in the garret (or in the stately home) and how their position within an economic system affected the way in which they wrote. Rather than simply accept a writer's position, Marxism will read them 'against the grain'. So, what might this look like? Let's take a writer like Virginia Woolf, whose novels are now regarded as classics of modernist literature. In a novel like *Mrs Dalloway* most critics would choose to focus on the eponymous heroine and Woolf's exploration of issues of time, consciousness and urban life. If they were to focus on a minor character it would be Septimus Smith, who represents the first literary representation of shell shock. A Marxist critic would start elsewhere, perhaps with the character of Doris Kilman, the teacher of Mrs Dalloway's daughter Elizabeth. She is portrayed in the novel as an unattractive and bitter woman of German ancestry who has no money. A minor character, she reveals certain preconceptions that Woolf has about class and money and can be read as the character whose negative portrayal reveals the most about Woolf's own particular middle-class worldview. The Marxist critic can then turn the text upside down and look at character relations not from the centre (Clarissa Dalloway) but the periphery, revealing the limited world of London life that Woolf tries to present as some sort of microcosm for experience. The Marxist critic will also think about who Woolf was writing for and why. Her readers were largely middle class and she had set up her own publishing imprint (Hogarth Press), which published this novel. Where was it sold? Who could afford it? How many copies were printed? Who bought them? These questions treat a novel not just as a work of imaginative creation, but as a commodity embedded in a system of relations of production that will determine how it was both written and received.

As this example has shown, Marxism is useful for calling into question the ways in which literature is written, but also how it is read. It can provide you, as students of literature, with a powerful tool for reading texts from marginal perspectives so that you see them as having a series of perspectives, even biases, which may not be apparent on first reading.

Further reading

Althusser, Louis. *Lenin and Philosophy and Other Essays*. Trans. Ben Brewster. New York: Monthly Review Press, 1976.

Althusser, Louis. *For Marx*. London: Allen Lane, 1969.

Gramsci, Antonio. *Selections from the Prison Notebooks*. London: Lawrence & Wishart, 2007.

Laclau, Ernesto and Chantal Mouffe. *Hegemony and Socialist Strategy: Towards a Radical Democratic Politics*. London: Verso, 1985.

Lukács, Georg. *History and Class Consciousness: Studies in Marxist Dialectics*. Trans. R. Livingstone. London: Merlin, 1971.

Marx, Karl. *Capital: A Critique of Political Economy, Volume 1*. Trans. Ben Fowkes. London: Penguin, 1990.

McLennan, David. *Marxism after Marx*, 3rd edn. London: Macmillan, 1998.

Osborne, Peter. *How to Read Marx*. London: Granta, 2005.

Thompson, E. P. *The Making of the English Working Class*. Harmondsworth: Penguin, 1980.

Williams, Raymond. *Marxism and Literature*. Oxford: Oxford University Press, 1977.

Structuralism

Alex Murray

The critical theory known as structuralism is used to define a broad series of critical methods for looking at a whole host of objects, from a poem through to advertisements. As a student of literature there is a good chance you will encounter it in a range of guises, along with the related critical position, post-structuralism. In short, structuralism sees languages as a system in which the meaning given to a word is dependent not on anything intrinsic to the word (whether written or spoken) but to the **contexts**, the series of relations in which it was presented. In studying literary texts you should always be attuned to the different meanings of words, and structuralism can help you to develop that awareness by grounding it in linguistics.

Structuralism and language

Structuralism emerged with the work of the French linguist Ferdinand de Saussure in the early twentieth century. From the years 1906 to 1911 Saussure gave a series of lectures on linguistics. From this course, two of his students copied down notes that were later posthumously published as *Course in General Linguistics*. In the *Course*, Saussure argues that language needs to be studied as a system as it exists in any one moment. In studying language as a system, Saussure began to call into question how words signify, and how this meaning is always determined in a structure.

The crux of Saussure's work is an investigation of the nature of the sign. Saussure suggested that signs don't necessarily mean anything, but that their meaning emerges in relation to other signs. In many cases this is simple, so for instance when you see a traffic light you know that red means stop, green means go, and amber means warning. But there is nothing about these colours that gives them these meanings. If we all stopped driving every time we saw the colour red, driving would be impossible. But in a traffic light system we all share a common understanding: red has a meaning only because it signifies as not being green or amber. So if a general system of signs, what is known as **semiotics**, relies on context and difference to create meaning, then how about in the case of language?

Saussure suggested that the linguistic sign (a word) needs to be broken down into two parts – the sound image and the thought image, or the **signifier** and the **signified** as they are commonly referred to. The signifier is the word that we hear, for instance 'cat'. The signified is what that word or sound conjures up in our mind, in this case a small fluffy domestic animal. Saussure suggested that these two parts of the sign do not mean intrinsically. For instance, if I am in France the signifier becomes 'chat', yet the signified hasn't changed. Or take the case of a term with different meanings across different contexts. Take the phrase 'We're rooting for you'. In the USA the phrase is one often deployed in a sporting context, with the term 'root' signifying support. In Australia, however, the term 'root' signifies copulation, and an unwitting American can encounter some rather strange stares. Or take the phrase, 'Alright, my lover'? A first-time visitor to the southwest of England would be initially a little confused and embarrassed before realizing it was a phrase of greeting, with the term 'lover' divested of its usual meaning. As simple as these examples are, they underpin the fact that words don't mean in and of themselves.

Saussure suggested that words instead take on their meaning through a pattern of relation within a system or structure. Take for instance the difference between the sounds 'a' and 'b'. For Saussure we don't register them as meaning in themselves; in fact they are seemingly arbitrary sounds. They only mean something because they have value in a system. This value comes from the fact that they are different from each other, not because they themselves mean anything as sounds. Take the word 'pain'. In English I automatically pronounce it with a stress on the 'i' so that it becomes, phonetically, more like 'y'. The phonetic use of the letters 'a' and 'i' become apparent only in a system. I know not to stress the 'a' and treat the 'i' as silent or I end up with the signifier 'pan'. Yet if I was in France that is precisely what I would do when using the term 'pain' (bread). Even though we do it innately in our mother tongue, we give letters meaning based upon their relation to other letters and those letters' relation to a word, and that word's relation to a sentence, and so on. The key point to take from Saussure's analysis, then, is that it is the structures and forms of **discourse** that determine meaning, not anything intrinsically related to the signs themselves.

Using structuralism to read a text

In many ways structuralism is easy for us to understand as students of literature because we are always doing it. How do I make sense of a poem? By being aware that the meaning of a word depends on its place in relation to the other words in the poem. Any time we encounter a metaphor we have to take the word (the signifier) and suspend our conclusions as to its meaning (the signified) until we can work out how the structure of the poem imparts a certain meaning. And even then the structure of a poem may not provide us with the answers, with an author using structure to halt our processes of interpretation. Take for instance Ezra Pound's early imagist poem 'In a Station of the Metro':

> The apparition of these faces in the crowd:
> Petals on a wet, black bough.

The meaning of each of these words is fairly obvious – you could use the *OED* to provide me with definitions of them all, but would that help? Not really. It is a very simple use of metaphor: Pound is getting off the metro in Paris and sees a number of beautiful faces, one after another. He is so struck by the experience that he tries to capture it in a poem, but the words he comes up with fail. Instead the emotion comes to him as splotches of colour and he doesn't know, as a poet, how to put that into art. Pound initially wrote a 30-line poem before coming up with this one-sentence hokku. The meaning of the words remains ambivalent because of the structure. Does apparition mean ghostly, unreal, fleeting, unclear? The poem can support readings of all of these, but the meaning of this one word will give you a totally different poem. It will in fact alter the metaphor, turning it from haunting and empty to vivid and sensual. The multiple and contradictory meanings of this one word illustrate, in a precise fashion, the central thesis of structuralist thought. It also suggests that structuralism is never going to provide 'solutions' or answers, but will provide the basis for conflicting and contradictory meanings to emerge from texts.

Semiology

The magnitude of Saussure's breakthrough only really became apparent when those who followed his work began the task of constructing a general science of signs which Saussure gestured towards, naming it semiology. A general science of signs was not concerned simply with language and meaning, but with a much broader use of signs. In our everyday life we use signs, such as a non-smoking sign, street signs, the keypads on our mobile phones, etc. Like language we use these signs without realizing precisely how they operate. One of the key proponents of semiology and structuralism was the French philosopher Roland Barthes. Barthes undertook an analysis of everyday symbols and sought to understand the structure through which we attach associative meaning. One of his famous examples is a bunch of roses, which signifies romance. Here the roses become a signifier and passion or romance become the signified. The roses in themselves are flowers, they mean nothing. Through a combination of social convention, tradition and my intention, that bunch of roses takes on a symbolic meaning.

Barthes then began to map exactly how these instances of investing signs with meaning relate to our larger sense of existence. In his study of advertising and consumer societies, *Mythologies* (1957), Barthes took to deconstructing an array of signs that make up something like a contemporary belief system (our own secular capitalist mythology). From steak and chips and detergents, to wrestling and striptease, Barthes sought to understand our investment in images and symbols by reading them within a larger structure of meaning. The book concluded with the important essay 'Myth Today', in which Barthes identified myth as a form of speech, what he would term a 'meta-language'. By this he meant that myth is an organizing principle in the structure of human forms that seeks to limit and control meaning. Myths tend to portray ideological values as timeless, rather than constructed, investing objects with a limited meaning. What structuralism helps us to do is to decode this meta-language of myth, to see its operation right down to the level of advertising and daily habit, and to thus see our own complicity in consuming an **ideology**.

During the 1950s and 1960s structuralism emerged as the leading intellectual movement in France. It perhaps reached its apex with the work of the French historian Michel Foucault, whose work attempted to work out exactly how we group together ideas of knowledge. Foucault believed we use systems and structures to organize and categorize the world around us. Take a discipline like sociology: it presents itself as an empirical science that can provide us with a broad knowledge of the world in which we live based upon research and observation. For Foucault, such claims attempt to cover over the fact that social science is about attempting to categorize, compartmentalize and seal off small areas of knowledge. His interest was in discovering exactly how this attempt to order and control knowledge had come about, and the consequences for how we obtain an understanding of the world and our place within it. Take examples such as the **discourse** of public health and statistics. The study of population health and its influence on governmental policy has had a massive influence on all of our lives, for the most part positive. Foucault was interested in how these sciences of population had come about, and in the interests and assumptions that underpinned the construction of the grid in which human life was turned into ordered and structured knowledge.

As you study literature you will no doubt come into contact with Saussure, Barthes and Foucault. While they often introduce a complex new vocabulary, the insights of their work can provide you with useful ways of reading texts, from poetry, to novels, to popular culture. The idea of meaning being determined not through any intrinsic value to a word, text or object, but to the system of relations, the structure that it finds itself in, is in many ways a good starting point for the entire endeavour of literary criticism.

3

Further reading

Barthes, Roland. *Image, Music, Text*. Ed. and trans. Stephen Heath. London: Fontana Press, 1977.

Benveniste, Emile. *Problems in General Linguistics*. Trans. Mary Elizabeth Meek. Miami: University of Miami Press, 1971.

Culler, Jonathan. *Saussure*. New York: Fontana, 1978.

Eco, Umberto. *A Theory of Semiotics*. Bloomington: Indiana University Press, 1975.

Hawkes, Terence. *Structuralism and Semiotics*. London: Methuen, 1980.

Jakobsen, Roman. *Six Lessons on Sound and Meaning*. Trans. John Mepham. Hassocks: Harvester Press, 1978.

Kurtzwell, Edith. *The Age of Structuralism: From Lévi-Strauss to Foucault*. London: Transaction,1996.

Lane, Michael. *Structuralism: A Reader*. London: Jonathan Cape, 1970.

Lévi-Strauss, Claude. *Structural Anthropology*. Trans. C. Jacobson and B. Grunfest Schoepf. London: Allen Lane, 1968.

Sturrock, John. *Structuralism*. Intro. Jean-Michele Rabaté. Oxford: Blackwell, 2003.

Psychoanalysis

Brian Jarvis

Put simply, psychoanalysis is a theory that focuses on the dynamic relationship between the body, mind and social order. This theory was first developed in the work of Sigmund Freud, a psychologist who ran a medical practice in Vienna from 1886 until he left for London in June 1938, dying there just over a year later in September 1939. Whilst the popular myth suggests that psychoanalysis is 'all about sex', Freud in fact studied and wrote about a range of subjects that included religion (in *The Future of an Illusion*, 1927, and *Moses and Monotheism*, 1939), occultism (in *Totem and Taboo*, 1913), trauma (in *Beyond the Pleasure Principle*, 1920) and humour (in *Jokes and their Relationship to the Unconscious*, 1905). Freud was not fixated on one subject; however, it is true to say that sexuality is central to much psychoanalytical thinking about the self, the family and society. Even if you do not agree with psychoanalysis (and many have their doubts) it is still necessary to recognize the huge impact of Freud's theories on Western culture, from the arts and academic disciplines to advertising and popular culture.

Perhaps *the* key concept underpinning psychoanalysis is the 'unconscious', or 'id', which Freud defined as 'the dark, inaccessible part of our personality' (Freud 1953–73, vol. 22: 328). According to this model there are parts of the mind – thoughts, **desires** and memories – that we cannot access but which nonetheless shape our identity and behaviour. To explain the development of the unconscious Freud went back to the beginning. Psychoanalysis contends that from the moment of our birth and then throughout infancy, we are governed by the 'pleasure principle'. The infant seeks only to obtain pleasure and this search for physical gratification inevitably centres upon her own body. Subsequently, as the child develops, she has to learn to give up the desire for immediate gratification. Society demands that we control our desires. The **pleasure principle** is repressed by what Freud termed the 'reality principle'. However, the story does not end here because desire is unruly. Repressed wishes do not simply disappear. Desires that have been denied reside in the unconscious and if too much sexual energy is repressed the subject can become mentally ill or 'neurotic'. Freud developed psychoanalysis as a tool which, he hoped, could cure mental illness, explain sexual development and shed light on the 'dark [and] inaccessible' parts of the mind. To achieve these goals the psychoanalyst focuses intently on language. Psychoanalysis is a form of 'talking cure'. The patient is encouraged to articulate their problems, to engage in word play (so-called 'free association') and to talk about their dreams. For Freud, dreams were the 'royal road' to the unconscious. A dream is the imaginary dramatization of wishes and fears that have been repressed in the waking world. According to Freud, the dream offers a complex code of images and symbols that has to be deciphered. The dream has a 'manifest content' (what we remember and narrate when awake) and a latent content (the secret meaning of these stories).

Because of its focus on language, storytelling and symbols, psychoanalysis lends itself to literary studies. The psychoanalyst offers close readings of the meaning hidden in the 'texts' offered by the patient when they talk about their feelings, their relationships and their dreams; or if they use one word when they intended to use another (the so-called 'Freudian slip'). Like many literary critics, the psychoanalyst suspects that deeper meanings are often hidden but can be uncovered by the work of interpretation. An excellent introduction to the twin practices of psychoanalysis and literary criticism is provided by Freud's own essay, 'The "Uncanny"' (1919). Here you will find Freud exploring the etymology of his keyword – 'uncanny', or *unheimlich* in German – alongside a reading of Hoffmann's gothic short story, 'The Sandman' (1816). Freud's work has inspired many literary critics and psychoanalytical concepts have been used to analyse authors, characters in novels and plays, literary language and history. For an introduction to one of the more rudimentary forms of psychoanalytical reading you might consult readings of 'In Winter in my Room' by the nineteenth-century American poet Emily Dickinson. This poem begins as follows:

> In Winter in my Room –
> I came upon a Worm –
> Pink, lank and warm – (Dickinson 1975: 682–3)

Following this discovery the female persona in the poem attempts to tie the worm up with string only for it to transform magically into a snake 'ringed with power'. In the poem's closing line this episode is revealed as a 'dream'. Practically every critical encounter with this poem has focused on its sexual symbolism. The 'worm/snake' has been interpreted as a phallic symbol that signifies the poet's 'penis envy' and repressed heterosexual **desire**, but also as a dream image that expresses her fear of and hostility towards male sexuality. In *Sexual Personae*, Camille Paglia underlines the extent to which psychoanalysis has become common currency, by suggesting that '[a]fter Freud, this poem would be unwritable, except by a child or psychotic. Its unself-conscious clarity is astounding' (Paglia 1992: 644).

Only a relatively small percentage of psychoanalytical critics content themselves with playing 'hunt the phallus'! If you develop your understanding of this critical approach it will become clear that psychoanalysis is a broad church. Freudian, or 'classical', psychoanalysis has been critiqued and developed and integrated with other critical approaches. Whilst Freud focused predominantly on the 'Oedipal' phase of development (typically between three and five years), his contemporary Melanie Klein concentrated on the formative significance of the pre-Oedipal phase (infancy). Klein proposed that one's earliest experiences with the mother's body formed a template for all future relationships, and her 'object relations theory' provided a platform for the development of feminist psychoanalysis. Without doubt the most significant revision of classical psychoanalysis was conducted by Jacques Lacan. Lacanian psychoanalysis combines Freudian theory with Saussurean linguistics and insists on the critical role played by language in our social and sexual development. Lacan's work is both highly influential and notoriously difficult, so you would be well advised to begin your investigation with an introductory guide. In addition to feminism and linguistics, psychoanalysis has also been joined with Marxist theory and has played a critical role in the evolution of gay and lesbian studies and film theory. For recommendations on where to begin your analysis of psychoanalysis, please see the 'further reading' section below.

Further reading

Ellmann, Maud. *Psychoanalytical Literary Criticism*. London: Longman, 1994.

Felman, Shoshana, ed. *Psychoanalysis and Literature: The Question of Reading, Otherwise*. New Haven, CT: Yale University Press, 1977.

Kofman, Sarah. *Freud and Fiction*. Oxford: Blackwell, 1990.

Lacan, Jacques. *Ecrits: The First Complete Edition in English*. New York. Norton, 2007.

Laplanche, J. and J. B. Pontalis. *The Language of Psycho-analysis*. London: Hogarth, 1973.

Mitchell, Juliet. *Psychoanalysis and Feminism*. Harmondsworth: Penguin, 1975.

Psychoanalytic Electronic Publishing: www.Pep-web.org

Thurschwell, Pamela. *Sigmund Freud*. London and New York: Routledge, 2001.

Wright, Elizabeth. *Psychoanalytical Criticism: A Reappraisal*. Oxford: Polity, 1998.

Žižek, Slavoj. *How to Read Lacan*. London: Granta, 2006.

Deconstruction

3

Maria-Daniella Dick

Although deconstruction is considered a branch of continental philosophy, it has also had a radical influence on the study of English Literature, within literary theory courses and the consideration of such concepts as the author and the book in period-specific study. While writing his 'Letter to a Japanese Friend' (1987), the French philosopher Jacques Derrida considers the meanings that surround the term that is associated primarily with his name and work. It is a piece often read as a summary of deconstruction and is the ideal introduction to its study, emphasizing as it does what many consider to be central to deconstruction considered as a critical approach: the contradiction of definitions. Derrida makes the point quite clearly: deconstruction is not a method and cannot be transformed into one. Deconstruction is, rather, something that *takes place*, within the text (Derrida in Kamuf, 1991).

The language and ideas which constitute a text and which may appear to represent one particular, stable meaning – the meaning we should take away from our reading as if we have 'solved' it – are shown when subjected to a close reading to be open to subversion. This challenges assumptions about the possibility of fixing one meaning on a text to the exclusion of others, especially where that meaning coincides with beliefs about the world: for example, that there is a 'masculine' way to write, and that that is how men write. Deconstruction seeks to show that such a preconception brought to reading is merely a fiction we do not acknowledge because we think it natural, while actually it is a culturally constructed idea based upon founding power structures that are so ingrained as to go unrecognized. A reading proceeding on the basis of these inherent myths is thus more likely to ignore differences within a text, because it looks only for those examples and themes which would support preconceptions, illusions mistaken as truths.

Critics of deconstruction, as well as some practitioners, misrepresent it as a unified subject area, rather than a collection of readings and practices which, though they can draw on a critical vocabulary, must always begin anew by responding to the singularity of each engagement. 'Singularity' is here a term given much weight by Derrida, referring to the condition that a text, like an event, is *singular*; that is to say, while it may bear surface similarities to other texts or events, it is, if not unique, then encountered in a given way one time only. Each reading of a text, of the same text, may well prove a singular experience, but this is something Derrida cautions cannot be programmed through a repeatable act of reading.

Some critics contend, incorrectly, that deconstruction is characterized by a fascination with language play and has no application in the outside world, alleging that the term points to a nihilistic concept of there being *no* meaning, no truth, recuperable through language in a text. This is a misunderstanding of the term; deconstruction, if we can say 'it' exists, tries to expose patiently the various meanings and truths inherent in a text, however internally contradictory or anomalous they may seem, while challenging a reading which does not attend to the complexities of that text but seeks to close off its potential prematurely, by imposing a limited meaning on it. To illustrate this, we may say that certain, obviously politicized forms of reading – Marxism or feminism, for example – have aims and goals. They set out, in their acts of reading, to look for particular representations, aspects of cultural, historical and social existence given **aesthetic** form in the literary text. In looking for those elements that conform to their reading and political perspective, they ignore those elements, aspects of narrative, images and so forth, which are not, apparently, germane to their sense of the political. This is to read according to a programme, and to impose, however unconsciously, on a novel, play or poem, a limit, a set of meanings, which are merely being tracked down, sought for, before the text is ever opened. For example, a Marxist critic (see MARXISM) might read William Faulkner's *As I lay Dying* in order to consider its representation of rural agrarian working-class members of the southern states of the USA, seeking in the novel the signs of the ways in which economic oppression brought about by capitalism have certain predictable effects. What the Marxist would, in all probability, not consider is the proliferation of references to food, and to eating, seeing these as mere 'colour' to aid in promoting the more realistic aspects of storytelling, and therefore 'only' formal, aesthetic. Similarly, a feminist critic (see FEMINISM) of Dickens's *Pickwick Papers* might examine the novel for the ways in which it promotes a benign **patriarchy**, in which men with money have the leisure to move around the country, whilst women are confined by economic circumstances to dependency on men, or the limited resources of education. Such a narrative, the feminist might conclude, demonstrates symbolically, as a mystification of the economic structures that inform patriarchal and capitalist culture, how 'man' is the aggressor, the hunter, adopting an active role, while women are passive, subject to men's **desires**. What the feminist would fail to notice, perhaps, is the anomalous trope that has little, apparently, to do with the male/female, active/passive dialectic; the trope less read, however, might be noted in the frequency with which eyes, optical devices, metaphors of vision and visibility, and other related matters pepper the text. The reader, reading after the 'deconstruction' that might take place in the text, would ask after such seeming anomalies, wondering why they appear so frequently when they seem to have little to do with narrative or what some might consider the dominant **tropes** of the text. Yet, once seen, such anomalous figures both serve to structure the text as it is and yet also destabilize any apparent, homogeneous meaning.

Derrida, deconstruction

Jacques Derrida was born in El-Biar, Algeria. He travelled to Paris in 1949 to study at the Lycée Louis-le-Grand, and then the École Normale Supérieure, remaining there until 1983 when he became director of studies at the École des Hautes Études en Sciences Sociales. A visiting professor at Yale from 1975, he and his colleagues – among them Paul de Man and J. Hillis Miller – were erroneously identified as the 'Yale School' of deconstruction, a name they rejected because it implied that each was practising the same methodology, rather than their own unique deconstructions. It is from a 1966 conference he attended in Baltimore that the movement is dated, and, however arbitrary such a date may be, as critics moved away from the limitations of a structuralist theory that sought to designate each aspect of a text within a totalizing system, Derrida agreed that the word 'deconstruction' was compelling. There was a general movement, after the movement known as structuralism (see STRUCTURALISM), towards viewing the text in terms of a multiplicity of meanings working together and against each other, rather than as an object to be assimilated within a system and its one particular and exclusive meaning decided upon (see, for example, BAKHTIN AND DIALOGIC CRITICISM, PSYCHOANALYSIS and GAY STUDIES AND QUEER THEORY, all of which demonstrate in different modes how various voices and meanings are available in the same text, often writing against the apparently evident 'message' of the work). Thus to deconstruct 'is a structuralist and anti-structuralist gesture at the same time' (Derrida 1992: 83), and deconstruction was to demonstrate that those oppositions themselves are necessarily deconstructable, always open to being overturned, as well as insisting on the obligation to read a text systematically.

His conference paper was published in *Writing and Difference* (1967), a collection of philosophical and literary engagements; with that book, published in the same year as *Speech and Phenomena* and *Of Grammatology*, he introduced the terminology which, along with that of three further publications in 1972 – *Positions*, *Margins of Philosophy* and *Dissemination* – would come to determine 'deconstruction'.

Concepts of deconstruction

Of Grammatology (1967) radicalizes the concept of writing, and illustrates the presumptions that we employ in analysing the world and the text. Through questioning the dominance of speech over writing in Western philosophy, it examines **binary oppositions** and demonstrates how the privileged part of a binary is reliant upon the relegated term, the seemingly stronger actually unable to function without the one which it subsumes. Language is thus always open to that which it at first appears not to contain. If you are an advanced student, you might wish to know that Derrida calls this haunting of language by other meanings the 'trace': it is always 'under erasure' as deconstructions call into question the illusion of presence upon which the foundational premises of Western **metaphysical** philosophy rest. One can never assert that a concept, or that language, can be fastened to only one authoritative statement of its meaning, though this is not through a lack of confidence or a view that language finally means nothing. It is, rather, to say that the concept, or language, must always remain open to the other meanings that inhabit it, so we can understand it better in its richness. If a meaning is absolutely present to the word, then that admits of no other meanings that might also be there. What deconstruction holds is that no meaning is ever fully present and identical with a word or concept, for there is always the trace of another, and thus meanings can be present and absent at the same time, never fully there nor ever fully away.

On investigating this concept, you may wish to note that where Western philosophy takes its origins from the Word, or *logos*, which is associated with the word of God, deconstruction holds that there is no stable original authority which can be said to be wholly present and on which we can base other meanings. This fiction of the origin is a fiction of presence, implying that there are certain founding truths that are absolutely available and absolutely stable, untainted by any intervention between thought and its expression. For example, in questioning the apparent binary opposition of speech over writing, Derrida identified the concept of *phonocentrism* as a key term within what he called *logocentrism*. Logocentrism is the illusion under which Western philosophy labours, that the *logos* – the fiction of a male Western idiom based on concepts of authority tracing back to the word of God – is at the centre of philosophy as its truth. Considering writing to be a secondary and pure formalization (see FORMALISM), phonocentrism presumes that speech need only be represented in writing, and that writing can be easily controlled by authorial intention, as a medium which can represent without introducing its own ambiguities. This questioning of the relegation of writing has a wide-reaching influence for the study of literature, by interrogating the authority of the author and the basis upon which the reader makes assumptions about a text.

Deconstructions are marked by what Derrida termed **différance**, a progression from structuralism and from Ferdinand de Saussure's concept of language as a differential system, in that it connotes not only *difference* – I am called a cat, because I am not called a dog – but also *deferral*. There is always a temporal and a spatial difference at work in the language of a text, so that the 'trace' of language is always inhabited by other meanings. In an often cited example from 1972's *Dissemination*, Derrida shows that in the text of Plato's *Phaedrus*, the word *'pharmakon'* is translated *either* as 'remedy' *or* 'poison' depending on its **context** in the discussion: the word is relegated to a presumed and prior 'truth' which underlies the text, illustrating the presumption that language follows a truth that comes before the text rather than itself creating a means by which the world may be understood. A translation which chooses to erase the **ambiguity** of the word, saying it can be *either* 'remedy' *or* 'poison' but not both simultaneously, is, Derrida argues, still inhabited by the 'other' meaning; an exclusive decision is impossible, for any attempt at closure will be opened to the exteriority of the trace, neither meaning exclusively present nor ever absent. Thus, while 'remedy' may at times seem to be the dominant term, the other term, 'poison', cannot be erased from the mind, and one can see that there is a more complicated ambiguity over the property of the *pharmakon* which a conventional reading would try to obscure by imposing a reading that elides this complication. This impurity is also characteristic of any figure which would pretend to refer to a stable and present totality, such as the archive, which, as Derrida shows in *Archive Fever* (1995), operates not on a principle of remembering but one of forgetting, as there is always something that will be unrecoverable to the archive, absent within it.

Derrida asserted that 'deconstruction' was never intended as a privileged term, but takes its place in a chain of other terms which reading relies on, such as *différance, arche-écriture, hymen,* all of which he employs graphically and conceptually in his writings to interrogate the fiction that structures are built on original truths. The hymen, for example, is discussed in 'The Double Session', an essay within *Dissemination* (1972), as a term which complicates distinctions between that which is 'inside' and that which is 'outside' the body: the hymen forms a boundary and is neither only inside nor outside the female body but both at the same time. This Derrida then relates to misconceptions about the world being 'outside' of the text which merely represents it, showing that the text cannot close itself off, cannot separate itself from the context which is seemingly 'outside' of it. The text is not an object set apart from the world, but rather partakes in shaping it and being shaped in turn by preconceptions about how the world operates and which are brought to our reading.

Deconstruction, then, is not a formula that can be applied or learned as a methodology, in order to be grafted onto each text in the same way. It is something that occurs differently in each text, and there is no method of deconstruction, for as reading happens it must respond to the singularity – the uniqueness – of each individual text. This is why there can be no description or definition of deconstruction, because the *is* upon which that explanation would be predicated – deconstruction *is* x, or *is* y – remains undecidable. Although there are guides which purport to illustrate how to 'do' deconstruction – by isolating the **binary oppositions** in a text (black and white, male and female, language and speech), then showing how the supposedly minor term in the binary can be coaxed out in order to challenge the major term – this is a crude approximation of what is, in the event, a patient and always singular operation.

Deconstruction takes place as a close reading, attending scrupulously to that which is latent, which is going against the grain and subverting a unified meaning. The work of Julian Wolfreys and Nicholas Royle should be consulted for an example of how such a reading can be effected, especially Wolfreys' *Deconstruction•Derrida* (1997), which provides a detailed account of deconstruction and its concepts, illustrated, among other readings, by a discussion of Joseph Conrad's *Heart of Darkness*.

Concerns of deconstruction

Recent studies that perceive particular strands in deconstruction, such as John D. Caputo's 1997 *Deconstruction in a Nutshell: A Conversation with Jacques Derrida*, which argues for a strain of religious messianism in the later writings, and Simon Critchley's 1992 *The Ethics of Deconstruction: Derrida and Lévinas*, which provides an account of an engagement by Derrida with the thought of Emmanuel Lévinas on justice, have helped to isolate certain concerns within deconstruction. Commonly characterized as the *ne plus ultra* of textualism and the '**linguistic turn**' in literary theory, deconstruction is often mistaken as rejecting the politics and issues of the world for a concentration on language; this limited view sees a partial correction of that course by the so-called 'ethical turn' in the 1980s towards ideas of law and global community; then, in 1993, to an explicit political engagement by Derrida in *Specters of Marx*.

The misconception of non-engagement with the world serves only to elide the ethical imperative which impels all deconstructions from Derrida's earliest readings, and those of other 'good readers' such as J. Hillis Miller. It ignores the fact that any reading which examines writing with respect for the '**other**', or difference which is being occluded by an impulse towards simple unity, is necessarily ethical: the distinction seems to be based, once again, on a false binary which seeks to demarcate an 'outside' of the text which cannot exist. This simple binary is also invoked in much criticism to impose a delineation between that in deconstruction which treats of 'literature' and that which is 'philosophy', or 'religion' or 'psychoanalysis'. *Deconstruction: a Reader* (2000), edited by Martin McQuillan, provides an overview of influences upon deconstruction, and discussions of deconstructions in areas of sexual difference, politics, literature, philosophy, ethics and culture, through essays by Peggy

Kamuf, Phillippe Lacoue-Labarthe, Geoffrey Hartmann and others investigating the several areas of concern in which deconstructions converge rather than being confined to one academic discipline. Derek Attridge's edited collection of essays, *Acts of Literature* (1992), shows that though Derrida has always engaged explicitly with literature, those engagements are always inflected by a desire to examine its concerns rigorously, and without confining 'literature' to a narrow interpretation.

Derrida's last writings interweave such concepts as 'the gift', 'senses', 'mourning', 'forgiveness' and 'the secret' towards a more contemplative reading in the wake of the earlier technical advancements, when a critical vocabulary has been established which refers to other readings, other deconstructions; the terms must be singular to that text, yet maintain the element of 'iterability' which recognizes the *différance*, the trace, of the singular with the iterable. That is to say, the terms must always be specific to the texts with which they are engaged, yet must always also be capable of repetition. The investigation, for example, of the 'name', another Derridean term, will not be the same in *Romeo and Juliet* – see 'Aphorism, Countertime' (Derrida in Attridge 1992: 414–33) – as it will be in his readings of his own name, which are well introduced in '"*As If* I were Dead": An Interview with Jacques Derrida', in John Brannigan, Ruth Robbins and Julian Wolfreys' *Applying: to Derrida* (1996: 212–26). The 'name', discussed over a number of texts, becomes a term which can take its part in a lexicon as its significance increases, the reader recalling other texts in which Derrida has invoked the term and its particular import within each. In the aforementioned interview, Derrida considers the implications of applying his name to his self and the 'death' that it effects, relatable to his pronouncements that how to live 'finally' when learning how to live ultimately signals that one has accepted one's own mortality. Jacques Derrida died, in Paris, in 2004.

Further reading

Caputo, John D. *Deconstruction in a Nutshell: A Conversation with Jacques Derrida*. New York: Fordham University Press, 1997.

Derrida, Jacques. *Writing and Difference*. Trans. Alan Bass. London: RKP, 1967.

Derrida, Jacques. *Speech and Phenomena and Other Essays on Husserl's Theory of Signs*. Trans. David B. Allison (1973). Evanston: Northwestern University Press, 1967.

Derrida, Jacques. *Of Grammatology*. Trans. Gayatri Chakravorty Spivak. Baltimore, MD: The Johns Hopkins University Press, 1967.

Derrida, Jacques. *Positions*. Trans. Alan Bass (1982). Chicago: University of Chicago Press, 1972.

Derrida, Jacques. *Margins of Philosophy*. Trans. Alan Bass. Chicago: University of Chicago Press, 1972.

Derrida, Jacques. *Dissemination*. Trans. Barbara Johnson. Chicago: University of Chicago Press, 1972.

Derrida, Jacques. *Specters of Marx: The State of the Debt, the Work of Mourning, and the New International*. Trans. Peggy Kamuf. London and New York: Routledge, 1993.

Derrida, Jacques. *Archive Fever: A Freudian Impression*. Trans. Eric Prenowitz. Chicago: University of Chicago Press, 1995.

Wolfreys, Julian. *Deconstruction•Derrida*. London: Macmillan, 1997.

Postcolonialism

Jenni Ramone

Graeme Harper claims that 'the colonial condition' is 'a contradictory one': this contradiction he summarizes as being caused by either 'the imposition of one cultural perspective on top of another, or the promotion of imperial law over an indigenous one, or the engagement of a set of exploitative economic possibilities over and above an established set of communal ones' (Harper 2002: 1). Postcolonialism aims to represent and interrogate these contradictions, by examining texts and contexts including 'colonialist, modern anti-colonial and contemporary postcolonial writings; theoretical explorations of nineteenth-century **imperialism** and late twentieth-century neo-colonialism', which might take place in 'the geo-political regions of Latin America, India, the Caribbean, the Pacific, Africa, Anglo-America, and the United Kingdom' (Chrisman and Parry 2000: vii).

Homi Bhabha's keyword 'hybridity', a key concept in postcolonialism, was forged in relation to postcolonial migrations. The migration process culminates, for Bhabha, in a '"splitting" of the national subject' (Bhabha 1990: 298). For Frantz Fanon, another key figure in postcolonialism, the notion of this split self is 'a direct result of colonialist subjugation' (Fanon 1986: 17). Frantz Fanon is the figure most prominently associated with postcolonial thinking on race. Fanon describes the synthesis of black and white consciousnesses, and suggests that the cultural dominance of the white colonizer over the black colonized leads to psychological disorder. According to postcolonial critiques of colonial writing, the colonies had been thought of as 'children' of the 'mother country', and they were expected both to emulate that European location and to remain subordinate to it. This symbolism problematically endows the colony with notions of underdevelopment and indiscipline. Postcolonialism was forged to identify and then counteract this method of representation.

Edward Said is perhaps the most famous commentator on colonial representations. For Said, 'the Orient was almost a European invention, and had been since antiquity a place of romance, exotic beings, haunting memories and landscapes, remarkable experiences' (Said 1991: 1). Said suggested that the Orient is 'the place of Europe's greatest and richest and oldest colonies, the source of its civilizations and languages, its cultural contestant, and one of its deepest and most recurring images of the Other' (ibid.). Said's work led to an emphasis on binaries between the colonizer and colonized in postcolonialism, an approach which is now questioned as somewhat crude by contemporary postcolonial theorists. For Gayatri Spivak, the **Other** is the subaltern, or the marginal.

Later approaches to postcolonial literature by Laura Chrisman, Benita Parry, Neil Lazarus and others have suggested that the ideas of hybridity and the binaries examined by Bhabha, Fanon and Said are limiting. Perhaps one of the most exciting recent developments in Postcolonial Studies has been the expansion of the term to include 'the neocolonial operations of global capitalism' (Chrisman and Parry 2000: x). Chrisman and Parry suggest that there has been a change to an interdisciplinary focus for postcolonialism (ibid.): colonial and postcolonial literatures are approached from an interdisciplinary, postcolonial framework. This means that the literary texts are not studied in isolation, nor are they studied solely through those established voices of postcolonialism. Instead, the literary texts are approached in the **context** of other disciplines, which include historical, cultural and linguistic perspectives.

Further reading

Bhabha, Homi K., ed. *Nation and Narration*. London: Routledge, 1990.

Boehmer, Elleke. *Stories of Women: Gender and Narrative in the Postcolonial.* Cambridge: Cambridge University Press, 2005.

Chrisman, Laura and Benita Parry, eds. *Postcolonial Theory and Criticism*. The English Association Essays & Studies. Cambridge: DS Brewer, 2000.

Fanon, Frantz. *Black Skin, White Masks*. London: Pluto, 1986.

Lazarus, Neil. *The Cambridge Companion to Postcolonial Literary Studies*: *Nation*. Manchester: Manchester University Press, 2004.

Said, Edward. *Orientalism*. London: Penguin, 1991.

Spivak, Gayatri. *The Post-Colonial Critic*. London: Routledge, 1990.

New historicism

Christopher Ringrose

The origins of new historicism as a theoretical and critical movement are usually dated to the early 1980s, and in particular to the influential work of the American scholar Stephen Greenblatt in *Renaissance Self-Fashioning* (1980), but its intellectual roots lie within the poststructuralist developments of the previous two decades. Its approach to literature and 'context' is often contrasted with the more traditional, homogeneous view of history presented in E. M. W. Tillyard's 1943 study *The Elizabethan World Picture* (e.g., in Barry 1995: 174; Selden et al. 1997: 187). New historicism proposes a more provisional and conflict-based model of the past, emphasizing competing discourses, ideological differences and the pervasive exercise of **power**. Its highly productive methodology has been to elide the distinction between literary **discourse** and the fascinating and diverse range of texts produced contemporaneously with it. These can include legal documents, travel writing, conduct books, pamphlets, cookery books, church records, household accounts, popular tales and songs, medical treatises or even inscriptions on cigarette cases (as in Christopher Craft's subtle study of *The Importance of Being Earnest* in Craft 1994: 106–39).

New historicism does not use these materials as the 'historical background' against which literature can be seen more clearly, but as part of the extensive web of **textuality** within which poetry, plays and fiction also operate. Through that textuality, power relations are negotiated and maintained, and selfhood constructed. Such an emphasis on tracing power relations might imply that new historicism sees its conjunction of literary and historical scholarship as a tool for political liberation. However, H. Aram Veeser's oft-cited definition in the Introduction to *The New Historicism* (1989) includes the claim that 'every act of unmasking, critique and opposition uses the tools it condemns and risks falling prey to the practices it exposes' – a proposition which draws upon the work of the French theorist Michel Foucault, and which, as John Brannigan observes in one of the best introductions to the topic, makes new historicism 'often ... grim reading with its insistence that there is no effective space of resistance' (Brannigan 1998: 8). For this reason it is frequently contrasted with the British-based cultural **materialism**, which is presented as more politically engaged and optimistic (Hawthorn 1996: 5; Selden et al. 1997: 191; Brannigan 1998: 10).

In its early days, new historicism's influence was felt most strongly in Renaissance studies, through the work of Louis Montrose ('"Eliza, Queene of Shepheardes" and the Pastoral of Power'), Jonathan Goldberg (*James I and the Politics of Literature*) and Greenberg himself. Since then, however, the University of California's important series *The New Historicism* (Stephen Greenblatt, General Editor) has included books on a wide range of historical and cultural politics, from nineteenth-century American selfhood and domesticity to Irish nationalism, and male homosexual **desire** in English discourse. Students interested in seeing how a new historicist reading of a familiar text can be constructed by reading an 'anecdote', or small piece of text, in conjunction with it, should find illuminating John Brannigan's reading of Joseph Conrad's *Heart of Darkness* alongside a fragment from Mary Kingsley's *Travels in West Africa* (Brannigan 1998: 133–54).

Further reading

Barry, Peter. *Beginning Theory: An Introduction to Literary and Cultural Theory*. Manchester: Manchester University Press, 1995.

Brannigan, John. *New Historicism and Cultural Materialism*. London: Macmillan, 1998.

Craft, Christopher. *Another Kind of Love: Male Homosexual Desire in English Discourse, 1850–1920*. Berkeley: University of California Press, 1994.

Goldberg, Jonathan. *James I and the Politics of Literature: Jonson, Shakespeare, Donne and Their Contemporaries*. Baltimore, MD: Johns Hopkins University Press, 1983.

Greenblatt, Stephen. *Renaissance Self-Fashioning: From More to Shakespeare*. Chicago: University of Chicago Press, 1980.

Hawthorn, Jeremy. *Cunning Passages: New Historicism, Cultural Materialism and Marxism in the Contemporary Literary Debate*. London: Arnold, 1996.

Montrose, Louis. "'Eliza, Queene of Shepherds" and the Pastoral of Power'. In *The New Historicism*, ed. Aram H. Veeser, 88–115. London: Routledge, 1989.

Selden, Raman et al. *A Reader's Guide to Contemporary Literary Theory*, 4th edn. London: Harvester Wheatsheaf, 1997.

Tillyard, E. M. W. *The Elizabethan World Picture*. London: Pimlico, 1998.

Veeser, H. Aram, ed. *The New Historicism*. London: Routledge, 1989.

Cultural materialism

Alex Murray

If historical materialism was Marxism's way of determining human history from the 'ground' up, then cultural materialism is a Marxist-influenced means of viewing cultural production (see MARXISM). Historically, Literary Studies had a propensity to view the production of literature as part of a narrative that reveals something intrinsic or essential about the language/tradition in which it was produced, or of human nature more generally. This understanding of literature, also influential in the creation of a literary **canon**, seeks to plot an abstracted, essentializing view of literature, with literary texts deracinated, removed from their social and historical **contexts**. The material conditions under which literature was produced, the precise and complex cultural contexts became irrelevant: literature was timeless. This sense of a timeless English literature was coupled with a hermetic notion of literary texts. During the 1950s, 1960s and for the majority of the 1970s, literary criticism in the United States and the United Kingdom was dominated by forms of formalist analysis (see FORMALISM). In the United States critics such as Cleanth Brooks and W. K. Wimsatt argued that the context, biography and psychology of the author was immaterial to the literary work itself, and that literary critics had only an obligation to examine the work from the standpoint of literary technique, **genre**, etc. This view of examining literature is terribly limiting, and would deny, for instance, the importance of the English Civil War to an understanding of Milton's *Paradise Lost*.

With the emergence of literary theory as an important feature of literary studies, cultural materialism became one of the most pronounced perspectives for viewing cultural production. The central contention of a cultural materialist view of culture is that each and every cultural producer works within a specific political and economic context. Cultural materialism is tied closely with the emergence of new historicism; indeed there is much debate over the differences, if any, between them in their contextual analysis of cultural production. That context, whether consciously or unconsciously, has a certain impact upon the literary production of writers, whether that be explicit, in the case of writers such as Pope, or heavily obscured in the case of modernist writers such as Joyce and Eliot. For the cultural materialist literary critic it is essential to know the precise means by which a writer subsisted, and by which culture circulated more generally, so that we can understand literary production in something like its true context. Like Marxist critics, they believe that the place of writers within an economic system has a profound effect on their perception of such a system, and that their work, right down to the minutiae of literary technique, must be seen as influenced by these contexts.

There were a number of key figures in the development of cultural materialism, perhaps the foremost being Raymond Williams. Williams had a long and distinguished career as an English (or Welsh, to be accurate) academic and public intellectual. Having served in the Second World War following his studies at Trinity College Cambridge, he went on to become a Professor at Cambridge where he published many influential works of criticism. Perhaps the most influential in the development of cultural materialism was *Marxism and Literature* (1977). In it Williams developed his most strident response to the Cambridge model of English championed by F. R. Leavis. For Leavis and his followers literature was a means of accessing 'immediate living experience', and its appreciation was a direct response to the language of the text itself and what it represented. In opposition to this idea of meaning being expressed in literature, Williams was concerned to show how it was produced, and the numerous ideological conceits at work if one is to limit analysis to a superficial study of expression. As he states, no expression – that is to say, no account, description, portrait – is 'natural' or 'straightforward'. These are at best socially relative terms. Language is not a pure medium through which the reality of an event or an experience or the reality of a society can 'flow' (Williams 1977: 166). Williams's Marxian call for an analysis of the cultural conditions in which a text was produced was part of a much larger push for a more contextual analysis of literary texts.

The most predominant critics in the subsequent development of cultural materialism were Jonathan Dollimore and Alan Sinfield. In 1985, they together published a collection of essays entitled *Political Shakespeare: Essays in Cultural Materialism*. The development of cultural materialist analyses of the greatest figure in the English 'canon' was a bold statement of the challenge that the more theoretically inflected shift in literary studies was making to the old Leavisite tradition, an antagonism often referred to as the culture or theory wars. In the introduction to part I, Dollimore outlines the general contention of the volume's intervention into studies of the Renaissance theatre. On one level it is a challenge to what he refers to as the 'idealist' critics 'preoccupied with supposedly universal truths which find their counterpart in "man's" essential nature; the criticism in which history, if acknowledged at all, is seen as inessential or a constraint transcended in the affirmation of a transhistorical human condition' (Dollimore and Sinfield 1994: 4).

On the other hand, the volume set out to establish the ways in which literary and cultural production could act as a subversion of dominant cultural, social and political **hegemonies**. The term 'subversion' is essential as it suggests that literature can act as a 'challenge to the principles upon which authority is based' (1994: 13). So an analysis of *Richard III*, for instance, is not only interested in the construction of dialogue, dramatic tension, metaphor, etc. but instead asks us to consider the ways in which the play anatomizes and challenges the notion of the 'great chain of being' that naturalized oppression during the period. The volume, in part II, also seeks to place into context the reproduction and reinvention of Shakespeare in a more contemporary context. Here the blasé reception of Shakespeare as the great English dramatist is challenged through an attempt to examine the persistence of Shakespeare and the politics of its cultural reception. As Sinfield suggests, 'There is no determinate entity called Shakespeare's play... and we should consider the implications, which are inescapably political, of rival claims to have the privileged perspective' (1994: 154). Here the politics of competing claims for cultural value become an important factor as we see cultural materialism examining the field of cultural production, to use Pierre Bourdieu's term, within which we consume culture, rather than privileging the inherently bourgeois forms of conservative **aesthetic** judgement.

Here we can also see the affinities between cultural materialism and cultural studies. Cultural materialism has become an essential part of literary studies used now to examine English literature from Chaucer through to contemporary fiction. This politicization and contextualization of literary and cultural production has provided the ground for a far greater diversity both in the texts studied and also the scope with which they are examined. The effect of this is, for example, that the study of Shakespeare today is far more historical and less universal than it was 20 years ago. As a student you will find far more emphasis given to questions of how the play was staged, who would have seen it and how it related to a broader social and political **context** – rather than seeing these plays as timeless works of literature which can 'speak' to you today. You are also likely to think about Shakespearean afterlives as you study (examining plays such as Tom Stoppard's *Rosencrantz and Guildenstern Are Dead* in relation to *Hamlet*, for example), keeping in mind that a text exists only as it is read/performed.

Further reading

Bourdieu, Pierre. *The Field of Cultural Production: Essays on Art and Literature*. Ed. Randall Johnson. New York: Columbia University Press, 1993.

Brannigan, John. *New Historicism and Cultural Materialism*. Basingstoke: Palgrave Macmillan, 1998.

Drakakis, John, ed. *Alternative Shakespeares*. London: Methuen, 1985.

Greenblatt, Stephen. *Shakespearean Negotiations: The Circulation of Social Energy in Renaissance England*. Oxford: Clarendon Press, 1990.

Hawthorn, Jeremy. *Cunning Passages: New Historicism, Cultural Materialism and Marxism in the Contemporary Literary Debate*. London: Arnold, 1996.

Higgins, John. *Raymond Williams: Literature, Marxism and Cultural Materialism*. London: Routledge, 1999.

Kiernan Ryan, ed. *New Historicism and Cultural Materialism: A Reader* London: Arnold, 1996.

Milner, Andrew. *Cultural Materialism*. Melbourne: Manchester University Press, 1993.

Milner, Andrew. *Re-imagining Cultural Studies: The Promise of Cultural Materialism*. London: Sage, 2002.

Sinfield, Alan. *Faultlines: Cultural Materialism and the Politics of Dissident Reading*. Oxford: Clarendon Press, 1992.

Wilson, Scot. *Cultural Materialism: Theory and Practice*. Oxford: Blackwell, 1995.

African American criticism

Andrew Dix

The first task confronting African American critics in the twentieth century was to establish a **canon** of primary texts *on which to practise criticism*. In the face of a racist bias which warped literary study as it did many other cultural and social activities in the United States, African American scholars necessarily devoted much of their energy to the basic work of identifying and celebrating a body of black-authored writing. This process gathered momentum with contributions such as Richard Wright's essay, 'The Literature of the Negro in the United States' (1957), and might be said to have culminated in the publication in 1997 of the first edition of Gates and McKay's monumental *Norton Anthology of African American Literature*.

On the basis of such endeavours, the African American canon is now both securely rooted and wide ranging. Thus, in your courses, you will be likely to study not only black-authored poetry, drama and literary fiction, but also an array of popular and generic verbal productions, extending from rap lyrics and Martin Luther King's speeches to African American science fiction and the crime novels of Chester Himes and Walter Mosley. You can also expect to engage with the long and varied tradition of black women's writing in the United States. Here you will be beneficiaries of the work of African American feminist critics who, two decades ago, had to fight canon wars of their own against masculine forces then prevailing in both the production and the evaluation of black literature in the United States. Key feminist interventions from this period include Barbara Christian's *Black Feminist Criticism* (1985), Hazel Carby's *Reconstructing Womanhood: The Emergence of the Afro-American Woman Novelist* (1987) and Sandi Russell's *Render Me My Song: African-American Women Writers from Slavery to the Present* (1990).

It will become apparent to you in your study of materials ranging historically from nineteenth-century slave narratives to the latest novels by Toni Morrison and Alice Walker that African American criticism has developed various models for conceptualizing the texts that make up its canon. At the start of his groundbreaking cultural survey *The Souls of Black Folk* (1905), W. E. B. Du Bois evokes a condition of 'double-consciousness', which he argues is peculiar to African Americans. As Du Bois writes: 'One ever feels his two-ness – an American, a Negro; two souls, two thoughts, two unreconciled strivings; two warring ideals in one dark body, whose dogged strength alone keeps it from being torn asunder' (1999: 11). Du Bois writes at a time well before

African American criticism was institutionalized and generated its own conferences, journals, book series and university modules; nevertheless, this branch of literary studies continues to owe much to his pioneering insight into African Americans' 'two-ness'. It would not be overstating the case, in fact, to represent the history of black literary criticism in the United States as a set of responses – variously affirmative or rejectionist – to Du Bois's thesis.

For some twentieth-century African American critics, seeking to rebut Du Bois, a distinctively black writing in the United States only occurs when texts are considered to show no traces of white-authored literature. Often responding to moments of heightened assertiveness in black American politics, critics working in this vein exemplify a form of *cultural separatism*. You may well encounter a number of vivid separatist manifestos, one being Langston Hughes's 'The Negro Artist and the Racial Mountain' (1926), which refutes the power of the white Anglo-American literary tradition and aims to ground African American writing instead in black popular speech and the rhythms of jazz and blues. The reader of Hughes's essay, or of other incendiary documents – including those produced by the 1960s Black Arts Movement – will find a strain of African American criticism which aims primarily to mobilize its own ethnic constituency rather than appeal to a mixed-race audience. For all their conceptual weaknesses, such assertions of the autonomy of black writing powerfully remind us that African American literary study is not a leisure pursuit but, rather, a practice which is part and parcel of the community's struggle to counter structural racism in the United States and achieve a sense of voice.

Much African American critical work, however, locates itself in Du Bois's lineage and is concerned less with developing theories of 'autonomy' or 'authenticity' than with exploring how black writing combines and negotiates multiple inheritances (white-authored as well as those emerging from the black community's folklore, speech and music). Although Richard Wright convicts the earliest black-authored texts in the United States of servile politeness – 'prim and decorous ambassadors who went a-begging to white America' (Gates and McKay 2004: 1403) – he scrupulously acknowledges his own indebtedness to, and strategic reworking of, the white literary tradition. As you study *Native Son* (1940), Wright's devastating novel about racist and capitalist America, you will observe its connections to both the gothic writing of Poe and the naturalistic fiction of white authors such as Theodore Dreiser and Jack London. More recently, major black theorists have been similarly concerned to question the notion of a pure or authentic African American literature. Henry Louis Gates's influential book, *The Signifying Monkey* (1988) begins by placing black writing of the United States in a line of descent from African and Afro-Caribbean traditions of verbal play, but goes on to argue that this writing's distinctiveness consists in productively *fusing* these models with influences from the white literary canon. Meanwhile, another key secondary text in this field, Paul Gilroy's *The Black Atlantic* (1993), insists from its very title onwards upon the importance of ideas of mediation, crossing and hybridity.

Gilroy's work in particular has helped to inaugurate a new internationalism in African American criticism. Just as American Studies more broadly has moved away from concepts of national autonomy and situated the United States instead in a nexus of international relationships, so criticism of black US literature has shown increasing interest in a *global* flow of texts, forms and ideas. Among suggestive recent work in this vein which you may encounter is John Gruesser's *Confluences* (2005). Rather than placing Toni Morrison alongside other black writers of the United States, Gruesser juxtaposes her with such ethnically diverse producers of postcolonial fiction as Jean Rhys and Salman Rushdie. His aim is certainly not to imply that African American and postcolonial literatures are identical in their formation, but rather to indicate the interpretive benefits of bringing these two bodies of work into contact with one another. Once again, the effect is to *hybridize* African American writing at the expense of models of black literary purity, which, politically important as they were at moments in the past, now risk seeming both theoretically outmoded and ideologically suspect.

Further reading

Baker, Houston A. *Blues, Ideology and Afro-American Literature: A Vernacular Theory*. Chicago: University of Chicago Press, 1985.

Balshaw, Maria. *Looking for Harlem: Urban Aesthetics in African American Literature*. London: Pluto Press, 1998.

Diedrich, Maria, Henry Louis Gates, Jr. and Carl Pedersen, eds. *Black Imagination and the Middle Passage*. New York: Oxford University Press, 1999.

Ervin, Hazel Arnett, ed. *African American Literary Criticism, 1773–2000*. New York: Twayne, 1999.

Graham, Maryemma, ed. *The Cambridge Companion to the African American Novel*. Cambridge: Cambridge University Press, 2004.

Morrison, Toni. *Playing in the Dark: Whiteness and the Literary Imagination*. Cambridge, MA: Harvard University Press, 1992.

Napier, Winston, ed. *African American Literary Theory: A Reader*. New York: New York University Press, 2000.

Smethurst, James Edward. *The Black Arts Movement: Literary Nationalism in the 1960s and 1970s*. Chapel Hill: University of North Carolina Press, 2005.

Sollors, Werner. *Ethnic Modernism*. Cambridge, MA: Harvard University Press, 2008.

Wall, Cheryl A. *Worrying the Line: Black Women Writers, Lineage, and Literary Tradition*. Chapel Hill: University of North Carolina Press, 2005.

Chicano/a studies

Jenni Ramone

The terms 'Chicano' and 'Chicana' refer to men and women, respectively, of Mexican origin who live in the United States, and 'Chicano/a literature' to writing in English by men or women of Mexican origin. Prominent writers include Sandra Cisneros, Rudolfo Anaya, Gloria Anzaldúa, Ron Arias, Ana Castillo, Lorna Dee Cervantes, Denise Chavez and Cherríe Moraga. For Chicano/a studies, the Mexico/United States border is a potent symbol: crossing the border has been a continuing theme in Chicano/a writing since the late nineteenth-century novels by María Amparo Ruíz de Burton, *Who Would Have Thought it?* (1872) and *The Squatter and the Don* (1885).

The broader category of Latino and Latina Studies includes a Nuyorican (Puerto Rican American) strand, offering a Northeastern perspective, where Chicana and Chicano writing is largely based in the Southern and Western states, including New Mexico and California. Nuyorican literature is located in the urban barrios, the neighbourhoods populated by Latin American communities. This writing often looks back to Puerto Rico as a rural – and racially neutral – idyll, as in Tato Laviera's and Judith Ortiz Cofer's poetry. Other Latino and Latina literatures include Cuban-American and Dominican-American writers, like Cristina García and Julia Alvarez.

The now dominant feminist focus of Chicana studies began with its separation from Chicano/a studies as a whole. Chicana studies has its origins in the Chicana feminist movement in the 1970s. The first National Chicana Conference took place in 1971, where over 600 women attended workshops on sex, marriage and religion, resulting in powerful resolutions stating that sex is good and healthy, demanding free and legal abortions, promoting gender equality, and insisting that the Catholic church revolutionize to accept these ideas, or that it 'get out of the way'.

Chicano/a studies is a much more common field in America, where there are numerous degree programmes, and there are modules on Literature and on Women's Studies degrees. In British universities the field is less well established, though American Studies and English/Literary Studies degrees sometimes offer modules on Chicano/a studies, or include novels written by Chicano/a writers.

How do you analyse Chicano/a literature?

Reading literature from a Chicano/a studies approach involves paying attention to the historical and geographical **context** of the text, and to the feminist agenda of the field. The following extract is taken from the opening of a recent novel, *Caramelo*, by Chicana writer Sandra Cisneros. The analysis below includes some of the key points considered by a Chicano/a studies approach.

Extract

> We're all little in the photograph above Father's bed. We were little in Acapulco. We will always be little. For him we are just as we were then.
> Here are the Acapulco waters lapping just behind us, and here we are sitting on the lip of land and water. The little kids, Lolo and Memo, making devil horns behind each other's heads; the Awful Grandmother holding

them even though she never held them in real life. Mother seated as far from her as politely possible; Toto slouched beside her. The big boys, Rafa, Ito, and Tikis, stand under the roof of Father's skinny arms. Aunty Light-Skin hugging Antonieta Araceli to her belly. Aunty shutting her eyes when the shutter clicks, as if she chooses not to remember the future, the house on Destiny Street sold, the move north to Monterrey.

Here is Father squinting that same squint I always make when I'm photographed. He isn't *acabado* yet. He isn't *finished*, worn from working, from worrying, from smoking too many packs of cigarettes. [...]

I'm not here. They've forgotten about me when the photographer walking along the beach proposes a portrait, *un recuerdo*, a remembrance literally. No one notices I'm off by myself building sand houses. They won't realize I'm missing until the photographer delivers the portrait to Catita's house, and I look at it for the first time and ask, – When was this taken? Where?

Then everyone realizes the portrait is incomplete. It's as if I didn't exist. It's as if I'm the photographer walking along the beach with the tripod camera on my shoulder asking, – *¿Un recuerdo?* A souvenir? A memory? (2002: 3–4)

Analysis

Prominent Chicana writer Sandra Cisneros lived for alternate periods in both Mexico and the USA, and this impermanent geography emerges in the form of her works, a fragmentary style that characterizes much Chicano/a writing. Cisneros's novels are often composed from short pieces, scraps, quotations, like the opening of *Caramelo*. The description of a photograph taken just before the family's move from Acapulco to Monterrey locates the narrator and her family in a specific geographical space, on 'the lip of land and water', on a distinct border. This border recalls their subsequent move further north to the USA. For Chicano/a studies, the borderland is understood as part of the Chicano/a identity. For Lala, the narrator, the picture shows generations of her family located on the border. Yet this souvenir photograph is 'incomplete': Lala is missing. Its incompleteness indicates an uncertainty, a problem that the novel will attempt to solve: if Lala hasn't a place in the photograph, does she have a place in her geographical space, as a migrant in the United States, and as a visitor in Mexico, the place of her ancestors? Chicano/a literature discusses the hybrid identity of its characters, and aims to create a space for the Chicano/a voice. In this photograph, there is no space for Lala; she is absent. To create her own space, she tells her own story – the events are presented from her perspective. She delivers the narrative using many Spanish words, describing her father as *acabado*, and calling the photograph *un recuerdo*. Like many Chicano/a novels, the text might be described as more 'Spanglish' than English. Retelling the story of migration from Mexico to the United States, Cisneros questions dominant media perceptions of Chicano/a identity. The questioning of formal 'truths' is a consistent feature of the literary, historical, anthropological and socioeconomic writings which constitute Chicano/a studies.

Further reading

Anzaldúa, Gloria. *Borderlands/La Frontera: The New Mestiza*, 2nd edn. San Francisco: Aunt Lute Books, 1999.

Arredondo, Gabriela F. *Chicano Feminisms: A Critical Reader*. Durham, NC: Duke University Press, 2003.

Garcia, Alma M., ed. *Chicana Feminist Thought: The Basic Historical Writings*. New York: Routledge, 1997.

Pérez, Emma. *The Decolonial Imaginary: Writing Chicanas into History*. Bloomington: Indiana University Press, 1999.

Rodriguez, Clara E. *Latin Looks – Images of Latinas and Latinos in the US Media*. Oxford: Westview Press, 1997.

Torres, Eden E. *Chicana Without Apology: The New Chicana Cultural Studies*. New York: Routledge, 2003.

Villa, Raul Homero. *Barrio-Logos: Space and Place in Urban Chicano Literature and Culture*. Austin: University of Texas Press, 2000.

Gay studies and queer theory

Helen Davies

The theory and practices of lesbian and gay literary criticism are closely related to the politics of the gay rights movement, and so to begin to understand the agenda and process of lesbian and gay criticism it is useful to appreciate something of the history and development of the actual political movement.

Historical and social context

There has been a long and painful history of social, legal and cultural discrimination against gay and lesbian people in Western society. Laws dating back to the reign of Henry VIII made the practice of 'sodomy' illegal in England, and the Labouchere Amendment of the Criminal Law Amendment Act of 1885 specified that all 'indecent acts' between men, both in public and in private, were against the law. (It is worth noting, however, that although lesbians have suffered similar oppression and prejudice to gay men in a variety of ways, there have never actually been laws passed in the UK prohibiting same-sex relationships between women. Indeed, there is a possibly apocryphal rumour that Queen Victoria, when asked whether the Criminal Law Amendment Act should also rule against 'indecent acts' between women, implied that she didn't believe lesbians could exist.) This law remained in place in England until 1967, when, after much political and social debate, sexual activity between men was decriminalized. Similar legal prohibitions were in place for the first half of the twentieth century in North America, with laws against 'sodomy' operating in many states. (Laws against homosexuality in North America have varied from state to state; the 'sodomy' law was only nationally repealed in 2003.) The 1960s witnessed an explosion of social rights movements, such as the Black Power movement in the United States and the feminist movement throughout the Western world. In such a politically charged climate, gay rights also became a consideration. After a homophobia-fuelled police raid on a gay bar, the Stonewall Inn, in New York in June 1969, the persecuted gays and lesbians of the community fought back, leading to a series of riots and pro-gay demonstrations in the Greenwich Village area of New York. The effects of the Stonewall protests in America and the changes in the law in England, both occurring during the late 1960s, inaugurated the gay rights/gay liberation movement.

Politics into theory: the practices of lesbian and gay literary criticism

Apart from a few notable exceptions (for example, Jeanette H. Foster's *Sex Variant Women in Literature*, published in 1958), lesbian and gay literary criticism was largely absent from academic work prior to the political developments of the late 1960s. The new emphasis on gay rights in the social arena had an effect on literary research in universities, providing an incentive to highlight the long-neglected area of gay and lesbian literary criticism. Gay and lesbian critics from the 1970s onwards have sought to highlight and challenge the homophobia of traditional literary criticism, which can function overtly through condemnation of gay/lesbian authors, literary representations and themes, or covertly through either ignoring the sexual orientation of lesbian/gay authors or excluding them from the literary **canon** of academic study. Lesbian and gay literary criticism seeks to locate sexual identity as a central issue in interpreting literature, and to focus upon and celebrate the work of lesbian and gay authors.

Identifying the subject of study

There are several strategies through which a lesbian/gay analysis of a text can be conducted. Firstly, we could specifically identify authors whose biography could justify a sexuality-based interpretation of their work. An author such as Oscar Wilde is frequently studied in this way: Richard Ellmann's biography of Wilde (published in 1987) focused upon the influence Wilde's sexuality had upon his literary output, and paved the way for numerous analyses of Wilde's work through the lens of his same-sex relationships, and trials and conviction for 'acts of gross indecency' in 1895 . A biographically based lesbian/gay interpretation of an author and their work is thus strongly interdisciplinary; you might take into consideration historical documents (letters, diaries, etc.), and think about how sociological, psychological, legal and cultural attitudes towards sexuality impact upon the reading of a text. Oscar Wilde's sexual orientation is, however, well known; a comparable approach for a lesbian/gay biographical reading of an author's work is to reappropriate an ostensibly heterosexual author from a lesbian/gay perspective (see, for example, Terry Castle's article 'Was Jane Austen Gay?' [2002], where Castle analyses Austen's personal correspondence and suggests that there is a privileging of same-sex intimacy between women that is also displayed in Austen's novels). To conduct a lesbian/gay biographical reading of an author's work you could also recover authors whose homosexuality (either in their work or their life) have been broadly ignored by or marginalized from the traditional literary canon. An example of an author who would fall into this category is Natalie Clifford Barney, an American lesbian poet who lived in Paris during the first half of the twentieth century, but whose work is rarely included in undergraduate university courses.

Rethinking the canon

The reclaiming of lesbian/gay authors and texts can therefore lead towards the composition of a lesbian/gay literary **canon**; you could consider a collection of authors that are united by their marginalized sexuality and its impact upon their work, and that form an alternative to the tradition of hetero-centric authors that tend to be studied and taught in universities. (The formation of a lesbian/gay canon of authors and texts highlights the similarities and intersections between lesbian and gay literary criticism and other political motivated/ socially aware critical perspectives; the impulse to create an 'alternative canon' of literature is also apparent in feminist criticism, African American criticism and postcolonial studies.) Claude J. Summers, for example, has focused on establishing a canon of gay authors and writing in his 1990 study *Gay Fictions: Wilde to Stonewall: Studies in a Male Homosexual Literary Tradition*. He argues that a genealogy of gay literature can be traced from Wilde's work in the late nineteenth century through to Christopher Isherwood's novels in the 1960s. Though Summers certainly notes the development of gay literature, he also focuses on the similarities between the historical spectrum of authors, and this emphasis on sexuality as a universalizing, uniting theme for non-heterosexual authors is an important aspect of lesbian/gay textual analysis.

Reading against the grain: lesbian/gay readings of 'heterosexual' authors

Justification for including authors in a lesbian/gay canon of literature does not just rest on biographical information; a critic conducting a lesbian/gay interpretation can potentially analyse any text from a homosexual perspective. This could be through the identification of same-sex relationships that are based in sexual attraction (such as in Radclyffe Hall's 1928 novel *The Well of Loneliness*) or through same-sex connections that may not be conventionally understood as 'lesbian/gay' but can be interpreted as privileging same-sex relationships or friendships over heterosexual (see, for example, Barbara Smith's 1977 reading of Toni Morrison's 1974 novel *Sula*. Smith argues that although Morrison is a heterosexual author, and the female characters in her novel are not overtly lesbian, the plot and themes of the novel provide a critique of conventional heterosexual institutions that mean that the text can be read from a lesbian perspective). A lesbian/gay critical perspective may also focus upon revealing the *coded* representation of homosexuality in a text, particularly if a text was written during a historical period of discrimination against same-sex **desire**. This could include identifying the metaphorical use of figures from Ancient Greece or Rome to signify an interest in same-sex relationships (for example, Oscar Wilde's *The Picture of Dorian Gray* makes reference to Antinous, the male lover of the Roman Emperor Hadrian), or focusing on ambiguous imagery in the depiction of same-sex friendships (for example, Catharine Stimpson [1981] comments on the motif of the kiss between women in Virginia Woolf's work, suggesting that this generates a range of ambivalent interpretations – is the kiss sexual, or friendly?)

Lesbian/gay literary criticism therefore necessitates a careful and close reading of texts, but also an awareness of extra-textual material that can span across academic disciplines (historical, sociological, psychoanalytical, political, legal, cultural). It is not simply the analysis of gay texts by gay authors that is important, but a strategy of reading that attempts to unravel and combat the entrenched homophobia of academic criticism and broader social/cultural understandings of same-sex desire.

Queer theory: an introduction

Queer theory represents a collection of complex and diverse critical strategies for reading texts; its origins are not confined to literary studies but embrace a broad spectrum of theoretical perspectives that are strongly interdisciplinary. The work of Judith Butler is, for example, generally considered to have inaugurated the academic interest in 'queer theory', but her theories are not specifically based in literary criticism, and are largely grounded in philosophy, psychoanalysis and linguistics.

Throughout much of the twentieth century, the word 'queer' has been used in a pejorative **context**, an offensive term for designating the supposed 'abnormality' of lesbian women and gay men. In the late 1980s and early 1990s, however, the word was reclaimed by gay rights groups such as 'Act Up' and 'Queer Nation'. Used in this context, the term 'queer' becomes a reappropriation and celebration of non-heterosexual identities, but more specifically an encompassing term for both gay and lesbian sexualities. Although queer theory does have strong connections with this non-academic gay activism, it also represents a significant departure from the tenets of lesbian and gay politics and criticism. As implied above, one of the imperatives of lesbian/gay criticism is that lesbian and gay sexual identities should be recognized and accepted. Reading a text from a queer perspective poses a challenge to the notion that there are stable or inherent 'heterosexual' or 'homosexual' identities in society, culture and therefore texts, thus potentially questioning the veracity of identity politics in literary criticism.

The development of queer theory (1): Michel Foucault

The French academic Michel Foucault, whose work is a combination of philosophy, history and sociology, published a series of three books between 1976 and 1984 entitled *The History of Sexuality*. In the first volume of the collection, *The Will to Knowledge* (first published in French in 1976, and translated into English in 1977), Foucault argues that the concept of 'the homosexual' as a social and sexual identity first entered legal and medical **discourse** towards the end of the nineteenth century. Prior to this historical period, sexuality was conceptualized as specific acts and practices that did not actually define an individual's sense of self and social identity. During the proliferation of medical writings on sexual behaviour in the latter half of the nineteenth century, however, a new concept of socio-sexual identity was brought into being: sexual behaviour (e.g., sodomy) became understood as revealing a 'truth' about the individual self and identity (e.g., 'the sodomite'). Foucault's theory basically challenges the understanding of sexuality as being an essential, inherent or timeless 'fact' of an individual person's sense of self; he contends that sexual identity is historically and culturally specific and is constructed through language or discourse.

Although Foucault is not writing from a specifically literary perspective, his argument has had a profound influence on queer theory in literature. If we accept that the concept of 'homosexuality' as a social identity is a relatively recent historical development, then how can we read Shakespeare's sonnets that appear to be addressed to a young man, for example, as revealing that Shakespeare is 'gay'? If we understand that the **binary** system of heterosexual/homosexual is constructed through language, then how stable are the essential or inherent truths of these identities? Though lesbian/gay criticism certainly does take into account the historical context of textual production, it still generally rests on the assumption that there is a reasonably coherent and continuous way to understand what it means to be 'gay' – or, to put it another way, that sexuality is a defining or permanent factor in an individual's sense of self/identity. If, as Foucault's work implies, concepts of sexuality are not fixed categories but are mutable and change over time, how useful are conventional definitions of homosexual/heterosexual identity? In a similar way to lesbian and gay criticism, queer literary criticism places sexuality at the centre of textual interpretation, but to read from a queer perspective you would need to question the assumption that there is a stable sexual identity to be revealed in analysing a text, either of the text's author or of the text's representation of sexuality.

The development of queer theory (2): Judith Butler

Judith Butler's work, though again not specifically focusing on literary representations of sex, sexuality and **gender**, has been hugely influential in shaping the critical focus of literary queer theory. Her book *Gender Trouble* (1990) develops Foucault's theories into focusing on the relationship between 'biological' sex, gender and sexuality. She argues that all gender and sexual identity categories – 'woman', 'man', 'femininity', 'masculinity', 'heterosexual', 'gay' and 'lesbian' – are produced through socialization, which she interprets as the repetition of socially sanctioned 'acts' or 'performances'; in other words, there is no true essence behind 'heterosexual' identity (or, indeed, homosexual identity) because it is wholly socially and discursively produced. If gendered or sexual identity is constructed through repeated acts, then surely, Butler ponders, gender and sexuality can be performed in alternative ways? This leads her to examine drag performance and 'camp' as methods of subverting conventional expectations of gender and sexuality, and such overt performances reveal the dissonances between the supposedly natural relationship between sex, gender and sexuality. Implicit in Butler's theory is that there are a spectrum of genders and sexualities that cannot be encompassed by the homosexual/heterosexual dichotomy or through a criticism that focuses on identifying what it means to be 'lesbian' or 'gay', since basically there is no static or stable norm of sexual identity.

Identifying a spectrum of sexual identities

Following Butler's emphasis on drag performance, queer theorists might focus on a wide range of sexual identities and practices that cannot necessarily be categorized as heterosexual or homosexual, such as cross-dressing, bisexuality, transgendered/transsexual identities, 'camp', the complexity of sexual fantasies, masturbation and a myriad of other non-conventional, potentially sexually dissident configurations of **desire**. This recognition of the plurality of sexual desires and identities may become manifest in a queer reading that challenges the status of an author or text that is usually understood as being simply 'heterosexual' or 'homosexual'. Joseph Allan Boone, writing on Djuna Barnes's novel *Nightwood* (1936), exemplifies this impulse to pluralize sexualities in queer criticism. Although he notes that the depiction of same-sex relationships in *Nightwood*, and Barnes's own experience of same-sex desire, have led numerous critics to provide a valid 'lesbian' reading of the text, Boone argues that the sheer proliferation of polymorphous, dissident desires and identities represented in the novel (from androgynous women to transvestite homosexual men) transgresses the cultural binaries of woman/man, homo/hetero, marginal/central to create a veritable queer universe (Boone 1998: 234–8).

Dismantling 'homosexual/heterosexual' binaries

To analyse a text from a queer perspective, then, you should seek to challenge, dismantle and open up traditional **binary** systems of thinking about sexuality and gender. Another formative text of queer theory is Eve Kosofsky Sedgwick's *Between Men: English Literature and Male Homosocial Desire* (1985), providing an excellent example of the ways in which the interrogation of homo/hetero dichotomies can produce a wider vocabulary for discussing issues of sexuality in literature. The word 'homosocial', as Kosofsky Sedgwick recognizes, is conventionally used to describe the socially approved bonds between men within patriarchal culture, whereby male bonding is privileged, but characterized by intense homophobia. Kosofsky Sedgwick's amalgamation of the word 'homosocial' with 'desire' purposely implies that there is a 'continuum' between homosocial (ostensibly heterosexual) bonds and homosexuality – her emphasis is on a *spectrum* of *potential* orientations and impulses that cannot be easily quantified by discrete sexual identities.

Focusing on the historical/social specificity of sexual identity

A queer literary analysis influenced by the work of Foucault would highlight the cultural and historical specificity of the construction of sexual identity, and the impact that this has on our reading of an author and their work. For example, Alan Sinfield's study *The Wilde Century* (1994) acknowledges the effect that the trial and conviction of Oscar Wilde had on shaping ideas about male homosexuality in the twentieth century, but argues that Wilde should not uncomplicatedly be considered as a 'gay' writer, considering that the historical period in which he was writing was only just beginning to understand homosexuality as a potential sexual identity. Conducting an interpretation such as Sinfield's would also mean focusing closely on the use of language as a way of constructing historically specific meaning. Sinfield, for instance, focuses on the changing definition of the word 'effeminacy' (ranging from an eighteenth-century understanding of 'effeminacy' as representing 'men who liked the company of women' to the twentieth-century comprehension of 'effeminacy' as signifying homosexuality).

Exploring the potential ambiguity of language

The slipperiness of language is a repeated theme in queer literary interpretation, as the multiplicity of meanings that can be attached to certain expressions impacts on our interpretation of a text. In Donald E. Hall's analysis of Charlotte Perkins Gilman's short story 'The Yellow Wallpaper', for instance, he notes the repeated emphasis on the word 'rub' to portray the narrator's contact with the wallpaper in her room. Hall suggests that this use of language could have connotations of an auto-erotic (masturbatory) impulse in the protagonist's depiction of her confinement in her bedroom (a conventionally sexually charged space). Gilman's story, as Hall notes, is generally read from a feminist perspective, fuelled by biographical information about Gilman's interest in women's rights; Hall's queer reading does not contradict the overtly feminist potential of the story but creates a spectrum of possibilities for reading the text in another way that is not dependent on authorial intentions. A queer reading of a text can mean you have to explore the diverse, often conflicting implications of a literary production, and tend to resist the 'closure' or 'explanation' of traditional literary criticism, therefore having a similar tone to poststructuralist/deconstructionist textual interpretation.

Though this essay has highlighted the differences between lesbian/gay criticism and queer theory, it is very important not to lose sight of the intrinsic connections between the two theoretical perspectives: both are dedicated to an anti-homophobic attitude towards texts, and are committed to crossing the boundaries between academic understandings of sexuality and the social/political experience of individuals of all sexual orientations.

Further reading

Butler, Judith. *Gender Trouble: Feminism and the Subversion of Identity.* London: Routledge, 2006.

Castle, Terry. 'Was Jane Austen Gay?'. *Boss Ladies, Watch Out! Essays on Women, Sex and Writing.* New York and London: Routledge, 2002.

Ellmann, Richard. *Oscar Wilde.* London: Penguin, 1988.

Foster, Jeanette H. *Sex Variant Women in Literature.* Florida: The Naiad Press, 1985.

Foucault, Michel. *The History of Sexuality*, Volume I: *The Will to Knowledge.* London: Penguin, 1998.

Hall, Donald E. *Queer Theories.* Basingstoke: Palgrave Macmillan, 2003.

Sedgwick, Eve Kosofsky. *Between Men: English Literature and Male Homosocial Desire.* New York: Columbia University Press, 1985.

Sinfield, Alan. *The Wilde Century: Effeminacy, Oscar Wilde, and the Queer Moment.* London: Cassell, 1994.

Smith, Barbara. 'Towards a Black Feminist Criticism'. In Gloria T. Hull, Patricia Bell-Scott and Barbara Smith (eds), *All the Women Are White, All the Blacks Are Men, But Some of Us Are Brave: Black Women's Studies*, 157–75. New York: Feminist Press, 1982.

Summers, Claude J. *Gay Fictions: Wilde to Stonewall: Studies in a Male Homosexual Literary Tradition.* New York: The Continuum Publishing Company, 1990.

Cultural studies

Brian Jarvis

Why do literature students need to know about cultural studies? There are two main reasons. Firstly, cultural studies is partly responsible for the shape of the syllabus in many English departments in the twenty-first century. It was involved in the challenge to the traditional **canon** of 'Great Works' by DWEMs (Dead White European Males). Cultural studies, therefore, is partly responsible for the fact that somewhere in your department people will be studying (get ready either to cheer or sneer) *Harry Potter*, or Stephen King, or Candace Bushnell's *Sex and the City* (1997). Although this might not seem especially contentious nowadays, just a few decades ago the idea that students might study graphic novels (that's the posh term for comics) or Hollywood adaptations of Shakespearean drama would have made most academics apoplectic (that's the posh term for *very* angry). A second reason why cultural studies is relevant to literature students is that it has been at the forefront of developing a distinctive approach to texts which is interdisciplinary, self-consciously theoretical and politicized. The 'cultural studies approach' has been imported into literary criticism and you are certain to encounter it at some stage in your secondary reading.

What is cultural studies?

So we know now *why* cultural studies is important for literature students – but we don't know yet *what* it is. This is a little harder. Cultural studies is difficult to define succinctly because it incorporates a range of critical practices that cross disciplinary boundaries. The 'cultural studies approach' can be found in literary, film and media studies, sociology, politics and geography, the study of different racial and ethnic groups as well as women's studies, lesbian and gay studies. In addition to appearing in a variety of subject areas, cultural studies is also associated with a wide range of critical theories that includes Marxism and feminism, postcolonialism and psychoanalysis, structuralism and poststructuralism. This dizzying array of -isms and -ologies can be intimidating to the student, but fortunately there are some key words and common denominators that can help us to sketch a working definition of this field.

To begin with, cultural studies is characterized by an expansive definition of its own key term. Instead of seeing 'culture' as a restricted collection of **canonical** works (Shakespeare's tragedies, Beethoven's symphonies etc.), cultural studies embraces popular culture in all of its guises. Cultural studies thus offers a combative challenge to the notion that 'culture' means 'high culture' – the 'timeless' classics often associated with a privileged elite – and instead explores the everyday and often ephemeral cultural experiences of the masses. This approach is illustrated well by Roland Barthes's *Mythologies* (1957), a groundbreaking collection of essays that offers quirky and effervescent readings of, amongst other things, wrestling, steak and chips, the 'New Citroen' and the face of screen idol Greta Garbo.

Literary cultural studies

In the literary **context**, cultural studies encourages us to turn to genres that have traditionally been neglected within the academy: comic books and women's magazines, westerns and weblogs as well as a range of non-canonical fictions. Instructive examples of the turn to popular fiction can be found in Janice Radway's (1991) *Reading the Romance* and Michael Denning's (1987) *Mechanic Accents: Dime Novels and Working-class Culture in America*. Cultural studies does not turn its back entirely on the canonical and will sometimes manufacture jarring juxtapositions that place, for example, Shakespeare alongside *The Simpsons,* or *Heart of Darkness* next to *Tarzan of the Apes.* This latter combination appears in Antony Easthope's (1991) *Literary into Cultural Studies*. Easthope interweaves the seminal modernist novel by Joseph Conrad

(*Heart of Darkness*) with Edgar Rice Burroughs' pulp fiction (*Tarzan of the Apes*) to investigate the clash of high and popular culture, definitions of 'literariness' and literary value and how each text relates to racist **ideology** and the history of colonialism in Africa. In their assault on the canon and *belles lettres*, cultural studies critics like Easthope tend to approach all cultural production in terms of 'text' and '**discourse**', with a politically charged focus on categories such as class, **gender**, race and sexuality. Cultural studies can thus be succinctly defined as a mode of textual critique that concentrates on issues of **power**. This critical practice is underpinned by a sense of culture as a battlefield on which the dominant groups in society seek to impose their will whilst subordinate groups attempt to resist the powerful and invent new identities for themselves.

A brief history of cultural studies

The origins of cultural studies can be traced back to the 1950s and a trio of left-wing academics working in British universities. Richard Hoggart, E .P. Thompson and Raymond Williams, the founding fathers of British cultural studies, sought to recover and valorize working-class history and culture. Their work was given added urgency by a shared sense that, in the postwar period, working-class traditions and culture were under threat from a burgeoning mass media and culture industry that was increasingly transnational and 'Americanized'. It was partly to counter this development that Hoggart founded the Centre for Contemporary Cultural Studies (CCCS) at Birmingham University in 1964. Initially under the directorship of Hoggart (1964–8) and then the British-West Indian critic Stuart Hall (1968–79), the Centre became an institutional base for academics keen to offer critiques of contemporary British culture. Throughout the 1960s and 1970s, the CCCS exerted a powerful influence on British academic and cultural life. It is worth noting that the work produced by the CCCS was itself influenced by a number of continental critics. Alongside Barthes's *Mythologies* and the work of Michel Foucault, Marxist critical thinking continued to have a defining influence. British cultural studies incorporated work by Mikhail Bakhtin, the Frankfurt School (especially Theodor Adorno and Walter Benjamin), Louis Althusser and Antonio Gramsci to refine the Marxist understanding of culture. An increasingly sophisticated sense of the relationships between economics, culture, various institutions and ideology replaced the 'vulgar' Marxist notion of culture as merely a tool of social control deployed by the ruling classes to manufacture consent (the process of **hegemony**). In place of a static and monolithic entity, 'culture' came to be seen as a dynamic and contradictory realm in which 'dominant', 'residual' and 'emergent' forces collided (this model and these terms are explained by Raymond Williams in *Marxism and Literature*, 1977).

From the late 1960s onwards, British cultural studies began to move from a preoccupation with class towards issues of gender and sexuality, race and ethnicity. This broadening of range was a response to the social struggles and political movements of the 1960s and the 1970s (women's rights and gay liberation, the struggle for racial equality and postcolonial politics). Since the 1970s, cultural studies has become increasingly conspicuous, with new departments, courses, journals and criticism appearing in the United States and Latin America, Asia and Africa, Europe and Australia. This field will be of particular interest to students of literature who are keen to connect literary art to other forms of cultural production in relation to questions of politics and power.

Further reading

Brantlinger, Patrick. *Crusoe's Footprints: Cultural Studies in Britain and America*. London and New York: Routledge, 1990.

During, E. Simon. *The Cultural Studies Reader*, 3rd edn. London: Routledge, 2007.

Fiske, John. *Reading the Popular.* London and New York: Routledge, 1989.

Fiske, John. *Understanding Popular Culture*. London and New York: Routledge, 1989.

Hall, Stuart, ed. *Culture, Media, Language: Working Papers in Cultural Studies, 1972–79*. London and New York: Routledge, 1980.

Hall, Stuart, ed. *Representation: Cultural Representations and Signifying Practices*. London and New York: Routledge, 1997.

Williams, Raymond. *Culture and Society: 1780–1950*. Harmondsworth: Penguin, 1963.

Williams, Raymond. *Keywords: A Vocabulary of Culture and Society*. London: Fontana, 1983.

Wolfreys, Julian. *Critical Keywords in Literary and Cultural Theory.* Basingstoke and New York: Palgrave Macmillan, 2004.

Ecocriticism

Jenny Bavidge

Ecocriticism has its roots planted in the many forms of literature and literary criticism which have addressed nature, landscape and humanity's relationship to the environment. However, just as feminist literary theory and queer studies gained impetus and focus from contemporary political and social events, growing awareness of the critical state of the environment and threats to biodiversity have given ecocriticism's focus a new urgency. As a very broad starting definition, ecocriticism is 'an earth-centred approach to literary studies' (Glotfelty 1996: xix). However, there are diverse interpretations of what this approach might entail. A collection of essays published on the website of the Association for the Study of Literature and the Environment (ASLE, www. asle.umn.edu/), offers 16 different answers to the question 'What is ecocriticism?'.

What is ecocriticism?

Ecocriticism emerges from a meeting between writing about nature, environmental politics and literary theory. In his 2005 book *The Future of Environmental Criticism*, Buell differentiates between 'first wave' and 'second wave' ecocritics.

The first wave were influenced by the 'deep ecology' movement and were passionate about bringing an ethical, even *spiritual* approach to their thinking and writing about literature. They were primarily concerned with the promotion of nature writing and a celebration of the natural world in literature. The 'second wave' takes a more politicized and theorizing approach, connecting environmental politics with aspects of literary theory. Early environmental criticism is mostly concerned with the critical interpretation of works about the natural world and so tended to focus on literature such as travel writing, or with movements or styles for which natural settings were especially important, particularly romanticism and pastoral literature. While the encroachment of industrialization in the Western world was a crucial topic for modernist literature (in the writing of D. H. Lawrence, for example), ecocriticism has grown symbiotically with the newly politicized and radical 'green' thinking of the second half of the twentieth century. For an overview of this movement, see the essays collected in *The Green Studies Reader*, which begins with the 'romantic ecology' of Blake, Wordsworth, Coleridge and Thoreau and ends with ecocritcal discussions of, among others, ecopolitics, 'post-pastoral' and *Silence of the Lambs*. Ecocriticism may therefore focus on literary works *about* the environment or it may widen its scope to consider all the ways in which ideas about the natural world are constructed through language and literary representation, rhetoric, **genre**, imagery and narrative. This means that ecocriticism is not just concerned with literature, but with all representational practices. In his book on the representation of the environment in Hollywood cinema, for example, David Ingram shows how Disney movies co-opt narratives of a pristine natural world (*Bambi*) or deep ecology (*The Lion King*'s 'circle of life') whilst telling strictly anthropocentric stories (Ingram 2000: 18–24). You might therefore find connections with ecocritical ideas in different and unexpected areas of your English studies, from romanticism to postmodern cyberpunk. You can use ecocriticism as a critical approach to analyse rhetoric about nature or to identify how specific genres deal with particular place and space (think of road movies or American novels dealing with suburban angst such as Richard Ford's *Independence Day*). An ecocritical **context** can help to examine the writing of authors whose works are suffused with the landscapes in which they are set (famous examples might include Seamus Heaney and Ted Hughes). Ecocriticism might also highlight environmental politics and issues of environmental justice, perhaps through the discussion of recent works which represent environmental disaster or terrifying visions of the future, such as Cormac McCarthy's *The Road*.

Influence of environmental politics

The growth of political awareness about environmental issues which inspired these two waves of ecocriticism is often identified with the publication of Rachel Carson's *Silent Spring* in 1962. The book's specific subject was the detrimental effects of agricultural chemicals on ecosystems, but it had an impact beyond its immediate subject, influencing 'deep ecology' thinkers and philosophies. Pragmatic or utilitarian positions on the environment have argued for the protection of the planet for the benefit of humankind and the progression of civilization, but deep ecologists criticize such anthropocentricism. Instead, they posit an ethical system that values the non-human world in and of itself, and not just as a resource for humans (E. O. Wilson coined the term 'biophilia' to capture a sense of this deeper connection between humans and nature). Another important thinker in this field is James Lovelock, who popularized the term 'Gaia' (the idea that the earth exists in a system of harmonious balance), which likewise rejects the notion of human 'stewardship' or ownership of the natural world. These ideas may once have seemed eccentric, but prominent campaigns such as Al Gore's climate change documentary *An Inconvenient Truth* have focused international attention on climate change and threats to biodiversity. As economic and political shifts try to keep pace with the emerging science of climate change, the principles of environmentalism are now mainstream, if not universally adopted or acted upon.

Defining 'nature'

Such developments in environmental thinking can be allied with various strands in literary theory to provide an 'earth-centred approach' to literary studies. Structuralist approaches in ecocriticism identify how discussions about the environment are structured around the central dualism of nature/culture, in which the natural is only ever given an identity in relation to human activity. So 'wilderness' is only 'wilderness' because humans cannot survive there, despite the masses of animal and plant life that it supports. The very existence of the word 'nature' shows how humans differentiate themselves from the 'natural world'. Poststructuralist thinking, which attacks notions of unified identity and knowledge, exposes the presumptions of *all* our categories of definition and explanation (meta-narratives such as 'civilization' or progress) and can shake our very certainty about the centrality of the human and our definitions of what it is to be human. In the same way that postcolonial criticism has shown how Western literature operates through a **discourse** of what Edward Said famously called **orientalism**, ecocriticism critiques a worldview which puts the human as the entity around which everything else – animal, vegetable and mineral – must be defined. Ecofeminist approaches should be mentioned here, too, as they meld ecological and feminist politics to argue that a worldview run along Western, capitalist, **patriarchal** lines has marginalized and suppressed both women and the natural world. Women's struggle for self-determination and independence from masculine power and ownership is linked to the domination of animals and the earth's natural resources. The novels of Margaret Atwood, for example, often link environmental disaster with women's oppression and sexual exploitation (see *The Handmaid's Tale* and *Oryx and Crake*). Feminism has **deconstructed** the social construction of

gender in the same way as ecocritics seek to denaturalize our definitions of nature.

But, critics might argue, if you're so worried about the environment, why are you sitting around writing or reading criticism about what literature says about it? Shouldn't you be out there, campaigning or taking action to combat climate change and environmental degradation? Ecocritics can answer that in order to combat the attitudes that can carelessly use up the planet's resources, we have to understand the discursive practices that make such exploitation seem 'natural'. In his useful introduction to ecocriticism, Greg Garrard emphasizes the importance of discursive categories – or **tropes** – which structure and organize the natural world in linguistic and literary form. For example, environmental campaigners have attempted in recent years to replace the phrases 'global warming' and 'climate change', which sound fairly benign and non-dramatic, with the more dynamic and scary 'climate chaos'.

'Earth-centred' approaches to literature begin with the belief that we cannot think about ourselves without thinking critically about our relationship with the environment. Novelists, poets and filmmakers have always explored this relationship, consciously and unconsciously. Ecocriticism draws our attention to this tradition, and its new urgency in the face of our use and abuse of the natural world.

Further reading

Buell, Lawrence. *The Environmental Imagination: Thoreau, Nature Writing, and the Formation of American Culture*. Cambridge, MA: Belknap Press, 1995.

Buell, Lawrence. *The Future of Environmental Criticism: Environmental Crisis and Literary Imagination*. Oxford: Blackwell Publishing, 2005.

Carson, Rachel. *Silent Spring*. London: Penguin, 2000.

Coupe, Laurence, ed. *The Green Studies Reader: From Romanticism to Ecocriticism*. London: Routledge, 2000.

Garrard, Greg. *Ecocriticism*. London and New York, Routledge, 2007.

Glofelty, C. and H. Fromm, eds. *The Ecocriticism Reader: Landmarks in Literary Ecology*. London: University of Georgia Press, 1996.

Ingram, David. *Green Screen: Environmentalism and Hollywood Cinema*. Exeter: University of Exeter Press, 2000.

Postmodernism

Andrew Dix

Postmodernism is a concept you will encounter frequently in your study of recent and contemporary work in literature and other cultural forms. It is, however, a complex, unstable and even contradictory term, which you may find messily plural in its meanings. Part of the difficulty with this piece of the critical lexicon lies in its very reference to the cultural moment we are presently living through. How adequately can we hope to understand the culture of postmodernism while we are still located within it? Murray Siskind, a trendy 'lecturer on living icons' in Don DeLillo's novel *White Noise* (1984), sums up this problem: 'We can't get outside the aura. We're part of the aura. We're here, we're now' (DeLillo 2002: 13). Following Siskind's logic, our status as citizens of the postmodern era makes it hard, if not impossible, to grasp this cultural phase as completely and authoritatively as we might claim to comprehend earlier periods such as the Renaissance or the eighteenth century.

Much work of an archaeological kind has been carried out with regard to postmodernism, attempting to specify the moment in which this cultural formation began to take shape. Here, however, you will not find critical unanimity. One influential account proposes that distinctively postmodern production in literature and other art forms can be identified during the 1960s in the United States and elsewhere in the West. Yet the first citation of the word 'postmodern' in the *Oxford English Dictionary* dates from as long ago as 1925; the *OED* also quotes the historian Arnold Toynbee's comment, in 1939, that the cataclysm of the First World War has given birth to 'the "Post-Modern" Age'. Even more disorientatingly, the *OED*'s earliest citation of the word 'post-modernism' itself is from as far back as 1914, the term cropping up in a theology scholar's rather cryptic statement that 'The *raison d'etre* of Post-Modernism is to escape from the double-mindedness of Modernism by being thorough in its criticism.' Despite such murky phrasing, this writer can still be seen to anticipate later critical thought by characterizing postmodernism as something *reactive*, an adversary of that late nineteenth- and early twentieth-century body of cultural production labelled 'modernism'. Some critics, however, have sought to muddy these clean timelines by pushing the origins of the postmodern back much further even than the First World War. A case in point is Jay Clayton's startling book, *Charles Dickens in Cyberspace: The Afterlife of the Nineteenth Century in Postmodern Culture* (2003), which essentially sets modernism aside and argues that features of postmodernism can already be seen in the Victorian period. The uncanny effect of such work is to identify postmodernism before there is any modernism for it actually to be 'post' to.

You will discover, then, that dating the postmodern is the stuff of critical disagreement, even controversy. Fortunately, scholars in this field have tended to be more unanimous about what constitutes postmodernism's distinctive stylistic repertoire. Postmodern work across multiple artistic fields is viewed, for example, as collapsing distinctions between traditionally 'high' and 'low' forms, thereby correcting the monumental modernist seriousness of such figures of the first half of the twentieth century as Virginia Woolf and T. S. Eliot in literature, Paul Cézanne and Pablo Picasso in painting, and Igor Stravinsky and Arnold Schoenberg in music. The postmodern artefact may also quote self-consciously from an array of pre-existing cultural materials, seeming to aspire less to the impression of a unique authorial signature than to an effect of collage. It may substitute delight in surface shimmers and textures for the modernist valuation of depth. Postmodern work is also liable to be fragmented, with postmodern fiction, for instance, representing a decisive break from the totalizing narrative systems evidenced within modernism by such novel cycles as Marcel Proust's *A la recherche du temps perdu* (1913–27) or Robert Musil's *Der Mann ohne Eigenschaften* [The man without qualities] (1930–42).

Engagement with postmodernism during your English courses is likely to take you in a number of directions and to involve study beyond the narrowly literary. While it is implausible to characterize all cultural production that occurs in the present moment as postmodern – what is postmodern, after all, about *EastEnders* or *Emmerdale*? – postmodernism is still, in the useful phrase of the American theorist Fredric Jameson, 'a cultural dominant' (Jameson 1991: 4). Thus it does not merely embrace literature – the poetry of John Ashbery, say, or the fiction of numerous writers including DeLillo, Thomas Pynchon, Salman Rushdie and Martin Amis – but extends into many other arts and media. You may find yourself juxtaposing postmodern literature with instances of postmodern television, such as the playful citations of already existing culture that are evident in *The Simpsons* or *Buffy the Vampire Slayer*, or in Ricky Gervais's *The Office* and *Extras*. You might venture into film studies, assessing, say, the generic collages of Quentin Tarantino or the slippage in tone between horror and farce in the cinema of David Lynch. There may also be opportunities to consider relevant musical examples: postmodern music ranges from the programmatically non-symphonic minimalism of the American composer Philip Glass to the experimentation with multiple, plastic identities practised by such contemporary artists as Madonna, Gwen Stefani and Britney Spears. One could equally well identify postmodernisms in architecture, or stand-up comedy, or visual art, or even literary theory. Given the specific materials and histories of these various art forms, it would be unwise to see them simply as governed by a homogeneous postmodernism. Nevertheless, there are sufficient family resemblances to make possible the devising of interdisciplinary modules in postmodernism that will study Andy Warhol's silkscreen paintings of consumer items one week and Paul Auster's novels pastiching detective fiction, *The New York Trilogy* (1985–6), the next.

Concern with the *styles* of postmodernism should not be aridly formalist, but, rather, something which leads you on to explore and evaluate the social formation in which this type of culture occurs and assumes dominance. For Marxist theorists including Jameson, Terry Eagleton and David Harvey, postmodernism is, quite simply, the cultural packaging around a massively expanded capitalist economy: it is, in Jameson's phrase, 'the cultural logic of late capitalism'. From this gloomy political viewpoint, the utopian aspirations of previous artistic periods have all but disappeared. Modernist ambition has given way, anti-climactically, to a depleted culture characterized merely by play, pastiche and endlessly recycled quotation. Far from being the artwork's enemy, as in the past, consumerism is welcomed into the postmodern artwork itself (as in the contemporary US artist Jeff Koons's gaudy castings of toys and baubles). Yet you will encounter dissenting voices within the postmodern debate, since other writers have argued that, far from being politically reactionary, postmodernism has actually opened up liberating possibilities. The crisis of totalizing narrative, for example, is understood from this rival perspective as making space for representations by previously neglected or subordinate social subjects, such as women, the non-white and the non-straight. Just as the dating of postmodernism, then, is not settled but still contested, so too is postmodernism's **ideology**.

Further reading

Baudrillard, Jean. *Selected Writings*, 2nd edn. Ed. Mark Poster. Cambridge: Polity, 2001.

Bauman, Zygmunt. *Postmodernity and Its Discontents*. Cambridge: Polity, 1997.

Gregson, Ian. *Postmodern Literature*. London: Arnold, 2004.

Harvey, David. *The Condition of Postmodernity: An Enquiry into the Origins of Cultural Change*. Oxford and Malden, MA: Blackwell, 1989.

Hutcheon, Linda. *A Poetics of Postmodernism*. London and New York: Routledge, 1988.

Hutcheon, Linda. *The Politics of Postmodernism*, 2nd edn. London and New York: Routledge, 2002.

Jameson, Fredric. *Postmodernism, or, The Cultural Logic of Late Capitalism*. London and New York: Verso, 1991.

Jameson, Fredric. *The Cultural Turn: Selected Writings on the Postmodern, 1983–1998*. London and New York: Verso, 1998.

Lyotard, Jean-François. *The Postmodern Condition: A Report on Knowledge*. Manchester: Manchester University Press, 1984.

McGuigan, Jim. *Modernity and Postmodern Culture*. Buckingham and Philadelphia: Open University Press, 1999.

Abjection [333] ¦ Absence/presence [333] ¦ Absurd, Theatre of the [333] ¦ Aesthetic/aesthetic theory [333] ¦ Aestheticism [333] ¦ Affective fallacy/agency [334] ¦ Alienation [334] ¦ Alienation effect [334] ¦ Allegory [334] ¦ Alterity [334] ¦ Ambiguity/ambivalence [334] ¦ Analogy [334] ¦ Analytical criticism [335] ¦ Androgyny [335] ¦ Anthropomorphism [335] ¦ Archetype [335] ¦ Author/authorship [335] ¦ Base/superstructure [335] ¦ Bildungsroman [335] ¦ Binary opposition [335] ¦ Canon [336] ¦ Carnival/carnivalesque [336] ¦ Catharsis [336] ¦ Cathexis [336] ¦ Character [336] ¦ Chiasmus [336] ¦ Close reading [336] ¦ Commodification/commodity fetishism [336] ¦ Conceit [336] ¦ Condensation [336] ¦ Connotation/denotation [336] ¦ Context [337] ¦ Countertransference [337] ¦ Couplet [337] ¦ Criticism [337] ¦ Cultural capital [337] ¦ Culture [337] ¦ Death drive/drive [337] ¦ Deconstruction [337] ¦ Defamiliarization [337] ¦ Demystification [338] ¦ Desire [338] ¦ Dialectic [338] ¦ Dialogism [338] ¦ Diaspora [338] ¦ Différance [338] ¦ Difference [339] ¦ Dirty realism [339] ¦ Discourse [339] ¦ Écriture féminine [339] ¦ Ego [339] ¦ Elegy [339] ¦ Empiricism [339] ¦ Epic [339] ¦ Epistemology [339] ¦ Epistolary novel [339] ¦ Essentialism [339] ¦ Ethnocentrism [339] ¦

Existentialism [339] ¦ Fabula/syuzhet [340] ¦ False consciousness [340] ¦ Fantastic, the [340] ¦ Fantasy [340] ¦ Farce [340] ¦ Fetishism [340] ¦ Flâneur [340] ¦ Focalization [340] ¦ Foregrounding [340] ¦ Free indirect discourse [340] ¦ Gaze [341] ¦ Gender [341] ¦ Genre [341] ¦ Gynocriticism [341] ¦ Hegemony [341] ¦ Hermeneutics [341] ¦ Heteroglossia [341] ¦ Historicism [341] ¦ Humanism [341] ¦ Idealism [341] ¦ Id [341] ¦ Ideology [341] ¦ Imaginary/Symbolic/Real [342] ¦ Imperialism [342] ¦ Intentional fallacy [342] ¦ Interpellation [342] ¦ Intertextuality [342] ¦ Irony [342] ¦ Jouissance [343] ¦ Kitsch [343] ¦ Künstlerroman [343] ¦ Langue/parole [343] ¦ Linguistic turn [343] ¦ Literature [343] ¦ Masquerade [343] ¦ Mass culture [343] ¦ Materialism [343] ¦ Meaning [344] ¦ Meta-language [344] ¦ Metacriticism [344] ¦ Metaphor/metonymy [344] ¦ Metaphysics [344] ¦ Mimesis [344] ¦ Mode of production [344] ¦ Myth [344] ¦ Narrative [344] ¦ Nihilism [345] ¦ Nouveau roman [345] ¦ Novel [345] ¦ Objectification [345] ¦ Objective correlative [345] ¦ Ontology [345] ¦ Organic form [345] ¦ Orientalism [345] ¦ Other/otherness [345] ¦ Overdetermination [346] ¦ Palimpsest [346] ¦ Pathetic fallacy [346] ¦ Patriarchy [346] ¦ Pleasure principle [346] ¦ Power [346] ¦ Primal scene [346] ¦

4 key terms and concepts in English literature

Queer [347] ¦ **Realism [347]** ¦ Reification [347] ¦ **Repression [347]** ¦ Rhetoric [347] ¦ **Screen memory [347]** ¦ Semiotics [347] ¦ **Signifier/signified [347]** ¦ Simulacra/ simulacrum/simulation [348] ¦ **Stream of consciousness [348]** ¦ Structure of feeling [348] ¦ **Subject/subjectivity [348]** ¦ Sublimation [348] ¦ **Sublime [348]** ¦ Subtext [348] ¦ **Symptomatic reading [348]** ¦ Teleology [348] ¦ **Textuality [349]** ¦ Trope [349] ¦ **Uncanny [349]** ¦ Unconscious [349] ¦ **Unreliable narrator [349]** ¦ Use value/exchange value [349] ¦ **Writerly text/readerly text [349]** ¦

Introduction

The following glossary is not intended to be exhaustive. There are already many such volumes available, which, because they serve exclusively as dictionaries, lexicons and other similar reference works, can be far more comprehensive. Amongst those which are available, we would recommend any of the following: Martin Gray's *A Dictionary of Literary Terms* (Longman), J. Cuddon's *The Penguin Dictionary of Literary Terms and Literary Theory* (Penguin), Peter Childs and Roger Fowler's *Routledge Dictionary of Literary Terms* (Routledge), and Julian Wolfreys, Ruth Robbins and Kenneth Womack's *Key Concepts in Literary Theory* (Edinburgh University Press). After a good dictionary, a reference work of technical and specialist terminology in literary studies can be your most important acquisition, and a reference work for which you will find endless use. What does follow, though, is a brief glossary of certain words, mostly drawn from the vocabulary of literary theory and criticism, which should provide you with a useful starting point for definition.

Abjection   Term popularized by Julia Kristeva. The abject is identifiable with neither subject nor object, self or other. Instead, the process of becoming abject involves me psychically into a 'place' where the stability, and therefore the meaning, of any term gives way. Abjection can be apprehended as the process by which the boundaries or limits of selfhood are erased. As such, it names that which we seek to suppress and exclude, in order that we can function as 'healthy' individuals.

Absence/presence   Absence and presence figure a binary opposition, understood implicitly first in Aristotelian metaphysics, and subsequently in structuralist linguistics and structuralist literary and cultural analysis, as any pairing in which one term gains its meaning only in relation and reference to the other.

Absurd, Theatre of the   Term coined by Martin Esslin, referring to the work of various mid-twentieth-century playwrights, including Jean Genet, Eugene Ionesco and Samuel Beckett. In such works, humans can find little or no purpose or meaning in action or event, and communication is fraught with difficulty and misunderstanding, if not being altogether impossible.

Aesthetic / aesthetic theory   'Aesthetic' derives from the Greek, meaning perceptible to the senses. Aesthetic study concerns itself primarily with formal elements of a literary or other artistic work, instead of addressing matters of history, politics or other contexts and 'extratextual' or extrinsic elements. It names that branch of critical appreciation or philosophy that examines the conditions of sensuous perception, producing in turn a theory of taste.

Aestheticism   Movement in art and literature associated with Oscar Wilde, Algernon Charles Swinburne and Walter Pater, amongst various writers and artists of the last decades of the nineteenth century, whose credo was summed up by Pater as 'art

4

for art's sake'. According to the aestheticist philosophy, art should not be subservient to any purpose, political, historical or moral, but simply be its own expression in a quest for beauty.

Affective fallacy The phrase is first coined by North American critics W. K. Wimsatt and Monroe C. Beardsley. Their contention is that any analysis of a text grounded in the perception of the emotional effects it produces results in a misunderstanding of the difference between what a text is and what it does.

Agency When William Beckford writes, in his 1868 novel *Vathek*, 'an invisible agency arrested his progress', he signifies a force acting on a character. In such an example, the force can be either supernatural or psychological. On the other hand, agency is also understood as that force or power granted the individual by virtue of social, cultural or political position (a prime minister or president, an officer in the military, the director of a theatre or art gallery, and so on).

Alienation Predominantly used in Marxist theory but also used similarly in other politically inflected critical discourses, alienation names the experience of being estranged from the products of one's own labour and, by extension, from one's 'proper' sense of identity as a result of the structures and effects of capitalism. Alternative translations of Marx's term *Entäusserung* give the term 'dehumanization'. The term is taken up in existentialist writings of the 1940s and 1950s to indicate more broadly the alienation of the individual within modern, mechanistic, estranging societies as a result of their (largely) capitalist modes of production and fragmentation.

Alienation effect The phrase comes from a translation of the German *Verfremdungsef-*

fekt in the work of German playwright Bertolt Brecht. Sometimes given as 'estrangement' or 'defamiliarization' effect, Brecht's theatrical practice sought to break the illusion of theatrical verisimilitude or other conventions of the stage whereby audiences would identify and empathize with characters as if the latter were real, free individuals. Through the various aspects of this technique, Brecht sought to distance the audience, making them aware that, ideologically and historically, people play roles in society, thereby removing any sense in the audience of feeling or involvement.

Allegory Allegory involves the description of or commentary on a particular subject presented in the guise of another subject, by which process of narrative analogy and symbolism, the reader comes to grasp the secondary meaning rather than the principal signification of content.

Alterity Commonly misunderstood as merely a modern theoretical term, alterity, meaning a condition of otherness or difference, is to be found in literary and philosophical works dating back over several centuries.

Ambiguity/ambivalence Ambiguity names the uncertainty within a statement or utterance where more than one meaning is inferred. William Empson's study *Seven Types of Ambiguity* offers a comprehensive analysis of the complexity of ambiguity. Ambivalence is, in a certain sense, an intensification of ambiguity, signalling powerfully contradictory states of feeling over a particular subject, or being indicative of the indeterminacy with which one can be confronted.

Analogy An analogy is produced through comparison being made between two narratives, images, forms or concepts for the purposes of agreement, comparison and

4

explanation. Analogy also signifies resemblance between elements forming logical reasoning, or the process of reasoning itself along parallel lines.

Analytical criticism Also referred to as – and akin to – practical criticism in the UK and New Criticism in the United States, such criticism always begins by, and proceeds from, the exploration of a central idea, question, image or theme found primarily in the principal text, poem or novel being studied. The purpose of such close reading is to construct an argument grounded in the language of the text, which, in demonstrating the relationship between different aspects of the text, aims to produce a reading of the text as an organic whole.

Androgyny Having the qualities or physical attributes of both sexes in one person, otherwise referred to as hermaphroditism, androgyny is sometimes employed by writers to signal an ambiguity or indeterminacy about a character's identity. In mythical narrative, figures are represented as having the characteristics of both male and female, or having facial features presented in such a manner that it is impossible to decide on the gender of the person thus represented.

Anthropomorphism The attribution or presentation of something non-human, whether a deity or universal force, as in mythological narrative, or a machine or animal, with human form or characteristics; also the assumption of anything impersonal or irrational as having human qualities.

Archetype In the context of literary studies, archetypes are discussed through either the critical work of Northrop Frye or the pscyhoanlytic theories of Carl Jung. Archetypes are pervasive or apparently universal symbols, recurring transhistorically and across cultures.

Author/authorship The concepts of author and authorship have complex histories bound up with legal rights of ownership, copyright and philosophical reflections on identity. An author can be defined today as an individual who uses his or her imaginative and intellectual powers to produce a work of fiction or other literary form. In particular, in theoretical contexts authorship has come to be defined as the locus and product of multiple cultural, historical and social forces, institutions, practices and discourses, of which the literary text is a singular mediation and production.

Base/superstructure Two concepts first defined by Karl Marx in the Preface to *A Contribution to the Critique of Political Economy*. In this, Marx argues that the economic organization of society, described as the relations of production or base, serves as the foundation of all other social relations and modes of cultural production. The economic base makes possible and determines the various superstructural institutions, praxes and discourses of a given society, whether in the form of the law, politics, the arts, religion and other cultural manifestations.

Bildungsroman From the German, meaning education-novel. Any such novel is one that traces the formative years, the spiritual and moral education and growth of its protagonist. Novels typically defined as Bildungsroman are *Tom Jones*, *David Copperfield*, *The Sorrows of Young Werther* or *Jane Eyre*.

Binary opposition Any pair of terms appearing as the opposites of each other, thus: good/evil, day/night, centre/margin, man/woman. Such pairs or oppositions were first considered as conceptual absolutes by Aristotle in his *Metaphysics*. Binary oppositions were given prominence by Ferdinand de Saussure in his structural model of linguistics, and subsequently employed by

4

structuralist critics. Importantly, Saussure identified the semantic dependency of any given term on its opposite, meaning thereby being revealed as not intrinsic but contextually given.

Canon Originally referring to the books of the Bible that had been accepted by Church authorities as bearing the word of God, the notion of the canon in literary studies refers to 'great books' or the works of authors who are considered as central to a literary tradition.

Carnival/carnivalesque Terms drawn from Mikhail Bakhtin's studies of the novel. The carnivalesque is that aspect of narrative form where social hierarchies and power structures, often organized according to social notions of 'high' and 'low', are temporarily inverted or reversed, often through forms of parody (a pig or beggar being crowned a king, for example), in order to destabilize one's notions of social order or 'natural' relations.

Catharsis A term taken from Aristotle's definition of tragedy, catharsis is understood as the psychological purging of emotions caused by the experience of catastrophic events in tragedy. In a play, the protagonist is purified by tragic events, and the audience is caused to understand and so pity the protagonist.

Cathexis Somewhat free translation of Freud's term *Libidobesetzung*, the concept refers to the mental process of concentrating and channelling the psychic energy of the *libido* as this is made manifest in emotions such as anxiety, dread or fear. The concept refers also to the displacement of libidinal interest from one's desire to inanimate objects.

Character Those various aspects of a fictional person such as behaviour, the expression of social or moral values, and the seemingly psychological traits and their outward manifestation such as appearance, clothing, actions, which serve to make the fictional figure human and believable for the reader.

Chiasmus Grammatical term referring to inversion of word order from one clause to another.

Close reading The process of analysis grounded in the language and form of a given text, whereby thematic and formal aspects are deduced through detailed comprehension of textual elements.

Commodification/commodity fetishism Commodification is the process by which an object or person becomes viewed principally as an article for economic exchange – or as a commodity. The term also defines the transformation of materials into objects with economic value. Marxist critics define commodity fetishism as the process by which, under capitalism, objects acquire value beyond their immediate usefulness; the desire to own a particular brand is indicative of the fetishistic encoding of commodities.

Conceit Typically found in verse of the early modern period, a conceit is the figural and symbolic means of expressing subjective apprehension in a particularly artificial and complex, often indirect manner.

Condensation Psychoanalytic, specifically Freudian term, signifying the process whereby mental images assumed to have a common effect are combined into a single image.

Connotation/denotation A word's connotations are those feelings, associations or undertones, which, though not precisely part of meaning, are nonetheless related to it. Denotation signifies precise meaning.

Context   Whether historical, philosophical or semantic, context is understood as that by which meaning coheres, is perceived, or is transmitted in a particular text. Any phrase or expression, any statement, is only communicable if the context out of which it emerges is understood by reader or audience.

Countertransference   Coined by Freud to indicate the unconscious emotions or feelings on the part of psychoanalyst towards the analysand and vice versa.

Couplet   A pair of lines in English poetry connected by rhyme and being of the same length.

Criticism   The act of analysing and evaluating literary texts, films, paintings and other forms of semantic structures, cultural forms or phenomena.

Cultural capital   Term first employed by French cultural critic Pierre Bourdieu to describe the hidden value attached to learning and education under capitalism; also, the dissemination of literary knowledge for the express purpose of enhancing the moral sensibilities of a given nation or culture's readership.

Culture   Aesthetic and moral values accumulated over time that are shared by a dominant group, and maintained for the purposes of social control and replication, through reproduction in literary and other artistic works; patterns of human knowledge referring to customary or conventional beliefs, social formations and traits belonging to racial, religious or social groups.

Death drive/drive   Freudian concept concerning human desire to return to a state of non-conflictual stasis, equilibrium or lifelessness. Intensified misdirection of the death drive in terms of psychic internalization is hypothesized as producing masochism, while direction towards another can result in sadism. More generally, drive is associated with Freudian discourse, being a translation of the German *Trieb*, more usually translated into English as 'instinct'. The two principal drives for Freud are the libidinal and the death drive.

Deconstruction   Word associated with the work of French philosopher Jacques Derrida, usually with his earlier publications, and mistakenly assumed to name a method of critical analysis, a school of critical work, or an analytical programme. Despite Derrida's patient and rigorous efforts to show how deconstruction is not a method and cannot be made into one, many critics employing the term persist in the misunderstanding. Deconstruction, if it exists at all or if there is such a thing (to paraphrase Derrida), takes place within structures (linguistic, textual, institutional, political, and so on), as that which, other than the logic or economy of any institution or form, nevertheless makes the operation of these function. Deconstruction cannot be imposed from the outside of a system; neither does 'it' (if it is definable as having an identity, which is problematic) await human consciousness to perceive or operate 'it'. If anyone tells you differently, they are wrong, but are wrong strategically, in order to make Derrida's thought over in a reductive manner into a system for interpretation.

Defamiliarization   Concept first employed in Russian Formalism to indicate aspects of literary works or other works of art that communicate whilst also estranging one's relationship to semantic transparency, and from there to perceptions of what is 'normal' or 'natural'.

4

Demystification A term associated with philosophies of cultural materialism that maintain that only social contradictions and economic conditions, rather than literary criticism and theory, possess the capacity for altering the course of reality; hence, materialist philosophy attempts to 'demystify' bourgeois pretensions towards totality and completeness. Alternatively, demystification refers to critical praxis which aims to bring to consciousness the hidden ideological traces and modes of production, which combine either to produce a view of the world as 'natural' and the causes of its events as 'inevitable', or otherwise to examine the ways in which material objects are produced as commodities.

Desire Psychic force distinguished in psychoanalysis from need, understood to be an unconscious drive manifesting itself through behaviour. Jacques Lacan argues that desire is never fulfilable; it is always deferred because that which satisfies momentarily is never the desired thing itself, merely a substitute for what cannot be defined.

Dialectic A dialectic is an argument whereby truth is arrived at through exposing contradictions in a debate through systematic analysis. A term associated with Marxism, and derived from Hegel, dialectic indicates both a scientific (i.e., philosophical) method and the rules of antagonism governing the historical transformations of reality. The Hegelian dialectic is defined, in its simplest terms, as *thesis/antithesis/synthesis*: a position or argument, a historical condition or consciousness provides the starting point, the thesis, to which an antithesis is given, an opposition, and out of the struggle between the two arrives a third term, the synthesis, which subsumes and displaces all contradictions to produce a new unity. In the Hegelian system, the notion of a master/slave dialectic is propounded, which expresses the interaction between two consciousnesses and the manner in which each entity considers the other in terms of the self. In Marxist theory, dialectical materialism proposes that material reality, social organization, exists in a constant state of struggle and transformation. The three laws of dialectical materialism stress (i) the transformation from quantity to quality, thereby making possible revolutionary change; (ii) the constitution of material reality as a unity composed of opposites; (iii) the negation or sublation of the binary oppositions, as a result of their antagonism, out of which historical development takes place, and yet within which traces of the negated positions remain.

Dialogism Term derived from Bakhtin, signifying polyphonic play of different voices or discourses in a text, without assumption of dominant voice.

Diaspora Settling of peoples away from their homeland, initially used with reference to the dispersal of the Israelites in the Old Testament; now used to refer in cultural studies, postcolonial studies and race theory to refer to any displaced peoples, through slavery or other means.

Différance Neologism employed by Jacques Derrida, in which 'a' is substituted for 'e' in order to indicate how, when spoken, the 'a' sounds no different from the 'e', thereby illustrating how writing always bears a remainder or trace inaccessible to the voice. There is, for Derrida, something in writing that escapes human authority, presence or intention. Moreover, in adopting the spelling Derrida conflates concepts of both (temporal) deferral and (spatial) differentiation in the single word, thereby suggesting the production of meaning as being subject to both spatial and temporal determinants; in short, meaning is neither immediate, nor is it intrinsic or a given.

Difference Concept deriving from ideological and political necessity to recognize distinctions between differing identities, whether in terms of ethnicity, belief or sexual orientation.

Dirty realism A literary movement, originating in North America during the 1970s, the chief characteristics of which are narrative minimalism and the stripping of narrative of all extraneous descriptive and other related details. The focus is on an economical use of words and surface description. Adverbs are omitted, generally. Dirty realist narratives, typified by the work of writers such as Charles Bukowski, Richard Ford and Raymond Carver, address the lives of unremarkable characters as central protagonists.

Discourse Traditionally, logical and coherent discussion focusing on a specific topic or subject; in the work of Michel Foucault, and subsequently in various critical-theoretical texts, discourse is defined as a specific language practice determined and employed by various institutions such as the law, medicine, the church, in order to regulate the subject historically through discursive practice and acceptance of the codes of practice, and the truths they claim to bear.

Écriture feminine Meaning 'feminine' or 'female writing', and taken from the work of Hélène Cixous, the term signifies a mode of textual production, not necessarily written by women (Cixous uses James Joyce as one example), which escapes economies of textual semantics grounded on central or single truths, transparency of communication, and the logic of linear narrative semantics.

Ego Psychoanalytic term defining the fundamental, conscious sense of one's self.

Elegy Poetic genre dealing with mortality, musing on loss, and other modes of introspective mourning.

Empiricism Philosophical approach to knowledge, proposing that all knowledge is derived from experience rather than reason or logic.

Epic Usually a poetic, or occasionally prose, composition in which the heroic exploits of one character or a small group of characters are delineated in a single continuous narrative.

Epistemology Branch of philosophy addressing the grounds and forms of knowledge.

Epistolary novel A novel form, popular in the eighteenth century, the narrative of which is presented through a succession of letters, often between different characters, as in Samuel Richardson's *Clarissa* or Tobias Smollett's *The Expeditions of Humphrey Clinker*.

Essentialism Belief that mistakenly confuses biology with aspects of identity that are social or cultural.

Ethnocentrism Beliefs based on the assumption of culturally relative values as absolutes, by which one judges another culture based on one's own values and makes ideological and hierarchical distinctions accordingly.

Existentialism Philosophical movement involving study of human existence in an infinite, unfathomable universe. Literary works, such as those of Jean-Paul Sartre, Albert Camus or Samuel Beckett, address the absurd nature of human existence in the absence of any transcendental meaning, or consider the role of free will and responsibil-

4

ity towards other humans in making ethical or moral judgements.

Fabula/syuzhet Terms employed originally in Russian Formalist criticism in order to distinguish between aspects of the novel. *Fabula* refers to the basic components of any story, while *syuzhet* signifies the plot in its formal constitution, the narrative order of the story elements.

False consciousness Term used in Marxist theory to signify mistaken beliefs held by social groups; for example, the belief on the part of the middle classes that class-based interests are not ideological but universal.

Fantastic, the Literature depicting unreal events that appear as either psychological or supernatural in origin, but remain indeterminate as to their precise nature.

Fantasy Narratives and other forms which present worlds and events free from the constraints of reality.

Farce Comic drama employing caricature and absurd plotting, along with slapstick and mistaken understanding as a means of complicating plot.

Fetishism In Freudian terms, sexual excitement or desire focused on a specific object, body part or representation thereof.

Flâneur French word defining (mostly) male member of leisured classes, who has the free time to stroll idly around urban areas observing life. The *flâneur* enjoys the luxury of observing social life in a random manner.

Focalization Term largely associated with narratology, focalization was first used by Gerard Genette to signify the perspective of narrative presentation. In a novel such as James Joyce's *Portait of the Artist as a Young Man*, the narrative is being focused

through Stephen Dedalus's consciousness, so this would be described as being internally focalized. An omniscient narrator, such as is to be found in a novel by George Eliot or Henry James, would be described as externally focalized.

Foregrounding Literary and aesthetic concept first proposed by Viktor Shklovsky, in which the artist or writer regards production as a process and not an end in itself, the purpose of which is to produce in the audience or readership a new awareness of the object or subject represented and so to understand the world differently. One means of foregrounding the process of perception and its active role in the interpretation of art is through what Shklovsky termed *ostranenie* – defamiliarization or 'making strange' – whereby the form of the art-object is revealed rather than occluded by content or subject and so how one perceives comes to be foregrounded. The artfulness involved in the production rather than the object is what is of most importance. From such a theoretical premise, it might be argued that James Joyce's *Ulysses* defamiliarizes narrative convention and one's assumption that the form of prose narrative is transparent through its self-conscious techniques of drawing attention to how narrative and language as forms shape and mediate perception of the world.

Free indirect discourse Mode of narrative presentation, which, though not directly presented as a character's speech patterns, idioms or grammatical idiosyncrasies, presents thoughts, events or reflections as if the narrative were the character's point of view. An example of this is when James Joyce begins the story 'The Dead' with the sentence 'Lily, the caretaker's daughter, was literally run off her feet.' Though the words are the narrator's, the figure *literally* indicates that this is what Lily thinks or what she would say. She is not literally run off her

4

feet at all; it would be grammatically correct to say that she was figuratively run off her feet, as the phrase is a figure or idiom, obviously, for being extremely busy.

Gaze Psychoanalytic concept, developed by Jacques Lacan, following Jean-Paul Sartre's analysis of the 'look', and subsequently adopted by feminist criticism and in film studies, which theorize the ways in which one sees another subject and also comprehends how one is seen. The theory posits that, in understanding how one is looked at, the subject apprehends that the other, on whom the gaze is turned, is also a subject.

Gender Term denoting the cultural construction of notions concerning masculinity or femininity, and the ways in which these serve ideologically to maintain stable gendered identities, whether normative or 'deviant'. In much feminist thought, gender is defined in distinction from biological sex.

Genre Occasionally confused with the idea of form, genres are definable types or forms of art and literature. In art, *genre painting* refers to the depiction of everyday life. In literature, while there are three genres broadly speaking – prose, poetry and drama – other more precise genre distinctions are made, such as romance, gothic, epic, epistolary novel, science fiction, science fantasy, Bildungsroman, comedy, tragedy, and so on.

Gynocriticism Study of women's writing.

Hegemony Term often associated with the Marxist cultural criticism of Antonio Gramsci and Raymond Williams, and referring to the cultural or intellectual control of one social or cultural group. Hegemonic power is maintained through the non-coercive dissemination and maintenance of cultural values and beliefs, manifested in institutions such as the church, state, education and literature.

Hermeneutics Originally associated with biblical exegesis and the interpretation of religious texts, now more commonly employed to define principles and methods by which interpretation takes place.

Heteroglossia A term often associated with Russian theorist Mikhail M. Bakhtin that refers to the many discourses that occur within a given language on a microlinguistic scale; *'raznorechie'* in Russian, heteroglossia literally signifies as 'different-speech-ness'. Bakhtin employed the term as a means for explaining the hybrid nature of the modern novel and its many competing utterances.

Historicism The idea that all forms of thought and interpretation must be defined from an historical perspective.

Humanism Western European philosophical discourse, first appearing in the early modern period, and subsequently a mode of inquiry that centres interpretation on humanity, particularly from secular perspectives. Humanist values are asserted as vaguely universal.

Idealism Belief in transcendent or metaphysical truths as unalterable and outside the real or material world.

Id That part of the unconscious in psychoanalysis comprising instinctive, pre-rational or conscious impulses.

Ideology A system of cultural assumptions, or the discursive network of beliefs or values which uphold or oppose the social order; otherwise, those ideas that provide a coherent structure of thought intended to occlude contradictory elements in social and economic formations. In Marxist theory, human consciousness is determined by ideology, and our perception of reality is ideologically mediated by a concatenation of beliefs.

Imaginary/Symbolic/Real Jacques Lacan's psychoanalytic model posits three psychic realms. The psychic aim of a 'healthy' adult subject is to achieve mastery in the Symbolic realm, a realm of ordered, structured language, the realm of Law. However, the Symbolic is not ideal because language is merely conventional and arbitrary in its acts of signification. For Lacan language can only describe what is not there. Language is thus a means of negotiating with the Symbolic, but also a reminder that one is always separated from the Symbolic order. Joining the Symbolic order is initiated in what Lacan calls the mirror phase, which initiates in the child a recognition of itself in a mirror as a separate and distinct being, one which now knows itself to be separate from the rest of the world; hence the need to acquire language, so as to 'rejoin' the world. Lacan refers to this early recognition and acculturation as 'Imaginary', because the mirror image reveals the self as an image or, in Lacanian terms, a signifier, rather than a signified. Such recognition is for Lacan a misrecognition, therefore. No one ever escapes the linguistic realm, Lacan argues. There are always Imaginary residues in even the most powerful Symbolic forms. The Real is a term used by Lacan to refer to the merely contingent accidents of everyday life that impinge on our subjectivity, but which have no fundamental psychic causes or meanings. You may well hit your head or knee accidentally, and this will hurt, quite possibly, but it has no signifying potential, it refers to nothing other than the realm of the Real in which it takes place.

Imperialism Policies of territorial expansion by which one culture or nation appropriates the land, people and resources of another to further its colonial ends; additionally, the practices and discourses which promote and maintain cultural, economic and ideological assumptions underpinning the assumption of the right to dominate another culture or nation in the process of building an empire.

Intentional fallacy Term coined by North American New Critics W. K. Wimsatt and Monroe Beardsley to define the mistaken critical assumption by readers that one can judge a literary work according to an author's intentions, whether these are explicit or implicit. For New Critics, value is to be found only in the text, not in what an author seeks to achieve or in the historical contexts that produce that text.

Interpellation Marxist term, associated with Louis Althusser, which defines the ways in which subjects of an ideology are placed in false positions of knowledge regarding themselves, including the misperception of autonomy and individuality. The subject is interpellated or 'called' by ideology, and in 'hearing' that call, is produced by the ideological structure.

Intertextuality A term first used by Julia Kristeva, intertextuality refers to the ways in which all utterances refer not to reality directly but other utterances. Literature is understood, from this perspective, as always intertextual: that is, belonging to a self-referential structure or system.

Irony A figure of speech in which the intended meaning is opposite to that expressed, often used when sarcasm or condemnation is implied in a seemingly positive or affirmative statement; also the contradiction, incongruity or discrepancy between appearance or expectation and reality. Irony can be understood in terms of events, situations and the structural components of literature. *Dramatic irony* involves a situation in which a given character's statements come back to haunt him or her, while *tragic irony* refers to situations in which the protagonist's tragic end is foreshadowed by a sense of foreboding and misinformation.

Structural irony reflects a given author's attempt to establish an ironic layer of meaning throughout a text, often by virtue of the ironic distance provided by the narration of a literary work.

Jouissance French, meaning enjoyment, used by Roland Barthes to distinguish that experience of reading different from pleasure, and associated with sexual pleasure. There is also in the word the sense of the subject's right to the experience of sensual enjoyment.

Kitsch Something usually of little aesthetic worth, but used in postmodern contexts to signify works of art that ironically play on the worthless or vulgar.

Künstlerroman German, meaning 'artist novel'; typically, novels which describe the development and growth of an artist.

Langue/parole Both French terms, originally given specific determination by Ferdinand de Saussure in his *Course on General Linguistics*. *Langue* defines the system of language, while *parole* signifies specific utterances.

Linguistic turn The term first gained popularity in 1967 with the publication of an essay collection edited by philosopher Richard Rorty. It signifies a turn in various analytical discourses including philosophy and literary criticism, and broadly refers to the fact that language in some manner serves to 'constitute' or 'construct' reality. This is not to suggest that reality does not exist, as some have misunderstood the implication, but instead that in addressing the condition of reality, one has to deal with language, broadly defined, as that medium which mediates our apprehension and perception of what is real. To analyse history from the perspective of a linguistic turn would be to recognize that the past *as such*

is inaccessible, and can only be configured and represented through language, and that this, therefore, always constitutes an interpretation, however much one may desire to be objective.

Literature Broadly, any written textual production; more specifically, any work of prose or poetry involving what has been designated 'imaginative', 'creative' or 'fictional' writing; thus, those works defined by the major genres – epic, ode, drama, novel, lyric, and so forth. The idea of literature also implies an aesthetic consideration or value judgement – Charles Dickens might be considered 'literature' while Dan Brown might not – but more neutrally, it can be said that the term designates the use of language in particular ways that transform ordinary or everyday speech, thereby intensifying or estranging its normative usage.

Masquerade Term employed in contemporary gender theory, which is used to argue that gender is a performance rather than a natural or essential condition.

Mass culture The term is frequently associated with the work of British cultural theorist Richard Hoggart, and refers to a new commercialized social order that finds its roots in the mass dissemination of television, radio, magazines and a variety of other media; in Hoggart's view, mass culture shapes and reconstructs cultural, social and intellectual life in its image and via its mediated depiction of artificial levels of reality.

Materialism Doctrine or system of beliefs suggesting that consciousness or will are the result of material conditions rather than being spiritually determined; also, analysis of culture, history and society, and the reading of these through literary examples, with a focus on the material conditions of a society depicted in the literary work.

4

Meaning That which is signified by words, not the objects or phenomena themselves; for example, the words 'dog' or 'cat' are not the animals understood by these terms but the words are defined by our perception of the animals, to which the words refer. The word gives meaning to the animal because it names it. Similarly, 'happiness' defines the emotional experience, but is not itself 'happy'. The meaning of 'happiness' can be apprehended because your experience of happiness is broadly similar to mine.

Meta-language Language concerning itself with language, its operations and significations.

Metacriticism Criticism that discusses criticism, its interests, approaches, criticism's history and the theories that are advanced in criticism.

Metaphor/metonymy A metaphor is a figure of speech in which two unlike objects are situated in comparison to one another. Metaphors serve to define one thing, or state, in terms of another. In metaphor the comparison is implicit rather than explicit. Metonymy is a figure of speech in which a word signifying an attribute or quality of a thing stands in for the thing itself. Using an author's name – Dickens, for example – for his novels is a typical example. Referring to 'the law' for the police is another.

Metaphysics A division of philosophy that explores the fundamental nature of reality or being; includes such disciplines as ontology, cosmology and epistemology, among others. Originally derived from the order of Aristotle's writings, where all writings that did not fit within the various disciplines were collected together in a volume 'next to the physics'. Metaphysical systems, conceived as systems for presenting the nature of being and knowing, differ according to the relation they posit between ontology (the philoso-phy of the meaning of being), epistemology, ethics and politics, and inquire into the nature of being, substance, time and space. At the same time, metaphysics character-izes a thinking that determines the physical according to the conceptualization of prin-ciples residing beyond the physical world – 'God' for example, or notions of universal truth. One distinguishes between a *meta-physica specialis*, concerning questions of divine being, immortality and freedom, and a *metaphysica generalis*, which strives to determine the meaning of being as such and in general.

Mimesis From the Greek meaning 'imita-tion', mimesis, used by Aristotle to suggest that tragic drama was an imitation of real life, is employed critically to discuss art in terms of the truth of its representation of life.

Mode of production Marxist concept in the theory of historical materialism that accounts for the historical conditions by which productive forces such as labour, the work force, technology, materials and tools combine in particular, historically determined ways with distribution of wealth, social power structures, ownership and control of power relations in society, the law and class relations to form an organic total-ity, which maintains and sustains social and economic order.

Myth Traditional story of pseudo-historical events that functions as a fundamental element in the worldview of a given people, culture or nation. Myths are used to explain the nature of natural phenomena or events.

Narrative An account of events, whether real or fictional, in a given order. Ordering events implies perspective, structure and causal relationship. Narration creates a connection between events. Point of view, emphasis, narratorial voice, first- or third-person narrative are amongst the elements that give shape to narrative.

Nihilism Philosophical rejection of all systems of belief, whether religious or secular, and a denial of the meaning of moral systems. A term applied to the existential despair in the face of a presumed lack of meaning or purpose to life. Also, nihilism is interpreted as a destructive, or negative, hostile attitude towards institutions and structures of belief.

Nouveau roman French term that translates as 'new novel', it refers to a movement that developed in the 1950s and continued in the 1960s. Its practitioners included Phillipe Sollers, Nathalie Sarraute, Alain Robbe-Grillet, Marguerite Duras and Claude Simon. In the *nouveau roman* many of the conventions of realism and other traditional novel forms were abandoned in favour of more experimental narrative modes in order to convey more accurately the random and discontinuous nature of modern experience.

Novel From the Italian, meaning 'piece of news' or 'tale', the term *novel* identifies one of the three major genres (the other two being drama and poetry), consisting of a prose fiction narrative, of varying lengths, and a variety of subject matter so wide as to be impossible to define.

Objectification The manner in which various individuals or social groups treat others as objects and expressions of their own senses of reality; reducing another's sense of being into a form that can be experienced universally by other individuals and social groups.

Objective correlative Concept defined by T. S. Eliot to indicate the expression of emotion through aesthetic form. Eliot suggests that an emotion is produced in the reader through a particular pattern of objects, situation or chain of events, which, in Eliot's view, become the formula for that emotion.

Ontology Philosophical term referring to the study of being; used in literary contexts to identify the particular elements of a given work or text that make it singularly what it is and unlike other works.

Organic form Idea proposed by several romantic writers that a poem should generate its own form from within itself in the act of composition, rather than being made to conform to a pre-existing form.

Orientalism Term coined by Edward Said, naming the ensemble of Western, usually European discourses, practices and modes of representation of non-Western cultures. Said traces the history of Orientalist discourses in literature, the arts and other documents from the eighteenth century onwards.

Other/otherness The quality or state of existence of being other than or different from established norms and social groups. The terms are employed throughout critical discourse in different ways. Otherness is immediately invoked in any differentiation one makes between oneself and another, particularly in terms of sexual, ethnic and other relative notions of difference; in Lacanian psychoanalysis, there is both the other and the Other (lower- and upper-case O). The former signifies that which is not really other but is simply a reflection and projection of the ego; the latter signifies a radical alterity irreducible to any imaginary or subjective identification. In Luce Irigaray's work, the other indicates the position always occupied by woman within patriarchal culture and other masculinist cultures which privilege masculinity as self-sameness, or otherwise a signifier of presence, origin and centrality. In postcolonial discourse, the notion of otherness or the other is employed to signify

4

any individual or group not of Western European origin. Robinson Crusoe and Friday provide one such example of self/other, in which a binary opposition is established which is implicitly if not explicitly given a cultural and ideological weighting in favour of the position of self over that of the other. This in turn invokes a master/slave dialectic (see **dialectic**).

Overdetermination A term used of literary texts to indicate the ways in which a given text is available to multiple interpretations and readings from a variety of critical and theoretical perspectives, which might well be incommensurable with one another. The notion of overdetermination also has specialist use in Freudian psychoanalysis and Louis Althusser's Marxism to suggest the ways in which subjectivity is overdetermined, that is to say produced from the interaction of a range of discourses and cultural practices. For Freud, the mind is capable of generating images, dreams and so forth, the meanings of which are in excess of the subject's comprehension. Any dream, for example, is the result of the symbolic construction which is produced by the unconscious, but every signifying element, image, sign or representation, whether verbal or visual, is overdetermined by the work of the unconscious, inasmuch as meaning is always multiple, and therefore available to different interpretations. Althusser develops the notion of overdetermination from the writings of Mao Zedong, who formulated the historical situation of China in the 1930s, which is made up of multiple social contradictions that coexist.

Palimpsest Any writing surface on which an earlier writing has been erased or effaced and a later writing inscribed or overlaid on that surface, often with the traces of the former inscription appearing underneath.

Pathetic fallacy Term coined by John Ruskin to signify the attribution of nature with human emotions or the displacement of an emotional or psychic condition onto natural or human-made phenomena; in this schema, human passion might be signified by a thunderstorm or the rushing of a train into a tunnel.

Patriarchy Term used for the complex system of male dominance by which societies have been, and continue to be, run; such structures and institutions have ways of marginalizing women or otherwise limiting their agency.

Pleasure principle Freudian term, naming the psychic drive towards gratification that has to be repressed in order that humans can function in the social world or work and formal relations.

Power A common enough term given particular focus in the work of Michel Foucault. For Foucault, power constitutes one of three axes by which subjectivity is constituted, the other two being ethics and truth. For Foucault, power implies knowledge, and vice versa. However, power is causal, it is constitutive of knowledge, even while knowledge is constitutive of power reciprocally: knowledge gives one power, but one has the power in given circumstances to constitute bodies of knowledge as either valid or invalid. Power serves to make the world controllable through knowledge. Yet, Foucault argues, power is essentially proscriptive; it can only negate or impose limits.

Primal scene In Freudian psychoanalysis, desires, fears, needs and anxieties are primal, and are constitutive of the origins of the subject's psyche. The primal scene is that moment in Freudian discourse where the infant subject becomes aware of the sexual relations between its parents.

Queer Term often associated with the contemporary gay and lesbian studies movement, as in the phrase 'queer theory'. Queer denotes a sense of otherness, as well as a means for breaking with convention and theorizing sexuality and its significant place in the construction of transcultural models of homosexuality. 'Queer' is also deployed as an affirmative, rather than conventionally pejorative, **signifier**.

Realism Realism has many meanings, and is potentially unusable, since critics differ greatly over its use. It is often used somewhat loosely as a synonymous term with realistic portrayal in a novel or play, and so comes to signify a 'natural' or unexaggerated, mimetic portrayal of – or perspective on – the world and everyday life. Realism would thus be the artifices and conventions in writing by which literariness becomes transparent, an invisible medium for representing the world. George Eliot's *Middlemarch* is considered a realist text because the fictional characters who inhabit the fictional world of the town that gives the novel its name behave more or less as people 'in the real world'. Franz Kafka's short story 'Metamorphosis' is not considered 'realist' because, unlike its protagonist, Gregor Samsa, people tend not to turn into giant insects.

Reification The process or result of rendering some idea or philosophy into a material or concrete entity; the process by which philosophical or ideological concepts disappear to the extent that they become incorporated into the everyday as 'natural', 'inevitable', 'human nature', 'common sense', and so on. In Marxist discourse, humans are reified into things, and thereby depersonalized – the worker, for example, perceived primarily as a factor in production, or else as a commodity within capitalism to be used in the process of production.

Repression The psychoanalytic process by which subjects seek to rid themselves of desires linked to instincts and given form through the images of thought and memory, which are considered forbidden in a wider culture. Repression is thus a form of self-censorship. However, whatever is repressed does not disappear; it may manifest itself in certain behaviours, slips of the tongue and other symptoms.

Rhetoric The study of the art of effective speech and composition; a mode of language, oration or discourse. Rhetoric also refers to a given mode of language or aspect of verbal communication; generally, eloquence in speech or writing, or those forms of writing which aim to persuade primarily through elegant expression. Rhetoric is sometimes conflated with style or technique.

Screen memory In his essay 'Screen Memories', Freud explores how memory distorts, covers or 'screens' (hence the term) an event or experience in the past. Whilst something may occur at a given historical moment, the process by which I remember that is problematized by my psyche. Instead of remembering the experience as it was, I overlay it, screening the truth of the event, with a memory constructed at a later juncture. Thus memory substitutes fragments in acts of misremembering to screen over childhood memory of the significant experience.

Semiotics Theory and science of signs, addressing the complex patterns of human communication, and the signals constituting the networks, modes and structures of communication and signification.

Signifier/signified Linguist Ferdinand de Saussure argues that a word or image –known as the sign – has two parts, the signifier and the signified. The sound or graphic equivalent of the sound of a word

4

is the signifier, and the image it produces is the signified. According to Saussure, the relationship between signifier and signified is entirely arbitrary, so while 'cat' can refer to a feline quadruped, it can equally designate a spiteful person (usually a woman, from a sexist perspective) or a whip. The word itself has no intrinsic image; we receive the signified only in a context that determines meaning.

Simulacra/simulacrum/simulation Term often associated with French theorist Jean Baudrillard's notion of the reality effect, which relates to the ways in which reality is often established and becomes represented for some individuals and cultures through hyperreal media such as photography, film and other media; hence, simulacrum refers to the image, representation or reproduction of a concrete other, in which process the very idea of the real is no longer the signified of which the simulacrum is the sign. Simulation, the process whereby simulacra assume their function, belongs to what Baudrillard calls 'the second order': there is no anterior 'real', the idea of the 'real' only coming into existence through the cultural disseminations of simulacral signs and images (as in advertising).

Stream of consciousness Literary technique in which the consciousness of the narrator or narrated subject's consciousness is represented freed from logical order or the demands of external narrative events. The language of the subject's consciousness is articulated as a flow of inner experience and mediation.

Structure of feeling Phrase coined by Raymond Williams as a mediating concept between 'art' and 'culture', in order to denote the 'deep community', as Williams describes it, which makes communication possible. Neither universal nor class specific, the idea of structure of feeling is intended to embrace both that which is immediately experiential and that which is generationally specific.

Subject/subjectivity The concept of self-hood that is developed in and articulated through acculturation generally and through language acquisition. Subjectivity is the process of attaining and expressing selfhood in and through language or the location of the self situated and subjectified by cultural, epistemological, ideological and other social discourses, practices and institutions.

Sublimation Freudian term which expresses the ways in which sexual drives are rerouted into other creative and intellectual areas of activity that are socially acceptable in public expression.

Sublime An aesthetic category, that which in a work of art or nature produces responses of awe and strong emotion.

Subtext That which is implicit in any narrative or which lies behind the ostensible motivations of characters, but which is never fully expressed.

Symptomatic reading Refers to a kind of reading practice that accounts for the power/knowledge relations that exist when the notion of meaning is in intellectual or ideological conflict; symptomatic readers reconstruct a given text's discursive conditions in order to treat the text as a symptom, understand its internal relations, and comprehend – by challenging the text's intellectual properties – the ways in which it ultimately produces (or fails to produce) meaning.

Teleology A branch of inquiry that assumes purpose and design behind phenomena and their relations to one another; the study of perceived design in nature and the attempt to explain, and give meaning to, phenomena according to a belief in a larger controlling pattern or purpose.

Textuality The notion of the text, after Barthes, signifies a structure in process rather than a finished work, the implication being that the reader takes an active role in deciphering the text rather than merely reading and acquiring its meanings. A novel or other literary work may be referred to as a text, but textuality identifies, beyond immediate form, the interwoven discourses, phenomena and other groupings of signs, images, and so on, by which meaning is structured and produced.

Trope Rhetorical figure of speech consisting of the use of a word, term or phrase in a sense other than that which is conventionally proper for it; more generally, any figurative language. The notion of trope incorporates metaphors, simile, personification and so on.

Uncanny That which is inexplicably odd, disturbing or strange, and which often is assumed to have supernatural origins or otherwise to be the interaction between a particular state of mind (uncertainty, fear, anxiety) and a given location at particular times of day (an empty house or dark forest at night). Freud draws on the etymology of the word in German (*unheimlich*, lit. unhomely) to suggest that which produces sensations of discomfort, strangeness or hauntedness in the places that are supposed to be the most familiar or comfortable.

Unconscious In psychoanalysis, the unconscious is that mental realm into which those aspects of mental life related to forbidden desires and instincts are consigned through the process of repression. The unconscious is absolutely inaccessible to one, unless indirectly through the release of encrypted images in dreams, or where in moments of stress or pressure that which is

repressed ceases to remain so and becomes released, leading to inadvertent actions or expressions.

Unreliable narrator In a novel or short story, a narrator whose perspective is biased, or who is either limited in terms of knowledge or else psychologically unstable.

Use value/exchange value Marxist terms, though originating in Aristotle. For Marx, buildings, machinery – all materials in fact, whether in their raw state or transformed through labour – have use value. Exchange value, on the other hand, implies an aspect of desirability or otherwise a quality where the basic function is subsumed or assumes secondary importance: all watches tell the time, for example, but a Rolex becomes desired by some for reasons that are neither tangible nor logically expressible. Objects thus assume exchange value when they become 'capital', capable of commanding the work of people, in order that workers might acquire what they believe they want.

Writerly text / readerly text Translations of the French neologisms *scriptible* and *lisible* first employed by Roland Barthes. For Barthes, the readerly or *lisible* text is the most conventional literary work, realist in nature, and one which hides the signs of its being a work of fiction or literary production. It is a fixed product, conforming to the dominant cultural modes of literature during the time of its production. Barthes sees such a text as making the reader passive in his or her reception of it, leaving the reader only the choice either of accepting or rejecting it and its ideologically mystified perspective on the world. The writerly or *scriptible* text, on the other hand, draws attention to its own artifice, to the ways in which it is structured, to its **intertextuality** and its self-reflexivity or self-consciousness, for example, and so challenges the reader to engage actively in the interpretation of such a text.

4

5 career pathways

5.1   career pathways   353

5

5.1 **career pathways**

chapter contents

> Introduction 353
> Careers for English graduates 354
> The experience of a degree in English 359
> Interview 360
> Conclusion 361

Introduction

This, the final section of *The English Literature Companion*, offers some advice and gives evidence of what awaits you after an English degree. It also provies a reflection on the various aspects of an English degree that prove to be so valuable, not only in the workplace but also to your life, broadly speaking.

The voices you will find here, though few, offer a not untypical 'range' of people with degrees in English. Ruth Robbins, who has been teaching for a number of years, reflects on her own experiences of, and reasons for, studying English, and why it might matter. Claire Bowditch, currently a doctoral student just beginning her PhD, gained her BA just two years ago, and her experience of the ways in which a BA equipped her both for what she has chosen to do in the narrow sense of a career, and also in her orientation towards the world, makes an eloquent case for the intangibles of English as a degree subject.

Following Claire's reflective essay, you will find an interview, conducted by Claire with a contemporary of hers, Charlotte, who works as a photo editor for a magazine. This is only a small indication of what you might do, but if we were to sum up the transferrable skills you will learn, and the professions you might enter, a sketch might indicate the following:

You will develop:

> logical thinking
> analytical skills
> research-related abilities, such as gathering information
> the ability to assess and interpret information
> the ability to communicate lucidly complex ideas in an accessible fashion
> the ability to compare and contrast different forms of information in meaningful ways.

The professions and career paths for which a degree in English literature can prepare you are:

> teaching, and related administrative positions
> publishing
> editing
> writing and research
> careers in television, journalism and film
> work with charities
> the Civil Service
> personnel management
> social care

Careers for English graduates

Ruth Robbins

In a pub in a northern English city in the summer of 1984 I was working behind the bar, waiting for the exam results that would determine whether or not I would go to university. When the results were published I celebrated by buying the three regulars in the bar that lunchtime a pint, at which moment one of them – let's call him Stan (it was his name) – said: 'What are you going to university for? You'll only settle down and have babies. It'll be a waste. And why are you going to study English, for goodness' sake?' Putting aside his rank ingratitude (I'd just bought him a pint) and his die-hard sexism (he had just retired from the steel industry, and feminism was a very foreign concept to him), I tried to answer the second question. What is the point of studying English? More particularly, what is the point of studying it to university level? My honest answer was that my parents expected me to go to university; that if I was going to go, I might as well spend three years doing something I really like doing – reading books. So I said to Stan, 'I'm going to spend 40 years or so doing some job or another, like you did, and I might as well have three years for myself before I start.' So why not go to university, and why not English?

It was a rotten answer, but it had the virtue of being true. What happened to me when I studied English is slightly unusual, though, because my 'useless, pointless' subject became vocational. I 'stopped on' at university, one way or another for the intervening 25 years. I did an MA and a PhD and eventually I got a job teaching English literature, and I've been doing it ever since. (I did settle down, by the way, but I did not have any babies at all, not even of any kind, as Oscar Wilde might have put it.) I got hooked, and I got enthusiastic about some of the less-walked byways of the late nineteenth century. But Stan's question remains in my mind and different versions of it have been in the minds of my students ever since. What he was getting at was that he could not see the purpose of studying English. It is a version of a commentary that has haunted English since its inception as a university-level subject in the late nineteenth century. As one rather sharp commentator put it in the late nineteenth century when the British university system was debating whether to admit English to the canon of subjects it offered to undergraduates:

> We are told that the study of literature 'cultivates the taste, educates the sympathies and enlarges the mind.' These are all excellent things, only we cannot examine tastes and sympathies. Examiners must have technical and positive information to examine. (Freeman, quot. Barry 1995: 14)

These are the words of Edward Freeman speaking in 1887. He was a Professor of History and he disapproved of English because it lacked – to his mind – technical knowledge; it was subjective, and was all about preferences and tastes, not about rigorous, quasi-scientific data and its interpretation. Moreover, it was also problematic for commentators such as Freeman because it was a common assumption that reading widely in the literature of one's own country was what one would do 'naturally': why give degrees for a study that was basically a pleasure? (In different ways, this is also the argument that has haunted the establishment of media and cultural studies – people watch TV and films for fun: why give degrees for it?) What does a degree in English offer to its students and graduates?

The answers to this are various and it does depend largely on the kind of English programme one follows. The technical knowledge component is different if one has spent more time with language than with literature, for instance; and if one is a literature student, the type of literature that is emphasized ('the great books' or the canon versus a more 'cultural studies' course focused on written works – some not 'great' books – in their various social, political and economic contexts), the knowledge base, will be different (see Chapter 1.2, 'Your literature course'). That said, in the UK at least, there is a benchmark statement, provided by the government body QAA, the Quality Assurance Agency. It is of necessity a document that ranges broadly since, when it was written, it sought to describe what was already happening in English departments up and down the land, rather than prescribing what must happen. But in its outlines it establishes some solid principles about the knowledge component of an English degree. As well as that subject-specific knowledge and skills base, however, the benchmark statement also describes what the English subject community believes it trains its students to be able to do in transferable or generic skills. These include:

> ❯ advanced literacy and communication skills and the ability to apply these in appropriate contexts, including the ability to present sustained and persuasive written and oral arguments cogently and coherently
> ❯ the capacity to analyse [...] diverse forms of discourse [...]
> ❯ the capacity to adapt and transfer the critical methods of the discipline to a variety of working environments
> ❯ the ability to acquire substantial quantities of complex information of diverse kinds in a structured and systematic way involving the use of the distinctive interpretative skills of the subject [...]

> the capacity for independent thought and judgement [...]

> skills in critical reasoning and analysis

> the ability to comprehend and develop intricate concepts in an open-ended way which involves an understanding of purpose and consequences

> the ability to work with and in relation to others [...] and the collective negotiation of solutions

> the ability to understand, interrogate and apply a variety of theoretical positions and weigh the importance of alternative perspectives

> the ability to handle information and argument in a critical and self-reflective manner

> research skills, including the ability to gather, sift and organize material independently and critically, and evaluate its significance

> information technology (IT) skills broadly understood and the ability to access, work with and evaluate electronic resources [...]

> time management and organizational skills, as shown by the ability to plan and present conclusions effectively. (QAA: 2007)

For most students, English is not a vocational subject as such, but it does provide its graduates with a range of valuable skills and attributes, as this list attests. And these are in demand from employers. These are skills often called the 'soft skills'. It is not a fair description of them because they are extremely important in the world of employment. But one of the reasons they may feel 'soft' is that students do not always know that they are acquiring them as they go along: being reflective about how you learn as well as what you learn is one way of making sure you know what it is that you are getting from your degree. Many UK institutions try to help you with this by asking (or requiring) you to participate in activities that go by various names, but which are really about your personal development (see Chapter 1.3, 'Study skills for literature'). You may, for example, be asked to complete skills audits when you first arrive at university – which things are you good at? Which bad? How are you going to remedy the things that you are less good at? If you are asked to do this, try to do it reasonably seriously, and revisit your results regularly – you ought to be improving your information literacy skills, for example, pretty much from the outset (using the library, finding out how to do good online searching, evaluating source material – these are all research skills which also demonstrate your information literacy and you need to identify them as such). Feedback from essays and assessments as you go along will tell you if there are other things you need to improve on: if everyone says your grammar is poor, it might just be that it is, so don't ignore the advice you receive, even if you are annoyed by it. A badly written job application is going straight to the recycling bin. And having evidence that you identified a problem in your university life and solved it is actually quite useful when it comes to filling in a 'criterion-referenced' job application which will demand real-life examples of the skills that you are claiming to have.

You may also be asked as part of personal development training to perform activities such as compiling a CV and/or completing a mock job application form or interview process. This may be part of your course, but if it isn't, you should seek advice on these things early (in your first year – really!) from your careers advisory service. The advice you are likely to get is that job advertisements leading to worthwhile employment are written very carefully. The person specification will list attributes and skills: download some and have a look at what employers in your preferred areas of work are looking for. Your application needs to show that you can do the things that are being asked for, preferably with evidence and examples. Thus there may be specific requirements – 'candidate must have a good honours degree' – for which your degree certificate is evidence. But if the job description asks for examples of teamwork, where does the evidence for that come from? It may come from a specific assignment in your degree programme: a group project, for example. Or it may come from your activities beyond the classroom: 'I'm good at teamwork and can demonstrate this by offering the example of my work as a volunteer on a forestry commission project in the summer of my first year.' Finding the space to 'round' your experience to set yourself apart from the rest is what matters. For some competitive careers (publishing is an example), getting experience while you are still at university (as an intern, if you are lucky, or as an unpaid dogsbody if you are less lucky) will save you time later. And if you want to teach, it is essential to get some classroom experience as a volunteer, because without it your application will not even be considered. Why would an employer choose someone with no experience if there are a lot of candidates with very similar qualifications many of whom do have experience? (The QAA estimates that around 8500 students per annum graduate with degrees in English as a single honours subject; a similar number again graduate with English as a significant component of their programme. You are in competition with a very large number of graduates.) If you're any good in those kinds of roles, it will also broaden the range of people available to write you references: employers in part-time work and managers of volunteering projects will have real-life examples of your capacities to offer for your résumé. You need to stand out from the crowd, and that means thinking now about how you make this happen.

When I look at my friends and contemporaries from the English degree I did, I see a rather wide range of careers being pursued with success and single-minded determination, or with success and a quieter sense of achievement, or just being pursued (career does not mean everything to everyone and some folk prefer to work to make enough money to pursue their out-of-work interests). My friends are teachers in schools, administrators, librarians (in the public and private sectors – law firms need librarians, apparently), civil servants (some very senior indeed). They work in business and industry, including in accountancy and finance. One owns her own successful marketing business and is also a poet. In a very unscientific survey – because although I am friendly, my sample is small – I asked them what they'd got from their degree, the 'Stan' question: had it been worth it? Had there been any point? They answered 'yes', but there was always a 'but'. The first 'but' was that we graduated (as perhaps you will too) at a period of intense economic uncertainty (in the UK there were more than 3 million people unemployed in 1987). Most of us spent a while doing 'nothing' jobs; most of us had to take further qualifications to do what we wanted to do. This is also likely to be true for you. To that extent, with one or two exceptions, it was the fact of having a degree that mattered, not the subject; postgraduate qualifications in law, marketing, personnel, information technology and so on all require one to be a graduate as the entry requirement for admission.

The second 'but' – and this is the one that you may need to pay more attention to – was that what went on in the classroom was extremely important, but so was the other stuff we did: the experiences – of friendship, of taking responsibility, of campaigning in student and other political arenas, of doing crumby part-time jobs, of volunteering for worthy (and sometimes not worthy) causes, of working in student radio, or for the student counselling service – all added to our CVs. In a competitive jobs market, when there are lots of graduates with qualifications that are quite difficult to tell apart, the 'value-added' element to the new graduate's CV is the capacity to point to other experiences, the ability to differentiate oneself from others with similar degrees. And that's the bit you really do need to focus on for the future, almost as much as you need to focus on your degree.

The 'yes' part of their answers to my ad hoc questions was that, although they hadn't always noticed it at the time of actually doing their degrees, English really had been useful. It had taught them a lot about reading and interpreting information, and doing it quickly. It had demanded that they be fluent and effective communicators, mostly in writing, but also in person-to-person discussions. Almost all of my peers are responsible for writing high-level reports in their day-to-day work – bids for jobs, marketing communications, job adverts, marketing information, reports on students, and they are in turn acknowledged by their peers as accurate, fluent, sophisticated writers. They have become good at arguing a case, often using information that conflicted with itself. They know themselves to be persuasive, and put some of that down to their English training. They can think critically, and spot the flaws in an opposing case. Those who work with numbers (and English graduates can be very good indeed with numbers) are good at explaining numbers to those who aren't so numerate – a lot of my friends are now in training roles. They are good at working alone (which English degrees certainly demanded in my time); they are also good at being team members, because they can communicate clearly and empathize with different points of view. They have always got something to talk about in social/work situations. They still enjoy a good jaw about a good (or even a bad) book.

The experience of a degree in English

Claire Bowditch

'What is literature?'

I begin rhetorically because, in short, this question represents many of the questions and the existing views held by students preparing to study and, indeed, currently studying English Literature in higher education today. It invites challenge, debate and consensus. The experience of being asked this question during the first lecture, in the first week of my studies as an undergraduate, means it has remained with me (and will, I imagine, continue to do so) for many years. The question is both provocative and stimulating, and encourages various levels of response, engagement with literary cultures and practices, and reveals (often subconscious) individual preferences. In short, then, it engages with many of the nuances and traditions associated with and applied within the discipline of Literary Studies. In its extended application, the question 'What is literature?' also implies the broad range of writing that students can expect to encounter throughout their time studying for a BA in English; relatively recent additions of areas of study such as contemporary writing, women's writing, postcolonial writing and creative writing to university syllabi mean that undergraduates will often be given the opportunity to study **canonical** writings alongside those which have been more recently introduced onto the university curriculum.

The study of English literature, or English language and literature, during further education often means that the discipline is informed by and experienced alongside perhaps more diverse academic interests. The continuation of this experience is also encouraged at many higher education institutions as the field of Literary Studies engages with the findings, nature and ethos of seemingly separate disciplines, such as history, philosophy and politics. Students can expect to be offered a choice of modules (some examples of which are discussed in this collection), often relating to both the areas of interest of the academics with whom they work and by whom they are taught, and a range of compulsory courses within their degree programme. Compulsory courses are designed to equip all students with the necessary skills to critically engage with and interrogate primary and secondary reading materials, and to provide a foundation for wider interests to be explored. As you progress through your degree, the opportunities to focus on a specific area of study (a single author, a certain time period, etc.) increase, as intellectual freedom and interest is encouraged, and the skills required for successful and confident interrogation are expanded.

The experience of studying for a BA in English goes far beyond the texts studied as part of the course requirements and, perhaps more significantly, far beyond the duration of the course. The skills acquired as part of the study of literature, and their applications, are as far-reaching as the question with which this section begins. The level of critical engagement established and encouraged as part of the process of studying for a BA in English will invariably come to inform your thinking in a wider context. Skills such as analytical thinking, independent research and study, and organizational abilities are developed and refined alongside those more closely linked to the discipline, such as the ability to structure and present literary arguments and observations. In short, and as I rapidly came to discover, you will never think in the same way again! That said, of course, there is, as far as I know, no one-size-fits-all experience of both taking the decision to undertake and then to pursue a BA in English: upon their arrival in an English department, many first-year students (myself included) are surprised to see their timetables, which often have fewer scheduled hours per week than their school or further education establishment required of them per day. This is the primary illustration of the importance – and, indeed, necessity – of independent thought and study required for the successful completion of a BA in English. The relatively few timetabled hours for the degree programme do not, however, reflect the amount of time students studying for a BA in English are expected to dedicate to their studies. In order to achieve the best possible results, students are encouraged to spend time preparing for group discussion in their taught modules, and conducting independent research into their areas of study. The time spent engaged in such activities often proves invaluable in terms of undertaking and preparing for assessed elements of the course, and also in developing an awareness of and engagement with key critical and literary debates. As a first-year undergraduate, I was surprised by the dynamics of seminar interaction, as students are often expected to lead the debate and offer informed opinions on the topic of discussion. The rewards for participation of this nature, though, are invaluable, as students develop skills in confident communication, public speaking and argumentation. Many of the most provocative and stimulating ideas for further thought and exploration are often founded in lively seminar discussion, as students are encouraged to share their thoughts and ideas.

The experience of doing a BA in English is one that is simultaneously challenging and rewarding. The qualification can lead to further study for higher degrees, and will provide an excellent foundation for jobs in both the public and the private sectors due to the nature of the skills developed as part of the demands and intricacies of the course.

5 Interview

Claire Bowditch

The interview that follows with Charlotte, magazine photo editor, not only indicates a career that takes full advantage of the skills you learn in taking an English degree; it also highlights the ways in which English provides and develops broad, useful abilities, which are easily transferable, and thus make the English graduate someone who is highly valued in many facets of the work community.

How do you think studying for a BA in English helped to equip you to deal with the demands of your current job?

As a photo editor for an online magazine, I have to keep up with not only the fast-paced world of the internet, but also the immediacy associated with popular journalism. Although this seems far removed from my English BA, it was while studying for my degree that I learnt to mentally absorb and process large amounts of information in a relatively short period of time, as reading and evaluating materials from different genres and centuries meant that large quantities of information relating to study had to be remembered and recalled quickly. Studying English as an undergraduate also helped to prepare me for the pressure of deadlines experienced by those who work in the media. This, too, is invariably linked to the independent organizational skills required at BA level in order to manage the workload. Such skills come to seem invaluable when you are not only managing your own time, but also the time of others on your team, or in your department. Many employers actively seek graduates with a degree in a humanities subject as, having been encouraged for three years to consider the wider context of thought and method, such graduates have experience in judging the wider implications and consequences of decision making on behalf of themselves and others.

Is there any advice that you would offer to those considering undertaking a BA in English relating to study practices and how these are relevant for life after their BA?

Many universities offer courses in study skills, and I would encourage anyone thinking of enrolling on a BA course in English to be prepared to attend these sessions. Most are not compulsory, but not only will your attendance allow you to meet other students who are taking different courses and who have different interests, but it will also make you more aware of the practicalities of independent study. The fact that they provide a great chance to meet new people also helps for working life after you've finished your BA, as in industry it's beneficial to have a range of contacts to help with everything ranging from business advice to securing and maintaining contracts. It's also a really good idea to structure your time so as to allow you proactive and productive working hours, whilst still factoring in some time off! Many of my friends didn't go to university, so the fact that I approached my BA in a similar way to their approach to their working hours meant that we could still meet and have fun once we'd finished work. It's important to maintain a level of balance while ensuring that you meet the requirements of your course.

Conclusion

Taking an English degree means that multiple careers pathways are opened for you. Journalism, the Civil Service, marketing and the media all offer long-term opportunities. Typically, the careers obtained are wide-ranging, as we have already suggested. Leicester University has provided evidence of where just under 100 students found work, representing around 85% of a single cohort of students. Details of careers, job titles, employers, and the kinds of further education into which students progressed following an English degree can be found at: www2.le.ac.uk/offices/ssds/sd/careers/plan/destinations/dss/english

A brief summary of the areas includes: Cancer Research and British Heart Foundation, Leicester City Council, Leicestershire Constabulary, Ministry of Justice, Nottingham Council for Volunteer Services, PricewaterhouseCoopers, and Wiley-Blackwell, the academic publishers.

At these and other employers, the positions include Administrative Officer, Assistant Language Teacher, Author Relations Executive, Charity Fundraising Organizer, Event Co-ordinator, Marketing Manager, Research Assistant, Journalist, Trainee Chartered Accountant.

Further degrees include: Graduate Diploma in Law, International Public Policy; MAs in literature, political science and other disciplines; Postgraduate Diploma in Print Journalism, and Postgraduate Certificates of Education in primary and secondary education, in a range of subjects.

At Loughborough University, we have evidence to show that many of our graduates pursued similar careers and further degrees, with employers including the BBC, Friends Provident, the Highways Agency, Local Government, National Probation Service, Newsgroup, and the National Health Service, and positions such as News Correspondent, Multimedia Editor, Fashion Intern, Administrator, and Recruitment Specialist.

Most universities publish, or otherwise provide such information, and each will have a development or careers office through which you can gain specific information on particular careers. Additionally, universities hold careers fairs, where you can gain further information, meet prospective employers, talk with their representatives, and so on. When you get to the stage where you will be attending a Graduate Recruitment and Placement Fair, there are some important things to remember:

> Find out in advance which companies are attending; they are as interested in meeting you as you are them.
> Decide on who you want to focus on, but remember to take a look at who else will be present; a career might present itself to you that you had never considered.
> Do some research on specific companies; this will help in focusing the questions you want to ask.
> Have your CV ready; your university will have a Careers Centre which will be happy to help with this.
> Practise your questions in order to appear calm and organized.
> Dress formally and smartly.

6 learning resource

6.1   chronology   365

chronology

The following chronology is not exhaustive; rather it aims to provide the student with an introductory sketch to the writing, performance and publication of literary works, along with reference to particular works of art, and also to document a number of significant cultural moments and events, including major works of architecture, technological developments and the establishment of particular institutions. Births and deaths been excluded, as have the reigns of monarchs, the dating of political administrations, and major political and historical events.

1337	William Merlee of Oxford made first scientific weather forecasts
1350	First paper mill in England, Hertford
1353	*The Decameron*
1354	Mechanical clock developed at Strasbourg
c. 1381–85	*Troilus and Criseyde*
c. 1386–90	*Confessio Amantis*
1387	Chaucer begins *Canterbury Tales*; *Piers Plowman*
1422	Earliest record of Chester Plays
c. 1450–1500	Towneley Cycle
1453	Gutenberg prints Bible in Mainz, Germany
1474	Caxton's *History of Troy*, first book printed in English
1476	Establishment of Caxton's printing press
1484	Botticelli's *Birth of Venus*
1485	Caxton prints Malory's *Morte D'Arthur*
1499–1500	Erasmus meets Thomas More at Oxford
1500	First black lead pencils used in England
1503	Leonardo da Vinci's *Mona Lisa*; Canterbury Cathedral finished
c. 1510	*Everyman*
1513	Machiavelli, *The Prince*
1516	Thomas More, *Utopia*

6

1517	Martin Luther's 95 theses at Wittenberg; coffee first brought to Europe
1528	Castiglone, *The Courtier*
1531	*The Boke Named the Governour*; first complete edition of Aristotle's works published by Erasmus
1533	Ariosto, *Orlando Furioso*
1549	Book of Common Prayer
1551	First licensing of alehouses and taverns in England and Wales
1556	Stationers' Company of London granted monopoly of printing in England
1563	Foxe's Book of Martyrs
1565	Arthur Golding's translation of first four books of Ovid's *Metamorphoses*
1569	Mercator's map of the world; public lottery in London
1574	Richard Burbage licensed to open a theatre in London
1577	Blackfriars, Curtain, and playhouse at Newington Butts built; Holinshed's *Chronicles*
1579	Edmund Spenser's *Shepheardes Calendar*
1580	Last performance of miracle play in Coventry; John Lyly, *Euphues and his England*; Philip Sidney completes *Apologie for Poetrie* and *The Old Arcadia*
1581	Joseph Hall, *Ten Books of Homer's Iliads*; Philip Sidney begins work on *Astrophil and Stella*
1586	Christopher Marlow's *Doctor Faustus* performed
1589	George Puttenham, *The Art of English Poesie*
1590	Marlow, *Tamburlaine* Parts I and II published; Sidney, *The New Arcadia*; Spenser, *The Faerie Queene*, I–III
1591	John Harington translates Ariosto's *Orlando Furioso*; William Shakespeare, *Henry VI* Parts I and II performed; *The Two Gentlemen of Verona* performed; Sidney: posthumous publication of *Astrophil and Stella*; Spenser, *Complaints*
1592	John Lyly, *Galatea*; Marlow, *Edward II* performed; Rose Theatre opens
1593	Shakespeare, *Comedy of Errors* and *Richard III* performed; *Venus and Adonis*
1594	Shakespeare, *Titus Andronicus* performed; *Lucrece*; Michael Drayton, *Ideas Mirrour*; Thomas Nashe, *The Unfortunate Traveller*

6

1595	Mary Sidney, *The Tragedy of Antonie*; Shakespeare, *Love's Labour's Lost*, *Midsummer Night's Dream*, *Richard II*, and *Romeo and Juliet* performed; Spenser, *Amoretti*, *Epithalamion*, *Colin Clout's Come Home Again*
1596	Ben Jonson, *Everyman in his Humour* performed; William Shakespeare, *Merchant of Venice* and *King John* performed; Spenser, *The Faerie Queene IV–VI* and *Four Hymns*
1597	Francis Bacon, *Essays*
1598	George Chapman translates Homer's *Iliad* I–II and VII–XI; Shakespeare, *Henry IV* Parts I and II performed
1599	Johnson, *Every Man Out of His Humour* performed; Shakespeare, *Julius Caesar*, *Henry V* and *Much Ado about Nothing* performed
1600	Shakespeare, *The Merry Wives of Windsor*, *As You Like It* performed
1601	Shakespeare, *Hamlet* and *Twelfth Night* performed
1602	Shakespeare, *Troilus and Cressida* performed; Bodleian Library founded
1603	Jonson, *Sejanus* performed; Shakespeare, *All's Well That Ends Well* performed; *Hamlet* first quarto
1604	Marlowe, *Doctor Faustus* earliest surviving edition; Shakespeare, *Othello* performed; *Hamlet* second quarto
1605	Michael Drayton, *Poems*; Jonson, *Volpone* performed
1606	Shakespeare, *King Lear* and *Macbeth* performed
1607	Shakespeare, *Antony and Cleopatra* written
1608	Thomas Heywood, *Rape of Lucrece*; Shakespeare, *Coriolanus* and *Timon of Athens* written; *King Lear* two quartos published
1609	Jonson, *Epicoene or the Silent Woman* performed; Shakespeare, *Pericles* performed; *Troilus and Cressida* two quartos published; *Sonnets* published
1610	Chapman continues *Iliad*; Jonson, *The Alchemist* performed; John Donne, *Pseudo-Martyr*
1611	Complete translation of *Iliad* by Chapman published; Dekker and Middleton, *The Roaring Girl* published; Shakespeare, *Macbeth* first recorded performance
1612	Drayton, *Poly-Olbion* I; Webster, *The White Devil* published
1613	Shakespeare, *Henry VIII* performed; Globe Theatre burns down
1614	Chapman translates *Odyssey* I–XII; Jonson, *Bartholomew Fair* performed; Walter Ralegh, *The History of the World*
1615	Chapman translates *Odyssey* XIII–XXIV

6

1616	Jonson, *The Devil Is an Ass* performed; Webster, *The Duchess of Malfi* performed
1617	Rachel Speght, *A Mouzell for Melastomus*; Joseph Swetnam, *Arraignment of Women*
1620	Mary Wroth, *Love's Victory*
1621	Robert Burton, *Anatomy of Melancholy*; Mary Wroth, *Pamphila to Amphilanthus* published; *Urania* I published; *Urania* II completed in manuscript; Speght, *Mortality's Memorandum*
1622	Drayton, *Poly-Olbion* Part II; Middleton and Rowley, *The Changeling* performed
1623	Shakespeare, *Comedies, Histories and Tragedies* (the First Folio) published; Webster, *The Duchess of Malfi* performed
1624	Middleton, *A Game at Chess* performed
1627	First atlas compiled by John Speed
1631	Jonson, *The Devil Is an Ass* and *The Staple of News* published
1633	Donne, *Poems* published posthumously; John Ford, *'Tis Pity She's a Whore* published; George Herbert, *The Temple*
1634	John Milton, *Comus* performed
1637	Milton, *Of Reformation*
1642	Thomas Browne, *Religio Medici*; Milton, *Apology for Smectymnuus*
1644	Milton, *Areopagitica*; Jane and Elizabeth Cavendish, *The Concealed Fancies* and *Poems* completed in manuscript
1648	Robert Herrick, *Hesperides*
1650	Anne Bradstreet, *The Tenth Muse*; John Playford, *The English Dancing Master*; Henry Vaughan, *Silex scintillans*; tea first imported into England
1651	John Cleveland, *Poems*; William Davenant, *Leviathan*; Hobbes, *Leviathan*
1652	Playford, *Musics Recreation*; Otto von Guericke invents the air pump at Magdeburg; opening of the first London coffee-house
1653	Izaak Walton, *The Compleat Angler*; Margaret Cavendish, *Poems and Fancies*
1654	Roger Boyle, *Parthenissa*; John Milton, *Second Defence*
1656	Cavendish, *A True Relation*
1658	Thomas Browne, *Urne-Burial* and *The Garden of Cyrus*
1659	Thomas Hobbes, *De homine*; Lovelace, *Posthume Poems*; Molière, *Les Précieuses ridicules*; Pepys begins diaries

6

1660 . . . . John Dryden, *Astraea redux*; George Mackenzie, *Arentina*;

1661 . . . . Boyle, *Some Considerations*; Brome, *Songs and Other Poems*; Davenant, *The Siege of Rhodes* parts 1 and 2; Sir Percy Herbert, *The Princess Gloria*

1662 . . . . Butler, *Hudibras* part 1; *Book of Common Prayer*, rev. version; Molière, *L'Ecole des femmes*; Royal Society founded; Press Act (rigid censorship)

1663 . . . . Butler, *Hudibras* part 2; Corneille/Phillips, *Pompée*; Dryden, *The Wild Gallant*

1664 . . . . Dryden, *The Rival Ladies*; Dryden/R. Howard, *The Indian Queen*; Etherege, *Love in a Tub*; Evelyn, *Sylva*; R. Howard, *The Vestal Virgin*; Molière, *Le Tartuffe*

1665 . . . . Bunyan, *The Holy City*; Dryden, *The Indian Emperor*; Hooke, *Micrographia*; La Rochefoucauld, *Réflexions et maxims*

1666 . . . . Bunyan, *Grace Abounding*; Dryden, *Annus mirabilis*; Molière, *Le misanthrope*; Fire of London, 2–7 September

1667 . . . . Margaret Fell, *Women's Speaking Justified*; Milton, *Paradise Lost*; Racine, *Andromque*;

1668 . . . . Dryden, *Essay of Dramatick Poesie*; Etherege, *She Wou'd if She Cou'd*; Lafontaine, *Fables*; Racine, *Britannicus*; Dryden appointed Poet Laureate

1669 . . . . Pepys ends diary

1670 . . . . Aphra Behn, *The Forc'd Marriage*; Dryden, *The Conquest of Granada* part 1; Molière, *Le bourgeois gentilhomme*; Pascal, *Pensées*; Racine, *Bérénice*; Dryden appointed Historiographer Royal

1671 . . . . Dryden, *The Conquest of Granada* part 2; Milton, *Paradise Regained* and *Samson Agonistes*; Newton makes reflector telescope

1672 . . . . Dryden, *Marriage à la Mode*; Molière, *Les femmes savants*; Racine, *Bajazet*; first public concerts in London

1673 . . . . Aphra Behn, *The Dutch Lover*; Davenant, *Collected Works*; Milton, *Of True Religion*; Molière, *Le malade imaginaire*, Racine, *Mithridate*

1674 . . . . Milton, *Paradise Lost* (12-book version); Racine, *Iphigénie*; Wycherley, *The Country Wife*

1675 . . . . Rochester, *Satyr against Mankind*; Royal Observatory, Greenwich; Wren begins St Paul's Cathedral

1676 . . . . Etherege, *The Man of Mode*; Otway, *Don Carlos*; Shadwell, *The Virtuoso*; Wycherley, *The Plain Dealer*

1677 . . . . Behn, *The Rover* part 1; Dryden, *All for Love* and *The State of Innocence*; Lee, *The Rival Queens*; Racine, *Phèdre*

6

1678 . . . . Bunyan, *Pilgrim's Progress* part 1; Butler, *Hudibras* part 3; Madame de Lafayette, *La princess de Clèves*

1679 . . . . Dryden, *Troilus and Cressida*; Newton's calculation of lunar orbit

1680 . . . . Bunyan, *Life and Death of Mr Badman*; Butler, *Hudibras*; Cellier, *Malice Defeated*; Otway, *The Orphan*; Comédie française established; Henry Purcell, *Dido and Aeneas*; penny post instituted in London

1681 . . . . Aphra Behn, *The Rover* part 2; Dryden, *Absalom and Achitophel* and *Religio Iaici* part 1; Marvell, *Miscellaneous Poems*; Tate, *King Lear*

1682 . . . . Dryden, *MacFlecknoe*; Otway, *Venice Preserv'd*

1684 . . . . Bunyan, *Pilgrim's Progress* part 2; Dryden, *Religio Laici* part 2

1685 . . . . Dryden, *Albion and Albinus*; Tate, *The Cuckold-Haven*

1686 . . . . Behn, *The Lucky Chance*

1687 . . . . Dryden, *The Hind and the Panther*, 'Song for Saint Cecilia's Day'; Newton, *Philosophiae naturalis principia mathematica*

1688 . . . . Behn, *Oroonoko*; Dryden, *Britannia Rediviva*; Shadwell, *The Squire of Alsatia*

1689 . . . . Behn, *The History of the Nun*; Lee, *The Massacre of Paris*; John Locke, *On Civil Government*; Thomas Shadwell appointed Poet Laureate

1690 . . . . John Locke, *Essay Concerning Human Understanding*; Huyghens proposes wave theory of light

1691 . . . . Congreve, *Incognita*; Racine, *Athalie*; Rochester, *Poems*; Purcell, *King Arthur*

1692 . . . . Southerne, *The Wives Excuse*; Purcell, *Fairy-Queen*; Nahum Tate appointed Poet Laureate

1693 . . . . Congreve, *The Old Bachelor*; John Locke, *Ideas on Education*

1694 . . . . Congreve, *The Double Dealer*; Dryden, *Love Triumphant*; Southerne, *The Fatal Marriage*; Purcell, *Te Deum* and *Jubilate*

1695 . . . . Congreve, *Love for Love*; Leibniz, *Système nouveau de la nature*; Southerne, *Oroonoko*; Purcell, *The Indian Queen*; end of press censorship in England

1696 . . . . John Aubrey, *Miscellanies*; Vanbrugh, *The Relapse*; licensing of plays by the Lord Chamberlain

1697 . . . . Dryden, *Alexander's Feast*; Vanbrugh, *The Provok'd Wife*

1699 . . . . Farquhar, *Love and a Bottle*

1700 . . . . Congreve, *The Way of the World*; Dryden, *Secular Masque*

1701 . . . . Dryden, *Collected Plays*; Rowe, *Tamerlane*

1702	Bysshe, *Art of English Poetry*; *Daily Courant*, first English daily newspaper; Vanbrugh builds Castle Howard, Yorkshire
1703	Mary, Lady Chudleigh, *Poems on Several Occasions*
1704	Swift, *Tale of a Tub* and *The Battle of the Books*; Newton, *Optics*
1705	Centlivre, *The Basset-Table*; opening of The Queen's Theatre, Haymarket; Hailey calculates the cometary orbit; Vanbrugh builds Blenheim Palace
1706	Farquhar, *The Recruiting Officer*
1707	Farquhar, *The Beaux' Stratagem*; Locke, *An Essay for the Understanding of St. Paul's Epistles*; Union of England and Scotland
1708	Swift, *An Argument Against Abolishing Christianity*; Handel, *Agrippina*
1709	Berkeley, *An Essay Towards a New Theory of Vision*; Steele, *The Tatler*; first Copyright Act
1710	Berkeley, *Principles of Human Knowledge*; Swift, *Meditations upon a Broomstick*; Handel, *Rinaldo*; Christopher Wren finishes St Paul's Cathedral
1711	Gay, *The Present State of Wit*; Pope, *Essay on Criticism*; Steele and Addison, *The Spectator*; Handel comes to London
1712	Pope, *The Rape of the Lock* (2-canto version)
1713	Addison, *Cato*; Pope, *Windsor Forest*; Steele and Addison, *The Guardian*; Scriblerus Club formed; Swift becomes Dean of St Paul's
1714	Gay, *The Shepherd's Week*; Mandeville, *Fable of the Bees*; Pope, *Rape of the Lock* (5-canto version); Fahrenheit makes mercury thermometer
1715	Pope's translation of the *Iliad* begun; Nicholas Rowe appointed Poet Laureate
1717	Gay/Pope/Arbuthnot, *Three Hours After Marriage*; Pope, *Works*
1719	Defoe, *Robinson Crusoe*
1720	John Gay, *Collected Poems*; Defoe, *Captain Singleton*; Handel, *Esther*; Little Theatre in the Haymarket is built; Westminster Hospital founded, the first subscription hospital
1721	Montesquieu, *Lettres persones*; first smallpox inoculations introduced by Lady Mary Wortley Montagu
1722	Defoe, *Moll Flanders*; *Journal of the Plague Year*; *Colonel Jack*; Haywood, *British Recluse*; Guy's Hospital founded
1723	Mandeville, *Fable of the Bees* (2nd, expanded, edn)

6

1724 . . . . Defoe, *Roxana*; *Tour through Great Britain*; Haywood, *A Wife to be Lett*; *Works*

1725 . . . . Haywood, *Fantomina*; *The Tea Table*; Pope, edition of Shakespeare; trans. *Odyssey*; first circulating libraries open in Bath and in Edinburgh; Grosvenor Square, London, begun; Handel, *Rodelina*

1726 . . . . Jane Barker, *Lining of the Patch-Work Screen*; Haywood, *City Jilt*; *Mercenary Lover*; Swift, *Gulliver's Travels*; Thomson, *The Seasons: Winter*; Voltaire in England (−1729)

1727 . . . . Gay, *Fables*; Pope, Swift, Arbuthnot, *Miscellanies*; Thomson, *The Seasons: Summer*

1728 . . . . Defoe, *Captain Carleton*; Fielding, *Love in Several Masques*; Gay, *Beggar's Opera*; Pope, *The Dunciad*; Elizabeth Rowe, *Friendship in Death*; Thomson, *The Seasons: Spring*

1729 . . . . Gay, *Polly*; *Mother Goose* (English translation of Perrault); Pope, *Dunciad Variorum*; Swift, *Modest Proposal*

1730 . . . . Fielding, *Tom Thumb*; Thomson, *The Seasons* (inc. *Autumn* and *Hymn*); Colley Cibber appointed Poet Laureate; *The Grub Street Journal* (−1737); Methodist Society formed in Oxford

1731 . . . . Fielding, *Grub Street Opera*; Lillo, *London Merchant*; Pope, *Epistle to Burlington*; *The Gentleman's Magazine* launched, ed. by Edward Cave; Hogarth, *Harlot's Progress*; Dublin Society formed

1732 . . . . Berkeley, *Dialogues of Alciphron*; Fielding, *Covent Garden Tragedy*; Pope, *Epistle to Bathurst*; *The London Magazine* (−1785); John Rich opens new Opera House at Covent Garden with proceeds of *The Beggar's Opera*; Jonathan Tyers opens Vauxhall gardens to the public; Kay invents the flying shuttle

1733 . . . . Pope, *Essay on Man*; *Horace's Satire II.i*; Wortley Montagu, *Verses Address'd to the Imitator of Horace*

1734 . . . . Pope, *Horace's Satire II.ii*; *Epistle to Cobham*; Handel, *Ariodante*

1735 . . . . Pope, *Epistle to Dr Arbuthnot*; *Epistle to a Lady*; Thomson, *Liberty*; Hogarth, *Rake's Progress*; Handel, *Alcina*

1736 . . . . Haywood, *Adventures of Eovaii*; statutes against witchcraft repealed

1737 . . . . Cooper, *Muses Library*; Green, *The Spleen*; Pope, *Horace's Epistles, I.i, vi; II.ii*; Theatre Licensing Act gives a patent to only two theatres and compels all plays to be submitted to the Lord Chamberlain before performance; Wortley Montagu, *The Nonsense of Common Sense*

1738 . . . . Johnson, *London*; Pope, *Epilogue to Satires*; Swift, *Polite Conversation*; Handel, *Saul*; *Israel in Egypt*

1739 . . . . Collier, *Woman's Labour*; Swift, *Verses on the Death of Dr Swift*; circulating library opens in London; rooms to allow concerts and balls are built at Marylebone Gardens; London Foundling Hospital opens

1740 . . . . Cibber, *Apology for the Life of Mr Colley Cibber*; Dyer, *Ruins of Rome*; Richardson, *Pamela*; Horse-racing Act

1741 . . . . Fielding, *Shamela*; Hume, *Essays, Moral and Political*; Richardson, *Letters Written to and for Particular Friends*; *Pamela* (Part III); Garrick's London debut as Richard III

1742 . . . . Collins, *Persian Eclogues*; Fielding, *Joseph Andrews*; Pope, *New Dunciad*; Handel, *Messiah* first performed in Dublin

1743 . . . . Fielding, *Miscellanies*; *Jonathan Wild the Great*; *Journey from this World to the Next*; Pope, *Dunciad in Four Books*

1744 . . . . Akenside, *Pleasures of Imagination*; Sarah Fielding, *David Simple*; Johnson, *Life of Mr Richard Savage*; Thomson, *The Seasons* (ref.); Haywood, *The Female Spectator* (–1746)

1745 . . . . Akenside, *Odes on Several Subjects*; Hogarth, *Marriage-à-la-Mode* engravings; lying-in hospital, Dublin, founded

1746 . . . . Collins, *Odes on Several Descriptive and Allegoric Subjects*; Handel, *Judas Maccabaeus*

1747 . . . . Gray, *Ode on E Eton College*; Richardson, *Clarissa*; Thomas Warton, *Pleasures of Melancholy*; Walpole acquires lease of Strawberry Hill and plans its transformation; Hogarth, *Industry and Idleness*

1748 . . . . Cleland, *Memoirs of a Woman*; Hume, *Enquiry concerning Human Understanding*; Leapor, *Poems upon Several Occasions*; Smollett, *Roderick Random*; Thomson, *The Castle of Indolence*; ruins of Pompeii discovered; Handel, *Solomon*

1749 . . . . Henry Fielding, *Tom Jones*; Sarah Fielding, *The Governess, Remarks on Clarissa*; Johnson, *The Vanity of Human Wishes*; Handel, *Music for the Royal Fireworks* to commemorate the Peace of Aix-la-Chapelle

1750 . . . . Mary Jones, *Miscellanies in Prose and Verse*; Robert Paltock, *Peter Wilkins*; Johnson, *The Rambler* (–1752); Westminster Bridge built

1751 . . . . Cleland, *Memoirs of a Coxcomb*; Henry Fielding, *Amelia*; Gray, *Elegy in a Country Churchyard*; Haywood, *The History of Miss Betsy Thoughtless*; Leapor, *Poems*, Vol. II; Smollett, *Peregrine Pickle*; Hogarth, *The Four Stages of Cruelty*; *Beer Street*; *Gin Lane*; Gin Act forbids sale of spirits by small shopkeepers

1752 . . . . Lennox, *Female Quixote*; Smart, *Poems on Several Occasions*; Act requiring licensing of all places of popular entertainment in London; Fielding, *Covent-Garden Journal*; Britain adopts Gregorian calendar

6

1753 . . . . Richardson, *Sir Charles Grandison*; Smollett, *Ferdinand Count Fathom*; British Museum founded; Hogarth, *Analysis of Beauty*

1754 . . . . Jane Collier & Sarah Fielding, *The Cry*; Duncombe, *The Feminiad*

1755 . . . . Fielding, *Voyage to Lisbon*; Hutcheson, *System of Moral Philosophy*; Johnson, *Dictionary of the English Language*; Smollett's translation of *Don Quixote*

1756 . . . . *The Critical Review* (–1763)

1757 . . . . Burke, *Philosophical Enquiry into E the Sublime and the Beautiful*; Dyer, *The Fleece*; Gray, *Odes*; Smollett's *Complete History of England*; William Whitehead appointed Poet Laureate; Walpole's private printing press at Strawberry Hill established with Gray's *Odes* as first publication

1758 . . . . Carter's translation of Epictetus; John Upton and Ralph Church's edition of Spenser's *The Faerie Queene*; Johnson, *The Idler* (–1760); subscription library in Liverpool

1759 . . . . Sarah Fielding, *Countess of Dellwyn*; Johnson, *Rasselas*; Sterne, *Tristram Shandy* Vols I & II; British Museum opens

1760 . . . . Goldsmith, *Citizen of the World*; Lyttleton & Elizabeth Montagu, *Dialogues of the Dead*; Smollett, *Sir Launcelot Greaves*; Wedgwood opens pottery works in Staffordshire; Society of Artists of Great Britain founded

1761 . . . . Frances Sheridan, *Memoirs of Miss Sidney Bidulph*; Sterne, *Tristram Shandy* Vols III & IV, V & VI; Bridgwater Canal opens

1762 . . . . Garrick expands Drury Lane; Horace Walpole, *Anecdotes of Painting in England*

1763 . . . . Frances Brooke, *Lady Julia Mandeville*; Catherine Macaulay, *History of England*; Wortley Montagu, *Letters*

1764 . . . . Goldsmith, *The Traveller*; Walpole, *The Castle of Otranto*; formation of the 'Literary Club'; James Hargreaves invents spinning jenny; James Watt perfects steam engine

1765 . . . . Collins, *Poetical Works*; Johnson, edition of Shakespeare; Macpherson, *The Works of Ossian*; Percy, *Reliques of Ancient English Poetry*; Smollett, *Travels through France and Italy*; Sterne, *Tristram Shandy* Vols VII & VIII

1766 . . . . Colman & Garrick, *Clandestine Marriage*; Goldsmith, *Vicar of Wakefield*; Rousseau in England (–1767); Stubbs's engraved plates, *The Anatomy of the Horse*

1767 . . . . Frances Sheridan, *History of Nourjahad*; Sterne, *Tristram Shandy* Vol. IX; James Craig's plan for New Town, Edinburgh, chosen; Royal Crescent, Bath, begun

1768 . . . . Goldsmith, *The Good-Natur'd Man*; Gray, *Poems*; Wortley Montague, *Poems*; Sterne, *Sentimental Journey*; *Encyclopaedia Britannica* (–1771); Royal Academy of Art opens; Joseph Wright, *An Experiment on a Bird in the Air Pump*; Priestley, *Essay on the First Principles of Government*

1769 . . . . Smollett, *Adventures of an Atom*; *The Morning Chronicle* (–1862); Reynolds is made president of the Royal Academy; James Watt's steam engine patented

1770 . . . . Goldsmith, *Deserted Village*; *The Lady's Magazine*

1771 . . . . MacKenzie, *Man of Feeling*; Smollett, *Humphry Clinker*; Pantheon opens in London; Upper Assembly Rooms, Bath, opened

1772 . . . . *The Morning Post* (–1936)

1773 . . . . Barbauld, *Poems*; Cook, *Account of a Voyage round the World*; James Boswell, *Journal of a Tour to the Hebrides*; Chapone, *Letters on the Improvement of the Mind*; Goldsmith, *She Stoops to Conquer*; Phillis Wheatley, *Poems*; subscription library in Bristol

1774 . . . . Mary Scott, *Female Advocate*; *Letters Written by the Earl of Chesterfield to His Son*; perpetual copyright is declared invalid; Thomas Warton, *History of English Poetry*

1775 . . . . Hester Chapone, *Poems*; Gray, *Poems*; Johnson, *Journey to Western Islands*; *Poetical Amusements at a Villa near Bath*; Sheridan, *The Duenna*; *The Rivals*; *St Patrick's Day*; Sterne, *Letters*; Drury Lane Theatre redesigned by Robert Adam

1776 . . . . Gibbon, *Decline and Fall of the Roman Empire*, Vol. I; Paine, *Common Sense*; Smith, *Wealth of Nations*; Charles Burney, *General History of Music*, Vol. I

1777 . . . . Chatterton, *Poems E by Thomas Rowley and others*; Chapone, *Letter to a New-Married Lady*; Cook, *Voyage towards the South Pole*; Sheridan, *School for Scandal*; *Trip to Scarborough*; Thomas Warton, *Poems*

1778 . . . . Barbauld, *Lessons for Children*; Burney, *Evelina*; Mary Hamilton, *Munster Village*; Clara Reeve, *Old English Baron*

1779 . . . . Alexander, *History of Women*; Cowper, *Olney Hymns*; Hume, *Dialogues concerning Natural Religion*; Johnson, *Lives of the Poets*; Mungo Park, *Travels in the Interior Districts of Africa*; Sheridan, *The Critic*; first iron bridge built at Coalbrookdale

1790 . . . . Baillie, *Poems*; Blake, *The Marriage of Heaven and Hell*; Burke, *Reflections on the Revolution in France*; Radcliffe, *A Sicilian Romance*; Wollstonecraft, *A Vindication of the Rights of Men*; Forth–Clyde Canal opened; first steam-powered rolling mill in Britain

1791 . . . . Barbauld, *Epistle to William Wilberforce*; *An Address to the Opposers of the Repeal of the Test and Corporation Acts*; Cowper, transl. *The Iliad and Odyssey*; Darwin, *The Botanic Garden*; Inchbald, *A Simple Story*; Paine, *The Rights of Man*, pt.1; Robinson, *Poems*; Haydn visits England; Mozart, *The Magic Flute*; Galvani publishes results of electrical experiments on frogs' legs

1792 . . . . Barbauld, *Civic Sermons to the People*; Gilpin, *Essays on Picturesque Beauty*; Paine, *The Rights of Man*, pt. 2; Wollstonecraft, *A Vindication of the Rights of Woman*; London Corresponding Society formed

1793 . . . . Blake, *Vision of the Daughters of Albion*; Godwin, *An Enquiry Concerning Political Justice*; Smith, *The Old Manor House*; Wordsworth, *Descriptive Sketches*; *An Evening Walk*

1794 . . . . Blake, *Songs of Innocence and of Experience*; Godwin, *Caleb Williams*; Radcliffe, *The Mysteries of Udolpho*; Turner, *Interior of Tintern Abbey*

1795 . . . . Edgeworth, *Letters for Literary Ladies*; hydraulic pump patented; metric system adopted in France; Haydn, *London* symphony

1796 . . . . Coleridge, *Poems on Various Subjects*; Lewis, *The Monk*; Robinson, *Sappho and Phaon*; Seward, *Llangollen Vale, With Other Poems*; Yearsley, *The Rural Lyre*; Jenner conducts first smallpox vaccination; Beckford begins Fonthill Abbey in gothic style

1797 . . . . Radcliffe, *The Italian*; Young's *Night Thoughts* engraved by Blake; Turner's Lake District tour; high-pressure steam pump patented

1798 . . . . Baillie, *A Series of Plays*; Coleridge, *Fears in Solitude*; *France: An Ode*; *Frost at Midnight*; Godwin, *Memoirs of the Author of a Vindication of the Rights of Woman*; Inchbald (ed.), *Lovers' Vows*; Wordsworth and Coleridge, *Lyrical Ballads*; Haydn, *The Creation*; invention of lithography; Malthus publishes *An Essay on the Principle of Population*

1799 . . . . Lewis, *Tales of Terror*; Seward, *Original Sonnets*; Rosetta Stone discovered in Egypt; Constable enrols at Royal Academy

1800 . . . . Robinson, *Lyrical Tales*; Wordsworth and Coleridge, *Lyrical Ballads* (with Preface); Beethoven, Symphony No.1; Herschel discovers infra-red rays; Volta invents the first electrical battery; carriage road begun over the Alps at the Simplon Pass

1801 . . . . Hogg, *Scottish Pastorals, Poems and Songs*; Robinson, *Memoirs*; Haydn, *The Seasons*; Beethoven composes the *Moonlight* sonata

1802 . . . . Baillie, *Plays of the Passions* (II); Scott (ed.), *Minstrelsy of the Scottish Border*; Wordsworth and Coleridge, *Lyrical Ballads* (new Preface); foundation of Cobbett's *Weekly Political Register* and the *Edinburgh Review*; Telford begins road construction in the Scottish Highlands; discovery of ultra-violet rays

1803 . . . . Chatterton, *Collected Works*; Darwin, *The Temple of Nature*;
Trevithick builds first working railway steam engine in South Wales

1804 . . . . Smith, *Conversations Introducing Poetry*; Ann and Jane Taylor,
Original Poems for Infant Minds; British and Foreign Bible Society
founded; first Royal Horticultural flower show; English Water Colour
Society founded; Beethoven, *Eroica* symphony

1805 . . . . Scott, *The Lay of the Last Minstrel*; Hazlitt, *An Essay on the
Principles of Human Action*

1806 . . . . Byron, *Fugitive Pieces*; Robinson, *Poetical Works*; East India Docks
opened in London

1807 . . . . Byron, *Hours of Idleness*; Charles and Mary Lamb, *Tales from
Shakespeare*; Smith, *Beachy Head and Other Poems*; Wordsworth,
Poems in Two Volumes; Geological Society founded

1808 . . . . Baillie, *Constantine Paleologus*; Hemans, *England and Spain*;
Poems; Scott, *Marmion*; first issues of *The Examiner* (ed. Leigh
Hunt); Davy isolates magnesium, strontium, barium and calcium;
Dalton's *New System of Chemical Philosophy*, Pt I

1809 . . . . Byron, *English Bards and Scotch Reviewers*; Charles and Mary
Lamb, *Poetry for Children*; *Quarterly Review* founded; first gas
lighting in central London; Lamarck suggests theory of evolution

1810 . . . . Baillie, *The Family Legend*; Barbauld (ed.), *The British Novelists*;
Crabbe, *The Borough*; Scott, *The Lady of the Lake*; Seward, *Poetical
Works* (ed. Scott); Blake engraves *The Canterbury Pilgrims*;
invention of method for preserving food in tins

1811 . . . . Jane Austen, *Sense and Sensibility*; Shelley, *The Necessity of
Atheism*; Tighe, *Psyche*; Coleridge lectures on Shakespeare and
Milton

1812 . . . . Baillie, *Plays of the Passions* (III); Barbauld, *Eighteen Hundred and
Eleven*; Byron, *Childe Harold's Pilgrimage* I and II; Crabbe, *Tales*;
Hemans, *Domestic Affections, and Other Poems*; Southey and
Coleridge, *Omniana*

1813 . . . . Austen, *Pride and Prejudice*; Byron, *The Giaour*; *The Bride of Abydos*;
Moore, *The Two-Penny Postbag*; Scott, *Rokeby*

1814 . . . . Austen, *Mansfield Park*; Byron, *The Corsair, Lara*; Hunt, *Feast of the
Poets*; Scott, *Waverley*; Wordsworth, *The Excursion*; Beethoven,
Fidelio; Stephenson constructs steam locomotive

1815 . . . . Byron, *Hebrew Melodies*; Scott, *Guy Mannering*; Wordsworth,
Poems; Davy designs the safety lamp; Brighton Pavilion begun

1816 . . . . Austen, *Emma*; Byron, *Childe Harold's Pilgrimage* III; Coleridge,
Christabel, *Kubla Khan* and *The Pains of Sleep*; Scott, *The Antiquary*

6

1817 . . . . Byron, *Manfred: A Dramatic Poem*; Coleridge, *Biographia Literaria*; Cobbett, *English Grammar*; Godwin, *Mandeville*; Hazlitt, *Characters of Shakespeare's Plays*; Hemans, *Modern Greece*; Keats, *Poems*; Shelley, *Laon and Cythna*; Southey, *Wat Tyler*; first issues of *Blackwood's Magazine*; Ricardo, *Principles of Political Economy*

1818 . . . . Austen, *Northanger Abbey*; *Persuasion*; Byron, *Beppo*; *Childe Harold's Pilgrimage* IV; Hazlitt, *Lectures on the English Poets*; Hunt, *Foliage*; Keats, *Endymion*; Lamb, *Collected Works*; Mary Shelley, *Frankenstein*; first iron passenger ship on the Clyde; Institute of Civil Engineers established

1819 . . . . Byron, *Don Juan* I and II; Crabbe, *Tales of the Hall*; Hemans, *Tales and Historic Scenes in Verse*; Scott, *Ivanhoe*; Shelley, *The Cenci*; Wordsworth, *Peter Bell*; *The Waggoner*; stethoscope invented; first Macadam roads laid; Schubert, *The Trout* quintet

1820 . . . . John Clare, *Poems, Descriptive of Rural Life*; Hemans, *The Sceptic*; Keats, *Lamia, Isabella, The Eve of St Agnes and Other Poems*; Lamb, 'Essays of Elia'; Wordsworth, *The River Duddon: A Series of Sonnets*; *Vaudracour and Julia, and Other Poems*; Scott, *The Abbot*; Royal Astronomical Society founded; first issues of *London Magazine*

1821 . . . . Baillie, *Metrical Legends of Exalted Characters*; Byron, *Cain*; *Sardanapalus*; *The Two Foscari*; *Marino Faliero*; *Don Juan*, III–IV; Clare, *The Village Minstrel, and Other Poems*; De Quincey, 'The Confessions of an English Opium-Eater'; Shelley, *Adonais*; *Epipsychidion*; Scott, *Kenilworth*; Faraday develops principles of electric motor

1822 . . . . Byron, *The Vision of Judgement*; *Werner*; Hemans, *Welsh Melodies*; Scott, *The Fortunes of Nigel*; Shelley, *Hellas*; Wordsworth, *Ecclesiastical Sketches*; Caledonian Canal completed; Daguerre's *Diorama* opens in Paris

1823 . . . . Byron, *The Age of Bronze*; *The Island*; *Don Juan* VI–XIV; Hazlitt, *Liber Amoris*; Hemans, *The Siege of Valencia, and Other Poems*; Scott, *Quentin Durward*; Mechanics' Institutes founded in London and Glasgow; Macintosh develops rubberized cloth; first issues of *The Lancet*

1824 . . . . Hogg, *Confessions of a Justified Sinner*; Letitia Landon, *The Improvisatrice*; Scott, *Redgauntlet*; foundation of Royal Society for the Prevention of Cruelty to Animals; foundation of the National Gallery in London

1825 . . . . Barbauld, *Works* (ed. Aikin); Coleridge, *Aids to Reflection*; Hazlitt, *The Spirit of the Age*; Hemans, *The Forest Sanctuary*; Landon, *The Troubadour*; Scott, *The Betrothed*; first steam locomotive railway opens between Stockton and Darlington; foundation of Society for the Diffusion of Useful Knowledge

1826	Barrett, *An Essay on Mind, with Other Poems*; Hazlitt, *The Plain Speaker*; Scott, *Woodstock*; Shelley, *The Last Man*; foundation of University College London; Niepce takes the first photograph
1827	Clare, *The Shepherd's Calendar*; De Quincey, 'On Murder Considered as One of the Fine Arts'; Scott, *Chronicles of the Canongate*; Tennyson, *Poems by Two Brothers*; Niepce makes photographs on a metal plate; invention of sulphur matches; water turbine developed; Dalton, *New System of Chemical Philosophy* Pt. II
1828	Hemans, *Records of Woman, with Other Poems*; Hunt, *Lord Byron and Some Contemporaries*; Scott, *Tales of a Grandfather* Pt. I; Schubert, Symphony No. 9
1829	Hogg, *The Shepherd's Calendar*; Scott, *Tales of a Grandfather* Pt. II; Stephenson's Rocket under construction; Braille develops reading system for blind people; publication of the first Baedeker guide book; Rossini, *William Tell*
1830	Cobbett, *Rural Rides*; Hemans, *Songs of the Affections*; Moore, *Letters and Journals of Lord Byron, with Notices of his Life*; Scott, *Letters on Demonology and Witchcraft*; *Tales of a Grandfather* Pts III & IV: Tennyson, *Poems, Chiefly Lyrical*; opening of the Manchester–Liverpool Railway; foundation of the Royal Geographic Society; Lyell's *Principles of Geology*
1832	Harriet Martineau, *Illustrations of Political Economy*; Charles Babbage, *On the Economy of Machinery and Manufactures*; Byron (posth.), *The Works of Lord Byron*, 17 vols; Scott, *Tales of My Landlord*; Tennyson, *Poems*; Shelley, *The Mask of Anarchy*; Benjamin Disraeli, *Contrarini Fleming*; Wordsworth, *The Poetical Works*; Edward Bulwer-Lytton, *Eugene Aram*; Frances Trollope, *Domestic Manners of the Americans*; *Tait's Edinburgh Magazine* founded; Morse invents telegraph; Constable, *Waterloo Bridge from Whitehall Stairs*
1833	Charles Dickens's first published story, 'A Dinner at Poplar Walk', in *Monthly Magazine*; Barrett Browning, trans. *Prometheus Bound*; Caroline Bowles, *Tales of the Factories*; Hemans, *Hymns on the Works of Nature of the Use of Children*; Charles Lamb, *The Last Essays of Elia*; John Henry Newman, *Tracts for the Times* begins; Bulwer-Lytton, *England and the English*; the Oxford Movement begins; Charles Babbage describes the analytical engine
1834	Thomas Carlyle, *Sartor Resartus*; Maria Edgeworth, *Helen*; Bulwer-Lytton, *The Last Days of Pompeii*; De Quincey, *Recollections of the Lakes*; hansom cabs in London
1835	Browning, *Paracelsus*; Bulwer-Lytton, *Rienzi*; Clare, *The Rural Muse*; Wordsworth, *Yarrow Revisited & Other Poems*; Brunel's Great Western Railway between London and Bristol opened; Charles Darwin arrives at Galapagos Islands; Constable, *The Valley Farm*

6

1836 . . . . Dickens, *Sketches by Boz*; Baillie, *Dramas*, 3 vols; Disraeli, *Henrietta Temple*; Walter Savage Landor, *Pericles and Aspasia*; Frederick Marryat, *Mister Midshipman Easy*; London Working Men's Society founded

1837 . . . . Carlyle, *The French Revolution*; Dickens, *The Pickwick Papers*; Disraeli, *Venetia*; Martineau, *Society in America*; Frances Trollope, *The Vicar of Wrexhill*; Pitman invents shorthand; smallpox epidemic; Euston Station (first London railway station) opens

1838 . . . . Elizabeth Barrett, *The Seraphim and Other Poems*; Dickens, *Oliver Twist*; R. S. Surtees, *Jorrocks' Jaunts & Jollities*; Thackeray, *Yellowplush*; Frances Trollope, *The Widow Barnaby*; Charles Lyell, *Elements of Geology*; Wordsworth, *Sonnets*; National Gallery opens; Brunel's Great Western steamer crosses Atlantic; Abolition Act; public house licensing hours regulated

1839 . . . . Dickens, *Nicholas Nickleby*; Darwin, *Zoology of the Voyage of HMS Beagle* (5 vols); Sarah Stickney Ellis, *The Women of England*; Michael Faraday, *Experimental Researches in Electricity*; Carlyle, *Chartism*; Ainsworth, *Jack Sheppard*; Bulwer-Lytton, *Cardinal Richelieu*; Landon, *The Zenana & Minor Poems*; Shelley, *Poetical Works*, ed. Mary Shelley; Martineau, *Deerbrook*; first Grand National; invention of daguerrotype; first Henley Royal Regatta; Kirkpatrick Macmillan constructs first bicycle

1840 . . . . Frances Trollope, *Michael Armstrong, Factory Boy*; Browning, 'Sordello'; Shelley, *A Defence of Poetry*; Thackeray, *Catherine*; Dickens, *Master Humphrey's Clock* begins serial publication; Catherine Napier, *Women's Rights and Duties*; Baillie, *Fugitive Verses*; Botanical Gardens at Kew open to public; Fox Talbot invents collotype photography; Penny Post; Pugin and Barry begin building new Palace of Westminster; Nelson's Column erected

1841 . . . . Browning, 'Pippa Passes'; *Punch* begins publication; Dickens, *the Old Curiosity Shop*, *Barnaby Rudge*; Carlyle, *On Heroes, Hero Worship & the Heroic in History*; Macaulay, *Warren Hastings*; Thackeray, *Samuel Titmarsh & the Great Hoggarty Diamond*; first issue of Bradshaw's Railway Guide; London Library opens; Thomas Cook arranges first travel excursion; Fox Talbot awarded photographic process patent

1842 . . . . Tennyson, *Poems*, 2 vols; Browning, *Dramatic Lyrics*; Chadwick, *Report on the Sanitary Condition of the Labouring Population*; Dickens, *American Notes*; Bulwer-Lytton, *Last of the Barons*; Macaulay, *Lays of Ancient Rome*; Pentonville Prison opened; London–Manchester railway; *Illustrated News* begins publication

1843 . . . . Dickens, *A Christmas Carol*; Hood, 'Song of the Shirt'; Tennyson, 'Morte D'Arthur', 'Locksley Hall'; Carlyle, *Past & Present*; Ruskin, *Modern Painters, Vol. 1*; John Stuart Mill, 'Logic'; Barrett Browning, *The Cry of the Children*; Browning, *Return of the Druses*; Macaulay, *Essays*; Ainsworth, *Windsor Castle*; *The Economist* begins publication; Wordsworth appointed Poet Laureate; Theatre Regulation Act

1844 . . . . Disraeli, *Coningsby*; Thackeray, *Barry Lyndon*; Dickens, *Martin Chuzzlewit*; Barrett Browning, *Poems*; Coventry Patmore, *Poems*; Dickens, *The Chimes*; YMCA founded; Turner, *Rain, Steam and Speed*; first public telegraph line; first public baths

1845 . . . . Engels, *The Condition of the Working Class in England*; Disraeli, *Sybil, or the Two Nations*; Dickens, *The Cricket on the Hearth*; Browning, *Dramatic Romances*; Newman, *Essay on Development*; Carlyle, *Oliver Cromwell's Letters & Speeches*; De Quincey, *Suspiria De Profundis*; first submarine cable laid across English Channel; Oxford–Cambridge boat race staged at Putney for first time

1846 . . . . George Eliot, translation of Strauss, *Das Leben Jesu*; Dickens, *The Battle of Life*; G. W. M. Reynolds, *The Mysteries of London*; Edward Lear, *Book of Nonsense*; the Brontë sisters, *Poems by Currer, Ellis, & Acton Bell*; Dickens, *Pictures from Italy*; Dickens and Angela Burdett Coutts establish Home for Homeless Women; Elizabeth Barrett marries Robert Browning; planet Neptune discovered; protoplasm discovered; Turner, *Angel Standing in the Sun*

1847 . . . . Charlotte Brontë, *Jane Eyre*; Emily Brontë, *Wuthering Heights*; serialization of Thackeray's *Vanity Fair* begins; Tennyson, *The Princess*; Marryat, *The Children of the New Forest*; Disraeli, *Tancred*; Anthony Trollope, *The Macdermots of Ballycloran*; Rymer, *Varney the Vampire*; chloroform used as anaesthetic

1848 . . . . Dickens, *Dombey & Son*; Anne Brontë, *The Tenant of Wildfell Hall*; Elizabeth Gaskell, *Mary Barton*; Marx and Engels, *The Communist Manifesto*; Macauley, *History of England*; Mill, *Principles of Political Economy*; Newman, *Loss & Gain*; Jewsbury, *The Half Sisters*; Pre-Raphaelite Brotherhood founded by Rossetti, Holman Hunt, Millais; Cambridge University Fitzwilliam Museum completed; Millais, *Ophelia*; higher education for governesses opened at Oxford University;

1849 . . . . C. Brontë, *Shirley*; Henry Mayhew, *London Labour & the London Poor*; Ruskin, *The Seven Lamps of Architecture*; Bulwer-Lytton, *The Caxtons*; Matthew Arnold, *Strayed Reveller & Other Poems*; Baillie, *Ahalya Baee: A Poem*; Holman Hunt, *Rienzi*; Macaulay, *History of England*; Bedford College for Women founded; Karl Marx moves to London

6

1850 . . . . Charles Kingsley, *Alton Locke*; Tennyson, *In Memoriam A.H.H.*; Dickens, *David Copperfield*; Barrett Browning, *Sonnets from the Portuguese*; Browning, *Christmas-Eve and Christmas-Day*; Wilkie Collins, *Antonina, or the Fall of Rome*; Bunsen burner invented; Tennyson appointed Poet Laureate; Dickens founds *Household Words*; Pre-Raphaelites found *The Germ*; Dover and Calais connected by telegraph; Millais, *Christ in the House of His Parents*; Public Libraries Act for England and Wales

1851 . . . . Ruskin, *The King of the Golden River*; *The Stones of Venice*; Barrett Browning, *Casa Guidi Windows*; Ballie, *The Dramatic & Poetical Works of Joanna Baillie*; Meredith, *Poems*; Carlyle, *Life of John Sterling*; Le Fanu, *Ghost Stories and Tales of Mystery*; Harriet Taylor Mill, 'The Enfranchisement of Women'; George Eliot assistant editor of *Westminster Review*; Great Exhibition, Crystal Palace; William Thomson publishes first and second laws of thermodynamics

1852 . . . . Charles Reade, *Masks & Faces*; Houses of Parliament reopened; first women's public toilets opened in London; Great Ormond Street Hospital opened; Holman Hunt, *The Light of the World*

1853 . . . . Gaskell, *Cranford*; C. Brontë, *Villette*; Dickens, *Bleak House*; Arnold, *Poems*; Charlotte Yonge, *The Heir of Redcliffe*; Charles Dickens gives first public readings

1854 . . . . Dickens, *Hard Times*; Eliot, transl. of Feuerbach, *The Essence of Christianity*; Tennyson, 'The Charge of the Light Brigade'; Patmore, *The Angel in the House*; Wilkie Collins, *Hide & Seek*; London Underground begins construction; Working Men's College founded

1855 . . . . Browning, *Men and Women*; Gaskell, *North and South*; Trollope, *The Warden*; Jewsbury, *Constance Herbert*; Tennyson, *Maud & Other Poems*; *Daily Telegraph* est.

1856 . . . . Wilkie Collins, *After Dark*; Eliot, 'The Natural History of German Life', 'Silly Novels by Lady Novelists'; Jewsbury, *The Sorrows of Gentility*; National Portrait Gallery opened

1857 . . . . Eliot, *Scenes of Clerical Life*; Dickens, *Little Dorrit*; Thomas Hughes, *Tom Brown's School Days*; Trollope, *Barchester Towers*; David Livingstone, *Missionary Travels and Researches in South Africa*; Barrett Browning, *Aurora Leigh*; Collins, *The Dead Secret*; Gaskell, *The Life of Charlotte Brontë*; Thackeray, *The Virginians*; laying of Atlantic telegraph begun; Sheffield F.C., world's first football club; Charles Hallé founds Hallé Concerts in Manchester; Science Museum, South Kensington, founded

1858 . . . . Robert Ballantyne, *Coral Island*; Trollope, *The Three Clerks*, *Doctor Thorne*; *English Woman's Journal* begins publication; William Frith, *Derby Day*

1859 . . . . Darwin, *On the Origin of Species*; Tennyson, *Idylls of the King*; Eliot, *Adam Bede*; Dickens, *A Tale of Two Cities*; Mill, *On Liberty*; Samuel Smiles, *Self-Help*; Eliot, *The Lifted Veil*; Wilkie Collins, *The Queen of Hearts*; Suez Canal begins construction; Dickens founds *All the Year Round*; Big Ben first used

1860 . . . . Eliot, *The Mill on the Floss*; Wilkie Collins, *The Woman in White*; Ruskin, *Unto this Last*; Barrett Browning, *Poems before Congress*; Trollope, *Castle Richmond*; Braddon, *Three Times Dead*; *Cornhill Magazine* started

1861 . . . . Ellen Wood, *East Lynne*; Isabella Beeton, *Book of Household Management*; Dickens, *Great Expectations*, *The Uncommercial Traveller*; Palgrave, *Golden Treasury*; Trollope, *Framley Parsonage*; Braddon, *Trail of the Serpent*; Eliot, *Silas Marner*; Reade, *The Cloister & the Hearth*; first English cricket series in Australia; Royal Academy of Music founded

1862 . . . . Braddon, *Lady Audley's Secret*; Christina Rossetti, *Goblin Market*; Wilkie Collins, *No Name*

1863 . . . . Charles Lyell, *Antiquity of Man*; Reade, *Hard Cash*; Kingsley, *The Water Babies*; Thackeray, *The Roundabout Papers*; Eliot, *Romola*; Gaskell, *Sylvia's Lovers*; Trollope, *Rachel Ray*; Braddon, *Aurora Floyd*, *Eleanor's Victory*, *John Marchmont's Legacy*; Mill, *Utilitarianism*; D. G. Rossetti, *Beata Beatrix*; Whistler, *Little White Girl*

1864 . . . . Newman, *Apologia Pro Vita Sua*; Tennyson, *Idylls of the Hearth*; Trollope, *The Small House at Allington*; Herbert Spencer, *Principles of Biology*; Gaskell, *Wives and Daughters*; Braddon, *The Doctor's Wife*; Red Cross founded; first edition of *Wisden Cricketers' Almanack* published

1865 . . . . Dickens, *Our Mutual Friend*; Lewis Carroll, *Alice's Adventures in Wonderland*; Arnold, *Essays in Criticism*; Claude Bernard, *An Introduction to the Study of Experimental Medicine*; Trollope, *Miss Mackenzie, Can you Forgive Her?*; Swinburne, 'Atalanta in Calydon'

1866 . . . . Eliot, *Felix Holt*; Swinburne, *Poems and Ballads*; Ruskin, *Crown of Wild Olive*; Wilkie Collins, *Armadale*; Trollope, *The Belton Estate*; Braddon, *The Lady's Mile*; cholera epidemic; Royal Aeronautical Society founded; Dr T. J. Barnardo opens his first home for destitute children in Stepney, London

1867 . . . . Ouida, *Under Two Flags*; Arnold, 'Dover Beach'; Marx, *Das Kapital*; Walter Bagehot, *The English Constitution*; first public readings in USA by Dickens; Second Reform Act

1868 . . . . Wilkie Collins, *The Moonstone*; Eliza Linn Linton, *The Girl of the Period*; Browning, *The Ring and the Book*; Trollope, *Linda Tressel*; Eliot, *The Spanish Gypsy*

6

1869 . . . . Arnold, *Culture and Anarchy*; Mill, *On the Subjection of Women*; R. D. Blackmore, *Lorna Doone*; Trollope, *Phineas Finn, the Irish Member, He Knew He Was Right*; Girton College, Cambridge, admits women

1870 . . . . Dickens, *The Mystery of Edwin Drood* (unfinished); Herbert Spencer, *Principles of Psychology*; Wilkie Collins, *Man & Wife*

1871 . . . . Darwin, *Descent of Man*; Carroll, *Through the Looking-Glass*; James Maxwell Clark, *Theory of Heat*; Hardy, *Desperate Remedies*; James, *Watch & Ward*; Ruskin, *Fors Clavigera*; FA Cup est.; Rossetti, *The Dream of Dante*; Albert Hall opened; bank holidays introduced

1872 . . . . Hardy, *Under the Greenwood Tree*; Eliot, *Middlemarch*; Darwin, *The Expression of Emotions in Man*; Samuel Butler, *Brewhon*; Thomas Cook world travel packages est.; Whistler, *The Artist's Mother*

1873 . . . . Pater, *Studies in the Renaissance*; Mill, *Autobiography*; Hardy, *A Pair of Blue Eyes*; Wilkie Collins, *The New Magdalen*; Trollope, *The Eustace Diamonds*

1874 . . . . Hardy, *Far from the Madding Crowd*; James Thomson, *The City of Dreadful Night*; William B. Carpenter, *Principles of Mental Physiology*; Trollope, *Phineas Redux*

1875 . . . . Trollope, *The Way We Live Now*; London Medical School for Women founded

1876 . . . . Eliot, *Daniel Deronda*; Henry James, *Roderick Hudson*; Alexander Graham Bell invents the telephone; Sophia Jex Blake qualifies as a doctor

1877 . . . . Thomas Edison's phonograph; tennis at Wimbledon; Charles Bradlaugh and Annie Besant tried for obscenity for publishing information about contraception

1878 . . . . Hardy, *Return of the Native*

1879 . . . . Ibsen, *A Doll's House*

1880 . . . . Eliot, *The Mill on the Floss*; electric light bulb independently invented by Edison in the USA and Swan in Great Britain

1881 . . . . Henry James, *Portrait of a Lady*; Ibsen, *Ghosts*; D'Oyly Carte builds the Savoy Theatre, first to be lit by electricity

1882 . . . . Louis Stevenson, *Treasure Island*

1883 . . . . Oliver Schreiner, *The Story of an African Farm*

1884 . . . . Trollope, *An Autobiography*; *Oxford English Dictionary* begins publication

1885 . . . . Pater, *Marius the Epicurean*; H. Rider Haggard, *King Solomon's Mines*; internal combustion engine invented; Pasteur's vaccine against rabies

6

1886 . . . . George Gissing, *Demos*; Stevenson, *Dr Jekyll and Mr Hyde*; first translation of Marx's *Capital* published; Hardy, *Mayor of Casterbridge*; James, *The Bostonians*

1887 . . . . Rider Haggard, *She*; *Allan Quatermain*; Arthur Conan Doyle, *A Study in Scarlet*; Pater, *Imaginary Portraits*; Hardy, *The Woodlanders*; Goodwin invents celluloid film; the speed of light is measured for first time; Victoria's Golden Jubilee

1888 . . . . Rudyard Kipling, *Plain Tales from the Hills*; Kodak no. 1 camera and roll film invented and marketed; Forth Rail Bridge completed; Jack the Ripper murders

1889 . . . . Yeats, *The Wanderings of Oisin*; Charles Booth, *Life and Labour of the People in London*; Pater, *Appreciations*; Wilde, 'The Decay of Lying'; first London performance of Ibsen's *A Doll's House*; Eiffel Tower built

1890 . . . . Wilde, *The Picture of Dorian Gray*; J. G. Frazer, *The Golden Bough* begins publication; discovery of tetanus and diphtheria viruses; William James, *Principles of Psychology*

1891 . . . . Wilde, 'The Soul of Man under Socialism'; Gissing, *New Grub Street*; Hardy, *Tess of the D'Urbervilles*; William Morris, *New from Nowhere*

1892 . . . . Kipling, *Barrack-Room Ballads*; Wilde, *Lady Windermere's Fan*; Doyle, *The Adventures of Sherlock Holmes*; Diesel's internal combustion engine invented

1893 . . . . Wilde, *A Woman of No Importance*; Yeats, *The Celtic Twilight*; Gissing, *The Odd Women*; Arthur Wing Pinero, *The Second Mrs Tanqueray*; Henry Ford's first cars manufactured; flashbulb (for photography) invented

1894 . . . . George Moore, *Esther Waters*; Kipling, *The Jungle Book*; Arthur Morrison, *Tales of Mean Streets*; Mona Caird, *The Daughters of Danaus*; George Bernard Shaw, *Arms and the Man*; The *Yellow Book* founded; Emile Berliner invents gramophone disc

1895 . . . . Wilde, *The Importance of Being Earnest* and *An Ideal Husband*; Hardy, *Jude the Obscure*; Wells, *The Time Machine*; Allen, *The Woman Who Did*; English trans. of Max Nordau's *Degeneration*; London School of Economics founded; Röentgen discovers x-rays; Marconi invents wireless telegraph; Lumière brothers invent the cinematograph; Gillette safety razor; Oscar Wilde tried and imprisoned

1896 . . . . A. E. Housman, *A Shropshire Lad*; Morrison, *A Child of the Jago*; London School of Economics opens to students

6

1897 . . . . Bram Stoker, *Dracula*; Wells, *The Invisible Man* and *The War of the Worlds*; Gissing, *The Whirlpool*; Joseph Conrad, *The Nigger of the 'Narcissus'*; Sarah Grand, *The Beth Book*; Richard Marsh, *The Beetle*; Tate Gallery opens

1898 . . . . Wilde, *The Ballad of Reading Gaol*; Arnold Bennett, *A Man from the North*; Hardy, *Wessex Poems*; James, *The Turn of the Screw*; *Country Life* founded

1899 . . . . Kipling, *Stalky and Co*; Conrad, *Heart of Darkness* serialized; Arthur Symons, *The Symbolist Movement in Literature*

1900 . . . . Conrad, *Lord Jim*; Symons, *The Symbolist Movement in Literature*; Yeats, *The Shadowy Waters*; Max Planck publishes theories of quantum physics; Freud, *The Interpretation of Dreams*

1901 . . . . Kipling, *Kim*; Marconi transmits radio waves across the Atlantic

1902 . . . . Bennett, *Anna of the Five Towns*; William James, *Varieties of Religious Experience*; *Times Literary Supplement* founded

1903 . . . . Butler, *The Way of All Flesh*; Wright brothers succeed in flying; Pankhurst founds the Women's Social and Political Union

1904 . . . . Conrad, *Nostromo*; Freud, *The Psychopathology of Everyday Life*

1905 . . . . Wilde, *De Profundis*; Wells, *A Modern Utopia* and *Kipps*; Forster, *Where Angels Fear to Tread*; Einstein describes the special theory of relativity; Freud, *Three Essays on Sexuality*

1906 . . . . John Galsworthy, *The Man of Property*

1907 . . . . Conrad, *The Secret Agent*; Synge, *The Playboy of the Western World*; Forster, *The Longest Journey*; Picasso exhibits *Les Demoiselles d'Avignon*; first Cubist exhibition in Paris; Baden Powell founds Boy Scout movement

1908 . . . . Bennett, *The Old Wives' Tale*; Wells, *Tono-Bungay*; Forster, *A Room with a View*

1909 . . . . Wells, *Ann Veronica*; Blériot flies Channel

1910 . . . . Forster, *Howards End*; Bennett, *Clayhanger*; Wells, *The History of Mr Polly*; Yeats, *The Green Helmet and Other Poems*; Ford Madox Ford, *A Call*; Roger Fry mounts Post-Impressionist Exhibition in London

1911 . . . . D. H. Lawrence, *The White Peacock*; Ezra Pound, *Cantos*; Conrad, *Under Western Eyes*; Rupert Brooke, *Poems*; Wells, *The New Machiavelli*; Bennett, *Hilda Lessways* and *The Card*; Katherine Mansfield, *In a German Pension*; Amundsen reaches the South Pole; Rutherford publishes *Theory of Atomic Structure*

1912 . . . . C. G. Jung, *The Theory of Psychoanalysis*; Futurist exhibition, Paris; *Titanic* disaster

1913 . . . . Lawrence, *Sons and Lovers*; Pound, *Personae*; Freud, *Totem and Taboo*; Marcel Proust, *Swann's Way*; Thomas Mann, *Death in Venice*

1914 . . . . James Joyce, *Dubliners*; Yeats, *Responsibilities*

1915 . . . . Rupert Brook, *1914 and Other Poems*; Virginia Woolf, *The Voyage Out*; Pound, *Cathay*; Lawrence, *The Rainbow*; Dorothy Richardson, *Pilgrimage*; Ford, *The Good Soldier*

1916 . . . . Joyce, *A Portrait of the Artist as a Young Man*; H.D., *Sea Garden*; Apollinaire, *Le Poète Assassiné*; Picabia, *La Fille Née Sans Mère*; Dada and Cabaret Voltaire, Zurich

1917 . . . . T. S. Eliot, *Prufrock and Other Observations*; Pound, 'Three Cantos'; Duchamp, *Fountain*

1918 . . . . Apollinaire, *Calligrammes*; Joyce, *Exiles*; Lytton Strachey, *Eminent Victorians*; Woolf, *Night and Day*; Willa Cather, *My Antonia*; Rebecca West, *The Return of the Soldier*; Lewis, *Tarr*; Mansfield, *Prelude*; Berlin Dada launched; Tristan Tzara, 'Dada Manifesto, 1918'

1919 . . . . Pound, *Hugh Selwyn Mauberley*; Yeats, *The Wild Swans at Coole*; Eliot, 'Tradition and the Individual Talent'; Hardy, *Collected Poems*; El Lissitsky, *Beat the Whites with the Red Wedge*; Bauhaus founded, Weimar; 'Manifesto of the Bauhaus'

1920 . . . . Wilfred Owen, *Poems*; Freud, *Beyond the Pleasure Principle*; Roger Fry, *Vision and Design*; F. Scott Fitzgerald, *This Side of Paradise*; Jessie Weston, *From Ritual to Romance*; Eliot, *The Sacred Wood*; Yeats, *Michael Robartes and the Dancer*; Lawrence, *Women in Love*; Katherine Mansfield, *Bliss and Other Stories*; Edward Lutyens's Cenotaph erected

1921 . . . . John Dos Passos, *Three Soldiers*; Aldous Huxley, *Crome Yellow*

1922 . . . . Eliot, *The Waste Land*; Joyce, *Ulysses*; Woolf, *Jacob's Room*; Edith Sitwell, *Façade*; e. e. cummings, *The Enormous Room*; BBC founded

1923 . . . . Freud, *Ego and Id*; Stevens, *Harmonium*; Williams, *Spring and All*; e. e. cummings, *Tulips and Chimneys*; Mina Loy, *Lunar Baedecke*; Mary Butts, *Speed the Plough*; Leon Trotsky, *Literature and Revolution*; Schwitters' first 'Merzbau' built, Hanover; Bessie Smith's first record, 'Downhearted Blues'

1924 . . . . Woolf, 'Mr Bennett and Mrs Brown'; Marianne Moore, *Observations*; Forster, *A Passage to India*; Mann, *The Magic Mountain*; Harrison, *Mythology*; first Surrealist Manifesto; *Transatlantic Review*

6

1925.................... Woolf, *Mrs Dalloway* and *The Common Reader*; Stein, *The Making of Americans*; Fitzgerald, *The Great Gatsby*; Alain Locke (ed.), *The New Negro*; Yeats, *A Vision*; Franz Kafka, *The Trial*; Adolf Hitler, *Mein Kampf*; Ernest Hemingway, *In Our Time*; Williams, *In the American Grain*; Dos Passos, *Manhattan Transfer*; Theodor Dreiser, *An American Tragedy*; Hugh MacDiarmid, *Sangschaw*; Edwin Muir, *First Poems*; Neue Sachlichkeit exhibition, Berlin; Emily Dickinson, *Complete Poems*, post. published

1926.................... Langston Hughes, *The Weary Blues*; H.D., *Palimpsest*; Stein, 'Composition as Explanation'; Hemingway, *The Sun Also Rises*; Sean O'Casey, *The Plough and Stars*; MacDiarmid, *A Drunk Man Looks at the Thistle*; Fritz Lang, *Metropolis*

1927.................... Woolf, *To the Lighthouse*; Alfred Döblin, *Berlin Alexanderplatz*; Joyce, *Pomes Penyeach*; Kafka, *Amerika*; Lewis, *The Wild Body*; Hemingway, *Men without Women*; Eliot, *Journey of the Magi*; Jean Rhys, *The Left Bank*; Lindbergh flies Atlantic solo

1928.................... Yeats, *The Tower*; Lawrence, *Lady Chatterley's Lover* and *Collected Poems*; Woolf, *Orlando*; Djuna Barnes, *Ladies' Almanack*; René Magritte, *The Treason of Images*; Sergei Eisenstein, *October* (film); Radclyffe Hall's *The Well of Loneliness* banned for obscenity; George Gershwin, *An American in Paris*

1929.................... Bertolt Brecht, *The Threepenny Opera*; Robert Graves, *Goodbye to All That*; Woolf, *A Room of One's Own*; Hemingway, *A Farewell to Arms*; Lawrence, *Pansies*; William Faulkner, *The Sound and the Fury*; Jean Cocteau, *Les Enfants Terribles*; J. B. Priestley, *The Good Companions*; C. Day Lewis, *Transitional Poem*; Second Surrealist Manifesto

1930.................... Lewis, *The Apes of God*; Eliot, *Ash Wednesday*; Hart Crane, *The Bridge*; Dos Passos, *U.S.A.*; Faulkner, *As I Lay Dying*; Rhys, *After Leaving Mr Mackenzie*; Auden, *Poems*; F. R. Leavis, *Mass Civilisation and Minority Culture*; William Empson, *Seven Types of Ambiguity*

1931.................... Woolf, *The Waves* and *The Second Common Reader*; Eugene O'Neill, *Mourning Becomes Electra*

1932.................... Aldous Huxley, *Brave New World*; Nathanael West, *Miss Lonelyhearts*; Lew Grassic Gibbon, *A Scots Quair*

1933.................... Stein, *The Autobiography of Alice B. Toklas*; Eliot, *The Use of Poetry and the Use of Criticism*; Yeats, *The Winding Stair*; Woolf, *Flush*; Walter Greenwood, *Love on the Dole*; George Orwell, *Down and Out in Paris and London*

1934.................... Nathanael West, *A Cool Million*; Pound, *The A.B.C. of Reading*; Zora Neal Hurston, *Jonah's Gourd Vine*; Wyndham Lewis, *Men without Art*; Fitzgerald, *Tender is the Night*; Rhys, *Voyage in the Dark*; Graves, *I, Claudius*; Orwell, *Burmese Days*

1935 . . . . Stevens, *Ideas of Order*; Hurston, *Mules and Men*; Eliot, *Murder in the Cathedral* and *Four Quartets*; W. H. Auden and Christopher Isherwood, *The Dog Beneath the Skin*, *Mr Norris Changes Trans*; Patrick Hamilton, *Twenty Thousand Streets Under the Sky: A London Trilogy*

1936 . . . . Dylan Thomas, *Twenty-five Poems*; Stevie Smith, *Novel on Yellow Paper*; Alain Locke (ed.), *Negro Art Past and Present*; Walter Benjamin, *The Work of Art in the Age of Mechanical Reproduction*; Margaret Mitchell, *Gone with the Wind*; Charles Chaplin, *Modern Times*

1937 . . . . Stevens, *The Man with the Blue Guitar*; Woolf, *The Years*; Barnes, *Nightwood*; David Jones, *In Parenthesis*; Lewis, *Blasting and Bombardiering*; Isherwood, *Sally Bowles*; Orwell, *The Road to Wigan Pier*; Entartete Kunst (Degenerate Art) Exhibition, Munich; New Bauhaus, Chicago; Picasso, *Guernica*

1938 . . . . Stein, *Dr Faustus Lights the Lights*; Woolf, *Three Guineas*; Samuel Beckett, *Murphy*; Louis MacNeice, *The Agamemnon of Aeschylus*; Richard Wright, *Uncle Tom's Children*; Orwell, *Homage to Catalonia*

1939 . . . . Joyce, *Finnegans Wake*; Nathanael West, *The Day of the Locust*; Isherwood, *Goodbye to Berlin*; Eliot, *Old Possum's Book of Practical Cats*; Rhys, *Good Morning Midnight*; John Steinbeck, *The Grapes of Wrath*

1940 . . . . Eliot, *East Coker*; Christina Stead, *The Man Who Loved Children*; Carson McCullers, *The Heart Is a Lonely Hunter*; Orwell, *Inside the Whale*

1941 . . . . Fitzgerald, *The Last Tycoon*; Hamilton, *Hangover Square*; James Agee, *Let Us Now Praise Famous Men*; Rebecca West, *Black Lamb and Grey Falcon*

1942 . . . . Faulkner, *Go Down, Moses*; Eliot, *Little Gidding*; Albert Camus, *The Outsider*

1943 . . . . Jackson Pollock, *Guardians of the Secret*

1944 . . . . William Carlos Williams, *The Wedge*; H.D., *The Walls Do Not Fall*; Tennessee Williams, *The Glass Menagerie*; Saul Bellow, *Dangling Man*

1945 . . . . Pound, *Pisan Cantos*; Dylan Thomas, *Fern Hill*; Wright, *Black Boy*; Hughes, *The Big Sea*; Evelyn Waugh, *Brideshead Revisited*; Mitford, *The Pursuit of Love*; Larkin, *The North Ship*; Betjeman, *New Bats in Old Belfries*; Orwell, *Animal Farm*; Brittain, *Peter Grimes*

1946 . . . . Larkin, *Jill*; D. Thomas, *Deaths and Entrances*; Russell, *History of Western Philosophy*; Arts Council founded

1947 . . . . Ivy Compton Burnett, *Manservant and Maidservant*

6

1948 . . . . Graham Greene, *The Heart of the Matter*; Fry, *The Lady's Not for Burning*; Waugh, *The Loved One*; Rattigan, *The Browning Version*; F. R. Leavis, *The Great Tradition*; T. S. Eliot, *Notes Towards a Definition of Culture*

1949 . . . . Bowen, *The Heat of the Day*; Mitford, *Love in a Cold Climate*; Orwell, *Nineteen Eighty-Four*; Eliot, *The Cocktail Party*

1950 . . . . Cooper, *Scenes from Provincial Life*; Greene, *The Third Man*; Pym, *Some Tame Gazelle*; Waugh, *Helena*; Lessing, *The Grass Is Singing*

1951 . . . . Manning, *School for Love*; Larkin, *Poems*

1952 . . . . Christie, *The Mousetrap*; D. Thomas, *Collected Poems*; Lessing, *Martha Quest*; Rattigan, *The Deep Blue Sea*

1953 . . . . Hartley, *The Go-Between*; Lehmann, *The Echoing Grove*; Wain, *Hurry on Down*; Ian Fleming, *Casino Royale*; Hillary and Tenzing climb Everest

1954 . . . . D. Thomas, *Under Milk Wood*; Amis, *Lucky Jim*; Golding, *Lord of the Flies*; Lessing, *A Proper Marriage*; Lamming, *The Emigrants*

1955 . . . . Beckett, *Waiting for Godot*; R. S. Thomas, *Song at the Year's Turning*; Bowen, *A World of Love*; Greene, *The Quiet American*; Rattigan, *Separate Tables*; Larkin, *The Less Deceived*

1956 . . . . John Osborne, *Look Back in Anger*; Sam Selvon, *The Lonely Londoners*; Lewis, *The Chronicles of Narnia*; Wilson, *Anglo-Saxon Attitudes*; Behan, *The Quare Fellow*; Tolkien, *The Lord of the Rings*; transatlantic telephone service started

1957 . . . . Ted Hughes, *Hawk in the Rain*; Braine, *Room at the Top*; MacInnes, *City of Spades*; Waugh, *The Ordeal of Gilbert Penfold*; Naipaul, *The Mystic Masseur*; Osborne, *The Entertainer*; Murdoch, *The Sandcastle*; Larkin, *A Girl in Winter*; Hoggart, *The Uses of Literacy*; Wolfenden Report on sexuality

1958 . . . . H. E. Bates, *The Darling Buds of May*; Murdoch, *The Bell*; Delaney, *A Taste of Honey*; Sillitoe, *Saturday Night and Sunday Morning*; Behan, *The Hostage*; Pinter, *The Birthday Party*; Betjeman, *Collected Poems*; Scott, *The Alien Sky*; Galbraith, *The Affluent Society*; first stereo recordings

1959 . . . . Bradbury, *Eating People Is Wrong*; Wesker, *Rots*; P. H. Johnson, *The Unspeakable Skipton*; Laurie Lee, *Cider with Rosie*; MacInnes, *Absolute Beginners*; Peake, *Gormenghast Trilogy*; Sillitoe, *The Loneliness of the Long Distance Runner*; Waterhouse, *Billy Liar*; Arden, *Serjeant Musgrave's Dance*; first section of M1 motorway opened; C. P. Snow, *Two Cultures*

6

1960 . . . . Pinter, *The Caretaker*; L. R. Banks, *The L-Shaped Room*; Lessing, *In Pursuit of the English*; Barstow, *A Kind of Loving*; Durrell, *The Alexandria Quartet*; Harris, *The Palace of the Peacock*; Storey, *This Sporting Life*; Plath, *The Colossus*; *New Left Review* begins; heart pacemaker invented; *Coronation Street* begins; the *Lady Chatterley* trial

1961 . . . . Waugh, *Sword of Honour Trilogy*; Spark, *The Prime of Miss Jean Brodie*; Osborne, *Luther*; DNA structure detected; *Private Eye* begins

1962 . . . . Burgess, *A Clockwork Orange*; Lessing, *The Golden Notebook*; Alvarez (ed.), *The New Poetry*; Sampson, *The Anatomy of Britain*; Jamaica, Trinidad and Uganda become independent; end of national service

1963 . . . . Naipaul, *Mr Stone and the Knights Companion*; Plath, *The Bell Jar*; Theatre Workshop, *Oh, What a Lovely War*; Dunn, *Up the Junction*; Brittain, *War Requiem*

1964 . . . . Larkin, *The Whitsun Weddings*; Wilson, *Late Call*; Selvon, *The Housing Lark*; Orton, *Entertaining Mr Sloane*; Marcuse, *One Dimensional Man*

1965 . . . . Plath, *Ariel*; Manning, *The Balkan Trilogy*; Bond, *Saved*; Drabble, *The Millstone*

1966 . . . . Orton, *Loot*; Fowles, *The Magus*; Rhys, *Wide Sargasso Sea*; Greene, *The Comedians*; Stoppard, *Rosencrantz and Guildenstern Are Dead*; Bunting, *Briggflatts*; *Cathy Come Home* televised

1967 . . . . Carter, *The Magic Toyshop*; Pinter, *The Homecoming*; Henri, Gough, Patten, *The Mersey Sound*; Naipaul, *The Mimic Men*; Dunn, *Poor Cow*; Jennings, *Collected Works*; first heart transplant

1968 . . . . Hines, *A Kestrel for a Knave*; Bond, *Early Morning*; theatre censorship ends; C. Day Lewis succeeds John Masefield as Poet Laureate

1969 . . . . Fowles, *The French Lieutenant's Woman*; Greene, *Travels with My Aunt*; Lessing, *Children of Violence*; Horovitz (ed.), *Children of Albion*; US astronauts walk on the moon; human eggs fertilized *in vitro*; Booker prize started

1970 . . . . Hughes, *Crow*; Snow, *Strangers and Brothers*; computer 'floppy' disks invented

1971 . . . . Hill, *Mercian Hymns*; Naipaul, *in a Free State*; Bond, *Lear*; decimalization of sterling currency

1972 . . . . Stoppard, *Jumpers*; Drabble, *The Needle's Eye*; Carter, *The Infernal Desire Machines of Doctor Hoffman*; John Betjeman appointed Poet Laureate

6

1973 . . . . Peter Schaffer, *Equus*; Murdoch, *The Black Prince*; Greene, *The Honorary Consul*; M. Amis, *The Rachel Papers*

1974 . . . . Larkin, *High Windows*; Lessing, *The Memoirs of a Survivor*; Burgess, *The Enderby Novels*; Murdoch, *The Sacred and Profane Love Machine*

1975 . . . . Griffiths, *Comedians*; Bradbury, *The History Man*; Jhabvala, *Heat and Dust*; Lodge, *Changing Places*; Powell, *A Dance to the Music of Time*; Scott, *The Raj Quartet*; Sinclair, *Lud Heat*; Rushdie, *Grimus*; Selvon, *Moses Ascending*; M. Amis, *Dead Babies*

1976 . . . . Lehmann, *A Sea-Grape Tree*; Tennant, *Hotel de Dream*; Concorde begins passenger service; National Theatre completed

1977 . . . . Scott, *Staying On*; Stoppard, *Professional Foul*; Carter, *The Passion of New Eve*; first AIDS deaths recognized in New York; Tom Nairn, *The Break-Up of Britain*; Virago Press publishes first book

1978 . . . . Hare, *Plenty*; McEwan, *The Cement Garden*; Murdoch, *The Sea, the Sea*; Weldon, *Praxis*; Tennant, *The Bad Sister*; Hill, *Tenebrae*; first 'test tube' baby

1979 . . . . Tennant, *Wild Nights*; Golding, *Darkness Visible*; Raine, *A Martian Sends a Postcard Home*; Naipaul, *A Bend in the River*; medical profession confirms that smoking causes cancer

1980 . . . . Manning, *The Levant Trilogy*; Burgess, *Earthly Powers*; Golding, *Rites of Passage*; Brenton, *The Romans in Britain*; Swift, *The Sweet-Shop Owner*; L. K. Johnson, *Inglan is a Bitch*

1981 . . . . Rushdie, *Midnight's Children*; D. M. Thomas, *The White Hotel*; Swift, *Shuttlecock*; IBM launches personal computer

1982 . . . . Barker, *Union Street*; Churchill, *Top Girls*; Gray, *Lanark*; Mo, *Sour Sweet*; compact disk players introduced

1983 . . . . Weldon, *The Life and Loves of a She Devil*; Swift, *Waterland*; Selvon, *Moses Migrating*; Rushdie, *Shame*

1984 . . . . Carter, *Nights at the Circus*; K. Amis, *Stanley and the Women*; Lodge, *Small World*; Raine, *Rich*; M. Amis, *Money*; Ballard, *Empire of the Sun*; I. Banks, *The Wasp Factory*; Barnes, *Flaubert's Parrot*; Roberts, *The Wild Girl*; Ted Hughes appointed Poet Laureate; first success of gene cloning

1985 . . . . Peter Ackroyd, *Hawksmoor*; Brenton and Hare, *Pravda*; Winterson, *Oranges Are Not the Only Fruit*; Hill, *Collected Poems*; Phillips, *The Final Passage*

1986 . . . . K. Amis, *The Old Devils*; Crace, *Continent*; Ishiguro, *An Artist of the Floating World*; laptop computers introduced

6

1987 . . . . Ackroyd, *Chatterton*; Churchill, *Serious Money*; Drabble, *The Radiant Way*; Lively, *Moon Tiger*; McEwan, *The Child in Time*; Winterson, *The Passion*; Chatwin, *The Songlines*; Gilroy, *There Ain't No Black in the Union Jack*

1988 . . . . Larkin, *Collected Poems*; Chatwin, *Utz*; Rushdie, *The Satanic Verses*; Lodge, *Nice Work*; Warner, *The Lost Father*; Moorcock, *Mother London*; Swift, *Out of This World*; Hollinghurst, *The Swimming-Pool Library*; Hawking, *A Brief History of Time*

1989 . . . . M. Amis, *London Fields*; Ackroyd, *First Light*; Ishiguro, *The Remains of the Day*; Winterson, *Sexing the Cherry*

1990 . . . . Byatt, *Possession*; Kureishi, *The Buddha of Suburbia*; Bainbridge, *An Awfully Big Adventure*; human gene experimentation

1991 . . . . M. Amis, *Time's Arrow*; Carter, *Wise Children*; Sinclair, *Downriver*; Okri, *The Famished Road*; Mo, *The Redundancy of Courage*

1992 . . . . Unsworth, *Sacred Hunger*; Harrison, *The Common Chorus*; Hornby, *Fever Pitch*; Headley, *Yardie*; Roberts, *Daughters of the House*; polytechnics given university status

1993 . . . . Phillips, *Crossing the River*; T. Johnson, *Hysteria*; D'Aguiar, *British Subjects*

1994 . . . . Gunesekera, *Reef*; Hollinghurst, *The Folding Star*; Coe, *What a Carve Up*; D'Aguiar, *The Longest Memory*; Ackroyd, *Dan Leno and the Limehouse Golem*; Sinclair, *Radon Daughters*; National Lottery commenced

1995 . . . . Barker, *Regeneration Trilogy*; Rushdie, *The Moor's Last Sigh*; M. Amis, *The Information*; Channel Tunnel opened

1996 . . . . Swift, *Last Orders*; Bainbridge, *Every Man for Himself*; Ravenhill, *Shopping and Fucking*; Pinter, *Ashes to Ashes*

1997 . . . . Sinclair, *Lights Out for the Territory*; Phillips, *The Nature of Blood*; McEwan, *Enduring Love*

1998 . . . . McEwan, *Amsterdam*; Barnes, *England, England*; Barker, *Another World*; Hughes, *Birthday Letters*; Motion, *Selected Poems 1976–1997*; Andrew Motion appointed Poet Laureate

1999 . . . . Armitage, *Killing Time*; Ackroyd, *The Plato Papers*; Rushdie, *The Ground Beneath Her Feet*

2000 . . . . Zadie Smith, *White Teeth*; Matthew Kneale, *English Passengers*; Ishiguro, *When We were Orphans*; Fred D'Aguiar, *Bloodlines*; Trezza Azzopardi, *The Hiding Place*; AOL purchases Time Warner; Tate Modern, London, opens

2001 . . . . Ian McEwan, *Atonement*; David Mitchell, *number9dream*; Stevie Davies, *The Element of Water*; Philip Pullman, *The Amber Spyglass*; Rachel Seifert, *The Dark Room*

6

2002 . . . . Sarah Waters, *Fingersmith*; John Banville, *Shroud*; Rohinton Mistry, *Family Matters*

2003 . . . . Monica Ali, *Brick Lane*; Margaret Atwood, *Oryx and Crake*; Caryl Phillips, *A Distant Shore*; Graham Swift, *The Light of the Day*

2004 . . . . Alan Hollinghurst, *The Line of Beauty*; David Mitchell, *Cloud Atlas*; Susanna Clarke, *Jonathan Strange and Mr Norell*

2005 . . . . John Banville, *The Sea*; Ishiguro, *Never Let Me Go*; Julian Barnes, *Arthur and George*; Hilary Mantel, *Beyond Black*; Ian McEwan, *Saturday*; Zadie Smith, *On Beauty*

2006 . . . . Sarah Waters, *The Night Watch*; Peter Carey, *Theft: A Love Story*; Nadine Gordimer, *Get a Life*

2007 . . . . Nicola Barker, *Darkmans*; Anne Enright, *The Gathering*; Ian McEwan, *On Chesil Beach*

2008 . . . . Philip Hensher, *The Northern Clemency*; Amitav Ghosh, *Sea of Poppies*

2009 . . . . Hilary Mantel, *Wolf Hall*; J. M. Coetzee, *Summertime*; Sarah Waters, *The Little Stranger*

bibliography

Adams, James Eli. 1995. *Dandies and Desert Saints. Styles of Victorian Manhood*. London: Cornell University Press.

Adams, M. H. 1999. *A Glossary of Literary Terms*. Boston, MA: Heinle and Heinle.

Adler, Eve. 2003. *Vergil's Empire: Political Thought in the Aeneid*. Philadelphia: Rowman and Littlefield.

Agee, Joel. 2007. 'A Lie That Tells the Truth: Memoir and the Art of Memory'. *Harper's Magazine*, (November): 55.

Alexander, Michael. 2000. *A History of English Literature*. Basingstoke: Palgrave Macmillan.

Allen, Walter. 1954. *The English Novel: A Short Critical History*. London: Phoenix House.

Arac, Jonathan. 1987. *Critical Genealogies: Historical Situations for Postmodern Literary Studies*. New York: Columbia University Press.

Armstrong, Nancy. 1987. *Desire and Domestic Fiction*. Oxford: Oxford University Press.

Ashcroft, Bill, Gareth Griffiths and Helen Tiffin, eds. 1995. *The Postcolonial Studies Reader*. London: Routledge.

Attridge, Derek, ed. 1992. *Acts of Literature*. New York: Routledge.

Baines, Paul. 2007. *Daniel Defoe: Robinson Crusoe/Moll Flanders: A Reader's Guide to Essential Criticism*. Basingstoke: Palgrave Macmillan.

Baker, Peter. 2003. *An Introduction to Old English*. Oxford: Blackwell.

Bakhtin, Mikhail. 1968. *Rabelais and His World*. Trans. H. Iswoksky. Cambridge, MA: MIT Press.

Bakhtin, Mikhail. 1981. *The Dialogic Imagination*. Ed. M. Holquist, trans. C. Emerson and M. Holquist. Austin: University of Texas Press.

Bakhtin, Mikhail. 1984. *Problems of Dostoevsky's Poetics*. Trans. C. Emerson. Minneapolis, MN and Manchester: University of Minnesota Press and Manchester University Press.

Bakhtin, Mikhail. 1990. 'The Problem of Content, Material and Form'. In *Art and Answerability: Early Philosophical Essays by M. M. Bakhtin*, ed. M. Holquist and V. Liapunov, trans. K. Brostrom, 257–325. Austin: University of Texas Press.

Barry, Peter. 1995. *Beginning Theory: An Introduction to Literary and Cultural Theory*. Manchester: Manchester University Press.

Barthes, Roland. 1972. *Mythologies*. Trans. Annette Lavers. London: Cape.

Barthes, Roland. 1977. 'The Death of the Author'. *Image-Music-Text*. Trans. Stephen Heath, 142–9. New York: Noonday.

Becker, George J. 1963. *Documents of Modern Literary Realism*. Princeton, NJ: Princeton University Press.

Bennington, Geoffrey, and Jacques Derrida. 1991. *Jacques Derrida*. Trans. Geoffrey Bennington 1993. Chicago: University of Chicago Press.

Bentley, Joseph. 1967. 'Satire and the Rhetoric of Sadism'. *Centennial Review*, II: 387–404.

Bertens, Hans and Joseph Natoli, eds. 2002. *Postmodernism: The Key Figures*. Oxford and Malden, MA: Blackwell.

Bevir, Mark, Jill Hargis and Sara Rushing, eds. 2007. *Histories of Postmodernism*. Abingdon and New York: Routledge.

Bhabha, Homi. 1990. 'DissemiNation: Time, Narrative, and the Margins of the Modern Nation'. In Homi Bhabha (ed.), *Nation and Narration*. London: Routledge.

Bigsby, Christopher and Howard Temperley, eds. 2005. *A New Introduction to American Studies*. Harlow: Longman.

Blair, John. 2000. *The Anglo-Saxon Age: A Very Short Introduction*. Oxford: Oxford Paperbacks.

Boone, Joseph Allen. 1998. *Libidinal Currents: Sexuality and the Shaping of Modernism*. Chicago and London: The University of Chicago Press.

Bradbury, Malcolm and James McFarlane. 1991. 'The Name and Nature of Modernism'. In Malcolm Bradbury and James McFarlane (eds), *Modernism: A Guide to European Literature 1890–1930*, 19–55. London: Penguin.

Branigan, Edward. 1992. *Narrative Comprehension and Film*. London: Routledge.

Brannigan, John. 1998. *New Historicism and Cultural Materialism*. London: Macmillan.

Brannigan, John, Ruth Robbins and Julian Wolfreys, eds. 1996. *Applying: to Derrida*. London: Macmillan.

Brik, Osip. 1964. *Two Essays on Poetic Language*. Postscript Roman Jakobson. Ann Arbor: University of Michigan Press.

Brontë, Charlotte. 1985. *Villette*. Harmondsworth: Penguin.

Brontë, Charlotte. 1996. *Jane Eyre*. Harmondsworth: Penguin.

Brontë, Emily. 1992. *Wuthering Heights: A Case Study in Contemporary Criticism*. Ed. Linda H. Peterson. New York: Bedford Books.

Brooks, Cleanth. 1956. *The Well-Wrought Urn: Studies in the Structure of Poetry*. London: Mariner Books.

Brooks, Cleanth and Robert Penn Warren. 1976. *Understanding Poetry*, 4th edn. New York: Holt, Rinehart and Winston.

Brooks, Peter. 1992. *Reading for the Plot: Design and Intention in Narrative*. Cambridge, MA: Harvard University Press.

Burnley, J. D. 1998. *Courtliness and Literature in Medieval England*. Harlow: Longman.

Burrow, Colin. 1993. *Epic Romance: Homer to Milton*. Oxford: Clarendon Press.

Butler, Judith. 1990. *Gender Trouble: Feminism and the Subversion of Identity*. New York: Routledge.

Byron, Glennis. 2003. *Dramatic Monologue*. New York and London: Routledge.

Cairns, Francis. 2008. *Virgil's Augustan Epic*. New edn. Cambridge: Cambridge University Press.

Callinicos, Alex. 1990. *Against Postmodernism: A Marxist Critique*. Cambridge: Polity.

Campbell, Neil and Alasdair Kean. 2006. *American Cultural Studies*, 2nd edn. New York: Routledge.

Carby, Hazel. 1987. *Reconstructing Womanhood: The Emergence of the Afro-American Woman Novelist*. New York: Oxford University Press.

Carlson, Susan. 1991. *Women and Comedy: Rewriting the British Theatrical Tradition*. Ann Arbor: University of Michigan Press.

Chatman, Seymour. 1990. *Coming to Terms: The Rhetoric of Narrative in Fiction and Film*. Ithaca, NY: Cornell University Press.

Cheney, Patrick and Lauren Silberman, eds. 2000. *Worldmaking Spenser: Explorations in the Early Modern Age*. Lexington: University Press of Kentucky.

Chrisman, Laura and Benita Parry, eds. 2000. *Postcolonial Theory and Criticism*, The English Association Essays & Studies. Cambridge: D. S. Brewer.

Christian, Barbara. 1985. *Black Feminist Criticism: Perspectives on Black Women Writers*. New York: Pergamon Press.

Cisnersos, Sandra. 2002. *Caramelo*. London: Bloomsbury.

Clayton, Jay. 2003. *Charles Dickens in Cyberspace: The Afterlife of the Nineteenth Century in Postmodern Culture*. New York: Oxford University Press.

Clery, E. J. 2004. *The Feminization Debate in Eighteenth-Century England: Literature, Commerce, and Luxury*. Basingstoke: Palgrave Macmillan.

Connor, Steven, ed. 2004. *The Cambridge Companion to Postmodernism*. Cambridge and New York: Cambridge University Press.

Craft, Christopher. 1994. *Another Kind of Love: Male Homosexual Desire in English Discourse, 1850–1920*. Berkeley: University of California Press.

Crane, Susan. 1986. *Insular Romance: Politics, Faith, and Culture in Anglo-Norman and Middle English Literature*. Berkeley: California University Press.

Critchley, Simon. 1992. *The Ethics of Deconstruction: Derrida and Lévinas*. Oxford: Wiley-Blackwell.

Cross, Wilbur L. 1899. *The Development of the English Novel*. New York: Macmillan.

Culler, Jonathan. 1976. *Structuralist Poetics: Structuralism, Linguistics, and the Study of Literature*. Ithaca, NY: Cornell University Press.

Culler, Jonathan. 1997. *Literary Theory: A Very Short Introduction*. Oxford: Oxford University Press.

Curran, Stuart. 1986. *Poetic Form and British Romanticism*. Oxford: Oxford University Press.

Currie, Mark. 1998. *Postmodern Narrative Theory*. Basingstoke: Palgrave Macmillan.

Davidoff, Leonore and Catherine Hall. 1987. *Family Fortunes. Men and Women of the English Middle Class, 1780–1850*. Chicago: University of Chicago Press.

Day, Gary. 2001. *Class: The Critical Idiom*. London: Routledge.

De Man, Paul. 1983. 'Form and Intent in the American New Criticism'. *Blindness and Insight*, 20–35. Minneapolis: University of Minnesota Press.

DeLillo, Don. 2002. *White Noise*. London: Picador.

Denning, Michael. 1987. *Mechanic Accents: Dime Novels and Working-class Culture in America*. London: Verso.

Derrida, Jacques. 1991. 'Letter to a Japanese Friend'. Trans. David Wood and Andrew Benjamin. In Peggy Kamuf (ed.), *A Derrida Reader: Between the Blinds*, 270–6. New York: Columbia University Press.

Derrida, Jacques. 1992. *Acts of Literature*. Ed. Derek Attridge. New York: Routledge.

Derrida, Jacques. 1996. '"*As If* I were Dead": An Interview with Jacques Derrida'. In John Brannigan, Ruth Robbins and Julian Wolfreys (eds), *Applying: to Derrida*, 212–26. London: Macmillan.

Dickinson, Emily. 1975. 'In Winter in my Room'. *The Complete Poems*. Ed. Thomas H. Johnson, 682–3. London: Faber and Faber.

Dollimore, Jonathan and Alan Sinfield. 1994. *Political Shakespeare: Essays in Cultural Materialism*. Manchester: Manchester University Press.

Douglas, Ann. 1978. *The Feminization of American Culture*. New York: Farrar, Straus, Giroux.

Dronke, Peter. 2002. *The Medieval Lyric*. Woodbridge: D. S. Brewer.

Du Bois, W. E. B. 1999. *The Souls of Black Folk*. New York: Norton.

Eagleton, Terry. 1976. *Marxism and Literary Criticism*. London: Methuen.

Eagleton, Terry. 1982. *The Rape of Clarissa: Writing, Sexuality and Class Struggle in Samuel Richardson*. Oxford: Basil Blackwell.

Eagleton, Terry. 1996. *The Illusions of Postmodernism*. Oxford and Malden, MA: Blackwell.

Eagleton, Terry. 2005. *The English Novel: An Introduction*. Malden, MA: Blackwell.

Easthope, Antony. 1991. *Literary into Cultural Studies*. London and New York: Routledge.

Ellis, Steve, ed. 2005. *Chaucer: An Oxford Guide.* Oxford: Oxford University Press.

Empson, William. 2004. *Seven Types of Ambiguity.* London: Pimlico.

Erlich, Victor. 1980. *Russian Formalism: History – Doctrine.* Berlin: Mouton de Gruyter.

Esslin, Martin. 1987. *The Field of Drama.* London: Methuen.

Fanon, Frantz. 1986. *Black Skin, White Masks*. London: Pluto.

Featherstone, Mike. 2007. *Consumer Culture and Postmodernism*, 2nd edn. London and Thousand Oaks, CA: SAGE Publications.

Fetterley, Judith. 1978. *The Resisting Reader: A Feminist Approach to American Fiction*. Bloomington: Indiana University Press.

Figes, Eva. 1976. *Tragedy and Social Evolution.* New York: Persea Books.

Fisk, Deborah Payne, ed. 2000. *The Cambridge Companion to English Restoration Theatre*. Cambridge: Cambridge University Press.

Foucault, Michel. 1994. *The Order of Things: An Archaeology of the Human Sciences*. New York: Vintage.

Fowler, Alastair. 1982. *Kinds of Literature: An Introduction to the Theory of Genres and Modes*. Oxford: Clarendon.

Fox, Robin Lane. 2008. *Travelling Heroes: Greeks and Their Myths in the Epic Age of Homer*. London: Penguin.

Freud, Sigmund. 1953–73. *The Standard Edition of the Complete Works of Sigmund Freud*. 24 vols. London: Hogarth Press.

Freud, Sigmund. 1986. 'Femininity'. In *The Essentials of Psychoanalysis*. Ed. Anna Freud. Harmondsworth: Pelican.

Fry, Stephen. 2005. *The Ode Less Travelled: Unlocking the Poet Within.* London: Hutchinson.

Frye, Northrop. 2001. 'The Archetypes of Literature'. In *The Norton Anthology of Theory and Criticism*, ed. Vincent B. Leitch, 1445–57. New York: W. W. Norton.

Furst, Lilian R. 1969. *Romanticism*. London: Methuen.

Fussell, Paul, ed. 1972. *English Augustan Poetry*. New York: Doubleday.

Gates, Henry Louis, Jr. 1988. *The Signifying Monkey: A Theory of African-American Literary Criticism*. New York: Oxford University Press.

Gates, Henry Louis, Jr. and Nellie Y. McKay, eds. 2004. *The Norton Anthology of African American Literature*, 2nd edn. New York: Norton.

Genette, Gérard. 1980. *Narrative Discourse: An Essay in Method*. Trans. Jane E. Lewin. Ithaca, NY: Cornell University Press.

Gibbons, Brian. 1980. *Jacobean City Comedy: A Study of Satiric Plays by Jonson, Marston and Middleton*, rev. edn. London: Routledge.

Gilroy, Paul. 1993. *The Black Atlantic: Modernity and Double Consciousness*. London: Verso and Cambridge, MA: Harvard University Press.

Glofelty, Cheryl. 1996. 'Introduction'. In *The Ecocriticism Reader: Landmarks in Literary Ecology*, ed. C. Glofeltly and H. Fromm, xv–xxxvii. London: University of Georgia Press.

Goldman, Jane. 2004. *Modernism, 1910–1945: Image to Apocalypse*. Basingstoke: Palgrave Macmillan.

Grant, Damian. 1970. *Realism*. London: Methuen.

Greenblatt, Stephen and Abrams, M. H., eds. 2006. *The Norton Anthology of English Literature*, 8th edn. Vol. 1. New York: W. W. Norton & Co.

Griffin, Dustin. 2009. *Regaining Paradise: Milton and the Eighteenth Century*. Cambridge: Cambridge University Press.

Gruesser, John Cullen. 2005. *Confluences: Postcolonialism, African American Literary Studies, and the Black Atlantic*. Athens, GA: University of Georgia Press.

Hammond, Brean and Sean Regan. 2005. *Making the Novel: Fiction and Society in Britain, 1660–1789*. Basingstoke: Palgrave Macmillan.

Harper, Graeme, ed. 2002. *Comedy, Fantasy and Colonialism*. London: Continuum.

Heale, Elizabeth, ed. 1998. *Wyatt, Surrey and Early Tudor Poetry*. London: Longman.

Henderson, Carol E. 2002. *Scarring the Black Body: Race and Representation in African American Literature*. Columbia, MO: University of Missouri Press.

Herwitz, Daniel. 2008. *Aesthetics*. London and New York: Continuum.

Homer, Sean. 2004. *Jacques Lacan*. London and New York: Routledge.

Howe, Nicholas. 1989. Migration *and Mythmaking in Anglo-Saxon England*. New Haven, CT and London: Yale University Press.

Hunt, Peter. 1991. *Criticism, Theory, and Children's Literature*. Oxford: Blackwell.

Hunter, J. Paul. 2001. 'Couplets and Conversation'. In *The Cambridge Companion to Eighteenth-Century Poetry*, 11–35. Ed. John Sitter. Cambridge: Cambridge University Press.

Hunter Blair, Peter. 2003. *An Introduction to Anglo-Saxon England*, 3rd edn. Cambridge: Cambridge University Press.

Irigaray, Luce. 1985. *This Sex Which Is Not One*. Trans. Catherine Porter, Ithaca, NY: Cornell University Press.

Jakobson, Roman. 1990. *On Language*. Ed. Linda R. Waugh and Monique Monville-Burston. Cambridge, MA: Harvard University Press.

James, Henry. 2008. 'Preface'. *The Ambassadors.* Ed. Harry Levin. London: Penguin.

Jameson, Fredric. 1972. *Prison-House of Language: A Critical Account of Structuralism and Russian Formalism*. Princeton, NJ: Princeton University Press.

Jameson, Frederic. 1984. 'Postmodernism, or, The Cultural Logic of Late Capitalism'. *New Left Review*, 146 (July–August): 59–92.

Jenkins, Henry. 1998. *The Children's Culture Reader*. New York: New York University Press.

Jump, John. 1974. *The Ode*. London: Methuen.

Kaplan, Amy. 1992. *The Social Construction of American Realism*. Chicago: University of Chicago Press.

Kendrick, Laura. 1988. *Chaucerian Play: Comedy and Control in* The Canterbury Tales. Berkeley: University of California Press.

Kettle, Arnold. 1951. *An Introduction to the English Novel*, Volume 1: *Defoe to George Eliot*. New York: Harper Torchbooks.

Kettle, Arnold. 1951. *An Introduction to the English Novel*, Volume 2: *Henry James to the Present*. New York: Harper Torchbooks.

King, John N. 2001. 'Spenser's Religion'. In *The Cambridge Companion to Spenser*, ed. Andrew Hadfield, 200–16. Cambridge: Cambridge University Press, 2001.

Klein, Melanie. 1985. *The Selected Melanie Klein*. Ed. Juliet Mitchell. Harmondsworth: Penguin.

Knapp, Jeffrey. 1992. *An Empire Nowhere: England, America, and Literature from* Utopia *to* The Tempest. Berkeley: University of California Press.

Krieger, Murray. 1963. *The New Apologists for Poetry*. Bloomington: Indiana University Press.

Kristeva, Julia. 1982. *Powers of Horror: An Essay on Abjection*. New York. Columbia University Press.

Leitch, Vincent B., ed. 2001. *The Norton Anthology of Theory and Criticism*. New York: W. W. Norton.

Leitch, Vincent. 2009. *American Literary Criticism Since the 1930s*, 2nd edn. London: Routledge.

Lemon, Lee T. and Marion J. Reis, ed. and trans. 1965. *Russian Formalist Criticism: Four Essays*. Lincoln: University of Nebraska Press.

Lentricchia, Frank. 1980. *After the New Criticism*. Chicago: University of Chicago Press.

Lerer, Seth. 1993. *Chaucer and His Readers: Imagining the Author in Late Medieval England*. Princeton, NJ: Princeton University Press.

Lesnik-Oberstein, Karin. 1994. *Children's Literature: Criticism and the Fictional Child*. Oxford: Clarendon Press.

Lewalski, Barabara Keifer. 1979. *Protestant Poetics and the Seventeenth-Century Religious Lyric.* Princeton, NJ: Princeton University Press.

Linton, Eliza Lynn. 1868. 'The Girl of the Period'. *Saturday Review*, 14 March 1868: 356–60.

Lock, Graham and David Murray, eds. 2009. *Thriving on a Riff: Jazz and Blues Influences in African American Literature and Film*. New York: Oxford University Press.

Lucy, Niall, ed. 2000. *Postmodern Literary Theory: An Anthology*. Oxford and Malden, MA: Blackwell.

Lyotard, Jean-Francois. 1984. *The Postmodern Condition: A Report on Knowledge*. Trans Geoff Bennington and Brian Massumi. Manchester: Manchester University Press.

Maley, Willy. 1997. *Salvaging Spenser: Colonialism, Culture and Identity.* Basingstoke: Palgrave Macmillan.

Maley, Willy. 2003. *Nation, State and Empire in English Renaissance Literature: Shakespeare to Milton.* Basingstoke: Palgrave Macmillan.

Malpas, Simon. 2005. *The Postmodern*. Abingdon and New York: Routledge.

Malpas, Simon, ed. 2001. *Postmodern Debates*. Basingstoke: Palgrave Macmillan.

Mann, Jill. 1973. *Chaucer and Medieval Estates Satire*. Cambridge: Cambridge University Press.

Marlowe, Christopher. 1981. *Tamburlaine the Great*. Ed. J. S. Cunningham. Manchester. Manchester University Press.

Marsh, Joss. 1998. *Word Crimes: Blasphemy, Culture, and Literature in Nineteenth-Century England.* Chicago and London: Chicago University Press.

Marx, Karl and Friedrich Engels. 1985. *The Communist Manifesto*. Trans. A. J. P. Taylor. Harmondsworth: Penguin.

McCarthy, Terrence. 1988. *An Introduction to Malory*. Cambridge: D. S. Brewer.

McFarlane, Brian. 1996. *Novel to Film: An Introduction to the Theory of Adaptation*. Oxford: Oxford University Press.

McQuillan, Martin, ed. 2000. *Deconstruction: A Reader*. Edinburgh: Edinburgh University Press.

Medcalf, Stephen, ed. 1981. *The Later Middle Ages*. London: Methuen.

Medvedev, Pavel. 1978. *The Formal Method in Literary Scholarship: A Critical Introduction to Sociological Poetics*. Trans. A. Wehrle. Baltimore, MD and London: The Johns Hopkins University Press.

Mitchell, Bruce and Fred C. Robinson. 2006. *A Guide to Old English*, 7th edn. Oxford: Blackwell.

Morris, Pam. 2003. *Realism*. London: Routledge.

Mulvey, Laura. 1989. *Visual and Other Pleasures*. Basingstoke: Palgrave Macmillan.

Nietzsche, Friedrich Wilhelm. 2000. *The Birth of Tragedy*. Trans. and int. Douglas Smith. Oxford: Oxford University Press.

Paglia, Camille. 1992. *Sexual Personae: Art and Decadence from Nefertiti to Emily Dickinson*. London: Vintage.

Pater, Walter. 1967. *The Renaissance*. New York: Meridian Books.

Pavel, Thomas. 1983. 'The Borders of Fiction'. *Poetics Today*, 1.3 (Spring): 23.

Plasa, Carl and Betty J. Ring, eds. 1994. *The Discourse of Slavery: Aphra Behn to Toni Morrison*. London: Routledge.

Porter, Joy and Kenneth M. Roemer, eds. 2005. *The Cambridge Companion to Native American Literature*. Cambridge: Cambridge University Press.

Powell, Barry P. 2004. *Homer*. Oxford: Wiley-Blackwell.

Propp, Vladimir. 1968. *Morphology of the Folktale*, 2nd edn. Trans. Laurence Scott. Austin: University of Texas Press.

Putter, Ad. 1996. *An Introduction to the Gawain-Poet*. Harlow: Longman.

Quality Assurance Agency. 2007. English Subject Benchmark. Internet: www.qaa.ac.uk/academicinfrastructure/benchmark/statements/English07.asp#nature (accessed 18 April 2009).

Radway, Janice. 1991. *Reading the Romance: Women, Patriarchy and Popular Literature*. Chapel Hill: University of North Carolina Press.

Ransom, John Crowe. 2001. 'Criticism, Inc.'. In *Norton Anthology of Theory and Criticism*. Ed. Vincent Leitch, 1108–17. New York: Norton.

Russell, Gillian. 2004. 'Theatrical Culture'. In *The Cambridge Companion to English Literature, 1740–1830*, ed. Thomas Keymer and Jon Mee, 100–18. Cambridge: Cambridge University Press.

Russell, Sandi. 2001. *Render Me My Song: African-American Women Writers from Slavery to the Present*, 2nd edn. London: Pandora Press.

Said, Edward. 1991. *Orientalism*. London: Penguin.

de Saussure, Ferdinand. 1983. *Course in General Linguistics*. Trans. Roy Harris. London: Duckworth.

Sedgwick, Eve Kosofsky. 1985. *Between Men: English Literature and Male Homosocial Desire*. New York: Columbia University Press.

Shklovsky, Victor. 1990. *Theory of Prose*. Trans. Benjamin Sher. Elmwood Park, IL: Dalkey Archive Press.

Showalter, Elaine, ed. 1986. *The New Feminist Criticism: Essays on Women, Literature and Theory*, London: Virago.

Silverman, Kaja. 1992. *Male Subjectivity at the Margins*. New York: Routledge.

Sim, Stuart. 2002. *Irony and Crisis: A Critical History of Postmodern Culture*. Duxford: Icon.

Sim, Stuart, ed. 2001. *The Routledge Companion to Postmodernism*. London: Routledge.

Simpson, James, ed. 2007. *Piers Plowman: An Introduction*, 2nd rev. edn. Exeter: University of Exeter Press.

Smith, Grahame. 2003. *Dickens and the Dream of Cinema*. Manchester: Manchester University Press.

Stanzel, F. K. 1984. *A Theory of Narrative*. Trans. Charlotte Goedsche. Cambridge: Cambridge University Press.

Steiner, Peter. 1986. *Russian Formalism: A Metapoetics*. Ithaca, NY: Cornell University Press.

Stimpson, Catharine R. 1981. 'Zero Degree Deviancy: The Lesbian Novel in English'. *Critical Inquiry*, 8(2) (Winter), 'Writing and Sexual Difference', 363–79.

Sutherland, John. 1982. *Offensive Literature: Decensorship in Britain 1960–1982*. London: Junction Books.

Swift, Graham. 2008. *Waterland*. London: Picador.

Tew, Philip. 2007. *The Contemporary British Novel*, 2nd edn. London: Continuum.

Thomson, Peter. 2006. *The Cambridge Introduction to English Theatre, 1660–1900*. Cambridge: Cambridge University Press,

Todd, Janet. 1999. 'Introduction'. In *Aphra Behn*, ed. Janet Todd, 1–11. Basingstoke: Palgrave Macmillan.

Tompkins, Jane. 1986. *Sensational Designs: The Cultural Work of American Fiction, 1790–1860*. Oxford: Oxford University Press.

Turville-Petre, Thorlac. 1977. *The Alliterative Revival*. Cambridge: D. S. Brewer.

Veeser, H. Aram, ed. 1989. *The New Historicism*. London: Routledge.

Voloshinov, Valentin. 1993. *Marxism and the Philosophy of Languag*. Trans. L. Matejka and I. R. Titunik. Austin: University of Texas Press.

Waller, Gary. 1994. *Edmund Spenser: A Literary Life*. London: Macmillan.

Watt, Ian. 2001. *The Rise of the Novel: Studies in Defoe, Richardson and Fielding*. Berkeley: University of California Press.

Wilde, Oscar. 1891. 'The Decay of Laying'. *Intentions and the Soul of Man*, 2–57. London: Methuen.

Williams, Raymond. 1963. *Culture and Society 1780–1950*. Harmondsworth: Penguin.

Williams, Raymond. 1977. *Marxism and Literature*. Oxford: Oxford University Press.

Wimsatt, W. K. and Monroe C. Beardsley. 1982. 'The Intentional Fallacy'. *Sewanee Review*, 54 (1946): 468–88. Revised and republished in W. K. Wimsatt, *The Verbal Icon: Studies in the Meaning of Poetry*. 3–18. Lexington: University of Kentucky Press.

Wolfreys, Julian. 1997. *Deconstruction•Derrida*. London: Macmillan.

Woods, Tim. 1999. *Beginning Postmodernism*. Manchester: Manchester University Press.

Woolf, Viriginia. 1977. *A Room of One's Own*. London: Fontana.

Wright, Richard. 1995. *White Man, Listen!* New York: HarperCollins.

Wright, Richard. 2000. *Native Son*. London: Vintage.

Zipes, Jack. 2002. *Breaking the Magic Spell: Radical Theories of Folk and Fairy Tales*. Lexington: University Press of Kentucky.

notes on contributors

Hugh Adlington is a lecturer in Early Modern Literature at Birmingham University. His research interests are primarily in the area of early modern literature, particularly religious poetry and prose. He is currently working on a monograph on the significance of legal thought and language in the work of John Donne, and is co-editing *The Oxford Handbook of the Early Modern Sermon*.

Jan Baetens is professor at the University of Leuven (Belgium), where he mainly teaches word and image studies. He co-edits the literary journals *Formules, revue des littératures à contraintes* and *FPC/Formes poétiques contemporaines*, as well as the peer-reviewed e-journal *Image & Narrative*. As an author, he has published eight books of poetry, including *Vivre sa vie. Une novellisation en vers du film de Jean-Luc Godard* (Les Impressions Nouvelles, 2005). A collection of verse on basketball, *Slam*, appeared in June 2006 with the same publisher.

Jenny Bavidge is a lecturer in English at the University of Greenwich. She has published articles on children's literature, literary geography and teen culture. She is the editor (with Robert Bond) of *City Visions: The Work of Iain Sinclair* (Cambridge Scholars Publishing, 2007) and her *Theorists of the City* is forthcoming from Routledge.

Megan Becker-Leckrone is Associate Professor with the English Department at University of Nevada, Las Vegas, and specializes in literary theory and nineteenth- and twentieth-century literature. In 2006 she was awarded UNLV's Morris Award for Excellence in Research and Scholarship, and, in addition to various articles and essays, is the author of *Julia Kristeva and Literary Theory* (Palgrave Macmillan, 2005).

Claire Bowditch is a PhD student at Loughborough University. Her research is focused on the theatre of Aphra Behn in relation to the Court of Charles II and the writings of Behn's contemporaries, so as to more firmly establish Behn's literary reputation in the wider context of Restoration culture.

Doris Bremm received her MA from the Rheinische Friedrich-Wilhelms-Universität, Bonn, and her PhD from the University of Florida. She teaches at Auburn University, Alabama, and specializes in contemporary British and American literature, intersections between literature and the visual arts, and literary theory. Her research and teaching interests include twentieth-century American and British literature, visual culture, film, metafiction, and modes of urban representation.

Robert John Brocklehurst is a lecturer in Technical Theatre at Loughborough University. He is currently conducting research at the University of Manchester, focusing on the relation between visual language and communal memory within Yucatec Mayan communities, Central Yucatan, Mexico. He has also worked as both a visiting lecturer and filmmaker in California, Bosnia Herzegovina and Ghana, West Africa.

Jennifer Cooke is Lecturer in English at Loughborough University. Her research is located in three interrelated areas: twentieth-century writing and thinkers, political thought, and creative writing. Her specific interests lie in psychoanalysis, the Frankfurt School critical theorists, messianism, representations of the plague in literature, tone in women's prose and poetry, and the politics and poetics of writing intimacy in twentieth-century literature. Her monograph, *Legacies of Plague in Literature, Theory and Film*, is currently in press.

Helen Davies is a postgraduate student at Leeds Metropolitan University.

Maria-Daniella Dick is a PhD student at the University of Glasgow researching literary authority in Joyce and Dante, and co-compiler and co-editor of *Derrida: A Concordance, Glossary and Bibliography* (Edinburgh University Press, forthcoming).

Andrew Dix is Lecturer in American Studies in the Department of English and Drama, Loughborough University. He is the author of *Beginning Film Studies* (Manchester University Press, 2008), co-editor with Jonathan Taylor of *Figures of Heresy: Radical Theology in English and American Writing, 1800–2000* (Sussex Academic Press, 2006), and has written on other topics in nineteenth- and twentieth-century American literature, including the work of Mark Twain, John Steinbeck and Sherman Alexie.

Joan Fitzpatrick is Lecturer in English at Loughborough University. She has published articles on Shakespeare, Spenser, Ireland and gender and writes the 'Spenser and Sidney' section of *The Year's Work in English Studies* (Oxford University Press). Her third monograph, entitled *Food in Shakespeare: Early Modern Dietaries and the Plays*, was published in 2007 by Ashgate. She is currently writing an *Athlone Dictionary on Shakespeare and the Language of Food*.

Nick Freeman is Senior Lecturer in English at Loughborough University. He has published widely on Victorian literature and culture, and has also written about film, television and contemporary fiction. He is the author of *Conceiving the City: London, Literature, and Art 1870–1914* (Oxford University Press, 2007).

David Griffith is Senior Lecturer in Medieval Language and Literature at the University of Birmingham. His research interests are largely interdisciplinary. He writes on relations between literary and visual cultures in the later medieval period and is currently working on projects to catalogue and interpret the large corpus of inscriptions in the vernacular languages of medieval England.

Brian Jarvis is Senior Lecturer in American Literature and Film at Loughborough University. He is the author of *Postmodern Cartographies: The Geographical Imagination in Contemporary American Culture* (1998) and *Cruel and Unusual: Punishment and U.S. Culture* (2004), as well as essays on a wide range of topics that includes trauma in the Vietnam fiction of Tim O'Brien, the cinema of serial killing, optics in horror film, the 9/11 attacks in New York, TV prison dramas, cultural geography, detective fiction and dirty realism.

Carolyn Kelley is a PhD student at the University of Florida.

Professor Ian McCormick is a member of the School of the Arts at the University of Northampton. His recent work has been in the field of deconstruction and drama, and in pedagogical aspects of eighteenth-century studies. Professor McCormick's critical editions of Robert Graves's novels *Antigua, Penny, Puce* and *They Hanged My Saintly Billy* (Carcanet) were published in 2003.

Alex Murray is Lecturer in the Department of English at the University of Exeter, and is based at Exeter's Cornwall campus. His research interests include critical theory and contemporary London-based fiction, radical revisitings of the past, and the textual and cultural politics of such historiographical writing. His first monograph, *Recalling London: Literature and History in the Work of Peter Ackroyd and Iain Sinclair*, was published in 2007 (Continuum) and he is currently completing a book on Giorgio Agamben (Routledge), as well as co-editing a collection on Agamben (Edinburgh) and the *Continuum Handbook for Modernism*.

Bill Overton is Professor of Literary Studies at Loughborough University. His most recent books are his edition *A Letter to My Love: Love Poems by Women First Published in the Barbados Gazette, 1731–1737* (University of Delaware

Press and Associated University Presses, 2001), *Fictions of Female Adultery: Theories and Circumtexts 1684–1890* (Palgrave Macmillan, 2002), and *The Eighteenth-Century British Verse Epistle* (Palgrave Macmillan, 2007).

Lawrence Phillips is Principal Lecturer in English, Divisional Leader, English, Media and Culture, Field Chair in English, and Course Leader of the BA in English at Northampton University. His research focuses on two areas: culture and space in the literary representation of cities and the urban, and Victorian and early twentieth-century empire writing. He has published a number of articles, essays and books, including, most recently, *London Narratives: Post-War Fiction and the City* (Continuum, 2006), and two edited collections, *The Swarming Streets: Twentieth-Century Literary Representations of London* (Rodopi, 2004) and *A Mighty Mass of Brick and Smoke: Victorian and Edwardian Representations of London* (Rodopi, 2007). He is also founding editor of the journal *Literary London: Interdisciplinary Studies in the Representation of London*.

Jenni Ramone is Senior Lecturer in English at Newman University College, Birmingham. She is co-editor, with Gemma Twitchen, of *Boundaries* (Cambridge Scholars Publishing, 2007), and is currently working on the short story form and bilingualism in New York Puerto Rican literature.

Christopher Ringrose is Principal Lecturer in English and Learning and Teaching, and Co-ordinator, School of the Arts, at the University of Northampton. His research interests include life writing, postcolonial writing, children's literature and contemporary literature. Recent publications include 'Ben Okri's Fiction, 1995–2006', in *Contemporary British Novelists*, ed. Rod Mengham and Philip Tew (Continuum, 2006). His current research involves a study of the use of e-learning in higher education in the UK.

Ruth Robbins is Associate Dean and Head of the School of Cultural Studies at Leeds Metropolitan University. Her research interests centre on the late Victorian period in English literature, especially the literature of decadence such as the writings of Oscar Wilde, Arthur Symons and Vernon Lee. She has published numerous articles, essays and books including *Subjectivity* (Palgrave, 2005), *Pater to Forster, 1873–1924* (Palgrave, 2003) and *Literary Feminisms* (Palgrave, 2000). She is also editor of *CCUE News*, the newsletter of the Council for College and University English.

Philippa Semper is lecturer in medieval English at the University of Birmingham, where she is also Director of Education for the School of English, Drama and American and Canadian Studies. She convenes the Graduate Medievalists' Research Seminar within the College of Arts and Law. Her research focuses upon Old English literature and text–image relationships; she is currently writing one book on Old English poetry and another on Anglo-Saxon manuscripts.

Neal Swettenham lectures in drama at Loughborough University. His research into the role and status of narrative in contemporary theatre has examined both conventional story-based drama and avant-garde performance work and especially the theatre of Richard Foreman.

Julian Wolfreys is Professor of Modern Literature and Culture at Loughborough University. His most recent publication is *Literature, in Theory* (Continuum, 2010).

Kenneth Womack is Professor of English, and Head of the Division of Arts and Humanities at Pennsylvania State University, Altoona. He is editor and author of numerous essays and articles. Additionally, he has authored, co-authored and co-edited several books including, with Todd F. Davis, *Formalist Criticism and Reader-Response Theory, Mapping the Ethical Turn: A Reader in Ethics, Culture, and Literary Theory, Postmodern Humanism in Contemporary Literature and Culture, Reading the Beatles: Cultural Studies, Literary Criticism, and the Fab Four*. His monograph, *Postwar Academic Fiction*, was published by Palgrave Macmillan (2006) and with William Baker he has edited *Felix Holt: The Radical*, by George Eliot and Ford Madox Ford's *The Good Soldier*, both published by Broadview Press.

Nigel Wood is Professor of Literature at Loughborough University. He has written widely on satirists. His 'Harvester New Critical Readings' volume on *Swift* appeared in 1986, followed by the *Swift Longman Critical Reader* in 1999. His edition of essays on *John Gay and the Scriblerians* (with Peter Lewis) appeared in 1988, on Byron's *Don Juan* in 1993 and his edition of Fielding's *The Modern Husband* was included in his edition of *She Stoops to Conquer and Other Eighteenth-Century Comedies* (2007). He is at present editing (with Julian Ferraro, Valerie Rumbold and Paul Baines) the poems of Alexander Pope for the Longman Annotated Poets series.

Helen Wright is currently a PhD student at Loughborough University researching the notion of truth in mid-Victorian literature. Other research interests include critical theory, philosophy, late Victorian literature and culture, and the emergence of modernism.

Karine Zbinden is Honorary Research Fellow at The Bakhtin Centre, The University of Sheffield.

index

A

abjection 107–8, 333
absence/presence 333. *See* binary
 opposition
Absurd, Theatre of the (also 'Absurdism')
 148, 258, 333, 339
Ackroyd, Peter 199
 Chatterton 199
Acland, Charles 241
Addison, Joseph 98 105
 The Spectator 105
Aeschylus 135
 Oresteia (*Agamennon, Choephoroi* [The
  Libation Bearers], *Eumenides*) 135–6
Aesthetic/s xvi, 1, 9, 11, 12, 13, 102, 103,
 105, 106, 107, 120, 121, 123, 124,
 225, 240, 266, 275, 276, 282, 297, 308,
 333–4, 337, 340, 343, 345
Aesthetic movement, Aestheticism 117,
 268
African American literature and studies
 251, 309–11
Agee, Joel 228–9
 'A Lie That Tells the Truth' 228–9
agency/agent 116, 205, 221, 334, 346
Ainsworth, Harrison 211
Alcott, Louisa M. 254
 Little Women 254
Ali, Monica 200
 Brick Lane 200
allegory 75, 83, 91, 107, 160, 173, 174, 232,
 334
Allen, Richard 213
 Skinhead 213

alterity 334, 345. *See* other/otherness
ambiguity 121, 123, 272, 300
American Civil War 253
Amis, Martin 199
 London Fields 199
Ancrene Riwle (*Guide for Anchoresses*) 73
Andre, Carl 6
Anglo-Saxon Chronicle 67–8, 73
Annotated Bibliography of English Studies 36
archetypal criticism, archetype 234, 270–2
Aristophanes 144
 The Birds 144
Aristotle xvi, 136–7, 138, 140, 168, 194,
 287
Armitage, Simon 213
Armstrong, Nancy 223–4, 282
Arnold, Matthew 5, 246, 268
Artaud, Antonin 164
 Spurt of Blood 164
Ashbery, John 257
Attridge, Derek 302
 Acts of Literature 302
Atwood, Margaret 14–15, 326–7
 The Handmaid's Tale 14–15, 326
 Oryx and Crake 326
Austen, Jane 121, 135, 146, 153, 210, 244,
 316
 Northanger Abbey 121, 146, 153, 316
 Pride and Prejudice 244
Auster, Paul 259
Austin, J. L. 204

B

Bacon, Francis 91

Of the Proficience and Advancement of Learning, Divine and Human 91

Bakhtin, Mikhail 148, 149, 275–8
   The Dialogic Imagination 277
   Problems of Dostoevsky's Poetics 276
   Rabelais and His World 277
Balzac, Honoré de 223
   Sarrasine 223
Banville, John 130, 131
   Ghosts 130
Barnes, Djuna 319
   Nightwood 319
Barrett Browning, Elizabeth 115–16, 117
   Aurora Leigh 115–16, 117
Barrie, J. M. 239–40
   Peter Pan 239–40
Barthes, Roland 36, 129, 223, 292, 293, 322
   'The Death of the Author' 223
   Mythologies 292, 322
base/superstructure 288
Bassnett, Susan 26, 29, 30
   Comparative Literature 26, 30
Beardsley, Monroe C. 273, 274. *See* W. K. Wimsatt
Beat generation 256–7
Beaumont, Francis 84
Beckett, Samuel 129, 139, 140, 145, 148, 167, 226
   Krapp's Last Tape 145, 148
   Waiting for Godot 167
Bede 68
   Ecclesiastical History of the English People 68
Behn, Aphra 91, 94, 95, 152, 185
   Oroonoko 91, 94, 95, 152
Benedictsson, Victoria 138, 139
   The Enchantment 138
Bennett, Arnold 191
Beowulf 65, 69
Bergman, Ingmar 237
Bhabha, Homi K. 219, 303, 304
binary opposition 107, 204, 216, 299, 301, 318, 333, 335–6, 338, 346. *See* absence/presence

Black Mountain poets 257
Blackwood's Magazine 210
Blake, William 90, 101, 102, 103, 160, 174–5
   Jerusalem 175
   The Marriage of Heaven and Hell 175
   Milton 175
   Songs of Innocence and of Experience 160
Blanchot, Maurice 223
blank verse 90, 96, 160, 161, 174, 210
Boone, Joseph Allan 319
Borges, Jorge Luis 129
   The Book of Sand 129
Botshon, Lisa 37
Bourdieu, Pierre 308
Bowles, Paul 16
   The Sheltering Sky 16
Braddon, Mary Elizabeth 113–14
   Lady Audley's Secret 114
Brannigan, John 305
Brecht, Bertolt 139–40, 168
   Mother Courage and Her Children 139–40
Brenton, Howard 185
   Pravda 185
Brik, Osip 268
   'Sound Repetitions' 268
Brontë, Charlotte 112, 205–6, 280, 284, 285
   Jane Eyre 112, 205–6, 281, 284–5
   Villette 280, 281
Brontë, Emily 35–6, 211, 282, 283
   Wuthering Heights 35–6, 60, 64, 112, 129, 154, 211, 282–4
Brook, Peter 166
Brooks, Cleanth 267, 272, 306
   The Well-Wrought Urn 272
Browne, Thomas 91
   Religio Medici 91
Browning, Robert 114–15
   'Fra Lippo Lippi' 114–15
Bruner, Jerome S. 14
   Acts of Meaning 14
Bunyan, John 91
   The Pilgrim's Progress 91

Burke, Edmund 102, 104, 107
  A Philosophical Inquiry into the Origin
    of Our Ideas of the Sublime and the
    Beautiful 107
Burney, Frances (Fanny) 95
  Evelina 95
Burroughs, Edgar Rice 323
  Tarzan of the Apes 323
Burroughs, William 257
  Naked Lunch 257
Butler, Judith 203, 204, 235, 317, 318–19
  Gender Trouble 204, 318
Byron, George Gordon, Lord 28–9, 102,
    107
  Manfred 28–9

C
Calvino, Italo 199
  If on a Winter's Night a Traveller 199
canon 5–6, 9, 27, 60, 76, 82, 96, 120, 121,
    122, 124, 127, 196, 199, 200, 211, 219,
    231, 232–3, 247, 248, 281, 306, 309,
    310, 315, 316, 319, 321, 322, 323, 355,
    359
Caputo, John D. 301
  Deconstruction in a Nutshell 301
Carew, Thomas 88
carnivalesque 148, 277
Carroll, Lewis 232, 233
  Alice's Adventures in Wonderland 230, 232
Carter, Angela 108
Carver, Raymond 258–9
  Cathedral 258–9
Cary, Elizabeth, Lady Falkland 88
Castiglione, Baldassare 81–2
  The Book of the Courtier 81–2
Castle, Terry 316
  'Was Jane Austen Gay?' 316
Celan, Paul 130
Cervantes (Saavedra), Miguel de 95, 152
  Adventures of Don Quixote 95, 152
Cesaire, Aimé 216
  A Tempest 216
Charles I 174

Eikon Basilike 174
Chaucer, Geoffrey 72–9 *passim*, 144, 145,
    148, 159, 161, 209, 308
  The Book of the Duchess 75
  The Canterbury Tales 75–6, 148, 159
  Troilus and Criseyde 75, 76
  'The Wife of Bath's Prologue and Tale'
    144, 145, 148, 209
Chekhov, Anton 139
  The Cherry Orchard 139
  The Seagull 139
  Three Sisters 139
Chicano/a literature and studies 251–2,
    311–14
Christie, Agatha 114
Cisneros, Sandra 312–13
Clare, John 211
class 5, 19, 20, 64, 75, 96, 106, 111, 112,
    113, 114, 123, 128, 130, 138, 142, 143,
    153, 189, 205, 209–15, 246, 259, 278,
    279, 281, 282, 287–8, 289, 323
Coetzee, J. M. 201
Coleridge, Samuel Taylor 20, 102, 107, 160,
    227, 325
  'Dejection: An Ode' 227
  Lyrical Ballads (with William
    Wordsworth) 20, 103, 160, 210
  The Rime of the Ancient Mariner 107
Collins, Michael 213
Collins, William 177–8
  'Ode to Evening' 177–8
Collins, William Wilkie 113–14
  The Moonstone 114
comedy 98, 135, 140, 142–50, 210, 254,
    271, 329
comparative literature 25–30
Conan Doyle, Arthur 114
Conrad, Joseph 120, 123, 135, 301, 322–3
  Heart of Darkness 122, 301
Contemporary Literature 126
context xii, 20, 28, 29, 33, 34, 43, 45, 58, 60,
    62, 63, 83, 96, 122, 128, 139, 146, 155,
    167, 168, 177, 179, 184, 204, 205, 207,
    213, 215, 218, 219, 222, 224, 231, 245,

271, 274, 290, 300, 304, 306, 307, 308, 312, 314, 317, 318, 322, 325
Cowley, Abraham 89
Crashaw, Richard 88
creative writing 21–5
Criminal Law Amendment Act (1885) 314
Critchley, Simon 301
   The Ethics of Deconstruction 301
Cromwell, Oliver 90, 174
Culler, Jonathan 26
cultural materialism 286, 305, 306–9. *See* materialism
cultural studies 321–4
cummings, e. e. 13
Cursor Mundi 74

D

Daniel 69
Darwin, Charles 115, 190
   Descent of Man 115
   On the Origin of Species 115
De Beauvoir, Simone 61, 203
   The Second Sex 203
De Lauretis, Teresa 204
   Technologies of Gender 204–5
DeLillo, Don 328
   White Noise 328
De Man, Paul, 298
deconstruction 108, 230, 296–303
Defoe, Daniel 93, 95, 153, 189, 191, 227
   Moll Flanders 94
   Robinson Crusoe 94, 95, 153, 154, 189, 191, 227
Dench, Judi 168
Derrida, Jacques 36, 43, 108, 296–301
   Archive Fever 300
   Dissemination 299, 200
   'Letter to a Japanese Friend' 296
   Margins of Philosophy 299
   Of Grammatology 48
   Positions 299
   Specters of Marx 301
   Speech and Pheomena 298
   Writing and Difference 298

Desani, G. V. 216–17
   All About H. Hatterr 216–17
Descartes, René, 187, 223, 226
   Meditations on First Philosophy 223
desire 88, 117, 123, 124, 224, 234, 257, 269, 279, 284, 285, 294, 295, 298, 305, 317, 319–20
dialectic 288
Dickens, Charles 4, 6, 107, 111, 112, 113, 122, 146–7, 154, 196, 200, 211, 231, 238, 245, 297
   A Christmas Carol 112
   Great Expectations 107, 122
   Hard Times 113
   Household Words 113
   The Old Curiosity Shop 113
   Oliver Twist 112, 147, 231
   Our Mutual Friend 122
   The Pickwick Papers 111, 113, 147
Dickinson, Emily 295
   'In Winter in My Room' 295
Didion, Joan 12–13, 16
   The White Album 12–13
discourse xii, 40, 61–2, 144, 145, 241, 267, 268, 291, 293, 304, 305, 323, 326
Dollimore, Jonathan 307
   (with Alan Sinfield) *Political Shakespeare* 307
Donne, John 87–8
   'Batter my Heart' 88
   'The Canonization' 87
   'The Sun Rising' 87
   'To His Mistress Going to Bed' 87–8
   'A Valediction Forbidding Mourning' 88
Dos Passos, John 238, 255
   Manhattan Transfer 238, 255
   U.S.A. 238
The Dream of the Rood 69
Dryden, John 88, 90, 160, 163, 178, 179
   Absalom and Achitophel 160
   Mac Flecknoe 90
   'Threnodia Augustalis' 178
   'To the Memory of Mr Oldham' 179
Du Bois, W. E. B. 309–10

The Soul of Black Folk 309–10
Dürrenmatt, Friedrich 128
    The Visit 128

E

Eagleton, Terry 6, 8, 9, 209, 239, 288
    Literary Theory 6
    Marxism and Literary Criticism 288
Easthope, Anthony 322–3
    Literary into Cultural Studies 322–3
Eco, Umberto 130
    The Name of the Rose 130
ecocriticism 207, 324–7
eighteenth-century literature 93–100
Eikhenbaum (Eichenbaum), Boris 238–9,
    268–9
    'The Theory of a "Formal Method"' 269
Eisenstein, Sergei 238
elegy 9, 97, 173, 178–9
Eliot, George (Mary Ann Evans) 110, 111,
    113, 154, 190, 210
    Middlemarch 110, 111, 113, 154, 190,
    210
Eliot, T. S. 120, 121, 160, 256, 274, 328
    'The Love Song of J. Alfred Prufrock' 274
    'Tradition and the Individual Talent' 274
    The Waste Land 121, 160, 256
Ellis, Bret Easton 258
    American Psycho 258
    Glamorama 258
    Less than Zero 258
Emin, Tracy 6
Empson, William 272
    Seven Types of Ambiguity 272
Engels, Friedrich 209, 286–7. *See* Karl Marx
epic 26, 27, 60, 65, 69, 74, 83, 89–90, 97,
    171–7, 181, 184, 271, 276
epistolary fiction 94–5
Equiano, Olaudah 4, 6, 94
    The Interesting Narrative 4, 6, 94
Eugenides, Jeffrey 203
    Middlesex 203
Euripides 135, 136
    Electra 136

    Medea 136
    The Trojan Women 136
existentialism 130, 140, 148, 227

F

Faulkner, William 241, 255, 297
    Absalom! Absalom! 255
    As I Lay Dying 297
    The Sound and the Fury 241, 255
feminism xv n.2, xvi n.2, 59, 61, 64,111,
    129, 203, 222, 266, 278–86, 296, 297,
    322, 325, 326, 354
Fielding, Henry 91, 95, 135, 145, 153, 185,
    189, 227
    Amelia 95
    Joseph Andrews 95, 189
    The Modern Husband 185
    Rape upon Rape 185
    Shamela 95
    Tom Jones 94, 95, 145, 153, 227
Fielding, Sarah 94, 95
    The Adventures of David Simple 94, 95
Figes, Eva 140
    Tragedy and Social Evolution 140
Fitzgerald, F. Scott 255
    The Great Gatsby 255
Fletcher, John 84
Ford, Ford Madox 13–14
    The Good Soldier 13–14
formalism (Russian Formalism) 7–8, 267–
    9, 272, 275, 276, 299, 306
Forster, E. M. 27, 212
    Howards End 212
    A Passage to India 27
Foucault, Michel 204, 223, 292–3, 305,
    318–19, 320, 323
    The History of Sexuality 204, 292–3, 305,
    318
    The Order of Things 223
    The Will to Knowledge 318
Fowler, Alistair 178
Fowles, John 129
    The French Lieutenant's Woman 129
Frazer, James G. 270

The Golden Bough 270
Freeman, Edward 355
French Revolution 102, 210
Freud, Sigmund 61, 146, 149, 154, 192,
    224, 225–6, 240, 278, 283, 294, 295
  Beyond the Pleasure Principle 294
  The Future of an Illusion 294
  The Interpretation of Dreams 226
  Jokes and Their Relation to the Unconscious
    146
  Moses and Monotheism 294
  Totem and Taboo 294
  'The "Uncanny"' 295
Fry, Stephen 162
  The Ode Less Travelled 162
Frye, Northrop 270–1
  Anatomy of Criticism 271
Fussell, Paul 97
  English Augustan Poetry 97
futurism 123–4

G

Galsworthy, John 191
Garcia Márquez, Gabriel 129
  One Hundred Years of Solitude 129
Garrick, David 98
Gaskell, Elizabeth 43, 113, 153–4
  Cranford 43
  Mary Barton 153–4
  North and South 113
Gates, Henry Louis 310
  The Signifying Monkey 310
Gawain-poet 75
  Sir Gawain and the Green Knight 75
Gay, John 97, 185
  The Beggar's Opera 98, 185
  Polly 185
  Trivia 97
gay studies 111, 204, 207, 298, 314–21, 322
gender 19, 20, 64, 70, 72, 98, 104, 108, 111,
    124, 126, 127, 129, 136, 138, 143, 145,
    166, 202–9, 211, 213, 221, 222, 234,
    235, 254, 256, 271, 278–9, 282, 286,
    312, 318–19, 323, 327

Genesis 69
Genette, Gérard 9, 95
genre x, xiv, 37, 38, 39, 40, 42, 44, 58, 77,
    88, 89, 90, 92, 95, 97, 113, 114, 134,
    137, 142, 143, 148, 150, 151, 152, 161,
    167, 170, 186, 187, 189, 190, 192, 194,
    195, 199, 200, 216, 217, 223, 232, 240,
    244, 248, 250, 252, 253, 258, 271, 276,
    306, 325
Geoffrey of Monmouth 74
  Historia Regum Britanniae 74
Gibbon, Edward 9
  The Decline and Fall of the Roman Empire
    9
Gilbert, Sandra M. 206, 282
  (with Susan Gubar) *The Madwoman in*
    the Attic 206, 282
Gilman, Charlotte Perkins 320
  'The Yellow Wallpaper' 320
Gilroy, Paul 310
  The Black Atlantic 310–11
Ginsberg, Allen 256–7
  'Howl' 256–7
Gissing, George 190
  The Nether World 190
Godwin, William 102
Goethe, Johann Wolfgang von 27
  The Sorrows of Young Werther 27
Golding, William 128
  Lord of the Flies 128
Goldsmith, Oliver 98, 99
  She Stoops to Conquer 98
gothic x, 19, 94, 101–10 *passim*, 112, 113,
    146, 153, 205, 218, 252, 253, 259, 280,
    295, 310
Gower, John 75, 77
  Confessio Amantis 75
Grant, Damian 187
graphic novel 195, 244, 246
Grass, Günter 128
  The Tin Drum 128
Gray, Thomas 96, 178
  'The Bard' 178

'Elegy Written in a Country Churchyard'
178, 179
'The Progress of Poesy' 178
Greenaway, Peter 169
Greenblatt, Stephen 304
Renaissance Self-Fashioning 304
Gubar, Susan 206, 282. *See* Sandra M.
Gilbert
Gui de Warewic 75
Gutenberg, Johannes 80

H
H.D. (Hilda Doolittle) 121, 255–6
Haggard, H. Rider 215
King Solomon's Mines 215
Hall, Donald E. 320
Hall, Stuart 323
Hanks, Tom 241
Forrest Gump 241
Hardy, Thomas 135, 137, 156–7, 191
Hare, David 185
Stuff Happens 185
Harper, Graham 303
Harrison, Tony 213
Hawthorne, Nathaniel 253–4
The Scarlet Letter 253–4
Haywood, Eliza 94
Love in Excess 94
Heaney, Seamus 65
Henryson, Robert 77
Testament of Cresseid 77
Herbert, George 88
The Temple 88
Herrick, Robert 89
'Corinna's Going A-Maying', 89
Herwitz, Daniel 194
Hirst, Damien 6
Hoby, Thomas 81
Hoccleve, Thomas 76
The Regement of Princes 76
The Series 77
Hoffmann, E. T. A. 295
'The Sandman' 295
Hogarth, William 195

The Rake's Progress 195
Hogg, James 107
Hoggart, Richard 213, 323
Hollinghurst, Alan 127
Homer 171, 172
Iliad 171
Odyssey 171, 172
Hopkins, Gerard Manley 65
Horace 182, 183
Howard, Henry, Earl of Surrey 82
Howe, Susan 129
Frame Structures 129
Hughes, Langston 310
'The Negro Artist and the Racial
Mountain' 310
Hunt, Leigh 210
Hunt, Peter 232–3, 234

I
Ibsen, Henrik 138–9
Hedda Gabler 138
idealism 105, 187, 188, 190, 192
ideology 70, 106, 123, 189, 194, 195, 222,
277, 288, 292, 323, 330
Idle, Eric 146
imagism 121
imperialism 217, 303
intentional fallacy 274
intertextuality 26, 76, 239, 271, 277
Ionesco, Eugène 148
Rhinoceros 148
irony 130, 148, 179, 181, 199, 271, 272

J
Jacobean and Caroline drama 87
Jakobson, Roman 7–8
James, Henry 43, 192, 254
The Ambassadors 192, 254
The Portrait of a Lady 254
The Turn of the Screw 107
James, M. R. 107
Johnson, Samuel 6, 88, 96, 99, 105
Dictionary 6
London 183

Preface to Shakespeare 6
The Vanity of Human Wishes 183
Jonson, Ben 84, 89, 90, 142, 184
  'The Masque of Blackness' 89
  'To Penshurst' 89
  'Pleasure Reconciled to Virtue' 89
  Volpone 142
Joyce, James 120, 224, 225, 226, 244, 255
  Finnegans Wake 122, 224
  Ulysses 154, 155, 224, 225, 244
Judith 69
Jung, Carl Gustav 270
Juvenal 183

K

Kamuf, Peggy 204, 301–2
  'Writing like a Woman' 204
Kane, Sarah 167, 169
  Blasted 167
Keats, John 101, 102, 210
  The Eve of St Agnes 107
  Lamia 107
Kelman, James 213
  How Late it Was, How Late 213
Kemble, John Philip 98
Kempe, Margery 77
  Book of Margery Kempe 77
Kerouac, Jack 257
  On the Road 257
King, Martin Luther 309
Kipling, Rudyard 111
  'The Man Who Would Be King' 111
Klein, Melanie 295
Kristeva, Julia 107, 277
Kundera, Milan 130
  The Unbearable Lightness of Being 130
Kyd, Thomas 84, 138
  The Spanish Tragedy 138

L

Lacan, Jacques 36, 226, 295
Landow, George 38
  Victorian Web 38
Lane, Edward William 29

Langland, William 75
  Piers Plowman 75
Lanyer, Aemilia 88
  'Description of Cooke-ham' 88
Lawrence, D. H. 120, 124, 212–13
  The Ladybird 124
  Lady Chatterley's Lover 212
Layamon 74
  Brut 74
Leavis, F. R. 6, 246, 307
  The Great Tradition 6
Le Fanu, James Sheridan 107
Lennox, Charlotte 95
  The Female Quixote 95
Lesnick-Oberstein, Karin 234
Lewis, Matthew 105
  The Monk 105
Lewis, Percy Wyndham 120, 123
Licensing Act (1737) 185
Linton, Eliza Lynn 117
  'The Girl of the Period' 117
literary theory 6, 21, 61, 218, 219, 230, 233,
  265, 266, 270, 296, 301, 311, 324, 325,
  326, 329
Liu, Alan 37–8, 44
  'Voice of the Shuttle' 44
Locke, John 187
Lodge, Thomas 184
  Defence of Poetry 184
Longinus 28
  On the Sublime 28
Lonsdale, Roger 6, 96
Lovelock, James 326
Lowell, Amy 155–6
Lydgate, John 76, 77
  Troy Book 76
Lyotard, Jean-François 200
lyric 19, 77, 87–8, 97, 159–60, 175, 177–
  81, 239, 245

M

Mack, Maynard 182
MacPherson, James 27
Malory, Thomas 151

Le Mort D'Arthur 151
Mannyng, Robert 74
   Chronicle 74
Mansfield, Katherine 120, 124
Marinetti, Filippo Tommaso 123
Marlowe, Christopher 60, 84, 85, 87, 139,
   160
   Dr Faustus 84, 87, 139
   'The Passionate Shepherd to His Love'
     160
Marvell, Andrew 90, 178
   'An Horatian Ode: Upon Cromwell's
     Return from Ireland' 90, 178
Marx, Karl 61, 107, 209, 227, 286–89
   Capital 227
   The Communist Manifesto 107
Marxism xvi, 59, 61, 64, 266, 275, 286–90,
   297, 305, 306, 322
materialism/materiality 188, 190, 192, 201,
   279, 287, 305, 306–8, 338
Maturin, Charles 105
   Melmoth the Wanderer 105
Maxims 69
McEwan, Ian 131, 201
   Amsterdam 201
   Atonement 131
   Enduring Love 201
   Saturday 201
McKellen, Ian 168
McQuillan, Martin 301
   Deconstruction: A Reader 301
medieval literature 19, 72–9
Medvedev, P. N. 276
   The Formal Method in Literary Scholarship
     276
metaphysics 88, 130, 139, 140, 299
Middleton, Thomas 84
   Women Beware Women 138
Millais, John Everett 116
   Ophelia 116
Miller, J. Hillis 298, 301
Miller, Jonathan 166
Milton, John 6, 86, 89–91, 96, 159, 160,
   161, 163, 173, 174–5, 178, 306

Eikonoklastes 174
   'Lycidas' 178–9
   Paradise Lost 86, 89–91, 96, 159, 160,
     173, 174–5, 306
'minority' literatures 251–2
MLA Bibliography 36
modernism 19, 120–5, 129, 154, 155, 191,
   201, 238, 254, 255–6, 328, 329
Molière (Jean-Baptiste Poquelin) 142
   The Misanthrope 142
Montagu, Mary Wortley 97, 99
   'Epistle from Arthur G[ra]y to Mrs
     M[urra]y' 97
   'Epistle from Mrs Y[onge] to her
     Husband' 97
Monty Python's Flying Circus 146, 184
More, Thomas 81
   Utopia 81
Morris, Pam 189–90
Morrison, Toni 251, 271, 309, 311, 316–17
   Beloved 251
   Sula 316–17
Mulvey, Laura 205
   'Visual Pleasure and Narrative Cinema'
     205
Murdoch, Iris 12
   The Sovereignty of Good 12
Musil, Robert 329
   Der Mann ohne Eigenschaften 329
Mystery play cycles 167

N
Nabokov, Vladimir 15–16, 128
   Lolita 15–16, 128
Native American literature 250–1
Nesbit, Edith 51
   The Railway Children 51
New Criticism 267, 272–5
new historicism 26, 204, 304–6, 324
Nietzsche, Friedrich 137
   The Birth of Tragedy 137
Norton Anthology of African American
   Literature 309
Norton Anthology of Poetry 162

Norton Anthology of Theory and Criticism 269

Norton Anthology of World Literature 27–8, 29

novel, the x, 9, 13, 14, 15, 16, 20, 26, 27, 36, 43, 51, 52, 58, 60, 91, 93–6, , 97, 98, 105, 106, 111, 112–14, 117, 122, 126, 128, 129, 130, 131, 140, 143, 144, 146, 147, 150–6, 159, 175, 187, 188, 189, 190, 191, 192, 100–200, 203, 205, 206–7, 212, 216, 218, 222, 223, 224, 226, 227, 118, 229, 233, 237, 238, 240, 241, 244, 251, 253, 254, 255, 257, 275–7, 281, 282, 283, 285, 289, 297, 310, 313, 316, 317, 319, 322, 328, 329

O

O'Hara, Frank 257
Old English literature 19, 65–71
Olney, James 14
　Metaphors of Self 14
orientalism 218, 220, 235, 326
Orwell, George 9, 196, 213
　Animal Farm 196
　Down and Out in Paris and London 196
　Nineteen Eighty-Four 196, 213
　The Road to Wigan Pier 196, 213
Osborne, John 128
　The Entertainer 128
other, otherness 14, 108, 146, 147, 226, 301, 303, 345–6, 347, 348. *See* alterity
Ovid 84
　Metamorphoses 84
Owen, Wilfrid 182
　'Dulce et decorum est' 182

P

Paglia, Camille 295
　Sexual Personae 295
Paine, Thomas 102
Pamuk, Orhan 130–1
　The New Life 130–1
pastoral 9, 97, 160, 178, 184, 325
Pater, Walter 117, 224–5, 227

The Renaissance 225
Patmore, Coventry 117
　The Angel in the House 117
Pavel, Thomas 196
Pepys, Samuel 152
　The Diary 152
Petrarch 82, 87, 179
　Canzoniere 179–80
Philips, John 96
　The Splendid Shilling 96
Pindar 178
Pinero, Arthur Wing 117–18
　The Second Mrs Tanqueray 118
Pinter, Harold 129, 139
Pirandello, Luigi 148
　Six Characters in Search of an Author 148
Pizan, Christine de 77
Plath, Sylvia 129
　The Bell Jar 129
Plato 81
Plautus 84
　Menaechmi 84
Poe, Edgar Allan 108, 253
　'The Fall of the House of Usher' 253
　'The Tell-Tale Heart' 253
Pope, Alexander 4, 96, 99, 175, 182
　The Dunciad 96, 99
　The Dunciad Variorum 175
　Imitations of Horace 182
　The Rape of the Lock 96, 175
postcolonialism 111, 129, 215–21, 222, 286, 303–4, 322
postmodernism 125, 126, 155, 198–202, 327–31
Potter, Sally 237
　Orlando 237
Pound, Ezra 120, 121, 123, 255–6, 291–2
　Cantos 255–6
　Hugh Selwyn Mauberley 256
　'In a Station of the Metro' 291–2
power 20, 64, 70, 235, 305, 323
Prest, Thomas Preskett 211
　Varney the Vampire 211
Project Gutenberg 36

Propp, Vladimir 268
  Morphology of the Folk Tale 268
Proust, Marcel 15, 329
  Du côté de chez Swann 15
  À la recherche du temps perdu 15, 329
psychoanalysis xv n.2, 59, 61, 64, 126, 146,
  192, 266, 279, 280, 284, 293–6, 301,
  317, 322
Puttenham, George 184
  Arte of English Poesie 184
Pynchon, Thomas 198, 200

Q

Quarterly Review 210
Queer theory, 40, 111, 206, 207, 214–21,
  222, 298, 314–23

R

Radcliffe, Ann 105, 106, 107
  The Mysteries of Udolpho 105, 107
Raleigh, Walter 160, 173
Ransom, John Crowe 273–4
realism 94, 107, 151, 152, 153, 154, 186–
  93, 199, 200, 232, 253–4, 255
Reeve, Clara 151, 153
Reid, Thomas 187–8
Renaissance theatre 83–4
rhetoric 6, 14, 80, 88, 173, 175, 182, 196,
  231, 248, 252, 269, 272, 325
Rhys, Jean 129, 207, 311
  Wide Sargasso Sea 129, 207
Rice, Anne 110
Rich, Adrienne 204
  On Lies, Secrets, and Silence 204
Richards, I. A. 272
  Practical Criticism 272
  Principles of Literary Criticism 272
Richardson, Samuel 93, 94, 153, 189
  Clarissa 94
  Pamela 94, 153
Ricks, Christopher 227–8
Rimbaud, Arthur 226
Rimmon-Kenan, Shlomith 95
  Narrative Fiction 95

Ringrose, Christopher 33
Roberts, Julia 239
  Pretty Woman 239
romanticism 101–10
Rosenblatt, Louise M. 11
  The Reader, the Text, the Poem 11
Rossetti, Christina 115–16, 117
  Goblin Market 115–16, 117
  'In an Artist's Studio' 116
Rossetti, Dante Gabriel 116
Rousseau, Jean-Jacques 103
Roy, Arundhati 200
  The God of Small Things 200
Royal Literary Fund 23
  Royal Literary Fund Fellow 23
Royal Shakespeare Company 166
Royle, Nicholas 301
Rushdie, Salman 128, 130, 198, 217–19,
  244, 311
  Midnight's Children 218
  The Satanic Verses 130, 198, 244
  'Yorick' 217
Ruskin, John 117
Russian Revolution 123, 139

S

Said, Edward 219, 235, 303, 304, 326
Salinger, J. D. 257
  The Catcher in the Rye 257
Sallustius 172–3
  On the Gods and the World 172–3
Saramago, José 130, 131
  Blindness 130
satire 81, 90, 94, 95, 97, 98, 128, 142, 148,
  160, 162, 181–6, 195, 271
Saussure, Ferdinand de 36, 290–2, 293, 295
  Course in General Linguistics 290
Seafarer, The 69
Sedgwick, Eve Kosofsky 204, 319–20
  Between Men 204, 319–20
semiotics 165, 247, 290
Sendak, Maurice, 231
  Where the Wild Things Are 231
sensation novel 113–14

Seth, Vikram 159
  The Golden Gate 159
Shadwell, Thomas 90, 185
Shakespeare, William 4, 6, 8, 15, 82–3, 83–
    5, 86, 87, 98, 137, 138, 141, 165–6,
    167, 168, 177, 188–9, 195, 210, 216,
    226, 307–8
  As You Like It 177
  The Comedy of Errors 84
  Hamlet 138, 226
  Henry V 188
  King Lear 167, 188, 226
  Macbeth 138, 168, 210
  The Merchant of Venice 84
  A Midsummer Night's Dream 165–6
  Richard III 307–8
  Romeo and Juliet 188
  The Taming of the Shrew 145
  The Tempest 87, 216
  Titus Andronicus 84
  Twelfth Night 9
Sharp, Jane 4, 6
  The Midwives Book 4, 6
Shaw, George Bernard 118
  Mrs Warren's Profession 118
Shelley, Mary 104, 107
  Frankenstein 104, 107
Shelley, Percy Bysshe 102, 227
  'Mutability' 227
Sheridan, Richard Brinsley 98
  The Duenna 98
  The Rivals 98
  The School for Scandal 98
Shklovsky, Viktor 7, 268
Showalter, Elaine 279
Siddal, Elizabeth 116
Siddons, Sarah 98
Sidney, Philip 28–9, 81, 87, 173
  Apology for Poetry 81, 173
  Arcadia (*The Countess of Pembroke's
      Arcadia*) 81
  Astrophil and Stella 81
  The Old Arcadia 81
signifier/signified 290, 291, 292

Sinfield, Alan 307–8. *See* Jonathan
    Dollimore
  (with Jonathan Dollimore) *Political
      Shakespeare* 307
  The Wilde Century 320
Skelton, John 77
  The Garland of Laurel 77
Smith, Sidney 250
Smith, Zadie 200
  White Teeth 200–1
Smollett, Tobias 95
  The Adventures of Humphrey Clinker 95
Snyder, Gary 256–7
sonnet 8–9, 26, 78, 81, 82, 87, 88, 112, 116,
    177, 179–80, 187, 222, 227, 274, 318
Sophocles 135, 136, 166–7
  Oedipus Rex 136, 166–7, 226
Soueif, Ahdaf 200
  The Map of Love 200
Southey, Robert 6
Speght, Rachel 88
Spenser, Edmund 82, 87, 90, 173
  The Faerie Queene 83, 90, 173
Spielberg, Steven 239–40
  Hook 239
Spitting Image 148
Spivak, Gayatri Chakravorty 25, 219, 303
Spooner, W. A. 146
Stage Licensing Act 97
Stanzel, F. K. 95
Sterne, Laurence 95–96, 227–8
  The Life and Opinions of Tristram Shandy
      95–96, 227–8
Stevens, Wallace 11–12, 187, 256
  'A Duck for Dinner' 11–12, 13
Stevenson, Robert Louis 107, 193–4
  The Strange Case of Dr Jekyll and Mr Hyde
      107
Stoker, Bram 107
  Dracula 107
Storey, John 245
Stowe, Harriet Beecher 254
  Uncle Tom's Cabin 254

stream of consciousness 154, 191, 224, 225, 257

Strindberg, August 138, 139

structuralism 290–3

subjectivity 20, 59, 64, 129, 221–30, 268

Swift, Graham 198, 199
    Waterland 198, 199

Swift, Jonathan 94, 95, 97, 179, 182–3, 185, 231
    The Battel of the Books 185
    'Description of a City Shower' 97
    Gulliver's Travels 94, 95, 182, 231
    A Modest Proposal 182
    Tale of a Tub 182
    'Verse on the Death of Dr Swift' 179

Swinburne, Algernon Charles 190

T

Tennyson, Alfred Lord, 65, 114–15, 211
    In Memoriam, A. H. H. 115
    Ulysses 114

Tew, Philip 201

textuality 305

Thacker, Deborah Cogan 233

Thackeray, W. M. 211
    Vanity Fair 211

Thompson, E. P. 323

Thomson, James 96
    Seasons, The 96

Thousand and One Nights, The 29

Tillyard, E. M. W. 304
    The Elizabethan World Picture 304

Tolkien, J. R. R. 65
    The Lord of the Rings 65

Tolstoy, Leo 7

tragedy 61, 87, 135–42, 147, 167, 181, 189, 271

transcendentalism 253

trope 38, 76, 118, 199, 298, 327

Twain, Mark 254
    Adventures of Huckleberry Finn 254

U

uncanny 295, 328

unconscious 105, 146, 188, 210, 225, 226, 234, 270, 294, 297, 306
    collective unconscious (Jung) 270

United States of America 5, 21

universities
    Birmingham (Centre for Contemporary Cultural Studies) 323
    Calgary 38
    East Anglia 21
    Leicester 361
    Liverpool 126
    Loughborough 45, 59
    Manchester Metropolitan 24
    Melbourne 39
    Southampton 39

Updike, John 258

V

Vaughan, Henry 88

Verfremdungseffekt [alienation/distancing/ estrangement effect] 140, 334

Veeser, H. Aram 305
    The New Historicism 305

Victorian and nineteenth-century literature 110–19
    Victorian poetry 114–17

Virago 281

Virgil 90, 171, 172
    Aeneid 90, 171

Volosinov, V. N. 276
    Marxism and the Philosophy of Language 276

W

Wace 74
    Roman de Brut 74

Walker, Alice 251, 309
    The Colour Purple 251

Wallace, David Foster 258
    Infinite Jest 258

Waller, Edmund 89
    'Song (Go, lovely rose!)' 89

Walpole, Horace 94, 105
    The Castle of Otranto 94, 105

Wanderer, the 69
Ward, Mrs Humphrey (Mary Augusta) 154
   Robert Elsmere 154
Waters, Sarah 127, 131
   Night Watch 131
Watt, Ian 93, 94, 188, 189, 192
   The Rise of the Novel 93, 94
Webster, John 87
   The Duchess of Malfi 87
   The White Devil 138
Wellek, René, 25–26
West, Nathanael 255
   The Day of the Locust 255
White, Hayden 196
Wilde, Oscar 117, 315–16, 317
   'The Decay of Lying' 117
   The Importance of Being Earnest 117
   The Picture of Dorian Gray 117, 317
Williams, Raymond 184, 209, 207, 307,
   323, 341, 348
   The Country and the City 184
   Marxism and Literature 307
Williams, Robin 239
   Good Morning, Vietnam! 239
Williams, William Carlos 256
   Paterson 256
   'The Red Wheelbarrow' 256
Wilmot, John, Earl of Rochester 89
Wilson, E. O. 326
Wimsatt, W. K. 273, 274, 306
   'The Intentional Fallacy' (with Monroe
     C. Beardsley) 274
   The Verbal Icon (with Monroe C.
     Beardsley) 273

Winterson, Jeanette 127
Wolfreys, Julian 301
   Deconstruction • Derrida 301
Wollstonecraft, Mary 102
Women's Press, The 281
Woolf, Virginia 120, 124, 135, 191–2, 224–
   5, 226, 237–8, 255, 284, 289, 317, 328
   Between the Acts 122
   'Modern Fiction' 135
   'Mr Bennett and Mrs Brown' 191–2, 223
   Mrs Dalloway 154–5, 289
   Orlando 237
   A Room of One's Own 284
   To the Lighthouse 122, 224
Wordsworth, William 101, 102, 103, 104,
   111, 112, 115, 160, 175, 210, 211, 227,
   325
   Lyrical Ballads (with Samuel Taylor
     Coleridge) 20, 103, 160, 210
   The Prelude 104, 175, 227
Wright, Richard 310
   Native Son 310
Wroth, Mary 88
Wyatt, Thomas 78, 82

Y
Year's Work in English Studies, The 36

Z
Zipes, Jack 234
Zola, Émile 190–1, 192